GO!
with Microsoft® Office

Word 2003
Volume 1

**John Preston, Sally Preston,
Robert L. Ferrett**

Shelley Gaskin, Series Editor

PEARSON

Prentice
Hall

Upper Saddle River, New Jersey

Library of Congress Cataloging-in-Publication Data

Preston, John.
 Go! with Microsoft Office Word 2003. Volume 1 / John Preston, Sally Preston,
Robert L. Ferrett.
   p. cm.— (Go! with Microsoft Office 2003)
Includes index.
 ISBN 0-13-145102-2 (perfect bound : alk. paper)—ISBN 0-13-143431-4 (spiral : alk.
paper)
 1. Microsoft Word. 2. Word processing. I. Title: Word 2003. II. Preston, Sally.
III. Ferrett, Robert. IV. Title. V. Series.
Z52.5.M52P738 2004
005.52—dc22

                                                        2003026105

Vice President and Publisher: Natalie E. Anderson
Executive Acquisitions Editor: Jodi McPherson
Marketing Manager: Emily Williams Knight
Marketing Assistant: Nicole Beaudry
Associate Director IT Product Development: Melonie Salvati
Project Manager, Editorial: Jodi Bolognese
Project Manager, Supplements: Melissa Edwards
Senior Media Project Manager: Cathi Profitko
Editorial Assistants: Jasmine Slowik, Jodi Bolognese, Alana Meyers
Manager, Production: Gail Steier de Acevedo
Senior Project Manager, Production: Tim Tate
Manufacturing Buyer: Tim Tate
Design Manager: Maria Lange
Art Director: Pat Smythe
Cover Designer: Brian Salisbury
Cover Photo: Steve Bloom/Getty Images, Inc.
Interior Designer: Quorum Creative Services
Full Service Composition: Black Dot Group
Printer/Binder: Von Hoffmann Corporation
Cover Printer: Phoenix Color Corporation

10 9 8 7 6 5 4 3 2 1
ISBN 0-13-143431-4

What does this logo mean?

It means this courseware has been approved by the Microsoft® Office Specialist Program to be among the finest available for learning **Microsoft® Office Word 2003, Microsoft® Office Excel 2003, Microsoft® Office PowerPoint® 2003,** and **Microsoft® Office Access 2003.** It also means that upon completion of this courseware, you may be prepared to take an exam for Microsoft Office Specialist qualification.

What is a Microsoft Office Specialist?

A Microsoft Office Specialist is an individual who has passed exams for certifying his or her skills in one or more of the Microsoft Office desktop applications such as Microsoft Word, Microsoft Excel, Microsoft PowerPoint, Microsoft Outlook, Microsoft Access, or Microsoft Project. The Microsoft Office Specialist Program typically offers certification exams at the "Specialist" and "Expert" skill levels.* The Microsoft Office Specialist Program is the only program approved by Microsoft for testing proficiency in Microsoft Office desktop applications and Microsoft Project. This testing program can be a valuable asset in any job search or career advancement.

More Information:

To learn more about becoming a Microsoft Office Specialist, visit **www.microsoft.com/officespecialist**

To learn about other Microsoft Office Specialist approved courseware from Pearson Education, visit **www.prenhall.com/phit**

*The availability of Microsoft Office Specialist certification exams varies by application, application version, and language. Visit www.microsoft.com/officespecialist for exam availability.

GO!

Series for Microsoft® Office System 2003

Series Editor: Shelley Gaskin

Office
Getting Started
Brief
Intermediate
Advanced

Word
Brief
Volume 1
Volume 2
Comprehensive

Excel
Brief
Volume 1
Volume 2
Comprehensive

PowerPoint
Brief
Volume 1
Volume 2
Comprehensive

Access
Brief
Volume 1
Volume 2
Comprehensive

GO! Series Reviewers

We would like to thank the following "Super Reviewers" for both their subject matter expertise and attention to detail from the instructors' perspective. Your time, effort, hard work, and diligence has helped us create the best books in the world. Prentice Hall and your author partners thank you:

Rocky Belcher	Sinclair CC
Judy Cameron	Spokane CC
Gail Cope	Sinclair CC
Larry Farrer	Guilford Tech CC
Janet Enck	Columbus State CC
Susan Fry	Boise State
Lewis Hall	Riverside CC
Jeff Howard	Finger Lakes CC
Jason Hu	Pasadena City College
Michele Hulett	Southwest Missouri State U.
Donna Madsen	Kirkwood CC
Cheryl Reindl-Johnson	Sinclair CC
Jan Spaar	Spokane CC
Mary Ann Zlotow	College of DuPage

We would also like to thank our valuable student reviewers who bring us vital input from those who will someday study from our books:

Nicholas J. Bene	Southwest Missouri State U.
Anup Jonathan	Southwest Missouri State U.
Kimber Miller	Pasadena City College
Kelly Moline	Southwest Missouri State U.
Adam Morris	Southwest Missouri State U.
Robert Murphy	Southwest Missouri State U.
Drucilla Owenby	Southwest Missouri State U.
Vince Withee	Southwest Missouri State U.

Finally, we have been lucky to have so many of you respond to review our chapter manuscripts. You have given us tremendous feedback and helped make a fantastic series. We could not have done it without you.

Abraham, Reni	Houston CC	Challa, Chandrashekar	Virginia State University
Agatston, Ann	Agatston Consulting	Chamlou, Afsaneh	NOVA Alexandria
Alejandro, Manuel	Southwest Texas Junior College	Chapman, Pam	Wabaunsee CC
Ali, Farha	Lander University	Christensen, Dan	Iowa Western CC
Anik, Mazhar	Tiffin University	Conroy-Link, Janet	Holy Family College
Armstrong, Gary	Shippensburg University	Cosgrove, Janet	Northwestern CT Community
Bagui, Sikha	Univ. West Florida		Technical College
Belton, Linda	Springfield Tech. Com College	Cox, Rollie	Madison Area Technical College
Bennett, Judith	Sam Houston State University	Crawford, Hiram	Olive Harvey College
Bishop, Frances	DeVry Institute- Alpharetta (ATL)	Danno, John	DeVry University/
Branigan, Dave	DeVry University		Keller Graduate School
Bray, Patricia	Allegany College of Maryland	Davis, Phillip Md.	Del Mar College
Buehler, Lesley	Ohlone College	Doroshow, Mike	Eastfield College
Buell, C	Central Oregon CC	Douglas, Gretchen	SUNY Cortland
Byars, Pat	Brookhaven College	Driskel, Loretta	Niagara CC
Cacace, Rich	Pensacola Jr. College	Duckwiler, Carol	Wabaunsee CC
Cadenhead, Charles	Brookhaven College	Duncan, Mimi	University of Missouri-St. Louis
Calhoun, Ric	Gordon College	Duvall, Annette	Albuquerque Technical
Carriker, Sandra	North Shore CC		Vocational Institute

Reviewers continues

Ecklund, Paula	Duke University	Menking, Rick	Hardin-Simmons University
Edmondson, Jeremy	Mount Pisgah School	Meredith, Mary	U. of Louisiana at Lafayette
Erickson, John	University of South Dakota	Mermelstein, Lisa	Baruch College
Falkenstein, Todd	Indiana University East	Metos, Linda	Salt Lake CC
Fite, Beverly	Amarillo College	Meurer, Daniel	University of Cincinnati
Foltz, Brian	East Carolina University	Monk, Ellen	University of Delaware
Friedrichsen, Lisa	Johnson County CC	Morris, Nancy	Hudson Valley CC
Fustos, Janos	Metro State	Nadas, Erika	Wright College
Gallup, Jeanette	Blinn College	Nadelman, Cindi	New England College
Gentry, Barb	Parkland College	Ncube, Cathy	University of West Florida
Gerace, Karin	St. Angela Merici School	Nicholls, Doreen	Mohawk Valley CC
Gerace, Tom	Tulane University	Orr, Claudia	New Mexico State University
Ghajar, Homa	Oklahoma State University	Otieno, Derek	DeVry University
Gifford, Steve	Northwest Iowa CC	Otton, Diana Hill	Chesapeake College
Gregoryk, Kerry	Virginia Commonwealth State University	Oxendale, Lucia	West Virginia Institute of Technology
Griggs, Debra	Bellevue CC	Paiano, Frank	Southwestern College
Grimm, Carol	Palm Beach CC	Proietti, Kathleen	Northern Essex CC
Helms, Liz	Columbus State CC	Pusins, Delores	HCCC
Hernandez, Leticia	TCI College of Technology	Reeves, Karen	High Point University
Hogan, Pat	Cape Fear CC	Rhue, Shelly	DeVry University
Horvath, Carrie	Albertus Magnus College	Richards, Karen	Maplewoods CC
Howard, Chris	DeVry University	Ross, Dianne	Univ. of Louisiana in Lafayette
Huckabay, Jamie	Austin CC	Rousseau, Mary	Broward CC
Hunt, Laura	Tulsa CC	Sams, Todd	University of Cincinnati
Jacob, Sherry	Jefferson CC	Sandoval, Everett	Reedley College
Jacobs, Duane	Salt Lake CC	Sardone, Nancy	Seton Hall University
Johnson, Kathy	Wright College	Scafide, Jean	Mississippi Gulf Coast CC
Jones, Stacey	Benedict College	Scheeren, Judy	Westmoreland County CC
Kasai, Susumu	Salt Lake CC	Schneider, Sol	Sam Houston State University
Keen, Debby	Univ. of Kentucky	Scroggins, Michael	Southwest Missouri State University
Kirk, Colleen	Mercy College		
Kliston, Linda	Broward CC	Sever, Suzanne	Northwest Arkansas CC
Kramer, Ed	Northern Virginia CC	Sheridan, Rick	California State University-Chico
Laird, Jeff	Northeast State CC	Sinha, Atin	Albany State University
Lange, David	Grand Valley State	Smith, T. Michael	Austin CC
LaPointe, Deb	Albuquerque TVI	Smith, Tammy	Tompkins Cortland CC
Lenhart, Sheryl	Terra CC	Stefanelli, Greg	Carroll CC
Letavec, Chris	University of Cincinnati	Steiner, Ester	New Mexico State University
Lightner, Renee	Broward CC	Sterling, Janet	Houston CC
Lindberg, Martha	Minnesota State University	Stroup, Tracey	Pasadena City College
Linge, Richard	Arizona Western College	Sullivan, Angela	Joliet Junior College
Loizeaux, Barbara	Westchester CC	Szurek, Joseph	University of Pittsburgh at Greensburg
Lopez, Don	Clovis- State Center CC District		
Low, Willy Hui	Joliet Junior College	Taylor, Michael	Seattle Central CC
Lowe, Rita	Harold Washington College	Thangiah, Sam	Slippery Rock University
Lucas, Vickie	Broward CC	Thompson-Sellers, Ingrid	Georgia Perimeter College
Lynam, Linda	Central Missouri State University	Tomasi, Erik	Baruch College
		Toreson, Karen	Shoreline CC
Machuca, Wayne	College of the Sequoias	Turgeon, Cheryl	Asnuntuck CC
Madison, Dana	Clarion University	Turpen, Linda	Albuquerque TVI
Maguire, Trish	Eastern New Mexico University	Upshaw, Susan	Del Mar College
Malkan, Rajiv	Montgomery College	Vargas, Tony	El Paso CC
Manning, David	Northern Kentucky University	Vicars, Mitzi	Hampton University
Marghitu, Daniela	Auburn University	Vitrano, Mary Ellen	Palm Beach CC
Marks, Suzanne	Bellevue CC	Wahila, Lori	Tompkins Cortland CC
Marquez, Juanita	El Centro College	Wavle, Sharon	Tompkins Cortland CC
Marucco, Toni	Lincoln Land CC	White, Bruce	Quinnipiac University
Mason, Lynn	Lubbock Christian University	Willer, Ann	Solano CC
Matutis, Audrone	Houston CC	Williams, Mark	Lane CC
McCannon, Melinda (Mindy)	Gordon College	Wimberly, Leanne	International Academy of Design and Technology
McClure, Darlean	College of Sequoias		
McCue, Stacy	Harrisburg Area CC	Worthington, Paula	NOVA Woodbridge
McEntire-Orbach, Teresa	Middlesex County College	Yauney, Annette	Herkimer CCC
McManus, Illyana	Grossmont College	Zavala, Ben	Webster Tech

Dedications

We dedicate this book to our granddaughters, who bring us
great joy and happiness: Clara and Siena & Alexis and Grace.

—John Preston, Sally Preston, and Robert L. Ferrett

This book is dedicated to my students,
who inspire me every day, and to my husband, Fred Gaskin.

—Shelley Gaskin

About the Authors/Acknowledgments

About John Preston, Sally Preston, and Robert L. Ferrett

John Preston is an Associate Professor at Eastern Michigan University in the College of Technology, where he teaches microcomputer application courses at the undergraduate and graduate levels. He has been teaching, writing, and designing computer training courses since the advent of PCs and has authored and co-authored over 60 books on Microsoft Word, Excel, Access, and PowerPoint. He is a series editor for the *Learn 97*, *Learn 2000*, and *Learn XP* books. Two books on Microsoft Access that he co-authored with Robert Ferrett have been translated into Greek and Chinese. He has received grants from the Detroit Edison Institute and the Department of Energy to develop Web sites for energy education and alternative fuels. He has also developed one of the first Internet-based microcomputer applications courses at an accredited university. He has a BS from the University of Michigan in Physics, Mathematics, and Education and an MS from Eastern Michigan University in Physics Education. His doctoral studies were in Instructional Technology at Wayne State University.

Sally Preston is president of Preston & Associates, which provides software consulting and training. She teaches computing in a variety of settings, which provides her with ample opportunity to observe how people learn, what works best, and what challenges are present when learning a new software program. This diverse experience provides a complementary set of skills and knowledge that blends into her writing. Prior to writing for the *GO! series*, Sally was a co-author on the *Learn* series since its inception and has authored books for the *Essentials* and *Microsoft Office User Specialist (MOUS) Essentials* series. Sally has an MBA from Eastern Michigan University. When away from her computer, she is often found planting flowers in her garden.

Robert L. Ferrett recently retired as the director of the Center for Instructional Computing at Eastern Michigan University, where he provided computer training and support to faculty. He has authored or co-authored more than 60 books on Access, PowerPoint, Excel, Publisher, WordPerfect, and Word and was the editor of the *1994 ACM SIGUCCS Conference Proceedings*. He has been designing, developing, and delivering computer workshops for nearly two decades. Before writing for the *GO! series*, Bob was a series editor for the *Learn 97*, *Learn 2000*, and *Learn XP* books. He has a BA in Psychology, an MS in Geography, and an MS in Interdisciplinary Technology from Eastern Michigan University. His doctoral studies were in Instructional Technology at Wayne State University. For fun, Bob teaches a four-week Computers and Genealogy class and has written genealogy and local history books.

Acknowledgments from John Preston, Sally Preston, and Robert L. Ferrett

We would like to acknowledge the efforts of a fine team of editing professionals, with whom we have had the pleasure of working. Jodi McPherson, Jodi Bolognese, Mike Ruel, and Shelley Gaskin did a great job managing and coordinating this effort. We would also like to acknowledge the contributions of Tim Tate, Production Project Manager, and Emily Knight, Marketing Manager, as well as the many reviewers who gave invaluable criticism and suggestions.

About Shelley Gaskin

Shelley Gaskin, Series Editor, is a professor of business and computer technology at Pasadena City College in Pasadena, California. She holds a master's degree in business education from Northern Illinois University and a doctorate in adult and community education from Ball State University. Dr. Gaskin has 15 years of experience in the computer industry with several Fortune 500 companies and has developed and written training materials for custom systems applications in both the public and private sector. She is also the author of books on Microsoft Outlook and word processing.

Acknowledgments from Shelley Gaskin

Many talented individuals worked to produce this book, and I thank them for their continuous support. My Executive Acquisitions Editor, Jodi McPherson, gave me much latitude to experiment with new things. Editorial Project Manager Mike Ruel worked with me through each stage of writing and production. Emily Knight and the Prentice Hall Marketing team worked with me throughout this process to make sure both instructors and students are informed about the benefits of using this series. Also, very big thanks and appreciation goes to Prentice Halls' top-notch Production and Design team: Associate Director Product Development Melonie Salvati, Manager of Production Gail Steier de Acevedo, Senior Production Project Manager and Manufacturing Buyer Tim Tate, Design Manager Maria Lange, Art Director Pat Smythe, Interior Designer Quorum Creative Services, and Cover Designer Brian Salisbury.

Thanks to all!
Shelley Gaskin, Series Editor

Why I Wrote This Series

Dear Professor,

If you are like me, you are frantically busy trying to implement new course delivery methods (e.g., online) while also maintaining your regular campus schedule of classes and academic responsibilities. I developed this series for colleagues like you, who are long on commitment and expertise but short on time and assistance.

The primary goal of the **GO! Series**, aside from the obvious one of teaching **Microsoft® Office 2003** concepts and skills, is ease of implementation using any delivery method—traditional, self-paced, or online.

There are no lengthy passages of text; instead, bits of expository text are woven into the steps at the teachable moment. This is the point at which the student has a context within which he or she can understand the concept. A scenario-like approach is used in a manner that makes sense, but it does not attempt to have the student "pretend" to be someone else.

A key feature of this series is the use of Microsoft procedural syntax. That is, steps begin with where the action is to take place, followed by the action itself. This prevents the student from doing the right thing in the wrong place!

The *GO! Series* is written with all of your everyday classroom realities in mind. For example, in each project, the student is instructed to insert his or her name in a footer and to save the document with his or her name. Thus, unidentified printouts do not show up at the printer nor do unidentified documents get stored on the hard drives.

Finally, an overriding consideration is that the student is not always working in a classroom with a teacher. Students frequently work at home or in a lab staffed only with instructional aides. Thus, the instruction must be error-free, clearly written, and logically arranged.

My students enjoy learning the Microsoft Office software. The goal of the instruction in the *GO! Series* is to provide students with the skills to solve business problems using the computer as a tool, for both themselves and the organizations for which they might be employed.

Thank you for using the **GO! Series for Microsoft® Office System 2003** for your students.

Regards,

Shelley Gaskin

Shelley Gaskin, Series Editor

Preface

Philosophy

Our overall philosophy is ease of implementation for the instructor, whether instruction is via lecture, lab, online, or partially self-paced. Right from the start, the *GO! Series* was created with constant input from professors just like you. You've told us what works, how you teach, and what we can do to make your classroom time problem free, creative, and smooth running—to allow you to concentrate on not what you are teaching from but who you are teaching to—your students. We feel that we have succeeded with the *GO! Series*. Our aim is to make this instruction high quality in both content and presentation, and the classroom management aids complete—an instructor could begin teaching the course with only 15 minutes advance notice. An instructor could leave the classroom or computer lab; students would know exactly how to proceed in the text, know exactly what to produce to demonstrate mastery of the objectives, and feel that they had achieved success in their learning. Indeed, this philosophy is essential for real-world use in today's diverse educational environment.

How did we do it?

- All steps utilize **Microsoft Procedural Syntax**. The *GO! Series* puts students where they need to be, before instructing them what to do. For example, instead of instructing students to "Save the file," we go a few steps further and phrase the instruction as "On the **Menu** bar, click **File**, and then select **Save As**."

- A unique teaching system (packaged together in one easy to use **Instructor's Edition** binder set) that enables you to teach anywhere you have to—online, lab, lecture, self-paced, and so forth. The supplements are designed to save you time:

    - ***Expert Demonstration Document***—A new project that mirrors the learning objectives of the in-chapter project, with a full demonstration script for you to give a lecture overview quickly and clearly.

    - ***Chapter Assignment Sheets***—A sheet listing all the assignments for the chapter. An instructor can quickly insert his or her name, course information, due dates, and points.

    - ***Custom Assignment Tags***—These cutout tags include a brief list of common errors that students could make on each project, with check boxes so instructors don't have to keep writing the same error description over and over! These tags serve a dual purpose: The student can do a final check to make sure all the listed items are correct, and the instructor can check off the items that need to be corrected.

- **Highlighted Overlays**—These are printed and transparent overlays that the instructor lays over the student's assignment paper to see at a glance if the student changed what he or she needed to. Coupled with the Custom Assignment Tags, this creates a "grading and scoring system" that is easy for the instructor to implement.

- **Point Counted Chapter Production Test**—Working hand-in-hand with the Expert Demonstration Document, this is a final test for the student to demonstrate mastery of the objectives.

Goals of the GO! Series

The goals of the *GO! Series* are as follows:

- Make it *easy for the instructor to implement* in any instructional setting through high-quality content and instructional aids and provide the student with a valuable, interesting, important, satisfying, and clearly defined learning experience.

- Enable true diverse delivery for today's diverse audience. The *GO! Series* employs various instructional techniques that address the needs of all types of students in all types of delivery modes.

- Provide *turn-key implementation* in the following instructional settings:

  - Traditional computer classroom—Students experience a mix of lecture and lab.

  - Online instruction—Students complete instruction at a remote location and submit assignments to the instructor electronically—questions answered by instructor through electronic queries.

  - Partially self-paced, individualized instruction—Students meet with an instructor for part of the class, and complete part of the class in a lab setting.

  - Completely self-paced, individualized instruction—Students complete all instruction in an instructor-staffed lab setting.

  - Independent self-paced, individualized instruction—Students complete all instruction in a campus lab staffed with instructional aides.

- Teach—*to maximize the moment*. The *GO! Series* is based on the Teachable Moment Theory. There are no long passages of text; instead, concepts are woven into the steps at the teachable moment. Students always know what they need to do and where to do it.

Pedagogical Approach

The *GO! Series* uses an instructional system approach that incorporates three elements:

- *Steps are written in* **Microsoft Procedural Syntax**, which prevents the student from doing the right thing but in the wrong place. This makes it easy for the instructor to teach instead of untangle. It tells the student where to go first, then what to do. For example—"On the File Menu, click Properties."

- *Instructional strategies* including five new, unique ancillary pieces to support the instructor experience. The foundation of the instructional strategies is performance based instruction that is constructed in a manner that makes it *easy for the instructor* to demonstrate the content with the GO Series Expert Demonstration Document, guide the practice by using our many end-of-chapter projects with varying guidance levels, and assess the level of mastery with tools such as our Point Counted Production Test and Custom Assignment Tags.

- *A physical design* that makes it *easy for the instructor* to answer the question, "What do they have to do?" and makes it easy for the student to answer the question, "What do I have to do?" Most importantly, you told us what was needed in the design. We held several focus groups throughout the country where we showed **you** our design drafts and let you tell us what you thought of them. We revised our design based on your input to be functional and support the classroom experience. For example, you told us that a common problem is students not realizing where a project ends. So, we added an "END. You have completed the Project" at the close of every project.

Microsoft Procedural Syntax

Do you ever do something right but in the wrong place?

That's why we've written the *GO! Series* step text using Microsoft procedural syntax. That is, the student is informed where the action should take place before describing the action to take. For example, "On the menu bar, click File," versus "Click File on the menu bar." This prevents the student from doing the right thing in the wrong place. This means that step text usually begins with a preposition—a locator—rather than a verb. Other texts often misunderstand the theory of performance-based instruction and frequently attempt to begin steps with a verb. In fact, the objectives should begin with a verb, not the steps.

The use of Microsoft procedural syntax is one of the key reasons that the *GO! Series* eases the burden for the instructor. The instructor spends less time untangling students' unnecessary actions and more time assisting students with real questions. No longer will students become frustrated and say "But I did what it said!" only to discover that, indeed, they *did* do "what it said" but in the wrong place!

Chapter Organization—Color-Coded Projects

All of the chapters in every *GO! Series* book are organized around interesting projects. Within each chapter, all of the instructional activities will cluster around these projects without any long passages of text for the student to read. Thus, every instructional activity contributes to the completion of the project to which it is associated. Students learn skills to solve real business problems; they don't waste time learning every feature the software has. The end-of-chapter material consists of additional projects with varying levels of difficulty.

The chapters are based on the following basic hierarchy:

Project Name

> **Objective Name** (begins with a verb)

>> **Activity Name** (begins with a gerund)

>>> **Numbered Steps** (begins with a preposition or a verb using Microsoft Procedural Syntax.)

Project Name → **Project 1A Exploring Outlook 2003**

Objective Name → **Objective 1**
Start Outlook and Identify Outlook Window Elements

Activity Name → **Activity 1.1** Starting Outlook

Numbered Steps → **1** On the Windows taskbar, click the Start button, determine from your instructor or lab coordinator where the Microsoft Office Outlook 2003 program is located on your system, and then click Microsoft Office Outlook 2003.

A project will have a number of objectives associated with it, and the objectives, in turn, will have one or more activities associated with them. Each activity will have a series of numbered steps. To further enhance understanding, each project, and its objectives and numbered steps, is color coded for fast, easy recognition.

In-Chapter Boxes and Elements

Within every chapter there are helpful boxes and in-line notes that aid the students in their mastery of the performance objectives. Plus, each box has a specific title—"Does Your Notes Button Look Different?" or "To Open the New Appointment Window." Our GO! Series Focus Groups told us to add box titles that indicate the information being covered in the box, and we listened!

Alert!

Does Your Notes Button Look Different?

The size of the monitor and screen resolution set on your computer controls the number of larger module buttons that appear at the bottom of the Navigation pane.

Alert! boxes do just that—they alert students to a common pitfall or spot where trouble may be encountered.

Another Way

To Open the New Appointment Window

You can create a new appointment window using one of the following techniques:

• On the menu bar, click File, point to New, and click Appointment.

• On the Calendar Standard toolbar, click the New Appointment button.

Another Way boxes explain simply "another way" of going about a task or shortcuts for saving time.

Note — Server Connection Dialog Box

If a message displays indicating that a connection to the server could not be established, click OK. Even without a mail server connection, you can still use the personal information management features of Outlook.

Notes highlight additional information pertaining to a task.

More Knowledge — Creating New Folders

A module does not have to be active in order to create new folders within it. From the Create New Folder text box, you can change the type of items that the new folder will contain and then select any location in which to place the new folder. Additionally, it is easy to move a folder created in one location to a different location.

More Knowledge is a more detailed look at a topic or task.

Organization of the GO! Series

The *GO! Series for Microsoft® Office System 2003* includes several different combinations of texts to best suit your needs.

- **Word, Excel, Access, and PowerPoint 2003** are available in the following editions:

  - **Brief:** Chapters 1–3 (1–4 for Word 2003)

  - **Volume 1:** Chapters 1–6
    ~ Microsoft Office Specialist Certification

  - **Volume 2:** Chapters 7–12 (7–8 for PowerPoint 2003)

  - **Comprehensive:** Chapters 1–12 (1–8 for PowerPoint 2003)
    ~ Microsoft Office Expert Certification for Word and Excel 2003.

- Additionally, the *GO! Series* is available in four combined **Office 2003** texts:

  - **Microsoft® Office 2003 Getting Started** contains the Windows XP Introduction and first chapter from each application (Word, Excel, Access, and PowerPoint).

  - **Microsoft® Office 2003 Brief** contains Chapters 1–3 of Excel, Access, and PowerPoint, and Chapters 1–4 of Word. Four additional supplementary "Getting Started" books are included (Internet Explorer, Computer Concepts, Windows XP, and Outlook 2003).

  - **Microsoft® Office 2003 Intermediate** contains Chapters 4–8 of Excel, Access, and PowerPoint, and Chapters 5–8 of Word.

  - **Microsoft® Office 2003 Advanced** version picks up where the Intermediate leaves off, covering advanced topics for the individual applications. This version contains Chapters 9–12 of Word, Excel, and Access.

Microsoft Office Specialist Certification

The *GO! Series* has been approved by Microsoft for use in preparing for the Microsoft Office Specialist exams. The Microsoft Office Specialist program is globally recognized as the standard for demonstrating desktop skills with the Microsoft Office System of business productivity applications (Microsoft Word, Microsoft Excel, Microsoft Access, Microsoft PowerPoint, and Microsoft Outlook). With Microsoft Office Specialist certification, thousands of people have demonstrated increased productivity and have proved their ability to utilize the advanced functionality of these Microsoft applications.

Instructor and Student Resources

Instructor's Resource Center and Instructor's Edition

The *GO! Series* was designed for you—instructors who are long on commitment and short on time. *We asked you how you use our books and supplements and how we can make it easier for you and save you valuable time.* We listened to what you told us and created this Instructor's Resource Center for you—different from anything you have ever had access to from other texts and publishers.

What is the Instructor's Edition?

1) Instructor's Edition

New from Prentice Hall, exclusively for the *GO! Series*, the Instructor's Edition contains the entire book, wrapped with vital margin notes—things like objectives, a list of the files needed for the chapter, teaching tips, Microsoft Office Specialist objectives covered, and MORE! Below is a sample of the many helpful elements in the Instructor's Edition.

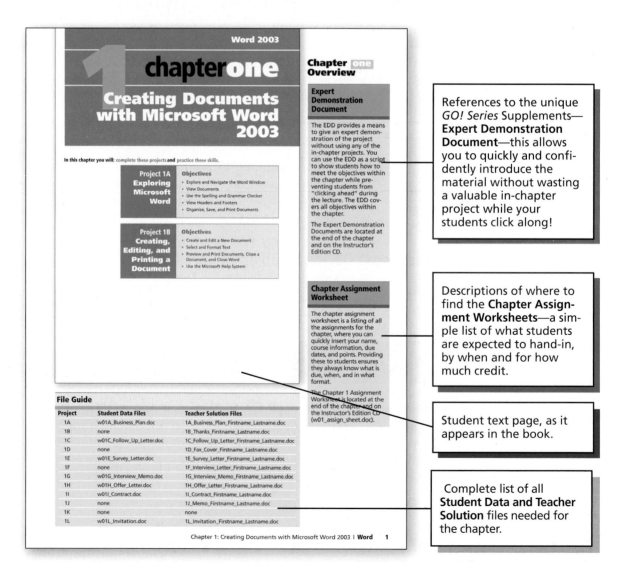

References to the unique *GO! Series* Supplements—**Expert Demonstration Document**—this allows you to quickly and confidently introduce the material without wasting a valuable in-chapter project while your students click along!

Descriptions of where to find the **Chapter Assignment Worksheets**—a simple list of what students are expected to hand-in, by when and for how much credit.

Student text page, as it appears in the book.

Complete list of all **Student Data and Teacher Solution** files needed for the chapter.

Reference to Prentice Hall's Companion Website for the *GO! Series*: **www.prenhall.com/go**

CW

www.prenhall.com/go

The Companion Website is an online training tool that includes personalization features for registered instructors. Data files are available here for download as well as access to additional quizzing exercises.

Each chapter also tells you where to find another unique *GO! Series* Supplement—the **Custom Assignment Tags**—use these in combination with the highlighted overlays to save you time! Simply check off what the students missed or if they completed all the tasks correctly.

Custom Assignment Tags

Custom Assignment Tags, which are meant to be cut out and attached to assignments, serve a dual purpose: the student can do a final check to make sure all the listed items are correct, and the instructor can quickly check off the items that need to be corrected and simply return the assignment.

The Chapter 1 Custom Assignment Tags are located at the end of the chapter and on the Instructor's Edition CD (w01_assign_tags.doc).

The Perfect Party

The Perfect Party store, owned by two partners, provides a wide variety of party accessories including invitations, favors, banners and flags, balloons, piñatas, etc. Party-planning services include both custom parties with pre-filled custom "goodie bags" and "parties in a box" that include everything needed to throw a theme party. Big sellers in this category are the Football and Luau themes. The owners are planning to open a second store and expand their party-planning services to include catering.

© Getty Images, Inc.

Getting Started with Microsoft Office Word 2003

Word processing is the most common program found on personal computers and one that almost everyone has a reason to use. When you learn word processing you are also learning skills and techniques that you need to work efficiently on a personal computer. Use Microsoft Word to do basic word processing tasks such as writing a memo, a report, or a letter. You can also use Word to do complex word processing tasks, including sophisticated tables, embedded graphics, and links to other documents and the Internet. Word is a program that you can learn gradually, adding more advanced skills one at a time.

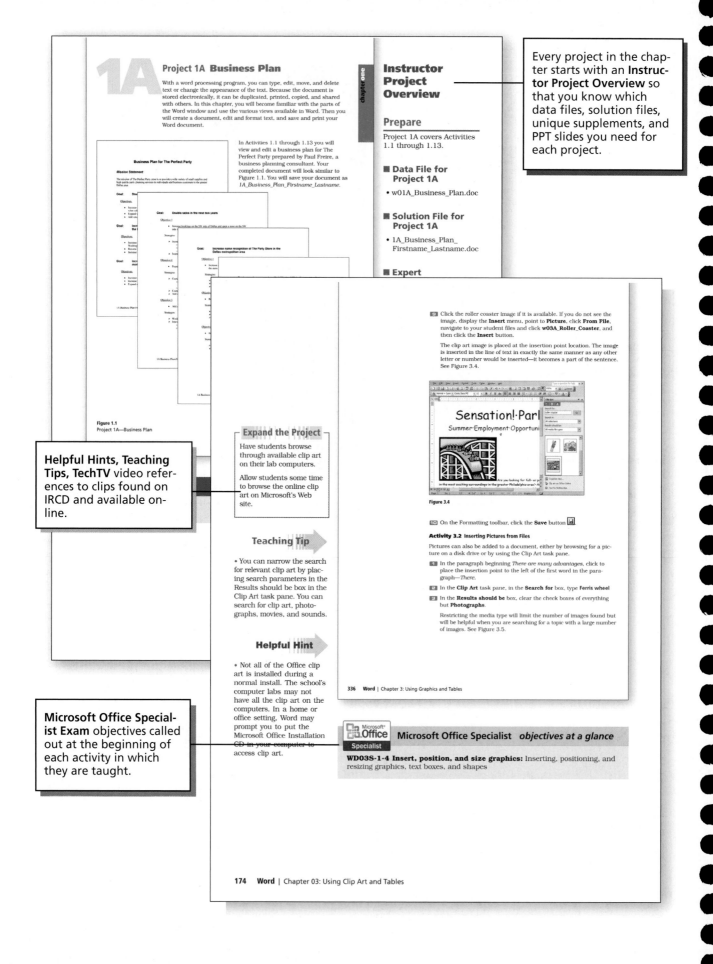

Every project in the chapter starts with an **Instructor Project Overview** so that you know which data files, solution files, unique supplements, and PPT slides you need for each project.

Helpful Hints, Teaching Tips, TechTV video references to clips found on IRCD and available online.

Microsoft Office Specialist Exam objectives called out at the beginning of each activity in which they are taught.

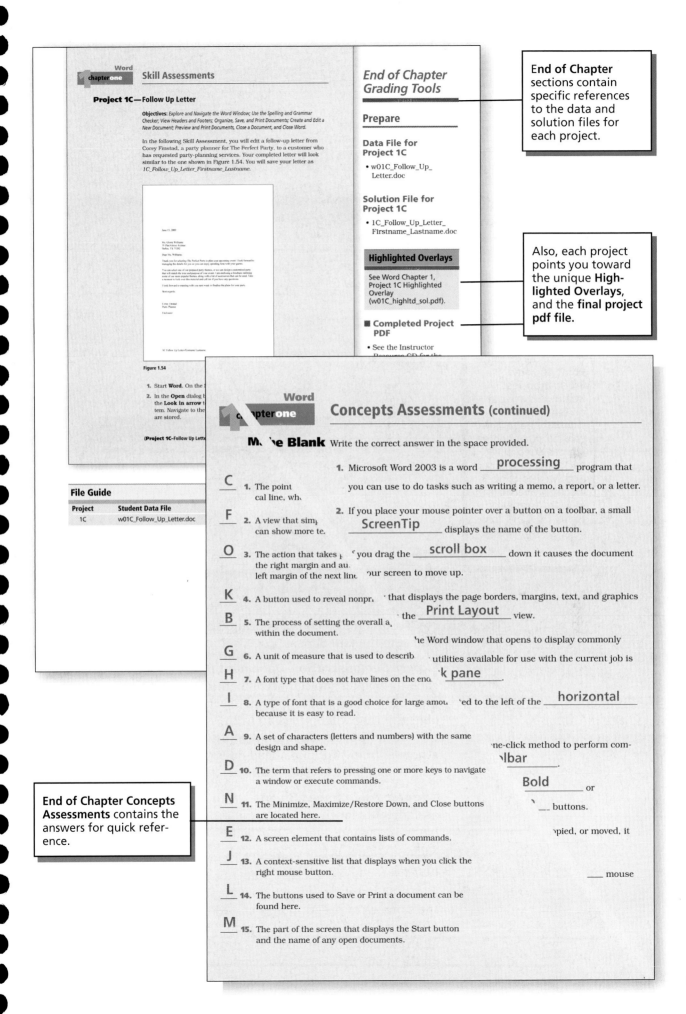

End of Chapter sections contain specific references to the data and solution files for each project.

Also, each project points you toward the unique **Highlighted Overlays**, and the **final project pdf file**.

End of Chapter Concepts Assessments contains the answers for quick reference.

Word

chapter **one**   **Skill Assessments**

Project 1C—Follow Up Letter

Objectives: Explore and Navigate the Word Window; Use the Spelling and Grammar Checker; View Headers and Footers; Organize, Save, and Print Documents; Create and Edit a New Document; Preview and Print Documents, Close a Document, and Close Word.

In the following Skill Assessment, you will edit a follow-up letter from Corey Finstad, a party planner for The Perfect Party, to a customer who has requested party-planning services. Your completed letter will look similar to the one shown in Figure 1.54. You will save your letter as *1C_Follow_Up_Letter_Firstname_Lastname.*

Figure 1.54

1. Start **Word**. On the
2. In the **Open** dialog
   the **Look in arrow** t
   tem. Navigate to the
   are stored.

(Project 1C–Follow Up Letter

File Guide

Project	Student Data File
1C	w01C_Follow_Up_Letter.doc

End of Chapter Grading Tools

Prepare

Data File for Project 1C
- w01C_Follow_Up_Letter.doc

Solution File for Project 1C
- 1C_Follow_Up_Letter_Firstname_Lastname.doc

Highlighted Overlays

See Word Chapter 1, Project 1C Highlighted Overlay (w01C_highltd_sol.pdf).

■ **Completed Project PDF**
- See the Instructor

Word

chapter **one**   **Concepts Assessments** (continued)

Fill in the Blank Write the correct answer in the space provided.

__C__ 1. The point
    cal line, wh

__F__ 2. A view that simp
    can show more te.

__O__ 3. The action that takes ʲ ʽyou drag the
    the right margin and au.
    left margin of the next line. ʲour screen to move up.

__K__ 4. A button used to reveal nonpr. ʲ that displays the page borders, margins, text, and graphics

__B__ 5. The process of setting the overall aʲ
    within the document.

__G__ 6. A unit of measure that is used to describ ʲ utilities available for use with the current job is

__H__ 7. A font type that does not have lines on the eno. ʲk pane

__I__ 8. A type of font that is a good choice for large amou. ʲed to the left of the
    because it is easy to read.

__A__ 9. A set of characters (letters and numbers) with the same
    design and shape.   ʲne-click method to perform com-

__D__ 10. The term that refers to pressing one or more keys to navigate ʲlbar
    a window or execute commands.

__N__ 11. The Minimize, Maximize/Restore Down, and Close buttons
    are located here.

__E__ 12. A screen element that contains lists of commands.

__J__ 13. A context-sensitive list that displays when you click the
    right mouse button.

__L__ 14. The buttons used to Save or Print a document can be
    found here.

__M__ 15. The part of the screen that displays the Start button
    and the name of any open documents.

1. Microsoft Word 2003 is a word _____processing_____ program that you can use to do tasks such as writing a memo, a report, or a letter.

2. If you place your mouse pointer over a button on a toolbar, a small _____ScreenTip_____ displays the name of the button.

3. The action that takes ʲyou drag the _____scroll box_____ down it causes the document

4. A button used to reveal nonpr. ʲthat displays the page borders, margins, text, and graphics _____Print Layout_____ view.

5. ʲhe Word window that opens to display commonly

6. _____k pane_____.

7. ʲed to the left of the _____horizontal_____

ʲlbar _____.

_____Bold_____ or

`_____ buttons.

ʲpied, or moved, it

_____ mouse

Chapter summary pages contain links to Glossary and Key Terms, as well as information about Online Courses and Prentice Hall's Train and Assess Generation IT—online training and assessment.

Another supplement exclusive to the *GO! Series* is the **Point Counted Production Test.** Reminders are put on each chapter summary page, the printed documents are provided in the back of each chapter, and we also provide electronic versions in Word format on the IE CD-ROM for easy customization.

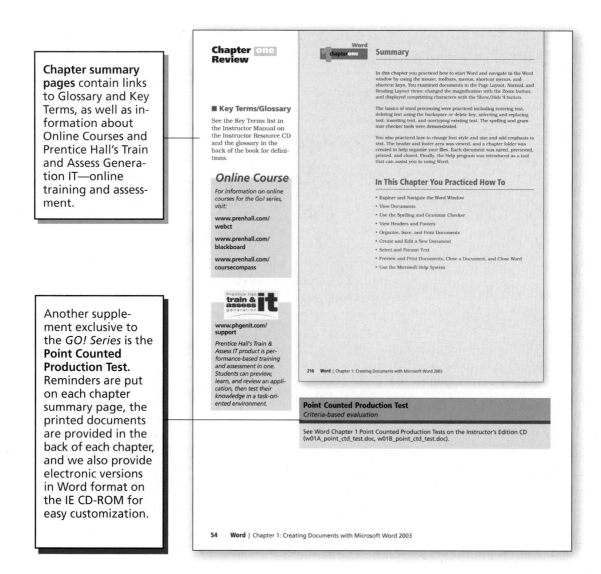

The Instructor's Edition also contains printed copies of these supplement materials *unique* to the *GO! Series*:

- *Expert Demonstration Document (EDD)*—A mirror image of each in-chapter project, accompanied by a brief script. The instructor can use it to give an expert demonstration of each objective that will be covered in the chapter, without having to use one of the chapter's projects. This EDD also prevents students from "working ahead during the presentation," as they do not have access to this document/project.

- *Chapter Assignment Sheets*—With a sheet listing all the assignments for the chapter, the instructor can quickly insert his or her name, course information, due dates, and points.

- *Custom Assignment Tags*—These cutout tags include a brief list of common errors that students could make on each project, with check boxes so instructors don't have to keep writing the same error description over and over! These tags serve a dual purpose: The student can do a final check to make sure all the listed items are correct, and the instructor can check off the items that need to be corrected.

- **Highlighted Overlays**—These are printed and transparent overlays that the instructor lays over the student's assignment paper to see at a glance if the student changed what he or she needed to. Coupled with the Custom Assignment Tags, this creates a "grading and scoring system" that is easy for the instructor to implement.
- **Point Counted Chapter Production Test**—Working hand-in-hand with the EDD, this is a final test for the student to demonstrate mastery of the objectives.

2) Enhanced Instructor's Resource CD-ROM

The Instructor's Resource CD-ROM is an interactive library of assets and links. The Instructor's Resource CD-ROM writes custom "index" pages that can be used as the foundation of a class presentation or online lecture. By navigating through the CD-ROM, you can collect the materials that are most relevant to your interests, edit them to create powerful class lectures, copy them to your own computer's hard drive, and/or upload them to an online course management system.

The new and improved Prentice Hall Instructor's Resource CD-ROM includes tools you expect from a Prentice Hall text:

- The Instructor's Manual in Word and PDF formats—includes solutions to all questions and exercises from the book and Companion Website
- Multiple, customizable PowerPoint slide presentations for each chapter
- Data and Solution Files
- Complete Test Bank
- Image library of all figures from the text
- TestGen Software with QuizMaster

  - TestGen is a test generator that lets you view and easily edit test bank questions, transfer them to tests, and print in a variety of formats suitable to your teaching situation. The program also offers many options for organizing and displaying test banks and tests. A built-in random number and text generator makes it ideal for creating multiple versions of tests that involve calculations and provides more possible test items than test bank questions. Powerful search and sort functions let you easily locate questions and arrange them in the order you prefer.

  - QuizMaster allows students to take tests created with TestGen on a local area network. The QuizMaster utility built into TestGen lets instructors view student records and print a variety of reports. Building tests is easy with TestGen, and exams can be easily uploaded into WebCT, Blackboard, and CourseCompass.

3) Instructor's Edition CD-ROM

The Instructor's Edition CD-ROM contains PDF versions of the Instructor's Edition as well as Word versions of the *GO! Series* unique supplements for easy instructor customization.

Training and Assessment—www2.phgenit.com/support

 Prentice Hall offers performance-based training and assessment in one product—Train&Assess IT. The training component offers computer-based training that a student can use to preview, learn, and review Microsoft Office application skills. Web or CD-ROM delivered, Train IT offers interactive, multimedia, computer-based training to augment classroom learning. Built-in prescriptive testing suggests a study path based not only on student test results but also on the specific textbook chosen for the course.

The assessment component offers computer-based testing that shares the same user interface as Train IT and is used to evaluate a student's knowledge about specific topics in Word, Excel, Access, PowerPoint, Outlook, the Internet, and Computing Concepts. It does this in a task-oriented environment to demonstrate proficiency as well as comprehension of the topics by the students. More extensive than the testing in Train IT, Assess IT offers more administrative features for the instructor and additional questions for the student.

Assess IT also allows professors to test students out of a course, place students in appropriate courses, and evaluate skill sets.

Companion Website @ www.prenhall.com/go

This text is accompanied by a Companion Website at www.prenhall.com/go. Features of this new site include an interactive study guide, downloadable supplements, online end-of-chapter materials, additional practice projects, Web resource links, and technology updates and bonus chapters on the latest trends and hottest topics in information technology. All links to Web exercises will be constantly updated to ensure accuracy for students.

CourseCompass—www.coursecompass.com

 CourseCompass is a dynamic, interactive online course-management tool powered exclusively for Pearson Education by Blackboard. This exciting product allows you to teach market-leading Pearson Education content in an easy-to-use, customizable format.

Blackboard—www.prenhall.com/blackboard

 Prentice Hall's abundant online content, combined with Blackboard's popular tools and interface, result in robust Web-based courses that are easy to implement, manage, and use—taking your courses to new heights in student interaction and learning.

WebCT—www.prenhall.com/webct

 Course-management tools within WebCT include page tracking, progress tracking, class and student management, gradebook, communication, calendar, reporting tools, and more. Gold Level Customer Support, available exclusively to adopters of Prentice Hall courses, is provided free-of-charge on adoption and provides you with priority assistance, training discounts, and dedicated technical support.

TechTV—www.techtv.com

 TechTV is the San Francisco-based cable network that showcases the smart, edgy, and unexpected side of technology. By telling stories through the prism of technology, TechTV provides programming that celebrates its viewers' passion, creativity, and lifestyle.

TechTV's programming falls into three categories:

1. **Help and Information**, with shows like *The Screen Savers*, TechTV's daily live variety show featuring everything from guest interviews and celebrities to product advice and demos; *Tech Live*, featuring the latest news on the industry's most important people, companies, products, and issues; and *Call for Help*, a live help and how-to show providing computing tips and live viewer questions.

2. **Cool Docs**, with shows like *The Tech Of...*, a series that goes behind the scenes of modern life and shows you the technology that makes things tick; *Performance*, an investigation into how technology and science are molding the perfect athlete; and *Future Fighting Machines*, a fascinating look at the technology and tactics of warfare.

3. **Outrageous Fun**, with shows like *X-Play*, exploring the latest and greatest in videogaming; and *Unscrewed* with Martin Sargent, a new late-night series showcasing the darker, funnier world of technology.

For more information, log onto www.techtv.com or contact your local cable or satellite provider to get TechTV in your area.

Visual Walk-Through

Project-based Instruction

Students do not practice features of the application; they create real projects that they will need in the real world. Projects are color coded for easy reference.

Projects are named to reflect skills the student will be practicing, not vague project names.

Word 2003

chapter**one**

Creating Documents with Microsoft Word 2003

In this chapter you will: complete these projects and practice these skills.

Project 1A Exploring Microsoft Word	**Objectives**
	• Explore and Navigate the Word Window
	• View Documents
	• Use the Spelling and Grammar Checker
	• View Headers and Footers
	• Organize, Save, and Print Documents

Project 1B Creating, Editing, and Printing a Document	**Objectives**
	• Create and Edit a New Document
	• Select and Format Text
	• Preview and Print Documents, Close a Document, and Close Word
	• Use the Microsoft Help System

Learning Objectives

Objectives are clustered around projects. They help students to learn how to solve problems, not just learn software features.

Each chapter opens with a story that sets the stage for the projects the student will create, not force them to pretend to be someone or make up a scenario themselves.

The Greater Atlanta Job Fair

The Greater Atlanta Job Fair is a nonprofit organization that holds targeted job fairs in and around the greater Atlanta area several times each year. The fairs are widely marketed to companies nationwide and locally. The organization also presents an annual Atlanta Job Fair that draws over 2,000 employers in more than 70 industries and generally registers more than 5,000 candidates.

©Getty Images, Inc.

Getting Started with Outlook 2003

Do you sometimes find it a challenge to manage and complete all the tasks related to your job, family, and class work? Microsoft Office Outlook 2003 can help. Outlook 2003 is a personal information management program (also known as a PIM) that does two things: (1) it helps you get organized, and (2) it helps you communicate with others efficiently. Successful people know that good organizational and communication skills are important. Outlook 2003 electronically stores and organizes appointments and due dates; names, addresses, and phone numbers; to do lists; and notes. Another major use of Outlook 2003 is its e-mail and fax capabilities, along with features with which you can manage group work such as the tasks assigned to a group of coworkers. In this introduction to Microsoft Office Outlook 2003, you will explore the modules available in Outlook and enter data into each module.

Each chapter has an introductory paragraph that briefs students on what is important.

Visual Summary

Shows students up front what their projects will look like when they are done.

Objective

The skills they will learn are clearly stated at the beginning of each project and color coded to match projects listed on the chapter opener page.

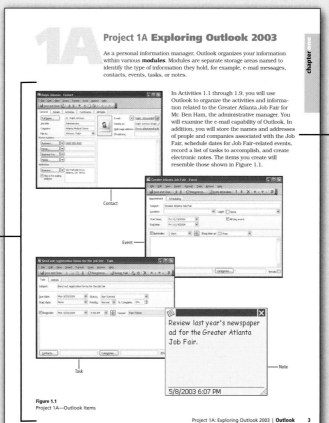

Project Summary

Stated clearly and quickly in one paragraph with the Visual Summary formatted as a caption so your students won't skip it.

Teachable Moment

Expository text is woven into the steps—at the moment students need to know it—not chunked together in a block of text that will go unread.

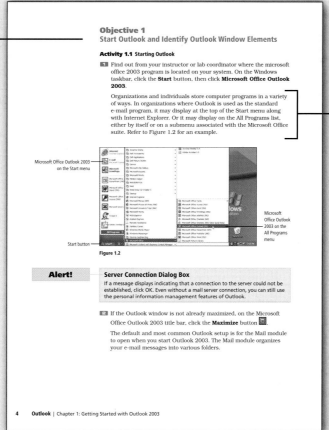

Steps

Color coded to the current project, easy to read, and not too many to confuse the student or too few to be meaningless.

Sequential Page Numbering

No more confusing letters and abbreviations.

End of Project Icon

All projects in the *GO! Series* have clearly identifiable end points, useful in self-paced or on-line environments.

Microsoft Procedural Syntax

All steps are written in Microsoft Procedural Syntax in order to put the student in the right place at the right time.

Objective 5
Organize, Save, and Print Documents

In the same way that you use file folders to organize your paper documents, Windows uses a hierarchy of electronic folders to keep your electronic files organized. Check with your instructor or lab coordinator to see where you will be storing your documents (for example, on your own disk or on a network drive) and whether there is any suggested file folder arrangement. Throughout this textbook, you will be instructed to save your files using the file name followed by your first and last name. Check with your instructor to see if there is some other file naming arrangement for your course.

Activity 1.12 Creating Folders for Document Storage and Saving a Document

When you save a document file, the Windows operating system stores your document permanently on a storage medium—either a disk that you have inserted into the computer, the hard drive of your computer, or a network drive connected to your computer system. Changes that you make to existing documents, such as changing text or typing in new text, are not permanently saved until you perform a Save operation.

1 On the menu bar, click **File**, and then click **Save As**.

The Save As dialog box displays.

2 In the **Save As** dialog box, at the right edge of the **Save in** box, click the **Save in arrow** to view a list of the drives available to you as shown in Figure 1.30. The list of drives and folders will differ from the one shown.

Figure 1.30

Activity 1.13 Printing a Document From the Toolbar

In Activity 1.13, you will print your document from the toolbar.

1 On the Standard toolbar, click the **Print** button.

One copy of your document prints on the default printer. A total of four pages will print, and your name and file name will print in the footer area of each page.

2 On your printed copy, notice that the formatting marks designating spaces, paragraphs, and tabs, do not print.

3 From the **File** menu, click **Exit**, saving any changes if prompted to do so.

Both the document and the Word program close.

Another Way

Printing a Document

There are two ways to print a document:

- On the Standard or Print Preview toolbar, click the Print button, which will print a single copy of the entire document on the default printer.
- From the File menu, click Print to display the Print dialog box, from which you can select a variety of different options, such as printing multiple copies, printing on a different printer, and printing some but not all pages.

End You have completed Project 1A

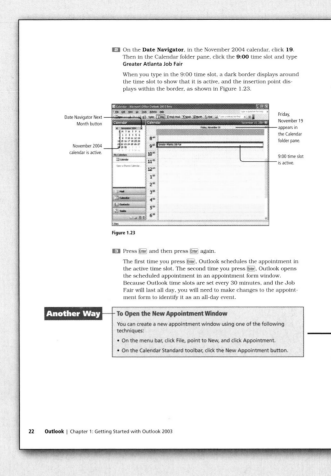

On the **Date Navigator**, in the November 2004 calendar, click **19**. Then in the Calendar folder pane, click the **9:00** time slot and type **Greater Atlanta Job Fair**

When you type in the 9:00 time slot, a dark border displays around the time slot to show that it is active, and the insertion point displays within the border, as shown in Figure 1.23.

Date Navigator Next Month button

November 2004 calendar is active.

Friday, November 19 appears in the Calendar folder pane.

9:00 time slot is active.

Figure 1.23

Press Enter and then press Enter again.

The first time you press Enter, Outlook schedules the appointment in the active time slot. The second time you press Enter, Outlook opens the scheduled appointment in an appointment form window. Because Outlook time slots are set every 30 minutes, and the Job Fair will last all day, you will need to make changes to the appointment form to identify it as an all-day event.

Another Way | **To Open the New Appointment Window**

You can create a new appointment window using one of the following techniques:

• On the menu bar, click File, point to New, and click Appointment.

• On the Calendar Standard toolbar, click the New Appointment button.

Alert box
Draws students' attention to make sure they aren't getting too far off course.

Another Way box
Shows students other ways of doing tasks.

More Knowledge box
Expands on a topic by going deeper into the material.

Note box
Points out important items to remember.

End-of-Chapter Material
Take your pick… Skills Assessment, Performance Assessment, or Mastery Assessment. Real-world projects with high, medium, or low guidance levels.

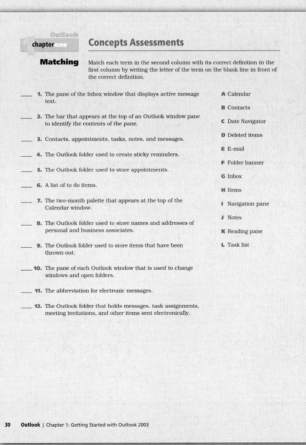

Outlook
chapter one

Concepts Assessments

Matching   Match each term in the second column with its correct definition in the first column by writing the letter of the term on the blank line in front of the correct definition.

_____ 1. The pane of the Inbox window that displays active message text.

_____ 2. The bar that appears at the top of an Outlook window pane to identify the contents of the pane.

_____ 3. Contacts, appointments, tasks, notes, and messages.

_____ 4. The Outlook folder used to create sticky reminders.

_____ 5. The Outlook folder used to store appointments.

_____ 6. A list of to do items.

_____ 7. The two-month palette that appears at the top of the Calendar window.

_____ 8. The Outlook folder used to store names and addresses of personal and business associates.

_____ 9. The Outlook folder used to store items that have been thrown out.

_____ 10. The pane of each Outlook window that is used to change windows and open folders.

_____ 11. The abbreviation for electronic messages.

_____ 12. The Outlook folder that holds messages, task assignments, meeting invitations, and other items sent electronically.

A Calendar

B Contacts

C Date Navigator

D Deleted items

E E-mail

F Folder banner

G Inbox

H Items

I Navigation pane

J Notes

K Reading pane

L Task list

Objectives List

Each project in the GO! Series end-of-chapter section starts with a list of the objectives covered, in order to easily find the exercises you need to hone your skills.

Performance Assessments

Project 1D—Creating Folders for College Fairs

Objectives: *Start Outlook and Create Outlook Folders.*

The fairs for Mercer College and Georgia Tech have been set for April 2005. As a result, you need to create folders to hold vendor information for the fairs. When you have created the contact folders for these two fairs, your Contacts list will appear as in Figure 1.35.

Figure 1.35

1. Start Outlook, open the **Contacts** module, open the main **Contacts** folder, and on the menu bar, click **File**, point to **Folder**, and click **New Folder** to open the **Create New Folder** dialog box.

2. In the **Name** text box, type **Mercer College Fair 2005** ensure that **Contact Items** appears in the **Folder contains** text box, and click **OK**.

3. Repeat the procedures in Steps 1 and 2 to create another contacts folder named **Georgia Tech Fair 2005**

End You have completed Project 1D

End of Each Project Clearly Marked

Groups of steps that the student performs; the guided practice in order to master the learning objective.

On the Internet

In this section, students are directed to go out to the Internet for independent study.

On the Internet

Locating Friends on the Web

The World Wide Web not only stores information about companies, Web sites for bidding on items, and so forth, but it also contains telephone book information as well as e-mail addresses for many people—especially those who are students at universities! Search the Web for the colleges that three of your friends attend. After you locate the sites, search each university's e-mail directory for one of your friends. Then record these friends and their university e-mail addresses in your contacts list. Print a copy of each contact form as you create it.

GO! with Help

Training on Outlook

Microsoft Online has set up a series of training lessons at its online Web site. You can access Microsoft.com and review these training sessions directly from the Help menu in Outlook. In this project, you will work your way through the links on the Microsoft Web site to see what training topics they currently offer for Outlook. Log onto the required networks, connect to the Internet, and then follow these steps to complete the exercise.

1. If necessary, start Outlook. On the menu bar, click **Help** and then click **Office on Microsoft.com**.

   The Microsoft Office Online Web page opens in the default browser window.

2. On the left side of the Microsoft Office Online Web page, click the **Training** link.

   The Training Home Web page opens.

3. On the Training Home page, under Browse Training Courses, click **Outlook**.

   The Outlook Courses Web page opens.

4. On the Outlook Courses Web page list, click **Address your e-mail: Get it on the To line fast**.

   The Overview Web page displays information about the training session, identifies the goals of the session, and displays links for continuing the session. Navigation buttons appear in a grey bar toward the top of the Overview page for playing, pausing, and stopping the session. Yellow arrows appear above the navigation bar to advance to the next session page.

5. In the upper right side of the Overview page, on the gray navigation bar, click **Play**.

GO! with Help

A special section where students practice using the HELP feature of the Office application.

Contents in Brief

Table of Contents

chapterone

Creating Documents with Microsoft Word 2003

In this chapter you will: complete these projects **and** practice these skills.

Project 1A
Exploring Microsoft Word

Objectives

- Explore and Navigate the Word Window
- View Documents
- Use the Spelling and Grammar Checker
- View Headers and Footers
- Organize, Save, and Print Documents

Project 1B
Creating, Editing, and Printing a Document

Objectives

- Create and Edit a New Document
- Select and Format Text
- Preview and Print Documents, Close a Document, and Close Word
- Use the Microsoft Help System

The Perfect Party

The Perfect Party store, owned by two partners, provides a wide variety of party accessories including invitations, favors, banners and flags, balloons, piñatas, etc. Party-planning services include both custom parties with pre-filled custom "goodie bags" and "parties in a box" that include everything needed to throw a theme party. Big sellers in this category are the Football and Luau themes. The owners are planning to open a second store and expand their party-planning services to include catering.

© Getty Images, Inc.

Getting Started with Microsoft Office Word 2003

Word processing is the most common program found on personal computers and one that almost everyone has a reason to use. When you learn word processing you are also learning skills and techniques that you need to work efficiently on a personal computer. Use Microsoft Word to do basic word processing tasks such as writing a memo, a report, or a letter. You can also use Word to do complex word processing tasks, including sophisticated tables, embedded graphics, and links to other documents and the Internet. Word is a program that you can learn gradually, adding more advanced skills one at a time.

Project 1A **Business Plan**

With a word processing program, you can type, edit, move, and delete text or change the appearance of the text. Because the document is stored electronically, it can be duplicated, printed, copied, and shared with others. In this chapter, you will become familiar with the parts of the Word window and use the various views available in Word. Then you will create a document, edit and format text, and save and print your Word document.

In Activities 1.1 through 1.13 you will view and edit a business plan for The Perfect Party prepared by Paul Freire, a business planning consultant. Your completed document will look similar to Figure 1.1. You will save your document as *1A_Business_Plan_Firstname_Lastname*.

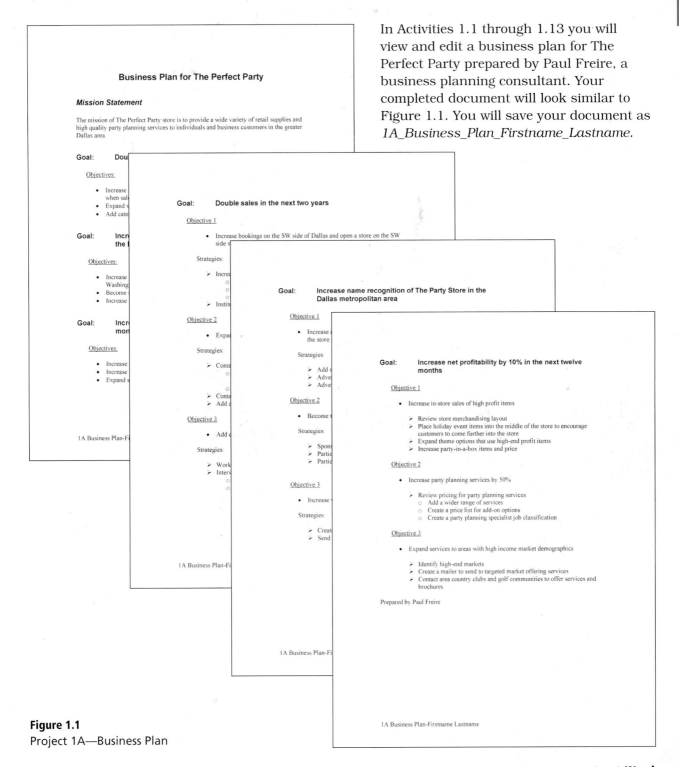

Figure 1.1
Project 1A—Business Plan

Objective 1
Explore and Navigate the Word Window

Activity 1.1 Starting Word and Identifying Parts of the Word Window

1 On the left side of the Windows taskbar, point to and then click the **Start** button [start].

The Start menu displays.

2 On the computer you are using, locate the Word program and then click **Microsoft Office Word 2003**.

Organizations and individuals store computer programs in a variety of ways. The Word program might be located under All Programs or Microsoft Office or at the top of the main Start menu. Refer to Figure 1.2 as an example.

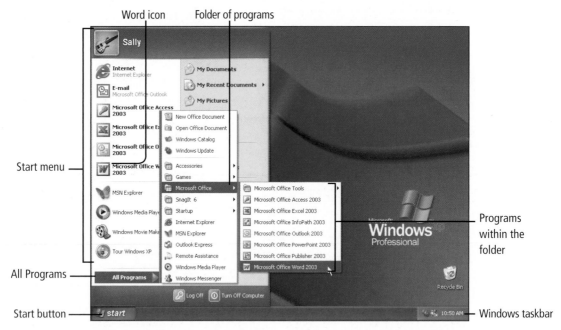

Figure 1.2

3 Look at the opening Word screen, and then take a moment to study the main parts of the screen as shown in Figure 1.3 and described in the table in Figure 1.4.

Alert!

Does your screen differ?

There are several ways to look at a document in the Word window. The appearance of the screen depends on various settings that your system administrator established when the program was installed and how the program has been modified since installation. In many cases, whether a screen element displays depends on how the program was last used.

4 On the Formatting toolbar, click the **Toolbar Options** button ■. If the Standard and Formatting toolbars are on two separate rows as shown in Figure 1.3, move the pointer into the Word document window and click to close the list without making any changes. If the toolbars are sharing a single row, click **Show Buttons on Two Rows**.

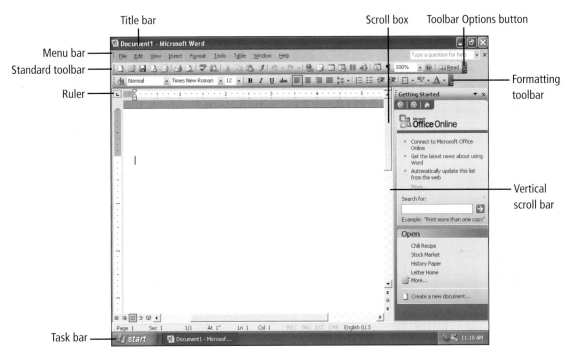

Figure 1.3a

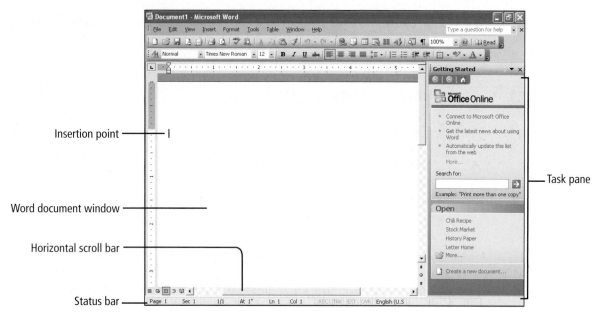

Insertion point ———— |

Task pane

Word document window ————

Horizontal scroll bar ————

Status bar ————

Figure 1.3b

It is easier to use the toolbars if all of the most commonly used buttons are displayed. Most Word users keep the Standard and Formatting toolbars displayed on separate rows.

More Knowledge — Turning on Toolbars

If a toolbar is missing entirely, point to an existing toolbar or to the menu bar and click the right mouse button (also known as right-clicking). On the shortcut menu that displays, point to the name of the toolbar you want to display and click the left mouse button. A shortcut menu is a context-sensitive menu of commands relevant to the particular item. Alternatively, display the View menu, click Toolbars, and then click the name of the toolbar you want to display. If a toolbar is open, a check mark displays to the left of the toolbar name.

Microsoft Word Screen Elements

Screen Element	Description
Title bar	Displays the program icon, the name of the document, and the name of the program. The Minimize, Maximize/Restore Down, and Close buttons are grouped on the right side of the title bar.
Menu bar	Contains a list of commands. To display a menu, click on the menu name.
Standard toolbar	Contains buttons for some of the most common commands in Word. It may occupy an entire row or share a row with the Formatting toolbar.
Formatting toolbar	Contains buttons for some of the most common formatting options in Word. It may occupy an entire row or share a row with the Standard toolbar.
Ruler	Displays the location of margins, indents, columns, and tab stops.
Vertical scroll bar	Enables you to move up and down in a document to display text that is not visible.
Horizontal scroll bar	Enables you to move left and right in a document to display text that is not visible.
Scroll box	Provides a visual indication of your location in a document. It can also be used with the mouse to drag a document up and down.
Toolbar Options button	Displays a list of all of the buttons associated with a toolbar. It also enables you to place the Standard and Formatting toolbars on separate rows or on the same row.
Word document window	Displays the active document.
Insertion point	Indicates, with a blinking vertical line, where text or graphics will be inserted.
Task pane	Displays commonly used commands related to the current task.
Taskbar	Displays the Start button and the name of any open documents. The taskbar may also display shortcut buttons for other programs.
Status bar	Displays the page and section number and other Word settings.

Figure 1.4

Activity 1.2 Opening an Existing Document

1 On the Standard toolbar, click the **Open** button 📂.

The Open dialog box displays.

2 In the **Open** dialog box, click the **Look in arrow** at the right edge of the **Look in** box to view a list of the drives available on your system. See Figure 1.5 as an example—the drives and folders displayed on your screen will differ.

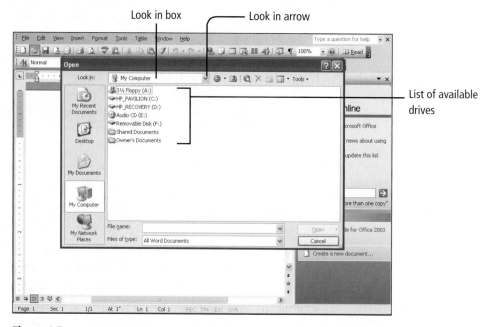

Figure 1.5

3 Navigate to the location where the student files for this textbook are stored.

4 Locate **w01A_Business_Plan** and click once to select it. Then, in the lower right corner of the **Open** dialog box, click the **Open** button. Alternatively, *double-click* the file name to open it—click the left mouse button twice in rapid succession.

The document displays in the Word window. See Figure 1.6.

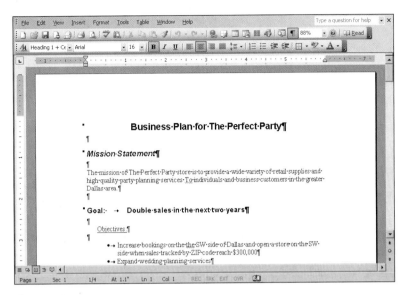

Figure 1.6

Note — Turning Off the Office Assistant

One of Word's Help features is an animated object called the Office Assistant. Many people like to turn this feature off. To hide the Office Assistant, click the right mouse button on the Office Assistant. In the menu that displays, click Hide with the left mouse button. The instruction in this textbook assumes that the Office Assistant is turned off.

Activity 1.3 Accessing Menu Commands and Displaying the Task Pane

Word commands are organized in *menus*—lists of commands within a category. The *menu bar* at the top of the screen provides access to the Word commands. The buttons on the toolbars provide one-click short-cuts to menu commands.

1 On the menu bar, click **View**.

The View menu displays in either the short format as shown in Figure 1.7, or in the full format, which displays all of the menu commands. If the full menu does not display, you can do one of three things:

- Wait a moment and the full menu will display if your system is set to do so.

- At the bottom of the menu, click the double arrows to expand the menu to display all commands.

- Before opening a menu, point to the menu name in the menu bar, and then double-click. This ensures that the full menu displays.

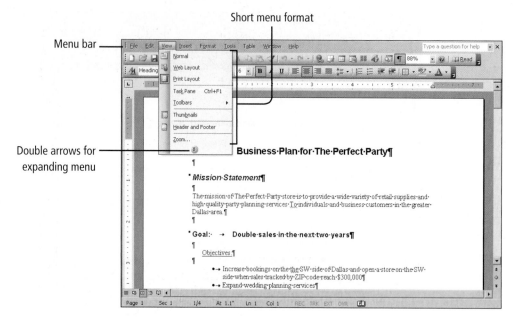

Menu bar

Short menu format

Double arrows for
expanding menu

Figure 1.7

> **Note** — **Turning On Full Menus**
>
> The instruction in this textbook assumes that the full menus display when you click a menu command. To turn on full menus, go to the menu bar, click Tools, and then click Customize. In the Customize dialog box, click the Options tab, and then click the *Always show full menus* check box. Click the Close button to close the dialog box.

2 Be sure that the full menu is displayed as shown in Figure 1.8, and notice to the right of some commands there is a **keyboard shortcut**; for example, *Ctrl+F1* for the task pane.

A keyboard shortcut enables you to perform commands using a combination of keys from your keyboard. For example, if you press and hold down Ctrl and then press F1, the result is the same as clicking View on the menu bar and then clicking Task Pane. Many commands in Word can be accomplished in more than one way.

Keyboard shortcut

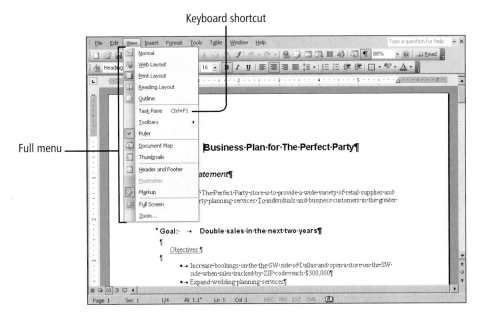

Full menu

Figure 1.8

3 On the displayed **View** menu, to the left of some command names, notice the image of the button that represents this command on a toolbar.

This is a reminder that you can initiate the command with one click from a toolbar, rather than initiating the command with multiple clicks from the menu.

4 On the displayed **View** menu, pause the mouse pointer over **Toolbars** but do not click.

An arrow to the right of a command name indicates that a submenu is available. When you point to this type of menu command, a submenu displays. See Figure 1.9.

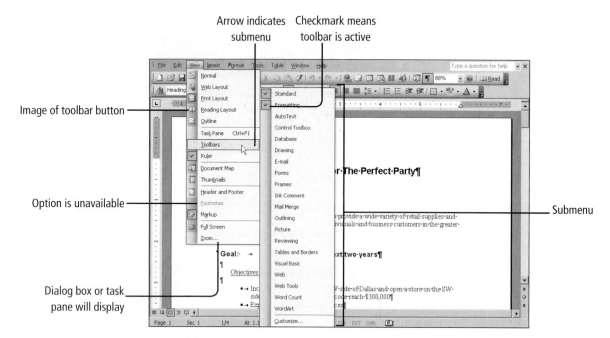

Figure 1.9

5 Look at the full **View** menu on your screen, and notice the various symbols and characters. These are standard across all Microsoft products. Take a moment to study the table in Figure 1.10 for a description of these elements.

Word Menu Characteristics

Characteristic	Description	Example
… (ellipsis)	Indicates that either a dialog box requesting more information or a task pane will display.	Zoom…
▶ (right arrow)	Indicates that a submenu—another menu of choices—will display.	Toolbars ▶
No symbol	Indicates that the command will perform immediately.	Web Layout
✔ (check mark)	Indicates that a command is turned on or active.	✔ Ruler
Gray option name	Indicates that the command is currently unavailable.	Footnotes

Figure 1.10

6 With the **View** menu still displayed, click **Task Pane**.

The Getting Started task pane displays as shown in Figure 1.11. If the task pane was already displayed, it will close. If the task pane was not visible, it will display on the right side of the screen. As you progress in your study of Word, you will see various task panes to assist you in accomplishing Word tasks.

Task Pane

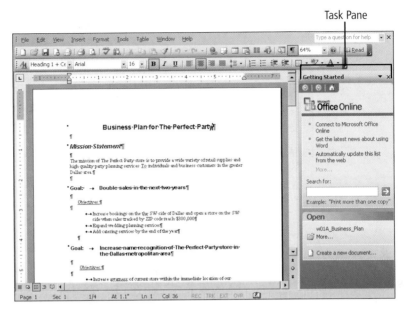

Figure 1.11

7 On the menu bar, click **View**, and then click **Task Pane** again to close the task pane.

For the remainder of this book the task pane should be closed, except when otherwise instructed.

Activity 1.4 Navigating a Document Using the Vertical Scroll Bar

Most Word documents are larger than the Word window. Therefore, there are several ways to *navigate* (move) in a document.

1 At the right of your screen, in the vertical scroll bar, locate the down arrow at the bottom of the bar as shown in Figure 1.12. Then, click the **down scroll arrow** five times.

Notice that the document scrolls up a line at a time. In this document, Word has flagged some spelling and grammar errors (red and green wavy lines), which you will correct in Activity 1.9.

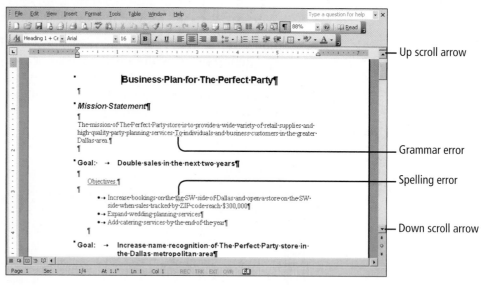

Up scroll arrow

Grammar error

Spelling error

Down scroll arrow

Figure 1.12

2 Point to the **down scroll arrow** again, and then click and hold down the mouse button for several seconds.

The document text scrolls up continuously, a line at a time.

3 At the top of the vertical scroll bar, point to the **up scroll arrow**, and then click and hold down the mouse button until you have scrolled back to the top of the document. As you do so, notice that the scroll box moves up in the scroll bar.

4 At the top of the vertical scroll bar point to the scroll box, and then press and hold down the left mouse button.

A **ScreenTip**—a small box that displays information about, or the name of, a screen element—displays. In this instance, the ScreenTip indicates the page number and the first line of text at the top of the page. See Figure 1.13.

ScreenTip

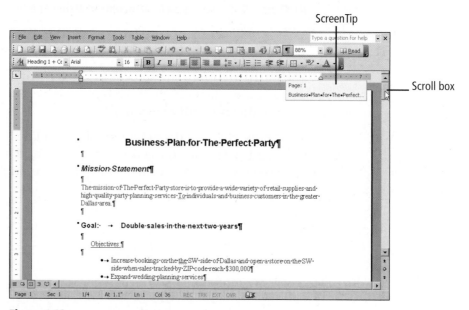

Scroll box

Figure 1.13

5 **_Drag_** (hold down the left mouse button while moving your mouse) the scroll box down to the bottom of the scroll bar. As you do so, watch the ScreenTip.

The ScreenTip changes as each new page reaches the top of the screen. See Figure 1.14.

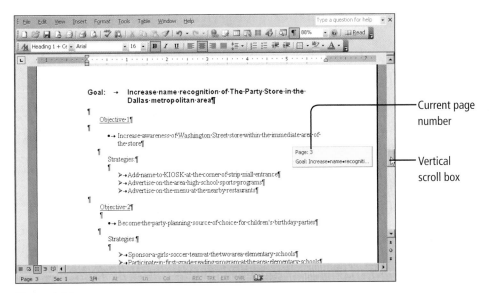

Figure 1.14

6 Release the mouse button, and then click in the gray area above the scroll box.

The document scrolls up one screen.

7 Practice clicking in the area above and below the scroll box.

This is a quick way to scan a document.

Another Way — **Using the Wheel Button on the Mouse**

If your mouse has a small wheel button between the left and right mouse buttons, you can scroll up and down in the document by rotating the wheel.

Activity 1.5 Navigating a Document Using the Keyboard

Keyboard shortcuts are another way to navigate your document quickly. Keyboard shortcuts provide additional navigation techniques that you cannot accomplish with the vertical scroll bar. For example, using keyboard shortcuts, you can move the insertion point to the beginning or end of a word or line.

1 On your keyboard, hold down Ctrl and press Home.

The top of the document displays, and the insertion point moves to the left of the first word in the document.

2 Hold down Ctrl and press End.

The text at the bottom of the last page in the document displays, and the insertion point moves to the right of the last word in the document.

3 Press Page Up.

The document scrolls up one screen.

4 Press End.

The insertion point moves to the end of the current line of text. Take a moment to study the table shown in Figure 1.15, which lists the most commonly used keyboard shortcuts.

Navigating a Document Using Keyboard Shortcuts

To Move	Press
To the beginning of a document	Ctrl + Home
To the end of a document	Ctrl + End
To the beginning of a line	Home
To the end of a line	End
To the beginning of the previous word	Ctrl + ←
To the beginning of the next word	Ctrl + →
To the beginning of the current word (if insertion point is in the middle of a word)	Ctrl + ←
To the beginning of the previous paragraph	Ctrl + ↑
To the end of the next paragraph	Ctrl + ↓
To the beginning of the current paragraph (if insertion point is in the middle of a paragraph)	Ctrl + ↑
Up one screen	Page Up
Down one screen	PageDown

Figure 1.15

5 Hold down Ctrl and press Home to position the insertion point at the beginning of the document.

Objective 2
View Documents

In addition to different document views, there is a method to view characters on your screen that do not print on paper. Examples of these characters include paragraph marks, tabs, and spaces.

Activity 1.6 Displaying Formatting Marks

When you press Enter, Spacebar, or Tab on your keyboard, characters are placed in your document to represent these keystrokes. These characters do not print, and are referred to as ***formatting marks*** or ***nonprinting characters***. Because formatting marks guide your eye in a document like a map and road signs guide you along a highway, these marks will be displayed throughout this instruction.

1 In the displayed document, look at the document title *Business Plan for The Perfect Party* and determine if a paragraph symbol (¶) displays at the end of the title as shown in Figure 1.16. If you do *not* see the paragraph symbol, on the Standard toolbar, click the **Show/Hide ¶** button to display the formatting marks.

Paragraph marks display at the end of every paragraph. Every time you press Enter, a new paragraph is created, and a paragraph mark is inserted. Paragraph marks are especially helpful in showing the number of blank lines inserted in a document. Spaces are indicated by dots, and tabs are indicated by arrows as shown in Figure 1.16.

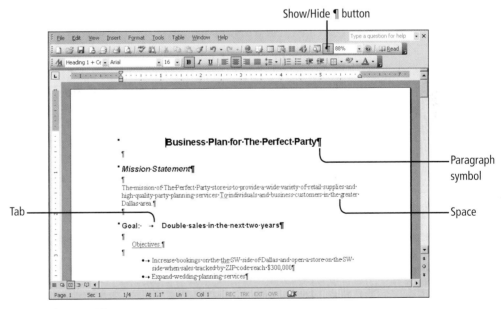

Figure 1.16

2 Click the **Show/Hide ¶** button. This turns off the display of nonprinting characters. Then, click the **Show/Hide ¶** button once more to turn it on again.

Viewing Documents

There are five ways to view your document on the screen. Each view is useful in different situations.

- The Print Layout view displays the page borders, margins, text, and graphics as they will look when you print the document. Most Word users prefer this view for most tasks, and it is the default view.

- The Normal view simplifies the page layout for quick typing, and shows a little more text on the screen than the Print Layout view. Graphics, headers, and footers do not display.

- The Web Layout view shows how the document will look when saved as a Web page and viewed in a Web browser.

- The Reading Layout view creates easy-to-read pages that fit on the screen to increase legibility. This view does not represent the pages as they would print. Each screen page is labeled with a screen number, rather than a page number.

- The Outline view shows the organizational structure of your document by headings and subheadings and can be collapsed and expanded to look at individual sections of a document.

Activity 1.7 Changing Views

1 To the left of the horizontal scroll bar, locate the **View buttons**.

These buttons are used to switch to different document views. Alternatively, you can switch views using the commands on the View menu.

2 Click the **Normal View** button ▤.

The work area covers the entire width of the screen. See Figure 1.17. Page margins are not displayed, and any inserted graphics, **headers**, or **footers** do not display. A header is information at the top of every page, and a footer is information at the bottom of every printed page.

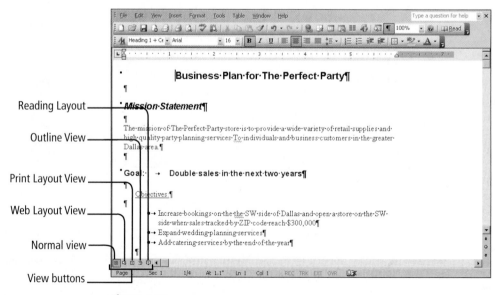

Reading Layout
Outline View
Print Layout View
Web Layout View
Normal view
View buttons

Figure 1.17

3 Click the **Reading Layout** button.

An entire page is displayed, and the text reaches nearly to the bottom. However, this is only about half of the text that is actually on the page as it is formatted and if it were printed. This view has its own toolbars and is optimized for easy reading. You can display side-by-side pages in longer documents, and you can *edit*—make changes to—the document in this view.

Note — Opening the Reading Layout view

The Reading Layout view is also accessible by clicking the Read button [📖 Read] on the Standard toolbar.

4 At the top of the screen, in the Reading Layout toolbar, click **Close** button [📖 Close].

Closing the Reading Layout view returns you to the previous view, which was Normal view.

5 At the left of the horizontal scroll bar, click the **Print Layout View** button.

In this view you can see all of the elements that will display on paper when you print the document. The instruction in this textbook will use the Print Layout View for most documents.

Activity 1.8 Using the Zoom Button

To *zoom* means to increase or to decrease the viewing area of the screen. You can zoom in to look closely at a particular section of a document, and then zoom out to see a whole page on the screen. It is also possible to view multiple pages on the screen.

1 On the Standard toolbar, click the **Zoom button arrow** [100% ▾].

The Zoom list displays as shown in Figure 1.18.

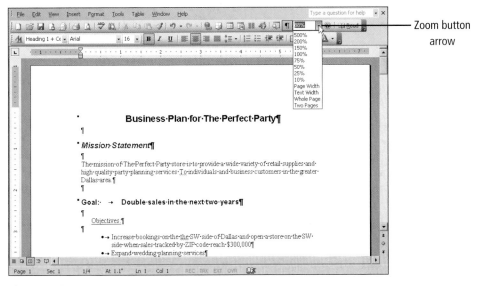

Zoom button arrow

Figure 1.18

2 On the displayed list, click **150%**.

The view of the text is magnified. See Figure 1.19.

Zoom changed to 150%

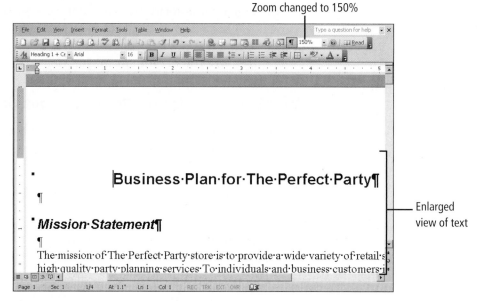

Enlarged
view of text

Figure 1.19

3 On the Standard toolbar, click the **Zoom button arrow** [100% ▾] again and then click **Two Pages**.

Two full pages display on the screen. This magnification enables you to see how the text is laid out on the page and to check the location of other document elements, such as graphics.

4 On the vertical scroll bar, click the down scroll arrow five times.

Notice that you can now see parts of four pages, and you can see how the text flows from one page to another. See Figure 1.20.

Two page view

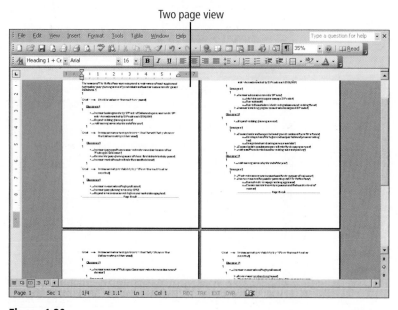

Figure 1.20

5 On the Standard toolbar, click the **Zoom button arrow** `100%` and from the displayed list click **Page Width**.

This is a flexible magnification, displaying the maximum page width, regardless of the size of your screen. The size shown in the Zoom box will vary depending on screen size and resolution.

6 On the Standard toolbar, click on the number in the Zoom box to highlight the number currently displayed. Type **100** and then press Enter.

Typing a number directly into the Zoom box is another method of changing the zoom level.

Objective 3
Use the Spelling and Grammar Checker

As you type, Word compares your words to those in the Word dictionary and compares your phrases and punctuation to a list of grammar rules. Words that are not in the Word dictionary are marked with a wavy red underline. Phrases and punctuation that differ from the grammar rules are marked with a wavy green underline. Because a list of grammar rules applied by a computer program can never be exact, and because a computer dictionary cannot contain all known words and proper names, you will need to check any words flagged by Word as misspellings or grammar errors.

Finally, Word does not check for usage. For example, Word will not flag the word *sign* as misspelled, even though you intended to type *sing a song* rather than *sign a song*, because both are legitimate words contained within Word's dictionary.

Activity 1.9 Checking Individual Spelling and Grammar Errors

One way to check spelling and grammar errors flagged by Word is to right-click the flagged word or phrase and, from the displayed shortcut menu, select a suitable correction or instruction.

1 Hold down Ctrl and press Home to move the insertion point to the top of the document. Scan the text on the screen to locate green and red wavy underlines.

Note — Activating Spelling and Grammar Checking

If you do not see any wavy red or green lines under words, the automatic spelling and/or grammar checking has been turned off on your system. To activate the spelling and grammar checking, display the Tools menu, click Options, and then click the Spelling & Grammar tab. Under Spelling, click the *Check spelling as you type* check box. Under Grammar, click the *Check grammar as you type* check box. There are also check boxes for hiding spelling and grammar errors. These should not be checked. Close the dialog box.

---

2 In the second line of the *Mission Statement*, locate the word *To* with the wavy green underline. Position your mouse pointer over the word and right-click.

A shortcut menu displays as shown in Figure 1.21. A suggested replacement is shown in the top section of the shortcut menu. In this instance, Word has identified an incorrectly capitalized word in the middle of a sentence.

Word underlined in text ⎯⎯⎯⎯⎯

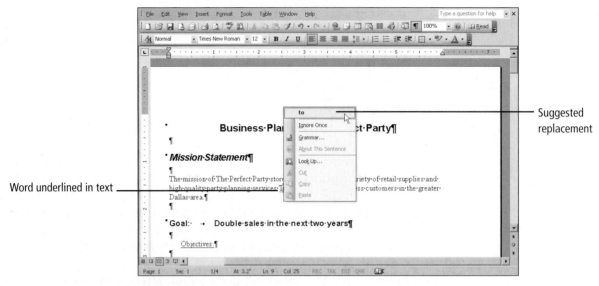

Suggested replacement

Figure 1.21

3 On the shortcut menu, click **to**.

The incorrect word is replaced.

4 In the first bullet point, find the word *the* with a wavy red underline. Position the mouse pointer over the word and right-click.

Word identified a duplicate word, and provides two suggestions—*Delete Repeated Word* or *Ignore*. See Figure 1.22. The second option is included because sometimes the same word will be used twice in succession.

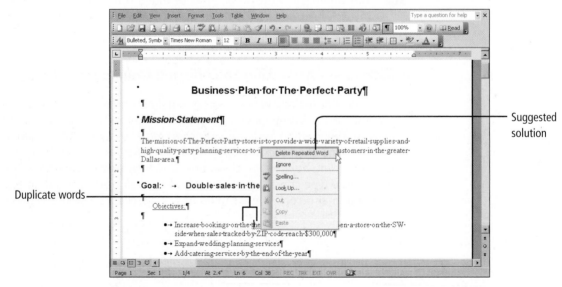

Suggested solution

Duplicate words ⎯⎯⎯⎯⎯

Figure 1.22

5 On the displayed shortcut menu, click **Delete Repeated Word**.

The repeated word is deleted.

Activity 1.10 Checking Spelling and Grammar in an Entire Document

Initiating the spelling and grammar checking feature from the menu or toolbar displays the Spelling and Grammar dialog box, which provides more options than the shortcut menus.

1 On the Standard toolbar, click the **Spelling and Grammar** button to begin a check of the document. If necessary, move your mouse pointer to the title bar of the dialog box, and drag the dialog box out of the way so you can see the misspelled word *awarness*.

The Spelling and Grammar dialog box displays. Under Not in Dictionary, a misspelled word is highlighted, and under Suggestions, two suggestions are presented. See Figure 1.23.

2 Take moment to study the spelling and grammar options available in the **Spelling and Grammar** dialog box as shown in the table in Figure 1.24.

Word not in dictionary ——————

Suggested alternatives ——————

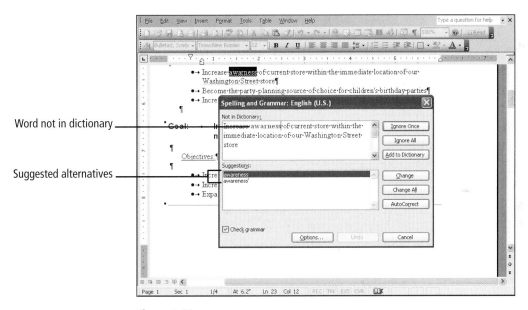

Figure 1.23

Spelling and Grammar Dialog Box Buttons

Button	Action
Ignore Once	Ignores the identified word one time, but flags it in other locations in the document.
Ignore All	Discontinues flagging any instance of the word anywhere in the document.
Add to Dictionary	Adds the word to a custom dictionary, which can be edited. This option does not change the built-in Microsoft Office dictionary.
Change	Changes the identified word to the word highlighted under Suggestions.
Change All	Changes every instance of the word in the document to the word highlighted under Suggestions.
AutoCorrect	Adds the flagged word to the AutoCorrect list, which will subsequently correct the word automatically if misspelled in any documents typed in the future.
Ignore Rule (Grammar)	Ignores the specific rule used to determine a grammar error and removes the green wavy line.
Next Sentence (Grammar)	Moves to the next identified error.
Explain (Grammar)	Displays the rule used to identify a grammar error.
Options	Displays the Spelling and Grammar tab of the Options dialog box.

Figure 1.24

3 Under **Suggestions**, make sure *awareness* is selected, and then click the **Change** button.

The correction is made and the next identified error is highlighted, which is another misspelled word, *merchandixing*.

4 Under **Suggestions**, make sure *merchandising* is selected, and then click the **Change** button.

The misspelled word is corrected, the next identified error is highlighted, and a number of suggestions are provided. This time the word is a proper noun, and it is spelled correctly. You could add this word to your dictionary, or choose to ignore it. See Figure 1.25.

Proper noun

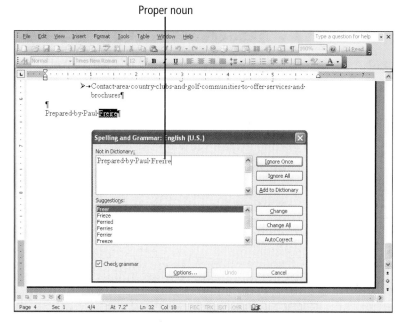

Figure 1.25

5 Click the **Ignore Once** button.

A dialog box displays indicating that the spelling and grammar check is complete. See Figure 1.26.

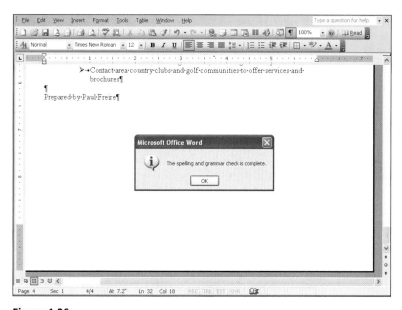

Figure 1.26

6 Click **OK** to close the dialog box.

Objective 4
View Headers and Footers

Headers and footers are areas reserved for text and graphics that repeat at the top (header) or bottom (footer) of each page in a document.

Activity 1.11 Accessing Headers and Footers

1 Display the **View** menu, and then click **Header and Footer**.

The first page of the document displays with the Header area outlined with a dotted line. By default, headers and footers are placed 0.5 inch from the top and bottom of the page, respectively. The Header and Footer toolbar displays, floating on your screen as shown in Figure 1.27.

Header area

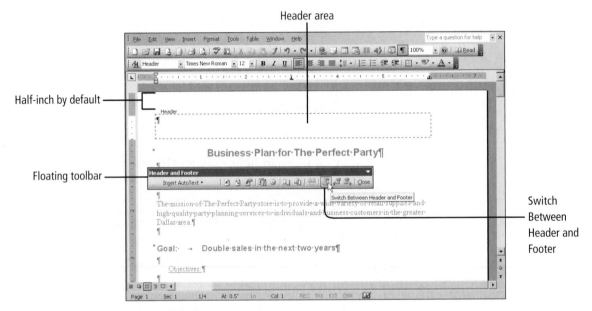

Half-inch by default

Floating toolbar

Switch Between Header and Footer

Figure 1.27

2 On the Header and Footer toolbar, click the **Switch Between Header and Footer** button.

The footer area displays with the insertion point blinking at the left edge of the footer area.

3 In the footer area, using your own name, type **1A Business Plan-Firstname Lastname** as shown in Figure 1.28.

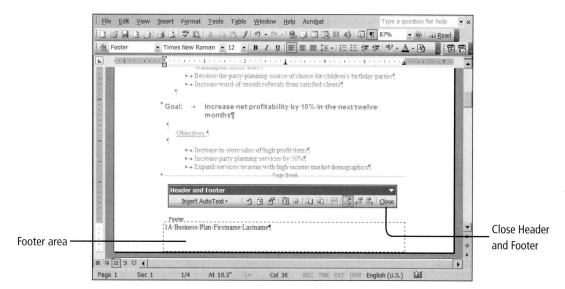

Footer area

Close Header
and Footer

Figure 1.28

4 On the Header and Footer toolbar, click the **Close** button. Alternatively, double-click anywhere in the text area of the document to close the Header and Footer toolbar.

5 Scroll down until you can see the footer on the first page.

The footer displays in light gray as shown in Figure 1.29. Because it is a proper name, your name in the footer may display with wavy red lines.

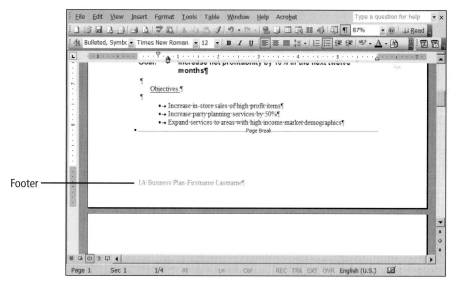

Footer

Figure 1.29

More Knowledge — Moving to the Header or Footer

A quick way to edit an existing header or footer is to double-click in the header or footer area. This will display the Header and Footer toolbar, and also place the insertion point at the beginning of the header or footer.

Objective 5
Organize, Save, and Print Documents

In the same way that you use file folders to organize your paper documents, Windows uses a hierarchy of electronic folders to keep your electronic files organized. Check with your instructor or lab coordinator to see where you will be storing your documents (for example, on your own disk or on a network drive) and whether there is any suggested file folder arrangement. Throughout this textbook, you will be instructed to save your files using the file name followed by your first and last name. Check with your instructor to see if there is some other file naming arrangement for your course.

Activity 1.12 Creating Folders for Document Storage and Saving a Document

When you save a document file, the Windows operating system stores your document permanently on a storage medium—either a disk that you have inserted into the computer, the hard drive of your computer, or a network drive connected to your computer system. Changes that you make to existing documents, such as changing text or typing in new text, are not permanently saved until you perform a Save operation.

1 On the menu bar, click **File**, and then click **Save As**.

The Save As dialog box displays.

2 In the **Save As** dialog box, at the right edge of the **Save in** box, click the **Save in arrow** to view a list of the drives available to you as shown in Figure 1.30. Your list of drives and folders will differ from the one shown.

Save in box

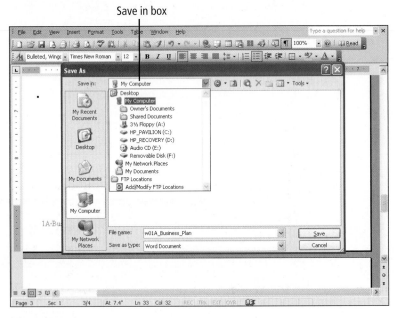

Figure 1.30

3 Navigate to the drive on which you will be storing your folders and projects for this chapter—for example, 3½ Floppy (A:) or the drive designated by your instructor or lab coordinator.

4 In the **Save As** dialog box toolbar, click the **Create New Folder** button [].

The New Folder dialog box displays.

5 In the **Name** box, type **Chapter 1** as shown in Figure 1.31, and then click **OK**.

The new folder name displays in the Save in box, indicating that the folder is open and ready to store your document.

Create New Folder button

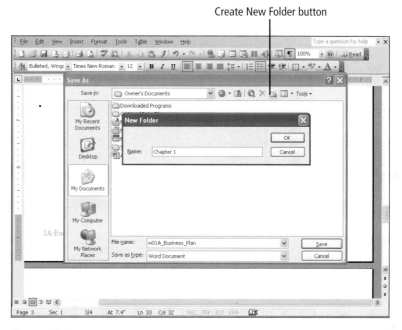

Figure 1.31

6 In the lower portion of the **Save As** dialog box, locate the **File name** box.

The file name *w01A_Business_Plan* may be highlighted in blue, in which case your new typing will delete the existing text.

More Knowledge — Renaming a Folder

You can rename folders as well as files. To rename a folder, right-click the folder in the Save As dialog box, click Rename from the shortcut menu, and then type a new folder name. This procedure also works in My Computer or Windows Explorer.

7 If necessary, select or delete the existing text, and then in the **File name** box, using your own first and last name, type **1A_Business_Plan_Firstname_Lastname** as shown in Figure 1.32.

The Microsoft Windows operating system recognizes file names with spaces. However, some Internet file transfer programs do not. To facilitate sending your files over the Internet using a course management system such as Blackboard, eCollege, or WebCT, in this textbook you will be instructed to save files using an underscore instead of a space. The underscore key is the shift of the ⊟ key, located two keys to the left of ⌫ Bksp .

Underscore
characters
in file name
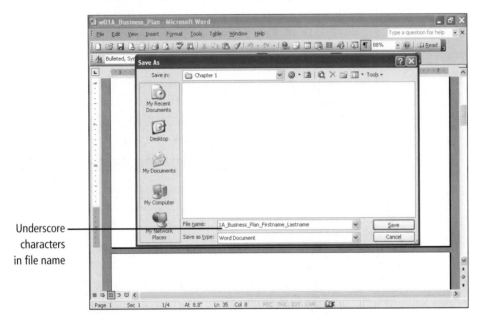

Figure 1.32

8 In the lower portion of the **Save As** dialog box, click the **Save** button, or press Enter .

Your file is saved in the new folder with the new file name.

More Knowledge — Saving Your Document Often

Save your documents frequently to avoid losing the information you have created in a new document or the changes you have made to an existing document. In rare instances, problems arise with your computer system or your electrical power source. After a document is saved, hardware or electrical problems will not harm your document. However, you could lose any new editing that you performed on the document after the last save operation.

Activity 1.13 Printing a Document from the Toolbar

In Activity 1.13, you will print your document from the toolbar.

1 On the Standard toolbar, click the **Print** button 🖨.

One copy of your document prints on the default printer. A total of four pages will print, and your name will print in the footer area of each page.

2 On your printed copy, notice that the formatting marks designating spaces, paragraphs, and tabs do not print.

3 From the **File** menu, click **Exit**, saving any changes if prompted to do so.

Both the document and the Word program close.

Another Way

Printing a Document

There are two ways to print a document:

- On the Standard or Print Preview toolbar, click the Print button, which will print a single copy of the entire document on the default printer.

- From the File menu, click Print to display the Print dialog box, from which you can select a variety of different options, such as printing multiple copies, printing on a different printer, and printing some but not all pages.

End You have completed Project 1A ———————————————————

Project 1B **Thank You Letter**

In Project 1A you opened and edited an existing document. In Project 1B you will create and edit a new document.

In Activities 1.14 through 1.22 you will create a letter from Gabriela Quinones, a co-owner of The Perfect Party, to Paul Freire, a business consultant who was involved in preparing the business plan. Your completed document will look similar to Figure 1.33. You will save your document as *1B_ Thanks_Firstname_Lastname.*

September 12, 2005

Mr. Paul Freire
Business Consulting Services
123 Jackson Street, Suite 100
Dallas, TX 75202

Dear Paul:

Subject: Your participation in the planning retreat

Thank you for participating in the planning retreat for **The Perfect Party**. We are very excited about the next two years. One of the reasons our future looks so bright is because of the contributions you have made!

I would also like to thank you personally for taking notes and summarizing the ideas expressed at the retreat.

Yours truly,

Gabriela Quinones

1B Thanks-Firstname Lastname

Figure 1.33
Project 1B—Thank you letter

Objective 6
Create and Edit a New Document

In Activities 1.14 through 1.17, you will practice the basic skills needed to create a new document, insert and delete text, and edit text.

Activity 1.14 Creating a New Document

1 Start Word. If necessary, close the Getting Started task pane by clicking the small Close button 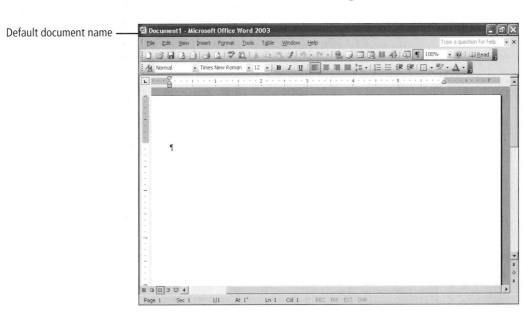 in the upper right corner of the task pane.

When Word is started, a new blank document displays.

2 In the blue title bar, notice that *Document1* displays.

Word displays the file name of a document in both the blue title bar at the top of the screen and on a button in the taskbar at the lower edge of the screen—including new unsaved documents. The new unsaved document displays *Document1* or *Document2* depending on how many times you have started a new document during your current Word session. See Figure 1.34.

Default document name ⎯⎯

Figure 1.34

Opening a New Document

There are five ways to begin a new document in Word:

- Start the Word program; a new blank document displays.

- On the Standard toolbar, click the New Blank Document button.

- From the menu bar, click File, and then click New.

- From the Getting Started task pane, under Open, click *Create a new document*.

- From the New Document task pane, under New, click *Blank document*.

Activity 1.15 Entering Text and Inserting Blank Lines

1 Verify that formatting marks are displayed. If necessary, click the Show/Hide ¶ button **¶** to display them. With the insertion point blinking in the upper left corner of the document to the left of the default first paragraph mark, type **Sept**

A ScreenTip displays *September (Press ENTER to Insert)* as shown in Figure 1.35. This feature, called **AutoComplete**, assists in your typing by suggesting commonly used words and phrases after you type the first few characters.

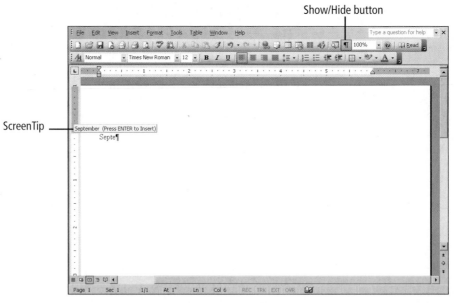

Figure 1.35

2 To finish the word *September*, press [Enter]. Press [Spacebar] once and then type **12, 2005** and press [Enter]. (If you are completing this activity during the month of September, AutoComplete may offer to fill in the current date. To ignore the suggestion, type as indicated.)

The first paragraph is complete and the insertion point is positioned at the beginning of the next line. A paragraph is created when you press [Enter]. Thus, a paragraph can be a single line like the date line, or a blank line.

A purple dotted underscore beneath the date indicates that Word has flagged this as a ***recognizer***. A recognizer indicates that Word recognizes this as a date. As you progress in your study of Microsoft Office, you will discover how dates such as this one can be added to other Office programs like Microsoft Outlook.

3 Press [Enter] three more times.

Three empty paragraphs, which function as blank lines, display below the typed date.

4 Type **Mr. Paul Freire** and then press [Enter].

5 On three lines, type the following address:

Business Consulting Services

123 Jackson Street, Suite 100

Dallas, TX 75202

6 Press [Enter] twice. Type **Dear Paul:** and then press [Enter] twice.

7 Type **Subject: Your participation in the planning retreat** and press [Enter] twice.

Compare your screen to Figure 1.36. The purple dotted line under the street address is another recognizer, indicating that you could add the address to your Microsoft Outlook address book or perform other useful tasks with the address. Additionally, the proper name *Freire* is flagged as misspelled because it is a proper name not contained in the Word dictionary.

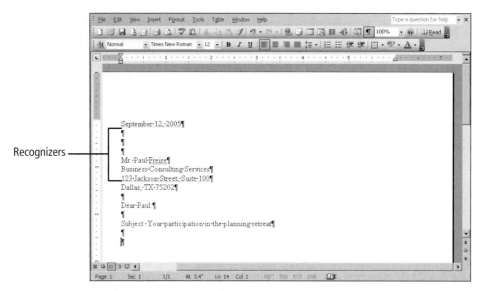

Recognizers

Figure 1.36

8 As you type the following text, press the [Spacebar] only once at the end of a sentence: **Thank you for participating in the retreat for The Perfect Party. We are really very excited about the next two years. One of the reasons our future looks so bright is because of the contributions you have made!** Press [Enter] twice.

As you type, the insertion point moves to the right, and when it reaches the right margin, Word determines whether or not the next word in the line will fit within the established right margin. If the word does not fit, Word will move the whole word down to the next line. This feature is **_wordwrap_**.

Note — Spacing at the End of Sentences

Although you may have learned to press [Spacebar] twice at the end of a sentence, it is common practice now to space only once at the end of a sentence.

9 Type **I would also like to thank you personally for taking notes and also for summarizing the ideas expressed at the retreat.**

10 Press [Enter] two times. Type **Your** and when the ScreenTip *Yours truly, (Press ENTER to Insert)* displays, press [Enter] to have AutoComplete complete the closing of the letter.

11 Press [Enter] four times, and then type **Angie Nguyen**

Compare your screen to Figure 1.37.

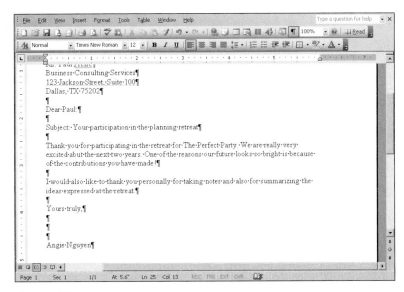

Figure 1.37

12 On the Standard toolbar, click the **Print Preview** button. If necessary, change the Zoom setting on the Print Preview toolbar to Whole Page to see the entire page as it will print.

Your document displays as it will print on paper. Notice that there is a large amount of blank space at the bottom of this short letter.

13 On the Print Preview toolbar, click **Close**. Display the **File** menu, and then click **Page Setup**.

14 On the displayed **Page Setup** dialog box, click the **Layout tab**. Under **Page**, click the **Vertical alignment arrow**. From the displayed list, click **Center** as shown in Figure 1.38.

Print Preview button   Layout tab

File menu

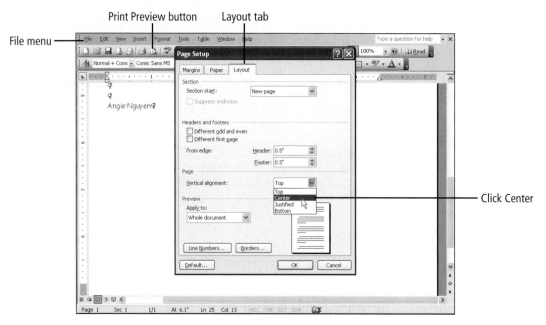

Figure 1.38

15 In the lower right corner of the **Page Setup** dialog box, click **OK**. On the Standard toolbar, click the **Print Preview** button .

Your document displays as it will print on paper. The text is centered on the page between the top and bottom margin. You can see that vertically centering one-page letters results in a more attractive and professional looking document.

16 On the Print Preview toolbar, click the **Close** button Close . On the Standard toolbar, click the **Save** button .

Because this document has never been saved, the Save As dialog box displays.

17 Use the **Save in arrow** to navigate to the **Chapter 1 folder** that you created in your storage location. In the lower portion of the **Save As** dialog box, in the **File name** box, delete any existing text and then type **1B_Thanks_Firstname_Lastname**

Make sure you type your own first name and last name as the last two parts of the new file name.

18 In the lower right portion of the **Save As** dialog box, click the **Save** button or press Enter.

Your file is saved in your Chapter 1 folder with the new file name.

Activity 1.16 Editing Text with the Delete and Backspace Keys

1 Scroll as necessary to view the upper portion of your document. In the paragraph beginning *Thank you*, at the end of the first line, click to position your insertion point to the left of the word *very*.

The insertion point is blinking to the left of the word *very*.

2 Press ⌫Bksp once.

The space between the words *really* and *very* is removed. See Figure 1.39.

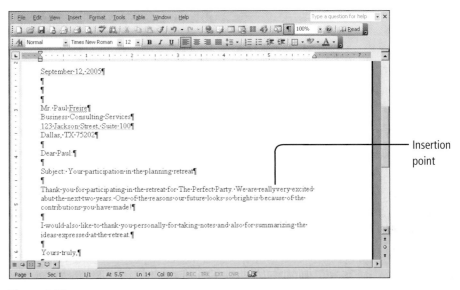

Insertion point

Figure 1.39

3 With the insertion point between the two words, press ⌫Bksp six times.

The word *really* is removed. Make sure there is only one dot (dots are the formatting marks that indicate spaces) between *are* and *very*. You can see that when editing text, it is useful to display formatting marks.

4 In the paragraph beginning *I would*, in the first line, locate the phrase *for summarizing* and then click to position the insertion point to the left of the word *for*.

5 Press ⌫Bksp five times.

The word *also* and the space between the words is removed.

6 Press Delete four times.

The word *for* to the right of the insertion point is removed, along with the space following the word. Make sure there is only one dot (space) between *and* and *summarizing*. See Figure 1.40.

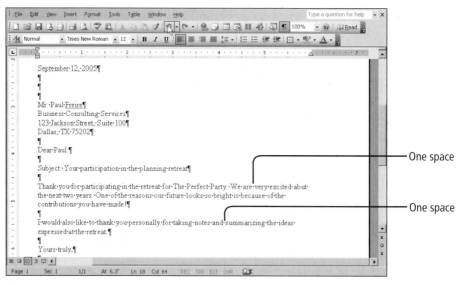

One space

One space

Figure 1.40

7 On the Standard toolbar, click the **Save** button 🖫 to save the changes you have made to your document since your last save operation.

Another Way

Removing Characters

There are two ways to remove individual characters in a document:

- Press [Delete] to remove characters to the right of the insertion point.
- Press [←Bksp] to remove characters to the left of the insertion point.

Activity 1.17 Inserting New Text and Overtyping Existing Text

When you place the insertion point in the middle of a word or sentence and start typing, the existing text moves to the right to make space for your new keystrokes. This is called ***insert mode*** and is the default setting in Word. If you press the [Insert] key once, ***overtype mode*** is turned on. In overtype mode, existing text is replaced as you type. When overtype mode is active, the letters *OVR* display in black in the status bar. When insert mode is active, the letters *OVR* are light gray.

1 In the paragraph beginning *Thank you*, in the first line, click to place the insertion point to the left of the word *retreat*.

The space should be to the left of the insertion point.

2 Type **planning** and then press $\boxed{\text{Spacebar}}$.

As you type, the existing text moves to the right to make space for your new keystrokes, and the overtype indicator (OVR) in the status bar is gray. See Figure 1.41.

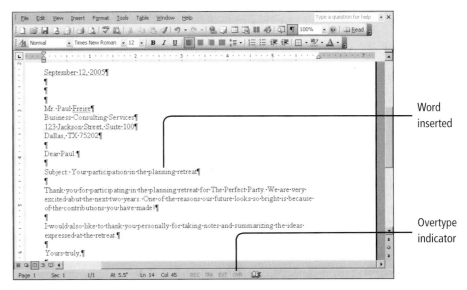

September·12,·2005¶
¶
¶
¶
Mr.·Paul·Freire¶
Business·Consulting·Services¶
123·Jackson·Street,·Suite·100¶
Dallas,·TX·75202¶
¶
Dear·Paul:¶
¶
Subject·:·Your·participation·in·the·planning·retreat¶
¶
Thank·you·for·participating·in·the·planning·retreat·for·The·Perfect·Party.·We·are·very·excited·about·the·next·two·years.·One·of·the·reasons·our·future·looks·so·bright·is·because·of·the·contributions·you·have·made.¶
¶
I·would·also·like·to·thank·you·personally·for·taking·notes·and·summarizing·the·ideas·expressed·at·the·retreat.¶
¶
Yours·truly,¶

Word inserted

Overtype indicator

Figure 1.41

3 In the last line of the document, click to place the insertion point to the left of *Angie Nguyen*.

4 Press $\boxed{\text{Insert}}$, and notice that in the status bar, the OVR indicator is black, indicating that overtype mode is active.

When you begin to type, the new text will replace the old text, rather than move it to the right.

5 Type **Gabriela Quinones**

Notice that as you type, the characters replace the existing text.

6 Press $\boxed{\text{Insert}}$ to turn off overtype mode. Alternatively, double-click the overtype indicator in the status bar.

7 On the Standard toolbar, click the **Save** button 🔲 to save the changes you have made to your document.

Objective 7
Select and Format Text

Selecting text refers to highlighting, by dragging with your mouse, areas of text so that the text can be edited, formatted, copied, or moved. Word recognizes a selected area of text as one unit, to which you can make changes. ***Formatting text*** is the process of setting the overall appearance of the text within the document by changing the color, shading, or emphasis of text.

Activity 1.18 Selecting Text

To perform an action on text—for example, to move, delete, or emphasize text—you must first select it. You can select text using either the mouse or the keyboard.

1 In the paragraph beginning *Thank you*, position the I-beam pointer ⌶ to the left of *Thank*, hold down the left mouse button, and then drag to the right to select the first sentence including the ending period and its following space as shown in Figure 1.42. Release the mouse button.

The first sentence of the paragraph is selected. Dragging is the technique of holding down the left mouse button and moving over an area of text. Selected text is indicated when the background and color of the characters are reversed—the characters are white and the background is black as shown in Figure 1.42. Selecting takes a steady hand. If you are not satisfied with your result, click anywhere in a blank area of the document and begin again.

Period and space included in the selection

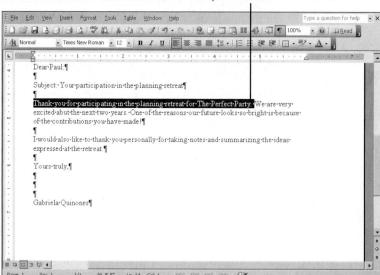

Figure 1.42

2 Click anywhere in the document to deselect the sentence. Then, in the same sentence, move the pointer over the word *Perfect* and double-click the mouse button.

The entire word is selected. Double-clicking takes a steady hand. The speed of the two clicks is not difficult (although you only have about a second between clicks), but you must hold the mouse perfectly still between the two clicks. If you are not satisfied with your result, try again.

3 Click anywhere to deselect the word *Perfect*. Then, move the pointer over the word *Perfect* and triple-click the mouse button.

The entire paragraph is selected. Recall that keeping the mouse perfectly still between the clicks is critical.

4 Hold down Ctrl and press A.

The entire document is selected. See Figure 1.43. There are many shortcuts for selecting text. Take a moment to study the shortcuts shown in the table in Figure 1.44.

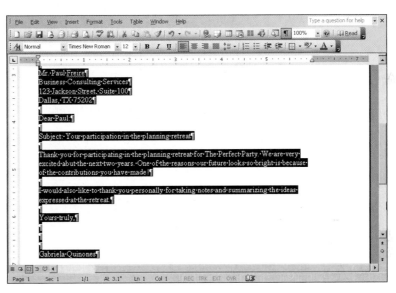

Figure 1.43

Selecting Text in a Document

To Select	Do This
A portion of text	Click to position the insertion point at the beginning of the text you want to select, hold down Shift, and then click at the end of the text you want to select. Alternatively, hold down the left mouse button and drag from the beginning to the end of the text you want to select.
A word	Double-click the word.
A sentence	Hold down Ctrl and click anywhere in the sentence.
A paragraph	Triple-click anywhere in the paragraph; or, move the pointer to the left of the line, into the margin area. When the pointer changes to a right-pointing white arrow, double-click.
A line	Move the pointer to the left of the line. When the pointer turns to a right-pointing white arrow, click once.
One character at a time	Position the insertion point at the left of the first character, hold down Shift and press → or ← as many times as desired.
A string of words	Position the insertion point to the left of the first word, hold down Shift and Ctrl, and then press → or ←.
Consecutive lines	Hold down Shift and press ↑ or ↓.
Consecutive paragraphs	Hold down Shift and Ctrl and press ↑ or ↓.
The entire document	Hold down Ctrl and press A or move the pointer to the left of the line. When it turns to a right-pointing white arrow, triple-click.

Figure 1.44

5 Click anywhere in the document to cancel the text selection.

Activity 1.19 Changing Font and Font Size

A *font* is a set of characters with the same design and shape. There are two basic types of fonts—serif and sans serif. *Serif fonts* contain extensions or lines on the ends of the characters and are good choices for large amounts of text because they are easy to read. Examples of serif fonts include Times New Roman, Garamond, and Century Schoolbook. *Sans serif fonts* do not have lines on the ends of characters. Sans serif fonts are good choices for headings and titles. Examples of sans serif fonts include Arial, Verdana, and Comic Sans MS. The table in Figure 1.45 shows examples of Serif and Sans Serif fonts.

Examples of Serif and Sans Serif Fonts

Serif Fonts	Sans Serif Fonts
Times New Roman	Arial
Garamond	Verdana
Century Schoolbook	Comic Sans MS

Figure 1.45

1 Move the mouse pointer anywhere over the subject line in the letter and triple-click.

The entire paragraph is selected. Recall that a paragraph is defined as one paragraph mark and anything in front of it, which could be one or more lines of text or no text at all in the case of a blank line.

2 On the Formatting toolbar, locate the **Font Size button arrow** `12 ▼` and click the arrow. On the displayed list, click **14** as shown in Figure 1.46.

Font size

Selected text ————

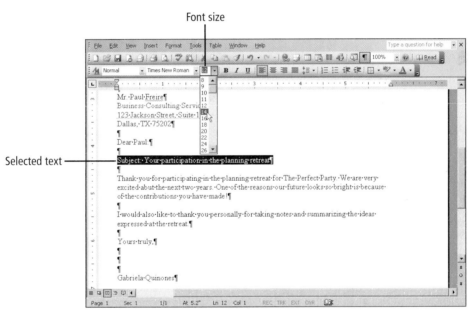

Figure 1.46

Fonts are measured in **points**, with one point equal to 1/72 of an inch. A higher point size indicates a larger font size. For large amounts of text, font sizes between 10 point and 12 point are good choices. Headings and titles are often formatted using a larger font size. The word *point* is abbreviated as **pt**.

3 On the Formatting toolbar, locate the **Font button arrow** Times New Roman and click the arrow.

On the displayed list, the fonts are displayed in alphabetical order. Word assists in your font selection by placing fonts recently used on this computer at the top of the list.

4 Scroll the displayed list as necessary and then click **Arial**. Click anywhere in the document to cancel the selection.

5 Hold down Ctrl and press A to select the document.

6 With the document selected, click the **Font button arrow** Times New Roman. On the displayed list, scroll as necessary and then click **Comic Sans MS**.

The selected text changes to the Comic Sans MS font. In a letter, it is good practice to use only one font for the entire letter. This font is less formal than the default font of Times New Roman.

7 With the entire document selected, click the **Font Size button arrow** 12 and change the font size to **11**. Alternatively, you can type **11** in the Font Size box. Click anywhere in the document to cancel the text selection.

8 Compare your screen to Figure 1.47.

Font name ——————— Font Size

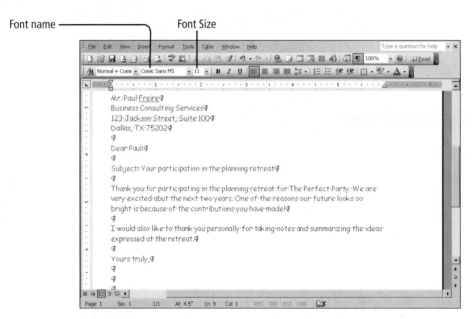

Figure 1.47

9 On the Standard toolbar, click the **Save** button 🖫 to save the changes you have made to your document. Leave the document open for Activity 1.20.

Activity 1.20 Adding Emphasis to Text

Font styles emphasize text and are a visual cue to draw the reader's eye to important text. Font styles include bold, italic, and underline, although underline is not commonly used for emphasis. You can add emphasis to existing text, or you can turn the emphasis on before you start typing the word or phrase and then turn it off.

1 Move the pointer over the subject line and triple-click to select the paragraph.

2 On the Formatting toolbar, click the **Italic** button 𝐼.

Italic is applied to the paragraph that forms the Subject line.

3 In the paragraph beginning *Thank you*, use any method to select the text *The Perfect Party*.

Another Way ── **Applying Font Styles**

There are three methods to apply font styles:

- On the Standard toolbar, click the Bold, Italic, or Underline button.
- From the menu bar, click Format, click Font, and apply styles from the Font dialog box.
- From the keyboard, use the keyboard shortcuts of Ctrl + B for bold, Ctrl + I for italic, or Ctrl + U for underline.

4 On the Formatting toolbar, click the **Bold** button 𝐁. Click anywhere in the document to cancel the selection.

5 On the Standard toolbar, click the **Print Preview** button 🔍 and compare your screen to Figure 1.48.

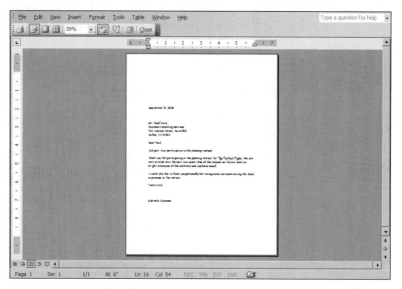

Figure 1.48

6 On the Print Preview toolbar, click **Close**.

7 In the inside address, right-click *Freire* and then click **Ignore All**. Correct any other spelling or grammar errors in your document.

8 On the Standard toolbar, click the **Save** button 🖫 to save your changes.

More Knowledge — Using Toggle Buttons

The bold, italic, and underline buttons are toggle buttons; that is, you can click the button once to turn it on and again to turn it off.

Objective 8
Preview and Print Documents, Close a Document, and Close Word

While creating your document, it is helpful to check the print preview to make sure you are getting the result you want. Before printing, make a final check with print preview to make sure the document layout is exactly what you want.

Activity 1.21 Previewing and Printing a Document and Closing Word

1 From the **View** menu, click **Header and Footer**. (The large header area at the top is a result of vertically centering the document on the page.) On the displayed Header and Footer toolbar, click the **Switch Between Header and Footer** button 🖭.

The footer area displays. The insertion point is at the left edge of the footer area.

2 In the footer area, using your own name, type **1B Thanks-Firstname Lastname** as shown in Figure 1.49.

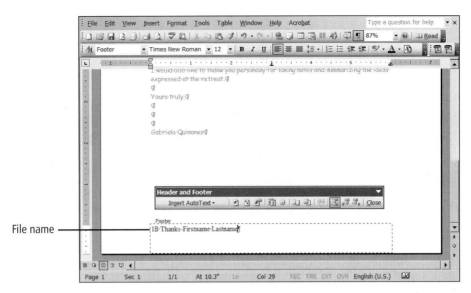

File name

Figure 1.49

3 Double-click anywhere in the text area of the document to close the Header and Footer toolbar. Alternatively, on the Header and Footer toolbar, click the Close button Close.

4 On the Standard toolbar, click the **Print Preview** button.

Your document displays exactly as it will print. The formatting marks, which do not print, are not displayed.

5 In the **Print Preview** window, move the mouse pointer anywhere over the document.

The pointer becomes a magnifying glass with a plus in it, indicating that you can magnify the view. See Figure 1.50.

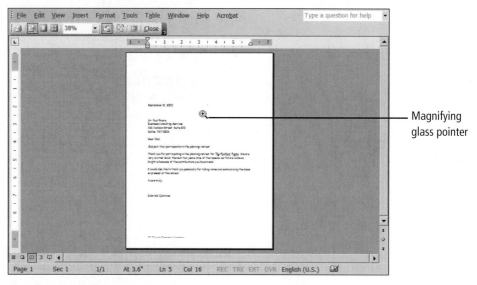

Magnifying glass pointer

Figure 1.50

6 Move the pointer over the upper portion of the document and click once.

The top portion of the document is magnified, and is easier to read. The pointer changes to a magnifying glass with a minus sign.

7 Click anywhere on the document.

The full page displays again.

8 On the Print Preview toolbar, click **Close**. On the Standard toolbar, click the **Save** button to save your changes.

9 Display the **File** menu, and then click **Print**.

The Print dialog box displays. See Figure 1.51. Here you can specify which pages to print and how many copies you want. Additional command buttons for Options and Properties provide additional printing choices. The printer that displays will be the printer that is selected for your computer.

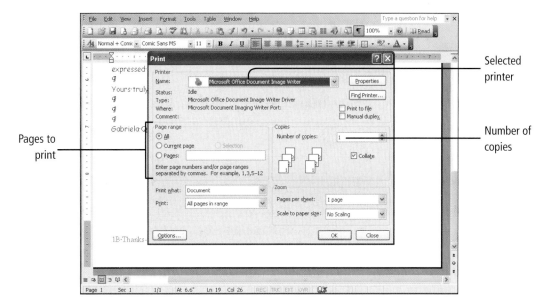

Pages to print

Selected printer

Number of copies

Figure 1.51

10 In the displayed **Print** dialog box, under **Copies**, change the number of copies to 2 by either typing **2** in the text box or clicking the **up arrow** in the spin box. See Figure 1.51. At the bottom of the **Print** dialog box, click **OK**.

Two copies will print.

11 From the **File** menu, click **Close**, saving any changes if prompted to do so. At the far right edge of the blue title bar, click the **Close** button ⊠.

The Word program is closed.

Objective 9
Use the Microsoft Help System

As you work with Word, you can get assistance by using the Help feature. You can ask questions and Help will provide you with information and step-by-step instructions for performing tasks.

Activity 1.22 Typing a Question for Help

The easiest way to use Help is to type a question in the *Type a question for help* box, located at the right side of the menu bar.

1 If necessary, start Word. Move your pointer to the right side of the menu bar and click in the **Type a question for help** box. With the insertion point blinking in the box, type **How do I open a file?** and then press Enter.

The Search Results task pane displays a list of topics related to opening a file. Your list may be quite different than the one shown in Figure 1.52.

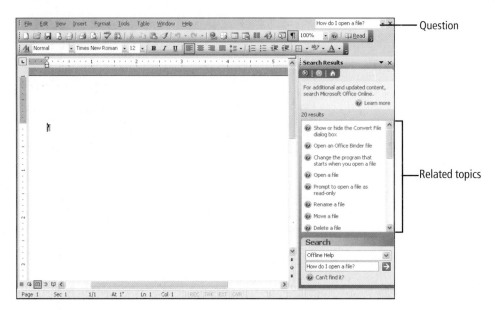

Figure 1.52

2 On the displayed list in the task pane, point to and then click **Open a file**.

The Microsoft Word Help window opens at listing instructions for opening a file. Text in blue at the bottom of the Help window indicates links to related instructions or related information.

3 At the bottom of the **Microsoft Office Word Help** window, click **Tips** to display additional information about opening files.

4 In the second bulleted item, point to and then click the blue highlighted words **task pane** to display a green definition of a task pane as shown in Figure 1.53.

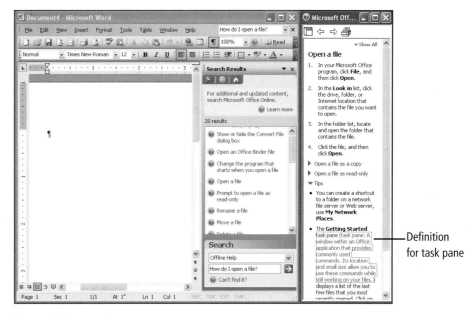

Figure 1.53

5 Click **task pane** again to close the definition.

6 In the **Microsoft Office Word Help** window, click the **Close** button ⊠.

On the **Search Results** task pane, click the **Close** button ⊠.

7 From the **File** menu, click **Exit** to close the Word program.

Another Way

Getting Help Using the Task Pane and the Office Assistant

You can access Help by clicking the Microsoft Word Help button on the Standard toolbar. This action opens the Help task pane. In the Search box, type a topic that you want to learn more about and then press Enter. Results are displayed in the Search Results task pane. The Office Assistant, an animated character that provides tips as you work, can be displayed from the Help menu by clicking Show the Office Assistant.

End You have completed Project 1B

Summary

In this chapter you practiced how to start Word and navigate in the Word window by using the mouse, toolbars, menus, shortcut menus, and shortcut keys. You examined documents in the Page Layout, Normal, and Reading Layout views; changed the magnification with the Zoom button; and displayed nonprinting characters with the Show/Hide ¶ button.

The basics of word processing were practiced including entering text, deleting text using the backspace or delete key, selecting and replacing text, inserting text, and overtyping existing text. The spelling and grammar checker tools were demonstrated.

You also practiced how to change font style and size and add emphasis to text. The header and footer area was viewed, and a chapter folder was created to help organize your files. Each document was saved, previewed, printed, and closed. Finally, the Help program was introduced as a tool that can assist you in using Word.

In This Chapter You Practiced How To

- Explore and Navigate the Word Window
- View Documents
- Use the Spelling and Grammar Checker
- View Headers and Footers
- Organize, Save, and Print Documents
- Create and Edit a New Document
- Select and Format Text
- Preview and Print Documents, Close a Document, and Close Word
- Use the Microsoft Help System

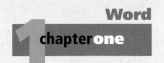

Concepts Assessments

Matching Match each term in the second column with its correct definition in the first column by writing the letter of the term on the blank line in front of the correct definition.

_____ 1. The point in the Word window, indicated by a blinking vertical line, where text will be inserted when you start to type.

_____ 2. A view that simplifies the page layout for quick typing and can show more text on a smaller screen.

_____ 3. The action that takes place when the insertion point reaches the right margin and automatically moves down and to the left margin of the next line.

_____ 4. A button used to reveal nonprinting characters.

_____ 5. The process of setting the overall appearance of the text within the document.

_____ 6. A unit of measure that is used to describe the size of a font.

_____ 7. A font type that does not have lines on the ends of characters.

_____ 8. A type of font that is a good choice for large amounts of text because it is easy to read.

_____ 9. A set of characters (letters and numbers) with the same design and shape.

_____ 10. The term that refers to pressing one or more keys to navigate a window or execute commands.

_____ 11. The Minimize, Maximize/Restore Down, and Close buttons are located here.

_____ 12. A screen element that contains lists of commands.

_____ 13. A context-sensitive list that displays when you click the right mouse button.

_____ 14. The buttons used to Save or Print a document can be found here.

_____ 15. The part of the screen that displays the Start button and the name of any open documents.

A Font

B Formatting

C Insertion point

D Keyboard shortcuts

E Menu bar

F Normal

G Point

H Sans serif

I Serif

J Shortcut menu

K Show/Hide ¶

L Standard toolbar

M Taskbar

N Title bar

O Wordwrap

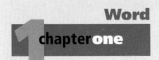
Fill in the Blank Write the correct answer in the space provided.

1. Microsoft Word 2003 is a word _____ program that you can use to do tasks such as writing a memo, a report, or a letter.

2. If you place your mouse pointer over a button on a toolbar, a small _____ displays the name of the button.

3. If you drag the _____ down it causes the document on your screen to move up.

4. The view that displays the page borders, margins, text, and graphics is known as the _____ view.

5. The portion of the Word window that opens to display commonly used commands or utilities available for use with the current job is known as the _____.

6. The View buttons are located to the left of the _____ scroll bar.

7. A row of buttons that provides a one-click method to perform common commands is called a _____.

8. To add emphasis to text, use the _____ or _____ or _____ buttons.

9. Before text can be edited, changed, formatted, copied, or moved, it must first be _____.

10. To display a shortcut menu, click the _____ mouse button.

Project 1C— Follow Up Letter

Objectives: *Explore and Navigate the Word Window; Use the Spelling and Grammar Checker; View Headers and Footers; Organize, Save, and Print Documents; Create and Edit a New Document; Preview and Print Documents, Close a Document, and Close Word.*

In the following Skill Assessment, you will edit a follow-up letter from Corey Finstad, a party planner for The Perfect Party, to a customer who has requested party-planning services. Your completed letter will look similar to the one shown in Figure 1.54. You will save your letter as *1C_Follow_Up_Letter_Firstname_Lastname.*

June 15, 2003

Ms. Gloria Williams
35 Pine Grove Avenue
Dallas, TX 75202

Dear Ms. Williams:

Thank you for selecting The Perfect Party to plan your upcoming event. I look forward to managing the details for you so you can enjoy spending time with your guests.

You can select one of our prepared party themes, or we can design a customized party that will match the tone and purpose of your event. I am enclosing a brochure outlining some of our more popular themes, along with a list of accessories that can be used. Take a moment to look over this material and call me if you have any questions.

I look forward to meeting with you next week to finalize the plans for your party.

Best regards,

Corey Finstad
Party Planner

Enclosure

1C Follow Up Letter-Firstname Lastname

Figure 1.54

1. Start **Word**. On the Standard toolbar, click the **Open** button.

2. In the **Open** dialog box, at the right edge of the **Look in** box, click the **Look in arrow** to view a list of the drives available on your system. Navigate to the location where the student files for this textbook are stored.

(Project 1C–Follow Up Letter continues on the next page)

(Project 1C–Follow Up Letter continued)

3. Locate and click the file **w01C_Follow_Up_Letter**. In the lower portion of the **Open** dialog box, click the **Open** button.

4. If necessary, on the Standard toolbar click the **Show/Hide ¶** button to display formatting marks.

5. On the menu bar, click **File**, and then click **Save As**. In the **Save As** dialog box, click the **Save in arrow**, and then navigate to the location where you are saving your projects for this chapter. Recall that you created a Chapter 1 folder for this purpose.

6. In the **File name** box, using your own first and last name, type **1C_Follow_Up_Letter_Firstname_Lastname**

7. In the lower portion of the **Save As** dialog box click the **Save** button.

8. Be sure the insertion point is positioned to the left of the blank line at the top of the document. If necessary, hold down Ctrl and press Home to move the insertion point to the top of the document.

9. Begin typing today's date and let AutoComplete assist in your typing by pressing Enter when the ScreenTip displays. Press Enter four times. Notice the purple dotted line under the date, which is the recognizer that could add this date to your Outlook calendar. Type the following on three lines:

Ms. Gloria Williams

35 Pine Grove Avenue

Dallas, TX 75202

10. Press Enter twice, type **Dear Ms. Williams:** and then press Enter once.

11. Hold down Ctrl and press End to move the insertion point to the end of the document. Press Enter twice, type **Best regards,** and then press Enter four times.

12. Finish the letter by typing the following on two lines:

Corey Finstad

Party Planner

13. Press Enter twice and type **Enclosure**

14. On the Standard toolbar, click the **Spelling and Grammar** button. The first error—a duplicated word—is highlighted, unless you made a typing error earlier in the document.

15. In the **Spelling and Grammar** dialog box, click the **Delete** button to delete the second occurrence of *the*. The next error is highlighted.

(Project 1C–Follow Up Letter continues on the next page)

(Project 1C–Follow Up Letter continued)

16. Under **Suggestions**, the first suggestion is correct. Click the **Change** button to change the misspelled word to the highlighted suggestion of *brochure*. The next error is highlighted.

17. Be sure *themes* is highlighted under **Suggestions**, and then click the **Change** button. Correct the next two errors, and then click **Ignore Once** to ignore the name *Finstad*. Click **OK** to close the box indicating the check is complete.

18. Drag the vertical scroll box to the top of the scroll bar to display the top of the document. In the paragraph beginning *Thank you*, double-click the word *handle* to select it and type **plan**

Notice that your typing replaces the selected word.

19. In the paragraph beginning *You can select*, locate the first occurrence of the word *party*, click to the left of the word, type **prepared** and then press ⌜Spacebar⌝ once.

20. On the menu bar, click **View**, and then click **Header and Footer**. Click the **Switch Between Header and Footer** button. In the footer area, using your own name, type **1C Follow Up Letter-Firstname Lastname**

21. On the Header and Footer toolbar, click the **Close** button.

22. Display the **File** menu, click **Page Setup**, and then in the displayed **Page Setup** dialog box, click the **Layout tab**. Under **Page**, click the **Vertical alignment arrow**, and from the displayed list, click **Center**. Recall that vertically centering one-page letters results in a more attractive letter. In the lower right corner of the dialog box, click **OK**.

23. On the Standard toolbar, click the **Save** button to save the changes you have made to your document.

24. On the Standard toolbar, click the **Print Preview** button to make a final check of your letter before printing. On the Print Preview toolbar, click the **Print** button, and then on the same toolbar, click the **Close** button.

25. From the **File** menu, click **Close** to close the document, saving any changes if prompted to do so. Display the **File** menu again and click **Exit** to close Word. Alternatively, you can close Word by clicking the **Close** button at the extreme right end of the blue title bar.

End **You have completed Project 1C** ━━━━━━━━━━━━━━━

Project 1D—Fax Cover

Objectives: *Explore and Navigate the Word Window; Create and Edit a New Document; View Documents; View Headers and Footers; Select and Format Text; Preview and Print Documents, Close a Document, and Close Word.*

In the following Skill Assessment, you will create a cover sheet for a facsimile (fax) transmission. When sending a fax, it is common practice to include a cover sheet with a note describing the pages that will follow. Your completed document will look similar to Figure 1.55. You will save your document as *1D_Fax_Cover_Firstname_Lastname*.

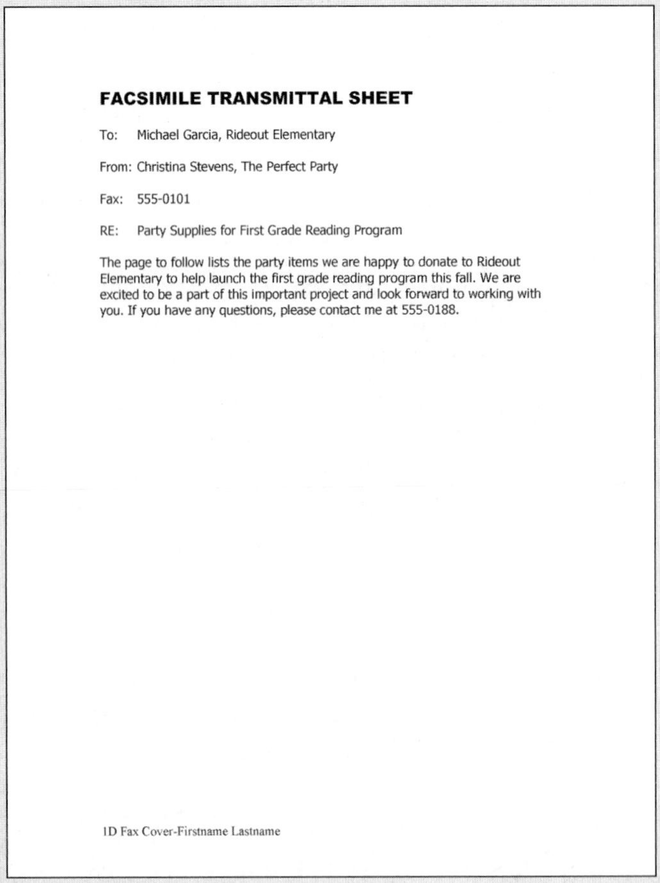

FACSIMILE TRANSMITTAL SHEET

To: Michael Garcia, Rideout Elementary

From: Christina Stevens, The Perfect Party

Fax: 555-0101

RE: Party Supplies for First Grade Reading Program

The page to follow lists the party items we are happy to donate to Rideout Elementary to help launch the first grade reading program this fall. We are excited to be a part of this important project and look forward to working with you. If you have any questions, please contact me at 555-0188.

1D Fax Cover-Firstname Lastname

Figure 1.55

1. Start **Word** and make sure the **Show/Hide ¶** button is active so you can view formatting marks. If necessary, close the task pane.

2. On your keyboard, press CapsLock. With the insertion point at the top of the document, type **FACSIMILE TRANSMITTAL SHEET** and then press Enter twice. Press CapsLock again to turn the feature off.

(Project 1D–Fax Cover continues on the next page)

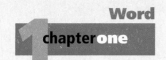
(Project 1D–Fax Cover continued)

3. On the Standard toolbar click the **Save** button. Because this new document has never been saved, the **Save As** dialog box displays. Click the **Save in arrow**, and then navigate to the location where you are saving your projects for this chapter. In the **File name** box type **1D_Fax_Cover_Firstname_Lastname** and in the lower portion of the **Save As** dialog box, click the **Save** button.

4. Type **To:** press ⎣Tab⎦, type **Michael Garcia, Rideout Elementary** and then press ⎣Enter⎦ twice. Type the remainder of the fax headings as follows, pressing ⎣Tab⎦ after each colon (:) and pressing ⎣Enter⎦ twice at the end of each line. Refer to Figure 1.55.

   From: Christina Stevens, The Perfect Party

   Fax: 555-0101

   RE: Party Supplies for First Grade Reading Program

5. Type the following, and as you do so, remember to let wordwrap end the lines for you and to press the ⎣Spacebar⎦ only once at the end of a sentence:

   The page to follow lists the party items we are happy to donate to Rideout Elementary to help launch the first grade reading program this fall. We are excited to be a part of this important project and look forward to working with you. If you have any questions, please contact me at 555-0188.

6. On the Standard toolbar click the **Save** button to save your work.

7. Press ⎣Ctrl⎦ + ⎣A⎦ to select the entire document. On the Formatting toolbar, click the **Font arrow**, scroll as necessary, and then click **Tahoma**. Click anywhere in the document to cancel the selection.

8. Move the mouse pointer into the margin area to the left of *FACSIMILE TRANSMITTAL SHEET* until the pointer displays as a white arrow. Click to select the title line only. On the Formatting toolbar, click the **Font arrow**, scroll as necessary, and then click **Arial Black**. You can also type the first letter of the font to move quickly in the Font box. With the text still selected, click the **Font Size arrow**, and then click **16**. Click anywhere to cancel the text selection.

(Project 1D–Fax Cover continues on the next page)

(Project 1D–Fax Cover continued)

9. On the menu bar, click **View**, and then click **Header and Footer**. On the Header and Footer toolbar, click the **Switch Between Header and Footer** button. In the footer area, type **1D Fax Cover-Firstname Lastname** using your own name. On the Header and Footer toolbar, click the **Close** button.

10. On your screen, notice that the word *Rideout*, which appears twice, is flagged as misspelled, and *The* is flagged as a grammar error. On the Standard toolbar, click the **Spelling and Grammar** button.

11. At the first occurrence of *Rideout*, click **Ignore All**. This action will remove the red flag from the second occurrence of the word. For the grammar error *The*, click **Ignore Once**. Because the word *The* is part of the proper name of the company, it is correct as written. If the Spelling and Grammar checker stops on your name, click **Ignore Once**. Click **OK** when the check is complete or, if necessary, click the **Close** button on the title bar of the **Spelling and Grammar** dialog box.

12. On the Standard toolbar, click the **Save** button to save your changes.

13. On the Standard toolbar, click the **Print Preview** button. On the Print Preview toolbar, click the **Print** button, and then click the **Close** button. From the **File** menu, click **Close**.

14. At right end of the title bar, click the **Close** button to close Word.

 You have completed Project 1D ———————————————

Project 1E—Survey Letter

Objectives: *Explore and Navigate the Word Window; View Documents; Create and Edit a New Document; Use the Spelling and Grammar Checker; Select and Format Text; View Headers and Footers; Organize, Save, and Print Documents; Preview and Print Documents, Close a Document, and Close Word.*

In the following Skill Assessment, you will edit a cover letter that will be sent with a survey to clients. Your completed document will look similar to Figure 1.56. You will save your document as *1E_Survey_Letter_Firstname_Lastname.*

November 23, 2005

Dear Customer:

Subject: We want to hear your opinion!

Thank you for using The Perfect Party services for your recent event. We hope that the party exceeded your expectations and that you will recommend us to your friends and associates.

As a new business, we are always looking for ways to expand our services. We know that our customers are our best advertising, and often they provide excellent suggestions that can help us develop our services. Please take a few moments to complete the short survey that is enclosed. Your candid comments and feedback are welcomed.

We look forward to working with you again when you want to throw another *Perfect Party.*

Best regards,

Angie Nguyen
Owner

Enclosure

1E Survey Letter-Firstname Lastname

Figure 1.56

1. Start **Word**. On the Standard toolbar, click the **Open** button.

2. In the **Open** dialog box, at the right edge of the **Look in** box, click the **Look in arrow** to view a list of the drives available on your system. Navigate to the location where the student files for this textbook are stored.

(Project 1E–Survey Letter continues on the next page)

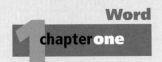

(Project 1E–Survey Letter continued)

3. Locate and click the file **w01E_Survey_Letter**. In the lower portion of the **Open** dialog box, click the **Open** button.

4. If necessary, on the Standard toolbar, click the **Show/Hide ¶** button to display formatting marks.

5. On the menu bar, click **File**, and then click **Save As**. In the **Save As** dialog box, click the **Save in arrow**, and then navigate to the location where you are saving your projects for this chapter.

6. In the **File name** box, using your own first and last name, type **1E_Survey_Letter_Firstname_Lastname** and then click the **Save** button.

7. Move the pointer into the left margin to the left of the subject line until the pointer takes the shape of a white arrow. Click once to select the subject line. On the Formatting toolbar, click the **Font arrow**, and then click **Arial Black**.

8. In the sentence beginning *We once again*, drag to select the phrase *We once again want to* and then press Delete to remove this phrase. Press Delete to delete the *t* in *thank*, and then type **T**

9. In the same paragraph, select the phrase *hopes and dreams* and then type **expectations** and adjust spacing if necessary.

10. In the same paragraph, click to place your insertion point to the left of the word *recommend* and type **will** and then press Spacebar.

11. In the paragraph beginning *As a new*, right-click *adverticing*, which is flagged as a spelling error. On the displayed shortcut menu, click *advertising*. In the same sentence double-click *ideas* to select it, and then type **suggestions** to replace it. In the same sentence replace the word *expand* with **develop**

12. In the same paragraph, right-click *moment*, which is flagged as a grammar error. From the displayed shortcut menu, click *moments*.

13. In the paragraph beginning *We look*, click to position the insertion point to the left of *Perfect Party*. Hold down Shift and Ctrl and then press → twice to select *Perfect* and then *Party*. Recall that this is a keyboard shortcut for selecting a string of words. On the Formatting toolbar, click the **Italic** button to apply the Italic font style to this phrase.

(Project 1E–Survey Letter continues on the next page)

(Project 1E–Survey Letter continued)

14. In the closing of the letter, click to position the insertion point to the left of *Sincerely* and then press [Insert] on your keyboard to activate Overtype mode. The OVR indicator on the status bar displays in black. Type **Best regards,** and then press [Delete] three times to delete the remaining unnecessary characters. Press [Insert] again to turn off Overtype mode and dim the OVR indicator.

15. Hold down [Ctrl] and press [End] to position the insertion point at the end of the document. Press [Enter] twice and then type **Enclosure**

16. On the menu bar, click **View**, and then click **Header and Footer**. On the Header and Footer toolbar, click the **Switch Between Header and Footer** button. In the footer area, type **1E Survey Letter-Firstname Lastname** and then on the Header and Footer toolbar, click the **Close** button.

17. From the **File** menu, click **Page Setup**, and then on the displayed **Page Setup** dialog box, click the **Layout tab**. Under **Page**, click the **Vertical alignment arrow**, and then click **Center**. In the lower right corner of the dialog box, click **OK**. Recall that one-page letters are commonly centered vertically on the page to give a more professional appearance.

18. On the Standard toolbar, click the **Save** button to save the changes you have made to your document. On the Standard toolbar, click the **Print Preview** button to view your document as it will print. On the Print Preview toolbar, click the **Print** button to print the letter, and then on the same toolbar, click the **Close** button.

19. From the **File** menu, click **Close** to close the document. At the right edge of the blue title bar, click the **Close** button to close Word.

End **You have completed Project 1E**

Project 1F — Interview Letter

Objectives: *View Headers and Footers; Create and Edit a New Document; Organize, Save, and Print Documents; and Preview and Print Documents, Close a Document, and Close Word.*

In the following Performance Assessment, you will create a letter to schedule an interview for Gabriela Quinones with a catering service. Your completed document will look similar to Figure 1.57. You will save your document as *1F_Interview_Letter_Firstname_Lastname.*

The Perfect Party
700 Washington Street
Dallas, TX 75202

September 22, 2005

Louise's Catering
2302 Boardwalk
Dallas, TX 75202

RE: Catering Services

Dear Ms. Gomez:

We have received a tremendous response to our ad for catering services. Your resume
and sample menus are outstanding and seem to fit with the vision for our business. We
would like to interview you and give you a chance to ask us questions. We will be
conducting interviews the week of October 10. My assistant, Ms. Finstad, will call to
schedule a time that will be convenient for you.

For the interview, we would invite you to bring a sample of your favorite dishes so we
can have an opportunity to taste your creations. There will be only two people conducting
the interview so a small sample would be appropriate.

We are looking forward to meeting with you.

Cordially,

Gabriela Quinones
Owner

1F Interview Letter-Firstname Lastname

Figure 1.57

(Project 1F–Interview Letter continues on the next page)

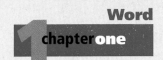
(Project 1F–Interview Letter continued)

1. Start **Word** and, if necessary, close the task pane. Beginning at the top of the page type the address on three lines as shown:

   The Perfect Party
   700 Washington Street
   Dallas, TX 75202

2. Press Enter four times. Type **September 22, 2005** and press Enter twice. Type the following on three lines:

   Louise's Catering
   2302 Boardwalk
   Dallas, TX 75202

3. Press Enter two times and then type **RE: Catering Services**
   Press Enter two times and type the salutation **Dear Ms. Gomez:**

4. Press Enter twice and type the body of the letter as follows, pressing Enter two times at the end of each paragraph:

   We have received a tremendous response to our ad for catering services. Your resume and sample menus are outstanding and seem to fit with the vision for our business. We would like to interview you and give you a chance to ask us questions. We will be conducting interviews the week of October 10. My assistant, Ms. Finstad, will call to schedule a time that will be convenient for you.

   For the interview, we would invite you to bring a sample of your favorite dishes so we can have an opportunity to taste your creations. There will be only two people conducting the interview so a small sample would be appropriate.

   We are looking forward to meeting with you.

5. Press Enter twice and type **Cordially,** create three blank lines (press Enter four times), and then type the following on two lines:

   Gabriela Quinones
   Owner

(Project 1F–Interview Letter continues on the next page)

(Project 1F–Interview Letter continued)

6. On the Standard toolbar, click the **Save** button. In the **Save As** dialog box, navigate to the location where you are saving your projects for this chapter. In the **File name** box, using your own name, type **1F_Interview_Letter_Firstname_Lastname** and then click the **Save** button.

7. Display the **View** menu, and then click **Header and Footer**. Click the **Switch Between Header and Footer** button. In the footer area, using your own information, type **1F Interview Letter-Firstname Lastname**

8. Double-click in the body of the document to close the Header and Footer toolbar and return to the document.

9. Display the **File** menu, click **Page Setup**, and then click the **Layout tab**. Under **Page**, click the **Vertical alignment arrow**, and then click **Center**. Click **OK** to center the letter on the page.

10. Proofread the letter to make sure it does not contain any typographical or spelling errors. Use the Spelling and Grammar checker to correct any errors.

11. On the Standard toolbar, click the **Print Preview** button to see how the letter will print on paper. On the Print Preview toolbar, click the **Print** button to print the letter. Close Print Preview and then click the **Save** button to save your changes. Close the document and close Word.

End You have completed Project 1F ───────────────

Project 1G — Interview Memo

Objectives: *Create and Edit a New Document; Select and Format Text; View Headers and Footers; and Organize, Save, and Print Documents.*

In the following Performance Assessment, you will edit a memo for Corey Finstad to Gabriela Quinones listing interviews that The Perfect Party has scheduled with catering firms. Your completed document will look similar to Figure 1.58. You will save your document as *1G_Interview_Memo_Firstname_Lastname.*

INTEROFFICE MEMORANDUM

To: Gabriela Quinones

From: Corey Finstad

RE: Interviews with Caterers

Date: September 30

cc: Angie Nguyen

As requested, I contacted the catering firms we discussed and have scheduled interviews with the selected candidates. I reserved the conference room and have cleared your calendar. The interview schedule is as follows:

Louise's Catering   October 12, 9:00 – 10:00
Sara's Gourmet   October 13, 9:00 – 10:00
Nancy's Pastries   October 13, 2:00 – 3:00
Feasts by Renee   October 14, 9:00 – 10:00

1G Interview Memo-Firstname Lastname

Figure 1.58

(Project 1G–Interview Memo continues on the next page)

(Project 1G–Interview Memo continued)

1. Start **Word**. On the Standard toolbar, click the **Open** button. Navigate to the location where the student files for this textbook are stored. Locate and open the file *w01G_Interview_Memo*.

2. From the **File** menu, click **Save As**. In the **Save As** dialog box, navigate to the location where you are saving your projects for this chapter. In the **File name** box, type **1G_Interview_Memo_Firstname_Lastname** and then click the **Save** button.

3. Click after the colon in the word *To:* then press Tab and type **Gabriela Quinones**

   Press ↓ twice to move to right of *From:* then press Tab and type **Corey Finstad**

4. Use the same keystroke technique to complete the heading portion of the memo as shown:

   RE: Interviews with Caterers

   Date: September 30

   CC: Angie Nguyen

5. Click to position the insertion point at the beginning of the third empty line in the body of the memo, and then type the following:

   As requested, I contacted the catering firms we discussed and have scheduled interviews with the selected candidates. I reserved the conference room and have cleared your calendar. The interview schedule is as follows:

6. Press Enter twice. Type **Louise's Catering** Press Tab and type **October 12, 9:00 –10:00** and then press Enter. Repeat this pattern to enter the remainder of the interview dates.

Sara's Gourmet	**October 12, 9:00–10:00**
Chef Michelangelo	**October 13, 9:00–10:00**
Nancy's Pastries	**October 13, 2:00–3:00**
Feasts by Renee	**October 14, 9:00–10:00**

(Project 1G–Interview Memo continues on the next page)

(Project 1G–Interview Memo continued)

7. On the Standard toolbar, click the **Spelling and Grammar** button. Click **Ignore Once** to ignore the any proper names that are flagged and correct any other errors that may be identified.

8. Beginning with the paragraph *As requested*, select all of the text of the memo and change the font to **Tahoma**, which is the same font used in the top portion of the memo.

9. Navigate to the top of the document and select the text *INTEROFFICE MEMORANDUM*. Change the font to **Arial Black** and the font size to **18** point.

10. Display the **View** menu and click **Header and Footer**. Click the **Switch Between Header and Footer** button. In the footer area, using your own information, type **1G Interview Memo-Firstname Lastname**

   Select the text you just typed in the footer and change the font to **Tahoma**, **12** point. Double-click the body of the document to close the Header and Footer toolbar and return to the document.

11. On the Standard toolbar, click the **Save** button to save your changes. On the Standard toolbar, click the **Print Preview** button to preview the document before it is printed. Print the document. Close the file and close Word.

End **You have completed Project 1G** ——————————————————

Project 1H—Offer Letter

Objectives: *Explore and Navigate the Word Window; View Documents; Use the Spelling and Grammar Checker; View Headers and Footers; Create and Edit a New Document; Select and Format Text; and Preview and Print Documents, Close a Document, and Close Word.*

In the following Performance Assessment, you will edit a letter for Gabriela Quinones to Sara's Gourmet requesting a follow-up meeting to discuss a possible business partnership. Your completed document will look similar to Figure 1.59. You will save your letter as *1H_Offer_Letter_Firstname_Lastname.*

The Perfect Party
700 Washington Street
Dallas, TX 75202

October 20, 2005

Sara's Gourmet
3200 Penny Lane
Dallas, TX 75202

Dear Sara:

We enjoyed meeting with you last week and were absolutely delighted with the appetizers you brought to the interview. You presented some unique ideas for party food, and demonstrated skill in the art of food presentation.

We would like to meet with you again before the end of the month to explore some possible business arrangements that would be mutually satisfying. As we stated in the interview, we are interested in working with someone on a contract basis initially, with a view to a longer term relationship that could include becoming a partner in *The Perfect Party*. We would like to discuss how your plans to grow your business might intersect with our need to add a catering component to our party planning business.

Please call my office at (214)-555-0188 to set up a time when you could meet with us. My partner, Angie Nguyen, is looking forward to meeting you.

Yours truly,

Gabriela Quinones
Owner

1H Offer Letter-Firstname Lastname

Figure 1.59

1. Start **Word**. On the Standard toolbar, click the **Open** button. Navigate to the location where the student files for this textbook are stored. Locate and open the file *w01H_Offer_Letter*.

2. Display the **File** menu, click **Save As**, and then use the **Save in arrow** to navigate to the location where you are storing your projects for this chapter. In the **File name** box, using your own information, type **1H_Offer_Letter_Firstname_Lastname**

(Project 1H–Offer Letter continues on the next page)

(Project 1H–Offer Letter continued)

3. In the paragraph that begins *We enjoyed meeting*, select *liked* and type **were absolutely delighted with** and then adjust the spacing if necessary.

4. In the same paragraph, select *interesting* and replace it with **unique** In the same sentence delete the word *alternatives*. In the same sentence, select the phrase *are very skillful* and replace it with **demonstrated skill**

5. In the paragraph that begins *We would like*, delete the word *once*. In the same sentence, replace the word *consider* with **explore** In the same sentence, place the insertion point at the end of the word *mutual* and type **ly**

6. There are some grammar and spelling errors that need to be corrected. Right-click on the duplicate or misspelled words and correct as necessary.

7. In the paragraph that begins with *We would like*, use the technique of Ctrl + Shift + → to select the three words *The Perfect Party* and then change the font to **Lucida Calligraphy**. If you do not have that font, choose a similar font from the list. Change the font size to **11** point. With the name still selected, click the **Bold** button.

8. Click in the blank line following *Yours truly* and add two more blank lines by pressing Enter two times. Three blank lines is the standard space allotted for a signature in a letter. Display the Page Setup dialog box and center the letter vertically on the page.

9. Display the **View** menu and then click **Header and Footer**. Click the **Switch Between Header and Footer** button. In the footer area, using your own information, type **1H Offer Letter-Firstname Lastname** Double-click in the body of the document to close the Header and Footer toolbar and return to the document.

10. Use Ctrl + Home to navigate to the top of the letter. On the Standard toolbar, click the **Read** button to display the document in Reading Layout view. Proofread the letter to make sure it is correct. In this format, two pages display to make the reading easier, but recall that this is not the page preview. When printed, the document will print on one page.

11. On the Reading Layout toolbar, click the **Close** button to return to the Page Layout view. Click the **Save** button to save your changes. Preview the letter in Print Preview and then print the document. Close the file and then close Word.

End **You have completed Project 1H** ⎯⎯⎯⎯⎯⎯⎯⎯⎯⎯⎯⎯⎯⎯⎯⎯

Project 1I—Contract

Objectives: *Explore and Navigate the Word Window; View Documents; View Headers and Footers; Create and Edit a New Document; Use the Spelling and Grammar Checker; Select and Format Text; Organize, Save, and Print Documents; and Preview and Print Documents, Close a Document, and Close Word.*

In the following Mastery Assessment, you will complete a contract that is given to clients of The Perfect Party. Your completed document will look similar to Figure 1.60. You will save your document as *1I_Contract_Firstname_Lastname*.

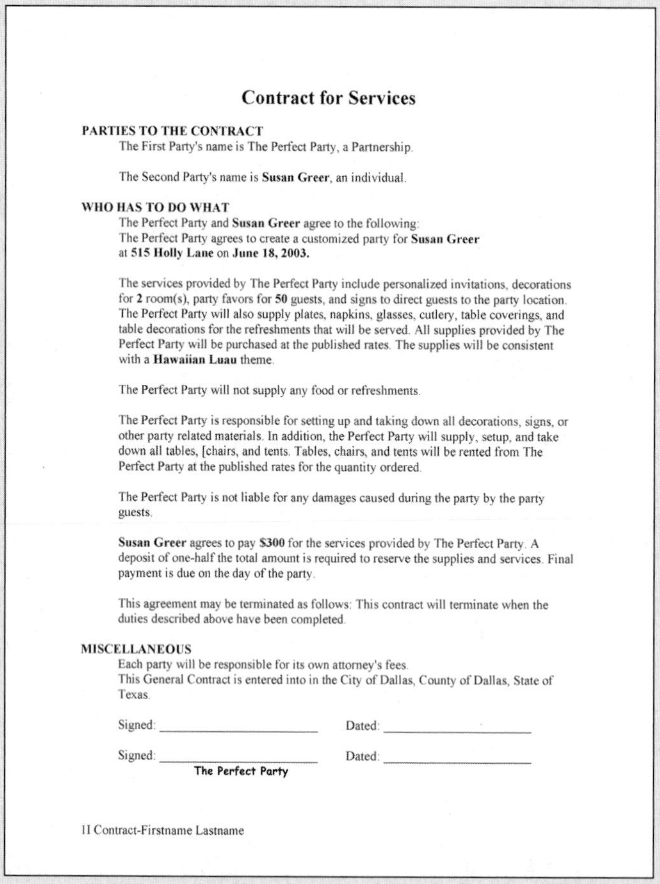

Contract for Services

PARTIES TO THE CONTRACT
The First Party's name is The Perfect Party, a Partnership.

The Second Party's name is **Susan Greer**, an individual.

WHO HAS TO DO WHAT
The Perfect Party and **Susan Greer** agree to the following:
The Perfect Party agrees to create a customized party for **Susan Greer**
at **515 Holly Lane** on **June 18, 2003.**

The services provided by The Perfect Party include personalized invitations, decorations for **2** room(s), party favors for **50** guests, and signs to direct guests to the party location. The Perfect Party will also supply plates, napkins, glasses, cutlery, table coverings, and table decorations for the refreshments that will be served. All supplies provided by The Perfect Party will be purchased at the published rates. The supplies will be consistent with a **Hawaiian Luau** theme.

The Perfect Party will not supply any food or refreshments.

The Perfect Party is responsible for setting up and taking down all decorations, signs, or other party related materials. In addition, the Perfect Party will supply, setup, and take down all tables, [chairs, and tents. Tables, chairs, and tents will be rented from The Perfect Party at the published rates for the quantity ordered.

The Perfect Party is not liable for any damages caused during the party by the party guests.

Susan Greer agrees to pay **$300** for the services provided by The Perfect Party. A deposit of one-half the total amount is required to reserve the supplies and services. Final payment is due on the day of the party.

This agreement may be terminated as follows: This contract will terminate when the duties described above have been completed.

MISCELLANEOUS
Each party will be responsible for its own attorney's fees.
This General Contract is entered into in the City of Dallas, County of Dallas, State of Texas.

Signed: _____   Dated: _____

Signed: _____   Dated: _____
　　　　　The Perfect Party

1I Contract-Firstname Lastname

Figure 1.60

1. Display the **Open** dialog box. Navigate to the student files, and then locate and open the file *w01I_Contract*. Display the **File** menu, click **Save As**, and then use the **Save in arrow** to navigate to the location where you are storing your projects for this chapter. In the **File name** box, type **1I_Contract_Firstname_Lastname**

2. Click the **Read** button to view this document and read through the contents of the contract. In the reading view, text size is increased to ease your reading of the document on the screen. Notice that there are three headings that are shown in all uppercase letters.

(Project 1I–Contract continues on the next page)

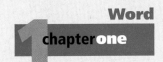
(Project 1I–Contract continued)

3. On the Reading View toolbar, click the **Close** button to return to the Print Layout view. Use the **Spelling and Grammar** checker to correct the errors in the document. The last error flagged shows *State*, and suggests that this needs to be changed to *and State*. Click **Ignore Once** to ignore this occurrence.

4. Locate the three headings in uppercase letters. Select each one and add bold emphasis.

5. Locate the black lines in the document that represent blanks to be filled in. Press Insert on your keyboard to turn on the overtype feature. Alternatively, double-click the **OVR** button displayed in the Status bar at the bottom of the Word Window.

6. In the line beginning *The Second Party's name*, click to position your insertion point after the space following *is*. Type **Susan Greer** and notice that as you type, your typing will be displayed in bold. Make sure you do not type over any of the words in the contract. Then, use Delete or ←Bksp to remove the unused portion of the black line. On the next two black lines, type **Susan Greer** again and delete the rest of both black lines. On the fourth black line, following the word *at*, type **515 Holly Lane** and delete the rest of the black line. At the beginning of the next black line, type the current date followed by a period and delete the rest of the black line. Delete unused portions of the black lines using Delete or ←Bksp as needed in the remaining steps.

7. In the paragraph that begins with *The services provided*, type **2** for the number of rooms to be decorated, and type **50** for the number of guests. On the last black line in this paragraph, type **Hawaiian Luau** as the theme for the party.

8. Locate the next black line, and type **Susan Greer** and in the next black line type **300** following the dollar sign.

9. At the end of the contract, under *Signed*, select *The Perfect Party* and change the font size to **10**, change the font to **Comic Sans MS**, and add bold emphasis.

10. Display the footer area, and then, using your own information, type **1I Contract-Firstname Lastname**

11. Save the changes. Preview the document and then print it. Close the file. On the Status bar, double-click the **OVR** button to turn off the overtype feature. Close Word.

End **You have completed Project 1I**

Project 1J—Memo

Objectives: *Create and Edit a New Document; View Documents; View Headers and Footers; Organize, Save, and Print Documents; Select and Format Text; Preview and Print Documents, Close a Document, and Close Word.*

In the following Mastery Assessment, you will create a memo for Christina Stevens requesting a copy of a contract from another Perfect Party employee and asking him to work at an upcoming event. Your completed memo will look similar to Figure 1.61. You will save your document as *1J_Memo_Firstname_Lastname*.

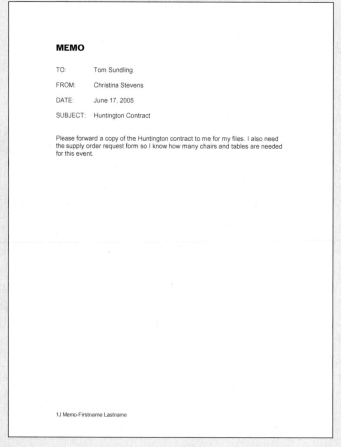

MEMO

TO: Tom Sundling

FROM: Christina Stevens

DATE: June 17, 2005

SUBJECT: Huntington Contract

Please forward a copy of the Huntington contract to me for my files. I also need the supply order request form so I know how many chairs and tables are needed for this event.

1J Memo-Firstname Lastname

Figure 1.61

1. Open **Word** and begin with a new document. Change the font to **Arial Black**, and the font size to **16**. Press CapsLock, type **MEMO** and press Enter twice. Change the font to **12-point Arial**.

2. Save the project in your storage location as **1J_Memo_Firstname_Lastname**

(Project 1J–Memo continues on the next page)

(Project 1J–Memo continued)

3. Change the font to **12-point Arial**. Type **TO:** and press `Tab` twice. Type **Tom Sundling** and press `Enter` twice. Follow the same pattern to enter the remainder of the heading, pressing `Enter` twice to create a blank line between each heading line. You will need to press `Tab` twice after *DATE* and then type the current date for the date line. Use the appropriate number of tabs to line up the text. Press `CapsLock` to turn it off.

   FROM: **Christina Stevens**

   DATE:

   SUBJECT: Huntington Contract Party

4. Make sure the information entered in the memo heading aligns as shown in Figure 1.61. Save your document.

5. At the end of the Subject line, press `Enter` three times and type the body of the memo as follows:

   Please forward a copy of the Huntington contract to me for my files. I also need the supply order request form so I know how many chairs and tables are needed for this event.

6. Save your document. Create a footer and type **1J Memo-Firstname Lastname** and then format the text in the footer to **10-point Arial** font.

7. Proofread the document and use the Spelling and Grammar checker to correct any errors if necessary.

8. Print the memo, save your changes, and close the file.

End **You have completed Project 1J** ———————————

Project 1K — Party

Objectives: *Create and Edit a New Document; View Headers and Footers; Organize, Save, and Print Documents; Select and Format Text; Preview and Print Documents, Close a Document, and Close Word.*

Using the information provided, draft a letter for the owners of The Perfect Party describing the services available to potential customers. Save your document as *1K_Party_Firstname_Lastname*.

1. Open **Word**. Type the current date and press Enter four times to create two blank lines. Type **Dear** and then create a blank line.

2. Compose a letter that explains the services offered by The Perfect Party. The tone of the letter should be positive and sales oriented. The letter should answer the question "why do I need this service?" As you write the letter, use your own imagination along with the information in the beginning of the chapter that describes the company. The letter should contain three paragraphs—an introductory paragraph, a second paragraph describing the services offered, and a closing paragraph.

3. Add an appropriate closing, such as **Sincerely** Create three blank lines and then type:

   Angie Nguyen

   Owner

4. Proofread the letter and correct any spelling or grammar errors.

5. Change the font of the letter to a font and font size of your choosing.

6. Create a footer and, using your own information, type **1K Party-Firstname Lastname**

7. Preview the letter. Use the **Page Setup** dialog box to center the letter vertically on the page.

8. Save the letter in your storage location as **1K_Party_Firstname_Lastname** Print the letter. Close the file and close Word.

End You have completed Project 1K

Project 1L — Invitation

Objectives: *Create and Edit a New Document; View Headers and Footers; Organize, Save, and Print Documents; Select and Format Text; Preview and Print Documents, Close a Document, and Close Word.*

Create a sample invitation for The Perfect Party that could be used for birthday parties. Save your invitation as *1L_Invitation_Firstname_Lastname.*

1. From your student files, open the file *w01L_Invitation* and save it in your storage location as **1L_Invitation_Firstname_Lastname**. This document contains only a title. On separate lines add labels for information that is typically found on an invitation, such as who the party is for; when, where, and why it is being held; any party theme; refreshments provided; and an R.S.V.P line. Place a blank line between each line of information.

2. Change the font of the title to **Batang** and increase the font size so the title is large and easy to read. Add bold emphasis to the title. If Batang is not available on your computer, choose another font.

3. Format the labels to **12-point Batang**. Add bold emphasis to the labels.

4. Next to each label, add a statement in brackets that describes the information to enter in each empty space; for example, **[Enter address of party]**

5. Change the font of the instructions on each line to a font of your choice in an appropriate font size.

6. View the footer area and, using your own information, type **1L Invitation-Firstname Lastname**

7. Save your changes and print the invitation. Close the file and close Word.

End **You have completed Project 1L**

On the Internet

Microsoft Word Specialist Certification

As you progress through this textbook, you will practice skills necessary to complete the Microsoft certification test for Word 2003. Access your Internet connection and go to the Microsoft certification Web site at **www.microsoft.com/traincert/mcp/officespecialist/requirements.asp**. Navigate to the Microsoft Word objectives for the certification exam. Print the Core (Specialist) objectives for the Microsoft Word user certification and any other information about taking the test.

GO! with Help

Getting Help While You Work

The Word Help system is extensive and can help you as you work. In this exercise, you will view information about getting help as you work in Word.

1. Start **Word**. On the Standard toolbar, click the **Microsoft Office Word Help** button 🔘. In the **Search for** box, on the **Microsoft Word Help** task pane type **help**. Click the green **Start searching** button to the right of the *Search for* box.

2. In the displayed **Search Results** task pane, click *About getting help while you work*. Maximize the displayed window, and at the top of the window, click the **Show All** link. Scroll through and read all the various ways you can get help while working in Word.

3. If you want, print a copy of the information by clicking the printer button at the top of Microsoft Office Word Help task pane.

4. Close the Help window, and then close Word.

2 chaptertwo

Formatting and Organizing Text

In this chapter, you will: complete these projects **and** practice these skills.

Project 2A **Changing the Appearance of a Document**	**Objectives**
	• Change Document and Paragraph Layout
	• Change and Reorganize Text

Project 2B **Working with Lists and References**	**Objectives**
	• Create and Modify Lists
	• Work with Headers and Footers
	• Insert Frequently Used Text
	• Insert References

Lake Michigan City College

Lake Michigan City College is located along the lakefront of Chicago—one of the nation's most exciting cities. The college serves its large and diverse student body and makes positive contributions to the community through relevant curricula, partnerships with businesses and nonprofit organizations, and learning experiences that allow students to be full participants in the global community. The college offers three associate degrees in 20 academic areas, adult education programs, and continuing education offerings on campus, at satellite locations, and online.

© Getty Images, Inc.

Formatting and Organizing Text

Typing text is just the beginning of the process of creating an effective, professional-looking document. Microsoft Word also provides many tools for formatting paragraphs and documents; tools to create shortcuts for entering commonly used text; and quick ways to copy, cut, and move text.

Word also provides tools to create specialized formats, such as endnotes, bulleted and numbered lists, and indented paragraphs.

In this chapter you will edit a report about a groupware database and how it is being used.

Project 2A **Campus Software**

You have practiced opening existing documents and creating and editing new documents. In this chapter you will go further and learn how to change paragraph layouts, work with lists, headers and footers, and references.

In Activities 2.1 through 2.12 you will edit a document that describes the groupware software used by Lake Michigan City College. Your completed document will look similar to Figure 2.1. You will save your document as *2A_Campus_Software_Firstname_Lastname.*

TSF Database 4
Background and Usage Within the Academic Counseling Department
Lake Michigan City College

Presented to the Database Development Committee
of the Intensive English Department

TSF Database 4 is the platform used to make information of the Academic Counseling Department at the College available internally to staff, faculty, and students at the main campus and satellite campuses. The College previously conducted much of the administration of this department at the main campus, but recent budget redistributions and staff changes have shifted much of the responsibility for the administration to the satellite campuses.

TSF Database 4 is a program that captures unstructured information created by diverse entities and allows it to be viewed and manipulated by users within the system. It is considered a form of groupware—programs that help some work together collectively while located remotely from each other. Groupware services can include:

shared calendars

shared information

collaborative writing

e-mail

electronic meetings with shared information

TSF Database 4 is a database, workflow engine, document store, client/server environment, electronic mail service, and data distribution system.

TSF 4 collects information with the goal of collecting knowledge. "Information taking data and putting it into a meaningful pattern. Knowledge is the ability to use that information." Since much information is stored in various places, TSF Database 4 attem collect the information in an accessible manner available to the entire organization.

How is information collected?

TSF Database 4 is a collection of databases, but the databases consist of docume just data that must be manipulated in some way to make sense. This concept is called do oriented data modeling. "Data modeling is the analysis of data objects that are used in a or other context and the identification of the relationships among these data objects." Ea document contains keyword fields that allow it to be sorted and retrieved. Documents al contain fields called rich text fields that can contain formatted text, sounds, pictures, an other programs. Such fields are designed to contain loosely structured information.

2A_Campus_Software_Firstname_Lastname

How is information shared?

TSF Database 4 clients connect to a database server and to each other. Each client and server has a unique ID file that establishes their identity and is also used for security purposes. Replication manages changes to documents and keeps their contents synchronized on various servers and clients. (Database replication is the copying and maintenance of data on multiple servers.) During replication, only information that has changed is moved across the network. This allows users working online to see the latest information almost instantly, and users working offline can update, or replicate, their work to the network very quickly.

Mail enabling is another important feature of TSF Database 4. It allows servers to route documents as messages and allows users to send information to a database.

How does the ACD use TSF Database 4?

The five main types of applications, discussion, broadcasting, reference, tracking, and workflow/approval, are all used by the Academic Counseling Department. Broadcasting refers to using the system to deliver non-critical college-wide information. Reference refers to using the system to replace printed reference materials, such as policy manuals, class information, and so forth. For tracking applications, the replication and security features make the system a useful tool for applications such as personnel and student tracking. Workflow/approval refers to applications where it is necessary to route knowledge according to defined protocols.

TSF Database 4 is not suited for applications requiring heavy analysis of numbers, real time analysis, or relational linking or record locking. It is, however, useful for collecting the results of such analysis and manipulation and presenting it in a format easily accessed by users throughout the College, including students. It is well suited, therefore, for use by the department.

Training Schedule:

Training will begin in May, and should be finished by the end of the month. The tentative training schedule follows.

2A_Campus_Software_Firstname_Lastname

Figure 2.1
Project 2A—Campus Software Document

Objective 1
Change Document and Paragraph Layout

Document layout includes *margins*—the space between the text and the top, bottom, left, and right edges of the page. Paragraph layout includes line spacing, indents, tabs, and so forth. Information about paragraph formats is stored in the paragraph mark at the end of a paragraph. When you press the Enter key, the new paragraph mark contains the formatting of the previous paragraph.

Activity 2.1 Setting Margins

You can change each of the four page margins independently. You can also change the margins for the whole document at once or change the margins for only a portion of the document.

1 Start Word. On the Standard toolbar, click the **Open** button. Navigate to the location where the student files for this textbook are stored. Locate **w02A_Campus_Software** and click once to select it. Then, in the lower right corner of the **Open** dialog box, click **Open**.

The *w02A_Campus_Software* file opens. See Figure 2.2.

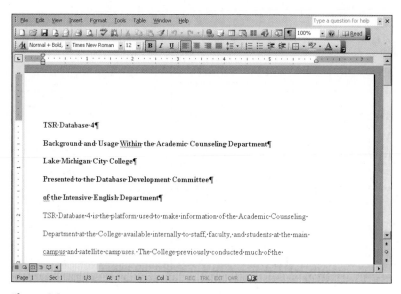

Figure 2.2

2 If your formatting marks are not displayed as shown in Figure 2.2, on the Standard toolbar, click the **Show/Hide ¶** button to display the formatting marks on your screen.

3 On the **File** menu, click **Save As**.

The Save As dialog box displays.

4 Use the **Save in arrow** to navigate to the location where you are saving your files. In the **File name** box, delete the existing text, and using your own name, type **2A_Campus_Software_Firstname_Lastname**

5 Click **Save**.

The document is saved with a new name.

6 On the Standard toolbar, click the **Zoom button arrow** ⌐100% ▾⌐ and click **Page Width**.

7 On the **File** menu, click **Page Setup**.

The Page Setup dialog box displays.

8 In the **Page Setup** dialog box, if necessary, click the **Margins tab**. Under **Margins**, with *1"* highlighted in the **Top** box, type **1.5**

This will change the top margin to 1.5 inches on all pages of the document. (Note: You do not need to type the inch (") mark.)

9 Press ⌐Tab⌐ two times to highlight the measurement in the **Left** box, type **1** and then press ⌐Tab⌐ again. With the measurement in the **Right** box highlighted, type **1**

The new margins will be applied to the entire document. Compare your Page Setup dialog box to Figure 2.3.

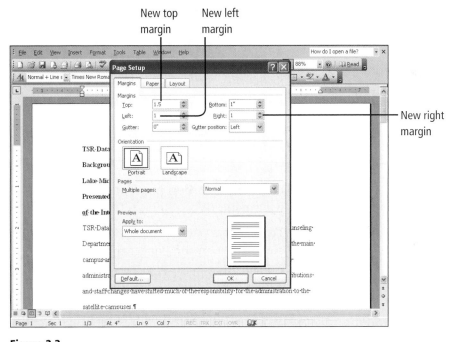

Figure 2.3

10 In the lower right corner of the dialog box, click **OK**.

The dialog box closes, and the new margins are applied to your document. The width of the document is displayed on the ruler. If the ruler is not displayed, from the View menu, click Ruler. With 1" left and right margins, the document width will be 6.5".

Activity 2.2 Aligning Text

Alignment is the placement of paragraph text relative to the left and right margins. Most paragraph text is ***aligned left***—aligned at the left margin, leaving the right margin uneven. Three other types of paragraph alignment are available: ***center alignment***, which is centered between the left and right margin, ***right alignment***, which is aligned on the right margin, and ***justified alignment***, which is text aligned on both the left and right margins. Examples are shown in the table in Figure 2.4.

Paragraph Alignment Options		
Alignment	**Button**	**Description and Example**
Align Left	🗐	Align Left is the default paragraph alignment in Word. Text in the paragraph aligns at the left margin and the right margin is ragged.
Center	🗐	The Center alignment option aligns text in the paragraph so that it is centered between the left and right margins.
Align Right	🗐	Align Right is used to align text at the right margin. Using Align Right, the left margin, which is normally even, is ragged.
Justify	🗐	The Justify alignment option adds additional space between words so that both the left and right margins are even. Justify is often used when formatting newspaper-style columns.

Figure 2.4

1 Place the insertion point anywhere in the first line of text in the document.

To format a paragraph, you only need to have the insertion point somewhere in the paragraph—you do not need to select all of the text in the paragraph.

2 On the Formatting toolbar, click the **Center** button 🗐.

The first paragraph, which is a title, is centered.

3 Move the pointer into the left margin area, just to the left of the second line of text. When the pointer changes to a white arrow, drag down to select the second, third, fourth, and fifth lines of text as shown in Figure 2.5.

Recall that a paragraph consists of a paragraph mark and all the text in front of it. To format multiple paragraphs, they need to be selected.

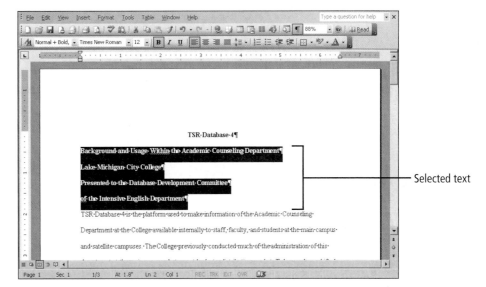

Figure 2.5

4 On the Formatting toolbar, click the **Center** button 🔲.

All five of the title lines of bold text are centered. The last four lines are still selected. See Figure 2.6.

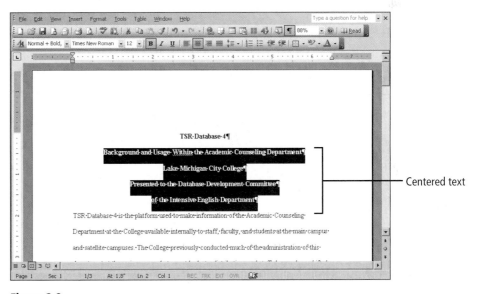

Figure 2.6

5 Click the down arrow at the bottom of the vertical scrollbar until you can see all of the paragraph that begins *TSR Database 4 is the platform* and click anywhere in this paragraph. Make sure that you can see the first two or three lines of the following paragraph also.

6 On the Formatting toolbar, click the **Justify** button 🔲.

Both the left and right edges of the paragraph are even. The other paragraphs are not affected. See Figure 2.7.

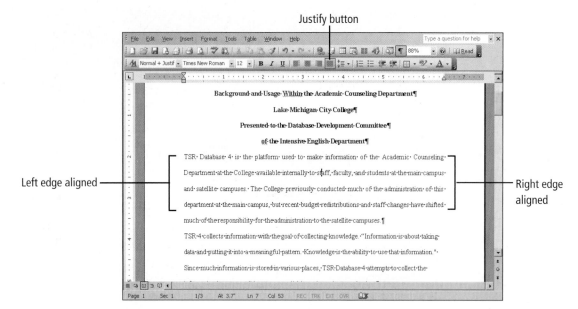

Justify button

Left edge aligned

Right edge aligned

Figure 2.7

7 On the Formatting toolbar, click the **Align Left** button.

The paragraph is returned to the left aligned format.

Activity 2.3 Changing Line Spacing

Line spacing is the distance between lines of text in a paragraph. A single-spaced paragraph of 12-point text has six lines per vertical inch. If you double-space the same text, each line will be 24 points high (12 points of text, 12 points of space), or three lines per inch. See Figure 2.8.

Line Spacing Options

Spacing	Example
Single (1.0)	Most business documents are single spaced. This means that the spacing between lines is just enough to separate the text.
Double (2.0)	Many college research papers and reports, and many draft documents that need room for notes are double spaced; there is room for a full line of text between each document line.

Figure 2.8

1 Move the pointer to the left margin just to the left of the first title line. When the pointer changes to a white arrow, drag downward to highlight the first and second lines of the title.

2 On the Formatting toolbar, click the arrow on the right of the **Line Spacing** button.

A list displays. A check mark next to 2.0 indicates that the selected paragraphs are double spaced. See Figure 2.9.

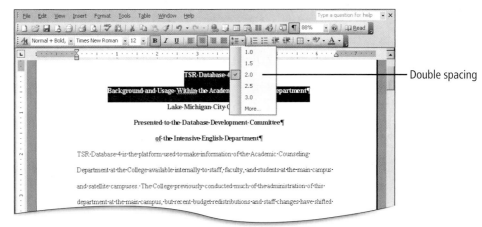

Double spacing

Figure 2.9

3 On the displayed **Line Spacing** list, click **1.0**.

The selected paragraphs are single spaced. The third title line is part of the first group of titles, so its spacing was left as double spaced to separate it from the following title lines. See Figure 2.10.

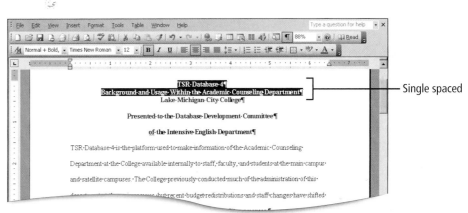

Single spaced

Figure 2.10

4 Click to place the insertion point anywhere in the fourth line of the title. On the **Formatting** toolbar, move the pointer over the **Line Spacing** button.

A ScreenTip displays, indicating *Line Spacing (1)*. This means that the last operation performed using this button is now the default when you click the button.

5 On the Formatting toolbar, click the **Line Spacing** button. Make sure you click the button and not the arrow on the right side of the button.

The line is single spaced.

6 In the paragraph that begins *TSR Database 4 is the platform*, click to place the insertion point to the left of the first word in the paragraph.

7 Use the vertical scrollbar to scroll to the bottom of the document, position the I-beam pointer ⟨I⟩ to the right of the last word in the text, hold down ⟨Shift⟩ and click.

All text between the insertion point and the point at which you clicked is selected. This ⟨Shift⟩ + click technique is convenient to select a block of text between two points that span several pages.

8 On the Formatting toolbar, click the **Line Spacing** button ⟨≣·⟩.

The selected text is formatted with single spacing.

9 Scroll to the top of the document and click anywhere to cancel the text selection.

Compare your screen to Figure 2.11.

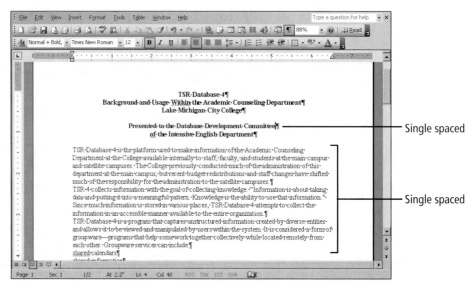

Figure 2.11

10 On the Standard toolbar, click the **Save** button ⟨💾⟩.

Activity 2.4 Adding Space After Paragraphs

Adjusting paragraph spacing from the Paragraph dialog box gives you the most control, because you can control the space before or after paragraphs using points as the unit of measure. Remember, there are 72 points per inch.

1 Click anywhere in the paragraph that begins *TSR Database 4 is the platform.*

2 On the **Format** menu, click **Paragraph**.

The Paragraph dialog box displays. You can also open this dialog box by clicking the arrow on the Line Spacing button ⟨≣·⟩ and clicking More from the displayed list.

3 If necessary, click the Indents and Spacing tab. Under **Spacing**, in the **After** box, click the up arrow twice.

The value in the box changes from 0 pt. to 12 pt. The up and down arrows, called *spin box arrows*, increment the point size by six points at a time. Alternatively, type a number of your choice directly into the text box. See Figure 2.12.

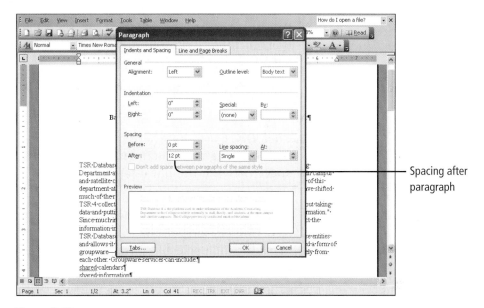

Spacing after paragraph

Figure 2.12

4 Click **OK**.

A 12-point space is added to the end of the paragraph. See Figure 2.13.

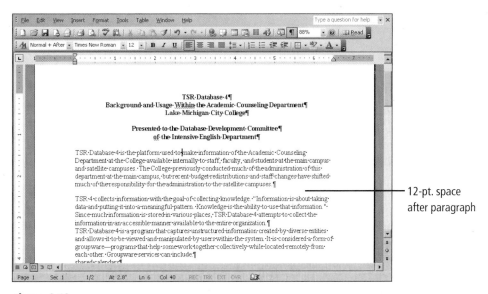

12-pt. space after paragraph

Figure 2.13

5 In the paragraph that begins *TSR 4 collects information*, click to the left of first word in the paragraph. Use the vertical scrollbar to scroll to the end of the document, position the I-beam pointer $\boxed{I}$ to the right of the last word in the document, hold down $\boxed{\text{Shift}}$ and click.

The text between the insertion point and the end of the document is selected.

6 With the text selected, display the **Format** menu, and then click **Paragraph**. Alternatively, you can right-click in the selected text and then click Paragraph from the shortcut menu.

7 In the displayed **Paragraph** dialog box, under **Spacing**, in the **After** box, click the **up spin arrow** twice.

The value in the box changes from 0 pt. to 12 pt.

8 Click **OK**. Click anywhere in the document to cancel the selection. Scroll through the document to examine the result of adding extra space between the paragraphs.

Recall that paragraph formatting instructions are stored in the paragraph marks at the end of each paragraph. When you select more than one paragraph, these instructions are placed in the paragraph mark for each selected paragraph but not for any other paragraphs in the document. Compare your screen to Figure 2.14.

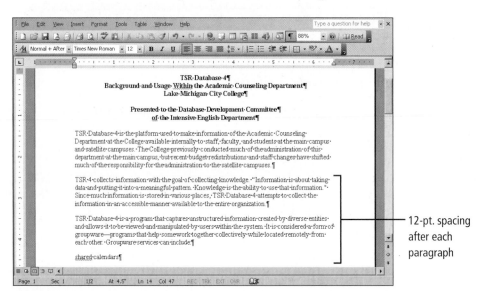

12-pt. spacing after each paragraph

Figure 2.14

9 On the Standard toolbar, click the **Save** button 🖫.

Another Way ── **Adding Space**

You can add space to the end of a paragraph in the following ways:

- Press Enter to add a blank line.

- Change the line spacing to double.

- From the Paragraph dialog box, adjust the spacing after the paragraph.

Activity 2.5 Indenting Paragraphs

In addition to adding space at the end of paragraphs, indenting the first lines of paragraphs provides visual cues to the reader to help break the document up and make it easier to read.

1 Hold down Ctrl and press Home to move to the top of page 1. Then, click anywhere in the paragraph that begins *TSR Database 4 is the platform.*

2 On the **Format** menu, click **Paragraph**.

The Paragraph dialog box displays.

3 Be sure that the **Indents and Spacing tab** is displayed. Under **Indentation**, click the **Special arrow**, and from the displayed list, click **First line**.

4 Under **Indentation**, in the **By** box, make sure *0.5"* is displayed. See Figure 2.15.

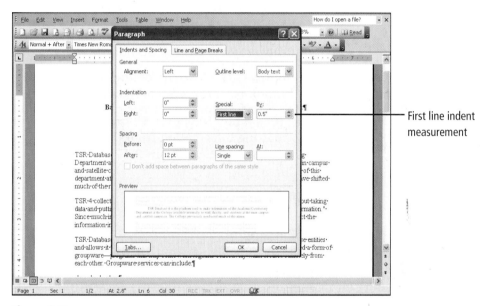

First line indent measurement

Figure 2.15

5 In the lower right corner of the dialog box, click **OK**.

The first line of the paragraph is indented by 0.5 inch, and the First Line Indent marker on the ruler moves to the 0.5 inch mark. See Figure 2.16.

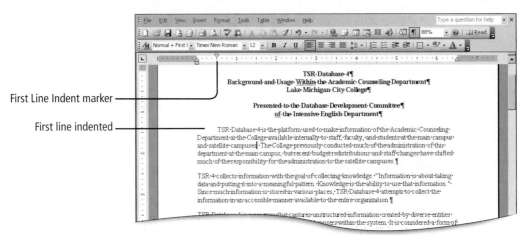

First Line Indent marker

First line indented

Figure 2.16

6 On the Standard toolbar, click the **Save** button 🖫.

Activity 2.6 Using the Format Painter

1 Click anywhere in the paragraph that begins *TSR Database 4 is the platform*. On the Standard toolbar, click the **Format Painter** button ⬛. Move the pointer over the next paragraph, beginning *TSR Database 4 collects information*.

The pointer takes the shape of a paintbrush, and contains the formatting information from the paragraph where the insertion point is positioned. See Figure 2.17.

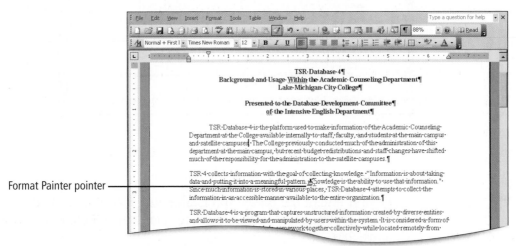

Format Painter pointer

Figure 2.17

2 Click once.

The paragraph is formatted with the same formatting as the previous paragraph.

The pointer returns to its normal I-beam 🔳 shape.

3 On the Standard toolbar, *double-click* the **Format Painter** button. Move the pointer over the paragraph that begins *TSR Database 4 is a program that captures*.

4 Click once.

The paragraph is indented, but this time the Format Painter paintbrush remains active.

5 Scroll down using the down scroll arrow and move the pointer over the paragraph that begins *TSR Database 4 is a database*. Click once.

6 Scroll down and click once in each of the remaining paragraphs that are not bold subheadings.

This is much faster than clicking on each paragraph and then opening the Paragraph dialog box to set the indentation parameters.

7 On the Standard toolbar, click the **Format Painter** button.

The Format Painter feature is turned off. You can also turn it off by pressing Esc.

8 On the Standard toolbar, click the **Save** button.

Objective 2
Change and Reorganize Text

Changing and reorganizing text is accomplished using Word tools such as the *Office Clipboard*, a temporary storage area that holds text. Text can be moved to the Office Clipboard by *copying* existing text, which leaves the original text in place, or by *cutting* text, which removes it from its original location. You can then *paste* the contents of the clipboard in a new location. There are keyboard shortcuts for many of these tools, as shown in Figure 2.18.

Activity 2.7 Finding and Replacing Text

Finding and then replacing text is a quick way to make a change in a document that occurs more than one time. For example, if you misspelled someone's last name, Word can search for all instances of the name and replace it with the correct spelling.

Keyboard Shortcuts for Editing Text

Keyboard Shortcut	Action
Ctrl + X	Cut text or graphic and place it on the Office Clipboard
Ctrl + C	Copy text or graphic and place it on the Office Clipboard
Ctrl + V	Paste the contents of the Office Clipboard
Ctrl + Z	Undo an action
Ctrl + Y	Redo an action
Ctrl + F	Find text
Ctrl + H	Find and replace text

Figure 2.18

1 Press `Ctrl` + `Home` to position the insertion point at the beginning of the document.

When you initiate a find-and-replace operation, it begins from the location of the insertion point and proceeds to the end of the document. If you begin a search in the middle of a document, Word will prompt you to return to the beginning of the document and continue the search.

2 On the **Edit** menu, click **Replace**.

3 In the displayed **Find and Replace** dialog box, in the **Find what** box, type **TSR**

4 In the **Find and Replace** dialog box, in the **Replace with** box, type **TSF**

5 Click **Find Next**.

The first instance of *TSR* is highlighted, and the Find and Replace dialog box remains open. See Figure 2.19.

First instance of found text ———

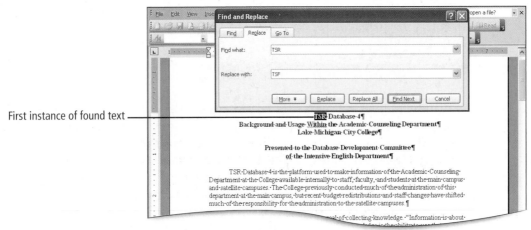

Figure 2.19

6 Click the **Replace** button.

The first instance of TSR is replaced by TSF, and the next instance of TSR is highlighted. See Figure 2.20.

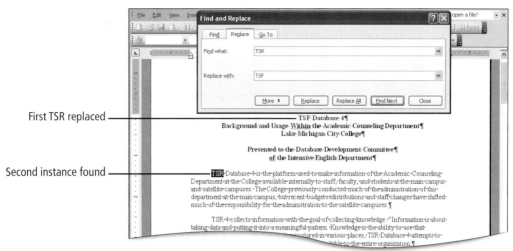

First TSR replaced

Second instance found

Figure 2.20

7 Click the **Replace All** button.

Every occurrence of TSR is replaced with TSF, and a dialog box indicates the number of replacements made. See Figure 2.21.

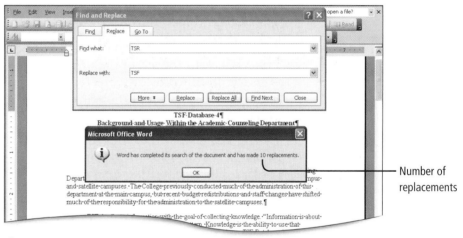

Number of replacements

Figure 2.21

8 Click **OK** to close the dialog box. In the **Find and Replace** dialog box click **Close**.

The Find and Replace dialog box closes.

Activity 2.8 Selecting and Deleting Text

You have practiced removing text one letter at a time using the Backspace key and the Delete key. For removing larger blocks of text, it is more efficient to select the block of text and then delete it.

1 Scroll down until you can see the lower portion of page 1 and locate the paragraph that begins *TSF Database 4 is a collection of databases.*

2 At the end of the fifth line in the paragraph, locate the word *can*, and then double-click to select the word. See Figure 2.22.

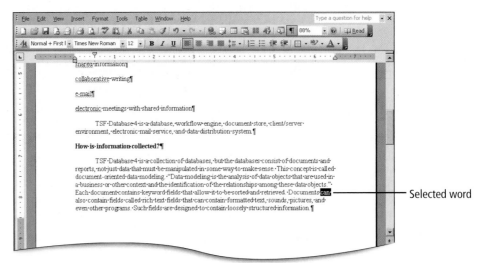

Selected word

Figure 2.22

3 Press Delete.

The word is removed from the paragraph.

4 Locate the phrase *and reports* in the first sentence of the same paragraph. Click to the left of the phrase, hold down Ctrl + Shift, and press → twice. Both words are selected. See Figure 2.23. Alternatively, you could click to the left of the phrase and drag to select both words, or you could click at the beginning of the phrase and Shift + click at the end of the phrase.

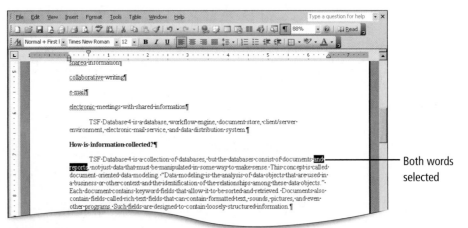

Both words selected

Figure 2.23

5 Press Delete.

Both words are deleted.

6 On the Standard toolbar, click the **Save** button.

Activity 2.9 Cutting and Pasting Text

You can move text from one location in a document to a different location in the same document with the commands cut and paste. The **cut** command moves text out of the document and onto the Office Clipboard—the temporary storage location for text or graphics. Then, use the **paste** command to paste the contents of the Office Clipboard into the new location.

1 Scroll down to view the upper portion of page 2, and locate the paragraph that begins *TSF Database 4 clients connect.*

2 Locate the second sentence, that begins with *Replication manages changes.* Hold down Ctrl and click anywhere in the sentence.

The entire sentence is selected. See Figure 2.24.

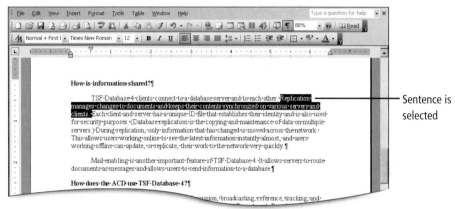

Sentence is selected

Figure 2.24

3 On the Standard toolbar, click the **Cut** button.

The sentence is removed from the document and moved to the Office Clipboard.

> ### Note — The Difference Between Using Delete, Backspace, and Cut
>
> When you use the Cut command to remove text, it is stored on the Office Clipboard and can be pasted into the same (or another) document. When you use Delete or Backspace to remove text, the text is not stored on the Office Clipboard. The only way you can retrieve text removed with Delete or Backspace is by using the Undo feature.

4 In the third line of the paragraph, click to position the insertion point to the left of the sentence that begins *(Database replication.* See Figure 2.25.

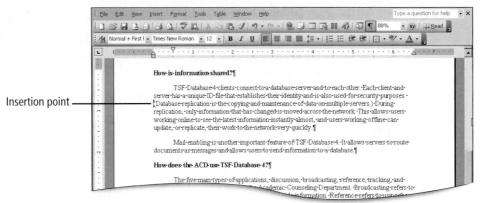

Insertion point

Figure 2.25

5 On the Standard toolbar, click the **Paste** button. Adjust the spacing before and after the sentence if needed.

The sentence is moved from the Office Clipboard and pasted into the document at the insertion point. A *smart tag* with a clipboard image also displays below the pasted sentence. A smart tag is a button that lets you control the result of certain actions, for example, a cut and paste operation.

6 Point to the smart tag until its ScreenTip *Paste Options* displays, and then click its small arrow.

A short menu provides commands related specifically to pasting, as shown in Figure 2.26. You can determine whether you want to format the pasted text the same as the surrounding text or retain its original formatting. Performing another screen action will cancel the display of the smart tag; alternatively press Esc to cancel its display.

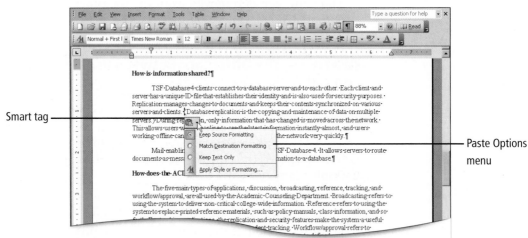

Smart tag

Paste Options menu

Figure 2.26

7 Click anywhere in the document to close the **Paste Options** menu.

8 Scroll up to position the insertion point at the top of page 1 on your screen, locate the paragraph that begins *TSF 4 collects information*, and then triple-click in the paragraph.

The entire paragraph is selected. Recall that double- and triple-clicking takes a steady hand. The speed of the clicks is important, but the mouse must also remain steady. If you did not select the entire paragraph, begin again. See Figure 2.27.

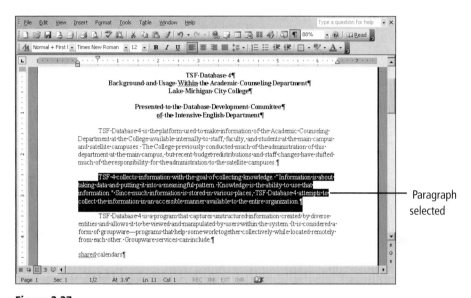

Paragraph selected

Figure 2.27

9 On the Standard toolbar, click the **Cut** button 🔏.

The paragraph is moved from the document onto the Office Clipboard.

Alert! | **If the Clipboard Task Pane Opens**

The Clipboard task pane may display on your screen depending on the options that have been set for the clipboard on your computer. If the Clipboard task pane opens, click the close button on the task pane title bar.

---

10 Scroll down as necessary and click to position the insertion point to the left of the word *How* in the subheading, *How is information collected?*

11 On the Standard toolbar, click the **Paste** button 📋.

The paragraph is pasted from the Office Clipboard into the document at the insertion point, and the Paste Options smart tag displays. See Figure 2.28.

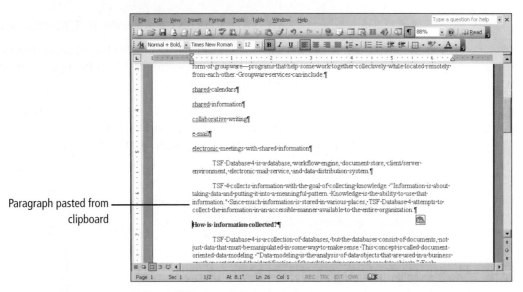

Paragraph pasted from clipboard

Figure 2.28

Activity 2.10 Copying and Pasting Text

The copy command places a copy of selected text on the Office Clipboard, which you can then paste to another location. Unlike the cut command, the copy command does not remove the selected text from its original location.

1 Be sure that the lower portion of page 1 is in view and then triple-click on the subheading *How is information collected?*

The subheading is selected. See Figure 2.29.

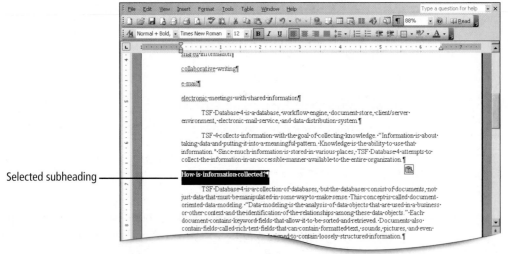

Selected subheading

Figure 2.29

2 On the Standard toolbar, click the **Copy** button. Alternatively, you can right-click on the selected text and click Copy from the shortcut menu, or press Ctrl + C.

The heading remains in its original location, but a copy has been moved onto the Office Clipboard.

3 Hold down [Ctrl] and press [End] to move to the end of the document.

4 In the last paragraph, click to position the insertion point to the left of the word *Training*. On the Standard toolbar, click the **Paste** button.

The text is copied from the Office Clipboard to the insertion point location. The spacing following the heading is also included because the information about the spacing following the paragraph is stored in its paragraph mark. See Figure 2.30.

Subheading pasted from clipboard

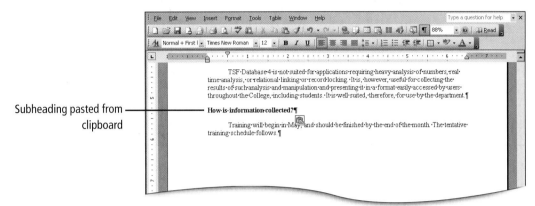

Figure 2.30

5 Triple-click on the new subheading to select it. Type **Training Schedule:** to replace the selected text.

The original text is replaced, but the formatting is retained. See Figure 2.31.

Replacement text — Format retained

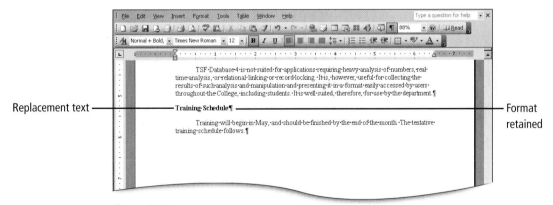

Figure 2.31

More Knowledge — Using the Office Clipboard Task Pane

If you use the copy command twice without pasting, a Clipboard task pane may open. This enables you to copy up to 24 pieces of text, graphics, and other objects into the Office Clipboard, and then paste them by selecting the desired item from the task pane. Clipboard task pane options are accessed by clicking the Options button at the bottom of the task pane. The Clipboard task pane can also be opened by clicking Edit on the menu bar, and then clicking Office Clipboard.

Activity 2.11 Dragging Text to a New Location

Another method of moving text is ***drag-and-drop***. This technique uses the mouse to drag selected text from one location to another. This method is useful if the text to be moved is on the same screen as the destination location.

1 Scroll as necessary to position the upper portion of page 2 at the top of your screen.

2 In the paragraph that begins *TSF Database 4 clients*, in the next to the last line, locate and select the word *almost*.

3 Move the pointer over the selected word.

The pointer becomes a white arrow that points up and to the left. This is the drag and drop pointer. See Figure 2.32.

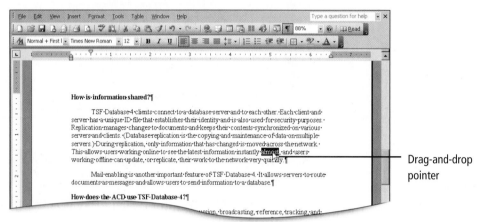

Figure 2.32

Note — Turning on the Drag-and-Drop Option

If you do not see the drag-and-drop pointer, you will need to turn this feature on. On the Tools menu, click Options, and then click the Edit tab. Under Editing options, select the *Drag-and-drop text editing* text box.

4 Hold down the left mouse button and drag to the left until the dotted vertical line that floats next to the pointer is positioned to the left of the word *instantly* and then release the left mouse button.

The word is moved to the insertion point location. The vertical line of the pointer assists you in dropping the moved text in the place where you want it. The small box attached to the pointer indicates that there is text attached to the pointer. See Figure 2.33.

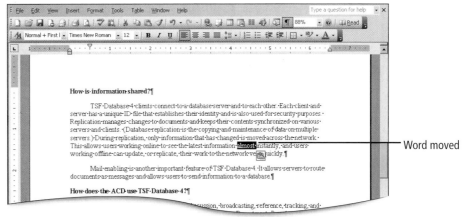

Figure 2.33

5 Press `Ctrl` + `End` to move to the end of the document. Then scroll as necessary so that you can view the last four paragraphs on your screen as shown in Figure 2.34.

6 Hold down `Ctrl` and click anywhere in the sentence *It is well suited, therefore, for use by the department* at the end of the second-to-last paragraph.

The sentence is selected.

7 Move the pointer over the selected sentence to display the drag-and-drop pointer, and then drag up to the paragraph above and position the vertical line to the right of the period at the end of *defined protocols.* as shown in Figure 2.34.

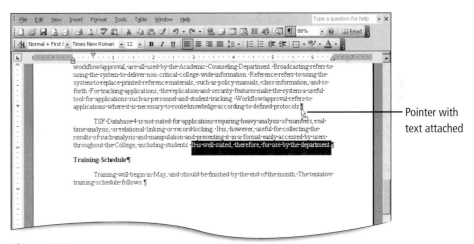

Figure 2.34

8 Release the mouse button. The sentence you moved becomes the last sentence in the paragraph. Notice that a space was automatically added before the sentence.

Activity 2.12 Undoing and Redoing Changes

You can Undo one or more actions that you made to a document since the last time you saved it. An Undo action can be reversed with the Redo command.

1 On the Standard toolbar, click the **Undo** button.

The sentence you dragged and dropped returns to its original location as shown in Figure 2.35.

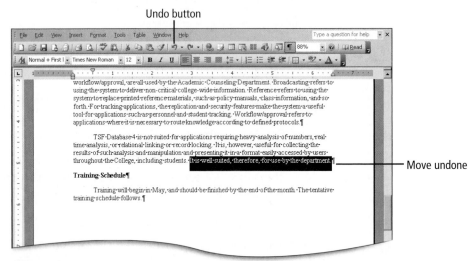

Undo button

Move undone

Figure 2.35

2 On the Standard toolbar, click the **Undo** button again.

The word you moved prior to moving the sentence returns to its original location.

3 On the Standard toolbar, click the **Redo** button.

The word is moved back. Clicking the Undo and Redo buttons changes one action at a time.

4 On the Standard toolbar, click the arrow on the right of the **Undo** button.

A list of changes displays showing all of the changes made since your last save operation. From the displayed list, you can click any of the actions and undo it, but all of the changes above the one you select will also be undone. See Figure 2.36.

Redo button

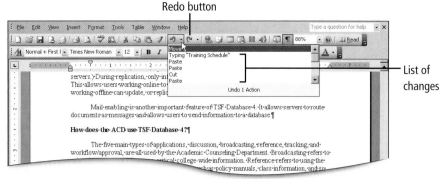

List of changes

Figure 2.36

5 Click anywhere in the document to close the Undo menu without selecting any actions.

6 From the **View** menu, click **Header and Footer**.

7 From the Header and Footer toolbar, click the **Switch Between Header and Footer** button 🔲. Using your own name, type **2A Campus Software_Firstname_Lastname** in the footer.

8 On the Header and Footer toolbar, click the **Close** button 𝘊𝘭𝘰𝘴𝘦.

9 On the Standard toolbar, click the **Save** button 🔲 and then click the **Print Preview** button 🔍 to preview the document. Close the Print Preview window. Use the P̲g̲U̲p̲ and P̲g̲D̲n̲ keys as necessary to view both pages in Print Preview. Make any necessary changes, and then click the **Print** button 🖨. Close the document saving any changes.

End **You have completed Project 2A** ──────────────

Project 2B **Software**

Word has numerous features to help you create a report. In this project, you will use report features such as lists, headers and footers, and footnote references.

In Activities 2.13 through 2.27 you will make further changes to a document that describes the groupware software being used by Lake Michigan City College. This document is similar to the one you worked on in Project 2A. Your completed document will look similar to Figure 2.37. You will save your document as *2B_Software_Firstname_Lastname*.

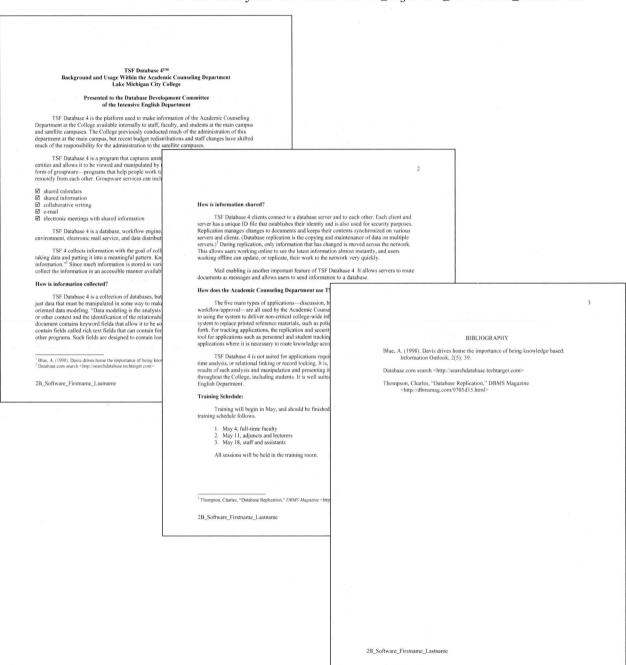

Figure 2.37
Project 2B—Software

Objective 3
Create and Modify Lists

Lists of information can be displayed two ways. A bulleted list uses bullets, which are text symbols such as small circles or check marks, to introduce each piece of information. Numbered lists use consecutive numbers to introduce each item in a list. Bulleted lists are used when the items in the list can be displayed in any order; numbered lists are used for items that have definite steps, a sequence of actions, or are in chronological order.

Activity 2.13 Creating a Bulleted List

1 Start Word. On the Standard toolbar, click the **Open** button. Navigate to the location where the student files for this textbook are stored. Locate **w02B_Software** and click once to select it. Then, in the lower right corner of the **Open** dialog box, click the **Open** button.

The *w02B_ Software* file opens.

2 If the formatting marks are not already displayed on your screen, on the Standard toolbar, click the Show/Hide ¶ button.

3 On the **File** menu, click **Save As**.

The Save As dialog box displays.

4 Use the **Save in arrow** to navigate to the location where you are saving your files. In the **File name** box, delete the existing text and, using your own name, type **2B_Software_Firstname_Lastname**

5 Near the bottom of the **Save As** dialog box, click **Save**.

The document is saved with a new name.

6 On the Standard toolbar, click the **Zoom button arrow** 100% and click **Page Width**.

7 Scroll as necessary to display the middle of page 1 on your screen, and locate the five short paragraphs that begin with *shared calendars*.

8 Move the pointer into the left margin to the left of *shared calendars*, and when the pointer changes to a white arrow, drag down to select the five short paragraphs as shown in Figure 2.38.

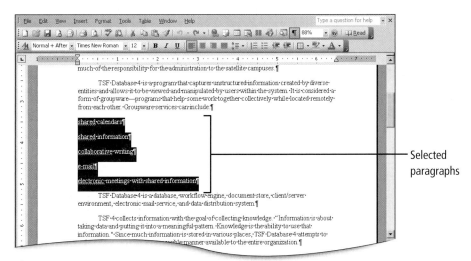

Selected paragraphs

Figure 2.38

To create a list from existing text, the paragraphs need to be selected.

9 On the Formatting toolbar, click the **Bullets** button 📃.

A symbol is placed to the left of each of the five paragraphs, and the text is moved to the right. The bullet symbol displayed on your screen depends on previous bullet usage of the computer at which you are seated. The default bullet is a large, round, black dot centered vertically on the line of text.

10 Click anywhere in the document to deselect the text. Click the **Show/Hide ¶** button 🔳.

This enables you to see the bulleted list without the formatting marks. Notice that the line spacing remains the same as it was before you created the list. See Figure 2.39.

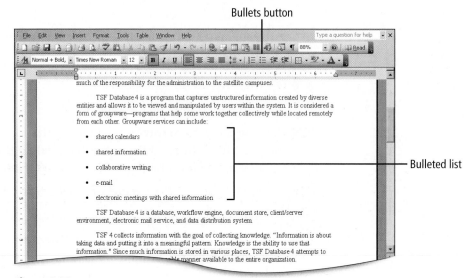

Figure 2.39

11 Click the **Show/Hide ¶** button 🔳 again to turn on formatting marks.

12 On the Standard toolbar, click the **Save** button 💾.

Activity 2.14 Creating a Numbered List

In the previous activity you created a list using existing text. You can also turn on the list feature and create a new list.

1 Press [Ctrl] + [End] to move to the end of the document and then press [Enter] once.

Notice that the insertion point is indented. This paragraph retains the formatting of the previous paragraph, which is stored in the paragraph mark you just created when you pressed [Enter].

2 On the Formatting toolbar, click the **Numbering** button 📊.

The number *1* is inserted to begin a numbered list as shown in Figure 2.40.

Numbering button

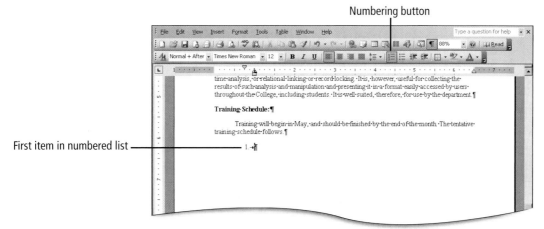

Figure 2.40

3 Type **May 4, full-time faculty** and press Enter.

The text is entered, and a second number is added.

4 Type **May 11, adjuncts and lecturers** and press Enter.

5 Type **May 18, staff and assistants** and press Enter.

Although this list will contain only the three lines you typed, the paragraph marker for the new paragraph retains the formatting of the previous paragraph, which is a numbered list. See Figure 2.41.

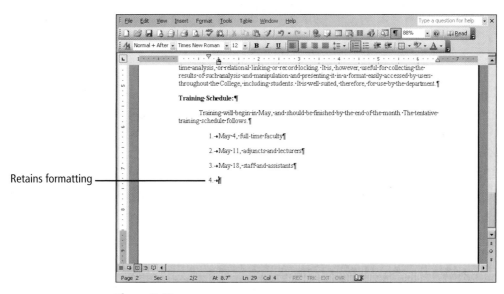

Figure 2.41

6 On the Formatting toolbar, click the **Numbering** button ▤ again.

The numbering format is turned off. Both list buttons, Numbering and Bullets, act as a ***toggle switch***; that is, clicking the button once turns the feature on, and clicking the button again turns the feature off.

7 Type **All sessions will be held in the training room.**

8 On the Standard toolbar, click the **Save** button ▣.

Activity 2.15 Formatting Lists

Lists are columns of paragraphs and can be formatted in the same way other paragraphs are formatted.

1 Move the pointer into the left margin to the left of *1.* and when the pointer changes to a white arrow, drag down to select the three numbered items.

The three items are selected, even though the list numbers are outside the highlighted area.

2 On the Formatting toolbar, click the **Decrease Indent** button [icon].

All of the items in the list move to the left, and the decreased indent is reflected in the ruler. See Figure 2.42.

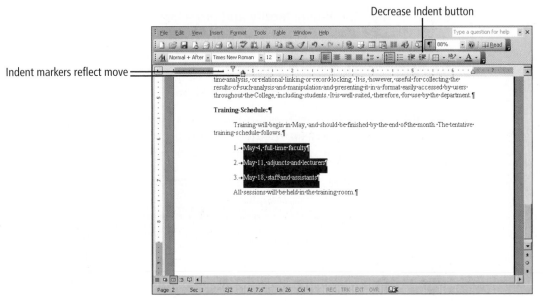

Figure 2.42

3 Select only the first two numbered items in the list.

4 On the **Format** menu, click **Paragraph**. If necessary, click the Indents and Spacing tab.

The Paragraph dialog box displays.

5 Under **Spacing**, in the **After** spin box, click the **down arrow** twice.

The value in the box changes from 12 pt. to 0 pt. as shown in Figure 2.43.

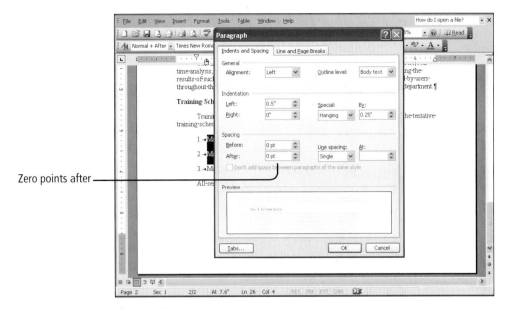

Zero points after

Figure 2.43

6 Click **OK**.

The extra spaces between the items in the list are removed resulting in single spacing. The space after the third item remains, because it was not selected. See Figure 2.44.

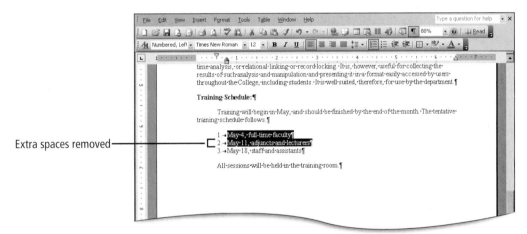

Extra spaces removed

Figure 2.44

7 Scroll up to view the bulleted list on page 1, position the pointer in the margin until it displays as a white arrow, and then drag downward to select the five bulleted items.

8 On the Formatting toolbar, click the **Decrease Indent** button.

All of the items in the list move to the left, and the ruler reflects the change.

9 Select the first four bulleted items in the list. On the **Format** menu, click **Paragraph**.

The Paragraph dialog box displays.

10 Under **Spacing**, in the **After** spin box, click the **down arrow** twice.

The value in the box changes from 12 pt. to 0 pt.

11 Click **OK**.

The bulleted list is now formatted in the same manner as the numbered list. The extra spacing after the last item remains to set it off from the next paragraph. See Figure 2.45.

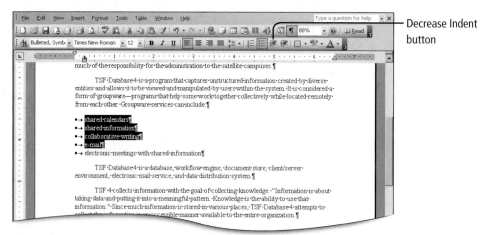

Figure 2.45

Activity 2.16 Customizing Bullets

You are not restricted to the bullet symbol that displays when you click the Bullets button. You can use any symbol from any font on your computer for your bullet character.

1 From the margin area to the left of the five bulleted items, drag to select the five items in the list.

2 On the **Format** menu, click **Bullets and Numbering**.

The Bullets and Numbering dialog box displays, showing you the most recently used bullets. Because the bullets displayed depend on previous usage at the computer at which you are seated, your screen may vary somewhat from Figure 2.46.

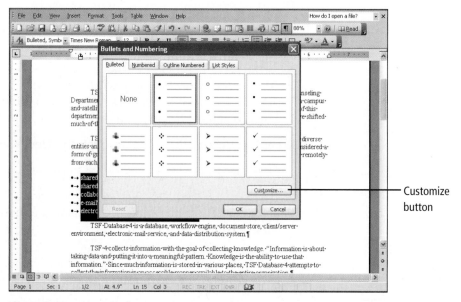

Figure 2.46

3 In the **Bullets and Numbering** dialog box, in the lower right corner click the **Customize** button.

The Customize Bulleted List dialog box displays, showing the options that are available for customizing a bullet character. See Figure 2.47.

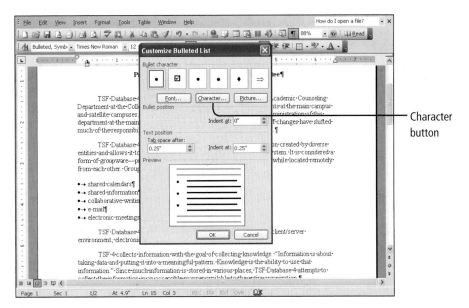

Character button

Figure 2.47

4 Under **Bullet character**, click the **Character** command button.

A table of characters displays in the Symbol dialog box. The character that is currently used for your list is highlighted. The font name of the current bullet symbol also displays. See Figure 2.48.

Font name of the current bullet symbol

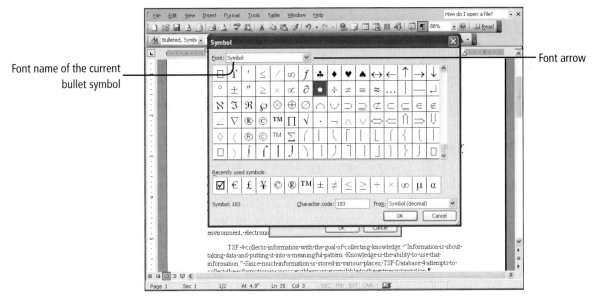

Font arrow

Figure 2.48

5 At the top of the dialog box, click the **Font arrow** at the right of the font box, scroll as necessary, and then click **Wingdings**.

6 Use the scroll bar on the right of the dialog box to scroll down the list of Wingding characters until you reach the end. Click the check mark in the last row as shown in Figure 2.49.

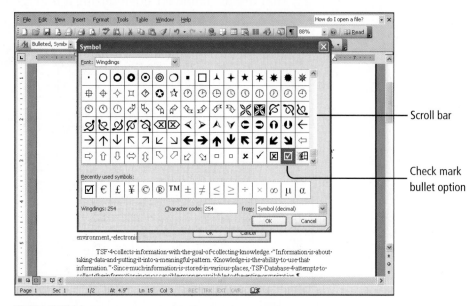

Scroll bar

Check mark
bullet option

Figure 2.49

7 Click **OK** to close the **Symbol** dialog box. Click **OK** again to close the **Customize Bulleted List** dialog box.

8 Click anywhere in the document to deselect the list.

The bullet character is changed to check marks in boxes, as shown in Figure 2.50.

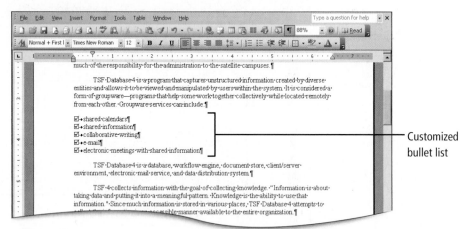

Customized
bullet list

Figure 2.50

9 On the Standard toolbar, click the **Save** button 🔲.

Objective 4
Work with Headers and Footers

Text or graphics that you insert into a header or a footer display on every page of a document. On the first page of a document, it is common practice to suppress (hide) the header or footer, and Word provides an easy way to accomplish this. Within a header or footer, you can add automatic page numbers, dates, times, the file name, and pictures.

Activity 2.17 Inserting and Formatting Page Numbers

1 Position the insertion point at the top of the document. On the **View** menu, click **Header and Footer**.

The Header area displays.

2 On the Formatting toolbar, click the **Align Right** button ▤.

The insertion point moves to the right edge of the header box.

3 On the Header and Footer toolbar, click the **Insert Page Number** button ⬚.

The page number, *1*, is inserted as shown in Figure 2.51.

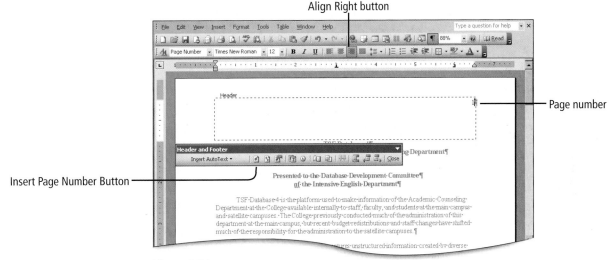

Align Right button

Page number

Insert Page Number Button

Figure 2.51

4 On the Header and Footer toolbar, click the **Page Setup** button ▨.

The Page Setup dialog box displays.

5 On the **Page Setup** dialog box, click the **Layout tab**. Under **Headers and footers**, select (click to place a check mark in) the **Different first page** check box as shown in Figure 2.52.

The Different first page option enables you to remove the header or footer information from the first page.

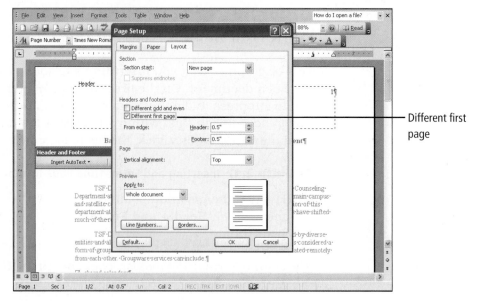

Figure 2.52

6 In the lower right corner of the dialog box, click **OK**.

The page number is removed from the header box and the name of the box changes to First Page Header.

7 Use the vertical scroll bar to scroll down and bring the top of page 2 into view.

The page number is displayed on the second page, and will be displayed on every page thereafter. This is an easy way to suppress the header on page 1. Notice that the name of the footer box at the end of page 1 has been changed to First Page Footer. This reflects the change you made to create a header and footer on the first page of your document that is different from those on the remaining pages. See Figure 2.53.

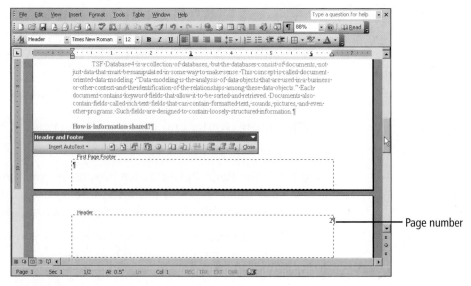

Figure 2.53

Activity 2.18 Inserting AutoText

1 On the Header and Footer toolbar, click the **Switch Between Header and Footer** button ⊞.

The insertion point is placed at the left edge of the First Page Footer box.

2 On the Header and Footer toolbar, click the **Insert AutoText** button Insert AutoText ▾. Take a moment to look at the items that can be inserted in the header or footer. See Figure 2.54.

Inserts file name ——

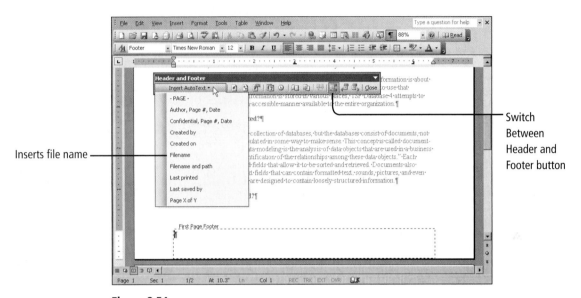

Figure 2.54

Switch Between Header and Footer button

3 Click **Filename**.

The file name displays in the First Page Footer. The file extension *.doc* may or may not display, depending on your Word settings. See Figure 2.55.

File name ——

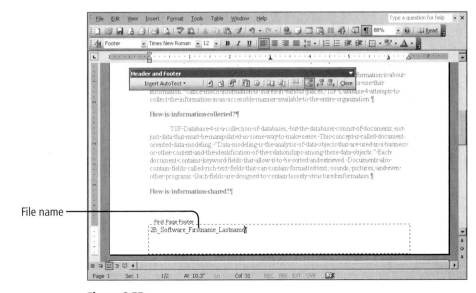

Figure 2.55

Activity 2.19 Inserting the Current Date and Time

1 Press Tab twice.

The insertion point moves to the right side of the footer box. Notice the location of the tab stop in the ruler bar.

2 On the Header and Footer toolbar, click the **Insert Date** button [image], and then type a comma and press the Spacebar once.

The current date displays.

3 On the Header and Footer toolbar, click the **Insert Time** button [image].

The current time displays. Your date and time will differ from the ones shown in Figure 2.56.

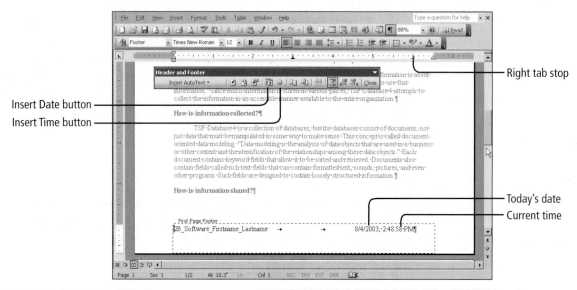

Insert Date button

Insert Time button

Right tab stop

Today's date

Current time

Figure 2.56

4 On the Header and Footer toolbar, click the **Close** button [Close].

5 Scroll down as necessary to view the bottom of the first page and the top of the second page.

Notice that the text in the header and footer is gray, while the text in the document is black. When you are working in the header and footer, the header and footer text is black (active) and the document text is gray (inactive). See Figure 2.57.

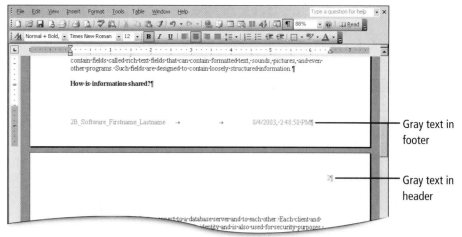

Figure 2.57

■ On the Standard toolbar, click the **Save** button 🖫.

Objective 5
Insert Frequently Used Text

AutoCorrect corrects common spelling errors as you type. When you type a word incorrectly, for example *teh*, Word automatically changes it to *the*.

If there are words that you frequently misspell, you can add them to the AutoCorrect list. Another feature, AutoText, lets you create shortcuts to quickly insert long phrases that are used regularly, such as a business name or your address, in a manner similar to AutoComplete.

Another type of frequently used text includes various symbols, such as the trademark symbol (™) or copyright symbol ©. These are accessed from the Insert Symbol dialog box.

Activity 2.20 Recording AutoCorrect Entries

You probably have words that you frequently misspell. You can add these to the AutoCorrect list for automatic correction.

■ On the **Tools** menu, click **AutoCorrect Options**.

The AutoCorrect dialog box displays as shown in Figure 2.58. All of the check boxes on the left of the dialog box are selected by default. Yours may be different.

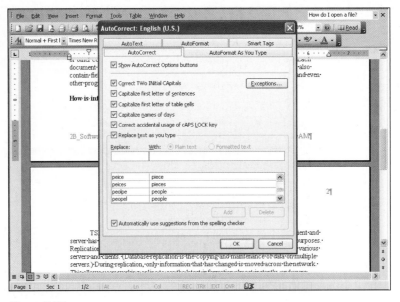

Figure 2.58

2 Under **Replace**, type **peepel**

3 Under **With**, type **people**

Your dialog box should be similar to Figure 2.59. If someone has already added this AutoCorrect entry, the Add button will change to a Replace button.

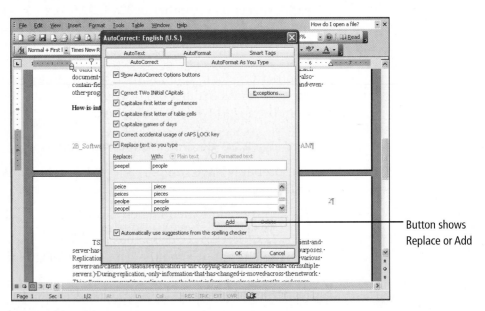

Button shows
Replace or Add

Figure 2.59

4 Click **Add**. If the entry already exists, click **Replace** instead, and then click **Yes**.

The new entry is added to the AutoCorrect list. See Figure 2.60.

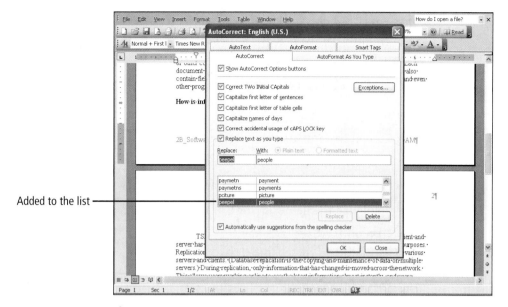

Added to the list ——

Figure 2.60

⑤ Click **OK**.

The dialog box closes.

⑥ Scroll to the top of page 1 and locate the paragraph that begins *TSF Database 4 is a program*, and then locate and double-click to select the word *some* in the third line.

⑦ Watch the screen, type **peepel** and then press Spacebar. If necessary, press ←Bksp to get rid of the extra space between words.

Notice that the misspelled word is automatically corrected.

⑧ Move the mouse pointer over the corrected word.

A blue line displays under the word. See Figure 2.61.

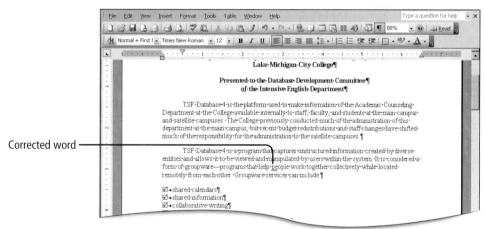

Corrected word ——

Figure 2.61

⑨ Move the pointer over the blue line until the **AutoCorrect Options** smart tag button displays, and then click the button.

The AutoCorrect options menu displays. Notice that you have several commands available. The Control AutoCorrect Options selection will display the AutoCorrect dialog box.

10 Click anywhere in the document to close the **AutoCorrect Options** menu without selecting a command.

More Knowledge — Other Uses of AutoCorrect

AutoCorrect can also be used to

- Correct two initial capital letters
- Capitalize the first letter of sentences
- Capitalize the first letter of table cells
- Capitalize the names of days of the week
- Turn off the Caps Lock key
- Create exceptions to automatic corrections
- Add your own AutoCorrect entries to the AutoCorrect list

Activity 2.21 Using AutoCorrect Shortcuts

The AutoCorrect replacement is most commonly used to correct spelling errors, but it can also be used to insert symbols or to expand shortcut text into longer words or phrases.

1 Scroll to the top of the document. In the fifth line of the title, select the words *Intensive English Department*.

Make sure you do not select the paragraph mark at the end of the title. See Figure 2.62.

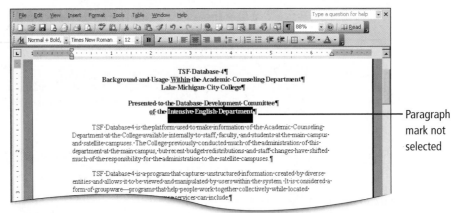

Paragraph mark not selected

Figure 2.62

2 On the **Tools** menu, click **AutoCorrect Options**.

The AutoCorrect dialog box displays. Notice that the selected text displays in the With box. See Figure 2.63.

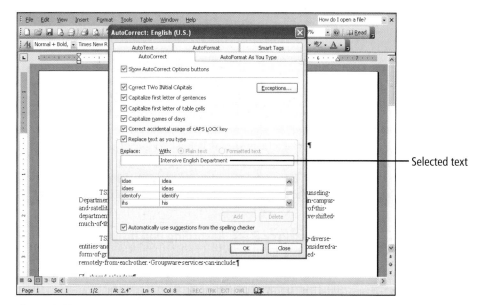

Figure 2.63

3 Under **Replace**, type **ied**, and then click **Add**. If this entry already exists, click the **Replace** button, and then click **Yes.**

The new shortcut is added to the list.

4 Click **OK** to close the **AutoCorrect** dialog box, and then press
[Ctrl] + [End] to move to the end of the document.

5 Locate the *Training Schedule:* subheading and at the end of the sentence just above this subheading select the word *department* and the period at the end of the sentence.

6 Type **ied.**

When you type the period, the AutoCorrect feature replaces the shortcut text with the text you defined. In order to activate the replace feature, you need to follow the shortcut with a space, a paragraph mark, or a punctuation mark. See Figure 2.64.

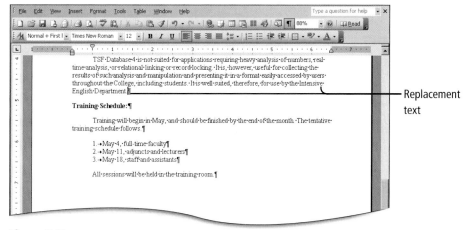

Replacement text

Figure 2.64

7 On the Standard toolbar, click the **Save** button 🖫.

More Knowledge — Creating AutoCorrect Shortcuts

When setting up an AutoCorrect shortcut, it is best not to use shortcut text that is an actual word or a commonly used abbreviation. Even though you can reverse an AutoCorrect replacement by using the AutoCorrect Options shortcut menu, it is best to avoid the problem by adding a letter to the shortcut text. For example, if you type both *LMCC* and *Lake Michigan City College* frequently, you might want to add *lmccx* (or just *lmx*) as an AutoCorrect shortcut for the text *Lake Michigan City College*.

Activity 2.22 Recording and Inserting AutoText

AutoText stores, with a unique name, text and graphics that you use frequently. For example, at Lake Michigan City College, individuals in the counseling department frequently type *Academic Counseling Department*.

1 Scroll to the top of the document. From the second title line, select *Academic Counseling Department*, but do not include the paragraph mark. See Figure 2.65.

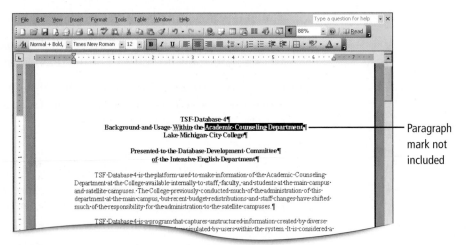

Paragraph mark not included

Figure 2.65

2 On the **Tools** menu, click **AutoCorrect Options**.

The AutoCorrect dialog box displays.

3 In the **AutoCorrect** dialog box, click the **AutoText tab**.

Notice that the selected text displays in the *Enter AutoText entries here* box. You can also type entries directly into this box. See Figure 2.66.

AutoText tab ——

Selected text ——

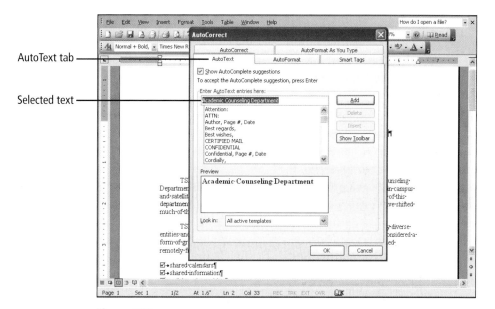

Figure 2.66

4 Click **Add**.

The phrase is added to the AutoText entries, and the AutoCorrect dialog box closes. If the entry has already been created on this computer, click Yes to redefine the entry.

5 Click outside the selected text to deselect it. On the **Edit** menu, click **Find**.

The Find and Replace dialog box displays. Using Find and Replace is not necessary to use AutoComplete—it just makes finding the text easier.

6 In the **Find what** box, type **acd** and then click **Find Next**.

The next (and only) instance of ACD is found in the third subheading. See Figure 2.67.

Found text ——

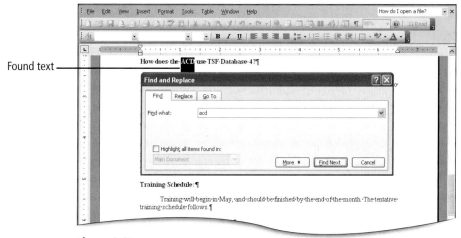

Figure 2.67

7 Click **Cancel** to close the Find and Replace dialog box.

ACD remains selected.

8 Type **acad** and look at the screen.

A ScreenTip displays the AutoCorrect entry that you just created. See Figure 2.68.

ScreenTip

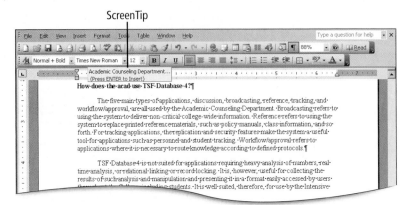

Figure 2.68

9 Press Enter.

ACD is replaced with the AutoText entry Academic Counseling Department. Notice that the text is bold, as it was in the document title. The character formatting of an AutoText entry is the same as its source text.

10 On the Standard toolbar, click the **Save** button 🖫.

Activity 2.23 Inserting Symbols

There are many symbols that are used occasionally, but not often enough to put on a standard keyboard. These symbols can be found and inserted from the Insert menu.

1 Scroll to view the middle of the second page, and locate the paragraph following the subheading *How does the Academic Counseling Department use TSF Database 4?*

2 After *The five main types of applications*, select the comma and space as shown in Figure 2.69.

Comma and space selected —

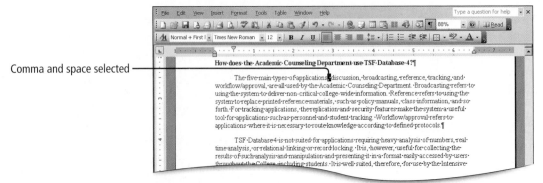

Figure 2.69

3 On the **Insert** menu, click **Symbol**.

The Symbol dialog box displays. This is the same dialog box you used when you formatted bullets.

4 Click the **Special Characters tab**.

A list of commonly used symbols displays. The keyboard shortcuts for inserting these commonly used symbols display to the right of the character name, as shown in Figure 2.70.

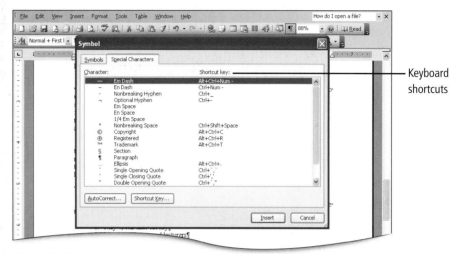

Keyboard shortcuts

Figure 2.70

5 Be sure the *Em dash* is selected. In the lower right corner of the dialog box, click **Insert**, and then click **Close**.

An em dash replaces the selected text. An ***em dash*** is the word processing name for a long dash in a sentence. An em dash in a sentence marks a break in thought, similar to a comma but stronger.

6 Select the em dash. On the Standard toolbar, click **Copy**.

7 Near the end of the same sentence, in the second line, select the comma and space after *workflow/approval*. Click **Paste**.

A second em dash is inserted in the sentence. Because you used a paste operation to insert the em dash, the Paste Options smart tag also displays. See Figure 2.71.

Em dash

Copied em dash

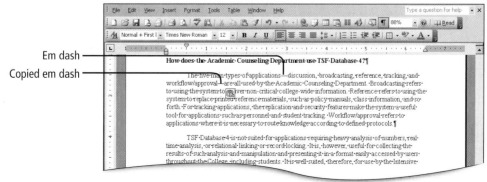

Figure 2.71

8 Navigate to the top of the document by pressing [Ctrl] + [Home]. Position the insertion point at the end of the first title line. Type **(tm)**

Although this symbol, which indicates a trademark, is available from the Symbol dialog box, it is also included in Word's AutoCorrect list. The parentheses are necessary for AutoComplete to insert a trademark symbol.

9 On the **Tools** menu, click **AutoCorrect Options** and then click the **AutoCorrect tab**.

Symbols that can be inserted automatically with AutoCorrect display at the top of the Replace With area. See Figure 2.72.

AutoCorrect symbols —

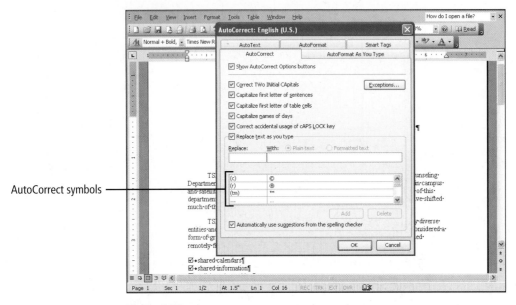

Figure 2.72

10 Scroll the list to view additional symbol shortcuts. When you are finished, click **OK** to close the dialog box. On the Standard toolbar, click the **Save** button [■].

Objective 6
Insert References

Reports frequently include information taken from other sources, and these need to be credited. Within report text, numbers mark the location of information that has been taken from another source, called **references**. The numbers refer to **footnotes** (references placed at the bottom of the page containing the reference), or **endnotes** (references placed at the end of a document or chapter).

When footnotes or endnotes are included in a report, a page listing the references is also usually included. Such a list is usually titled *Bibliography*, *Works Cited*, *Sources* or *References*.

Activity 2.24 Inserting Footnotes

Footnotes can be added when you type the document or after the document is complete. They do not need to be entered in order, and if one is removed, the rest are renumbered.

1 In the lower half of page 1, in the paragraph that begins *TSF 4 collects information*, locate the quotation mark in the third line of text. Click to right of the quotation mark.

Direct quotes always need to be referenced.

2 On the **Insert** menu, point to **Reference** and then click **Footnote**.

The Footnote and Endnote dialog box displays.

3 Under **Location**, be sure the **Footnotes** option button is selected and that **Bottom of page** is selected. Under **Format**, be sure **Start at** is at **1**, and **Numbering** is **Continuous**.

4 If necessary, under **Format** click the **Number format** arrow and, from the displayed list, click **1**, **2**, **3**.

The number format is selected.

Under Apply changes, *Apply changes to* the *Whole document* is selected by default. Compare your Footnote and Endnote dialog box to Figure 2.73.

Continuous numbering starting at 1

Applied to the whole document

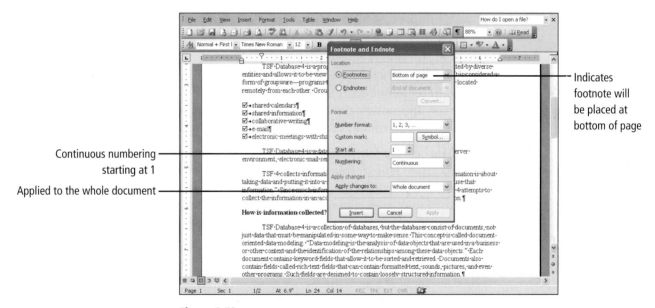

Indicates footnote will be placed at bottom of page

Figure 2.73

5 Click **Insert**.

A footnote area is created at the bottom of the page, and a footnote number is added to the text at the insertion point location. Footnote 1 is placed at the top of the footnote area, and the insertion point is moved to the right of the number. You do not need to type a footnote number.

6 Type **Blue, A. (1998). Davis drives home the importance of being knowledge based. Information Outlook, 2(5): 39.**

Footnote 1 is placed at the bottom of the page. See Figure 2.74.

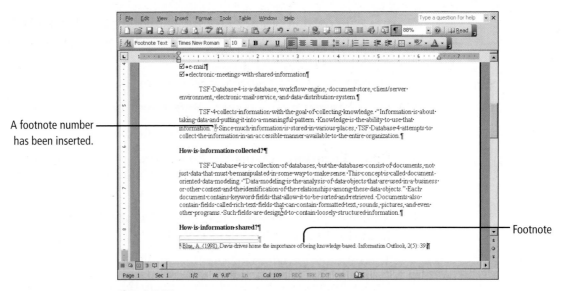

A footnote number has been inserted.

Footnote

Figure 2.74

7 Scroll as necessary to position the top of page 2 in view. In the paragraph that begins *TSF Database 4 clients connect*, in the fifth line, locate servers.) and click to the right of the parenthesis.

8 On the **Insert** menu, point to **Reference** and then click **Footnote**. Using the settings from your previous footnote, move to the bottom of the dialog box, click **Insert** and then in the inserted footnote box type **Thompson, Charles, "Database Replication," DBMS Magazine <http://dbmsmag.com/9705d15.html>**

The second footnote is placed at the bottom of the second page. The footnote feature places the footnote text on the same page as the referenced text and adjusts pages as necessary. The AutoCorrect feature may also replace straight quotes with curly quotes, depending on the settings on your computer. See Figure 2.75.

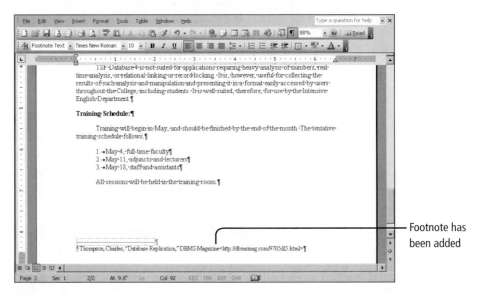

Footnote has been added

Figure 2.75

Alert! | **If the Web Address Changes to a Hyperlink**

If you press the spacebar after you type the Web address in the footnote, the Web address text may be displayed in blue with an underline. This is the common format used to display a *hyperlink*—which is a link that can be used to open the Web page on the Internet that is related to this address. If this happens, click the Undo button once to reverse the formatting.

9 In the lower half of page 1, in the paragraph that begins *TSF Database 4 is a collection of*, locate the closing quotation mark near the end of the fourth line and position the insertion point to the right of the quotation mark.

10 On the **Insert** menu, point to **Reference**, and then click **Footnote**. Click **Insert**, and then type:
Database.com search <http://searchdatabase.techtarget.com>

This new footnote number is 2, and the footnote on page 2 becomes footnote 3. In this manner, Word makes it easy to insert footnotes in any order within your report, because it automatically renumbers and adjusts page endings. Compare your screen to Figure 2.76.

New footnote on page 1 ⟶

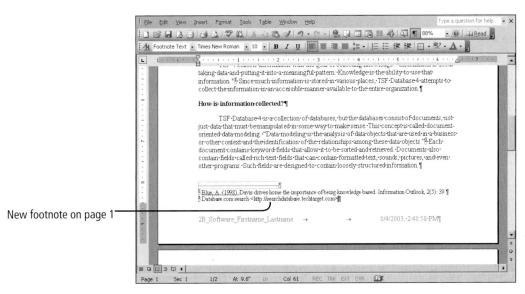

Figure 2.76

11 Click to see if the *How is information shared?* subheading is at the bottom of the page. If so, position the insertion point to the left of the subheading, hold down [Ctrl] and press [Enter].

A manual page break is inserted, the subheading is moved to the second page, but the footnotes remain on the proper page. See Figure 2.77.

Footnotes remain on page 1 —

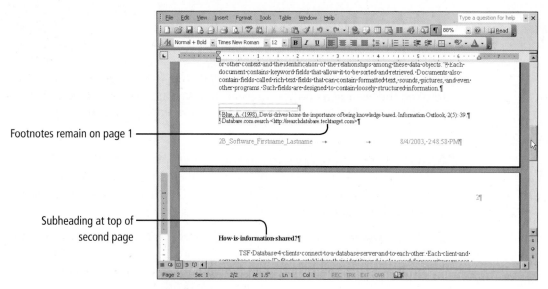

Subheading at top of second page —

Figure 2.77

12 On the Standard toolbar, click the **Save** button 🖫.

Activity 2.25 Formatting Footnotes

Some parts of footnotes require special formatting. Magazine and book titles, for example, need to be italicized.

1 At the end of the first page, in the first footnote, locate and select the magazine title, *Information Outlook*.

2 Click the **Italic** button 𝐼.

The magazine title is italicized as shown in Figure 2.78.

Italic button

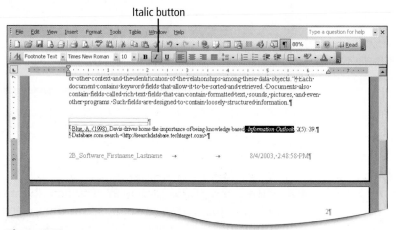

Figure 2.78

3 Scroll to the bottom of the document, locate and select the magazine title, *DBMS Magazine*.

4 Click the **Italic** button 𝐼.

The magazine title is italicized.

5 On the Standard toolbar, click the **Save** button 🖫.

Activity 2.26 **Creating a Reference Page**

In a long document, there will be many books, articles, and Web sites that have been referenced on the various pages. Some of them may be noted many times, others only once. It is common to include, at the end of a report, a single list of each source referenced. This list is commonly titled *References*, *Bibliography*, *Sources* or *Works Cited*.

1 Press Ctrl + End to navigate to the end of the document.

2 Hold down Ctrl and press Enter.

A manual page break is inserted, and a new page is created.

3 Press CapsLock, type **BIBLIOGRAPHY** and press Enter. Turn off CapsLock. See Figure 2.79.

The paragraphs are double spaced and indented because the paragraph mark for the last paragraph of the document contains those instructions. Notice the indents in the ruler.

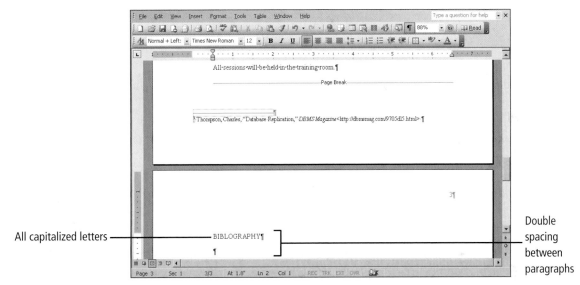

All capitalized letters

Double spacing between paragraphs

Figure 2.79

4 Type **Blue, A. (1998). Davis drives home the importance of being knowledge based. Information Outlook, 2(5): 39.** Press Enter.

5 Type **Thompson, Charles, "Database Replication," DBMS Magazine http://dbmsmag.com/9705d15.html** and then press Enter.

When you type the Internet address, it may change to blue. This means that you have created a live Internet link. If this happens, move the pointer over the link, point to the small blue box under the first letter in the Internet address to display a white arrow, click the displayed AutoCorrect Options smart tag, and from the displayed menu, click Undo Hyperlink.

6 Type **Database.com search <http://searchdatabase.techtarget.com>** and press Enter. If necessary, undo the hyperlink in the same manner as the previous step.

Compare your screen to Figure 2.80.

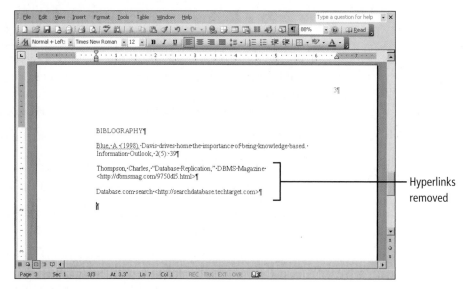

Hyperlinks removed

Figure 2.80

7 On the Standard toolbar, click the **Save** button 💾.

Activity 2.27 Formatting a Reference Page

Bibliographies have special formatting requirements. The title should be centered, the entries should be in alphabetical order, and the subsequent lines of an entry should be indented 0.5 inch to the right of the first line of the entry.

1 Click anywhere in the title *BIBLIOGRAPHY*.

2 On the Formatting toolbar, click the **Center** button ▤.

The title is centered, but the centering is between the first line indent of 0.5" (instead of the left margin) and the right margin.

3 On the **Format** menu, click **Paragraph**. On the **Indents and Spacing tab**, under **Indentation**, change the **Left** indent to 0. In the lower right corner of the dialog box, click **OK**.

4 Select all three bibliographic entries. On the **Format** menu, click **Paragraph**.

5 In the displayed **Paragraph** dialog box, under **Indentation**, change the **Left** indent to 0. Click the **Special arrow**, and from the displayed list, click **Hanging**. See Figure 2.81.

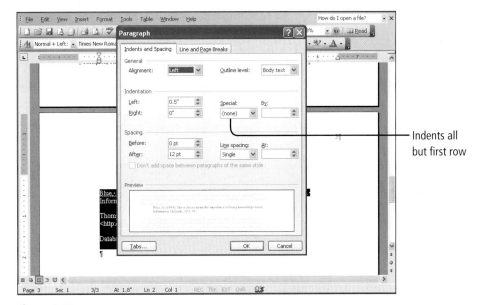

Indents all
but first row

Figure 2.81

6 Click **OK** to close the dialog box.

This paragraph style is called a ***hanging indent***, where the first line extends to the left of the rest of the lines in the same paragraph. Notice the indent markers on the toolbar. See Figure 2.82.

First Line Indent marker
Hanging Indent marker

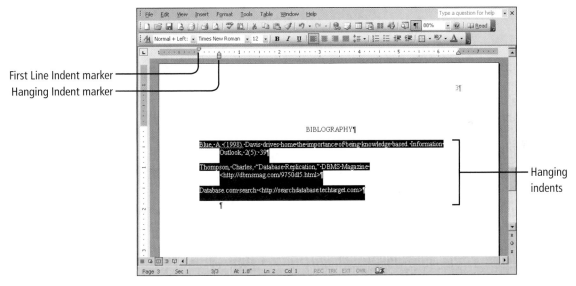

Hanging
indents

Figure 2.82

7 Be sure the three entries are still selected. From the **Table** menu, click **Sort**.

The Sort Text dialog box displays as shown in Figure 2.83.

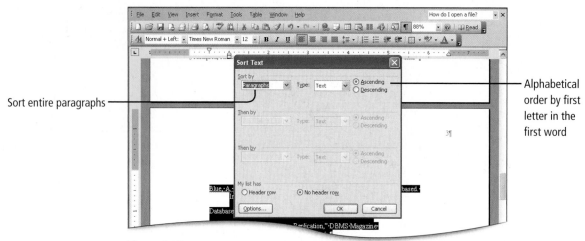

Sort entire paragraphs ——————

Alphabetical order by first letter in the first word

Figure 2.83

8 Accept the default sort options, which sort by paragraph in ascending (A-to-Z) order and click **OK**.

The paragraphs are sorted alphabetically.

9 Click anywhere in the document to deselect the text.

Compare your Bibliography page with Figure 2.84.

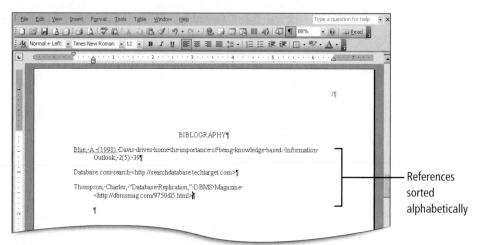

References sorted alphabetically

Figure 2.84

10 Move to page 2 and click anywhere in the text. From the **View menu**, display the **Header** and Footer toolbar, switch to the footer and on the Header and Footer toolbar, click **Insert AutoText**, and then click **Filename**. Close the **Header** and Footer toolbar.

This is necessary because the Different First Page option was selected, and the footer you added earlier displays only on page 1. Adding the filename to the footer of page 2 displays the footer in the rest of the document.

11 On the Standard toolbar, click the **Save** button and then click the **Print Preview** button to preview the document. Close the Print Preview window. Make any necessary changes, and then click the **Print** button . Close the document and save any changes.

End You have completed Project 2B ——————

Summary

In this chapter you practiced how to change the format of pages by setting the margins and how to change the format of paragraphs by changing indents, line spacing, and the spacing after paragraphs. You practiced applying the format from one paragraph to others using the Format Painter. Another paragraph formatting technique you used was creating bulleted and numbered lists and modifying the bullets from the Bullets and Numbering dialog box.

One of the most important features of word processing was presented in this chapter—moving and copying text. Both cut-and-paste and drag-and-drop techniques were demonstrated for moving text. You also practiced how to copy text and place it in a new location. You used the Find and Replace dialog box to locate text that you want to modify, and you practiced how to use the AutoCorrect, AutoText, AutoComplete, and Insert Symbols features.

In the header and footer areas, you accessed commands from the toolbar to add consecutive page numbers, the current date, the time, and the filename. Finally, you practiced how to add footnotes to a document, create a reference page with hanging indent paragraph format, and sort references in alphabetical order.

In This Chapter You Practiced How To

- Change Document and Paragraph Layout

- Change and Reorganize Text

- Create and Modify Lists

- Work with Headers and Footers

- Insert Frequently Used Text

- Insert References

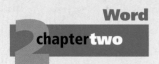

Matching   Match each term in the second column with its correct definition in the first column by writing the letter of the term on the blank line in front of the correct definition.

_____ **1.** Text that is aligned on both the left and right margins.

_____ **2.** A temporary storage location that is used for text that is cut or copied.

_____ **3.** The button that is used to reverse a previous action.

_____ **4.** A small symbol that is used to begin each line of information in a list.

_____ **5.** A reference that is placed at the bottom of a page.

_____ **6.** The alignment of text in the middle of the document between the left and right margin.

_____ **7.** The Word feature that is primarily responsible for correcting commonly misspelled words.

_____ **8.** A paragraph style that positions the first line of text to the left of the rest of the paragraph.

_____ **9.** In most documents, paragraphs are aligned on this side of the page.

_____ **10.** The action that leaves text in its original location but also makes it available to place in a new location.

_____ **11.** The name of a dialog box that you can use to locate specific text.

_____ **12.** The command activated by the keyboard shortcut Ctrl + X.

_____ **13.** The command activated by the keyboard shortcut Ctrl + V.

_____ **14.** The area at the bottom of a page that shows the same information, or same type of information on every page of a document, with the possible exception of the first page.

_____ **15.** The type of menu that displays by right-clicking on selected areas of a document.

A AutoCorrect

B Bullet

C Centered

D Copy

E Cut

F Find and Replace

G Footer

H Footnote

I Hanging indent

J Justified

K Left

L Office Clipboard

M Paste

N Shortcut menu

O Undo

Fill in the Blank Write the correct answer in the space provided.

1. The width between the text and the edge of the paper is known as the _____.

2. The placement of text relative to the left and right side of a paragraph is known as _____.

3. When you drag-and-drop text, it is _____ from one place to another.

4. When you paste text, the text is taken from the _____ and placed where the insertion point is positioned.

5. The keyboard shortcut used to copy text is
   Ctrl + _____.

6. If you need to create a list of items that is sequential, you should use a(n) _____ list.

7. When you click the Redo button, it reverses the action of the _____ _____.

8. If you want to create a shortcut that will automatically finish a frequently used phrase or name, use the _____ feature.

9. If you need to add a ™ ® or © to a document, display the _____ dialog box from the Insert menu.

10. A reference placed at the end of a document or a chapter is known as a(n) _____.

Project 2C—Computer Lab

Objectives: *Change Document and Paragraph Layout, Change and Reorganize Text, Create and Modify Lists, Work with Headers and Footers, Insert Frequently Used Text, and Insert References.*

In the following Skill Assessment, you will format and modify a document regarding the Computer Lab policies at Lake Michigan City College. Your completed document will look similar to the one shown in Figure 2.85. You will save your document as *2C_Computer_Lab_Firstname_Lastname.*

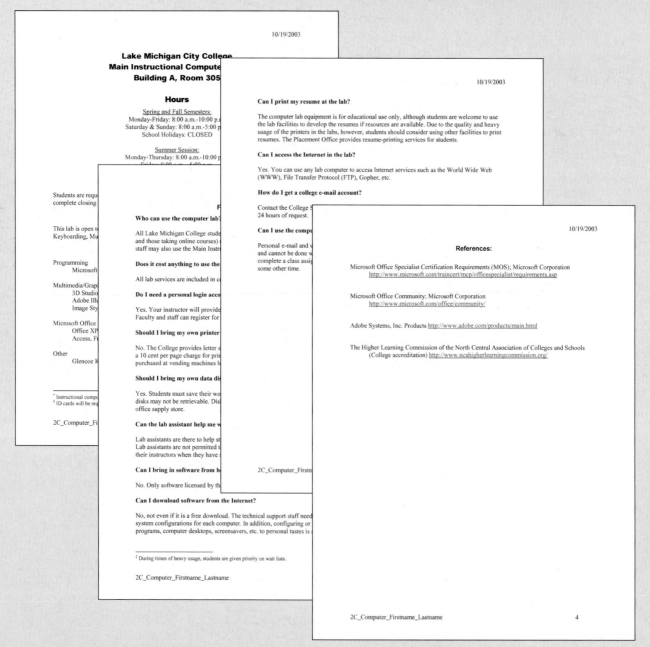

Figure 2.85

(Project 2C–Computer Lab continues on the next page)

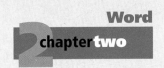
(Project 2C–Computer Lab continued)

1. Start Word. On the Standard toolbar, click the **Open** button. Navigate to the location where the student files for this textbook are stored. Locate and open **w02C_Computer_Lab**. Be sure that non-printing characters are displayed. This is a three-page document; take a moment to scroll through the document to familiarize yourself with the overall content and layout.

2. Display the **File** menu and then click **Save As**. Navigate to the location where you are saving your projects for this chapter. In the **File name** box, type **2C_Computer_Lab_Firstname_Lastname** and then in the lower portion of the **Save As** dialog box, click the **Save** button.

3. Select the first four lines of text in the document, which comprise the document's title, two subtitles, and *Hours*. On the Formatting toolbar, click the **Center** button. With the four lines still selected, click the **Font button arrow**, click **Arial Black**, click the **Font Size button arrow**, and then click **14**. The title is centered and looks more distinctive.

4. Click anywhere to deselect. Select the title line and the first subtitle line—the first two lines of the document. Click the **Line Spacing button arrow** and, from the displayed list, click **1.0**. The line spacing for the first two lines of the document is changed, but the third line remains double-spaced so that it creates a space after effect.

5. Select the four lines of text that begin *Spring and Fall Semesters*. On the Formatting toolbar, click the **Center** button. Select the five lines of text that begin *Summer Session*, and click the **Center** button again. On the Standard toolbar, click **Save**.

6. Scroll to view the bottom of page 1, and click to position the insertion point at the beginning of the heading *Frequently Asked Questions*. Because it is not good document design to strand a subheading at the bottom of the page without any of its following information, press Ctrl + Enter to insert a hard page break if necessary and move this subheading to the next page.

7. Scroll to view the bottom of page 3, click to the left of the *References:* heading, and then press Ctrl + Enter to insert a page break and move the References portion to a separate page. This becomes page 4. Click the **Save** button.

(Project 2C–Computer Lab continues on the next page)

(Project 2C–Computer Lab continued)

8. Hold down Ctrl and press Home to move the insertion point to the top of the document. Click to place the insertion point at the end of *Main Instructional Computer Lab*. Display the **Insert** menu, point to **Reference**, and then click **Footnote**. In the **Footnote and Endnote** dialog box, under **Location**, be sure the **Footnotes** option button is selected and **Bottom of page** is displayed in the Footnotes box. Under **Format**, click the **Number format arrow**, and then click the sixth item in list, which is a group of symbols beginning with an *. These are appropriate to use when you are not making a specific reference to a document, but are noting additional information. In the lower left of the **Footnote and Endnote** dialog box, click **Insert**.

9. The insertion point is moved to the new footnote created at the bottom of page 1. Type the following note: **Instructional computer labs are also located at satellite campuses. See catalog or call campus for details.** Recall that you do not have to type the footnote symbol—Word places the symbol in the correct location for you.

10. Scroll to view the middle of page 1, and in the paragraph under the subheading *Courses Supported*, click to the right of the word *enrolled*. Display the **Insert** menu, point to **Reference**, and then click **Footnote**. In the displayed dialog box, in the lower left corner, click the **Insert** button to accept the settings. A new footnote is inserted, and the insertion point moves to the bottom of page 1. Type **ID cards will be required for entrance to lab.**

11. Navigate to the top of page 2. In the paragraph beginning *All Lake Michigan College students*, in the third line, click to place the insertion point to the right of the period following *Main Instructional Computer Lab*. Display the **Footnote and Endnote** dialog box, click the **Insert** button, and then type the following: **During times of heavy usage, students are given priority on wait lists.** This footnote, the third one you have added to the document, is placed at the bottom of page 2.

12. Navigate to page 4—the References page. Select the two lines beginning *Microsoft Office Specialist*. Hold down Ctrl and select the two lines beginning *Microsoft Office Community*. Continue to hold down Ctrl and select the text lines that form the remaining two references. All four references are selected, but the blank lines between them are not selected. From the **Format** menu, click **Paragraph**, and then click the **Indents and Spacing tab**. Under **Indentation**, click the **Special arrow** and then click **Hanging**. Under **Spacing**, in the **After** box, click the up arrow in the spin box to change the spacing after the paragraph to 12 pt. Click **OK**. The references are displayed with a hanging line indent and 12 points of space after each paragraph.

(Project 2C–Computer Lab continues on the next page)

(Project 2C–Computer Lab continued)

13. Click anywhere to deselect. On the **View** menu, click **Header and Footer**. With the header area displayed, on the Formatting toolbar, click the **Align Right** button. On the Header and Footer toolbar, click the **Insert Date** button. The current date is placed on the right side of the header.

14. On the Header and Footer toolbar, click the **Switch Between Header and Footer** button. In the footer area, on the **Header and Footer** toolbar, click **Insert AutoText**, and then click **Filename**. Press Tab twice to move the insertion point to the right side of the footer. On the Header and Footer toolbar, click the **Insert Page Number** button, and then click the **Close** button.

15. On the Standard toolbar, click the **Save** button to save the changes you have made to your document.

16. Press Ctrl + Home. On the Standard toolbar, click the **Print Preview** button to make a final check of your document before printing. Use the scroll bar to view each page in the document, and notice how Word formatted and placed your footnotes on pages 1 and 2. On the Print Preview toolbar, click the **Print** button, and then, on the same toolbar, click the **Close** button.

17. From the **File** menu, click **Close** to close the document, saving any changes if prompted to do so. Display the **File** menu again and then click **Exit** to close Word. Alternatively, you can close Word by clicking the Close button at the extreme right end of the blue title bar.

 You have completed Project 2C ─────────────────────

Project 2D—AFV Proposal

Objectives: *Change Document and Paragraph Layout, Create and Modify Lists, Work with Headers and Footers, and Insert Frequently Used Text.*

In the following Skill Assessment, you will format and edit a proposal for an Alternative Fuel Project that is being cosponsored by the college and several energy-related businesses. Your completed document will look similar to Figure 2.86. You will save your document as *2D_AFV_Proposal_Firstname_Lastname.*

1. On the Standard toolbar, click the **Open** button. Navigate to the location where the student files for this textbook are stored. Locate and open **w02D_AFV_Proposal**. Be sure that nonprinting characters are displayed. This is a two-page document. Take a moment to scroll through the document to familiarize yourself with the content and layout.

(Project 2D–AFV Proposal continues on the next page)

(Project 2D–AFV Proposal continued)

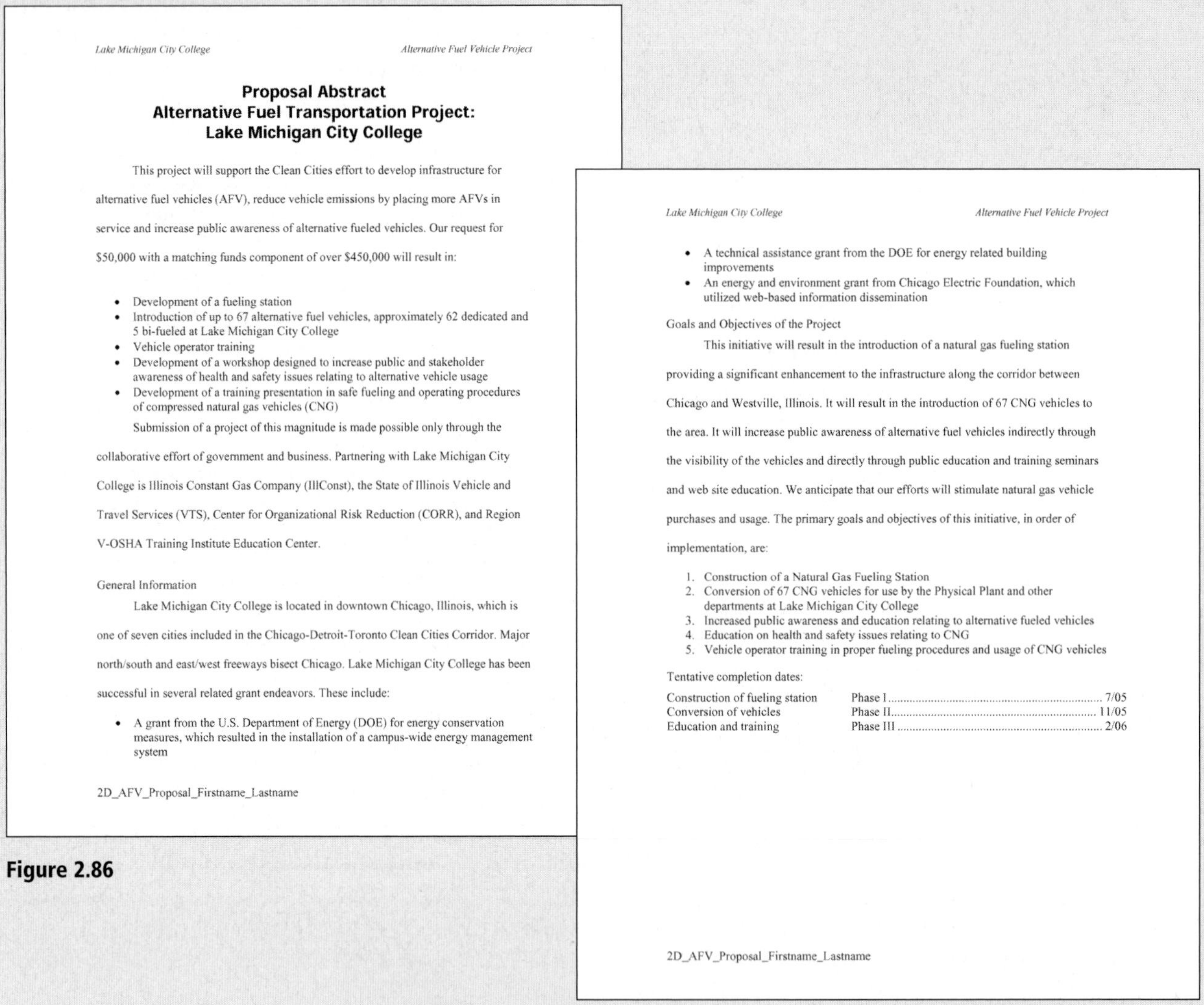

Lake Michigan City College   Alternative Fuel Vehicle Project

Proposal Abstract
Alternative Fuel Transportation Project:
Lake Michigan City College

This project will support the Clean Cities effort to develop infrastructure for

alternative fuel vehicles (AFV), reduce vehicle emissions by placing more AFVs in

service and increase public awareness of alternative fueled vehicles. Our request for

$50,000 with a matching funds component of over $450,000 will result in:

- Development of a fueling station
- Introduction of up to 67 alternative fuel vehicles, approximately 62 dedicated and 5 bi-fueled at Lake Michigan City College
- Vehicle operator training
- Development of a workshop designed to increase public and stakeholder awareness of health and safety issues relating to alternative vehicle usage
- Development of a training presentation in safe fueling and operating procedures of compressed natural gas vehicles (CNG)

Submission of a project of this magnitude is made possible only through the

collaborative effort of government and business. Partnering with Lake Michigan City

College is Illinois Constant Gas Company (IllConst), the State of Illinois Vehicle and

Travel Services (VTS), Center for Organizational Risk Reduction (CORR), and Region

V-OSHA Training Institute Education Center.

General Information

Lake Michigan City College is located in downtown Chicago, Illinois, which is

one of seven cities included in the Chicago-Detroit-Toronto Clean Cities Corridor. Major

north/south and east/west freeways bisect Chicago. Lake Michigan City College has been

successful in several related grant endeavors. These include:

- A grant from the U.S. Department of Energy (DOE) for energy conservation measures, which resulted in the installation of a campus-wide energy management system

2D_AFV_Proposal_Firstname_Lastname

Lake Michigan City College   Alternative Fuel Vehicle Project

- A technical assistance grant from the DOE for energy related building improvements
- An energy and environment grant from Chicago Electric Foundation, which utilized web-based information dissemination

Goals and Objectives of the Project

This initiative will result in the introduction of a natural gas fueling station

providing a significant enhancement to the infrastructure along the corridor between

Chicago and Westville, Illinois. It will result in the introduction of 67 CNG vehicles to

the area. It will increase public awareness of alternative fuel vehicles indirectly through

the visibility of the vehicles and directly through public education and training seminars

and web site education. We anticipate that our efforts will stimulate natural gas vehicle

purchases and usage. The primary goals and objectives of this initiative, in order of

implementation, are:

1. Construction of a Natural Gas Fueling Station
2. Conversion of 67 CNG vehicles for use by the Physical Plant and other departments at Lake Michigan City College
3. Increased public awareness and education relating to alternative fueled vehicles
4. Education on health and safety issues relating to CNG
5. Vehicle operator training in proper fueling procedures and usage of CNG vehicles

Tentative completion dates:

Construction of fueling station	Phase I	7/05
Conversion of vehicles	Phase II	11/05
Education and training	Phase III	2/06

2D_AFV_Proposal_Firstname_Lastname

Figure 2.86

2. From the **File** menu, click **Save As**. Navigate to the location where you are saving your projects for this chapter. In the **File name** box, type **2D_AFV_Proposal_Firstname_Lastname** and then in the lower portion of the **Save As** dialog box, click the **Save** button.

3. The name of the college needs to be added to the title and in several locations throughout the document. This will be easier if you first create an AutoText entry for Lake Michigan City College. From the **Tools** menu, click **AutoCorrect Options**. In the **AutoCorrect** dialog box, click the **AutoText tab**. In the **Enter AutoText entries here** box type **Lake Michigan City College** and click the **Add** button. (If the Add button is dimmed and *Lake Michigan City College* displays in the list, another student has already added this text to AutoText. Click Cancel and go on to the next step. You will be able to use the existing AutoText entry.) This AutoText is added to the list. In the lower portion of the **AutoText** dialog box, click **OK**.

(Project 2D–AFV Proposal continues on the next page)

(Project 2D–AFV Proposal continued)

4. On the second line of the document, click to place the insertion point following the colon after *Alternative Fuel Transportation Project:* and then press Enter. On the new line, start typing **Lake Michigan City College** When the AutoText ScreenTip displays, press Enter to finish the text.

5. Select the first three lines in the document and, on the Formatting toolbar, click the **Center** button. Click the **Font button arrow**, click **Tahoma**, click the **Font Size button arrow**, click **16**, and then click the **Bold** button. Click anywhere to deselect the title lines.

6. There are several places in the document where the phrase *the college* needs to be replaced with the phrase *Lake Michigan City College*. From the **Edit** menu, click **Replace**. In the **Find what** box type **the college** In the **Replace with** box type **Lake Michigan City College** In the **Find and Replace** dialog box, click the **Find Next** button. When the first occurrence of *the college* is highlighted, click **Replace**. When the second occurrence of *the college* is highlighted, click **Replace**. When the next occurrence is highlighted, click **Replace All**. When the message box displays that Word has finished searching the document, click **OK**, and then close the **Find and Replace** dialog box. Click the **Save** button.

7. Hold down Ctrl and press Home to move to the top of the document. In the paragraph beginning *This project will*, at the end of the fourth line, click at the end of the paragraph, to the right of *result in:* and then press Enter.

8. Beginning with *Development of a fueling*, select the next five short paragraphs—through *compressed natural gas vehicles (CNG)*. This is a list of results that are expected from the Alternative Fuel Project. With the list selected, on the Formatting toolbar, click the **Bullets** button.

9. The bullet symbol last used on your computer displays. With the list still selected, display the **Format** menu and then click **Bullets and Numbering**. In the first row, click the second box. If the second box is not solid black circles, in the lower left of the dialog box, click Reset and then click **Yes**. The selected box changes to its original setting—a solid black circle. Click **OK**.

10. Scroll as necessary to view the paragraphs below the bulleted list. Locate the subtitle *General Information*. Five lines below that, locate the paragraph that begins *A grant from*. Select the three paragraphs (five lines of text) beginning with *A grant from*. On the Formatting toolbar, click the **Bullets** button. The same bullet symbol that was used previously is applied to the list.

11. Scroll down to view the top portion of page 2. Select the six lines of text beginning with *Construction of a Natural*. On the Formatting toolbar, click the **Numbering** button. The result is five numbered items. Click the **Save** button.

(Project 2D–AFV Proposal continues on the next page)

(Project 2D–AFV Proposal continued)

12. Press [Ctrl] + [Home] to move to the top of the document, and then click to place the insertion point anywhere in the paragraph that begins *This project.* From the **Format** menu, click **Paragraph**. In the **Paragraph** dialog box, under **Indentation**, click the **Special arrow**, and then click **First line**. Under **Spacing**, click the **Line spacing arrow**, click **Double**, and then in the **Before** box, click the spin box up arrow once to display **6 pt**. Click **OK**.

13. The paragraph format that you just set will be applied to the other main paragraphs in the document. With the insertion point still in the formatted paragraph, on the Formatting toolbar, double-click the **Format Painter** button. Move the mouse pointer into a text portion of your document and verify that it takes on the shape of a paint brush. On this page, use the scroll bar to scroll down slightly below the first bulleted list, locate the paragraph that begins *Submission of a project* and then click in the paragraph. The paragraph format is applied, and the mouse pointer retains the paint brush. (If your mouse pointer no longer displays the paintbrush, double-click the Format Painter button again.)

14. Use the scroll arrow to move down slightly to view the paragraph beginning *Lake Michigan City College is located*—click in the paragraph to apply the formatting. Use the scroll bar to move to page 2, locate the paragraph that begins *This initiative will result*, and click in the paragraph. On the Formatting toolbar, click the **Format Painter** button once to turn it off.

15. Press [Ctrl] + [Home] to move to the top of the document. From the **View** menu, click **Header and Footer**. In the header area, type **Lake Michigan City College** (use AutoText to complete the entry if it displays), press [Tab] twice, and type **Alternative Fuel Vehicle Project** Select the text in the header and then, on the Formatting toolbar, click the **Italic** button.

16. On the Header and Footer toolbar, click the **Switch Between Header and Footer** button. On the Header and Footer toolbar, click the **Insert AutoText** button, point to **Header/Footer**, and then click **Filename** from the list that displays. Close the Header and Footer toolbar.

17. Click the **Save** button, then click the **Print Preview** button to see the document as it will print. Click the **Print** button, then close the file saving changes if prompted to do so.

End **You have completed Project 2D** ————————————

Project 2E—Delivery Suggestions

Objectives: *Change Document and Paragraph Layout, Change and Reorganize Text, Create and Modify Lists, Work with Headers and Footers, and Insert Frequently Used Text.*

In the following Skill Assessment, you will format and edit a paper that discusses technology needed for delivering online courses at Lake Michigan City College. Your completed document will look similar to Figure 2.87. You will save your document as *2E_Delivery_Suggestions_Firstname_Lastname.*

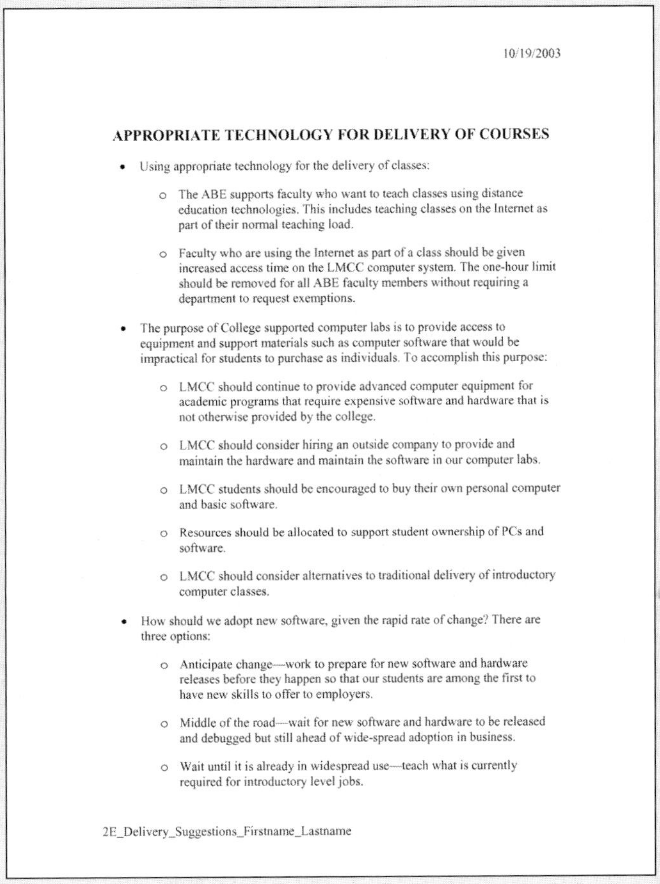

Figure 2.87

(Project 2E–Delivery Suggestions continues on the next page)

(Project 2E–Delivery Suggestions continued)

1. On the Standard toolbar, click the **Open** button. Navigate to the location where the student files for this textbook are stored. Locate and open **w02E_Delivery_Suggestions**. Be sure that nonprinting characters are displayed.

2. From the **File** menu, click **Save As**. Navigate to the location where you are saving your projects for this chapter. In the **File name** box, type **2E_Delivery_Suggestions_Firstname_Lastname** and then in the lower portion of the **Save As** dialog box, click the **Save** button.

3. Select the first line of the document and then, on the Formatting toolbar, click the **Center** button. From the **Format** menu, click **Change Case**. In the **Change Case** dialog box, click the **UPPERCASE** option button and then click **OK**. With the title still selected, on the Formatting toolbar, click the **Font Size button arrow**, click **14**, and then click the **Bold** button.

4. Click anywhere in the line beginning *1. Using*. Click the **Bullets** button. The last bullet symbol used on the computer at which you are seated is applied. Display the **Format** menu, and then click **Bullets and Numbering**. In the **Bullets and Numbering** dialog box, in the first row, click the second box. If the second box is not solid black circles, in the lower left of the dialog box, click Reset, and then click **Yes**. The selected box changes to its original setting—a solid black circle. Click **OK**.

5. On the Formatting toolbar, double-click the **Format Painter** button. When moved into the text area, the mouse pointer takes the shape of a paint brush. Use the scroll bar to scroll down until you see the next numbered paragraph beginning *1. The purpose of College supported* and then click in the numbered paragraph. A bullet replaces the number. Scroll down the document and click once in the next numbered paragraph, which begins *1. How should we*. On the Formatting toolbar, click the **Format Painter** button once to turn it off.

6. Scroll to position the second bulleted item and its following paragraphs into view on your screen. Select the paragraph that begins *Students should be*. On the Standard toolbar, click the **Cut** button. Click to place the insertion point at the beginning of the paragraph that begins *Resources should be allocated*. On the Standard toolbar, click the **Paste** button. The paragraph is moved.

7. Locate the paragraph under the second bulleted item that begins *We should consider hiring an outside company*. Select the word *software*, point to the selected word and drag it to the right of *hardware* and then release the mouse button. In the same sentence, select the second *and*, point to the selected word and drag it to the right of hardware, dropping it between *hardware* and *software*. Click to the left of *software*, and type **maintain the** The sentence should now read *...provide and maintain the hardware and maintain the software in our computer labs.*

(Project 2E–Delivery Suggestions continues on the next page)

(Project 2E–Delivery Suggestions continued)

8. Press Ctrl + Home to move to the top of the document. Under the first bulleted item, locate the paragraph that begins *Faculty who are using*. In the second line, select the text *LMCC* and click the **Copy** button.

9. In the second bulleted item, locate the paragraph that begins *The college should*. At the beginning of the paragraph, select the text *The college* and then click the **Paste** button. LMCC replaces the selected text.

10. In the first line of the next paragraph, select *We* and click the **Paste** button. In the next paragraph, select the *S* in *Students* click the **Paste** button, and then type **s** to provide the lower case letter at the beginning of the word *students*. Finally, select *We* at the beginning of the last paragraph under this bullet point and then click the **Paste** button.

11. Navigate to the top of the document and select the two paragraphs under the first bullet point. From the **Format** menu, click **Bullets and Numbering**. In the displayed dialog box, in the first row, click the third box, which should be a hollow circle. (If this bullet is not a hollow circle, in the lower left of the dialog box, click Reset. In the message box that displays, click Yes to reset the gallery position to the default setting. This resets the selected symbol to the default setting, which for the third box is a hollow circle.) Click **OK**. The selected text is formatted with a hollow circle bullet and is indented to the right under the first bullet.

12. Under the second bulleted item, select the five paragraphs that begin *LMCC should continue to provide*. On the Formatting toolbar, click the **Bullets** button and then click the **Increase Indent** button. When the bulleted text is indented, the bullets change to the hollow circle style.

13. Repeat this process to create the same style of bulleted list for the paragraphs that are listed under *How should we adopt*.

14. In the three bulleted items you just formatted, you will replace a colon (:) with an em dash. Position the bottom of the page into view on your screen. In the first bulleted item that begins *Anticipate*, select the colon and space following the text *Anticipate change*. From the **Insert** menu, click **Symbol**. In the **Symbol** dialog box, click the **Special Characters tab**. Make sure that **Em Dash** is highlighted, and then in the lower portion of the dialog box click **Insert**. The **Symbol** dialog box remains open on your screen.

(Project 2E–Delivery Suggestions continues on the next page)

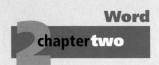

(Project 2E–Delivery Suggestions continued)

15. Point to the title bar of the **Symbol** dialog box, and then drag it to the right of your screen so that you can view the last two bulleted items on the page. Select the colon and space that follows *Middle of the road*, and then in the **Symbol** dialog box, click **Insert**. Moving the dialog box as necessary, repeat this process to replace the colon and space in the final bulleted item, found after *widespread use*. Close the **Symbol** dialog box. Click **Save** to save your changes.

16. From the **View** menu, click **Header and Footer**. In the header area, press twice. On the Header and Footer toolbar, click the **Insert Date** button.

17. On the Header and Footer toolbar, click the **Switch Between Header and Footer** button. On the Header and Footer toolbar, click the **Insert AutoText** button, and then from the displayed list, click **Filename**. Close the Header and Footer toolbar.

18. From the **File** menu, click **Page Setup**. In the displayed **Page Setup** dialog box, click the **Margins tab**. Under **Margins**, click in the **Top** box and type **1.5** In the lower right corner of the dialog box, click **OK**.

19. On the Standard toolbar, click the **Save** button to save the changes to the document.

20. On the Standard toolbar, click the **Print Preview** button to view your document as it will print. On the Print Preview toolbar, click the **Print** button to print the document, and then on the same toolbar, click the **Close** button. Close the document and then close Word.

End You have completed Project 2E

Project 2F—Computer Virus Policy

Objectives: *Change Document and Paragraph Layout, Change and Reorganize Text, Create and Modify Lists, Work with Headers and Footers, Insert Frequently Used Text, and Insert References.*

In the following Performance Assessment, you will format and edit a report regarding the Lake Michigan City College computer virus policy. Your completed document will look similar to Figure 2.88. You will save your document as *2F_Computer_Virus_Firstname_Lastname.*

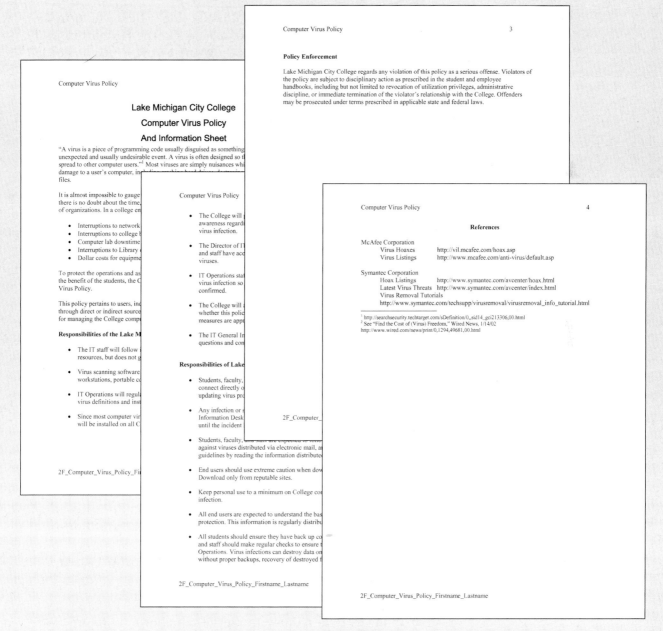

Figure 2.88

(Project 2F–Computer Virus continues on the next page)

(Project 2F–Computer Virus Policy continued)

1. Click the **Open** button. Navigate to the location where the student files for this textbook are stored. Locate and open **w02F_Computer_Virus_Policy**. From the **File** menu click **Save As**. Navigate to the location where you are saving your projects for this chapter. In the **File name** box, and using your own name, type **2F_Computer_Virus_Policy_Firstname_Lastname** and then click the **Save** button.

2. From the **File** menu, click **Page Setup**. In the **Page Setup** dialog box, change the left margin to **1"** and the right margin to **1"** and then click **OK**.

3. At the top of the document, select the first line, which will form the title and begins *Lake Michigan City College*. On the Formatting toolbar, click the **Center** button. Click the **Font arrow**, scroll as needed and click **Arial Unicode MS**, click the **Font Size arrow**, and then click **16**. On the Formatting toolbar, click the **Bold** button. Place the insertion point at the end of the word *College* and press Enter. Place the insertion point at the end of the word *Policy* and press Enter again. The title is on three lines and is easier to read. If necessary, on the Standard toolbar, click the Show/Hide ¶ button to display nonprinting characters. Delete the spaces at the beginning of the second and third lines of the title.

4. The first two sentences in this document—beginning with *"A virus—* is a quote and needs to be referenced. In the third line of this paragraph, place the insertion point after the closing quote mark following *computer users."* From the **Insert** menu, point to **Reference**, and then click **Footnote**. In the **Footnote and Endnote** dialog box, under **Location**, click the **Endnotes** option button, and be sure **End of document** displays in the box to its right. Under **Format**, click the **Number format arrow**, and then click **1, 2, 3** from the list. Click **Insert**. In the endnote area type **http://searchsecurity.techtarget.com/sDefinition/0,,sid14_gci213306,00.html** but do not type a space or press Enter.

5. Because this is an Internet address, the Word program may automatically format it as a hyperlink—in blue and underlined—if you follow it with a space or Enter. If Word formats the address as a hyperlink, right-click on the address and click Remove Hyperlink.

6. Press Ctrl + Home. Locate the paragraph of text that begins *It is almost impossible* and place the insertion to the right of *viruses each year*—before the comma. Display the **Footnote and Endnote** dialog box again, click **Insert**, and then, without pressing Enter, but placing a space after the date, type **See "Find the Cost of (Virus) Freedom," Wired News, 1/14/02 http://www.wired.com/news/print/0,1294,49681,00.html**

   Your text may wrap at a different place than shown in Figure 2.88. Click the **Save** button.

(Project 2F–Computer Virus continues on the next page)

(Project 2F–Computer Virus Policy continued)

7. Near the top of the document, select the five one-line paragraphs starting with the paragraph that begins *Interruptions to network* and then click the **Bullets** button. (If the bullet that displays is not a solid round symbol, display the Format menu, click Bullets and Numbering, click the solid round bullet example, and then click OK.)

8. Position the lower portion of page 1 into view. In the paragraph beginning *The IT staff will follow,* click to left of the first word in the paragraph. Use the scroll arrow to view the top of the next page. Hold down Shift and, in the seventh line down, click after the period following the word *College.* This will select all the text paragraphs that follow this subheading. With these paragraphs selected, apply a solid round bullet. Display the **Format** menu, click **Paragraph**, and increase the spacing after to **12 pt**.

9. Using the technique in the previous step, select the paragraphs of text following the subheading *Responsibilities of Lake Michigan City College Students, Faculty, and Staff,* and use the same procedure to add solid round bullets and increase the space after to **12 pt**.

10. Navigate to the bottom of page 3, click to place the insertion point to the left of the word *References* and then press Ctrl + Enter to insert a page break and move this title to the next page. Select *References* and click the **Center** button.

11. On page 4, select *McAfee Corporation* and the two references listed under it. Click the **Cut** button. Place the insertion point to the left of *Symantec* and press the **Paste** button. The references are reordered. Insert an empty line between the Symantec and McAfee references.

12. Select the four lines listed under *Symantec Corporation.* Display the **Table** menu and then click **Sort**. In the **Sort Text** dialog box, under **Sort by**, be sure *Paragraphs* displays and then click **OK**. The references are resorted in alphabetical order. Right-click on any Web references that are formatted as hyperlinks (blue and underlined) and click **Remove Hyperlink**. Remove any empty paragraphs between the last reference and the beginning of the endnotes.

13. Display the **View** menu and then click **Header and Footer**. In the header area, type **Computer Virus Policy**, press Tab twice, and then click the **Insert Page Number** button. Switch to the footer area, click the **Insert AutoText** button, and insert the **Filename**. Close the Header and Footer toolbar.

14. Click the **Save** button, then click the **Print Preview** button. Compare the layout of your document to the figure. Click the **Print** button and then close the Print Preview window. Close the document, saving any changes and then close Word.

End You have completed Project 2F

Project 2G—Interview Questions

Objectives: *Change Document and Paragraph Layout, Change and Reorganize Text, Create and Modify Lists, Work with Headers and Footers, Insert Frequently Used Text, and Insert References.*

In the following Performance Assessment, you will edit and format a list of questions from Lisa Huelsman, Associate Dean of Adult Basic Education, for use in an interview with candidates for a new Director of Distance Education at Lake Michigan City College. Your completed document will look similar to Figure 2.89. You will save your document as *2G_Interview_Questions_Firstname_Lastname.*

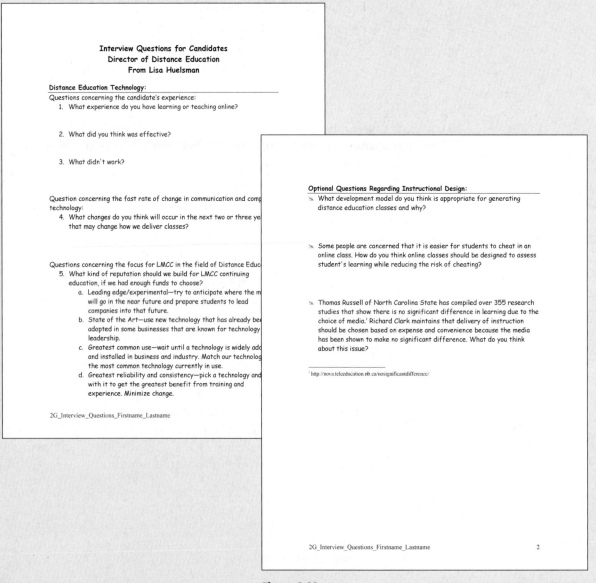

Figure 2.89

(**Project 2G**–Interview Questions continues on the next page)

(Project 2G–Interview Questions continued)

1. Click the **Open** button. Navigate to the location where the student files for this textbook are stored. Locate and open **w02G_Interview_Questions**. From the **File** menu, click **Save As**. Navigate to the location where you are saving your projects for this chapter. In the **File name** box, using your own name, type **2G_Interview_Questions_Firstname_Lastname** and then click the **Save** button. Make sure that nonprinting characters are displayed and take a moment to scroll through this two-page document to familiarize yourself with the layout and content.

2. In the first line of the document that begins *Interview Questions*, place your insertion point after *Candidates* and press Enter. Type **Director of Distance Education** and then press Enter again. There are now three title lines. Delete the space to the left of the third line.

3. Select the three title lines. On the Formatting toolbar, click the **Center** button and then click the **Bold** button. Change the **Font Size** to **14**.

4. Locate the first question beginning with *What experience*. Three questions are listed concerning the experience of the candidate. Select the three questions and, on the Formatting toolbar, click the **Line Spacing** arrow and then click **3.0**. This increases the spacing between the questions, which will provide space for the interviewer to make notes during the interview.

5. With the three questions still selected, on the Formatting toolbar, click the **Numbering** button.

6. Position the middle of page 1 into view. Select the paragraph that begins *What changes*. From the **Format** menu, click **Paragraph** and then click the **Indents and Spacing tab**. Under **Spacing**, change the **After** box to **36**. You can either type 36 or use the spin box arrow to increase the number displayed. Click **OK** to close the **Paragraph** dialog box. Notice that in this instance, the Line Spacing button was not used, because doing so would increase the space between the two wrapped lines of the paragraph. Because the goal is to add some space after the question for handwritten notes, the Spacing After paragraph feature is useful here.

7. With the question still selected, on the Formatting toolbar, click the **Numbering** button. The question is numbered 1, starting the numbering sequence over again, and the AutoCorrect Options button displays. Point to the **AutoCorrect Options** button, click its arrow to display the list of options available, and then, from the displayed list, click **Continue Numbering**. The number for this question is changed to 4.

8. Scroll down a few lines, select the question beginning *What kind of reputation*, and then click the **Numbering** button. The question is numbered 5, continuing the numbering sequence.

(Project 2G–Interview Questions continues on the next page)

(Project 2G–Interview Questions continued)

9. Select the four paragraphs following question 5, beginning with *Leading Edge*. Click the **Numbering** button. The numbering sequence continues—6 through 9. However, these paragraphs are a subset of question 5. With the four paragraphs still selected, on the Formatting toolbar, click the **Increase Indent** button. The paragraphs are indented and the numbers changed to letters a through d.

10. On the Standard toolbar, click the **Save** button. Each of the four paragraphs now labeled a. through d. has a colon followed by a space in the first line. In the paragraph beginning *a. Leading edge*, select the colon and its following space. From the **Insert** menu, click **Symbol**. In the **Symbol** dialog box, click the **Special Characters tab**; be sure that **Em Dash** is highlighted. Click **Insert**. The dialog box remains open on your screen. Select the colon and following space found in the first line of the paragraphs labeled, b., c., and d. and replace it by inserting an em dash from the **Symbol** dialog box. Move the dialog box on your screen as necessary and then close the dialog box.

11. Scroll as necessary to view page 2 on your screen. Select the paragraphs under *Instructional Design* including the two empty paragraphs between the questions. Display the **Paragraph** dialog box and increase the spacing after to **18**. Click **OK**. The space after formatting was applied to all of the paragraphs, including those without text.

12. With the paragraphs still selected, display the **Bullets and Numbering** dialog box and click the **Bulleted tab**. If necessary, click any bullet syles to activate the **Customize button**. In the lower right corner, click the **Customize button**. In the **Customize Bulleted List** dialog box, click the **Character button**. In the displayed **Symbol** dialog box, click the **Font** arrow, click **Wingdings**, scroll to the top of the list, and in the third row, click the first symbol-a hand with a pencil. Click **OK** twice. Then, click the **Decrease Indent** button as many times as necessary to align the bullets at the left margin.

If the numbers continue sequentially with the number 6 from the previous list, instead of restarting at number 1, open the **Bullets and Numbering** dialog box and click again to select the **Restart Numbering** option button. Click **OK**.

13. From the **View** menu, click **Header and Footer**. Switch to the footer area and then, on the **Header and Footer** toolbar, click **Insert AutoText**. From the displayed list, click **Filename**. Press Tab and click the **Insert Page Number** button. Close the Header and Footer toolbar.

(Project 2G–Interview Questions continues on the next page)

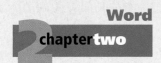
(Project 2G–Interview Questions continued)

14. Press Ctrl + Home to move to the top of the document. In the first group of questions, the second and third questions need to be reversed. Select the question *What did you think was effective?* The number will not be highlighted. Point to the highlighted text. When the mouse pointer is in the shape of the white move arrow, drag the question and place the vertical line at the beginning of question 2— in front of the *W*—and then release the mouse button. The questions are reversed. On the Standard toolbar click the **Undo** button and then click the **Redo** button. Notice that the numbers stay in sequence.

15. Press Ctrl + End to move to the end of the document. In the paragraph beginning *Thomas Russell*, in the third line, click to place the insertion point following the period after the word *media.* From the **Insert** menu, point to **Reference** and then click **Footnote**. In the **Footnote and Endnote** dialog box, under **Location**, click the **Endnotes** option button and be sure **End of document** is displayed in its box. Under **Format**, click the **Number format arrow** and then click **i, ii, iii** from the list that displays. Click the **Insert** button. In the endnote area, type **http://nova.teleeducation.nb.ca/nosignificantdifference/**

16. Click the **Save** button and then click the **Print Preview** button to view the document. From the Print Preview toolbar, click the **Print** button and then, on the same toolbar, click the **Close** button. Close the document, saving changes if prompted to do so.

End You have completed Project 2G

Performance Assessments (continued)

Project 2H—Virtual Tour

Objectives: *Change Document and Paragraph Layout, Change and Reorganize Text, Work with Headers and Footers, and Insert Frequently Used Text.*

In the following Performance Assessment, you will edit and format a report written by students of the Advanced Web Design class, regarding a Web site they plan to create for members of the local community. Your completed document will look similar to Figure 2.90. You will save your document as *2H_Virtual_Tour_Firstname_Lastname.*

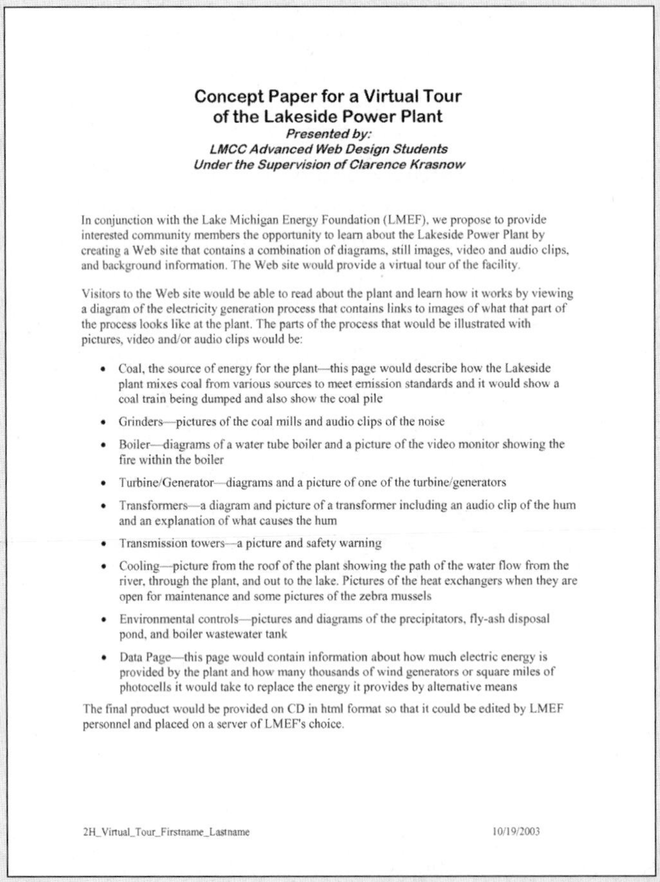

Concept Paper for a Virtual Tour of the Lakeside Power Plant
Presented by:
LMCC Advanced Web Design Students
Under the Supervision of Clarence Krasnow

In conjunction with the Lake Michigan Energy Foundation (LMEF), we propose to provide interested community members the opportunity to learn about the Lakeside Power Plant by creating a Web site that contains a combination of diagrams, still images, video and audio clips, and background information. The Web site would provide a virtual tour of the facility.

Visitors to the Web site would be able to read about the plant and learn how it works by viewing a diagram of the electricity generation process that contains links to images of what that part of the process looks like at the plant. The parts of the process that would be illustrated with pictures, video and/or audio clips would be:

- Coal, the source of energy for the plant—this page would describe how the Lakeside plant mixes coal from various sources to meet emission standards and it would show a coal train being dumped and also show the coal pile
- Grinders—pictures of the coal mills and audio clips of the noise
- Boiler—diagrams of a water tube boiler and a picture of the video monitor showing the fire within the boiler
- Turbine/Generator—diagrams and a picture of one of the turbine/generators
- Transformers—a diagram and picture of a transformer including an audio clip of the hum and an explanation of what causes the hum
- Transmission towers—a picture and safety warning
- Cooling—picture from the roof of the plant showing the path of the water flow from the river, through the plant, and out to the lake. Pictures of the heat exchangers when they are open for maintenance and some pictures of the zebra mussels
- Environmental controls—pictures and diagrams of the precipitators, fly-ash disposal pond, and boiler wastewater tank
- Data Page—this page would contain information about how much electric energy is provided by the plant and how many thousands of wind generators or square miles of photocells it would take to replace the energy it provides by alternative means

The final product would be provided on CD in html format so that it could be edited by LMEF personnel and placed on a server of LMEF's choice.

2H_Virtual_Tour_Firstname_Lastname 10/19/2003

Figure 2.90

(Project 2H–Virtual Tour continues on the next page)

(Project 2H–Virtual Tour continued)

1. Click the **Open** button. Navigate to the location where the student files for this textbook are stored. Locate and open the file **w02H_Virtual_Tour**. From the **File** menu, click **Save As**. Navigate to the location where you are storing your projects for this chapter. In the **File name** box, using your own name, type **2H_Virtual_Tour_Firstname_Lastname**

2. From the **File** menu, click **Page Setup**. Change the left and right margin boxes to **1"**.

3. From the **Tools** menu, click **AutoCorrect Options** and then click the **AutoCorrect tab**. In the **Replace** box type: xlmef and in the **With** box type **Lake Michigan Energy Foundation**. Click the **Add** button and then click **OK**. If another student has already added this AutoCorrect entry, the Replace button will be indicated instead of the Add button. Click Replace, click Yes, and then click OK.

4. In the paragraph that begins with *In conjunction with*, in the first line, place the insertion point to the left of LMEF. Type **xlmef** and then press the spacebar. The name of the foundation replaces the shortcut you typed. Enclose *LMEF* in parentheses.

5. In the same paragraph, at the end of the third line, select *still images,*—be sure you include the comma and the space. Point to the selected text and drag it to the left of *video and audio clips* in the same sentence. Adjust the spacing if necessary.

6. Select the two paragraphs above the bulleted list, beginning with *In conjunction with*, point anywhere in the selected text and right-click, and then click **Paragraph** from the shortcut menu. Under **Spacing**, change the **After** box to **12**. Click **OK**.

7. In the bulleted list, rearrange the items into the following order: Coal, Grinders, Boiler, Turbine/Generator, Transformers, Transmission towers, Cooling, Environmental Controls, Data Page.

8. Press Ctrl + Home to move to the top of the document. Press Ctrl + H to open the **Find and Replace** dialog box. In the **Find what** box, type **web** In the **Replace with** box, type **Web** Click **Replace All**. Four replacements are made. Close the dialog box.

9. From the **View** menu, click **Header and Footer**. Switch to the footer area on the Header and Footer toolbar, click **Insert AutoText** and then click **Filename**. Press Tab two times to move to the right side of the footer area and then click the **Insert Date** button. Select the text in the footer and change the font size to **10 pt**. Close the Header and Footer toolbar.

10. Click the **Save** button and then click the **Print Preview** button. From the Print Preview toolbar, click the **Print** button and then, on the same toolbar, click the **Close** button. Close the document.

 End You have completed Project 2H

Project 2I — Organizations

Objectives: *Change Document and Paragraph Layout, Change and Reorganize Text, Create and Modify Lists, and Work with Headers and Footers.*

In the following Mastery Assessment, you will format and reorganize a list of the student organizations at LMCC. Your completed document will look similar to Figure 2.91. You will save your document as *2I_Organizations_Firstname_Lastname.*

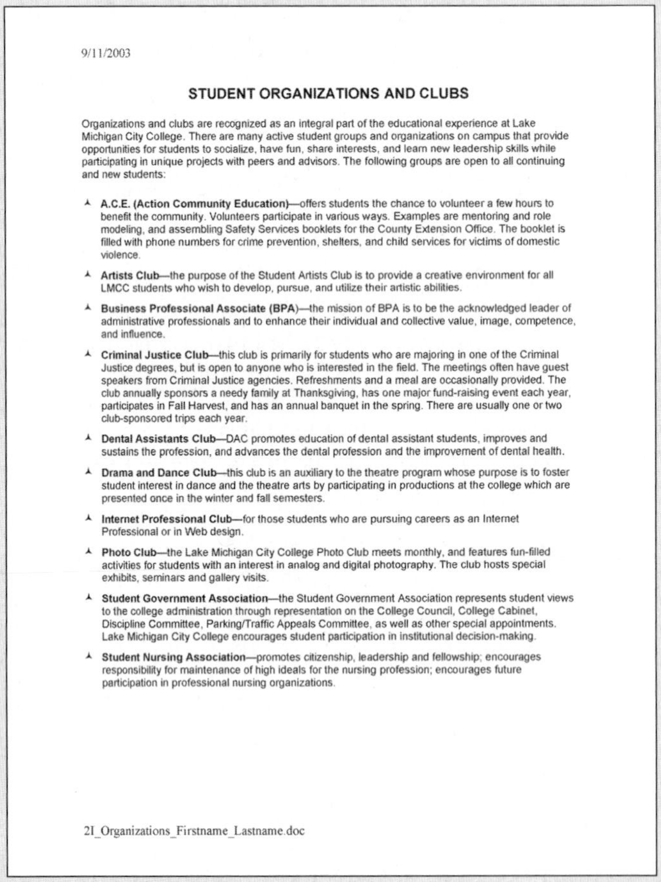

9/11/2003

STUDENT ORGANIZATIONS AND CLUBS

Organizations and clubs are recognized as an integral part of the educational experience at Lake Michigan City College. There are many active student groups and organizations on campus that provide opportunities for students to socialize, have fun, share interests, and learn new leadership skills while participating in unique projects with peers and advisors. The following groups are open to all continuing and new students:

- **A.C.E. (Action Community Education)**—offers students the chance to volunteer a few hours to benefit the community. Volunteers participate in various ways. Examples are mentoring and role modeling, and assembling Safety Services booklets for the County Extension Office. The booklet is filled with phone numbers for crime prevention, shelters, and child services for victims of domestic violence.
- **Artists Club**—the purpose of the Student Artists Club is to provide a creative environment for all LMCC students who wish to develop, pursue, and utilize their artistic abilities.
- **Business Professional Associate (BPA)**—the mission of BPA is to be the acknowledged leader of administrative professionals and to enhance their individual and collective value, image, competence, and influence.
- **Criminal Justice Club**—this club is primarily for students who are majoring in one of the Criminal Justice degrees, but is open to anyone who is interested in the field. The meetings often have guest speakers from Criminal Justice agencies. Refreshments and a meal are occasionally provided. The club annually sponsors a needy family at Thanksgiving, has one major fund-raising event each year, participates in Fall Harvest, and has an annual banquet in the spring. There are usually one or two club-sponsored trips each year.
- **Dental Assistants Club**—DAC promotes education of dental assistant students, improves and sustains the profession, and advances the dental profession and the improvement of dental health.
- **Drama and Dance Club**—this club is an auxiliary to the theatre program whose purpose is to foster student interest in dance and the theatre arts by participating in productions at the college which are presented once in the winter and fall semesters.
- **Internet Professional Club**—for those students who are pursuing careers as an Internet Professional or in Web design.
- **Photo Club**—the Lake Michigan City College Photo Club meets monthly, and features fun-filled activities for students with an interest in analog and digital photography. The club hosts special exhibits, seminars and gallery visits.
- **Student Government Association**—the Student Government Association represents student views to the college administration through representation on the College Council, College Cabinet, Discipline Committee, Parking/Traffic Appeals Committee, as well as other special appointments. Lake Michigan City College encourages student participation in institutional decision-making.
- **Student Nursing Association**—promotes citizenship, leadership and fellowship; encourages responsibility for maintenance of high ideals for the nursing profession; encourages future participation in professional nursing organizations.

2I_Organizations_Firstname_Lastname.doc

Figure 2.91

(Project 2I–Organizations continues on the next page)

(Project 2I–Organizations continued)

1. Display the **Open** dialog box. Navigate to the student files and then locate and open the file **w02I_Organizations**. In the **File name** box, type 2I_Organizations_Firstname_Lastname Display nonprinting characters. Display the **File** menu and click **Save As**. Navigate to the location where you are storing your projects for this chapter.

2. From the **File** menu, display the **Page Setup** dialog box. Change the left and right margins to **1 inch**, and close the dialog box. Center the title of the document.

3. Select the list of student organizations, beginning with *Student Government* and continuing down through the end of the document. Recall that you can click at the beginning point in the text, scroll to the end, press Shift, and then click at the end to select all of the text rather than dragging. Display the **Paragraph** dialog box, click the **Indents and Spacing tab**, and then, under **Spacing**, change the **After** box to **6**.

4. With the list of organizations still selected, display the **Bullets and Numbering** dialog box. Click the **Bulleted tab** and then click any of the bullet options. Click the **Customize** button and then click the **Character** button. In the **Symbol** dialog box, click the **Font arrow**, scroll, and then click **Wingdings**. Click a symbol of your choice that would serve as a bullet and then click **OK** twice to apply the bullet. Click the **Decrease Indent** button once to move the list to the left.

5. With the list of organizations still selected, from the **Table** menu, click **Sort**. Sort the list alphabetically by paragraph.

6. Display the footer area and then, using the **Insert AutoText** button, insert the **Filename**. Switch to the header area and insert the date at the left side of the header.

7. Save the changes. Preview and then print the document. Close the file.

End You have completed Project 2I ────────────────────────

Project 2J — Online Article

Objectives: *Change Document and Paragraph Layout, Change and Reorganize Text, Create and Modify Lists, Work with Headers and Footers, Insert Frequently Used Text, and Insert References.*

In the following Mastery Assessment, you will edit and format an article about one of the professors at LMCC who offers online classes. The completed article will look similar to Figure 2.92. You will save your document as *2J_Online_Article_Firstname_Lastname.*

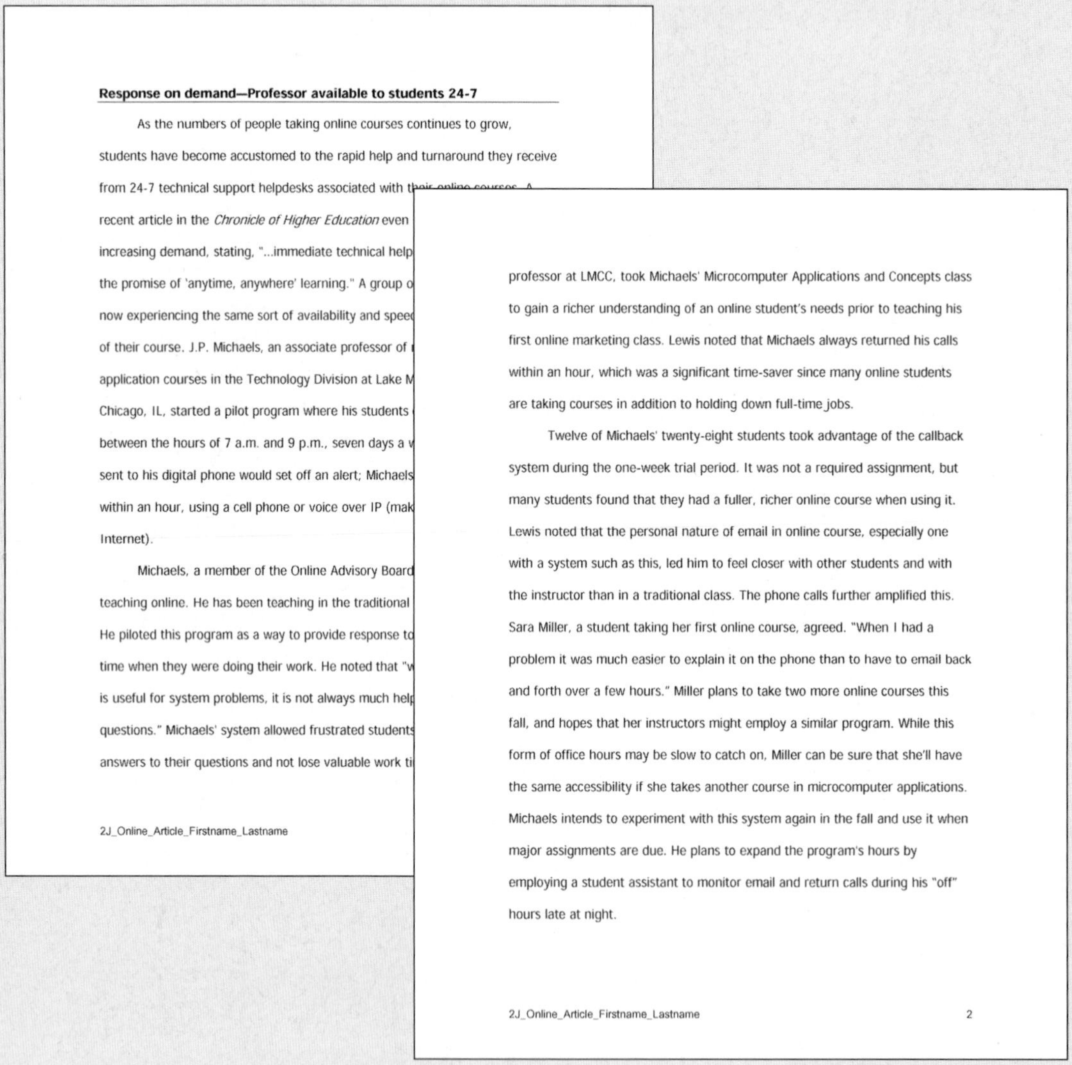

Response on demand—Professor available to students 24-7

As the numbers of people taking online courses continues to grow, students have become accustomed to the rapid help and turnaround they receive from 24-7 technical support helpdesks associated with their online courses. A recent article in the *Chronicle of Higher Education* even [...] increasing demand, stating, "...immediate technical help [...] the promise of 'anytime, anywhere' learning." A group o[...] now experiencing the same sort of availability and speed [...] of their course. J.P. Michaels, an associate professor of [...] application courses in the Technology Division at Lake M[...] Chicago, IL, started a pilot program where his students [...] between the hours of 7 a.m. and 9 p.m., seven days a w[...] sent to his digital phone would set off an alert; Michaels [...] within an hour, using a cell phone or voice over IP (mak[...] Internet).

Michaels, a member of the Online Advisory Board[...] teaching online. He has been teaching in the traditional [...] He piloted this program as a way to provide response to [...] time when they were doing their work. He noted that "w[...] is useful for system problems, it is not always much help[...] questions." Michaels' system allowed frustrated students [...] answers to their questions and not lose valuable work ti[...]

2J_Online_Article_Firstname_Lastname

professor at LMCC, took Michaels' Microcomputer Applications and Concepts class to gain a richer understanding of an online student's needs prior to teaching his first online marketing class. Lewis noted that Michaels always returned his calls within an hour, which was a significant time-saver since many online students are taking courses in addition to holding down full-time jobs.

Twelve of Michaels' twenty-eight students took advantage of the callback system during the one-week trial period. It was not a required assignment, but many students found that they had a fuller, richer online course when using it. Lewis noted that the personal nature of email in online course, especially one with a system such as this, led him to feel closer with other students and with the instructor than in a traditional class. The phone calls further amplified this. Sara Miller, a student taking her first online course, agreed. "When I had a problem it was much easier to explain it on the phone than to have to email back and forth over a few hours." Miller plans to take two more online courses this fall, and hopes that her instructors might employ a similar program. While this form of office hours may be slow to catch on, Miller can be sure that she'll have the same accessibility if she takes another course in microcomputer applications. Michaels intends to experiment with this system again in the fall and use it when major assignments are due. He plans to expand the program's hours by employing a student assistant to monitor email and return calls during his "off" hours late at night.

2J_Online_Article_Firstname_Lastname   2

Figure 2.92

(Project 2J–Online Article continues on the next page)

(Project 2J–Online Article continued)

1. Display the **Open** dialog box. Navigate to the student files and then locate and open the file **w02J_Online_Article**. Display the **File** menu, click **Save As**, and navigate to the location where you are storing your projects for this chapter. In the **File name** box, type **2J_Online_Article_Firstname_Lastname**

2. From the **File** menu, display the **Page Setup** dialog box. Change the left and right margins to **1.25"**.

3. Beginning with the paragraph *As the numbers*, select the entire body of the article, click the arrow on the **Line Spacing** button, and then click **2.0**.

4. With the text still selected, display the **Paragraph** dialog box, and then click the **Indents and Spacing tab**. Under **Indentation**, click the **Special arrow** and then click **First line**.

5. Position the insertion point at the top of the document and then display the **Find and Replace** dialog box. In the **Find what** box type **e-mail** and in the **Replace with** box type **email** Find and replace this word throughout the document.

6. Use the **Find and Replace** dialog box to locate **College of Technology** and replace it with **Technology Division** Make sure the insertion point is at the top of the document. Use the **Find and Replace** dialog box to locate the second occurrence of *Lake Michigan City College* and replace it with **LMCC** Finally, use the **Find and Replace** dialog box to find **Rosenthal** and replace each occurrence with **Miller**.

7. Move to the top of the document. In the paragraph beginning *As the numbers*, in the middle of the seventh line, locate the phrase *speed and availability*. Use drag-and-drop or cut-and-paste techniques to reword this to read *availability and speed*.

8. Press Ctrl + End to move to the end of the document. Select the last sentence in the document beginning with *Miller plans to take* (do not select the ending paragraph mark). In the same paragraph, locate the sentence that begins *While this form* and then use the drag-and-drop technique to move the selected sentence in front of the *While this form* sentence. Adjust the spacing if necessary. Be sure that you did not create a new paragraph.

9. View the footer area, click the **Insert AutoText** button, and then insert the **Filename**. Tab to the right side of the footer and insert the page number.

10. Save the changes. Preview and then print the document. Close the file.

End **You have completed Project 2J**

Project 2K — Holidays

Objectives: *Change Document and Paragraph Layout, Change and Reorganize Text, Create and Modify Lists, Work with Headers and Footers.*

You will write a memo listing the holidays that will be taken during the calendar school year at Lake Michigan City College. You will save your document as *2K_Holidays_Firstname_Lastname.*

1. Open Word. Use the **Page Setup** dialog box to set the margins to **2 inches** at the top margin, and **1 inch** on the left and right sides.

2. Create a MEMO heading at the top of the document. Format the heading in a distinctive manner and align it on the right side of the page. Press [Enter] four times.

2. Type the heading of the memo as follows:

   MEMO TO: **James Smith, Vice President of Student Affairs**
   FROM: **Henry Sabaj, Vice President of Academic Affairs**
   DATE: **August 1**
   SUBJECT: **College Holidays**

3. Format the heading to be double-spaced and indent 1 inch from the left margin. Format the headings in uppercase bold.

4. Write one or two introductory sentences indicating that this is the list of holiday dates agreed to by the faculty and administration for the upcoming college year.

5. Use a calendar and create a bulleted list of official holiday names and dates for the September through May college year. Look at your own college calendar and include the dates for any winter or spring breaks that may be scheduled.

6. Format the list of holidays using a bullet symbol of your choice.

7. Save the memo in your storage location with the name **2K_Holidays_Firstname_Lastname**

8. View the footer area and insert the filename using AutoText.

9. Switch to the header area and type **Academic Affairs**

10. Preview and then print the memo. Close the file and close Word.

End **You have completed Project 2K**

Project 2L — Computer Information Memo

Objectives: *Change Document and Paragraph Layout, Change and Reorganize Text, Create and Modify Lists, Work with Headers and Footers.*

In this Problem Solving assessment, you will write a memo to the Vice President of Academic Affairs listing the Computer Information Systems courses at LMCC. You will save your memo as *2L_Computer_Information_Memo_Firstname_Lastname.*

1. Open Word. Use the **Page Setup** dialog box to set the margins to **2"** at the top margin, and **1"** on the left and right sides.

2. Create a MEMO heading at the top of the document. Format the heading in a distinctive manner and center it on the page. Press Enter four times.

3. Type the heading of the memo as follows:

   MEMO TO: **Henry Sabaj, Vice President of Academic Affairs**
   FROM: **Lisa Huelsman, Associate Dean of Adult Basic Education**
   DATE: **September 30**
   SUBJECT: **Computer Information Systems Courses**

4. Format the heading area to be double-spaced and indent 1" from the left margin. Format the headings in uppercase bold.

5. Write one or two introductory sentences explaining that the list includes the current Computer Information Systems courses required for a certificate or degree at LMCC.

6. Using the course catalog and other information available via your college's Web site, create a bulleted list of the course numbers and names that are required as Computer Information Systems—or similar—classes at your college.

7. Add a closing to the memo requesting that Mr. Sabaj review the list for possible adjustments or modifications.

8. Save the memo in your storage location with the name **2L_Computer_Information_Memo_Firstname_Lastname**

9. View the footer area and insert the filename using AutoText.

10. Preview and then print the memo. Close the file and close Word.

End You have completed Project 2L ────────────

On the Internet

Finding More Bullet Styles To Use

The bullet symbols that display in the Symbols dialog box are used throughout Microsoft Office programs. You can also download and use symbols from other sites on the Internet.

1. Open your Web browser and go to a search engine such as www.google.com or www.yahoo.com. Type the key words **bullets** and **free** in the search box.

2. Look through the various sites for one you like that has a variety of interesting graphics that may be used for bullets. There are several that do not require that you sign up for advertising or provide your e-mail address.

3. Pick a bullet you like and right-click it. Click the **Save as Picture** option from the shortcut menu and save it to your disk.

4. Open a Word document and create a short bulleted list to demonstrate your new bullet.

5. Select the list and, on the Formatting toolbar, click the **Bullet** button.

6. From the **Format** menu, choose **Bullets and Numbering**. Click **Customize** and then **Picture**.

7. Click **Import**. In the **Add Clips to Organizer** dialog box, find the picture you saved to your disk, click it, and then click **Add**. Select your new picture, if necessary, click **OK**, and then click **OK** again to close the dialog boxes.

8. Close the file without saving the changes and then close Word.

GO! with Help

Restoring the Default Bullets and Numbering

If you have used a number of customized bullets in the Bullets and Numbering dialog box, you may want to restore the dialog box to its original configuration. The Word Help program gives you step-by-step instructions on how to restore a customized list format to its original setting.

1. Start Word. On the menu bar, in the *Type* a question for help box, type **How do I restore customized bullet list** and then press Enter.

2. Locate and then click the topic **Restore a customized list format to its original setting.**

3. Read the instructions that display and then follow the steps to restore the original settings to the Bullets and Numbering dialog box on your computer.

4. Close the Microsoft Word Help pane and then close the Search Results task pane.

3 chapterthree

Using Graphics and Tables

In this chapter, you will: complete these projects **and** practice these skills.

Project 3A **Creating a Flyer**	**Objectives**
	• Insert Clip Art and Pictures
	• Modify Clip Art and Pictures
	• Work with the Drawing Toolbar

Project 3B **Formatting a Report**	**Objectives**
	• Work with Tab Stops
	• Create a Table
	• Format Tables
	• Create a Table from Existing Text

Sensation! Park

Sensation! Park is a "family fun center" theme park designed for today's busy families. The park offers traditional amusement park rides and arcade games along with new and popular water rides, surf pools, laser tag, video games, and a racetrack for all ages.

Situated on 100 acres, the park's mission is to provide a safe, clean, exciting environment where children and adults of all ages can find a game, ride, or event that suits their interests or discover something completely new!

© Getty Images, Inc.

Adding Graphics and Tables to a Document

Adding graphics can greatly enhance the effectiveness of documents. Digital images, such as those obtained from a digital camera or a scanner, can be inserted into documents. A **clip** is a media file, including art, sound, animation, or movies. **Clip art** images—which are predefined graphic images included with Microsoft Office or downloaded from the Web—can be effective if used appropriately. You can also create your own graphic objects by using the tools on the Drawing toolbar.

Tabs can be used to horizontally align text and numbers. The Tab key is used to move to **tab stops**, which mark specific locations on a line of text. You can set your own tab stops and specify the alignment of each stop.

Tables are used to present data effectively and efficiently. The row and column format makes information easy to find and easy to read and helps the reader organize and categorize the data. The Word table feature has tools that enable you to format text, change column width and row height, change the background on portions or all of the table, and modify the table borders and lines.

Project 3A **Job Opportunities**

In this chapter, you will create a document and add a picture from a file and a clip art image provided by Microsoft. You will format, resize, and move the images. You will add tab stops, and you will create and format two tables.

In Activities 3.1 through 3.9, you will edit a job announcement flyer for Sensation! Park. You will add a picture and a clip art image. You will also add objects from the Drawing toolbar. Your completed document will look similar to Figure 3.1. You will save your document as *3A_Job_Opportunities_Firstname_Lastname.*

Sensation! Park
Summer Employment Opportunities

Are you looking for full- or part-time work in the most exciting surroundings in the greater Philadelphia area? Are you self-motivated, ambitious, friendly? Do you like working with people? If so, Sensation! Park has the job for you!

There are many advantages to working at Sensation! Park, including a strong benefits package, flexible hours, competitive wages, a friendly working environment, and the use of park facilities during off-peak hours.

We have jobs available in the following areas:
- Food service
- Ride management
- Security
- Transportation
- Clerical
- Maintenance

Some full- and part-time jobs are available immediately. Other jobs will begin in May. The park opens this year on May 20, the week before Memorial Day. Training sessions begin the week of May 13. There are also summer jobs available for college and high school students (minimum age 16).

The SuperSpeed Ferris Wheel, one of the new rides at Sensation! Park

Call 215.555.1776

3A_Job_Opportunities_FirstName_Lastname

Figure 3.1
Project 3A—Job Opportunity Flyer

Objective 1
Insert Clip Art and Pictures

Graphic images can be inserted into a document from many sources. Clip art can be inserted from files provided with Microsoft Office or can be downloaded from the Microsoft Office Web site. Pictures can be scanned from photographs or slides, taken with a digital camera, or downloaded from the Web.

Activity 3.1 Inserting Clip Art

1 On the Standard toolbar, click the **Open** button. Navigate to the location where the student files for this textbook are stored. Locate **w03A_Job_Opportunities** and click once to select it. Then, in the lower right corner of the **Open** dialog box, click **Open**.

The w03A_Job_Opportunities file opens. See Figure 3.2.

Figure 3.2

2 From the **File** menu, click **Save As**. In the **Save As** dialog box, click the **Save in** arrow and navigate to the location where you are storing your files for this chapter, creating a new Chapter 3 folder if you want to do so.

3 In the **File name** box, type **3A_Job_Opportunities_Firstname_Lastname** and then click **Save**.

The document is saved with a new name. Make sure you substitute your name where indicated.

4 If necessary, on the Standard toolbar, click the Show/Hide ¶ button to display the nonprinting characters.

5 In the paragraph near the top of the document beginning *Are you looking*, click to place the insertion point to the left of the first word in the paragraph—*Are*.

6 From the **Insert** menu, point to **Picture**, and then click **Clip Art**.

The Clip Art task pane opens.

7 In the **Search in** box, verify that *All collections* displays and, if necessary, click the arrow, and then select the **Everywhere** check box. In the **Results should be** box, verify that *All media file types* displays and, if necessary, click the arrow, and then select the **All media types** check box.

8 In the **Search for** box, delete any existing text, type **roller coaster** and then click the **Go** button. Locate the roller coaster image from the task pane as shown in Figure 3.3. Use the scroll bar if necessary.

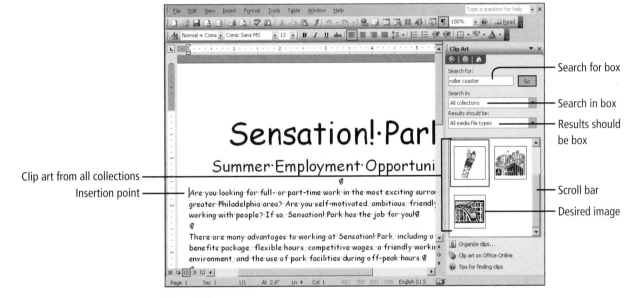

Figure 3.3

Alert!

Is the Image Missing from your Task Pane?

Many colleges perform minimum installations of software, including Microsoft Office. This means that little or no clip art is included with the program. When the program searches for an image, it looks on the hard drive and also tries to access the clip libraries on the Microsoft Office Web site. If you are not connected to the Web, your screen will not display the images shown in Figure 3.3.

If you do not see the appropriate image, click Organize clips at the bottom of the Clip Art task pane. From the File menu, point to Add Clips to Organizer, and then click Automatically. After a few minutes, all images on your computer are identified and organized. If the appropriate image is still not available, display the Insert menu, point to Picture, click From File, navigate to the location in which your student files are stored, click w03A_Roller_Coaster and then click the Insert button. Alternatively, use a similar image from the task pane.

9 Click the roller coaster image if it is available. If you do not see the image, display the **Insert** menu, point to **Picture**, click **From File**, navigate to your student files and click **w03A_Roller_Coaster**, and then click the **Insert** button.

The clip art image is placed at the insertion point location. The image is inserted in the line of text in exactly the same manner as any other letter or number would be inserted—it becomes a part of the sentence. See Figure 3.4.

Figure 3.4

10 On the Formatting toolbar, click the **Save** button 🖫.

Activity 3.2 Inserting Pictures from Files

Pictures can also be added to a document, either by browsing for a picture on a disk drive or by using the Clip Art task pane.

1 In the paragraph beginning *There are many advantages*, click to place the insertion point to the left of the first word in the paragraph—*There*.

2 In the **Clip Art** task pane, in the **Search for** box, type **Ferris wheel**

3 In the **Results should be** box, clear the check boxes of everything but **Photographs**.

Restricting the media type will limit the number of images found but will be helpful when you are searching for a topic with a large number of images. See Figure 3.5.

Search for photos   Type of photo

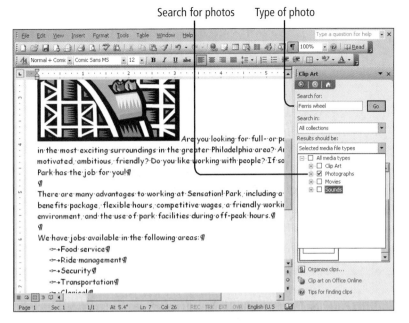

Figure 3.5

4 Click **Go**.

One or more Ferris wheel photographs display.

5 Click the Ferris wheel with the blue background. If the image is not available, select another similar image or display the **Insert** menu, point to **Picture**, click **From File**, navigate and click **w03A_Ferris_Wheel**, and click **Insert**. Scroll to the top of the second page.

The photograph is inserted at the insertion point location and the document expands to a second page. See Figure 3.6.

Task pane
Close button

Starts search

Figure 3.6

6 On the **Clip Art** task pane title bar, click the **Close** button ⊠.

7 From the **View** menu, click **Header and Footer**.

The Header and Footer dialog box displays.

8 On the Header and Footer toolbar, click the **Switch Between Header and Footer** button ⊞.

The insertion point is positioned in the footer box.

9 On the Header and Footer toolbar, click the **Insert AutoText** button `Insert AutoText ▾`, and then click **Filename**.

The file name is inserted in the footer. The file extension .doc may or may not display, depending on your Word settings. See Figure 3.7.

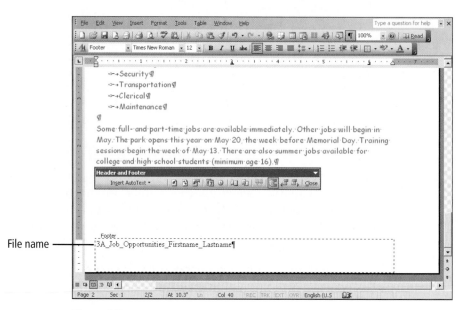

File name ─── 3A_Job_Opportunities_Firstname_Lastname¶

Figure 3.7

10 On the Header and Footer toolbar, click the **Close** button `Close`.

11 On the Standard toolbar, click the **Save** button 🖫. Alternatively, press `Ctrl` + `S` to save your changes.

Objective 2
Modify Clip Art and Pictures

You can format clip art or pictures once you have placed them in a document. When images are placed in documents, they are placed inline. *Inline images* are just like characters in a sentence. You can change them to *floating images*—images that can be moved independently of the surrounding text—by changing the wrapping options. You can also change the size of an image to make it fit better in your document.

Activity 3.3 Wrapping Text around Graphic Objects

Pictures and clip art images that are treated as characters in a sentence can cause awkward spacing in a document. To avoid this awkward spacing, you can format any graphic to move independently of the surrounding text.

1 Locate and click the first image (the roller coaster) that you inserted.

Sizing handles, small black boxes, display around the image border. These handles are used to increase or decrease the size of the image. The sizing handles also indicate that the image is selected. The Picture toolbar may also open, either floating over the document, or added to the other toolbars. See Figure 3.8.

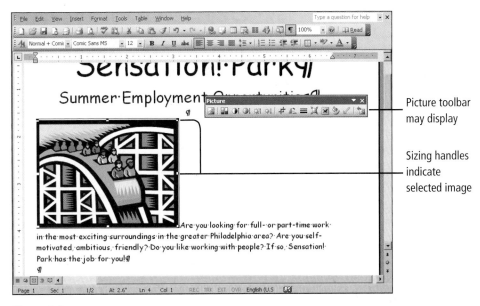

Picture toolbar may display

Sizing handles indicate selected image

Figure 3.8

2 From the **Format** menu, click **Picture**. Alternatively, you can right-click the image and click Format Picture from the shortcut menu.

The Format Picture dialog box displays.

3 In the **Format Picture** dialog box, click the **Layout tab**

The wrapping and alignment options display on the Layout tab. See Figure 3.9.

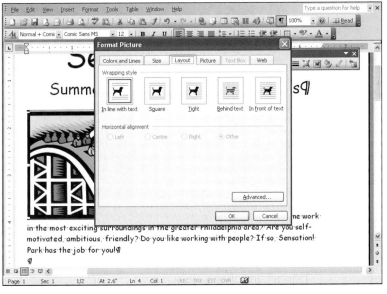

Figure 3.9

4 Under **Wrapping style**, click **Tight**, and then click **OK**.

The text wraps tightly around the image, and the ferris wheel picture moves up from the second page. See Figure 3.10.

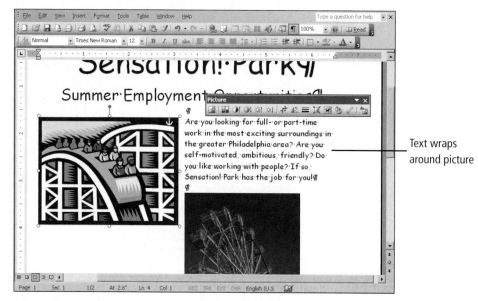

Figure 3.10

5 Scroll down and click the Ferris wheel picture.

6 From the **Format** menu, click **Picture**, and then click the **Layout tab**.

7 Under **Wrapping style**, click **Tight**, and then click **OK**.

The text wraps around the second image. See Figure 3.11. Because the spaces to the right of the pictures are used to display text, the document now occupies one page instead of two.

Figure 3.11

8 On the Standard toolbar, click the **Save** button 🖫.

Activity 3.4 Resizing a Graphic Object

Usually you will want to adjust the size of the clip art and pictures that you place in documents. Use the sizing handles to resize images.

1 Locate and click the first image you inserted (the roller coaster). Drag the image to the right side of the page so that its right edge aligns at approximately **6.5 inches on the horizontal ruler**.

Sizing handles, a *rotate handle*, and an **anchor** all display on or near the image. If your ruler is not displayed, from the View menu, click Ruler. You may need to use the horizontal scrollbar to move left to see the anchor. The table in Figure 3.12 describes the purpose of each of these formatting tools. Then refer to Figure 3.13 for placement of the image.

Graphic Formatting Marks, Handles, and Anchors

Mark	Purpose
Corner-sizing handles	Resizes images proportionally
Side-sizing handles	Stretches or shrinks the image in one direction
Rotate handle	Rotates the image clockwise or counterclockwise
Anchor	Indicates that the image is attached to the nearest paragraph

Figure 3.12

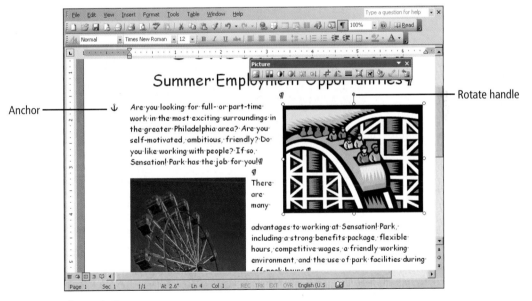

Anchor

Rotate handle

Figure 3.13

2 Locate the sizing handle in the middle of the lower edge of the roller coaster image and drag it up until the image is about an inch high. Check the ruler height on the vertical ruler, although it need not be exact.

Notice that the image shape is distorted. See Figure 3.14.

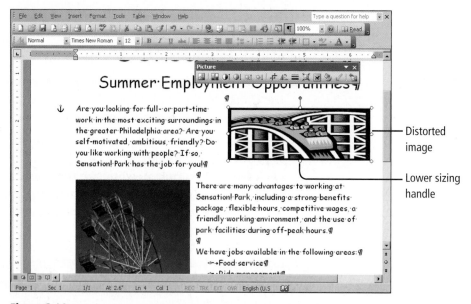

Figure 3.14

3 From the Standard toolbar, click the **Undo** button.

The image returns to its original size.

4 Locate the sizing handle on the lower right corner of the image and drag it up and to the left until the image is about an inch high.

Notice that the image is resized proportionally and not distorted. Do not be concerned if the words do not wrap exactly as shown in Figure 3.15.

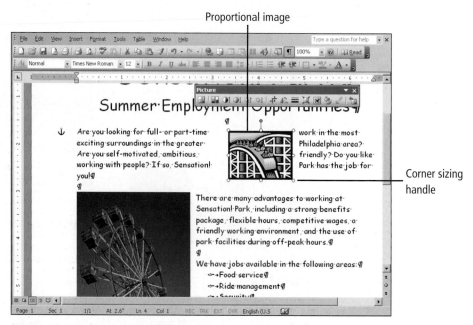

Figure 3.15

5 On the Standard toolbar, click the **Save** button.

Activity 3.5 Moving a Graphic Object

Once you have chosen one of the image wrapping options, you can move the image anywhere on the page.

1 Move the pointer to the middle of the roller coaster image but do not click.

The move pointer displays. See Figure 3.16.

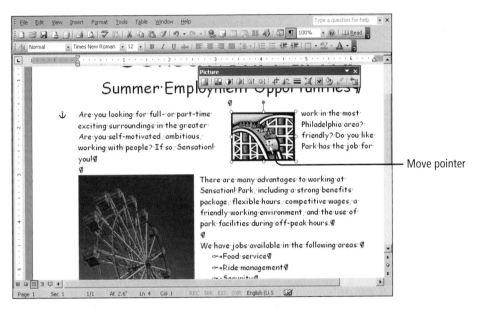

Move pointer

Figure 3.16

2 Click in the middle of the image and, as shown in Figure 3.17, drag it to the right of the paragraph beginning *Are you looking for*.

A dashed border around the pointer indicates the potential position of the image. See Figure 3.17.

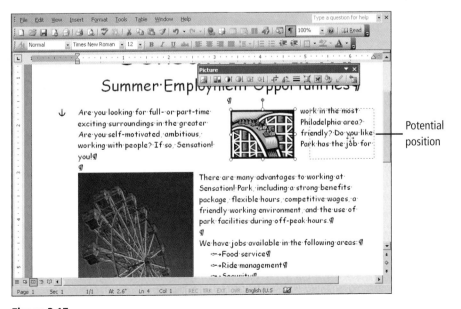

Potential position

Figure 3.17

3 Release the mouse button.

The image moves to the pointer location, and the text wraps at the left border of the image.

4 On the Standard toolbar, click the **Save** button 🖫.

Objective 3
Work with the Drawing Toolbar

The Drawing toolbar has tools to add text boxes, lines, arrows, boxes, circles, and predefined shapes to your document. Many of these drawing objects can be formatted; that is, you can increase line thickness and color, change font colors, and change the background colors and patterns. A drawing canvas is provided as a work area for complex drawings; however, when inserting and formatting simple drawing objects, it is more convenient to turn the drawing canvas off.

Activity 3.6 Inserting a Text Box

A *text box* is a movable, resizable container for text or graphics. A text box is useful to give text a different orientation from other text in the document because it is can be placed anywhere in the document. A text box can be moved around the document just like a floating image. A text box is a drawing object and, as such, can be placed outside the document margin, resized, and moved. This is easier if you first turn off the drawing canvas. As you progress in your study of Word, you will learn more about using the drawing canvas.

1 From the **Tools** menu, click **Options**, and then click the **General tab**.

2 Under **General options**, locate the last check box, **Automatically create drawing canvas when inserting AutoShapes** and, if necessary, clear (click to remove the check mark). Click **OK** to close the **Options** dialog box.

The drawing canvas is turned off.

3 Check to see the if your Drawing toolbar is displayed at the bottom of your screen. If it is not, right-click either toolbar to activate the Toolbars shortcut menu and then click Drawing.

The Drawing toolbar displays, usually at the bottom of the screen. You can also open the Drawing toolbar by clicking the Drawing button on the Standard toolbar.

4 Position your document so the bulleted list is near the top of your screen. On the Drawing toolbar, click the **Text Box** button 🔲 and then move the pointer into the document window.

The pointer changes to a crosshair. See Figure 3.18.

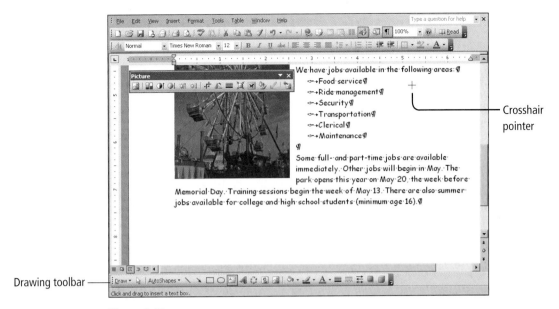

Crosshair pointer

Drawing toolbar

Figure 3.18

5 Position the crosshair pointer slightly to the right of *Food service* and then drag down and to the right to form an approximately 1½-inch square. Release the mouse button. Your measurement need not be exact.

A text box displays with the insertion point in the upper left corner, and the Text Box toolbar displays.

6 Type **The SuperSpeed Ferris Wheel, one of the new rides at Sensation! Park**

The text wraps within the text box. See Figure 3.19.

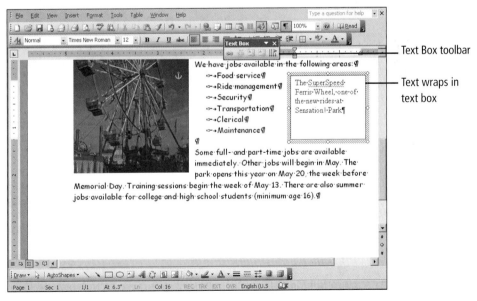

Text Box toolbar

Text wraps in text box

Figure 3.19

Activity 3.7 Moving and Resizing a Text Box

1 On the Standard toolbar, click the **Zoom button arrow** 100% ▾ , and then click **Page Width**.

2 Move the pointer over a border of the text box until a four-headed arrow pointer displays.

The pointer changes to a move pointer, which looks like a four-way arrow.

3 Drag the text box down to the empty area below the paragraph beginning *Some full- and part-time* as shown in Figure 3.20. A dashed border around the pointer indicates the potential position of the image.

4 Release the mouse button.

The text box is moved to the new location. See Figure 3.20.

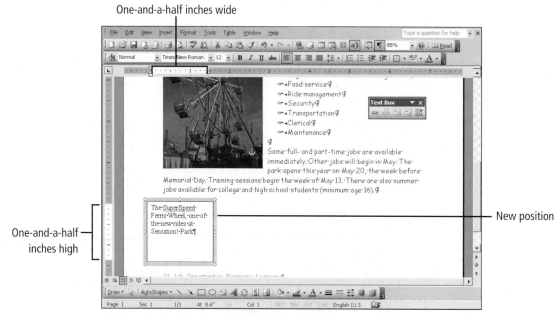

One-and-a-half inches wide

One-and-a-half inches high

New position

Figure 3.20

5 Scroll down until you can see the whole text box. If necessary, position the pointer over the center right sizing handle to display a two-headed pointer and then drag to the right to adjust the text box size until all the text in the box displays on three lines. Drag the lower center handle up slightly to remove excess white space in the text box.

6 On the Formatting toolbar, click the **Center** button ▤.

The text is horizontally centered within the text box. Compare your screen to Figure 3.21.

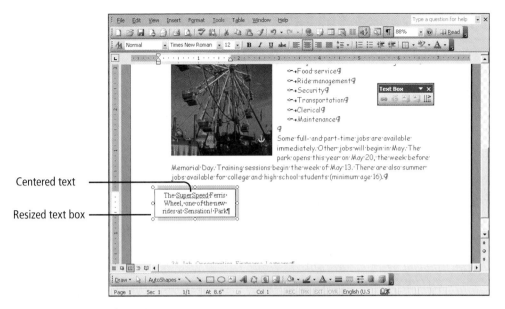

Centered text

Resized text box

Figure 3.21

7 On the Standard toolbar, click the **Save** button.

Activity 3.8 Inserting an Arrow

Buttons on the Drawing toolbar enable you to create shapes—circles, boxes, lines, and arrows. Arrows are very useful to point out features in graphic objects such as photographs and maps.

1 On the Drawing toolbar, click the **Arrow** button and move your pointer into the document window.

The pointer changes to a crosshair.

Alert!

Does a Large Drawing Box Display?

If you did not deactivate the drawing canvas earlier, clicking buttons on the Drawing toolbar results in the insertion of a large *drawing canvas*, which is a work area for creating drawings. This work area is very handy for combining several graphic objects but gets in the way when you try to add simple shapes to a document. To turn off the drawing canvas, click the Close button on the Drawing Canvas toolbar and click in the drawing canvas area.

The drawing canvas can be deactivated by choosing Tools, Options from the menu. Click the General tab. Clear the *Automatically create drawing canvas when inserting AutoShapes* check box.

2 Position the crosshair pointer at the center of the left border of the text box.

3 Drag up and to the right to draw a line to the Ferris wheel picture and then release the mouse button.

The arrowhead points in the direction you dragged the arrow. See Figure 3.22.

Inserted arrow ──

Arrow button ──

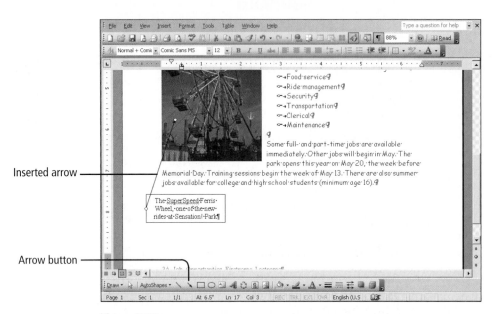

Figure 3.22

4 With the arrow still selected, move your pointer over the white sizing handle on the lower end of the arrow to display a two-headed pointer and then drag up to shorten the arrow until its lower end is near the left edge of the top border of the text box as shown in Figure 3.23.

End of arrow repositioned ──

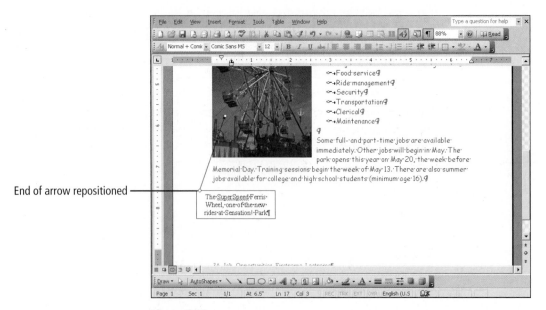

Figure 3.23

5 Move the pointer over the selected arrow and right-click. From the shortcut menu, click **Format AutoShape** and, in the displayed **Format AutoShape** dialog box, click the **Colors and Lines tab**.

6 Under **Line**, click the **Weight spin** box up arrow three times to select **1.5 pt**.

7 Under **Arrows**, click the **End Size** arrow and, from the displayed menu, click the largest arrowhead—**Arrow R Size 9**.

Compare your dialog box to Figure 3.24.

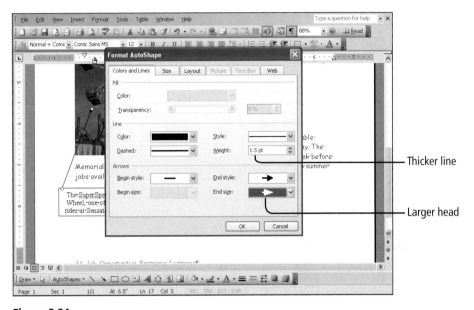

Figure 3.24

8 Click **OK**.

The arrow is thicker and has a larger arrowhead.

9 On the Standard toolbar, click the **Save** button 📖.

Activity 3.9 Inserting an AutoShape

More than 150 predefined AutoShapes are available to use in documents. These include stars, banners, arrows, and callouts.

1 On the Drawing toolbar, click the **AutoShapes** button AutoShapes ▾.

Point to the **Stars and Banners** button 🖼.

Sixteen star and banner shapes display. See Figure 3.25.

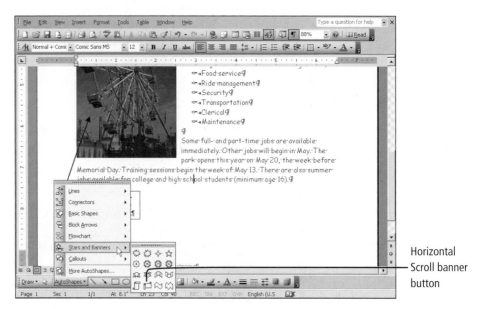

Horizontal
Scroll banner
button

Figure 3.25

2 In the fourth row of the **Stars and Banners** menu, click the second shape, the **Horizontal Scroll** banner button ▢, and move your pointer into the document window.

A crosshair pointer displays.

3 Position the crosshair to the right of the text box approximately **3 inches on the horizontal ruler**. As shown in Figure 3.25, drag down and to the right until the banner is about ¾ inch high and 3½ inches wide and release the mouse button. Use the horizontal and vertical rulers to help you determine the size of the banner. If you are not satisfied with your result, click Undo and begin again.

A banner is placed at the bottom of the flyer. See Figure 3.26.

Three-and-a-half inches wide

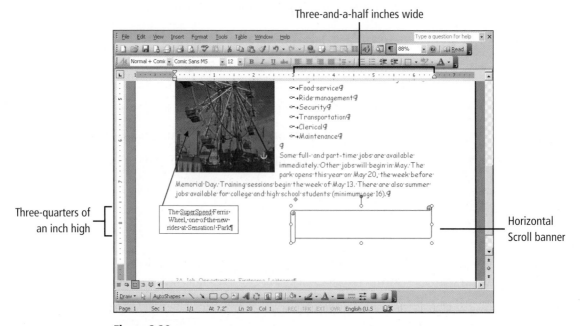

Three-quarters of
an inch high

Horizontal
Scroll banner

Figure 3.26

4 Move the pointer over the banner and right-click. From the shortcut menu, click **Add Text**.

The insertion point is placed in the banner, and a slashed border surrounds the shape.

5 Type **Call 215.555.1776**

6 Select the text you just typed. From the Formatting toolbar, click the **Font Size arrow** and click **28**, as shown in Figure 3.27.

7 Be sure the text is still selected and then on the Formatting toolbar, click the **Bold** button **B**. Adjust the height and width of the AutoShape as necessary.

8 On the Formatting toolbar, click the **Center** button. Use the sizing handles to adjust the banner until it looks similar to Figure 3.27. Click outside the banner to deselect it.

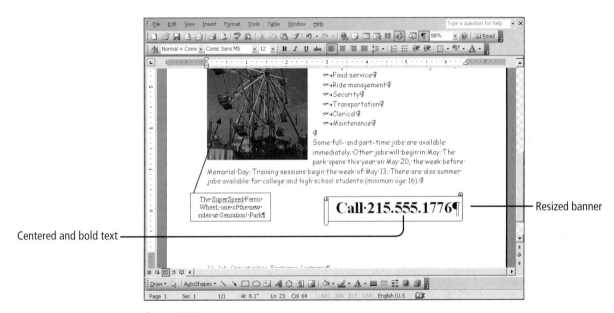

Centered and bold text ⎯⎯⎯⎯⎯

Resized banner

Figure 3.27

8 On the Standard toolbar, click the **Save** button. Then, on the Standard toolbar, click the **Print Preview** button to view your document.

9 On the Print Preview toolbar, click the **Print** button. Close the document.

End You have completed Project 3A ⎯⎯⎯⎯⎯⎯⎯⎯⎯⎯⎯⎯

Project 3B **Park Changes**

In Project 3A you worked with clip art and the drawing features of Word. Now you will use tabs and tables to align and organize lists of information.

In Activities 3.10 through 3.24 you will edit a list of changes in age and height restrictions for the rides and other attractions for the coming Sensation! Park season. You will add a tabbed list and two tables. Your completed document will look similar to Figure 3.28. You will save your document as *3B_Park_Changes_Firstname_ Lastname.*

MEMO TO: Dana Brothers, Vice President, Marketing

FROM: McNeal Blackmon

DATE: February 25

SUBJECT: Final Changes in Hours of Operation, Ticket Prices, and Restrictions

Here are the final changes in hours of operation, ticket prices, and restrictions for the new season. I know you are in a deadline crunch for the brochure, so please take a look at these changes and let me know if you see any problems. If you are comfortable with everything, go ahead and finish the brochure. Let's see if we can get it printed before the New Employee Orientation meetings.

The hours of operation are very similar to last year; the Sunday opening time is the only change:

Monday–Thursday	1 p.m.	10 p.m.
Friday	1 p.m.	11 p.m.
Saturday and Holidays	11 a.m.	11 p.m.
Sunday	NOON	11 p.m.

Admission charges are significantly different, with the price of season passes reduced by $20 for Adults, and increased by $20 for Juniors. Let's hope the 15% increase in revenue is realistic!

	Age	One Day	Season Pass
Toddler	3 & under	Free	Free
Junior	4 to 11	$19	$89
Adult	12 to 59	$39	$129
Senior	60+	$29	$99

Height and age restrictions are unchanged for most of the activities, with the following exceptions:

Activity	Minimum height/age:	To be able to:
	52" tall	Drive alone
Speedway Go-Karts	16 years old	Drive with a passenger
	40" tall	Ride as a passenger
	44" tall	Drive alone
Bumper Boats	14 years old	Drive with a passenger
	32" tall	Ride as a passenger
	10 years old	Play without parent/guardian
Miniature Golf	No age limit	Play with parent/guardian
	5 years old	Play with 12+ year old companion

3B_Park_Changes_Firstname_Lastname

Figure 3.28
Project 3B—Park Changes Memo

Objective 4
Work with Tab Stops

Tab stops are used to indent and align text. By default, tab stops are set every half inch, although the stops are not displayed on the horizontal ruler. Each time you press the tab key, the insertion point moves across the page a half inch. You can also customize tab stops by designating the location and characteristics of the tab stops. Custom tab stops override default tab stops that are to the left of the custom tab stop position. When you create a custom tab stop, its location and tab stop type is displayed on the ruler, as shown in Figure 3.29. The types of tab stops are shown in the table in Figure 3.29.

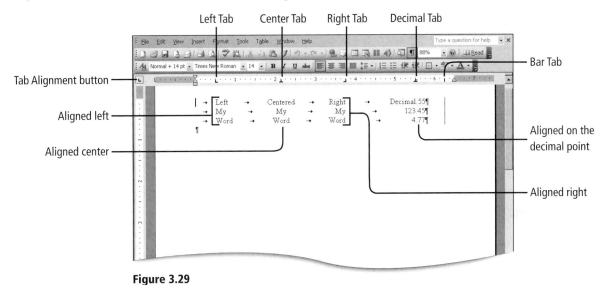

Figure 3.29

Tab Alignment Options

Type	Tab Alignment Button Displays This Marker	Description
Left		Text is left aligned at the tab stop and extends to the right.
Center		Text is centered around the tab stop.
Right		Text is right aligned at the tab stop and extends to the left.
Decimal		The decimal point aligns at the tab stop.
Bar		A vertical bar is inserted in the document at the tab stop.
First Line Indent		Indents the first line of a paragraph.
Hanging Indent		Indents all lines but the first in a paragraph.

Figure 3.30

Activity 3.10 Setting Tab Stops

Tab stops enable you to position text on a line. Tab stops can be set before or after typing text, but it is easiest to set them before you type the text.

1 On the Standard toolbar, click the **Open** button . Navigate to the location where the student files for this textbook are stored. Locate **w03B_Park_Changes** and click once to select it. Then, in the lower right corner of the **Open** dialog box, click **Open**.

The w03B_Park_Changes file opens. See Figure 3.31.

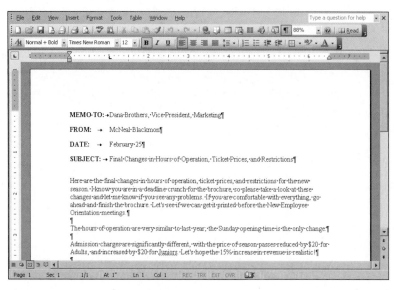

Figure 3.31

2 From the **File** menu, click **Save As**. In the **Save As** dialog box, click the **Save in** arrow and navigate to the location in which you are storing your files for this chapter.

3 In the **File name** box, type **3B_Park_Changes_Firstname_Lastname** and click **Save**.

The document is saved with a new name. Make sure you substitute your name where indicated.

4 In the paragraph beginning *The hours of operation*, position the insertion point after the colon at the end of the paragraph. Press Enter two times.

5 At the left end of the horizontal ruler, position the pointer over the **Tab Alignment** button .

A ScreenTip displays showing the type of tab currently selected, as shown in Figure 3.32.

Options for tab alignment ———

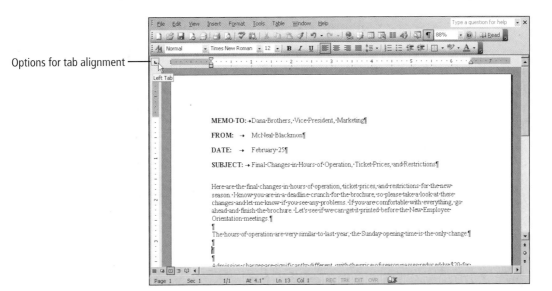

Figure 3.32

6 Click the **Tab Alignment** button ⌞ once, move the mouse pointer away, and then point to the button again to display the next ScreenTip—*Center Tab*. Repeat this process to cycle through and view the ScreenTip for each of the types of tab stops, and then stop at the **Left Tab** button ⌞.

7 Move the pointer over the horizontal ruler and click at the **1 inch mark**.

A left tab stop is inserted in the ruler. See Figure 3.33. Left tab stops are used when you want the information to align on the left.

Left alignment tab at the 1-inch mark

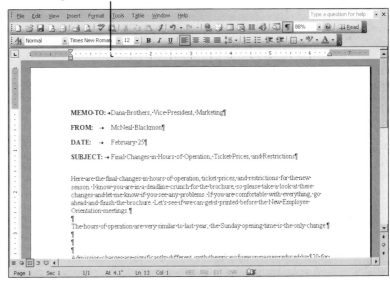

Figure 3.33

8 Click the **Tab Alignment** button ⌞ two times to display the **Right Tab** button ⌟.

9 At the **4 inch mark on the horizontal ruler**, click once.

A right tab stop is inserted in the ruler. See Figure 3.34. Right tab stops are used to align information on the right. As you type, the information will extend to the left of the tab stop.

Right alignment tab

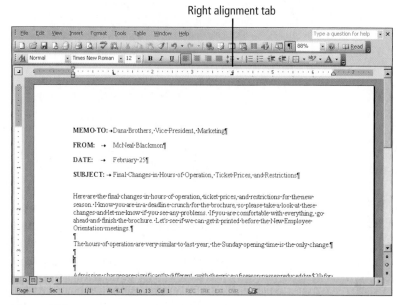

Figure 3.34

10 Click the **Tab Alignment** button six times to display the **Center Tab** button .

11 Click at the **5 inch mark on the horizontal ruler**, and then click again at the **6 inch mark**.

Two center tab stops are inserted in the ruler. See Figure 3.35. Center tab stops are used when you want the information to be centered over a particular point.

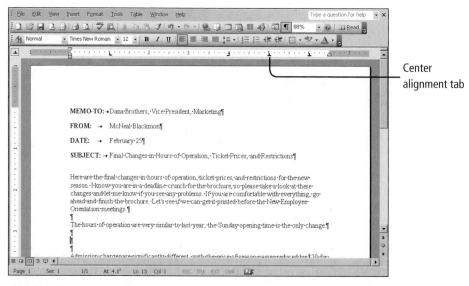

Center alignment tab

Figure 3.35

Activity 3.11 Formatting and Removing Tab Stops

The Tabs dialog box enables you to add, remove, and format tab stops. You can also change the alignment of a tab stop.

1 From the **Format** menu, click **Tabs**.

The Tabs dialog box displays. The tabs you just added to the ruler for the paragraph at the insertion point location are displayed under the *Tab stop position*, as shown in Figure 3.36.

Tabs you set on the ruler ——

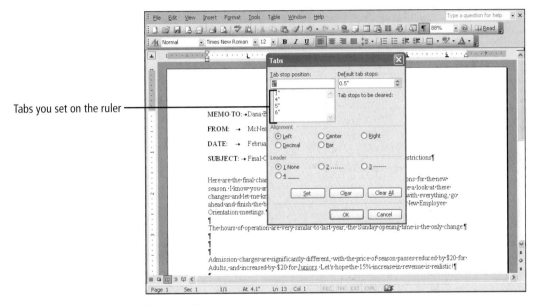

Figure 3.36

2 Under **Tab stop position**, click **4"**.

The tab stop at the 4-inch mark is selected.

3 At the bottom of the **Tabs** dialog box, click the **Clear** button.

The tab stop is ready to be removed, although it won't be removed until you close the dialog box. See Figure 3.37.

Tab stop removed ——

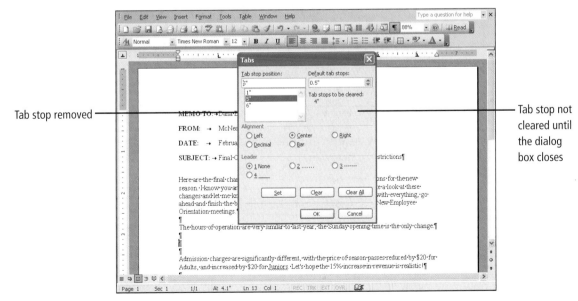

Tab stop not cleared until the dialog box closes

Figure 3.37

4 Under **Tab stop position**, click **5"**.

5 Under **Leader**, click the **2** option button. Near the bottom of the **Tabs** dialog box, click **Set**.

The Set button saves the change. The tab stop at the 5 inch mark now has a *dot leader*. Dot leader tabs are used to help draw the reader's eye across the page from one item to the next. Later, when you tab to this spot, a row of dots will display. See Figure 3.38.

Selected tab stop —

Dot leader —

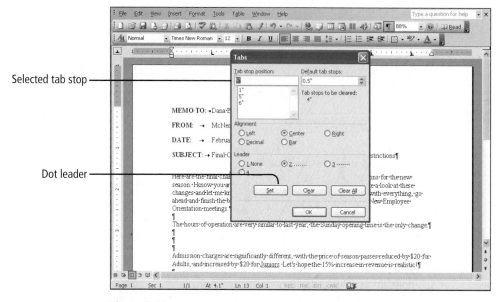

Figure 3.38

6 Under **Tab stop position**, click **5"**.

7 Under **Alignment**, click the **Right** option button. Near the bottom of the **Tabs** dialog box, click **Set**. Repeat this process to change the tab stop at the **6 inch mark** to a **Right** align tab stop as shown in Figure 3.39.

The tab stops at the 5- and 6-inch marks will be right aligned when the dialog box is closed.

Two tab stops changed to right alignment —

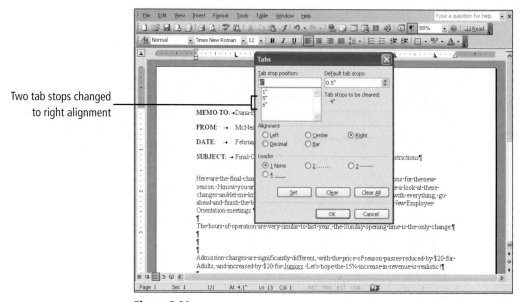

Figure 3.39

8 At the bottom of the **Tabs** dialog box, click **OK**.

Notice that the changes are reflected in the ruler. See Figure 3.40.

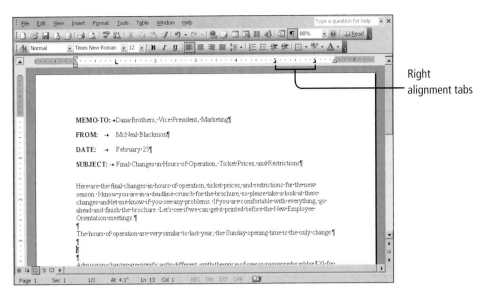

Right
alignment tabs

Figure 3.40

9 From the **View** menu, click **Header and Footer**. On the Header and Footer toolbar, click the **Switch Between Header and Footer** button.

10 On the Header and Footer toolbar, click the **Insert AutoText** button Insert AutoText, and then click **Filename**.

The filename is inserted in the footer. The file extension .doc may or may not display, depending on your Word settings.

11 On the Header and Footer toolbar, click the **Close** button Close.

12 On the Standard toolbar, click the **Save** button.

Activity 3.12 Using Tab Stops to Enter Text

1 With the insertion point positioned at the beginning of the line with the new tab stops, press Tab.

The insertion point moves to the first tab, which is at the 1 inch mark, and the nonprinting character for a tab (a small arrow) displays. See Figure 3.41.

Tab stop

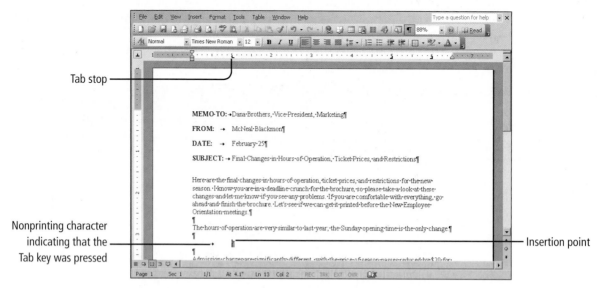

Nonprinting character indicating that the Tab key was pressed

Insertion point

Figure 3.41

2 Type **Monday-Thursday**

Notice that the left edge of the text stays aligned with the tab stop.

3 Press Tab.

The insertion point moves to the tab stop at the 5 inch mark, and a dot leader is added, helping to draw your eye across the page to the next item. See Figure 3.42.

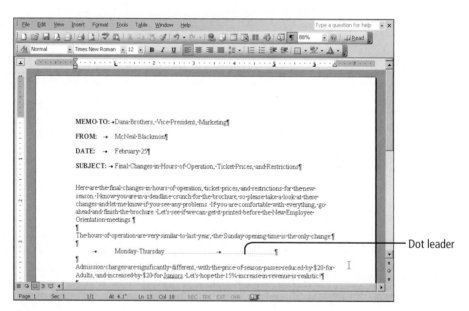

Dot leader

Figure 3.42

More Knowledge — Using Dot Leaders

A String of Periods Is Not the Same Thing

It is sometimes tempting to hold down the Period key on the keyboard to create a string of dots. This is not a good idea for several reasons. The periods, because of proportional spacing, may be spaced differently between rows, the periods will not line up, and, most importantly, the column on the right side of the string of periods may look lined up, but will be crooked when printed. If you need a string of dots, always use a tab with a dot leader.

4 Type **1 p.m.**

With a right tab, the right edge of the text stays aligned with the tab mark, and the text moves to the left. See Figure 3.43.

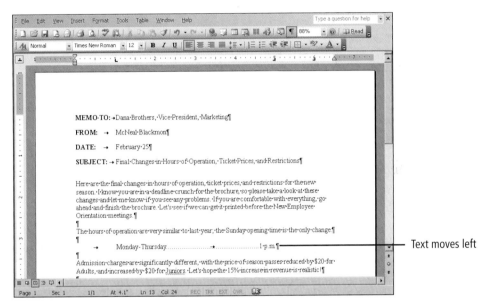

Text moves left

Figure 3.43

5 Press Tab. Type **10 p.m.**

The right edge of the text is aligned on the tab mark.

6 Press Enter.

Recall that when you press Enter, the formatting of the previous paragraph, including tab stops, is copied to the new paragraph. Tab stops are a form of paragraph formatting, and thus, the information about them is stored in the paragraph mark to which they were applied.

7 Type the following to complete the park schedule:

Friday	1 p.m.	11 p.m.
Saturday and Holidays	11 a.m.	11 p.m.
Sunday	NOON	11 p.m.

Compare your screen to Figure 3.44.

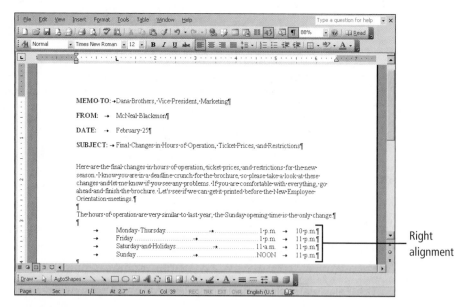

Figure 3.44

Right alignment

8 On the Standard toolbar, click the **Save** button 🖫.

Activity 3.13 Moving Tab Stops

If you are not satisfied with the arrangement of your text after setting tab stops, it is easy to reposition the text by moving tab stops.

1 In the four lines of tabbed text, disregard any wavy green lines or right-click them and click **Ignore Once** to remove them. Move the pointer into the left margin area, to the left of the first line of tabbed text. When the pointer changes to a white arrow, drag down to select the four lines of text as shown in Figure 3.45.

By selecting all of the lines, changes you make to the tabs will be made to the tabs in all four rows simultaneously.

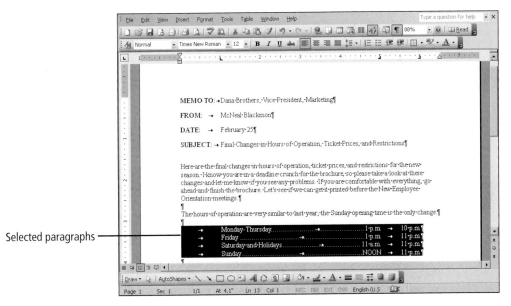

Selected paragraphs ——

Figure 3.45

2 With the four lines of tabbed text selected, move the pointer into the horizontal ruler and position it so the tip of the pointer arrow is touching the 1 inch tab stop mark.

3 When you see the ScreenTip *Left Tab*, drag the tab stop mark to the left to the **0.5 inch mark on the ruler** as shown in Figure 3.46 and then release the mouse button.

The first column of text is moved to the new location, as shown in Figure 3.46.

Note — Selecting Tab Stop Marks

Selecting and moving tab stop marks on the horizontal ruler requires fairly exact mouse movement. The tip of the pointer needs to touch the tab mark. If you miss it by even a little, you will probably insert another tab stop. One way to tell if you are in the right position to move a tab stop on the ruler is to look for a ScreenTip showing the tab type. To remove an accidental tab stop when you are trying to select an existing one, click the Undo button and try again. Alternatively, you can drag the unwanted tab stop marker below the ruler and release the mouse button.

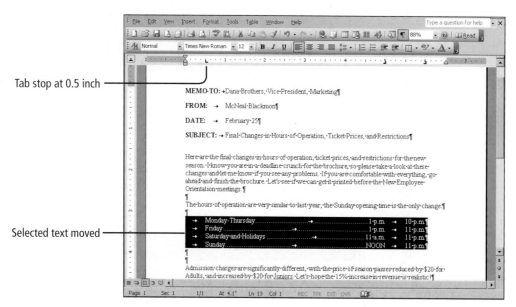

Tab stop at 0.5 inch

Selected text moved

Figure 3.46

4 Move the pointer into the ruler, and position it so the tip of the pointer arrow is touching the 5 inch tab stop mark and you see the ScreenTip *Right Tab*. Drag the tab stop mark to the left to the **4.5 inch mark on the ruler**.

Compare your screen to Figure 3.47.

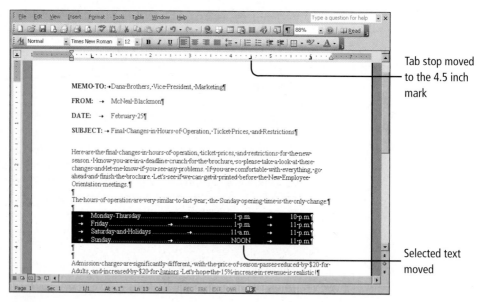

Tab stop moved to the 4.5 inch mark

Selected text moved

Figure 3.47

5 Click anywhere to deselect and then, on the Standard toolbar, click the **Save** button.

Objective 5
Create a Table

The table feature in Word processing programs has largely replaced the use of tabs because of its flexibility and ease of use. **Tables** consist of rows and columns and are used to organize data. You can create an empty table and then fill in the boxes, which are also called **cells**. You can also convert existing text into a table if the text is properly formatted.

If a table needs to be adjusted, you can add rows or columns and change the height of rows and the width of columns. The text and numbers in the cells can be formatted, as can the cell backgrounds and borders.

Activity 3.14 Creating a Table

1 In the paragraph beginning *Admission charges*, position the insertion point after the exclamation point at the end of the second sentence. Press [Enter] two times.

2 On the Standard toolbar, click the **Insert Table** button [icon].

3 Move the pointer down to the cell in the third row and third column of the **Insert Table** menu.

The cells are highlighted, and the table size is displayed at the bottom of the menu, as shown in Figure 3.48.

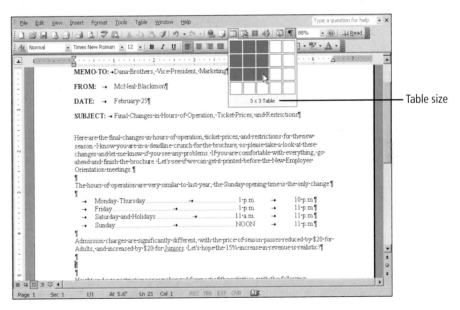

Figure 3.48

4 Click the mouse button.

A table with three rows and three columns is created at the insertion point location and the insertion point is placed in the upper left cell. The table fills the width of the page, from the left margin to the right margin, as shown in Figure 3.49.

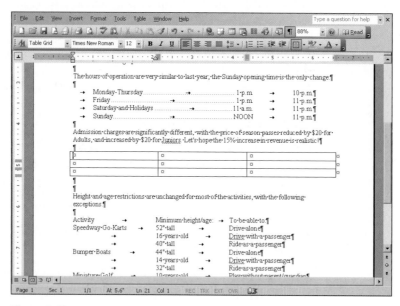

Figure 3.49

5 Press ⌨Tab to the second cell in the first row of the table.

Note — **Moving Between Cells in a Table**

Using the Tab Key Rather than the Enter Key

The natural tendency is to press Enter to move from one cell to the next. In a table, however, pressing Enter creates another line in the same cell, similar to the way you add a new line in a document. If you press Enter by mistake, you can remove the extra line by pressing the Backspace key.

---

6 Type **Age** and press ⌨Tab.

7 Type **One Day** and press ⌨Tab.

The text displays in the top row, and the insertion point moves to the first cell in the second row, as shown in Figure 3.50.

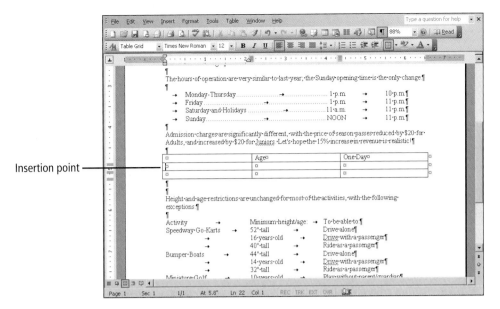

Insertion point ────

Figure 3.50

◙ Type the following to complete the table (do not press Enter or Tab after the last item):

| Toddler | 3 & under | Free |
| Adult | 12 to 59 | $39 |

Compare your screen to Figure 3.51.

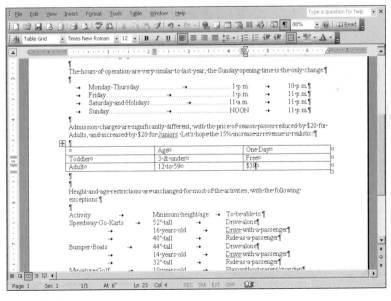

Figure 3.51

9 On the Standard toolbar, click the **Save** button 🔲.

Activity 3.15 Adding a Row to a Table

You can add rows to the beginning, middle, or end of a table.

1 With the insertion point in the last cell in the table, press Tab.

A new row is added to the bottom of the table. See Figure 3.52.

New row —

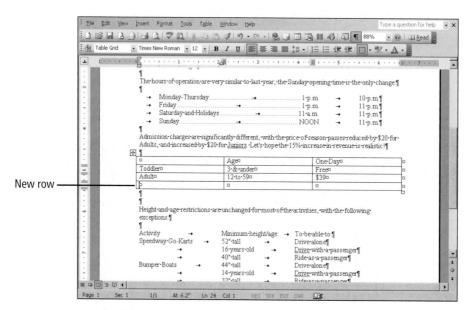

Figure 3.52

2 In the first cell of the new row, type **Senior** and then press Tab.

3 Type **60+** and press Tab. Type **$29**

Compare your new row to Figure 3.53.

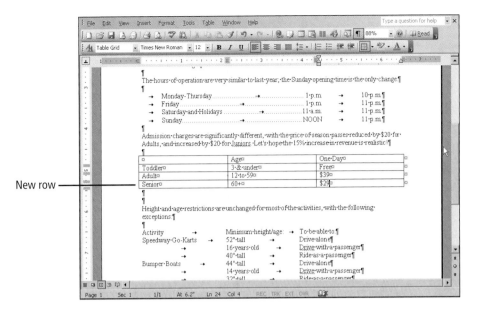

New row

Figure 3.53

4️⃣ In the table row beginning *Adult*, click anywhere to place the insertion point.

5️⃣ From the **Table** menu, point to **Insert** and then click **Rows Above**.

A new row is added above the row containing the insertion point. See Figure 3.54.

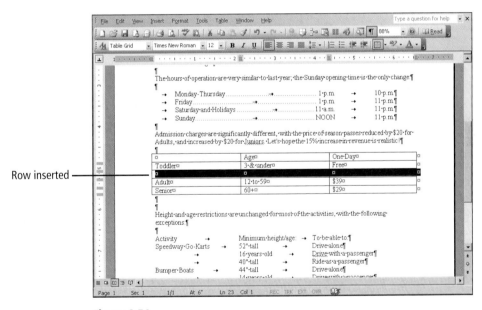

Row inserted

Figure 3.54

6️⃣ Type **Junior** and press Tab.

When the entire row is selected, text is automatically placed in the cell on the left.

7️⃣ Type **4 to 11** and press Tab. Type **$19**

Compare your table to Figure 3.55.

New row

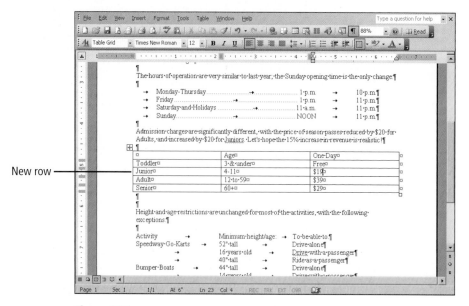

Figure 3.55

8 On the Standard toolbar, click the **Save** button .

Activity 3.16 Changing the Width of a Table Column

In Word tables, you can change the column widths easily and quickly and adjust them as often as necessary to create a visually appealing table.

1 Move the pointer over the right boundary of the first column until the pointer changes to a left- and right-pointing resize arrow, as shown in Figure 3.56.

Resize pointer

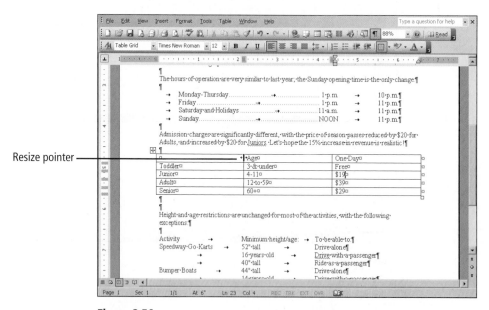

Figure 3.56

2 Drag the boundary to the left until the first column is about 1-inch wide, to approximately the **1 inch mark on the horizontal ruler**.

Use the horizontal ruler as a guide. If only one row resizes, click the Undo button and start again.

3 Drag the right boundary of the second column to the left until the column is about 1-inch wide, to approximately the **2 inch mark on the horizontal ruler**.

4 Drag the right boundary of the third column to the left until the column is about 1-inch wide, to approximately the **3 inch mark on the horizontal ruler**.

Compare your table to Figure 3.57.

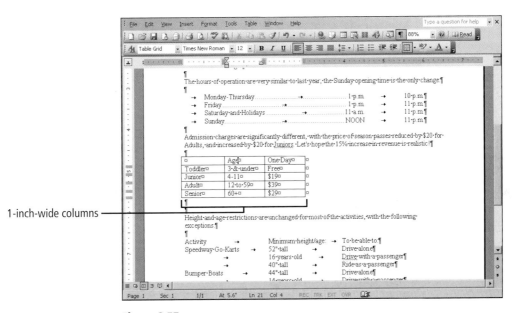

1-inch-wide columns

Figure 3.57

5 On the Standard toolbar, click the **Save** button.

Activity 3.17 Adding a Column to a Table

1 In the last column of the table, click anywhere in the column to position the insertion point.

2 From the **Table** menu, point to **Insert**, and then click **Columns to the Right**.

A new column is added to the right of the column containing the insertion point and is the same width as that column. See Figure 3.58.

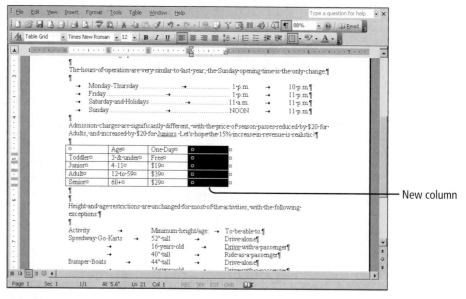

Figure 3.58

3 Type **Season Pass**

In a selected column, text is entered in the top cell when you type. If necessary, drag the column slightly to the right so that the text displays on one line.

4 Complete the column with the following information. Compare your table with Figure 3.59.

Toddler	**Free**
Junior	**$89**
Adult	**$129**
Senior	**$99**

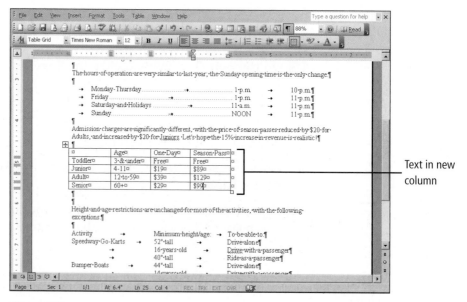

Figure 3.59

5 On the Standard toolbar, click the **Save** button ▦.

More Knowledge — Using Tabs in Tables

You can also add tabs to a table column so you can indent items within a table cell. The easiest way to add a tab is to click on the ruler to set the location within a column. Then you can drag the tab stop indicator to change the location of the tab within the column or add the hanging indent marker so multiple lines in a list are evenly indented. To move to the tabbed location within the cell, press Ctrl + Tab.

Objective 6
Format Tables

Formatted tables are more attractive and easier to read. When you type numbers, for example, they line up on the left of a column instead of on the right until you format them. With Word's formatting tools, you can shade cells, format the table borders and grid, and center the table between the document margins. All of these features make a table more inviting to the reader.

Activity 3.18 Formatting Text in Cells

In addition to aligning text in cells, you can also add emphasis to the text.

1 Click anywhere in the cell containing the word *Age*, hold down the left mouse button, and then drag to the right until the second, third, and fourth cells in the top row are selected. See Figure 3.60.

Selected cells —

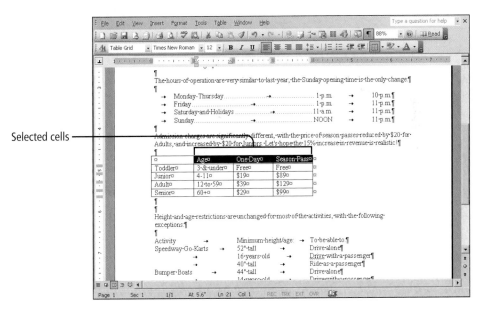

Figure 3.60

2 On the Formatting toolbar, click the **Bold** button B, and then click the **Center** button.

The text in the first row of cells is bold and centered, as shown in Figure 3.61.

Bold, centered text ———

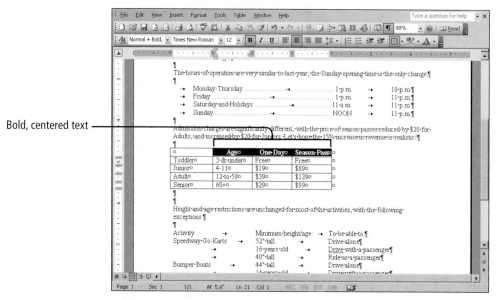

Figure 3.61

3 Click in the cell containing the word *Toddler* and then drag down to select the second, third, fourth, and fifth cells in the first column.

4 On the Formatting toolbar, click the **Bold** button B.

5 In the third column, click in the cell containing *Free*, drag down and to the right until all of the cells in the last two columns, except the first row, are selected.

6 From the Formatting toolbar, click the **Align Right** button.

Compare your table to Figure 3.62.

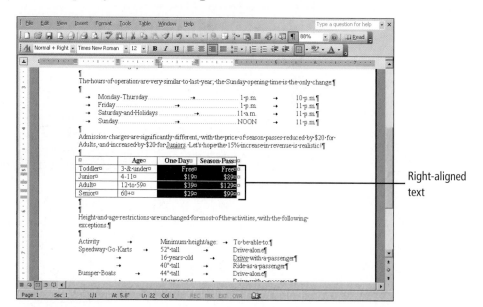

Right-aligned text

Figure 3.62

7 Click anywhere to deselect, and then on the Standard toolbar, click the **Save** button 🖫.

Activity 3.19 Shading Cells

Backgrounds can be added to cells to differentiate them from other cells.

1 In the cell containing the word *Age*, drag to the right to select the second, third, and fourth cells in the top row.

2 From the **Format** menu, click **Borders and Shading**.

The Borders and Shading dialog box displays.

3 In the **Borders and Shading** dialog box click the **Shading tab**.

4 Under **Fill**, in the second row, click the third button as shown in Figure 3.63.

The name of the shading option—*Gray-10%*—displays to the right of the shading option buttons, and the Preview area shows what the shading will look like in the table.

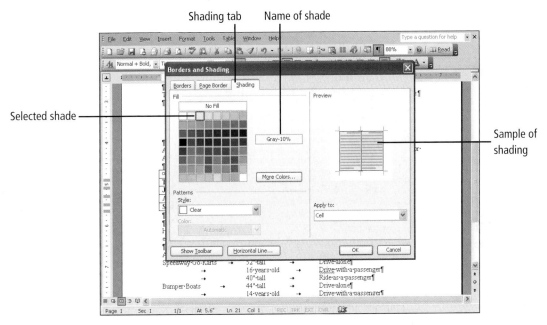

Shading tab   Name of shade

Selected shade

Sample of shading

Figure 3.63

5 Click **OK**. Click anywhere in the document to deselect the text.

A light gray background is applied to the three column headings. See Figure 3.64.

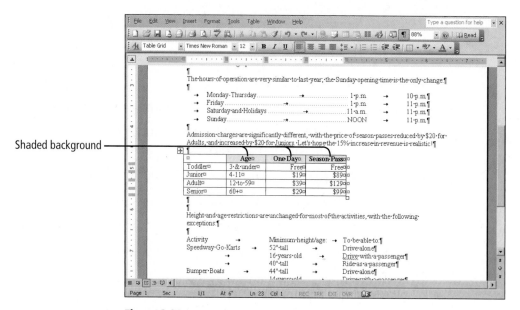

Shaded background

Figure 3.64

6 Click in the cell containing the word *Toddler*, drag down until the second, third, fourth, and fifth cells in the first column are selected.

7 From the **Format** menu, click **Borders and Shading**. Under **Fill**, click the same shading option you chose for the row headings—Gray-10%. Click **OK**. Click anywhere in the document to deselect so you can see the shading.

Compare your table to Figure 3.65.

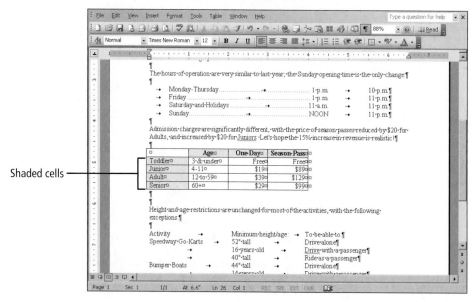

Shaded cells

Figure 3.65

8 On the Standard toolbar, click the **Save** button.

Activity 3.20 Changing the Table Border

You can modify or remove the border from the entire table, a selected cell, or individual boundaries of a cell.

1 Click in any cell in the table. From the **Format** menu, click **Borders and Shading**.

The Borders and Shading dialog box displays.

2 In the **Borders and Shading** dialog box, click the **Borders tab**.

3 Under **Setting**, click **Grid**.

The Preview area in the right portion of the dialog box displays the current border settings, and the line width is displayed in the Width box, as shown in Figure 3.66.

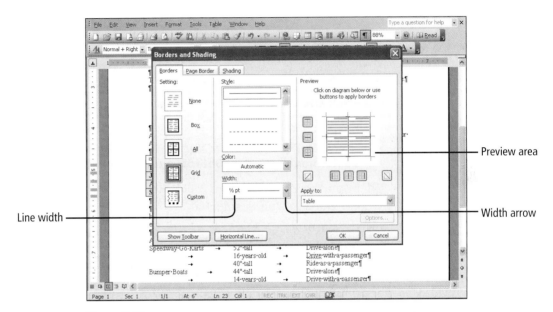

Figure 3.66

4 Click the **Width arrow**, and then from the displayed list, click **1½ pt**.

Notice, under Preview, the outside border is changed to a thicker 1½ point width, while the inner grid lines remain at ½ point width. See Figure 3.67.

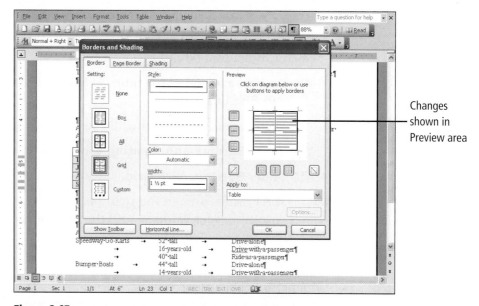

Changes shown in Preview area

Figure 3.67

5 Click **OK**, and then click anywhere in the document to deselect the table.

6 In the empty cell at the upper left of the table, click once. From the **Table** menu, point to **Select**, and then click **Cell**.

7 From the **Format** menu, click **Borders and Shading**. Be sure that the **Borders tab** is selected.

8 In the **Preview** area, point to and then click the top border twice to remove all borders.

The first click returns the border to ½ point, the second click removes the border. See Figure 3.68.

Top border line removed

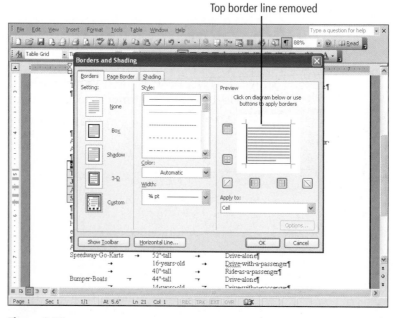

Figure 3.68

9 In the **Preview** area, click the left border twice, until there is no border displayed.

The left border is removed.

10 Click the **Width arrow**, and from the displayed list, click **1½ pt**.

11 In the **Preview** area, click the bottom border once.

The bottom border is widened to 1½ point.

12 In the **Preview** area, click the right border once.

The right border is widened to 1½ point, as shown in Figure 3.69.

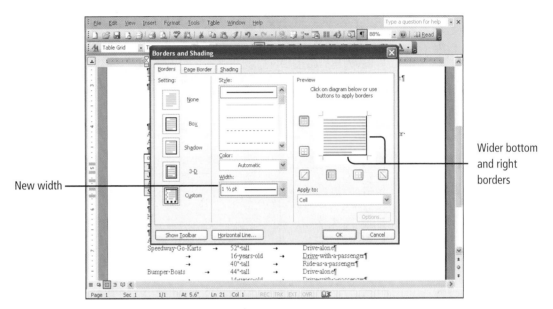

New width ——

Wider bottom and right borders

Figure 3.69

13 Click **OK**. Click anywhere in the document to deselect the table.

Compare your table to Figure 3.70.

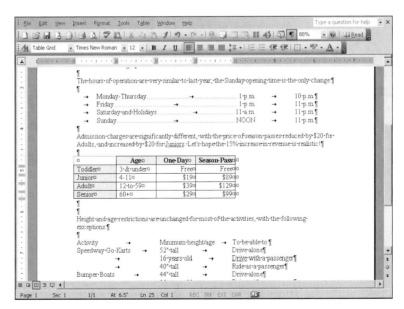

Figure 3.70

14 On the Standard toolbar, click the **Save** button 🖫.

Activity 3.21 Centering a Table

1 Click anywhere in the table.

2 From the **Table** menu, click **Table Properties**.

The Table Properties dialog box displays.

3 In the **Table Properties** dialog box click the **Table tab**.

4 Under **Alignment**, click **Center**. See Figure 3.71.

Table tab

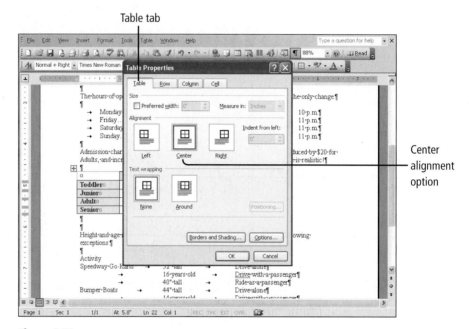

Center
alignment
option

Figure 3.71

5 Click **OK**.

The table is centered horizontally between the left and right margins.

Another Way ── **Centering a Table**

You can center a table by clicking the Center button on the Formatting tool-bar. First you must select the entire table. To select a table, from the Table menu, point to Select and then click Table. Alternatively, in Print Layout view, rest the pointer on the upper left corner of the table until the table move handle appears, and then click the table move handle to select the table. After the table is selected, on the Formatting toolbar, click the Center button.

6 Place the insertion point in the blank line just below the table and press ⏎Delete.

There should be only one empty paragraph before and one empty paragraph after the table.

7 Click the **Show/Hide ¶** button ![¶].

The nonprinting characters are hidden. Your table should look like Figure 3.72.

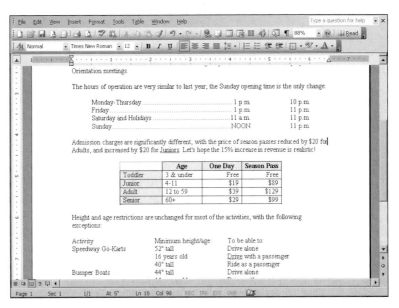

Figure 3.72

8 Click the **Show/Hide ¶** button ![¶] to redisplay the nonprinting characters.

9 On the Standard toolbar, click the **Save** button ![save].

Objective 7
Create a Table from Existing Text

The Insert Table feature is useful if you are beginning a new table, but Word also provides a tool that enables you to convert existing text into a table. The text needs to be marked using ***separator characters***—usually tabs or commas that separate the text in each line. When you convert text to a table, you can have Word optimize the column widths at the same time. You can also add blank rows or columns, if needed.

Activity 3.22 Converting Text to Tables

If text is separated with a recognized separator character, and the text is selected, converting text to a table is an easy process.

1 Scroll as necessary to view the lower portion of the document on your screen. In the block of text at the end of the document, beginning with *Activity* and continuing to the end of the document, notice the tab marks indicating where the ⌧ Tab ⌧ key was pressed.

The tab marks can act as separator characters for the purpose of converting text to a table. See Figure 3.73.

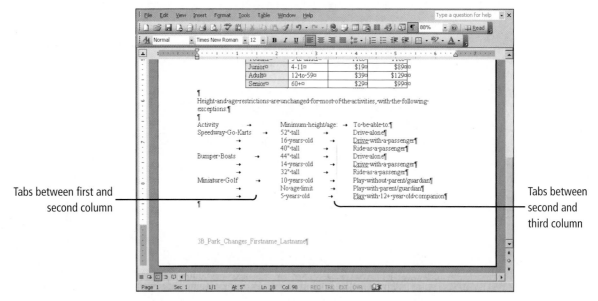

Tabs between first and second column

Tabs between second and third column

Figure 3.73

More Knowledge — Formatting Text to Convert to a Table

If you have text you would like to convert into a table, you will need to separate the columns using a separator character. Tabs and commas are the most commonly used separators, but you can specify a number of different marks, including dashes, dollar signs, or colons. You must be consistent, however. Word will not recognize a mixture of tabs and commas as separators in the same block of text.

2 Click to position the insertion point to the left of the word *Activity*, hold down Shift, and then click at the end of the last line, after the word *companion*.

3 With the text selected, from the **Table** menu, point to **Convert**, and then click **Text to Table**.

The Convert Text to Table dialog box displays. Under Table size, the Number of columns should be 3.

4 In the **Convert Text to Table** dialog box, under **AutoFit behavior**, click the **AutoFit to contents** option button.

5 Under **Separate text at**, click the **Tabs** option button, if necessary.

Compare your dialog box to Figure 3.74.

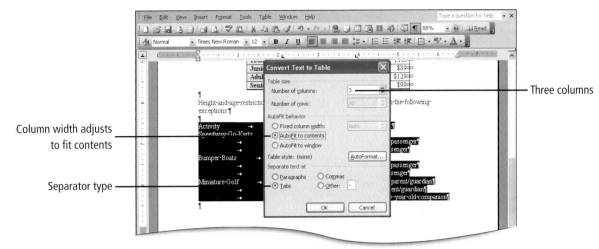

Column width adjusts to fit contents ——

Separator type ——

Three columns

Figure 3.74

More Knowledge — Make Sure There Is Only One Separator Between Columns

Before you convert your text to a table, make sure there is only one separator between each column item. If you are using tabs, for example, each tab will move the subsequent item one more column to the right. An extra tab between items will mean that the item will eventually end up in the wrong column. There is an exception to this rule. If you have an empty cell, an extra tab will move the following item to the correct column. Always turn on the nonprinting characters in your document and visually scan the text for extra separators. Also, check the table once you have completed the conversion to make sure everything is in the right column.

6 At the bottom of the **Convert Text to Table** dialog box, click **OK**. Click anywhere in the document to deselect the table.

Compare your table to Figure 3.75.

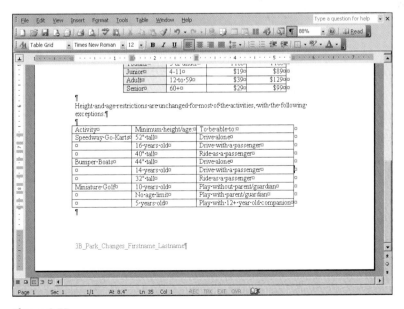

Figure 3.75

7 On the Standard toolbar, click the **Save** button 🖫.

Activity 3.23 Applying a Predefined Format to a Table

You can format each of the table elements independently, but there is also a quick way to *AutoFormat* the whole table at one time, using predefined formats.

1 In the table you just created, click anywhere to position the insertion point within the table.

You do not need to select the entire table to use the AutoFormat feature.

2 From the **Table** menu, click **Table AutoFormat**.

3 In the displayed **Table AutoFormat** dialog box, under **Table styles**, click any of the table styles and, under **Preview**, notice the style. Click several of the AutoFormat styles to see what types of formatting are available.

4 Under **Table styles**, scroll toward the bottom of the list and click **Table Professional**. Under **Apply special formats to**, select the check boxes as necessary so that all four are selected, as shown in Figure 3.76.

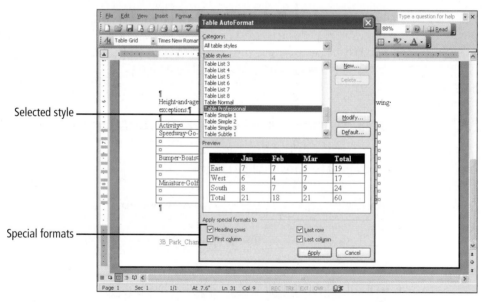

Selected style ———

Special formats ———

Figure 3.76

5 At the bottom of the **Table AutoFormat** dialog box, click **Apply**.

Compare your table to Figure 3.77.

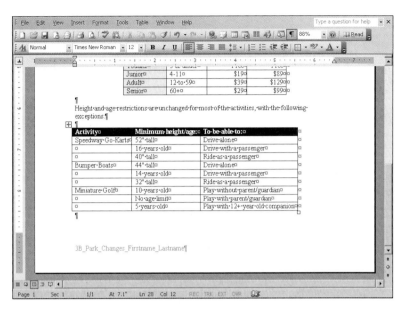

Figure 3.77

6 On the Standard toolbar, click the **Save** button.

Activity 3.24 Merging Cells and Aligning Text Vertically

Sometimes a title looks better if it spans two or more columns or rows. This can be accomplished by merging cells.

1 In the table you just formatted, position your pointer over the second cell in the first column—the *Speedway Go-Karts* cell—and then drag down to select the cell and the two empty cells below.

Because of the formatting in the first row, it will appear that four cells are selected, but if you look closely, you will see that the selection area is indented slightly. See Figure 3.78.

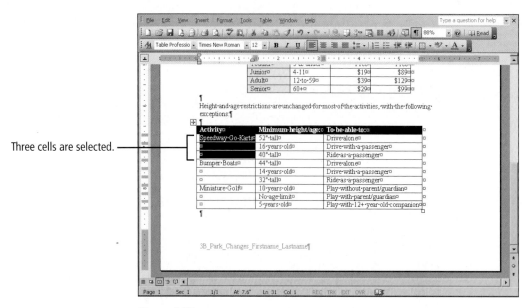

Three cells are selected.

Figure 3.78

2 On the Formatting toolbar, click the **Bold** button **B**. From the **Table** menu, click **Merge Cells**.

The cells are merged, and the cell borders are removed. Notice that making the text bold also increased the width of the cell. The widths of all of the cells in the first column increased slightly.

3 Repeat the procedure used in Steps 1 and 2 to bold and merge the three *Bumper Boats* cells and the three *Miniature Golf* cells.

Compare your table to Figure 3.79.

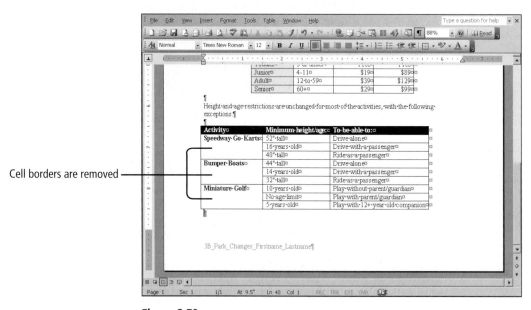

Cell borders are removed

Figure 3.79

4 In the *Speedway Go-Karts* cell, click once to position the insertion point.

5 From the **Table** menu, click **Table Properties**.

The Table Properties dialog box displays.

6 In the **Table Properties** dialog box, click the **Cell tab**. Under **Vertical alignment**, click **Center**. See Figure 3.80.

Cell tab

Vertical center option

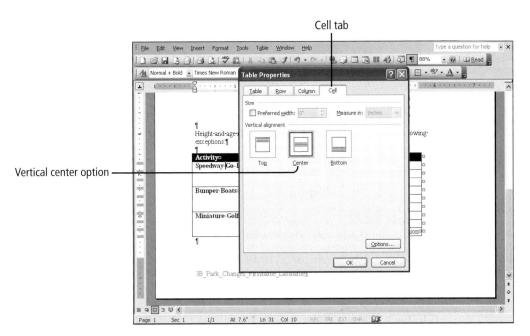

Figure 3.80

7 At the bottom of the **Table Properties** dialog box, click **OK**.

The text is centered vertically.

Another Way

Aligning Text in a Table

Use the Shortcut Menu

You can use shortcut menus to align text in a table. Right-click the cell, point to Cell Alignment on the shortcut menu, and then click the alignment style you want from the Cell Alignment palette that displays. You can choose from both vertical and horizontal cell alignment options using the Cell Alignment palette.

8 Drag to select the *Bumper Boats* and the *Miniature Golf* cells, display the **Table** menu, click **Table Properties**, and on the **Cell tab** under **Vertical alignment**, click **Center**. Click **OK**. Click anywhere in the document to deselect the selected cells.

Compare your table to Figure 3.81.

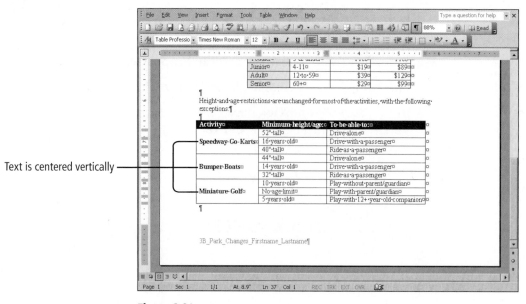

Text is centered vertically ——

Figure 3.81

9 From the **Table** menu, point to **Select** and then click **Table**.

10 On the Formatting toolbar, click the **Center** button. Click anywhere in the document to deselect the table.

The table is centered horizontally on the page. Compare your finished table to Figure 3.82.

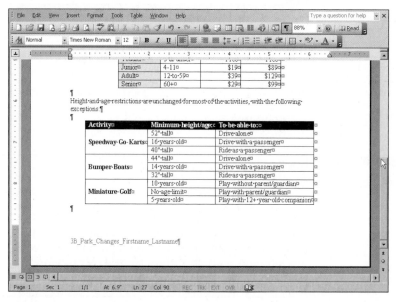

Figure 3.82

11 Press Ctrl + S to save your changes. On the Standard toolbar, click the **Print Preview** button to view your document.

12 On the Print Preview toolbar, click the **Print** button. Close Print Preview and close your document.

End You have completed Project 3B ——

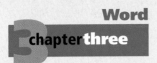

Summary

Many graphical elements can be used with Word. In this chapter you practiced inserting, moving, and resizing clip art and pictures. You also worked with the Drawing toolbar and learned how to create basic shapes using the AutoShapes, line, and text box tools. You modified shapes by changing the size, shape, and background color.

An effective way to present information is with a tabbed list or a table. You have used tabs to display information in single rows with multiple columns. A variety of tabs can be used, such as dot-leader, decimal, centered, or right-aligned. You practiced setting, moving, and changing tabs, as well as entering text in a tabbed list.

Tables also have a row and column format, but have the advantage of displaying multiple lines of text in a cell and still maintaining a horizontal relationship with the other cells in the same row. Tables can be formatted to display the information in a manner that emphasizes certain parts of the table. You practiced how to format individual cells or an entire table, using both the Formatting toolbar and the AutoFormat with other commands found under the Table menu. Finally, you practiced how to convert text to a table.

In This Chapter You Practiced How To

- Insert Clip Art and Pictures
- Modify Clip Art and Pictures
- Work with the Drawing Toolbar
- Work with Tabs
- Create a Table
- Format Tables
- Create a Table from Existing Text

Matching   Match each term in the second column with its correct definition in the first column by writing the letter of the term on the blank line in front of the correct definition.

_____ **1.** A tool that is used to resize an image proportionally.

_____ **2.** Images that can be moved independently of the surrounding text.

_____ **3.** A tool that is used to move an image in a clockwise or counterclockwise direction.

_____ **4.** The term used to identify commas or tabs when they are used to separate text in a line so it can be converted into a table.

_____ **5.** The general term used for any media file such as art, sound, animation, or movies.

_____ **6.** A button on the Drawing toolbar that can be used to insert and to draw a variety of forms.

_____ **7.** A mark on the ruler that indicates the location where the insertion point will be placed when you press Tab.

_____ **8.** The symbol that indicates that an image is attached to the nearest paragraph.

_____ **9.** A group of cells organized in rows and columns.

_____ **10.** Images that behave just like characters in a sentence.

_____ **11.** This button can be used to change the type of tab stop that will be set, before clicking on the ruler.

_____ **12.** The term used to refer to the boxes in a table where information is typed.

_____ **13.** Before you can move an image on your screen you first need to change this property.

_____ **14.** To change the color of the outside border on a table you would open this dialog box.

_____ **15.** To move vertically down a column in a table you can use this key.

A Anchor

B AutoShapes

C Borders and Shading

D Cells

E Clip

F Corner sizing handles

G Down arrow

H Floating images

I Inline images

J Rotate handle

K Separator characters

L Tab Alignment button

M Tab stop

N Table

O Wrapping

Fill in the Blank Write the correct answer in the space provided.

1. To create a table in Word, you can click on the _____ _____ button found on the Standard toolbar.

2. Predefined graphics such as those that come with the Word program or that can be downloaded from the Web are known as _____.

3. When a graphic image is selected, _____ _____ display around the edge of the image.

4. To align text to the contours of an irregularly shaped graphic, you would choose the _____ wrapping option.

5. A type of drawing object in which you can insert text, which can be placed outside of the document margin, is known as a _____ _____.

6. A series of dots following a tab that serve to guide the reader's eye is known as a dot _____.

7. A work area used for combining several graphic objects, known as the drawing _____, can also be turned off when adding simple shapes to a document.

8. To move from cell to cell across a table as you enter text, press _____.

9. To align a table on a page, you can use the _____ _____ dialog box.

10. A quick way to format a table is to use the _____ command found on the Table menu.

Project 3C—Teacher Promotion

Objectives: *Create a Table, Format Tables, and Create a Table from Existing Text.*

In the following Skill Assessment, you will add a table to a planning meeting memo for the upcoming Teacher Appreciation Day at Sensation! Park. Your completed memo will look like the one shown in Figure 3.83. You will save your document as *3C_Teacher_Promotion_Firstname_Lastname*.

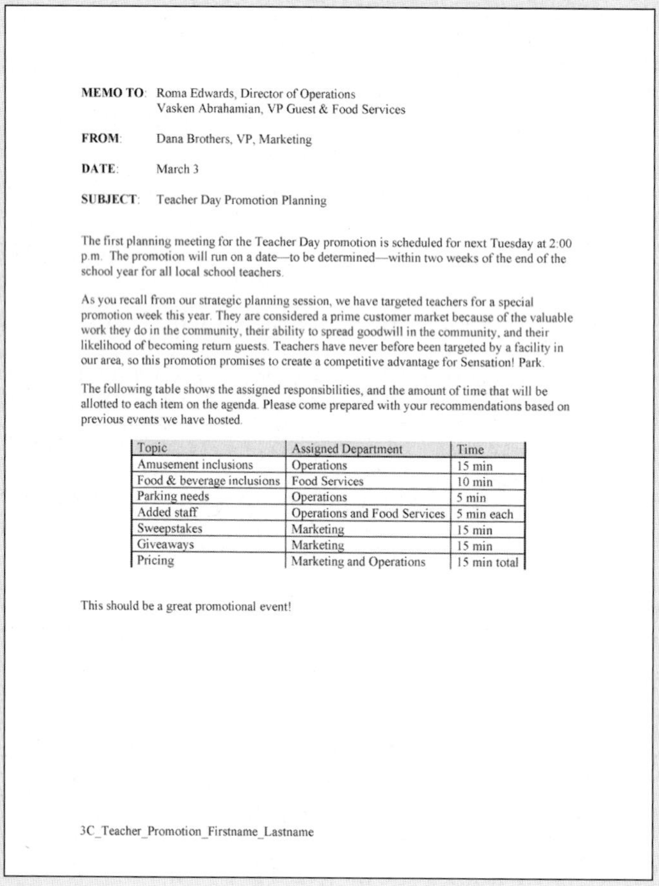

MEMO TO: Roma Edwards, Director of Operations
Vasken Abrahamian, VP Guest & Food Services

FROM: Dana Brothers, VP, Marketing

DATE: March 3

SUBJECT: Teacher Day Promotion Planning

The first planning meeting for the Teacher Day promotion is scheduled for next Tuesday at 2:00 p.m. The promotion will run on a date—to be determined—within two weeks of the end of the school year for all local school teachers.

As you recall from our strategic planning session, we have targeted teachers for a special promotion week this year. They are considered a prime customer market because of the valuable work they do in the community, their ability to spread goodwill in the community, and their likelihood of becoming return guests. Teachers have never before been targeted by a facility in our area, so this promotion promises to create a competitive advantage for Sensation! Park.

The following table shows the assigned responsibilities, and the amount of time that will be allotted to each item on the agenda. Please come prepared with your recommendations based on previous events we have hosted.

Topic	Assigned Department	Time
Amusement inclusions	Operations	15 min
Food & beverage inclusions	Food Services	10 min
Parking needs	Operations	5 min
Added staff	Operations and Food Services	5 min each
Sweepstakes	Marketing	15 min
Giveaways	Marketing	15 min
Pricing	Marketing and Operations	15 min total

This should be a great promotional event!

3C_Teacher_Promotion_Firstname_Lastname

Figure 3.83

1. On the Standard toolbar, click the **Open** button. Navigate to the location where the student files for this textbook are stored. Locate and open **w03C_Teacher_Promotion**. On the Standard toolbar, click the **Show/Hide ¶** button if necessary to display the nonprinting characters.

2. From the **File** menu, click **Save As**. In the **Save As** dialog box, use the **Save in arrow** to navigate to the location where you are storing your files for this chapter. In the **File name** box, type **3C_Teacher_Promotion_Firstname_Lastname** using your own name. Click the **Save** button.

(Project 3C–Teacher Promotion continues on the next page)

(Project 3C–Teacher Promotion continued)

3. Scroll down to the middle of the document and locate the tabbed list. Click to place the insertion point to the left of *Amusement inclusions* in the list. Move the mouse pointer to the right of *Marketing and Operations*, the last item in the tabbed list, hold down ⬚Shift⬚, and then click to select the entire list.

4. Display the **Table** menu, point to **Convert**, and then click **Text to Table**.

5. In the **Convert Text to Table** dialog box, under **Table size**, be sure **2** displays in the **Number of columns** box. Under **AutoFit behavior**, click the **AutoFit to contents** option button. Under **Separate text at** be sure **Tabs** is selected. Click **OK**. The tabbed list is converted to a table.

6. Click anywhere in the second column of the table. Display the **Table** menu, point to **Insert**, and then click **Columns to the Right**. In the newly inserted column (which may be quite narrow), position the mouse pointer over the right border until the left-right arrow pointer displays, and then drag the border to the right to approximately **5.25 inches on the horizontal ruler**.

7. Click in the first cell of the third column and type **15 min** Press ⬚↓⬚ to move to the second cell in the third column and type **10 min** Continue to use the ⬚↓⬚ to move down the column and enter the remaining time blocks that have been allotted for each topic as follows:

Parking needs	**5 min**
Added Staff	**5 min each**
Sweepstakes	**15 min**
Giveaways	**15 min**
Pricing	**15 min total**

8. Click anywhere in the first row of the table, display the **Table** menu, point to **Insert**, and then click **Rows Above**. In the first cell of the new row, type **Topic** and then press ⬚Tab⬚, type **Assigned Department** and then press ⬚Tab⬚ and then type **Time**

9. With the insertion point anywhere in the table, display the **Table** menu and then click **Table AutoFormat**. In the **Table AutoFormat** dialog box, scroll down and click the **Table Grid 4** format. In the lower portion of the dialog box, under **Apply special formats to**, be sure there is no check mark in the Last row and Last column check boxes. Clear them, if necessary. Click **Apply**. The table is formatted.

10. With the insertion point still in the table, display the **Table** menu, point to **AutoFit**, and then click **AutoFit to Contents**.

(Project 3C–Teacher Promotion continues on the next page)

(Project 3C–Teacher Promotion continued)

11. Display the **Table** menu again and then click **Table Properties**. In the **Table Properties** dialog box, click the **Table tab** if necessary. Under **Alignment**, click the **Center** button and then click **OK**. The table is horizontally centered on the page.

12. Display the **View** menu and then click **Header and Footer**. On the Header and Footer toolbar, click the **Switch Between Header and Footer** button. With the insertion point positioned in the footer area, on the Header and Footer toolbar click the **Insert AutoText** button and then click **Filename**. Close the Header and Footer toolbar.

13. On the Standard toolbar, click the **Save** button and then click the **Print Preview** button to see the document as it will print. Click the **Print** button and then close Print Preview and close the file, saving changes if prompted to do so.

End You have completed Project 3C _____

Project 3D — Announcement Meeting

Objectives: *Insert Clip Art and Pictures, Modify Clip Art and Pictures, and Work with the Drawing Toolbar.*

In the following Skill Assessment, you will add graphics to an announcement for the upcoming Teacher Day promotion at Sensation! Park. Your completed announcement will look like the one shown in Figure 3.84. You will save your document as *3D_Announcement_Firstname_Lastname*.

1. On the Standard toolbar, click the **Open** button. Navigate to the location where the student files for this textbook are stored. Locate and open **w03D_Announcement**. The document opens at 75% zoom.

2. From the **File** menu, click **Save As**. In the Save As dialog box, use the **Save in arrow** to navigate to the location where you are storing your files for this chapter. In the **File name** box, type **3D_Announcement_Firstname_Lastname** using your own name. Click the **Save** button.

3. From the **File** menu, display the **Page Setup** dialog box and click the **Margins tab**. Under **Orientation**, click **Landscape**. Under **Margins**, change the **Top** and **Bottom** boxes to **1.0** and then click **OK**.

4. From the **Tools** menu, click **Options**. Click the **General tab**. Under **General options**, locate the last check box—**Automatically create drawing canvas when inserting AutoShapes**—and be sure that it is unchecked. Clear the check box if necessary. Click **OK**. Recall that to use simple drawing tools, it is useful to turn off the drawing canvas.

(Project 3D–Announcement Meeting continues on the next page)

(Project 3D–Announcement Meeting continued)

Figure 3.84

5. Check to see if your Drawing toolbar is displayed at the bottom of your screen. If it is not, right-click on one of the toolbars and, from the displayed list, click Drawing. Click to place the insertion point to the left of the line that begins *It's been a LONG*. On the Drawing toolbar, click the **Line** button. Drawing a line is similar to drawing an arrow. Drag the crosshair pointer to draw a line under the text *Teacher Appreciation Day*. With the line still selected, on the Drawing toolbar, click the **Line Style** button and then click **2¼ pt**.

6. You can change the color of a line using the Line Color button, which is two buttons to the left of the Line Style button on the Drawing toolbar. With the line still selected, on the Drawing toolbar, locate the **Line Color** button and click its arrow to display a palette of colors. In the second row, click the **fourth color—green**.

7. Place the insertion point on the empty line under *And teachers deserve a break!* From the **Insert** menu, point to **Picture** and then click **Clip Art** from the submenu. In the **Clip Art** task pane, in the **Search for** box, type **teacher** In the **Search in** box, click the arrow and be sure **Everywhere** is selected. In the **Results should be box**, click the arrow and be sure **All media file types** are selected and then click the **Go** button. Locate the clip art image shown in Figure 3.84 and click the image to insert it. If you cannot locate that image, choose another image of a classroom teacher or insert the file **w03D_Teacher**. Close the Clip Art task pane.

(Project 3D–Announcement Meeting continues on the next page)

(Project 3D–Announcement Meeting continued)

8. Place the insertion point to the left of the line that begins *Come on June 22*. On the Drawing toolbar, click **AutoShapes**, point to **Stars and Banners** and then click the first shape—**Explosion 1**. Position the crosshair pointer at approximately **2.5 inches on the vertical ruler** and at the left margin in the horizontal ruler. Drag down so that one of the points is near the word *Come*, as shown in Figure 3.84. The size and placement need not be exact, but if you are not satisfied with your result, click Undo and begin again.

9. Right-click on the **Explosion 1 AutoShape** and, from the displayed shortcut menu, click **Add Text**. Type **Sweepstakes** and then select the text you typed. From the Formatting toolbar, change the font to **Comic Sans MS** and the font size to **16**. Point to a sizing handle and drag to expand the size of the shape until the text is displayed on one line.

10. With the Sweepstakes shape selected, locate the **Fill** button (paint can image) on the Drawing toolbar. Click the button's arrow and, on the displayed color palette, in the last row, click the **first color—Rose**. Click the arrow on the **Line Color** button and, from the displayed palette, click **Rose**. The line around the shape is the same color as the background color. Click the **Save** button.

11. Using the techniques you have just practiced, and using Figure 3.84 as a guide, create three more shapes as listed below. Use the Comic Sans MS 16-pt. font. Use the sizing handles to enlarge or to shrink your AutoShape, and recall that you can drag an AutoShape to a different position. Do not be concerned about exact placement.

AutoShape	Placement	Text	Fill Color	Line Color
24-point star	Lower left corner	**Door Prizes**	Light Yellow	Green
24-point star	Lower right corner	**BBQ Lunch**	Light Yellow	Green
Explosion 1	Right of date	**Discount Prices**	Bright Green	Bright Green

12. Select *Sweepstakes* and, on the Formatting toolbar, click the **Center** button. Repeat this process to center the text in each of the other three AutoShapes.

13. Click the **Sweepstakes shape**. Drag the **Rotate** button to the right until the shape is pointing to the date as shown in Figure 3.84. Adjust the position and sizes of the other shapes so they resemble the arrangement shown in the figure.

(Project 3D–Announcement Meeting continues on the next page)

(Project 3D–Announcement Meeting continued)

14. Display the **View** menu, and then click **Header and Footer**. On the Header and Footer toolbar, click the **Switch Between Header and Footer** button. With the insertion point positioned in the footer area, on the Header and Footer toolbar, click the **Insert AutoText button** and then click **Filename**. Close the Header and Footer toolbar.

15. On the Standard toolbar, click the **Save** button and then click the **Print Preview** button to see the document as it will print. Make sure none of the shapes are outside of the margin area. Click the **Print** button, close Print Preview, and then close the file saving changes if prompted to do so.

End You have completed Project 3D

Project 3E — Budget

Objectives: *Work with Tabs and Work with the Drawing Toolbar.*

In the following Skill Assessment, you will finish a memo by adding the results of the Teacher Promotion day at Sensation! Park. Your completed memo will look like the one shown in Figure 3.85. You will save your document as *3E_Budget_Firstname_Lastname*.

1. On the Standard toolbar, click the **Open** button. Navigate to the location where the student files for this textbook are stored. Locate and open **w03E_Budget**.

2. From the **File** menu, click **Save As**. In the **Save As** dialog box, use the **Save in arrow** to navigate to the location where you are storing your files for this chapter. In the **File name** box, using your own name, type **3E_Budget_Firstname_Lastname** Click the **Save** button.

3. If necessary, click the **Show/Hide ¶** button so you can see the non-printing characters as you complete this exercise. Place the insertion point at the end of the last paragraph—after the period following the word *below*—and press Enter. Spacing is added because spacing of 12 pt. after the paragraph has been set in this document.

4. On the Formatting toolbar, click the **Center** button and then click the **Underline** button. From the **Format** menu, click **Paragraph** and, under **Spacing**, use the spin box arrows to change **After** to **0 pt**. Click **OK**. Type **Attendance** and press Enter twice.

5. On the Formatting toolbar, click the **Align Left** button to change the alignment from Center, click the **Underline** button to turn off underline, and then click the **Increase Indent** button twice. This action indents the insertion point to the 1 inch mark—notice the indicator shown on the ruler.

(Project 3E–Budget continues on the next page)

(Project 3E–Budget continued)

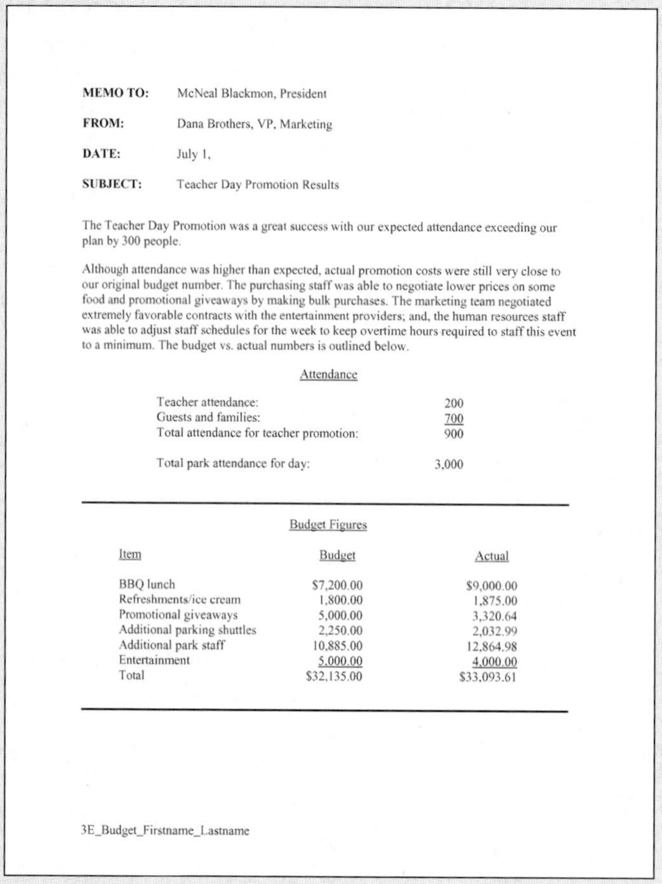

MEMO TO: McNeal Blackmon, President

FROM: Dana Brothers, VP, Marketing

DATE: July 1,

SUBJECT: Teacher Day Promotion Results

The Teacher Day Promotion was a great success with our expected attendance exceeding our plan by 300 people.

Although attendance was higher than expected, actual promotion costs were still very close to our original budget number. The purchasing staff was able to negotiate lower prices on some food and promotional giveaways by making bulk purchases. The marketing team negotiated extremely favorable contracts with the entertainment providers; and, the human resources staff was able to adjust staff schedules for the week to keep overtime hours required to staff this event to a minimum. The budget vs. actual numbers is outlined below.

Attendance

Teacher attendance:	200
Guests and families:	700
Total attendance for teacher promotion:	900
Total park attendance for day:	3,000

Budget Figures

Item	Budget	Actual
BBQ lunch	$7,200.00	$9,000.00
Refreshments/ice cream	1,800.00	1,875.00
Promotional giveaways	5,000.00	3,320.64
Additional parking shuttles	2,250.00	2,032.99
Additional park staff	10,885.00	12,864.98
Entertainment	5,000.00	4,000.00
Total	$32,135.00	$33,093.61

3E_Budget_Firstname_Lastname

Figure 3.85

6. At the left end of the horizontal ruler, click the **Tab Alignment** button until the **Decimal Tab** marker displays and then click the ruler at the **5 inch** mark. Type the following lines; press Tab after typing the text to move to the decimal tab stop and then press Enter at the end of each line. Refer to Figure 3.85.

Teacher attendance:	**200**
Guests and families:	**700**
Total attendance for teacher promotion:	**900**

7. Select 700 and, on the Formatting toolbar, click the **Underline** button. Position the insertion point to the right of 900, press Enter twice, and then type the following line pressing Tab before typing the number:

Total park attendance for day:	**3,000**

8. Press Enter twice. On the Formatting toolbar, click the **Decrease Indent** button twice to move the Left Indent indicator back to the left margin. On the Formatting toolbar, click the **Center** button and then click the **Underline** button. Type **Budget Figures** and press Enter twice.

(Project 3E–Budget continues on the next page)

(Project 3E–Budget continued)

9. On the Formatting toolbar, click the **Align Left** button to return to left alignment, click the **Underline** button to turn it off, and then click the **Increase Indent** button once.

10. From the **Format** menu, click **Tabs**. In the lower portion of the **Tabs** dialog box, click the **Clear All** button to remove any tabs from this line. In the **Tab stop position** box, type **3.5** Under **Alignment**, click **Center** and then click the **Set** button. This sets the first tab. In the **Tab stop position** box, type **5.5** and, under **Alignment**, click **Center** and then click **Set**. Two tabs have been set for this line of text. Click **OK** to close the dialog box, and notice the two Center tab stops indicated on the horizontal ruler.

11. Type the following, pressing Tab between each word:

    Item   Budget   Actual

12. Press Enter twice. From the **Format** menu, click **Tabs**. With **3.5** in the **Tab stop position** box, under **Alignment**, click **Decimal** and then click **Set**. Click the **5.5" tab** to select it, under **Alignment**, click **Decimal** and then click **Set**. The alignment of the two tabs is changed to Decimal. In a decimal tab stop, text aligns around the decimal point. Click **OK** to close the dialog box.

13. Type the following on separate lines, pressing Tab between the items listed in the columns:

BBQ lunch	$7,200.00	$9,000.00
Refreshments/ice cream	1,800.00	1,875.00
Promotional giveaways	5,000.00	3,320.64
Additional parking shuttles	2,250.00	2,032.99
Additional park staff	10,885.00	12,864.98
Entertainment	5,000.00	4,000.00
Total	$32,135.00	$33,093.61

14. On the Standard toolbar, click the **Save** button. On the line beginning with *Entertainment*, select **5,000.00**, click the **Underline** button, and then select **4,000.00** and click the **Underline** button.

15. The words *Budget* and *Actual* need to be better aligned over the columns of figures. Click anywhere on the line of headings above the budget figures. On the ruler, drag the first center tab stop one tick-mark (the tiny vertical lines between the numbers on the horizontal ruler) to the left between the 3 and 3.5 inch marks, so the word *Budget* is centered over the column of figures. Drag the second center tab stop one tick-mark to the left between the 5 and 5.5 inch marks to center the word *Actual* over the column of figures. When dragging tab stops, you can place the insertion point anywhere in the line.

(Project 3E–Budget continues on the next page)

(Project 3E–Budget continued)

16. From the **Tools** menu, click **Options** and then click the **General tab**. Under **General options**, in the last check box, if necessary, clear the *Automatically* create drawing canvas when inserting AutoShapes check box. Click **OK**. Recall that it is easier to create simple drawing objects with the drawing canvas turned off.

17. Check to see if your Drawing toolbar is displayed. If necessary, right-click on one of the toolbars and then click Drawing to display the Drawing toolbar. Place the insertion point on the empty line under *Total park attendance for day* and press Enter once. On the Drawing toolbar, click the **Line** button and then position the crosshair pointer at the left margin at approximately **5 inches on the vertical ruler**. Hold Shift, and then drag to form a line from the left to the right margin. Holding down the Shift key ensures that your line will be straight, and not jagged. With the line selected, on the Drawing toolbar, click the **Line Style** button and click **1½ pt**.

18. With the line still selected, on the Standard toolbar, click the **Copy** button and then click the **Paste** button. A copy of the line is pasted under the first line. Drag the second line to a position under the budget as shown in Figure 3.85.

19. Display the **View** menu and then click **Header and Footer**. On the Header and Footer toolbar, click the **Switch Between Header and Footer** button. With the insertion point positioned in the footer area, on the Header and Footer toolbar, click the **Insert AutoText** button and then click **Filename**. Close the Header and Footer toolbar.

20. On the Standard toolbar, click the **Save** button and then click the **Print Preview** button to see the document as it will print. Click the **Print** button, close Print Preview, and then close the file saving changes if prompted to do so.

End You have completed Project 3E ————————————————

Project 3F—Refreshments

Objectives: *Insert Clip Art and Pictures, Modify Clip Art and Pictures, Work with the Drawing Toolbar, and Work with Tabs.*

In the following Performance Assessment, you will create a poster for one of the refreshment stands at Sensation! Park. Your completed document will look like the one shown in Figure 3.86. You will save your publication as *3F_Refreshments_Firstname_Lastname.*

Figure 3.86

1. Start Word and display a blank document. If necessary, close the Getting Started task pane. Be sure that nonprinting characters are displayed; if necessary, click the **Show/Hide ¶** button. Make sure the document is in the **Print Layout** view. From the **Tools** menu, click **Options** and then click the **General tab**. Under General Options, if necessary, clear the check box next to Automatically create drawing canvas when inserting AutoShapes and then click **OK**. Recall that if you want to use a simple drawing object, it is best to turn off the drawing canvas. If necessary, right-click on one of the toolbars and click **Drawing** to display the Drawing toolbar.

(Project 3F–Refreshments continues on the next page)

(Project 3F–Refreshments continued)

2. On the Drawing toolbar, click **AutoShapes** and point to **Stars and Banners**. In the displayed menu, in the fourth row, click the second shape—**Horizontal Scroll**. Position the crosshair pointer at the paragraph mark and then drag down and to the right to approximately **2 inches on the vertical ruler** and **6 inches on the horizontal ruler**, as shown in Figure 3.86.

3. Right-click in the **Horizontal Scroll** shape and, from the displayed menu, click **Add Text**. On the Formatting toolbar, change the font to **Comic Sans MS**, the font size to **48**, and the alignment to **Center**. Type **Refreshments** The text is added to the banner in a large font that is centered in the banner. If necessary, drag a sizing handle to adjust the size of the banner so the text is displayed on one line.

4. With the banner shape selected, on the Drawing toolbar, click the arrow on the **Line Color** button. From the displayed palette, click **Red**. Click the **Line Style** button and then click **1½ pt**. The outline of the banner is changed to a thicker red border.

5. Click the **Save** button. In the **Save As** dialog box, navigate to the location where you are saving your files. In the **File name** box, using your own name, type **3F_Refreshments_Firstname_Lastname** and then click the **Save** button.

6. Move the I-beam pointer just below the banner's left edge and double-click to insert one or two paragraph marks and to place the insertion point under the banner. With the insertion point positioned in front of the final paragraph mark, change the font to **Comic Sans MS** and the font size to **16 pt**. Notice that the paragraph mark reflects the changes.

7. From the **Format** menu, click **Tabs**. In the **Tabs** dialog box, in the **Tab stop position** box, type **1** and then, under **Alignment**, click **Left**. Click the **Set** button. The first tab is set. Set a second **Left** tab at **1.3 inches** and a third tab at **4.5 inches** that is a **Right** tab with **Leader option 2**. Click **Set** and then click **OK**.

8. Press [Tab], type **Hot Dogs** press [Tab], type **$2.25** and then press [Enter]. Repeat this pattern to add the next two items shown below. Press [Enter] once after the last line.

> Chili Dogs   2.75
>
> Knockwurst   3.25

(Project 3F–Refreshments continues on the next page)

(Project 3F–Refreshments continued)

Press [Tab] twice and type **Add Kraut** Press [Tab] again and type **.50** and then press [Enter]. This add-on is listed under Knockwurst. Press [Tab] twice and type **Add Chili** Press [Tab] again, type **.50** and then press [Enter] twice. Add the rest of the items listed below, pressing [Tab] once at the beginning of each line and again between the item and the price.

Chips	1.00
Water/Pop	1.50
Child Size	1.25
Single Scoop	2.00
Double Scoop	3.25

9. Click to the left of *Chips*, press [Enter] twice, and then press [Tab] once to restore the alignment of *Chips* in the listed items. Click to the left of *Child Size*, press [Enter] three times, and then press [Tab] once to restore the alignment. The prices for ice cream are moved down the page so you can add a subheading. Click the empty line above *Child Size*, change the font size to **22** and the alignment to **Center**, and then type **Ice Cream** Click the **Save** button.

10. Click to the left of *Hot Dogs*, to the left of the first tab mark. Display the **Insert** menu, point to **Picture**, and then click **Clip Art**. In the **Results should be** box, check that *All media file types* is displayed. In the **Search in box**, check that *All collections* is displayed. In the **Clip Art** task pane, in the **Search for** box, type **hot dog** and then click the **Go** button. Scroll down the list and locate the hot dog displayed in Figure 3.86. If you cannot find the hot dog shown in the figure, select another one of your choice or insert from your student files the file w03F_Hot_Dog. Click the image to insert it.

11. Click the inserted image to select it. Right-click to display the shortcut menu, and then click **Format Picture**. Click the **Layout tab**, click **Square**, and then click **OK**. In this case, you want the text to be aligned vertically in a list and not to wrap to the contour of the image. Drag the hot dog image as necessary to the left of the list of hot dog options as shown in Figure 3.86. Use the corner sizing handles to adjust the size of your image if needed. The size of the hot dog graphic used in Figure 3.86 was not changed.

12. Move your insertion point to the right of *1.25* on the *Child Size* row. In the **Clip Art** task pane, in the **Search for** box, replace *hot dog* with **ice cream cone** and then click the **Go** button. Scroll down the list and locate the ice cream cone displayed in Figure 3.86. If you cannot find the ice cream cone shown in the figure, select another one of your choice or, from your student files, insert w03F_Ice_Cream. Click the image to insert it.

(Project 3F–Refreshments continues on the next page)

(Project 3F–Refreshments continued)

13. Click the inserted image. Display the **Format Picture** dialog box, click **Layout**, click **Square**, and then click **OK**. Position the ice cream cone image to the right of the list of ice cream cone choices as shown in Figure 3.86. Be sure the top of the image is anchored to the Child Size line and not to the Ice Cream heading. Use the corner sizing handles to adjust the size of the image if needed. The image used in Figure 3.86 was not resized. Close the Clip Art task pane.

14. Display the **View** menu and then click **Header and Footer**. Switch to the footer area, click the **Insert AutoText** button, and click **Filename**. Close the Header and Footer toolbar.

15. Click the **Save** button and then click the **Print Preview** button to see the document as it will print. Click the **Print** button, close Print Preview, and then close the file, saving changes if prompted to do so.

End **You have completed Project 3F** ——————————

Project 3G — Hours

Objectives: *Work with the Drawing Toolbar, Create a Table, and Format Tables.*

In the following Performance Assessment, you will create a poster listing the hours of operation at Sensation! Park. Your completed document will look like the one shown in Figure 3.87. You will save your document as *3G_Hours_Firstname_Lastname.*

1. On the Standard toolbar, click the **Open** button. Navigate to the location where the student files for this textbook are stored. Locate and open **w03G_Hours**.

2. From the File menu, open the **Save As** dialog box. Navigate to the location where you are storing your files for this chapter. In the **File name** box, type **3G_Hours_Firstname_Lastname** using your own name. Then click the **Save** button.

3. Click to the left of the first paragraph mark under *May Hours* to position your insertion point. On the Standard toolbar, click the **Insert Table** button, move the mouse pointer to select a table that is 3 columns wide by 4 rows high, and then click once to insert the table.

4. Enter the information in the table as shown below. Do not be concerned about the text alignment or formatting at this time.

Monday-Thursday	1 p.m.	10 p.m.
Friday	1 p.m.	11 p.m.
Saturday and holidays	11 a.m.	11 p.m.
Sunday	NOON	11 p.m.

(Project 3G–Hours continues on the next page)

(Project 3G–Hours continued)

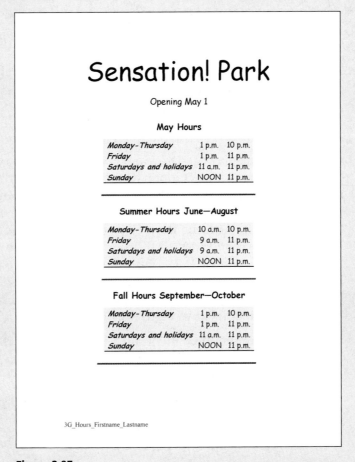

Figure 3.87

5. With your insertion point in the table, display the **Table** menu and then click **Table AutoFormat**. Under **Table styles**, scroll as necessary and then click **Table Colorful 2**. Under **Apply special formats to**, clear the **Heading rows** check box and, if necessary, clear the **Last column** check box. Click **Apply**.

6. Display the **Table** menu, point to **AutoFit**, and then click **AutoFit to Contents**.

7. Select the first column of the table. On the Formatting toolbar, click the **Align Left** button. From the **Table** menu, point to **Select** and then click **Table**. On the Formatting toolbar, click the **Center** button to center the table between the left and right margins.

8. With the table still selected, on the Standard toolbar, click the **Copy** button. Place the insertion point to the left of the first empty paragraph under *Summer Hours* and then click the **Paste** button. Click on the empty paragraph under *Fall Hours* and click the **Paste** button again. The table is copied to the two locations.

(Project 3G–Hours continues on the next page)

(Project 3G–Hours continued)

9. Change the hours in the table under *Summer Hours* as shown below:

Monday-Thursday	**10 a.m.**	**10 p.m.**
Friday	**9 a.m.**	**11 p.m.**
Saturday and holidays	**9 a.m.**	**11 p.m.**
Sunday	**NOON**	**11 p.m.**

10. On the Standard toolbar, click the **Save** button and then, if necessary, display the Drawing toolbar. If necessary, turn off the Drawing Canvas (Tools, Options, General tab). Click the **Line** button and drag a line under the first table between the two empty paragraph marks. Refer to Figure 3.87 to see where to position the line and how long to make it. With the line selected, click the **Line Color** arrow and click **Blue** (second row, sixth from the left) and then click the **Line Style** button and click **2¼**. With the line selected, click **Copy** and then click **Paste** two times. Drag the lines into position under the remaining two tables, similar to the position for the May table. Compare your document to Figure 3.87.

11. Display the **View** menu and click Header and Footer. Switch to the footer area, click the **Insert AutoText** button, and click **Filename**. Close the Header and Footer toolbar.

12. Click the **Save** button and then click the **Print Preview** button to see the document as it will print. Click the **Print** button, close Print Preview, and then close the file, saving changes if prompted to do so.

End You have completed Project 3G ————————————————

Project 3H — Prices

Objectives: *Create a Table from Existing Text and Format Tables.*

In the following Performance Assessment, you will create a poster with a list of prices for admission to Sensation! Park. Your completed document will look like the one shown in Figure 3.88. You will save your publication as *3H_Prices_Firstname_Lastname.*

1. On the Standard toolbar, click the **Open** button. Navigate to the location where the student files for this textbook are stored. Locate and open **w03H_Prices**.

2. From the **File** menu, open the **Save As** dialog box. Navigate to the location where you are storing your files for this Chapter. In the **File name** box, type **3H_Prices_Firstname_Lastname** using your own name. Then click the **Save** button.

(Project 3H–Prices continues on the next page)

(Project 3H–Prices continued)

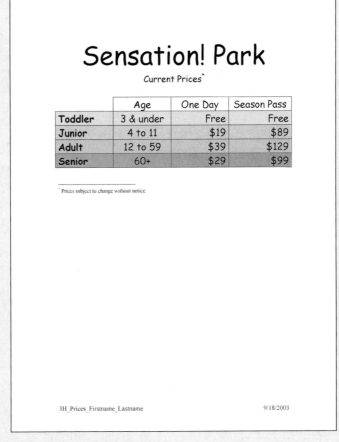

Figure 3.88

3. Click to the left of the first tab mark, left of *Age*, and select the five lines in the tabbed list. From the **Table** menu, point to **Convert** and then click **Text to Table**. In the **Convert Text to Table** dialog box, be sure **4** displays in the **Number of columns** box, and then click **OK**.

4. With the table still selected, using the Formatting toolbar, change the font to **Comic Sans MS** and the font size to **18**. Click anywhere to deselect the table.

5. Select the **first column** of the table and then click the **Bold** button. Select the **first row** of the table and then click the **Center** button. Select the four cells under *Age* and then click the **Center** button. In the last two columns, select the cells under the headings (do not select the headings) and click the **Align Right** button. Click the **Save** button.

(Project 3H–Prices continues on the next page)

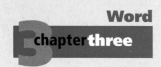
(Project 3H–Prices continued)

6. Click in the first cell of the table—the one that is empty. From the Format menu, click **Borders and Shading**. In the Borders and Shading dialog box, on the right side, click the **Apply to arrow** and then, from the displayed list, click **Cell**. In the **Preview** area, click the **top** and **left** borders to deselect them and then click **OK**. Click the **Print Preview** button to verify that the top and left borders on the first cell will not print. Close the Print Preview window.

7. Select the row beginning with *Toddler*. From the **Format** menu, click **Borders and Shading** and then click the **Shading tab**. Under **Fill**, in the last row of the color palette, click **Light Turquoise**—the fifth color from the left. The name of the color displays to the right of the color palette after it is selected. Click **OK**.

8. Repeat Step 7 to apply colors to the three remaining rows of the table as follows:

   Junior   Light Yellow

   Adult   Light Green

   Senior   Lavender

9. Place the insertion point to the right of *Current Prices*. From the **Insert** menu, point to **Reference** and then click **Footnote**. In the **Footnote and Endnote** dialog box, under **Location**, click the **Endnotes** option button. Under **Format**, click the **Number format arrow** and, from the displayed list, click the last item—symbols that begin with *. At the lower left of the dialog box, click **Insert**. In the new endnote box, type **Prices subject to change without notice**

10. Display the **View** menu and then click **Header and Footer**. Switch to the footer area, click the **Insert AutoText** button, and then click **Filename**. Press Tab twice and then, on the Header and Footer toolbar, click the **Insert Date** button. Close the Header and Footer toolbar.

11. Click the **Save** button and then click the **Print Preview** button to see the document as it will print. Click the **Print** button, close Print Preview, and then close the file, saving changes if prompted to do so.

End You have completed Project 3H ————————————————

Project 3I — Water Rides

Objectives: *Insert Clip Art and Pictures, Modify Clip Art and Pictures, Create a Table, Format Tables, and Create a Table from Existing Text.*

In the following Mastery Assessment, you will create a table announcing new water rides at Sensation! Park. Your completed document will look like the one shown in Figure 3.89. You will save your publication as *3I_Water_Rides_ Firstname_Lastname.*

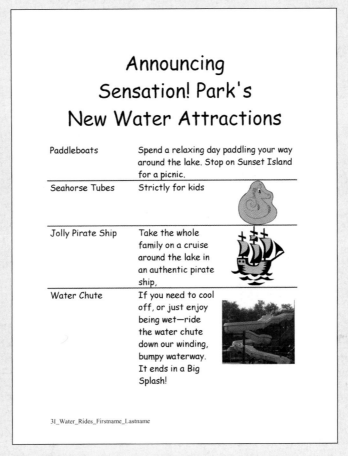

Figure 3.89

1. Start Word. From your student files, open **w03I_Water_Rides**. Save the file with the name **3I_Water_Rides_Firstname_Lastname** in the same location as your other files and using your own name. In the same manner as you have done in previous documents, display the footer and insert the AutoText filename.

2. Select the tabbed list, beginning with *Paddleboats* and ending with *Big Splash!* Convert this text to a two-column table.

3. Add a column to the right side of the table.

(Project 3I–Water Rides continues on the next page)

(Project 3I–Water Rides continued)

4. Drag to select the cell beginning with *Spend a relaxing day* and the empty cell to the right. Right-click the selected cells and click **Merge Cells** from the shortcut menu.

5. Click in the empty cell to the right of *Strictly for Kids*. Insert the file **w03I_Seahorse**. Use a corner sizing handle to resize the image to approximately 1 inch wide. With the image still selected, on the **Formatting** toolbar, click the **Center** button.

6. In the cell under the seahorse, insert file **03I_Pirate_Ship**. Resize the image so it is approximately 1 inch wide. With the image still selected, on the **Formatting** toolbar, click the **Center** button

7. Click in the empty cell in the last row. Press **Enter**, and then insert the **w03I_Waterride**.

8. Select the entire table and then display the **Borders and Shading** dialog box. Click the **Borders tab**. Under **Setting**, click **None** to remove all of the borders. In the lower middle of the dialog box, click the **Color arrow** and, from the displayed palette, in the second row, click the sixth color—**Blue**. Click the **Width arrow** and, from the displayed list, click **1½ pt**. In the Preview area, click the button that displays a **horizontal border line** between the rows. A horizontal border is added between the rows in the table preview graphic. Click **OK**.

9. Save the completed document. Preview the document and then print it.

End You have completed Project 3I ───────────────────

Project 3J—Events Memo

Objectives: *Create a Table, Format Tables, and Create a Table from Existing Text.*

In the following Mastery Assessment, you will add a table to a memo regarding the events that are planned for the upcoming season at Sensation! Park. In two columns in the memo, you will set tab stops and the hanging indent marker so you can create an indented list. Your completed document will look like the one shown in Figure 3.90. You will save your publication as *3J_Events_Memo_Firstname_Lastname.*

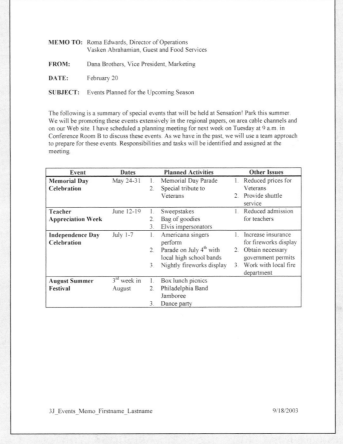

Figure 3.90

1. Start Word. From your student files, open **w03J_Events_Memo**. Save the file with the name **3J_Events_Memo_Firstname_Lastname** in the same location as your other files.

2. Click to position the insertion point to the left of the empty paragraph mark under the paragraph ending with *meeting* and insert a table that has four columns and four rows.

3. Be sure the ruler is displayed on your screen and the left tab indicator displays in the Tab Alignment button. Select the third

(Project 3J–Events Memo continues on the next page)

(Project 3J–Events Memo continued)

column of the table and then click on the ruler at the **3⅜** inch mark (third tick mark to the left of the 4 inch mark) to add a left tab. Point to the gray indent markers on the ruler until the *Hanging Indent* ScreenTip displays and then drag the hanging indent marker for that column to the **3⅜** inch position.

4. Select the fourth column of the table, click to place a left tab stop at **5.25** inches, and then drag the hanging indent marker to that tab stop.

5. Refer to Figure 3.90, and then in the first row of the table, type the information shown below. In the third cell, type **1.** and press Ctrl + Tab to move to the tab stop you created and then continue typing. Press Enter to move to the second line in this cell. Type **2.** press Ctrl + Tab and finish typing the information for the third cell.

Note that because numbers are used in this example, the AutoCorrect Options button may display to number the list for you. Click **Stop automatically creating numbered lists** from the displayed list. This will stop the AutoCorrect Options feature from creating a numbered list in each cell of the table.

| Memorial Day Celebration | May 24–31 | 1. Memorial Day Parade
2. Special tribute to Veterans | 1. Reduced prices for Veterans
2. Provide shuttle service |

Press Tab to move to the fourth cell and use same process to type the information so it aligns on the tab stop.

6. Enter the remaining information as shown in the table below. Use the same technique in the third and forth column—type the number and the period and then press Ctrl + Tab before continuing to type the rest of the data. Be sure to press Enter when multiple items are listed in a cell.

Teacher Appreciation Week	June 12–19	1. Sweepstakes 2. Bag of goodies 3. Elvis impersonators	1. Reduced admission for teachers
Independence Day Celebration	July 1–7	1. Americana singers perform 2. Parade on July 4th with local high school bands 3. Nightly fireworks display	1. Increase insurance for fireworks display 2. Obtain necessary government permits 3. Work with local fire department
August Summer Festival	3rd week in August	1. Box lunch picnics 2. Philadelphia Band Jamboree 3. Dance party	

(Project 3J–Events Memo continues on the next page)

(Project 3J–Events Memo continued)

7. Click in the first row of the table and insert a new row above. Type the following headings in this new first row:

   Event   Dates   Planned Activities   Other Issues

8. Select the table and use the **AutoFormat** dialog box to apply the **Table List 5** format to the table. Use **AutoFit** to fit the table to the contents and then center the column headings.

9. In the same manner as you have done in previous documents, display the footer and insert the **AutoText filename**. Press Tab to move to the right side of the footer. Notice that the right tab stop for the footer is not aligned with the right margin. On the ruler, drag the right tab stop to align with the right margin, and then click the **Insert Date** button.

10. Save the completed document. Preview the document and then print it.

End **You have completed Project 3J** —————————————————

Project 3K — Resume

Objectives: *Create a Table and Format Tables.*

The Table tool is convenient for creating resumes. In this Problem-Solving exercise, you will use a table to create your own resume. Your completed document will look similar to the one shown in Figure 3.91. You will save your resume as *3K_Resume_Firstname_Lastname*.

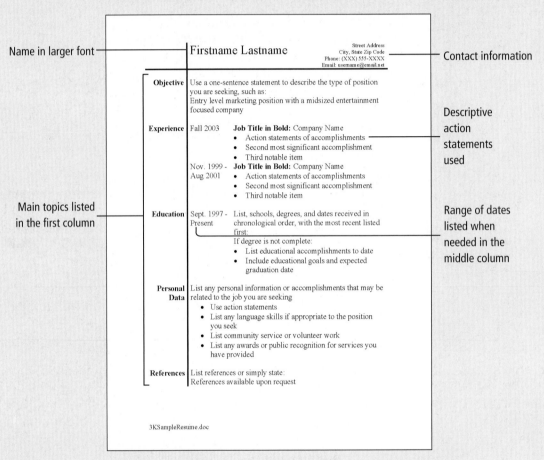

Figure 3.91

1. Examine Figure 3.91. This sample of a resume uses a three-column table with only a first column and first row border displayed. The middle column is used for dates when needed or merged with the third cell in the row to expand the text across a wider area.

2. Examine Figure 3.92, which displays the resume as it looks in Word. Notice the rows that have been added to increase space between major headings. The major topics in the left column have been aligned on the left and bold emphasis has been added.

(Project 3K–Resume continues on the next page)

(Project 3K–Resume continued)

First column border

First row border

Text right aligned

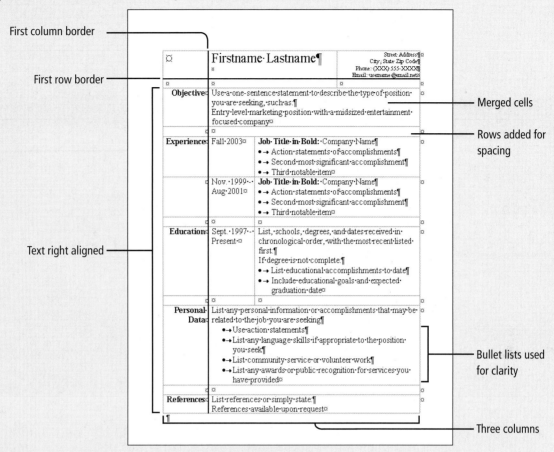

Merged cells

Rows added for spacing

Bullet lists used for clarity

Three columns

Figure 3.92

3. Create a three-column table with four rows to start—you can add more rows as needed. Remove all of the borders.

4. Select the top row and add a bottom border and then select the first column and add a right border. The bottom border of the first cell may be overwritten when you add the border to the right of the first column. Select the top left cell and re-apply the bottom border.

5. Fill in your name and personal information at the top of the table, formatting it appropriately.

6. The objective statement should be directed toward the job for which you are applying. You can write this as if applying for the job you already have, one you would like to have, or for a specific job posting.

7. Using the figures as a model, enter information for your own resume. The content of the figures provides tips on the type of information and format to use when writing a resume.

(Project 3K–Resume continues on the next page)

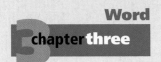
(Project 3K–Resume continued)

8. Proofread your resume and remove any spelling, grammar, or typographical errors. Save the document as **3K_Resume_Firstname_Lastname** In the footer area, using the AutoText button, insert the file name.

9. Print the document and then close the file, saving changes if prompted to do so.

 End You have completed Project 3K ————————————————

Project 3L — July 4th

Objectives: *Insert Clip Art and Pictures, Modify Clip Art and Pictures, Work with Tab Stops, Work with the Drawing Toolbar*

Sensation! Park has several events that it needs to promote for the upcoming season. In this Problem Solving exercise, you will create a promotional poster for the July 4th Celebration.

1. Type the name of the park at the top of the page and then use an AutoShape to create a banner for the event name. Add an event title in the shape you selected and format the font to a size and style that will make it stand out.

2. Using the skills you have practiced in this chapter and your imagination, create and format a table listing four to five planned activities and the scheduled day and times during the week of July 4.

3. Add clip art, such as fireworks, picnics, or pictures of parades to call attention to the events that are planned for the week.

4. Add a text box or a callout shape and draw a line to point out a special event or time.

5. Add a tabbed list of discounts that are offered for special groups or large parties.

6. Preview the document. Make sure the font style is consistent throughout and the various components are balanced on the page.

7. Save the document as **3L_July_4th_Firstname_Lastname** In the footer area, using the AutoText button, insert the file name.

8. Print the document and then close the file, saving changes if prompted to do so.

 End You have completed Project 3L ————————————————

Clip Art on the Internet

You do not have to limit your choice of clip art or pictures to those images that come with Microsoft Word. You can download clip art images or select pictures to use from the Web. You can also insert pictures from your own files into any Word document. If you use images from a proprietary Web site, such as National Geographic, you must provide proper credit and reference to the location where the images were found. In some cases, a Web site will state specifically that all content is copyrighted and cannot be used without written permission. Web sites offering free clip art images do not have that requirement.

1. Open your Web browser and go to a search engine such as www.google.com or www.yahoo.com. Type the key words **clip art** and **free** in the search box.

2. Look through the various sites for one you like that has a variety of interesting graphics. There are several that do not require that you sign up for advertising or provide your e-mail address.

3. Find a site you like and practice inserting images in a Word document. When you right-click on an image, you can either copy it or use the Save as option from the shortcut menu to save it to your disk.

4. Open a Word document and insert some new images you found on the Web. Try more than one site to sample the variety of Web sites available.

5. If you like a site you found, you can add it to your Favorite Sites list or bookmark it.

6. Close your browser and close Word.

Changing Text Orientation

You may want to change the orientation of text in a Word document so it is vertical instead of horizontal. You can do this in a table or by using a text box. There are several tutorials in the Word Help program that provide instructions on how to change the orientation of text.

1. Start Word. In the Type a Question for Help box, type **Text Orientation** Scroll through the list of topics that displays in the Search Results task pane. From this list of help topics, click **Change the orientation of text**.

2. In a blank document, create a text box and type your name. Follow the directions to practice changing the orientation in a text box.

3. Create a 3-by-2 (three columns by two rows) table and type random words in the table. Try changing the orientation of the first column of text in your table. Use Word Help if necessary to provide instructions. This process also works in drawing objects.

4. Close the Help task pane and exit Word.

chapterfour

Creating Documents with Multiple Columns and Special Formats

In this chapter, you will: complete these projects **and** practice these skills.

Project 4A **Creating a Newsletter**	**Objectives** • Create a Decorative Title • Create Multicolumn Documents • Add Special Paragraph Formatting • Use Special Character Formats
Project 4B **Creating a Web Page**	**Objectives** • Insert Hyperlinks • Preview and Save a Document as a Web Page
Project 4C **Creating a Memo**	**Objectives** • Locate Supporting Information • Find Objects with the Select Browse Object Button

The City of Desert Park

Desert Park, Arizona, is a thriving city with a population of just under 1 million in an ideal location serving major markets in the western United States and Mexico. Desert Park's temperate year-round climate attracts both visitors and businesses, and it is one of the most popular vacation destinations in the world. The city expects and has plenty of space for long-term growth, and most of the undeveloped land already has a modern infrastructure and assured water supply in place.

© Getty Images, Inc.

Creating Documents with Multiple Columns and Special Formats

Creating a newsletter is usually a job reserved for **desktop publishing** programs, such as Microsoft Publisher. Word, however, has a number of tools that enable you to put together a simple, yet effective and attractive newsletter.

Newsletters consist of a number of elements, but nearly all have a title—called a **masthead**—story headlines, articles, and graphics. The text is often split into two or three columns, making it easier to read than one-column articles. Column widths can be changed, text is usually justified, and lines can be inserted to separate columns.

Newsletters are often printed, but they can also be designed as Web pages. Links to other Web sites can be included and can be accessed by clicking words or graphics. Microsoft Word provides research tools to find information included in the Office package or information on the Web. These materials can be collected and then pasted into different parts of the document.

Project 4A **Garden Newsletter**

In this chapter, you will edit and format newsletters and add elements such as mastheads, borders, and shading. You will add links and save a document as a Web page. You will also use research tools to find information and place it in a document.

In Activities 4.1 through 4.10 you will edit a newsletter for the City of Desert Park Botanical Gardens. You will add a WordArt masthead and a decorative border line. You will also change the text of the articles from one column to two columns and then format the columns. Finally, you will use special text formatting features to change the font color and set off one of the paragraphs with a border and shading. Your completed document will look similar to Figure 4.1. You will save your document as *4A_Garden_Newsletter_Firstname_Lastname.*

Botanical Notes

GARDEN GETS NPS GRANT

The City of Desert Park received a $100,000 grant from the National Park Service (NPS) to be used in the Desert Park Botanical Garden. The grant comes from an NPS program entitled "Urban Park and Recreation Recovery" (UPARR).

UPARR grants can be used to renovate existing recreation areas and facilities. The grants highlight the importance of having safe and accessible neighborhood recreation facilities available for people of all ages.

To qualify for the grant, the Fine Arts and Parks Department followed the eligibility requirements and application procedures, which were posted in a Federal Register notice last January. Applications from around the nation were reviewed by NPS, and final selections were recently named by the NPS Director.

The UPARR program was established in 1978 to provide matching grants and technical assistance to urban communities. The law encourages systematic local planning and commitment to continuing operation and maintenance of recreation programs, sites, and facilities.

Additional information on the UPARR program can be found on the National Park Service's Web site at www.nps.gov/uparr.

OUTDOOR MUSIC

Classical music is alive and well in Desert Park! Since 1986, the Desert Park Botanical Garden Outdoor Concert Series has presented over 600 high-quality events to audiences from Desert Park and from around the nation. With steady growth, the series has  become a major public-private coalition of organizations. The series started with an idea of a group of music faculty members at Desert Park University and Desert Park Community College. During its history, the series has never compromised its level of world-class excellence, bringing to its audiences a mix of well-known and up-and-coming performers.

Please feel free to bring your picnic supper to enjoy in the Garden before the performance begins. Many of our attendees love to bring their bright table linens and vases of fresh flowers to accompany their picnics. (Due to fire danger, please no candles.)

4A_Garden_Newsletter_Firstname_Lastname

Figure 4.1
Project 4A—Garden Newsletter

Objective 1
Create a Decorative Title

The title at the top of a newsletter should be short and distinctive. Microsoft Word uses an Office program called *WordArt* to change text into a decorative graphic. WordArt can be formatted, even after the text has been changed to a graphic. Word also has attractive borders that can be used to separate the masthead from the articles.

Activity 4.1 Inserting WordArt

1 Start Word. On the Standard toolbar, click the **Open** button 📂. Navigate to the location where the student files for this textbook are stored. Locate **w04A_Garden_Newsletter** and click once to select it. Then, in the lower right corner of the **Open** dialog box, click **Open**.

The w04A_Garden_Newsletter file opens.

2 From the **File** menu, click **Save As**. In the **Save As** dialog box, click the **Save in arrow** and navigate to the location in which you are storing your files for this chapter, creating a new folder for chapter 4 if you want to do so.

3 Type **4A_Garden_Newsletter_Firstname_Lastname** in the **File name** box, using your own name, and click **Save**. On the Standard toolbar, click the Zoom button arrow ▐100% ▼▏, and then click Page Width.

4 Be sure that you have the nonprinting characters displayed and notice the two blank lines at the top of the document. With the insertion point positioned to the left of the first blank paragraph mark, display the **Insert** menu, point to **Picture**, and then click **WordArt**.

The WordArt Gallery dialog box displays.

5 Under **Select a WordArt style**, in the second row, click the fifth option as shown in Figure 4.2.

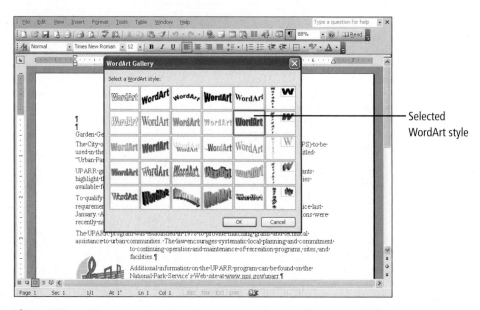

Selected WordArt style

Figure 4.2

6 At the bottom of the **WordArt Gallery** dialog box, click **OK**.

The Edit WordArt Text dialog box displays with placeholder text *Your Text Here*. As soon as you begin to type, the placeholder text will be replaced.

7 In the **Edit WordArt Text** dialog box, under **Text**, type **Botanical Notes**

The text you type displays. The default font size is 36 points, and the default font is Impact. Compare your Edit WordArt Text dialog box to Figure 4.3.

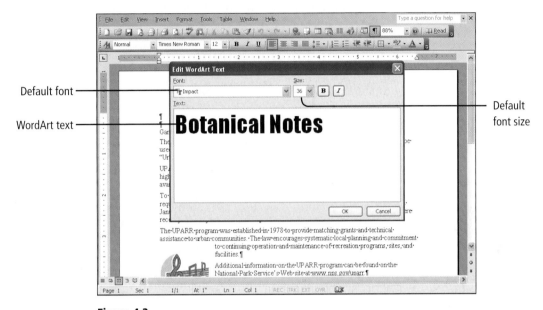

Default font ⎯⎯⎯⎯⎯

WordArt text ⎯⎯⎯⎯⎯

Default font size ⎯⎯⎯⎯⎯

Figure 4.3

8 At the bottom of the **Edit WordArt Text** dialog box, click **OK**.

The WordArt graphic is inserted at the insertion point location, as shown in Figure 4.4.

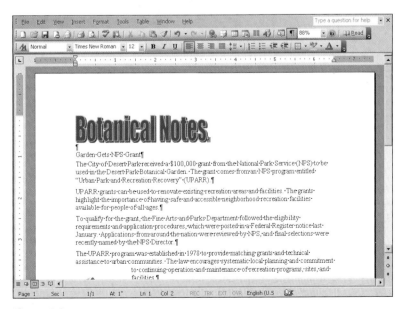

Figure 4.4

9 On the Standard toolbar, click the **Save** button ⊞.

Activity 4.2 Formatting WordArt

When you create a WordArt image, a good technique is to create the graphic at the default (36-point) font size and then adjust it after you see how it fits in the allotted space.

1 Click the **WordArt object** to select it, and notice that the WordArt toolbar displays, floating somewhere on your screen. Pause your mouse pointer over each button to display the ScreenTip and examine the description of each button in the table in Figure 4.5.

Buttons on the WordArt Toolbar

ScreenTip	Button	Description
Insert WordArt		Inserts a new WordArt object.
Edit Text	Edit Text...	Opens the Edit WordArt dialog box so that the text for an existing WordArt object can be modified.
WordArt Gallery		Opens the WordArt Gallery so that a new design can be applied to an existing WordArt object.
Format WordArt		Opens the Format WordArt dialog box so that fill colors, size, position, and layout can be modified.
WordArt Shape		Displays options for changing the shape of an existing WordArt object.
Text Wrapping		Displays the text wrapping menu.
WordArt Same Letter Heights	Aa	Changes the height of lowercase letters so that they are the same height as uppercase letters.
WordArt Vertical Text		Displays WordArt text vertically.
WordArt Alignment		Applies alignment options to a WordArt object.
WordArt Character Spacing	AV	Adjusts the amount of spacing between WordArt characters.

Figure 4.5

2 On the WordArt toolbar, click the **Edit Text** button Edit Text... . Alternatively, move the pointer over the new WordArt graphic and double-click.

The Edit WordArt Text dialog box displays.

3 In the **Edit WordArt Text** dialog box, click the **Size arrow** and then, from the displayed list, click **66**. Click **OK**.

The masthead of the newsletter you created using WordArt reaches nearly to the right margin.

4 Look at the horizontal ruler and locate the boundary of the right margin—the area at 6.5 inches where the shading changes. On the right edge of the masthead, drag the middle sizing handle to align approximately with the right margin. See Figure 4.6.

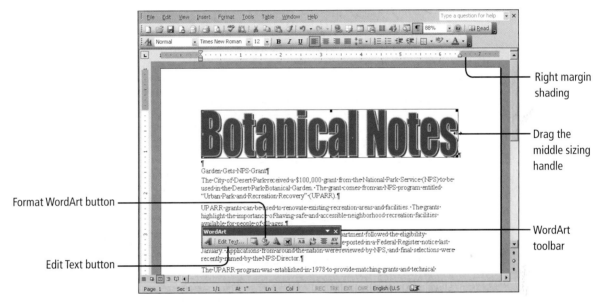

Figure 4.6

5 On the **WordArt** toolbar, click the **Format WordArt** button. If necessary, click the Colors and Lines tab.

6 Under **Fill**, click the **Color arrow**.

A color palette displays, as shown in Figure 4.7.

Colors and Lines tab —

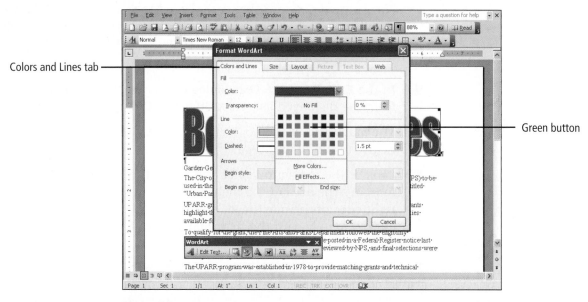

Green button

Figure 4.7

7 In the second row of color options, click the fourth color—**Green**. At the bottom of the **Format WordArt** dialog box, click **OK**.

The WordArt letters that form the newsletter's masthead letters change from blue to green.

8 On the Standard toolbar, click the **Save** button.

Activity 4.3 Adding a Border Line

A line between the masthead and the rest of the material makes the newsletter look more professional. Word provides many decorative line types that you can add to your document.

1 In the blank line below the masthead, click to position the insertion point.

2 From the **Format** menu, click **Borders and Shading**.

The Borders and Shading dialog box displays.

3 If necessary, click the Borders tab. Under **Setting**, click the **Custom** option.

4 Under **Style**, scroll down about halfway and click the double line with the heavy top and lighter bottom lines.

5 Under **Preview**, click the **Bottom Border** button.

Compare your dialog box to Figure 4.8.

Borders tab   Line style

Custom button

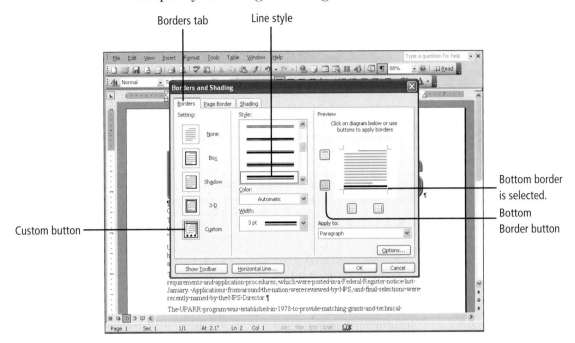

Bottom border is selected.

Bottom Border button

Figure 4.8

6 At the bottom of the **Borders and Shading** dialog box, click **OK**.

The double-line border is inserted at the bottom of the empty paragraph and stretches from the left margin to the right margin. See Figure 4.9.

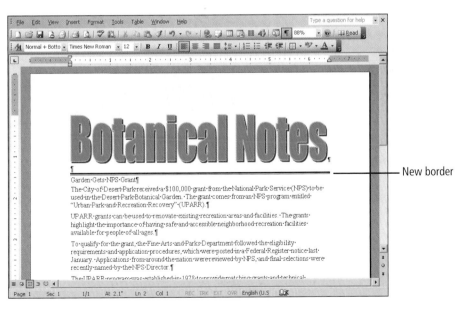

New border

Figure 4.9

7 On the Standard toolbar, click the **Save** button .

Objective 2
Create Multicolumn Documents

All newspapers and most magazines and newsletters use multiple columns for articles because text in narrower columns is easier to read than text that stretches across a page. Word has a tool that enables you to change a single column of text into two or more columns. The columns can be formatted, and a line can be added between columns. If a column does not end where you want, a ***manual column break*** can be inserted.

Activity 4.4 Changing One Column to Two Columns

Newsletters are nearly always two or three columns wide. It is probably not wise to create four or more columns because they are so narrow that word spacing looks awkward, often resulting in one long word by itself on a line.

1 Position the insertion point to the left of the first line of text, which begins *Garden Gets NPS Grant.* Use the Scroll bar to scroll down to the bottom of the document, hold down ⁅Shift⁆, and then click at the end of the last line.

All the text is selected. Do not be concerned about selecting the two pictures—they will be moved later, and they are not affected by changing the number of columns.

2 On the Standard toolbar, click the **Columns** button ⁅▦⁆.

A Columns menu displays, showing up to four possible columns.

3 Move the pointer over the second column.

Two columns are highlighted, and the bottom of the menu displays the number of columns, as shown in Figure 4.10.

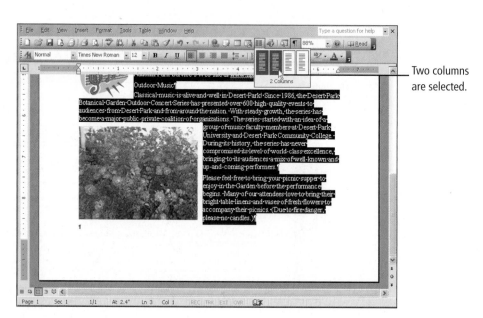

Two columns are selected.

Figure 4.10

4 Click the mouse button and then scroll up as necessary to view the top of your document.

The text is divided into two columns, and a section break is inserted below the masthead, dividing the one-column section from the two-column section. Do not be concerned with the placement of the pictures—one may be displayed on top of the other, or one may display outside the document margin. See Figure 4.11.

Two columns are created. ————

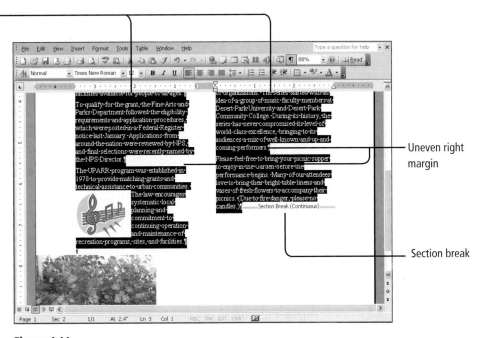

Uneven right margin

Section break

Figure 4.11

5 On the Standard toolbar, click the **Save** button.

Activity 4.5 Formatting Multiple Columns

The ragged right edge of a single page width column is readable. When you create narrow columns, justified text is preferable. The font you choose should also match the type of newsletter.

1 With the text still selected, on the Formatting toolbar, click the **Font button arrow** Times New Roman.

The Font menu displays.

2 From the **Font** menu, scroll to and click **Comic Sans MS**. Alternatively, you can press C to move to the first font beginning with that letter, and then scroll down to the desired font.

Because the Comic Sans MS font is larger than Times New Roman, the text expands to a second page.

3 On the Formatting toolbar, click the arrow **Font Size button arrow** 12 and then click **10**.

The document returns to a single page.

4 On the Formatting toolbar, click the **Justify** button ![justify icon]. Scroll to the top of the document and click anywhere in the document to deselect the text.

The font is changed to 10-point Comic Sans MS, an informal, easy-to-read font, and the text is justified. See Figure 4.12. The text at the top of the second column may differ from the figure because of the displaced pictures. This will be adjusted later.

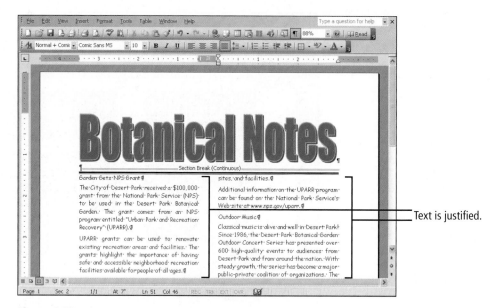

Text is justified.

Figure 4.12

5 From the **View** menu, click **Header and Footer**.

The Header and Footer toolbar displays.

6 On the Header and Footer toolbar, click the **Switch Between Header and Footer** button ![switch icon].

The insertion point is positioned in the footer box.

7 On the Header and Footer toolbar, click the **Insert AutoText** button ![Insert AutoText ▾], and then click **Filename**.

The file name is inserted in the footer. Do not be concerned if one of the pictures is covering your footer—this will be adjusted in a later activity.

8 On the Header and Footer toolbar, click the **Close** button ![Close].

9 On the Standard toolbar, click the **Save** button ![save icon].

Activity 4.6 Inserting a Column Break

Manual column breaks can be inserted to adjust columns that end or begin awkwardly or to make space for graphics or text boxes.

1 On the Standard toolbar, click the **Print Preview** button.

If the newsletter was printed at this point, the ends of the columns would be uneven.

2 On the Print Preview toolbar, click the **Close** button. Position the insertion point to the left of the paragraph at the bottom of the first column that begins *The UPARR program was established.*

3 From the **Insert** menu, click **Break**.

The Break dialog box displays. See Figure 4.13. Here you can insert column breaks, page breaks, or text-wrapping breaks. You can also set four types of section breaks. The *Next page* break moves the text after the break to the next page of your document, whereas a *Continuous break* creates a section break on the same page. *Even page* and *Odd page* breaks are used when you need to have a different header or footer for odd and even pages in a manuscript, manual, or other long document that will be printed on two-sided paper.

Column break option ———

This text will be moved to the next column.

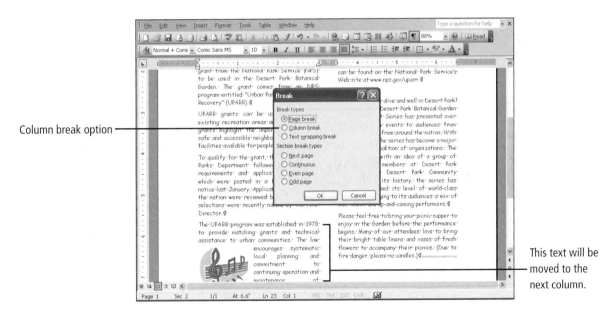

Figure 4.13

4 Under **Break types**, click the **Column break** option button.

5 At the bottom of the **Break** dialog box, click **OK**.

The column breaks at the insertion point, and the text following the insertion point moves to the top of the next column. See Figure 4.14.

Column break ——————

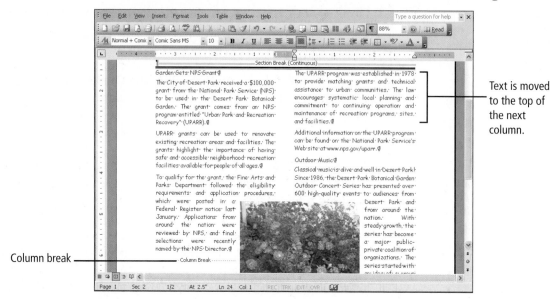

Text is moved to the top of the next column.

Figure 4.14

6 Position the document so that you can view the lower portion on your screen. Point to the picture of the flowers, hold down the left mouse button, and then drag the picture of the flowers slightly below the column break you just inserted at the bottom of the first column. Align the top edge of the picture at approximately **6 inches on the vertical ruler**.

7 In the second column, in the paragraph that begins *Classical music is alive and well*, drag the picture of the musical notes so the right border of the picture aligns with the right side of the column, then drag up or down as necessary to match Figure 4.15. Click anywhere to deselect the image.

Your newsletter should look similar to Figure 4.15.

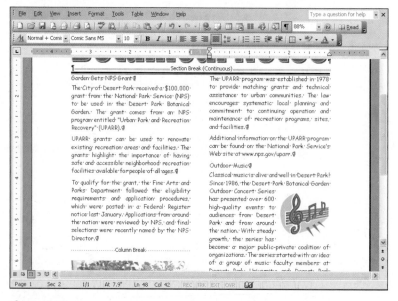

Figure 4.15

8 On the Standard toolbar, click the **Save** button 🖫.

More Knowledge — Balancing Column Breaks

You can also insert a column break to help balance columns so that they end evenly. This is important when the end of the columns is not the end of the document. If you want to balance the columns in a document, switch to Print Layout view, if necessary, and click at the end of the last column. On the Insert menu, click Break and then click the Continuous section break option. This will cause the end of the columns to be approximately even.

Objective 3
Add Special Paragraph Formatting

Sometimes you will want to call attention to specific paragraphs of text. One way to do this is to place a border around the paragraph. You can also shade a paragraph, although use caution not to make the shade too dark, because it will be hard to read the text.

Activity 4.7 Adding a Border to a Paragraph

Paragraph borders provide strong visual cues to the reader.

1 At the top of the second column, in the second paragraph that begins *Additional information on the UPARR program*, triple-click in the paragraph to select it.

The paragraph is selected.

2 From the **Format** menu, click **Borders and Shading**.

The Borders and Shading dialog box displays.

Note — Adding Borders to Text

Add Simple Borders Using the Outside Border Button

Simple borders, and border edges, can be added using the Outside Border button on the Formatting toolbar. This button offers very little control, however, because line thickness and color depends on the previous thickness and color chosen from the Borders and Shading dialog box.

3 Under **Setting**, click **Box**.

4 Under **Width**, click the arrow and then click **1½ pt**.

Compare your Borders and Shading dialog box to Figure 4.16. Notice that the Apply to box displays *Paragraph*. The Apply to box directs where the border will be applied—in this case, the border that has been set will be applied to the paragraph that is selected.

Box button

Width arrow

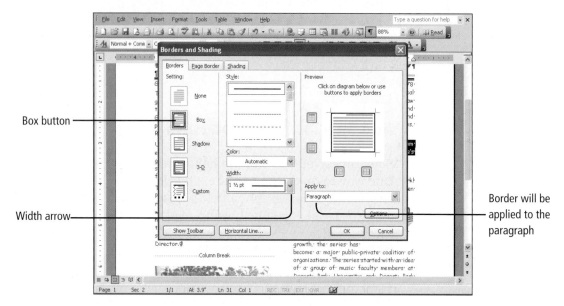

Border will be applied to the paragraph

Figure 4.16

5 At the bottom of the **Borders and Shading** dialog box, click **OK**.

A border has been placed around the paragraph, as shown in Figure 4.17.

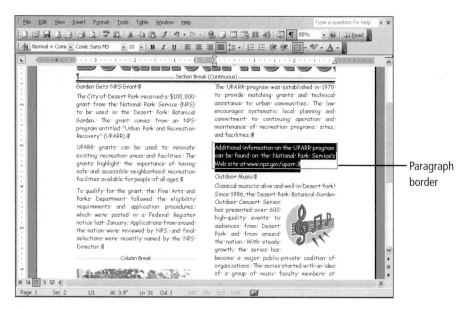

Paragraph border

Figure 4.17

6 On the Standard toolbar, click the **Save** button .

Activity 4.8 Shading a Paragraph

Shading can be used with or without borders. When used with a border, shading can be very effective.

1 With the paragraph still selected, from the **Format** menu, click **Borders and Shading**.

The Borders and Shading dialog box displays.

2 In the **Borders and Shading** dialog box, click the **Shading tab**.

3 Under **Fill**, in the first row of the color palette, click the third button.

A box to the right of the palette indicates *Gray-10%*. See Figure 4.18.

Selected shading

Shading tab

Shading intensity

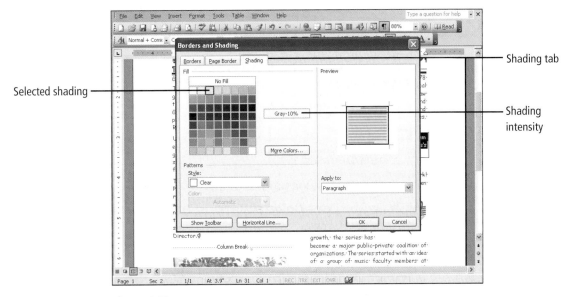

Figure 4.18

4 At the bottom of the **Borders and Shading** dialog box, click **OK**. Click anywhere in the document to deselect the text.

The paragraph is shaded and has a border, as shown in Figure 4.19.

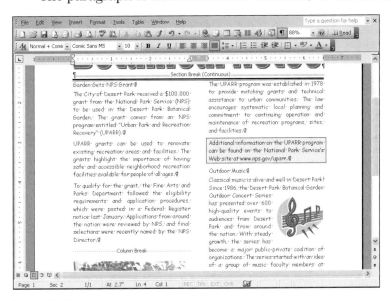

Figure 4.19

5 On the Standard toolbar, click the **Save** button.

Objective 4
Use Special Character Formats

Headlines and titles should be set off from the rest of the text in a distinctive manner. This is usually done by emphasizing the text with the use of bold or italics, different fonts, or increased font size. If you are going to use a color printer or post the document on the Web, changing the color is very effective.

Activity 4.9 Changing Font Color

1 At the top of the first column, select the *Garden Gets NPS Grant* headline.

This is the headline for the first story in the newsletter.

2 On the Formatting toolbar, click the **Bold** button **B**.

3 On the Formatting toolbar, click the **Font Size button arrow** 12, and then click **18**.

4 On the Formatting toolbar, click the arrow click the **Font Color button arrow** A.

The Font Color palette displays.

5 On the **Font Color palette**, in the second row, click the fourth color—**Green**.

The first headline is bold, 18 point, and green. The Font Color button retains the color that was just applied, which means that if you click the button, it will apply Green to whatever text has been selected.

6 Under the shaded paragraph, select the *Outdoor Music* headline. Repeat Steps 2 through 5 to apply the same format to the second headline. Alternatively, you could use the Format Painter to apply the format from the first headline to the second headline. Click anywhere in the document to deselect the text.

The second headline is formatted the same as the first, as shown in Figure 4.20.

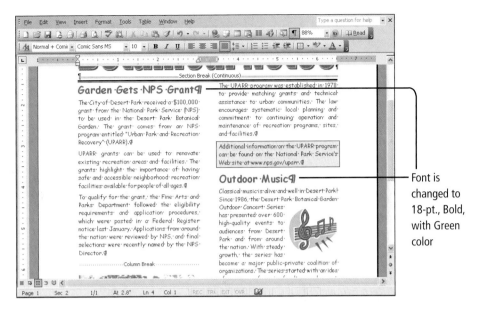

Figure 4.20

Font is changed to 18-pt., Bold, with Green color

---

7 On the Standard toolbar, click the **Save** button 🖫.

Activity 4.10 Using Small Caps

For headlines and titles, **small caps** is a useful font effect. Lower-case letters are changed to capital letters but remain the height of lower-case letters. Titles are often done in this style.

1 Select the *Outdoor Music* title again. From the **Format** menu, click **Font**.

The Font dialog box displays. See Figure 4.21. There are several special effects that can be applied to fonts using the Font dialog box.

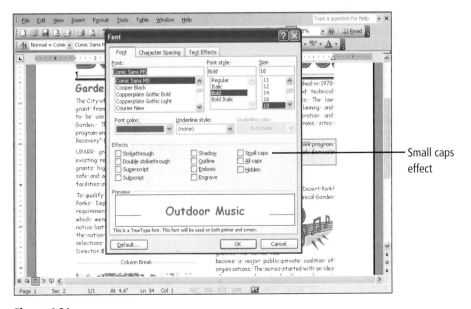

Small caps effect

Figure 4.21

2 Under **Effects**, select the **Small caps** check box.

3 At the bottom of the **Font** dialog box, click **OK**.

The second headline displays in small caps.

4 In the first title, *Garden Gets NPS Grant*, repeat Steps 1 through 3. Alternatively, use the Format Painter to apply the small caps effect to the first title. Click anywhere in the document to deselect the text.

Both headlines display in small caps, as shown in Figure 4.22.

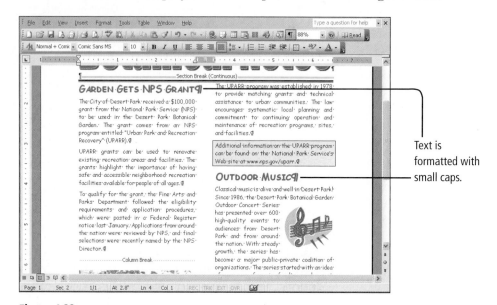

Figure 4.22

5 On the Standard toolbar, click the **Show/Hide ¶** button to turn off the nonprinting characters.

6 Click the **Zoom button arrow** [100% ▾], click the arrow and then click **Whole Page**.

The entire newsletter displays, as shown in Figure 4.23.

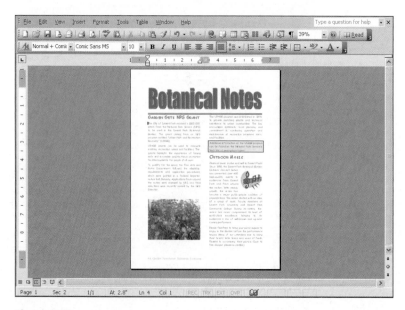

Figure 4.23

More Knowledge — Removing Blank Pages

If you created empty paragraphs at the end of a document by pressing the Enter key too often, the result might be an extra blank page. To remove this page, click at the bottom of the document and press the Backspace key until the extra page is removed. It is best to use the Show/Hide ¶ button to show hidden characters so you can view the formatting marks that should be deleted.

7 If your document looks different, make the necessary adjustments.

8 On the Standard toolbar, click the **Show/Hide ¶** button ¶ to redisplay nonprinting characters.

9 Click the **Zoom button arrow** , click the arrow and then click **Page Width**.

Page Width displays the document at its maximum width while still displaying the margins. The percent displayed in the Zoom box is affected by your screen resolution, and whether you are in Print Layout View or Normal View.

10 On the Standard toolbar, click the **Print** button.

If you are using a black-and-white printer, the colors will print as shades of gray.

11 On the Standard toolbar, click the **Save** button. Close the document.

End You have completed Project 4A ——————————

Project 4B **Water Matters**

In Project 4A you created titles and worked with paragraph and character formatting. In the following project, 4B, you will insert hyperlinks and practice saving documents as Web pages.

City of Desert Park

Water Matters

Runoff Management—Residents can visit the City's Web site to view the Urban Runoff Management Plan. The Plan details the City's action to protect and improve water quality of the lakes, rivers, and creeks in the region, and achieve compliance with the State Municipal Storm Water Permit.

The Urban Runoff Management Plan has been posted to allow public access and

 understanding of the overall efforts of the City Manager's office to improve water quality in the City of Desert Park. Implementing the plan is one of the six objectives of the City's Storm Water Pollution Prevention Program to help improve water quality.

The City Council approved the plan last January, and is effective through February of 2006. At the City's Web site, click on "City Services," and choose "Storm Water Pollution Prevention." See the EPA Watershed site.

Drinking Water—Regulations from the State Public Health Services Drinking Water Program and the Environmental Protection Agency (EPA) require all community water systems to deliver an annual Consumer Confidence Report (water quality report) to customers. The City of Desert Park Water Bureau began sending this information to all postal customers in 1996, before these regulations went into effect in 1999.

The most interesting information for most consumers is this: our drinking water supply

 continues to meet all state and federal regulations, without exception. This report includes other information of interest to many consumers: water quality test results; definitions; information on our sources of water supply; how to reduce exposure to lead in drinking water; and special notice for immuno-compromised persons. Copies of the report may also be ordered in Braille by calling the City Manager's office at 626-555-1234.

4B_Water_Matters_Firstname_Lastname

In Activities 4.11 through 4.15 you will edit a document that deals with water issues in the City of Desert Park. You will add links to text and graphics and then save the document as a Web page. Your completed document will look similar to Figure 4.24. You will save your document as *4B_Water_Matters_Firstname_Lastname.*

Figure 4.24
Project 4B—Water Matters

Objective 5
Insert Hyperlinks

Cities, businesses, and other organizations are publishing their important documents on the Web with increasing frequency. Web pages are easy to create using Microsoft Word features that enable the creation of Web pages directly from word processing documents. One of the strengths of using Web pages is that hyperlinks can be added to take the user to related sites quickly and easily. **Hyperlinks** are text or graphics that you click to move to a file, another page in a Web site, or a page in a different Web site.

You can create a Web page in Word, add text, graphics, and hyperlinks, and then preview the document in a Web browser to see how it looks. You can adjust the page to your satisfaction and then save the document as a Web page.

Activity 4.11 Inserting Text Hyperlinks

The type of hyperlink used most frequently is one that is attached to text. Text hyperlinks usually appear underlined and in blue.

1 On the Standard toolbar, click the **Open** button [icon]. Navigate to the location where the student files for this textbook are stored. Locate **w04B_Water_Matters** and click once to select it. Then, in the lower right corner of the **Open** dialog box, click **Open**.

The w04B_Water_Matters file opens.

2 From the **File** menu, click **Save As**. In the **Save As** dialog box, click the **Save in arrow** and navigate to the location in which you are storing your files for this chapter.

3 Type **4B_Water_Matters_Firstname_Lastname** in the **File name** box, using your own name, and click **Save**.

The document is saved with a new name.

4 On the Standard toolbar, click the **Show/Hide ¶** button [¶], if necessary, to display the nonprinting characters. On the Standard toolbar, click the Zoom button arrow [100% ▾], and then click Page Width.

5 Position the insertion point at the end of the paragraph beginning *The City Council approved*. Press [Spacebar] once and then type **See the EPA Watershed site.** In the sentence you just typed, select *EPA Watershed*.

6 From the **Insert** menu, click **Hyperlink**. Alternatively, right-click on the selected text and click Hyperlink from the shortcut menu or click the Insert Hyperlink 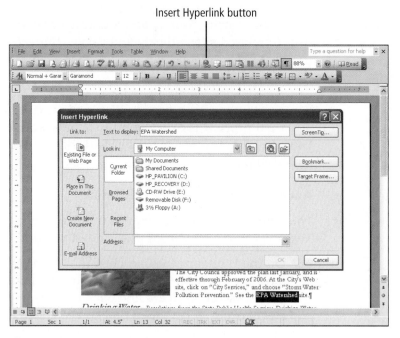 button on the Standard toolbar.

The Insert Hyperlink dialog box displays, as shown in Figure 4.25.

Insert Hyperlink button

Figure 4.25

7 Under **Link to**, click **Existing File or Web Page**. In the **Address** box, type **http://cfpub.epa.gov/surf/locate/map2.cfm** If another address displays while you are typing, ignore it and continue typing.

An address may display in the Address box as you type. This is AutoComplete at work. It displays the most recently used Web address for your computer.

8 On the upper-right corner of the **Insert Hyperlink** dialog box, click **ScreenTip**.

The Set Hyperlink ScreenTip dialog box displays.

9 In the **Set Hyperlink ScreenTip** dialog box, type **Watershed Map**

This is the ScreenTip that will display when the pointer is placed over the hyperlink. See Figure 4.26.

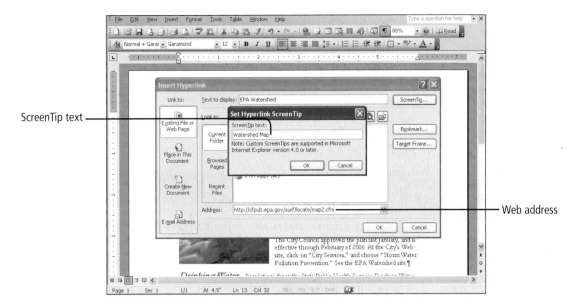

ScreenTip text

Web address

Figure 4.26

10 On the **Set Hyperlink ScreenTip** dialog box, click **OK**. At the bottom of the **Insert Hyperlink** dialog box, click **OK**.

The hyperlink is recorded, and the selected text changes to blue and is underlined.

11 In the next paragraph, in the second line, select *Environmental Protection Agency (EPA)*. Repeat Steps 6 through 10 to create a hyperlink, but type **http://www.epa.gov** for the address and **EPA Home Page** for the ScreenTip.

The hyperlink is recorded, and the selected text changes to blue and is underlined, as shown in Figure 4.27.

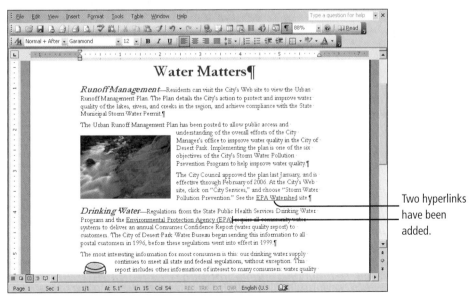

Two hyperlinks have been added.

Figure 4.27

12 On the Standard toolbar, click the **Save** button.

Activity 4.12 Adding a Hyperlink to a Graphic

When you move your pointer over a graphic on a Web page, and the pointer changes to a hand, it means a hyperlink has been added to the graphic. When you move your pointer over a hyperlink in a Word document, a ScreenTip displays with instructions for accessing the link.

1 Scroll to the bottom of the document.

2 Click the water cooler picture to select it.

3 From the **Insert** menu, click **Hyperlink**.

The Insert Hyperlink dialog box displays.

4 Under **Link to**, make sure **Existing File or Web Page** is selected. In the **Address** box, type **http://www.epa.gov**

5 On the upper-right corner of the **Insert Hyperlink** dialog box, click **ScreenTip**.

The Set Hyperlink ScreenTip dialog box displays.

6 In the **Set Hyperlink ScreenTip** dialog box, type **Drinking Water Standards**

Compare your dialog box with Figure 4.28.

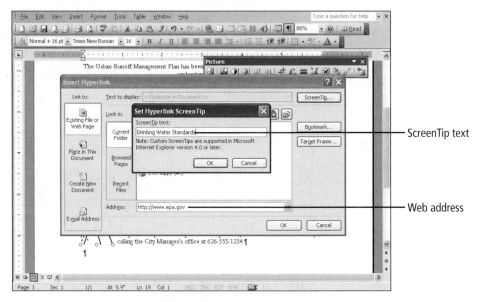

Figure 4.28

7 On the **Set Hyperlink ScreenTip** dialog box, click **OK**. At the bottom of the **Insert Hyperlink** dialog box, click **OK**.

The hyperlink is recorded, but there is no visual indication that the link has been added.

8 Move the pointer over the water cooler graphic.

The ScreenTip that you typed displays, as shown in Figure 4.29.

ScreenTip ——

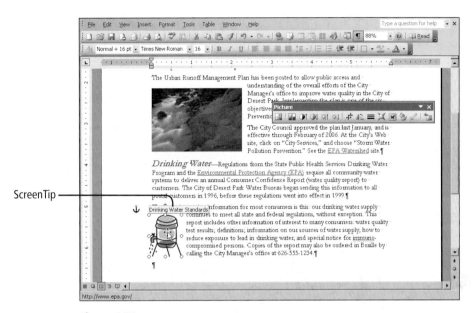

Figure 4.29

9 On the Standard toolbar, click the **Save** button.

Activity 4.13 Modifying Hyperlinks

If you need to change a hyperlink, you will use a dialog box similar to the one you used to create it.

1 Move the pointer over the water cooler and right-click.

A shortcut menu displays.

2 From the shortcut menu, click **Edit Hyperlink**.

The Edit Hyperlink dialog box displays. Its components are similar to those of the Insert Hyperlink dialog box.

3 At the bottom of the **Edit Hyperlink** dialog box, in the **Address** box, add **safewater** to the end of the Internet address.

Compare your dialog box to Figure 4.30.

> **Note** — **If the Text Displays Automatically**
>
> When you begin typing the text in the text boxes of the Edit Hyperlink dialog box, the complete text may display after only a few letters. This results from someone else using the same computer to do this exercise before you. The text is completed only if the AutoComplete feature is turned on.

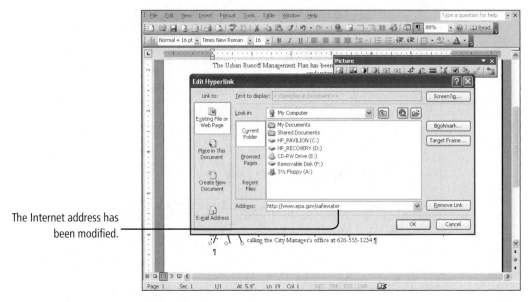

The Internet address has been modified.

Figure 4.30

4 At the bottom of the **Edit Hyperlink** dialog box, click **OK**.

The hyperlink address is changed.

5 From the **View** menu, click **Header and Footer**. On the Header and Footer toolbar, click the **Switch Between Header and Footer** button.

6 On the Header and Footer toolbar, click the **Insert AutoText** button Insert AutoText, and then click **Filename**.

The file name is inserted in the footer.

7 On the Header and Footer toolbar, click the **Close** button Close.

8 On the Standard toolbar, click the **Save** button.

9 On the Standard toolbar, click the **Print Preview** button. Take a moment to check your work. On the **Print Preview** toolbar, click the **Close Preview** button Close.

10 On the Standard toolbar, click the **Print** button.

Objective 6
Preview and Save a Document as a Web Page

After you have created a document to be used as a Web page, you can see what the page will look like when displayed in a **Web browser** such as Internet Explorer or Netscape. A Web browser is software that enables you to use the Web and navigate from page to page and site to site. You can adjust the image and preview it until you get it exactly right. Once you are satisfied with the way the document looks when displayed in a Web browser, you can save the document as a Web page.

Activity 4.14 Previewing a Document as a Web Page

1 From the **File** menu, click **Web Page Preview**.

Your Web browser opens, and your document displays as a Web page. Your screen may look different, depending on your screen size, screen resolution, and the Web browser you use.

2 Move your pointer over the *EPA Watershed* hyperlink.

The pointer changes to a hand, indicating that the text contains a link, as shown in Figure 4.31.

Document displayed in a Web browser

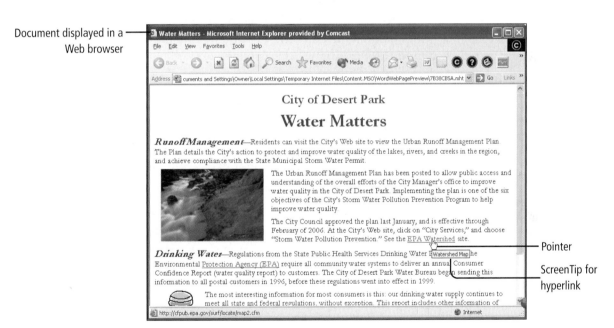

Pointer

ScreenTip for hyperlink

Figure 4.31

3 On the vertical scroll bar, click the down arrow to scroll down the page, if necessary.

On some high-resolution screens, you will not need to scroll down. Notice that the file name you placed in the footer does not display on the Web page.

4 Click the **water cooler image** to make sure your Web link works.

If you are connected to the Internet, you will see the *EPA Drinking Water* page.

If You Are Not Connected to the Internet

If you are not connected to the Internet, you will see a message box informing you that you are not connected, or the site could not be found. Click OK to acknowledge the message, and then resume with Step 6 of the instructions.

5 On the Browser title bar, click the **Close** button ☒. Make any changes that you feel are necessary and preview your Web page again.

6 On the Standard toolbar, click the **Save** button 🔲.

Activity 4.15 Saving a Document as a Web Page

Once you are satisfied with your document, you can save it as a Web page.

1 From the **File** menu, click **Save as Web Page**.

The Save As dialog box displays.

2 In the **Save in** dialog box, navigate to the location in which you are saving your files.

Notice in the File name box that the file extension has changed from .doc to .mht. This is the extension of a single Web page. If file extensions have been turned off on your computer, you will not see the extension. The Save as type box displays *Single File Web Page*, and the document title displays as the Page title.

3 Near the bottom of the **Save As** dialog box, click **Change Title**.

The Set Page Title dialog box displays. What you type here will become the Web page title; this is the title that displays in the browser title bar and shows up in the Web browser's history list.

4 Type **City of Desert Park Water Issues** See Figure 4.32.

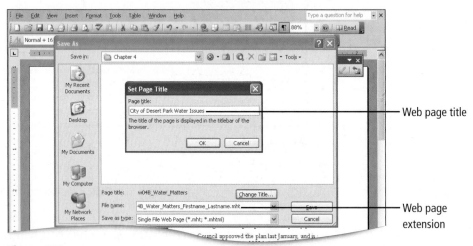

Figure 4.32

5 Click **OK** to close the **Set Page Title** dialog box.

In the Save as dialog box, the new title for your Web page displays as the Page title. Accept the default File name for the Web page. When you save it, the Web page will have a different file extension and file type icon to distinguish it from the Word document by the same name.

5 At the bottom of the **Save As** dialog box, click **Save**.

A dialog box displays stating that some of the elements in this page will not display properly on very early versions of Web browsers. See Figure 4.33.

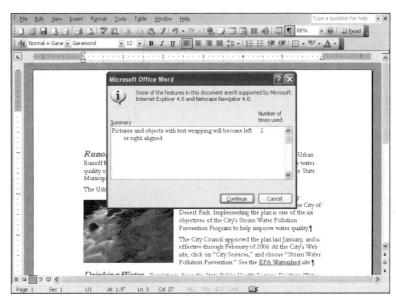

Figure 4.33

6 At the bottom of the dialog box, click **Continue**.

The file is saved and the document displays on your screen in the Web page format, with text across the full width of the screen—no margins, and both pictures displayed on the left side.

7 On the Standard toolbar, click the **Save** button 🔲. Close the document.

End You have completed Project 4B ————————————————

Project 4C Recreation Ideas

In Project 4B you practiced saving documents as Web pages. In Project 4C you will work with supporting information and objects.

In Activities 4.16 through 4.21, you will gather text and graphics that will be used in a Recreation Department newsletter. You will gather several documents and several pictures and then paste them from the Office Clipboard. You will use the **Thesaurus**—a language tool for finding alternative words with similar meanings—and then you will use special tools to browse a document. You will save your document as *4C_Recreation_Ideas_Firstname_Lastname*.

MEMO TO: Jane Romano

FROM: Ray Hamilton

DATE: March 5, 2005

SUBJECT: Ideas for the June Recreation Notes Newsletter

Here are some ideas for the June *Recreation Notes* newsletter, which should include the rough drafts of articles on Golf and Bicycling. I've also included some information on the history of each sport that you might be able to use for the *Did You Know?* boxes. Finally, I've added an image you might be able to use.

GOLF

Draft of article:
The Desert Park Fine Arts and Parks Department is hosting a golf clinic and nighttime golf benefit at the North Park Golf Course on Friday, August 21 to benefit the city's Youth Golf Program.
A PGA Tour Professional, recognized as one of the most accomplished golfers to play the game, will be at the North Park Golf Course to offer a free Golf Clinic. The clinic will run from 9 a.m. – 10:30 a.m. It's open to the public and there is no charge for admission. Come on out and learn some valuable tips from a pro!
Want to see how a pro applies those clinic techniques to an actual round of golf? As a follow-up to the clinic, our pro will join tournament guests in an exhibition round beginning at 12 noon. Plan to follow this foursome to see how they perform.
The nighttime event begins at 8 p.m. Pre-registration is required. The cost is $25 per person. Registration includes greens fees, glow balls, prizes, soft drinks, and pull carts. The tournament is a four-person scramble with a shotgun start at 8:15 p.m.
The tournament, which is played on the nine-hole course, is limited to the first 12 teams (48 players). The Youth Golf Program provides free golf lessons to youth at six of Desert Park's municipal golf courses. Funding makes it possible to provide year-round instruction, golf clubs, balls and other equipment for use during the classes. For more information, call 626-555-1131.
"The Golf Benefit is a fun and informal way to support hundreds of young people in Desert Park and the surrounding county," said Fred Stein, president of the Youth Golf Program Foundation. "The golf clinic is a great opportunity for children to learn about the game and be exposed to business leaders who can have an influence on their lives."
Last year the Youth Golf Program Foundation helped 145 young men and women learn to play the value of good sportspersonship. The organization is a non-profit organization that provides golf events through structured, school-based golf programs.

Information for Did You Know? boxes:
Some historians believe that golf originated in the Netherlands (the Dutch word *kolf* had a game played with a bent stick and a ball made of feathers that may have been It has been fairly well established, however, that the game that is known today was a the 14th or 15th century.

Image:

4C_Recreation_Ideas_Firstname_Lastname

BICYCLING

Draft of article:
The "Golden Age" of bicycling occurred during the development of Desert Park many years ago. Early photographs show street scenes with bicycles, horses, trolleys, and pedestrians. In fact, our first streets were arranged for these users. But Desert Park was ahead of its time, because this development pattern is actually an essential element of a livable community.
Desert Park is a city in which people can get around without cars, and the City hopes to make this a place where it is easier to ride a bicycle than to drive a car. Ideally, bicyclists should be able to circulate along city streets freely and safely. At the bicyclist's destination there should be safe, free, and accessible parking.
The City is working on a plan that identifies a network of bikeways that will connect bicycle riders to their destinations. The enhancements to the Agave Trail are an important part of this plan. The plan includes a list of other projects and programs, similar to the Agave Trail program, to be added to the Transportation Improvement Plan.

Information for Did You Know? boxes:
The bicycle was not invented by any one person. Rather, it is an outgrowth of ideas and inventions dating to the late 18th century. Some people claim the bicycle's history goes back even further, citing certain drawings by Leonardo da Vinci of a two-wheeled vehicle.
Image:

4C_Recreation_Ideas_Firstname_Lastname

Figure 4.34
Project 4C—Recreation Ideas

Objective 7
Locate Supporting Information

When you are writing, you may want to refer to information related to your topic. This **supporting information** could be located in other documents or on the Web. As you collect information for a new document, you can store all of the pieces (text and pictures) on the Office Clipboard. When you have all of the information pieces gathered, you can go to your document and paste the information one piece at a time. This feature is called **collect and paste**.

Word has a Thesaurus tool that enables you to find exactly the right word. Also, a special button can be used to quickly locate various elements in a document. For example, you can navigate through a document by moving from one section to the next or from one image to the next. It is recommended that you do these activities on a computer with an Internet connection. You will not be able to complete Activity 4.18 without a connection.

Activity 4.16 Using Collect and Paste to Gather Images

Recall that the Office Clipboard is a temporary storage area maintained by your Windows operating system. When you perform the Copy command or the Cut command, the text that you select is placed on the Clipboard. From this Clipboard storage area, you can paste text into another location of your document, into another document, or into another Office program.

You can copy and then paste a single selection of text without displaying the Clipboard task pane. Displaying the Clipboard is essential, however, if you want to collect a group of selected text pieces or images and then paste them. The Clipboard can hold up to 24 items, and the Clipboard task pane displays a short representation of each item.

1 On the Standard toolbar, click the **Open** button. Locate and open the **w04C_Recreation_Ideas** file.

2 From the **File** menu, click **Save As**. Navigate to the location where you are storing your files for this chapter. In the **File name** box, type **4C_Recreation_Ideas_Firstname_Lastname** and click **Save**.

The document is saved with a new name. Be sure you substitute your name where indicated.

3 From the **Edit** menu, click **Office Clipboard**.

The Clipboard task pane displays, as shown in Figure 4.35.

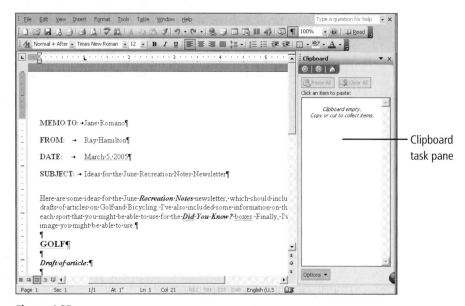

Clipboard task pane

Figure 4.35

Another Way — **Other Ways to Display the Clipboard Task Pane**

There are two other ways to display the Clipboard task pane:

- If a different task pane is displayed, click the Other Task Panes arrow and then click Clipboard.

- Select the first piece of text that you want to copy, hold down Ctrl, and then quickly press C two times.

4 If the Office Clipboard displays any entries, from the top of the Clipboard task pane, click the **Clear All** button. From the **Insert** menu, point to **Picture** and then click **Clip Art**.

The Clip Art task pane replaces the Clipboard task pane.

5 In the **Search for box**, type golf Click the **Search in arrow** and then select **Everywhere**. Click the **Results should be arrow**, be sure the **Clip Art** check box is selected, and then clear the other check boxes. Click **Go** twice.

6 In the **Clip Art** task pane, move the pointer over the image of a woman golfer.

If the image shown in Figure 4.36 is not available, choose another golf picture.

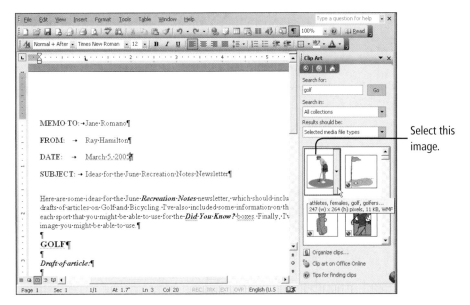

Select this image.

Figure 4.36

> ## Note — Inserting Clip Art Images from Your Student Files
>
> If you do not have an Internet connection, and if you have a minimum Office installation, you may not have any images of golf available. Both images used for this activity have been included with the files for this chapter. To access those files, from the bottom of the Clip Art task pane, click *Organize clips*. In the Favorites-Microsoft Clip Organizer dialog box, display the File menu, point to Add Clips to Organizer, and then click On My Own. Use the Look in arrow to navigate to the location of your student files and find *w04C_Golf*. Select it and then, in the lower right corner of the dialog box, click Add. When the image displays in the dialog box, move the pointer over the arrow on the right side of the image and then click Copy. Close the dialog box. When prompted, click the Yes button to copy the image to the Office Clipboard. Continue with Activity 4.16.

7 On the image of the woman golfer, click the arrow and then click **Copy**.

The image is copied to the Clipboard.

8 In the title bar of the **Clip Art** task pane, click the **Other Task Panes arrow**. From the task pane menu, click **Clipboard**.

The image you selected displays in the Clipboard task pane. When copying clip art, you need to redisplay the Clipboard after you copy an image; otherwise, the next image you copy will replace the current image.

9 In the title bar of the **Clipboard** task pane, click the **Other Task Panes arrow**. From the task pane menu, click **Clip Art**.

10 In the **Search for** box, type **cycling** and then click **Go**.

11 In the **Clip Art** task pane, move the pointer over the image of a cyclist on a trail.

If the image shown in Figure 4.37 is not available, choose another similar picture, or read the Note box for directions on how to find w04C_Cycling from your student files.

⌨12 On the image of the cyclist, click the arrow and then click **Copy**.

The image is transferred to the Clipboard.

⌨13 In the title bar of the **Clip Art** task pane, click the **Other Task Panes arrow**. From the task pane menu, click **Clipboard**.

Both images are displayed in the Clipboard task pane, with the most recently copied image on top. See Figure 4.37.

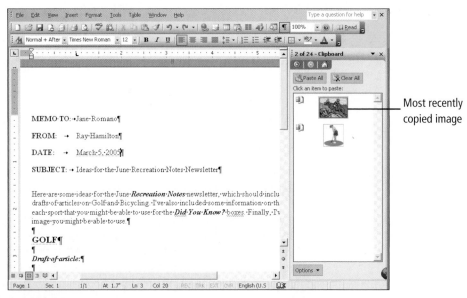

Most recently copied image

Figure 4.37

Activity 4.17 Collecting Information from Other Documents

If you need information from another document, you can open the source document, copy the text you need onto the Clipboard, and then paste it into your document later.

⌨1 Be sure **4C_Recreation_Ideas** is still displayed on your screen, and the Clipboard task pane displays the two images you have copied.

On the Standard toolbar, click the **Open** button 📂. Locate and open the **w04C_Golf** file.

⌨2 In the **w04C_Golf** file, hold down ⌈Ctrl⌉ and press ⌈A⌉.

All the text is selected.

⌨3 On the Standard toolbar, click the **Copy** button 📄.

The text is copied to the Clipboard, along with the two images.

⌨4 On the Standard toolbar, click the **Open** button 📂. Locate and open the **w04C_Bicycle** file.

⑤ In the **w04C_Bicycle** file, hold down Ctrl and press A to select the document.

⑥ On the Standard toolbar, click the **Copy** button 🔲.

The text is copied to the Clipboard along with the *Golf* text and the two images.

⑦ In the upper right corner of your screen, to the right of the *Type a question for help* box, click the **Close Window** button ⊠ to close the **w04C_Bicycle** file.

⑧ Click the Close Window button ⊠ to close the **w04C_Golf** file.

Compare your clipboard to Figure 4.38. Notice that as new items are copied to the Office Clipboard, the most recent item moves to the top of the list.

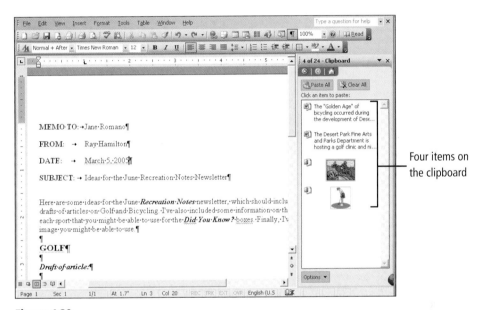

Four items on the clipboard

Figure 4.38

Activity 4.18 Finding Supporting Information Using the Research Tool

Word includes a research tool that enables you to search for information on a variety of topics. You will need an Internet connection to complete this activity.

① On the Standard toolbar, click the **Research** button 🔲.

The Research task pane displays.

② In the **Search for** box, type **Golf**

3 Under the **Search for** box, in the second box, click the arrow, and then click **Encarta Encyclopedia**.

Your screen may indicate only *Encyclopedia* or it may display the language and version of the active encyclopedia. A list of golf topics displays. See Figure 4.39.

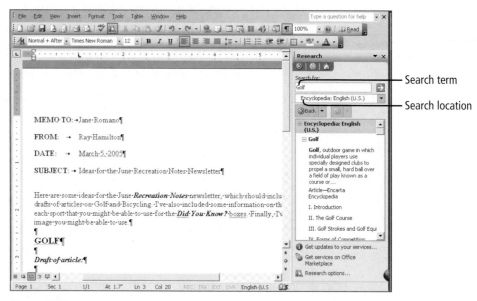

Figure 4.39

4 In the **Research** task pane list of topics, click **History**.

You may have to scroll down the list of topics. The program moves to the *MSN Learning & Research* site on the Web. The History section, which is in the middle of the document, displays at the top of the screen.

5 Move the pointer to the left of the top paragraph that begins *Some historians believe*. Drag to the end of the second sentence, which ends *the 14th or 15th century*.

Be sure you have only the two sentences selected. Your screen should look similar to Figure 4.40. Because the information on Web sites changes often, the information on your screen may look slightly different.

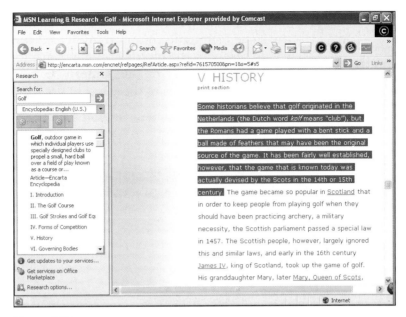

Figure 4.40

More Knowledge — Being Careful of Copyright Issues

Nearly everything you find on the Web is protected by copyright law, which protects authors of original works, including text, art, photographs, and music. If you want to use text or graphics that you find online, you will need to get permission. One of the exceptions to this law is the use of small amounts of information for educational purposes, which falls under Fair Use guidelines.

Copyright laws in the United States are open to different interpretations, and copyright laws can be very different in other countries. As a general rule, if you want to use someone else's material, always get permission first.

6 From the **Edit** menu, click **Copy**. Alternatively, right-click the selected text and from the shortcut menu click Copy.

The text is added to the Clipboard.

7 Close the *MSN Learning & Research* window.

8 In the title bar of the **Research** task pane, click the **Other Task Panes arrow**. From the task pane menu, click **Clipboard**.

The text you copied displays in the Clipboard task pane.

9 Click the **Other Task Panes arrow** again and click **Research**. Use the same technique you used in Steps 2 through 7 for researching golf to research the **bicycle** You may have to scroll down the topics area to find **History of the Modern Bicycle**. Select and copy the first three sentences of the **History** area.

You should have six items in your Clipboard task pane, as shown in Figure 4.41.

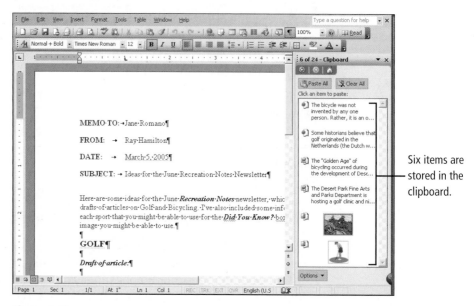

Six items are stored in the clipboard.

Figure 4.41

Activity 4.19 Pasting Information from the Clipboard Task Pane

Once you have collected text and images from other documents or sources, such as the Internet, you can paste them into your document.

1 With **4C_Recreation_Ideas_Firstname_Lastname** open, in the blank line under the **GOLF** *Draft of article*, click to position the insertion point.

2 On the Clipboard task pane, under **Click an item to paste**, click the fourth item in the item list, the one that begins *The Desert Park Fine Arts*.

The text is pasted into the document at the insertion point location, as shown in Figure 4.42.

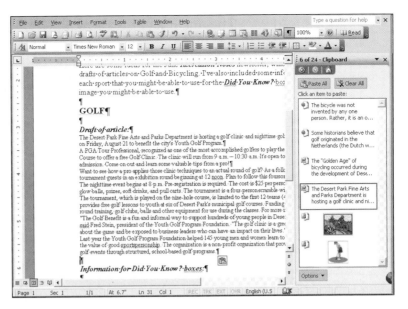

Figure 4.42

3 Position the insertion point in the blank line under the **GOLF** *Information for Did You Know? boxes*. From the **Click an item to paste** on the **Clipboard** task pane, click the second item in the item list, the one that begins *Some historians believe.*

The text is placed at the insertion point.

4 Position the insertion point in the blank line under the **GOLF** *Image*. From the **Click an item to paste** on the **Clipboard** task pane, click the sixth item in the item list, the graphic of the golfer.

The image is placed at the insertion point, as shown in Figure 4.43.

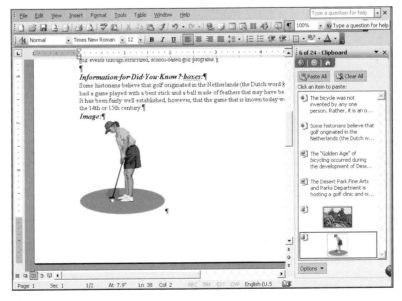

Figure 4.43

5 In the blank line under the BICYCLING Draft of article, click to position the insertion point. On the Clipboard task pane, under Click an item to paste, click the third item in the item list, the one that begins The "Golden Age" of bicycling. The text is pasted into the document at the insertion point location.

6 Position the insertion point in the blank line under the **BICYCLE** *Information for Did You Know? boxes.* From the **Click an item to paste** on the **Clipboard** task pane, click the text that begins *The bicycle was not invented.*

Compare your document to Figure 4.44.

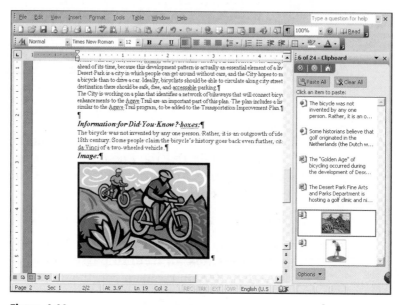

Figure 4.44

7 Position the insertion point in the blank line under the **Bicycling** *Image.* From the **Click an item to paste** on the **Clipboard** task pane, click the fifth item in the item list, the graphic of the bicyclists.

8 Under **Click an item to paste** on the **Clipboard** task pane, move the pointer over the first item in the list. Click the arrow.

9 From the menu, click **Delete**.

The item is removed from the list. You can remove one item from the Clipboard without disturbing the rest of the items stored there.

10 At the top of the **Clipboard** task pane, click **Clear All**.

All of the items are removed from the list.

11 In the title bar of the **Clipboard** task pane, click the Close button [X].

The Clipboard task pane closes.

12 On the Standard toolbar, click the **Save** button [💾].

Activity 4.20 Using the Thesaurus

The *thesaurus* is a language tool that assists in your writing by suggesting synonyms (words that have the same meaning) for words that you select.

1 From the **Edit** menu, click **Find**.

The Find and Replace dialog box displays.

2 In the **Find and Replace** dialog box, in the **Find what** box, type **training** and click **Find next**.

The word *training* in the Golf section is highlighted.

3 In the **Find and Replace** dialog box, click **Cancel**.

4 Right-click the selected word. From the shortcut menu, point to **Synonyms**.

A list of synonyms displays, as shown in Figure 4.45.

Selected word

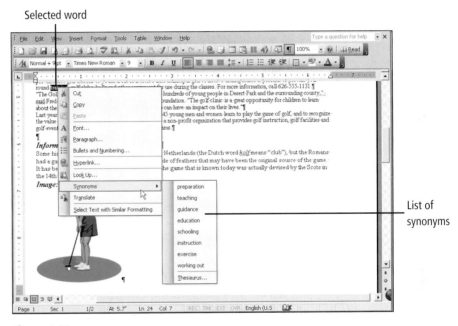

List of synonyms

Figure 4.45

5 In the list of synonyms, click **instruction**.

Instruction replaces *training* in the document.

6 From the **Edit** menu, click **Find**. In the **Find and Replace** dialog box, in the **Find what** box, type **impact** and click **Find next**.

The word *impact* in the Golf section is highlighted.

7 In the **Find and Replace** dialog box, click **Cancel** to close the dialog box.

8 Right-click the selected word. From the shortcut menu, point to **Synonyms**.

A list of synonyms displays. Sometimes the best word is not included in the list of synonyms.

9 At the bottom of the synonym list, click **Thesaurus**.

The Research task pane displays and lists words from the English Thesaurus. Notice that there are more options available. See Figure 4.46.

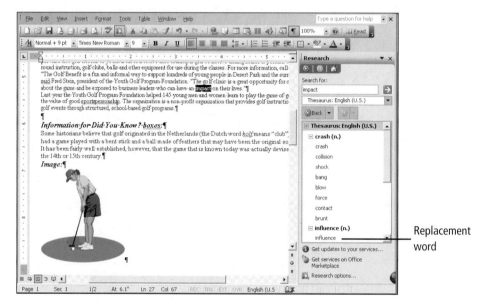

Figure 4.46

10 In the **Research** task pane, point to *influence*, click the down arrow on the right side of the word, and then, from the displayed list, click **Insert**.

Influence replaces *impact* in the document.

11 In the title bar of the **Research** task pane, click the **Close** button ☒.

On the Standard toolbar, click the **Save** button 🖫.

Objective 8
Find Objects with the Select Browse Object Button

The Select Browse Object button is located at the bottom of the vertical scroll bar and can be used to navigate through a document by type of object. For example, you can move from one footnote to the next or from one section to the next. This feature can be used on short documents but is most effective when you are navigating long documents. You can navigate using several different object elements, by graphic, table, section, footnote, or page.

Activity 4.21 Using the Select Browse Object Menu to Find Document Elements

1 With the **4C_Recreation_Ideas_Firstname_Lastname** open, at the bottom of the vertical scroll bar, click the **Select Browse Object** button.

The Select Browse Object palette displays, as shown in Figure 4.47. The order of the buttons in the Select Browse Object palette on your computer may be different from what is shown in the figure. Examine the Object buttons on the palette and compare them to the ones shown in the table in Figure 4.48 to identify each button and its purpose.

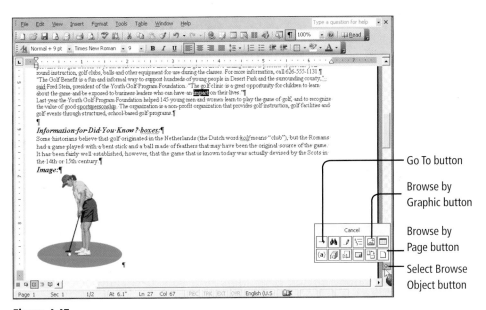

Go To button

Browse by Graphic button

Browse by Page button

Select Browse Object button

Figure 4.47

Buttons on the Select Browse Object Palette

ScreenTip	Button	Description
Browse by Field	{a}	Moves between objects in your document that have been defined as fields.
Browse by Endnote		Moves from one endnote to the next.
Browse by Footnote		Moves from one footnote to the next.
Browse by Comment		Moves between comments that have been inserted in your document.
Browse by Section		Moves from one section to the next.
Browse by Page		Moves by page in your document. This is the most common way to browse a document and is the default setting for the Select Browse Object button.
Go To	→	Moves to the next occurrence of an object as defined in the Go To page of the Find and Replace dialog box.
Find		Moves to the next word or phrase that has been entered in the Find and Replace dialog box.
Browse by Edits		Moves between Edits that have been made to your document using the Track Changes command.
Browse by Heading		Moves between Heading styles that have been applied to a document.
Browse by Graphic		Moves between graphic objects that have been inserted in your document.
Browse by Table		Moves between tables in your document.

Figure 4.48

2 On the **Select Browse Object** palette, click the **Browse by Page** button ▢.

The insertion point moves to the top of the second page.

3 Click the **Select Browse Object** button ⊙ again. On the **Select Browse Object** palette, click the **Go To** button →.

The Find and Replace dialog box displays. Notice that the Go To tab at the top of the Find and Replace dialog box is selected. This page of the dialog box enables you to go to a specific page, or navigate by various objects.

4 In the **Find and Replace** dialog box, under **Go to what**, scroll to the top of the list and click **Page**.

5 Under **Enter page number**, type **1**

Compare your Find and Replace dialog box to Figure 4.49.

Go To tab

Page number

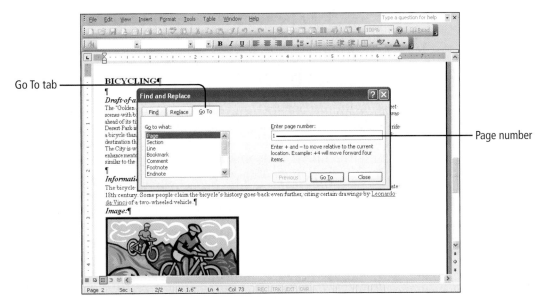

Figure 4.49

6 In the **Find and Replace** dialog box, click **Go To**.

The insertion point moves to the top of the first page of the document.

7 Close the **Find and Replace** dialog box. Click the **Select Browse Object** button. In the **Select Browse Object** palette, click the **Browse by Graphic** button.

The insertion point moves to the graphic of the golfer. The arrow buttons above and below the Select Browse Object button can be used to navigate to the next or previous object location. These buttons take on the name of the type of object that has been set with the Select Browse Object button.

8 Click the **Next Graphic arrow** below the **Select Browse Object** button.

The insertion point moves to the graphic of the bicyclists.

9 Click the **Select Browse Object** button ⊙. In the **Select Browse Object** palette, click the **Browse by Page** button ⬜.

This returns the Select Browse Object button to the Browse by Page function, which is the most common method for browsing a document. The Select Browse Object button retains the method of browsing that was last selected.

10 From the **View** menu, click **Header and Footer**. On the Header and Footer toolbar, click the **Switch Between Header and Footer** button ⬚.

11 On the Header and Footer toolbar, click the **Insert AutoText** button Insert AutoText ▾, and then click **Filename**.

The file name is inserted in the footer.

12 On the Header and Footer toolbar, click the **Close** button Close.

13 From the Standard toolbar, click the **Save** button 🖫.

14 On the Standard toolbar, click the **Print Preview** button 🔍. Take a moment to check your work. On the Print Preveiw toolbar, click the **Close Preview** button Close.

15 On the Standard toolbar, click the **Print** button 🖨. Close the document saving any changes.

End You have completed Project 4C ────────────────────────

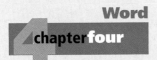

Summary

Microsoft Word includes many features that can be used to create a newsletter or a Web page, similar to those created by desktop publishing or Web design programs. In this chapter, you created a masthead by changing text into a graphic element with the WordArt program, added borders and shading to paragraphs for special effect, and used special character formats to create more distinctive headings. You learned how to change from a single- to a multiple-column document and to control where a column ends. You practiced adding hyperlinks to a Word document and saving it as a Web page.

Finally, you practiced gathering information from several resources to create a new document. This collect-and-paste process can involve using the Office Clipboard, the Microsoft Research tools to find supporting information, and such common but helpful tools as a thesaurus. The Select Browse Object button was introduced as a tool to help navigate within a document.

In This Chapter You Practiced How To

- Create a Decorative Title
- Create Multicolumn Documents
- Add Special Paragraph Formatting
- Use Special Character Formats
- Insert Hyperlinks
- Preview and Save a Document as a Web Page
- Locate Supporting Information
- Find Objects with the Select Browse Object Button

Matching   Match each term in the second column with its correct definition in the first column by writing the letter of the term on the blank line in front of the correct definition.

_____ **1.** A Microsoft Office subprogram used to change text into a decorative graphic.

_____ **2.** Text or graphic that you can click to move to a file, another page in a Web site, or a different Web site.

_____ **3.** Laws that protect authors of original works, including text, art, photographs, and music.

_____ **4.** The place where copied items are stored temporarily until they are pasted in another location.

_____ **5.** The alignment used, especially in columns of text, to create a flush edge of text on both the left and right side of a column.

_____ **6.** A button on the Standard toolbar that connects you to a group of resources for exploring information.

_____ **7.** A special font effect where the lower-case letters are changed to capital letters but remain the height of lowercase letters.

_____ **8.** The process of gathering various pieces of information together on the Office Clipboard for use in another document.

_____ **9.** A dialog box used to add special formats to a paragraph so it stands out from the rest of the text.

_____ **10.** A document that has been saved with a .mht extension so it can be viewed with a Web browser.

_____ **11.** A dialog box used to change the appearance of a WordArt graphic.

_____ **12.** The type of section break used when you want columns to end at approximately the same place on the page.

_____ **13.** A dialog box used to create a Hyperlink.

_____ **14.** An option used to expand a clip art search to include all possible locations.

_____ **15.** A Word window that provides commonly used commands; useful for searching for clip art, researching information, or collecting items on the clipboard.

A Borders and Shading

B Collect and Paste

C Continuous

D Copyright

E Everywhere

F Format WordArt

G Hyperlink

H Insert Hyperlink

I Justified

J Office Clipboard

K Research

L Small caps

M Task pane

N Web page

O WordArt

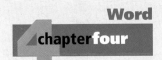
Fill in the Blank Write the correct answer in the space provided.

1. Netscape and Internet Explorer are examples of _____ _____.

2. To change the font size and style of a WordArt graphic, use the _____ _____ dialog box.

3. The title in a newsletter is known as a _____.

4. Microsoft Publisher is a _____ _____ program.

5. The Office Clipboard can store up to _____ items.

6. To artificially end a column and move the rest of the text in that column to the top of the next column, you can insert a _____ _____.

7. When you change from a two-column format to a one-column format, Word inserts a _____ _____.

8. To change one column of text into two columns, use the _____ button on the Standard toolbar.

9. To move in a document from one section to the next, or from one graphic to the next, use the _____ button.

10. If you want to substitute one word for another and need to look up a synonym, use the Word language tool called a _____.

Project 4D — Council News

Objectives: *Create a Decorative Title, Create Multicolumn Documents, Add Special Paragraph Formatting, Use Special Character Formats, and Find Objects with the Select Browse Object Button.*

In the following Skill Assessment, you will create a newsletter for the Desert Park City Council. Your completed document will look similar to Figure 4.50. You will save your publication as *4D_Council_News_Firstname_Lastname.*

Figure 4.50

1. On the Standard toolbar, click the **Open** button and then navigate to the location where the student files for this textbook are stored. Locate **w04D_Council_News** and click once to select it. Then, in the lower right corner of the **Open** dialog box, click **Open**.

2. From the **File** menu, click **Save As**. In the **Save As** dialog box, click the **Save in arrow** and then navigate to the location in which you are storing your files for this chapter. In the **File name** box type **4D_Council_News_Firstname_Lastname** and click **Save**.

(Project 4D–Council News continues on the next page)

(Project 4D–Council News continued)

3. Be sure that the nonprinting formatting marks are displayed and then be sure the insertion point is at the top of the document, to the left of the empty paragraph mark. From the **Insert** menu, point to **Picture** and then click **WordArt**. In the **WordArt Gallery** dialog box, in the first row, click the fourth style and then click **OK**.

4. In the **Edit WordArt Text** dialog box type **City Council News** and then change the **Size** box to **66** Click **OK**.

5. Click the WordArt graphic to select it, if necessary. On the floating WordArt toolbar, click the **Format WordArt** button. In the **Format WordArt** dialog box, under **Fill**, click the **Color arrow**. On the displayed color palette, in the second row, click the first color—**Dark Red**. Under **Line**, click the **Color arrow**, click **Dark Red**, and then click **OK**. Alternatively, under Line, click the Color arrow, click No Line, and then click OK. The letters will appear slightly narrower. The color of the WordArt graphic is changed. On the Standard toolbar, click the **Save** button.

6. On the line below your inserted WordArt, click to the left of *City Council Workshop Planned* and press Enter. Notice that when the WordArt is deselected, the WordArt toolbar is closed. Move the insertion point to the left of the empty line you just created and type **News from Desert Park City Council** Select the text you just typed, on the Formatting toolbar click the **Center** button, and then click the arrow on the **Font Color** button. From the displayed palette, click **Dark Red**.

7. With the line you typed still selected, from the **Format** menu, click **Borders and Shading**. In the **Borders and Shading** dialog box, click the **Borders tab**. Under **Setting**, click **Custom**. Under **Style**, scroll down and click the option with a thick bottom line and a thin line above it (refer to Figure 4.50). Click the **Color arrow** and then click **Dark Red**. In the **Preview** area, click the **bottom line** in the preview graphic and then click **OK**. On the Standard toolbar, click **Save** to save the changes you have made.

8. Select the text *City Council Workshop Planned* and, from the **Format** menu, click **Font**. In the **Font** dialog box, change the number in the **Size** box to **18**. Click the **Font Color arrow** and click **Dark Red**. Under **Effects**, select the **Outline** and **Small caps** check boxes and then click **OK**. Scroll down to view the lower half of the document and then repeat this process to apply the same font format to the headline *New City Council Committees Announced*. Alternatively, apply the font format by using the Format Painter.

(Project 4D–Council News continues on the next page)

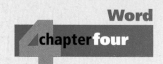

(Project 4D–Council News continued)

9. Scroll to view the upper portion of your document. Beginning with *Citizens are invited*, select the text between the two headlines. (Hint: Click to the left of *Citizens*, hold down Shift, and then click to the right of the period following *process*.) Do not include the paragraph mark at the end of the selected text. On the Standard toolbar, click the **Columns** button, drag to select **two columns**, and then release the left mouse button. The selected text is arranged into two columns, and section breaks are inserted before and after the selected text. Repeat this process to format the text under *New City Council*, beginning with *The Office of the City Clerk*, to a two-column format. On the Standard toolbar, click the **Save** button.

10. Place the insertion point to the left of *Aviation*. Type **New Council Committees:** and press Enter. Select the heading you just typed and the list of committees listed under it, including those in the second column, and then, on the Formatting toolbar, click the **Center** button.

11. Select *New Council Committees:* and, on the Formatting toolbar, click the **Font Color arrow** and then click **Dark Red**. Click the **Font Size arrow** and then click **14**. From the **Format** menu, display the **Borders and Shading** dialog box and click the **Borders tab**. Under **Style**, be sure the single line at the top of the style list is selected. Click the **Color arrow** and then click **Dark Red**. Click the **Width arrow** and then click **1 pt**. In the **Preview** area, click the **bottom line** and then click **OK**.

12. At the lower end of the vertical scroll bar, click the **Select Browse Object** button to display the menu. Point to the buttons until you locate the **Browse by Section** button and then click it. This sets the browse object so you can move from section to section and moves the insertion point to the next section. Point to the arrow below the Select Browse Object button; the ScreenTip displays *Next Section*. Point to the arrow above the Select Browse Object button; the ScreenTip displays Previous Section. Click the **Previous Section arrow**. The insertion point moves up the document to the previous section. Continue clicking the **Previous section arrow** until the insertion point is at the WordArt Graphic at the top of the document.

13. Click the **WordArt** graphic to select it and then, from the WordArt toolbar, click the **Format WordArt** button. In the **Format WordArt** dialog box, under **Line**, click the **Color arrow** and then click **black**—the first color in the first row. A graphic like WordArt has two parts—its surrounding line, and its interior fill. This action will change the surrounding line color to black. Click **OK**. Click in the body of the document to deselect the graphic.

(Project 4D–Council News continues on the next page)

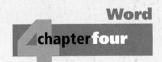
(Project 4D–Council News continued)

14. From the **View** menu, display the Header and Footer toolbar, switch to the footer, and then, on the Header and Footer toolbar, click **Insert AutoText**. From the displayed list, click **Filename**. Close the Header and Footer toolbar.

15. On the Standard toolbar, click the **Save** button and then click the **Print Preview** button to preview the document. Click the **Print** button. Close the Print Preview window and close the document, saving changes if prompted to do so.

 You have completed Project 4D ————————————

Project 4E — Public Safety

Objectives: *Insert Hyperlinks, Preview and Save a Document as a Web Page, and Locate Supporting Information.*

In the following Skill Assessment, you will create a Web page for the Desert Park Department of Public Safety. You will start with a file that contains the headings for the articles and then use the collect-and-paste technique to gather the necessary information for the article. You will add hyperlinks and save the document as a Web page. Your completed document will look similar to Figure 4.51. You will save your publication as *4E_Public_Safety_Firstname_Lastname.*

1. Be sure your computer is online and connected to the Internet. Start Word. On the Standard toolbar, click the **Open** button and navigate to the location where the student files for this textbook are stored. Locate **w04E_Public_Safety** and click once to select it. In the lower right corner of the **Open** dialog box, click **Open**.

2. From the **File** menu, click **Save As**. In the **Save As** dialog box, click the **Save in arrow** and navigate to the location in which you are storing your files for this chapter. In the **File name** box, type **4E_Public_Safety_Firstname_Lastname** and then click **Save**.

3. From the **Edit** menu, click **Office Clipboard**. If necessary, at the top of the Clipboard task pane, click the Clear All button to remove any items that display.

4. On the Standard toolbar, click the **Open** button. Locate and open the **w04E_Block_Clubs** file, and then press Ctrl + A to select all of the text. On the Standard toolbar, click the **Copy** button. The selected text is copied to the Office Clipboard. Close the w04E_Block_Clubs file.

5. Open and copy all of the text in the file **w04E_Fire**. Close the w04E_Fire file. The text is copied to the Clipboard.

(Project 4E–Public Safety continues on the next page)

(Project 4E–Public Safety continued)

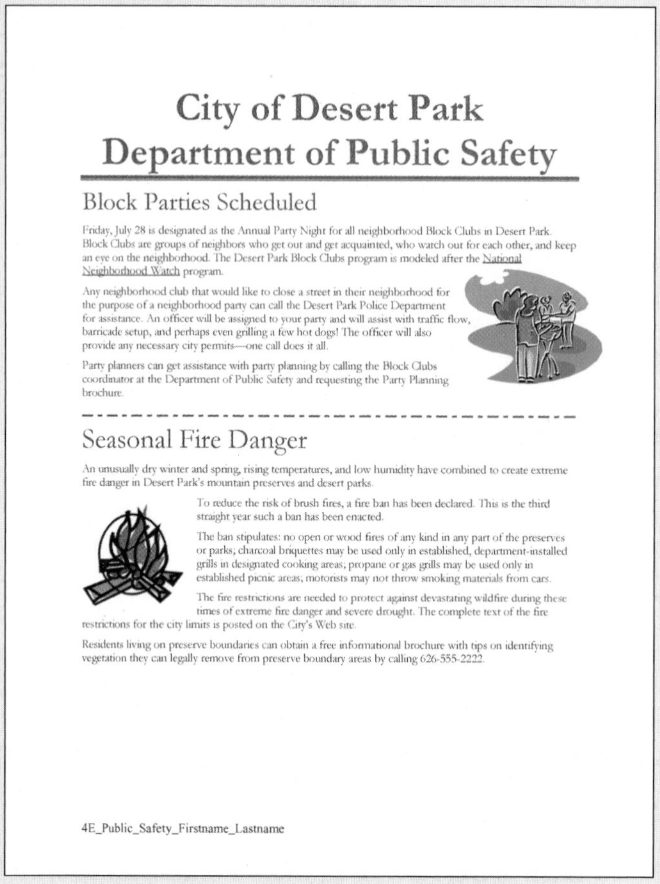

City of Desert Park
Department of Public Safety

Block Parties Scheduled

Friday, July 28 is designated as the Annual Party Night for all neighborhood Block Clubs in Desert Park. Block Clubs are groups of neighbors who get out and get acquainted, who watch out for each other, and keep an eye on the neighborhood. The Desert Park Block Clubs program is modeled after the National Neighborhood Watch program.

Any neighborhood club that would like to close a street in their neighborhood for the purpose of a neighborhood party can call the Desert Park Police Department for assistance. An officer will be assigned to your party and will assist with traffic flow, barricade setup, and perhaps even grilling a few hot dogs! The officer will also provide any necessary city permits—one call does it all.

Party planners can get assistance with party planning by calling the Block Clubs coordinator at the Department of Public Safety and requesting the Party Planning brochure.

Seasonal Fire Danger

An unusually dry winter and spring, rising temperatures, and low humidity have combined to create extreme fire danger in Desert Park's mountain preserves and desert parks.

To reduce the risk of brush fires, a fire ban has been declared. This is the third straight year such a ban has been enacted.

The ban stipulates: no open or wood fires of any kind in any part of the preserves or parks; charcoal briquettes may be used only in established, department-installed grills in designated cooking areas; propane or gas grills may be used only in established picnic areas; motorists may not throw smoking materials from cars.

The fire restrictions are needed to protect against devastating wildfire during these times of extreme fire danger and severe drought. The complete text of the fire restrictions for the city limits is posted on the City's Web site.

Residents living on preserve boundaries can obtain a free informational brochure with tips on identifying vegetation they can legally remove from preserve boundary areas by calling 626-555-2222.

4E_Public_Safety_Firstname_Lastname

Figure 4.51

6. From the **Insert** menu, point to **Picture** and then click **Clip Art**. In the **Clip Art** task pane, in the **Search for** box, type **BBQ** If the **Search in** box does not display *All Collections*, click the **Search in arrow** and select **Everywhere**. Click the **Results should be arrow**, be sure only **Clip Art** is selected, and then click the **Go** button. Scroll the list of available images and locate the one shown in Figure 4.51. (If you cannot locate that image, choose one that is similar; alternatively, use the w04E_BBQ image that is with the student files for this book.) Copy the image to the Office Clipboard as described in Activity 4.16, step 11. On the image of the BBQ, click the arrow and then click Copy from the displayed menu.

7. In the title bar of the **Clip Art** task pane, click the **Other Task Panes arrow** and then click **Clipboard**. The image you copied is displayed at the top of the clipboard. Recall that as you copy items to the Clipboard, the most recent item moves to the top of the list.

(Project 4E–Public Safety continues on the next page)

(Project 4E–Public Safety continued)

8. Place the insertion point to the left of the empty paragraph mark under *Block Parties Scheduled*. On the **Clipboard** task pane, click the block of text beginning with *Friday, July 28 is*. The text is pasted to the Public Safety document at the location of your insertion point.

9. Place the insertion point to the left of the empty paragraph mark under *Seasonal Fire Danger*. On the **Clipboard** task pane, click the block of text beginning with *An unusually dry winter*. The text is pasted to the Public Safety document. On the Standard toolbar, click the **Save** button.

10. In the Block Parties article, click to the left of the paragraph that begins *Any neighborhood club*. In the **Clipboard** task pane, click the **BBQ image** to insert it in the article. Click the inserted image to select it and, on the floating Picture toolbar, click the **Text Wrapping** button. From the displayed list, click **Tight**. Drag the image to the right, as shown in Figure 4.51, aligning the right sizing handles with the right margin and the top sizing handles at approximately **2.5 inches on the vertical ruler**. Do not be concerned if your text does not wrap exactly as shown in the figure. In the **Clipboard** task pane, click the **Clear All** button and then close the Clipboard task pane.

11. In the *Seasonal Fire* article, click to the left of the paragraph that begins *To reduce the risk*. From the **Insert** menu, point to **Picture** and then click **From File**. In the **Insert Picture** dialog box, navigate to the location where the student files for this textbook are stored and locate **w04E_No_Fire**. If you do not see the file, click the Files of type box arrow and then click All files from the displayed list. Click the file to select it and then click Insert.

12. Click the inserted image to select it and, on the floating Picture toolbar, click the **Text Wrapping** button. From the displayed list click **Square**. Compare your document to Figure 4.51.

13. Under the *Block Parties Scheduled* heading, at the end of the paragraph that begins *Friday, July 28*, select *National Neighborhood Watch* in the last sentence. (Hint: Double-click *National* to select it, hold down [Shift] and hold down [Ctrl], and then press [→] two times.) From the **Insert** menu click **Hyperlink**.

14. In the **Insert Hyperlink** dialog box, under **Link to**, click **Existing File or Web Page**. Under **Address**, type **http://www.nnwi.org/**

15. In the upper right corner of the **Insert Hyperlink** dialog box, click **ScreenTip**. In the **Set Hyperlink ScreenTip** dialog box, type **National Neighborhood Watch Institute** In the **Set Hyperlink ScreenTip** dialog box, click **OK**. At the bottom of the **Insert Hyperlink** dialog box, click **OK**. The hyperlink is recorded, and the selected text changes to blue and is underlined.

(Project 4E–Public Safety continues on the next page)

(Project 4E–Public Safety continued)

16. Right-click the **No Fire image** and then click **Hyperlink** from the shortcut menu. Repeat Steps 14 and 15, but type **http://www.smokey bear.com/** for the address and **Fire Safety Tips** for the ScreenTip.

17. From the **View** menu, display the Header and Footer toolbar, switch to the footer, and then, on the Header and Footer toolbar, click **Insert AutoText**. From the displayed list, click **Filename**. Close the Header and Footer toolbar. On the Standard toolbar, click the **Save** button.

18. From the **File** menu, click **Save as Web Page**. In the **Save As** dialog box, navigate to the location in which you are saving your files. In the lower portion of the **Save As** dialog box, click **Change Title**. The **Set Page Title** dialog box displays. Type **Public Safety** and then click **OK** to close the **Set Page Title** dialog box. In the lower right corner of the **Save As** dialog box, click **Save**. Click **Continue** to acknowledge the message box that displays. The Web page displays.

19. Point to the two hyperlinks you created to display the ScreenTips. Press Ctrl and click to go to the related Web site(s). Close the site(s) to return to your Web page.

20. On the Standard toolbar, click the **Print Preview** button. Take a moment to check your work. On the **Print Preview** toolbar, click the **Close Preview** button.

21. Click the **Print** button to print the Public Safety Web page and then close the document.

 You have completed Project 4E ———————————

Project 4F—IT Volunteers

Objectives: *Add Special Paragraph Formatting, Use Special Character Formats, Insert Hyperlinks, Locate Supporting Information, and Preview and Save a Document as a Web Page.*

In the following Skill Assessment, you will create a Web page notifying the citizens of Desert Park about an opportunity to volunteer their computer skills. Your completed document will look similar to Figure 4.52. You will save your publication as *4F_IT_Volunteer_Firstname_Lastname*.

1. On the Standard toolbar, click the **Open** button and navigate to the location where the student files for this textbook are stored. Locate **w04F_IT_Volunteer** and click once to select it. In the lower right corner of the **Open** dialog box, click **Open**.

2. From the **File** menu, click **Save As**. In the **Save As** dialog box, click the **Save in arrow** and navigate to the location in which you are storing your files for this chapter. In the **File name** box type **4F_IT_Volunteer_Firstname_Lastname** and click **Save**.

(Project 4F–IT Volunteers continues on the next page)

Skill Assessments (continued)

(Project 4F–IT Volunteers continued)

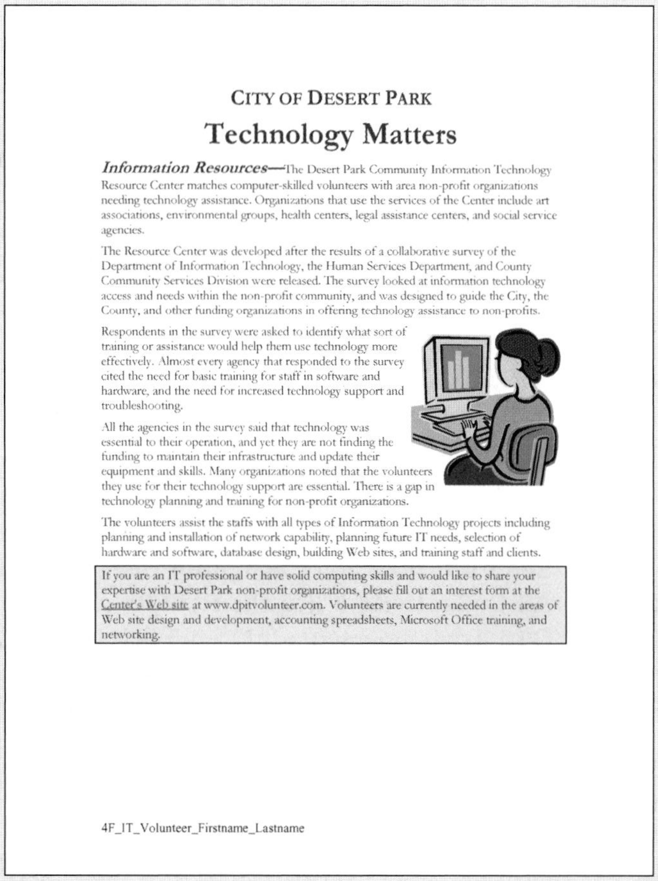
CITY OF DESERT PARK

Technology Matters

Information Resources—The Desert Park Community Information Technology Resource Center matches computer-skilled volunteers with area non-profit organizations needing technology assistance. Organizations that use the services of the Center include art associations, environmental groups, health centers, legal assistance centers, and social service agencies.

The Resource Center was developed after the results of a collaborative survey of the Department of Information Technology, the Human Services Department, and County Community Services Division were released. The survey looked at information technology access and needs within the non-profit community, and was designed to guide the City, the County, and other funding organizations in offering technology assistance to non-profits.

Respondents in the survey were asked to identify what sort of training or assistance would help them use technology more effectively. Almost every agency that responded to the survey cited the need for basic training for staff in software and hardware, and the need for increased technology support and troubleshooting.

All the agencies in the survey said that technology was essential to their operation, and yet they are not finding the funding to maintain their infrastructure and update their equipment and skills. Many organizations noted that the volunteers they use for their technology support are essential. There is a gap in technology planning and training for non-profit organizations.

The volunteers assist the staffs with all types of Information Technology projects including planning and installation of network capability, planning future IT needs, selection of hardware and software, database design, building Web sites, and training staff and clients.

If you are an IT professional or have solid computing skills and would like to share your expertise with Desert Park non-profit organizations, please fill out an interest form at the Center's Web site at www.dpitvolunteer.com. Volunteers are currently needed in the areas of Web site design and development, accounting spreadsheets, Microsoft Office training, and networking.

4F_IT_Volunteer_Firstname_Lastname

Figure 4.52

3. Press Ctrl + A to select all of the text in the document. Change the font to **Garamond 12 pt**. From the **Format** menu, display the **Paragraph** dialog box. Under **Spacing**, change the number in the **After** box to **6 pt**. and click **OK**.

4. Hold down Ctrl and press Home to place the insertion point at the top of the document. Press Enter to create an empty line preceding the text. Click to the left of the empty line and on two separate lines type

   City of Desert Park

   Technology Matters

5. Select *City of Desert Park* and, from the **Format** menu, click **Font**. In the **Font** dialog box, under **Font style**, click **Bold**. Under **Size**, click **20**. Click the **Font color arrow** and, in the second row, click the sixth color—**Blue**. Under **Effects**, select the **Small caps** check box and then click **OK**.

(Project 4F–IT Volunteers continues on the next page)

(Project 4F–IT Volunteers continued)

6. Select *Technology Matters* and, on the Formatting toolbar, use the **Font Size** button to change the font size to **28 pt**. Click the **Bold** button and then click the **Font Color arrow**. From the displayed palette, click **Blue**. Select the two title lines you just formatted and then, on the Formatting toolbar, click the **Center** button.

7. Under the two heading lines, click to the left of *The Desert Park Community* and type **Information Resources** From the **Insert** menu, click **Symbol**. Click the **Special Characters** tab, be sure **Em Dash** is selected, and then click **Insert**. Close the **Symbol** dialog box. Select *Information Resources* and the following dash and then, using the Formatting toolbar, change the font size to **16 pt.**, change the font color to **Blue**, and add **Bold** and **Italic** for emphasis.

8. Place the insertion point at the start of the paragraph beginning *Respondents in the survey.* Display the **Insert** menu, point to **Picture**, and then click **Clip Art**. In the **Clip Art** task pane, in the **Search for** box, type **computer** Be sure the **Search in box** displays **All Collections**. Click the **Results should be arrow**, be sure only **Clip Art** is selected, and then click the **Go** button. Locate the image of a woman at a computer as shown in Figure 4.52. Click the figure to insert it in the document. Alternatively, insert the file w04F_Computer from your student files by displaying the insert menu, pointing to Picture, and then clicking From File.

9. Close the **Clip Art** task pane. Click the inserted image to select it and, on the floating Picture toolbar, click the **Text Wrapping** button. From the displayed list, click **Square**. Drag the image to the right of the paragraphs as shown in Figure 4.52, aligning its right edge with the right margin and the top edge at approximately **3 inches on the vertical ruler**. Do not be concerned if your text does not wrap exactly as shown in the Figure. On the Standard toolbar, click the **Save** button.

10. Scroll down the document until you can see the last paragraph, which begins *If you are.* Select the paragraph. From the **Format** menu, click **Borders and Shading**. In the **Borders and Shading** dialog box, click the **Shading tab**. Under **Fill**, in the last row, click the fifth color—**Light Turquoise**. Click the **Borders tab** and then, under **Settings**, click **Box**. Click the **Width** arrow and click **1 pt**. Click the **Color arrow** and click **Black**, if necessary, and then click **OK**. Click anywhere to deselect the paragraph and view your formatting. The special format is applied to the last paragraph.

11. In the same paragraph, select *Center's Web site* and then, from the **Insert** menu, click **Hyperlink**. In the **Insert Hyperlink** dialog box, under **Link to**, be sure **Existing File or Web Page** is selected. In the **Address** box, type **http://www.dpitvolunteer.com/**

(Project 4F–IT Volunteers continues on the next page)

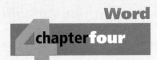
(Project 4F–IT Volunteers continued)

12. On the upper right corner of the **Insert Hyperlink** dialog box, click **ScreenTip**. In the **Set Hyperlink ScreenTip** dialog box, type **Click Here to Volunteer** and then click **OK**. At the bottom of the **Insert Hyperlink** dialog box, click **OK**. The hyperlink is recorded, and the selected text changes to blue and is underlined.

13. From the **Edit** menu, click **Find**. In the **Find and Replace** dialog box, in the **Find what** box, type **cooperative** and then click the **Find Next** button. If necessary, drag the dialog box away from the high-lighted word. Leave the **Find and Replace** dialog box open and click the document to make it active. Right-click the highlighted word *cooperative* and point to **Synonyms** on the shortcut menu. To view additional synonyms for the word *cooperative*, click **Thesaurus**. The **Research** task pane displays. Under joint (adj.), point to *collaborative* and then click the arrow on *collaborative*. From the displayed list, click **Insert**; *cooperative* is replaced with *collaborative*.

14. Using the technique in step 13, from either the list of suggested synonymns or by opening the Thesaurus and finding additional synonymns, locate and replace *vital* with *essential* and *efficiently* with *effectively*. Close the **Find and Replace** dialog box and close the **Research** task pane.

15. From the **View** menu, display the Header and Footer toolbar, switch to the footer, and, on the Header and Footer toolbar, click **Insert AutoText**. From the displayed list, click **Filename**. Close the Header and Footer toolbar. On the Standard toolbar, click the **Save** button.

16. From the **File** menu, click **Save As Web Page**. In the **Save As** dialog box, navigate to the location in which you are saving your files. In the lower portion of the **Save As** dialog box, click **Change Title**. The **Set Page Title** dialog box displays. Type **IT Volunteer** and then click **OK** to close the **Set Page Title** dialog box. In the lower right corner of the **Save As** dialog box, click **Save**. Click **Continue** to acknowl-edge the message box that displays. The Web page is displayed in Word.

17. On the Standard toolbar, click the **Print Preview** button. Take a moment to check your work. On the **Print Preview** toolbar, click the **Close Preview** button.

18. Click the **Print** button and then close the document.

End **You have completed Project 4F**

Project 4G—Youth

Objectives: *Create a Decorative Title, Add Special Paragraph Formatting, Use Special Character Formats, Insert Hyperlinks, and Preview and Save a Document as a Web Page.*

In the following Performance Assessment, you will finish formatting a document for the Family Services Department of Desert Park. The document will then be saved as a Web page. Your completed document will look similar to Figure 4.53. You will save your document as *4G_Youth_Firstname_Lastname.*

Figure 4.53

1. Click the **Open** button and navigate to the location where the student files for this textbook are stored. Locate and open **w04G_Youth**. From the **File** menu, display the **Save As** dialog box. Navigate to the location in which you are storing your files for this chapter. In the **File name** box, type **4G_Youth_Firstname_Lastname** and click **Save**.

(Project 4G–Youth continues on the next page)

(Project 4G–Youth continued)

2. With the insertion point at the top of the document, click the **Insert** menu, point to **Picture**, and then click **WordArt**. In the third row, click the first style and then click **OK**. In the **Edit WordArt Text** dialog box, type **Desert Park Family Services** and click **OK**.

3. Click the **WordArt** graphic and, on the WordArt toolbar, click the **WordArt Shape** button. In the first row of the displayed palette, click the fifth style—the **Chevron Up** style. The WordArt graphic changes to the selected shape. Drag the right center sizing handle to the right margin—approximately **6.5 inches on the horizontal ruler**.

4. In the paragraph beginning with *The fair will focus*, select *dental care* at the end of the first line and then, from the **Insert** menu, display the **Insert Hyperlink** dialog box. Under **Link to**, be sure **Existing File or Web Page** is selected. In the **Address** box, type **http://ada.org/public/topics/infants.html**

5. In the upper right corner of the dialog box, click **ScreenTip**. Type **American Dental Association Tips** and then click **OK**. At the bottom of the **Insert Hyperlink** dialog box, click **OK**. The hyperlink is recorded, and the selected text changes to blue and is underlined.

6. In the same paragraph select *immunization*. Following the instructions in Steps 4 and 5, add a hyperlink to immunization, but for the address type **http://www.cdc.gov.nip/vfc/** and for the **ScreenTip** type **CDC Immunization Recommendations** and then click **OK** twice.

7. Scroll to the bottom of the page. In the paragraph beginning with *There's something*, click to place the insertion point to the left of *You* at the beginning of the second sentence. Press Enter. Select the paragraph you just created, beginning with *You can pick*, and, from the **Format** menu, display the **Borders and Shading** dialog box. Under **Setting**, click **Box**, change the **Width** of the border to **2¼ pt.**, and then change the **Color** to **Bright Green**—the fourth color in the fourth row. Click **OK**. Save your changes.

8. Select the text within the border and, from the **Format** menu, open the **Font** dialog box. Change the **Size** to **16**, the **Font style** to **Bold**, and the **Font color** to **Blue**. Under **Effects**, select the **Small caps** check box. Click **OK**. On the Formatting toolbar, click **Center** to center the text horizontally.

(Project 4G–Youth continues on the next page)

(Project 4G–Youth continued)

9. Scroll to view the upper portion of your document. In the Child Health Fair article, in the paragraph beginning with *The Fair is part*, click to place the insertion point to the right of Desert Park Month. From the **Insert** menu, point to **Picture** and then click **Clip Art**. In the **Clip Art** task pane, search for **toothbrush** in the Clip Art collection. Locate the toothbrush image displayed in Figure 4.53. (If you cannot locate that image, select another image of a toothbrush; alternatively, use the w04G_Toothbrush image that is included the student files for this book.) Click the image to insert it. With the image selected, on the Picture toolbar, click the **Text Wrapping** button and then click **Tight**. Use the Rotate handle to rotate the image so it is on an angle as displayed in Figure 4.53 and then position it in the approximate location shown in the figure. Do not be concerned if your text wraps differently than shown in the figure. Close the **Clip Art** task pane.

10. From the **View** menu, display the Header and Footer toolbar, switch to the footer, click **Insert AutoText**, and then click **Filename**. Close the Header and Footer toolbar. Save your changes.

11. From the **File** menu, click **Web Page Preview**. The document displays as it will when you save it as a Web page. Notice that the toothbrush that you placed in the middle of the paragraph displays on the left side of the text. In the **Web Page** title bar, click the **Close** button to close your browser and return to your 4G_Youth Word file.

12. From the **File** menu, click **Save As Web Page**. Navigate to the location where you are saving your files. In the **Save As** dialog box, click **Change Title**, type **Youth Programs** and then click **OK** to close the **Set Page Title** dialog box. Save the Web page and click **Continue** to acknowledge the message box that displays.

13. **Print** the Web page view of your document and then close it.

 You have completed Project 4G

Project 4H—Cultural Affairs

Objectives: *Create a Decorative Title, Create Multicolumn Documents, Add Special Paragraph Formatting, and Locate Supporting Information.*

In the following Performance Assessment, you will gather information and create a newsletter concerning recent cultural activities in Desert Park. Your completed document will look similar to Figure 4.54. You will save your document as *4H_Cultural Affairs_Firstname_Lastname.*

(Project 4H–Cultural Affairs continues on the next page)

(Project 4H–Cultural Affairs continued)

City of Desert Park
Office of Cultural Affairs

Museum of Art Relocated

Thanks to a bond issue passed by the residents of Desert Park in 1998, the Desert Park Museum of Art has relocated to a new facility at 20th Street and Via Colinas. A gala dedication ceremony will be held on September 12, at 8:00 p.m. The ceremony is open to the public.

The new space was designed to allow a permanent exhibit area as well as changing exhibits area, museum store, collection storage, and children's museum. "I know that residents and visitors to the city will be impressed by the new museum," said Elizabeth Viejo, museum curator. "The space was specially designed with our collection in mind and it shows it off to the fullest."

This investment will ensure that the residents of Desert Park will have a beautiful museum to enjoy for many years to come. At the next meeting of the City Council, the various organizations that worked to get the bond measure passed will be recognized. They include the Heritage Commission, Friends of Fine Arts and Parks, Desert Park Citizens United, and many other individual citizens.

For exhibit information and museum hours, call 626-555-4ART or visit the Web site at www.desertparkmuseum.org.

Did you know...

An *exhibition*, or exhibit, is a display that incorporates objects and information to explain concepts, stimulate understanding, relate experiences, invite participation, prompt reflection, or inspire wonder.

Call for Artists

The Desert Park Fine Arts Commission is accepting applications from individual artists and artistic teams to design several public art projects for the City Hall Plaza mall. The goal of the public art projects is to provide an aesthetic link among intersections, bikeways, pedestrian bridges, and trails. Additionally, enhancements and artistic improvements to gateways to residential areas will be considered. The Commission hopes to add additional gardens, sculptures, walking paths, and pedestrian bridges to the area.

A team can include artists, architects, and landscape architects. A selection committee will choose finalists to develop a preliminary proposal. Selected finalists must present their conceptual approach at a City Council meeting, and will receive a $1,000 honorarium for the proposals. Local artists and architects are encouraged to apply.

Students from the departments of Art and of Landscape Architecture at Desert Park University will assist the Fine Arts Commission in organizing submissions for judging. Dr. Betty Frank, the university's president, said, "We are proud to be a part of this artistic endeavor."

The deadline to apply is 5 p.m. Friday, September 1. Each team member should include a resume and a portfolio of relevant work. For more information or detailed submission requirements, call the Cultural Affairs office at 626-555-1234.

4H_Cultural_Affairs_Firstname_Lastname

Figure 4.54

1. Make sure you have an active Internet connection, which is required to complete this exercise. Click the **Open** button and navigate to the location where the student files for this textbook are stored. Locate and open **w04H_Cultural_Affairs**. From the **File** menu, display the **Save As** dialog box. Navigate to the location in which you are storing your files for this chapter. In the **File name** box, type **4H_Cultural_Affairs_Firstname_Lastname** and click **Save**.

2. With the insertion point at the top of the document, from the **Insert** menu, point to **Picture** and then click **WordArt**. In the fourth row, click the second style and then click **OK**. In the **Edit WordArt Text** dialog box, type **City of Desert Park** and press Enter. Type **Office of Cultural Affairs** and then click **OK**.

3. Click the **WordArt** graphic. Drag the right center sizing handle to approximately **6.5 inches on the horizontal ruler** to expand the shape and stretch it to the right margin. Click anywhere to deselect the **WordArt**.

(Project 4H–Cultural Affairs continues on the next page)

(Project 4H–Cultural Affairs continued)

4. From the **Edit** menu, click **Office Clipboard**. At the top of the **Clipboard** task pane, click the **Clear All** button to remove any items that may be displayed. From your student files, open **w04H_Museum**, select all of the text, click the **Copy** button, and then close the document. The copied text displays as the first item on the Office Clipboard. Open **w04H_Artists**, select all of the text, click the **Copy** button, and then close the document. The text of both articles displays in the Clipboard task pane.

5. On the Standard toolbar, click the **Research** button. In the **Research** task pane, in the **Search for** box, type museum and then click the arrow on the second box. From the displayed list, click **Encyclopedia (or Encarta or Encarta Encyclopedia)**. Your system searches and then displays a list. Click the topic *Exhibitions*. In the Encyclopedia window, in the first paragraph starting with *An Exhibition*, select the first sentence and then press Ctrl + C to copy this sentence to the clipboard. Close the encyclopedia.

6. Now you will collect clip art and place it on the Office Clipboard. Click the **Other Task Panes arrow** on the title bar of the **Research** task pane and then click **Clip Art**. In the **Search for** box, type artist Be sure the **Search in** box displays **All collections**. Click the arrow on the **Results should be** box and be sure just **Clip Art** is selected. Click the **Go** button. Locate the image shown in Figure 4.54. Click the arrow on the image and then click **Copy**. (If you cannot locate the image shown, select another image of an artist. Alternatively, use the w04H_Artist_Picture that is with the student files for this book.)

7. Click the **Other Task Panes** arrow on the title bar of the **Clip Art** task pane and then click **Clipboard**. Place the insertion point on the empty line under *Museum of Art Relocated* and then click the Clipboard item beginning with *Thanks to a bond issue*. The article is inserted.

8. Place the insertion point on the empty line under *Call for Artists* and insert the article beginning with *The Desert Park Fine Arts.* The artist article is inserted.

9. Select all of the text in the document except the WordArt graphic and the line below the graphic. Click the **Columns** button and drag to select **two columns**. With the text selected, on the Formatting toolbar, click the **Justify** button. Click the **Save** button.

10. With the text still selected, on the **Format** menu, click **Columns**. The **Columns** dialog box displays. The Columns dialog box allows you to control the width of columns and offers some other formatting options. On the right side of the dialog box, select the **Line between** check box. Notice at the bottom of the dialog box, the **Applies to** box displays *Selected Text*. Click **OK**.

(Project 4H–Cultural Affairs continues on the next page)

(Project 4H–Cultural Affairs continued)

11. Position the insertion point to the left of the heading *Call for Artists*. From the **Insert** menu, click **Break** and, in the **Break** dialog box, click **Column break**. Click **OK**. The artist article moves to the top of the second column. On the Standard toolbar, click the **Print Preview** button to see the result of your work so far. On the Print Preview toolbar, click the **Close** button.

12. In the artist article, position the insertion point at the start of the paragraph that begins *A team can include*. From the **Clipboard**, click the artist image to insert it. Use the lower right corner sizing handle to reduce the size of the image to about one quarter of its original size. With the image selected, on the floating Picture toolbar, click the **Text Wrapping** button and then click **Square**. Position the image as shown in Figure 4.54. Do not be concerned if your text does not align exactly as shown in the figure. Click the **Save** button.

13. In the first column of text, position the insertion point to the left of the empty paragraph mark at the end of the museum article. Type **Did you know...** and then press Enter. From the **Clipboard**, click the Encarta information to insert it. Close the **Clipboard** task pane.

14. Select the *Did you know* heading and the inserted reference and change the font size to **11 pt**. From the **Format** menu, display the **Borders and Shading** dialog box. Under **Settings**, click **Shadow**, change the **Color** to **Plum**—the seventh color in the fourth row—and the **Width** to **2¼**. Click the **Shading tab** and, in the first row under **No Fill**, click the second color—**5% gray** shading. Click **OK**.

15. Select the text *Did you know...* and add **Bold** emphasis. Then change the font size to **14** and the font color to **Plum** to match the other headings. Move to the top of the newsletter. Select the *Museum of Art Relocated* title and click **Center**. The selected text is centered over the column. Center the title *Call for Artists* over its column in the same manner.

16. Click the **Print Preview** button to see how the document will look when it is printed. Be sure you do not have a stray second page and that the columns are balanced—that is, their bottom edges align at approximately the same place. If you have an empty second page, remove any stray paragraph marks at the end of the document. Add the filename to the footer and save your changes. Print the newsletter and close the document.

End **You have completed Project 4H**

Project 4I—Interns

Objectives: *Create a Decorative Title, Add Special Paragraph Formatting, Use Special Character Formats, and Preview and Save a Document as a Web Page.*

In the following Performance Assessment, you will create and format a document announcing the internship program for the city of Desert Park and then save the document as a Web page. Your completed document will look similar to Figure 4.55. You will save your document as *4I_Interns_Firstname_Lastname.*

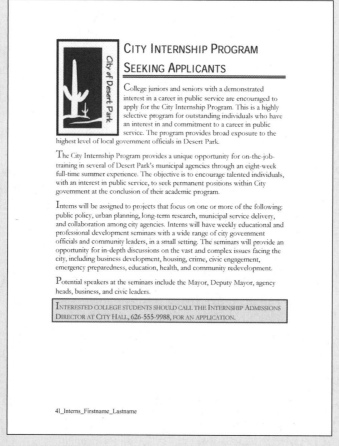

Figure 4.55

1. Click the **Open** button and navigate to the location where the student files for this textbook are stored. Locate and open **w04I_Interns**. From the **File** menu, display the **Save As** dialog box. Navigate to the location in which you are storing your files for this chapter. In the **File name** box type **4I_Interns_Firstname_Lastname** and click **Save**.

(Project 4I–Interns continues on the next page)

(Project 4I–Interns continued)

2. Select all of the text and change the font to **Garamond 14 pt**. From the **Format** menu, open the **Paragraph** dialog box and, under **Spacing**, increase the number in the **After** box to **6 pt**. Use the Spelling and Grammar Checker to correct the spelling errors in this document. Ignore grammar errors.

3. Select only the first letter in each paragraph and change the font size to **20** and the font color to **Dark Blue**—the sixth color in the first row. After you have formatted the first letter, use the **Format Painter** to copy the format to the first letter of each subsequent paragraph.

4. In the first paragraph, position the insertion point to the left of *College* and press Enter twice. Move the insertion point to the first empty line and type **City Internship Program** and press Enter. Type **Seeking Applicants**

5. Select the text you just typed and, from the **Format** menu, display the **Font** color dialog box. Change the **Font** to **Tahoma**, the **Size** to **24 pt.**, and the **Color** to **Dark Blue**. Under **Effects**, select the **Small caps** check box. Click **OK**.

6. With the title still selected, from the **Format** menu, display the **Borders and Shading** dialog box. Click the Borders tab if necessary. Under **Style**, scroll down and click the **double underline**, change the **Color** to **Dark Blue**, and then change the **Width** to **1½**. In the **Preview** area, be sure only the bottom line is displayed—click the left, right, and top lines to remove them from the preview if necessary. Check that **Paragraph** displays in the **Applies to** box and then click **OK**.

7. In the title, position the insertion point to the left of *City*. From the **Insert** menu, point to **Picture** and then click **From File**. Navigate to your student files and locate the **w04I_DPLogo** file. Click **Insert**. With the image selected, on the floating Picture toolbar, click the **Text Wrapping** button and then click **Square**. Remove the extra paragraph mark between the title and the first paragraph. The text moves up as shown in Figure 4.55. Save your changes.

8. Scroll to the bottom of the document and select the last paragraph. From the **Format** menu, display the **Borders and Shading** dialog box. Under **Setting**, click **Box**, change the **Color** to **Dark Blue** and the **Width** to **1½**. Be sure the preview area displays a dark blue border on all sides. Click the **Shading tab**. Under **Fill**, click **Light Yellow**—the third color in the last row. Click **OK**.

(Project 4I–Interns continues on the next page)

(Project 4I–Interns continued)

9. With the text still selected, open the **Font** dialog box. Change the **Font color** to **Dark Blue**. Under **Effects**, select the **Small caps** check box and then click **OK**.

10. From the **View** menu, display the Header and Footer toolbar, switch to the footer, click **Insert AutoText**, and then click **Filename**. Close the Header and Footer toolbar. Save your changes.

11. From the **File** menu, click **Save As Web Page**. Navigate to the location where you are saving your files. In the **Save As** dialog box, click **Change Title**, type **Intern Program** and then click **OK** to close the **Set Page Title** dialog box.

12. **Save** the Web page and click **Continue** to acknowledge the message box that displays. Print the Web page and then close it.

End You have completed Project 4I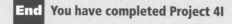

Project 4J — Desert Oasis

Objectives: *Create a Decorative Title, Create Multicolumn Documents, Add Special Paragraph Formatting, Use Special Character Formats, and Locate Supporting Information.*

In the following Mastery Assessment, you will create a newsletter published by the Parks and Recreation Department in Desert Park. Your completed newsletter will look like Figure 4.56. You will save your document as *4J_Desert_Oasis_Firstname_Lastname.*

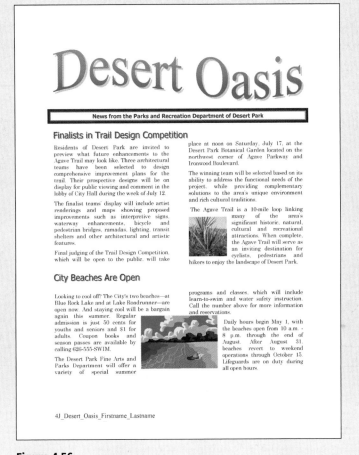

Figure 4.56

1. Start Word. In a blank document, open the **Page Setup** dialog box and change the left and right margins to 1 inch. Be sure you are in the **Print Layout View** and the nonprinting characters are displayed.

2. Display the **WordArt Gallery** dialog box and, in the third row, click the fifth style and click **OK**. In the **Edit WordArt Text** dialog box, type **Desert Oasis** Change the **Font Size** of the WordArt to **66** and then click **OK**.

(Project 4J–Desert Oasis continues on the next page)

(Project 4J–Desert Oasis continued)

3. With the WordArt graphic selected, drag the side sizing handle so it stretches between the left and right margins. Use the horizontal ruler to see the margins.

4. On the right side of the WordArt graphic, click in the margin to deselect and then press Enter twice to insert two paragraph marks at the left margin. Click the **Center** button and then type **News from the Parks and Recreation Department of Desert Park**

5. Select the text you just typed and change the font to **Tahoma**, **10 pt.**, **Bold**, and **Blue**. Open the **Borders and Shading** dialog box, click the **Box** setting, and then, in the **Style** list box, click the style that is third from the bottom. Change the color to **Teal** and click **OK**. Compare your banner to Figure 4.56.

6. Save your work as you have previously with the file name **4J_Desert_Oasis_Firstname_Lastname**

7. Position your I-beam pointer slightly below the banner at the left margin and double-click to place the insertion point just below the banner. Adjust as necessary so that two paragraph marks display and then position your insertion point to the left of the second paragraph mark and type **Finalists in Trail Design Competition**

   Select the text and change the font to **16-point Tahoma**. Change the font color to **Blue**. Open the **Font** dialog box and select the **Emboss** check box. Deselect the text.

8. Press Enter. Recall that paragraph marks retain the formatting of the preceding paragraph. To change the formatting, select the paragraph mark and open the **Font** dialog box. Change the font to **10-point Century Schoolbook** and change the font color to **Black**. Under **Effects**, clear the check box next to **Emboss**. Click **OK**. Now you will collect and paste the articles that will be used for this newsletter.

9. Display the **Office Clipboard** and click the **Clear All** button. From your student files, locate and open **w04J_Agave_Trail**. Select and copy all of the text and then close the file. Locate and open **w04J_Beaches**. Copy all of the text and then close the file.

10. Display the **Clip Art** task pane and search for *beaches*. Locate the beach image displayed in Figure 4.56, click the arrow on the image, and then click **Copy** to copy it to the Clipboard. (If you cannot locate the image that is shown in the figure, select another beach image; alternatively, use the w04J_Beach_Picture that is included with the student files for this book. Use the technique you practiced in Activity 4.16, step 11, to copy the picture from your student files to the Office Clipboard.) On the **Clip Art** task pane, click the **Other Task Panes arrow** and click **Clipboard** to see the image you copied and the two articles.

(Project 4J–Desert Oasis continues on the next page)

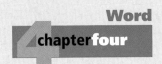

(Project 4J–Desert Oasis continued)

11. Display the **Research** task pane and type **Agave** and then select **Encyclopedia (or Encarta Encyclopedia)** as the research reference. In the list of choices displayed, under **Related items**, click *pictures of Agave plants*. In the MSN window that displays, locate the picture of a typical Agave type of plant. Right-click on the image and then click **Copy** to add the image to the Clipboard. Close the MSN window and then display the **Clipboard** task pane. Four items are displayed. Alternatively, insert the file w04J_Agave_Picture from your student files by displaying the Insert menu, pointing to Picture, and then clicking From File.

12. Position the insertion point in your document to the left of the last empty paragraph mark. From the **Clipboard** task pane, click the trail article that begins *Residents of Desert Park*. The article is inserted. Click the **Paste Options** button arrow that displays and click **Match Destination Formatting** to change the font to **Century Schoolbook, 10 pt**. Recall that the Paste Options button can be used to change the format of inserted text to match the formatting of the surrounding text.

13. Select the article text and change it to two columns, and then change the alignment to **Justify**. Display the **Paragraph** dialog box and add a **6-pt**. **Before** spacing to the article paragraphs. Save your changes.

14. To add the second article headline, click to the left of the empty paragraph mark on the left side of the screen, press (Enter), and type **City Beaches Are Open**

   Press (Enter) twice. Select the new headline and change the font so it matches the *Finalists in Trail Design Competition* headline.

15. Click to the left of the second paragraph mark under the *Beaches* headline and, from the Clipboard task pane, paste the beach article that begins *Looking to cool off?* Click the **Paste Options** button that displays and click **Match Destination Formatting**. Change the article to two columns and the alignment to **Justify**. Display the **Paragraph** dialog box and add a **6-pt**. **Before** spacing to the paragraphs.

16. In the *Finalists in Trail Design Competition* article, in the second column, place the insertion point to the left of the paragraph that begins *The Agave Trail*.

   From the clipboard, paste the image of the Agave plant. Use a corner sizing handle to increase the size of the image until it is approximately 1 inch square. On the Picture toolbar, click the **Text Wrapping** button and click **Square**. Drag the image to position it in the article as shown in Figure 4.56. Do not be concerned if the text does not wrap around the image exactly as shown in the figure.

(Project 4J–Desert Oasis continues on the next page)

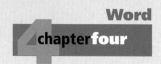
(Project 4J–Desert Oasis continued)

17. In the *City Beaches Are Open* article, place the insertion point at the beginning of the last paragraph that begins *Daily hours*. From the **Clipboard**, insert the beach picture. Set the **Text Wrapping** to **Square** and then position the image in the middle of the article as shown in Figure 4.56. If necessary, reposition the Agave plant image in the first article.

18. View the footer area and add the **AutoText file name** to the footer. Preview the document to be sure it is on one page. Make any necessary adjustments. Depending on your printer, the lines in the columns may be slightly different when compared to Figure 4.56. Print the newsletter, save your changes, and then close the document.

End You have completed Project 4J ─────────────

Project 4K — Recreation Notes

Objectives: *Create a Decorative Title, Create Multicolumn Documents, Add Special Paragraph Formatting, Use Special Character Formats, Insert Hyperlinks, and Locate Supporting Information.*

In the following Mastery Assessment, you will create a newsletter about upcoming sports events in Desert Park. Your completed newsletter will look similar to Figure 4.57. You will save your document as *4K_Recreation_Notes_Firstname_Lastname*.

1. Start Word. In a blank document open the **Page Setup** dialog box and set the left and right margins to 1 inch. Be sure you are in **Print Layout** view and that the nonprinting characters are displayed. If necessary, close the task pane.

2. Display the **WordArt Gallery** dialog box. In the fourth row, click the first style, click **OK**, and then type **Recreation Notes** Change the **Font Size** to **66** and then click **OK**. Select the **WordArt** graphic and open the **Format WordArt** dialog box. On the **Colors and Lines tab** of the dialog box, click the **Fill Color arrow** and then click **Fill Effects**. In the **Fill Effects** dialog box, click the **Texture tab** and then, in the first row, click the first texture—**Green marble**. Click **OK** twice.

3. On the right side of the **WordArt** graphic, click in the margin to deselect and then press twice to insert two paragraph marks at the left margin. Click the **Center** button and then type **Sports News from the Parks and Recreation Department of Desert Park**

Select the text you just typed and change the font to **Comic Sans MS, 10 pt., Bold**. Change the font color to **Green**. Open the **Borders and Shading** dialog box, click the **3-D setting**, and then, in the **Style** list box, click the line style that displays a heavy top line and a narrow bottom line. Change the line color to **Green** and click **OK**. Compare your banner to Figure 4.57.

(Project 4K–Recreation Notes continues on the next page)

(**Project 4K**–Recreation Notes continued)

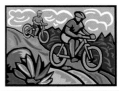

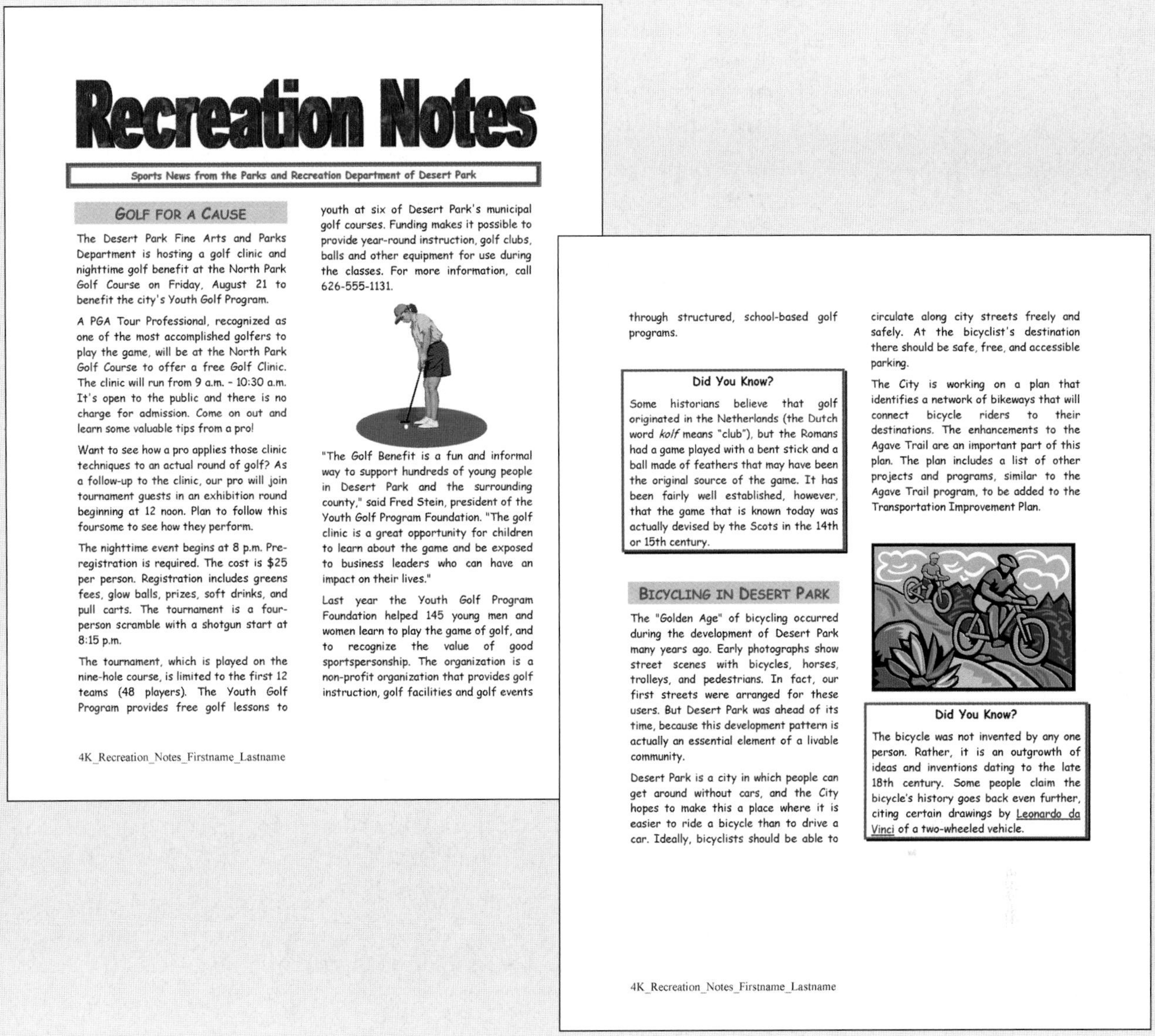

Recreation Notes

Sports News from the Parks and Recreation Department of Desert Park

Golf for a Cause

The Desert Park Fine Arts and Parks Department is hosting a golf clinic and nighttime golf benefit at the North Park Golf Course on Friday, August 21 to benefit the city's Youth Golf Program.

A PGA Tour Professional, recognized as one of the most accomplished golfers to play the game, will be at the North Park Golf Course to offer a free Golf Clinic. The clinic will run from 9 a.m. - 10:30 a.m. It's open to the public and there is no charge for admission. Come on out and learn some valuable tips from a pro!

Want to see how a pro applies those clinic techniques to an actual round of golf? As a follow-up to the clinic, our pro will join tournament guests in an exhibition round beginning at 12 noon. Plan to follow this foursome to see how they perform.

The nighttime event begins at 8 p.m. Pre-registration is required. The cost is $25 per person. Registration includes greens fees, glow balls, prizes, soft drinks, and pull carts. The tournament is a four-person scramble with a shotgun start at 8:15 p.m.

The tournament, which is played on the nine-hole course, is limited to the first 12 teams (48 players). The Youth Golf Program provides free golf lessons to youth at six of Desert Park's municipal golf courses. Funding makes it possible to provide year-round instruction, golf clubs, balls and other equipment for use during the classes. For more information, call 626-555-1131.

"The Golf Benefit is a fun and informal way to support hundreds of young people in Desert Park and the surrounding county," said Fred Stein, president of the Youth Golf Program Foundation. "The golf clinic is a great opportunity for children to learn about the game and be exposed to business leaders who can have an impact on their lives."

Last year the Youth Golf Program Foundation helped 145 young men and women learn to play the game of golf, and to recognize the value of good sportspersonship. The organization is a non-profit organization that provides golf instruction, golf facilities and golf events

4K_Recreation_Notes_Firstname_Lastname

through structured, school-based golf programs.

Did You Know?

Some historians believe that golf originated in the Netherlands (the Dutch word *kolf* means "club"), but the Romans had a game played with a bent stick and a ball made of feathers that may have been the original source of the game. It has been fairly well established, however, that the game that is known today was actually devised by the Scots in the 14th or 15th century.

Bicycling in Desert Park

The "Golden Age" of bicycling occurred during the development of Desert Park many years ago. Early photographs show street scenes with bicycles, horses, trolleys, and pedestrians. In fact, our first streets were arranged for these users. But Desert Park was ahead of its time, because this development pattern is actually an essential element of a livable community.

Desert Park is a city in which people can get around without cars, and the City hopes to make this a place where it is easier to ride a bicycle than to drive a car. Ideally, bicyclists should be able to circulate along city streets freely and safely. At the bicyclist's destination there should be safe, free, and accessible parking.

The City is working on a plan that identifies a network of bikeways that will connect bicycle riders to their destinations. The enhancements to the Agave Trail are an important part of this plan. The plan includes a list of other projects and programs, similar to the Agave Trail program, to be added to the Transportation Improvement Plan.

Did You Know?

The bicycle was not invented by any one person. Rather, it is an outgrowth of ideas and inventions dating to the late 18th century. Some people claim the bicycle's history goes back even further, citing certain drawings by Leonardo da Vinci of a two-wheeled vehicle.

4K_Recreation_Notes_Firstname_Lastname

Figure 4.57

4. Save your work as you have previously with the file name **4K_Recreation_Notes_Firstname_Lastname**

5. Position your I-beam pointer at the left margin and slightly under the banner you just created and then double-click to place the insertion point below the banner. Adjust as necessary so that two paragraph marks display, and then position your insertion point to the left of the second paragraph mark. Type **Golf for a Cause**

   Select the text you just typed and change the font to **16 pt.**, **Bold**, and **Green**. Deselect the text.

(**Project 4K**–Recreation Notes continues on the next page)

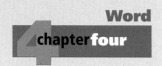

(Project 4K–Recreation Notes continued)

6. Press ⟨Enter⟩ and drag to select the empty paragraph mark you just created. Change the font size to **11 pt.**, remove **Bold**, and change the font color to **Black**. Recall that paragraph marks retain the formatting of the preceding paragraph. You are ready to collect and paste the articles that will be used for this newsletter.

7. Display the **Office Clipboard** and, if necessary, click the **Clear All** button to clear the Clipboard. From the student files, locate and open **w04K_Recreation_Ideas**. This memo contains information that was gathered by the director of the Parks Department. You will copy each part separately so you can control the placement of the articles in the newsletter. Copy the golf article, starting with the paragraph that begins *The Desert Park.* Copy the first Did You Know paragraph, starting with *Some historians believe.* Copy the image of the woman golfer. Copy the bicycling article, starting at the paragraph that begins *The "Golden Age."* Copy the second Did You Know paragraph starting with *The bicycle was not.* Finally, copy the image of the bicyclers. Close the document.

8. Place the insertion point to the left of the last empty paragraph mark. From the **Clipboard** task pane, click the golf article that begins *The Desert Park.* The article is inserted. Point to the displayed **Paste Options** button and click the arrow. From the displayed list, click **Match Destination Formatting** to change the font to **Comic Sans, 11 pt.**

9. Press ⟨Enter⟩ and type **Did You Know?** Press ⟨Enter⟩ again and, from the Clipboard task pane, click the paragraph that begins *Some historians believe.* Click the **Paste Options button arrow** and then click **Match Destination Formatting**. Your newsletter expands to a second page.

10. On page 1, place the insertion point at the start of the paragraph that begins *"The Golf Benefit* and insert the woman golfer image. Select the image. From the displayed Picture toolbar, click the **Text Wrapping** button and then click **Top and Bottom**.

11. Hold down ⟨Ctrl⟩ and press ⟨End⟩ to move the insertion point to the end of the document. Press ⟨Enter⟩ and then type the headline for the next article: **Bicycling in Desert Park**

   Press ⟨Enter⟩ and then select the headline. Format the text the same as the *Golf for a Cause* headline—try using Format Painter to copy the format. Save your changes.

(Project 4K–Recreation Notes continues on the next page)

(Project 4K–Recreation Notes continued)

12. Click to the left of the paragraph mark under the new headline and then paste the bicycle article, which begins The *"Golden Age."* Use the **Paste Options** button to match the destination formatting. Press Enter to add a blank line after the article and then paste the image of the bicyclers. Click to the right of the image, press Enter, and then type **Did You Know?** Press Enter again, paste the text beginning with *The bicycle was not*, and then use the **Paste Options** button to match the destination formatting. A third page may be created in your newsletter. Close the Clipboard.

13. Move to the top of the first page. Place the insertion point to the left of the *Golf for a Cause* headline. Select all of the text in the newsletter except the banner and the Word Art Graphic. Open the **Paragraph** dialog box, set the spacing after to **6 pt.**, and then click **OK**.

14. With the text still selected, change the columns to **two** and change the alignment to **Justify**. Deselect the text. The newsletter is now on two pages. On page 1, drag as necessary to visually center the image of the woman golfer horizontally within the column, between the two paragraphs. Compare the placement of the image to Figure 4.57.

15. On page 2, in the first column, select the *Did You Know?* heading. Change the font to **Comic Sans MS**, **12-pt.**, **Bold**, and center it. In the second column, below the bicycle image, do the same to the second Did You Know? heading.

16. Select the first *Did You Know?* heading and the paragraph that follows it. Open the **Borders and Shading** dialog box and add a **Shadow** style, **2¼ pt.**, **Green** border around the paragraph to draw the reader's eye to it. Do the same for the second *Did You Know?* heading and paragraph.

17. Select the *Golf for a Cause* headline, open the **Borders and Shading** dialog box, click the **Shading tab**, and then apply a **light green** shading to the paragraph. Open the **Font** dialog box, apply the **Small caps** effect, and then center the headline. On page 2, apply the same formatting to the *Bicycling in Desert Park* headline.

18. View the footer area and add the **AutoText file name** to the footer. Preview the document, pressing PgUp and PgDn to move between the pages—your newsletter should occupy two pages. Compare your document to Figure 4.57 and the print it. Save your changes and close the document.

End You have completed Project 4K

Project 4L — Tutoring Services

Objectives: *Create a Decorative Title, Add Special Paragraph Formatting, Use Special Character Formats, Insert Hyperlinks, and Preview and Save a Document as a Web Page.*

Use the skills you have learned in this and preceding chapters to create a one-page Word document to announce your services as a tutor for Microsoft Office applications. Save the document as a Web page with the file name *4L_Tutoring_Services_Firstname_Lastname.*

1. Start Word and create a headline to announce your services as a tutor. Use WordArt or any of the font characteristics you have practiced.

2. Write a paragraph or two to describe the skills you have acquired in Microsoft Word and other Microsoft programs. Include information about yourself that would make you qualified to be a tutor, such as patience or good listening skills. Think about the skills you would find helpful in a tutor. Format the text attractively so it is easy to read. When someone reads an announcement, they are usually seeking information about who, what, when, where, and why. Thus, be sure that your announcement describes who you are, what you do, when you are available to tutor, where tutoring can be held, and why you are qualified to be a tutor.

3. Add clip art or other pictures that are appropriate to the topic of tutoring using a computer.

4. Include a hyperlink to the Microsoft Web site— http://www.microsoft.com—or some other site appropriate to Microsoft Office programs.

5. Review your work and correct any errors. Be sure it is attractive and balanced on the page.

6. Save the document with the name **4L_Tutoring_Services_Firstname_ Lastname** Add the filename to the footer area. Then save the document as a Web Page. Print your results.

End **You have completed Project 4L** ───────────────────

Project 4M—Personal Newsletter

Objectives: *Create a Decorative Title, Create a Multicolumn Document, Add Special Paragraph Formatting, Use Special Character Formats, and Locate Supporting Information.*

Create a one-page personal newsletter to send to your friends and family. Save your document as *4M_Personal_Newsletter_Firstname Lastname.*

1. From a blank document, create a WordArt heading for your personal newsletter. Add a decorative banner line under the newsletter heading.

2. Write a few paragraphs to describe the significant events in your life over the last few months to share with your family or friends. Write about two or more significant topics for which you could create a headline; for example, Enrolled In a Computer Course!

3. Create headlines for the topics you have chosen and then format them appropriately.

4. Change the text of the articles to two columns.

5. Add appropriate clip art or pictures. Select a significant paragraph and format it to stand out from the rest of the text.

6. If necessary, insert a continuous break at the end of the newsletter so the columns are even.

7. Save the file as **4M_Newsletter_Firstname_Lastname** Add the file name to the footer area and then print the document.

End **You have completed Project 4M**

On the Internet

Locating Supporting Information on the Web

In this chapter, you were introduced to the Research feature of Microsoft Word. The Research button connects you to resources that you can use as you write. This includes the thesaurus and encyclopedia, which you used in the chapter, as well as many other tools. You can translate a word or a whole document into another language. Some of the resources that are displayed require that you pay a fee. Open Word and click the Research button. Explore the options available to you. Discover which ones are free, and which ones require you to sign up for the service and pay a fee. Try the translation feature, which will require that you have a document open. Think about how this compares to using your favorite Internet search engine to locate information. Also, think about how much you would be willing to pay for the resources available through the Research button.

GO! with Help

Special Column Formats

In the exercises in this chapter you created a simple one- or two-page newsletter. While desktop publishing software offers many more features for newsletter creation, Word can still be used—an advantage if you do not own desktop publishing software. Some additional features of Word can be applied to columns in a newsletter.

1. Start Word. On the menu bar, in the **Type a question for help** box, type **Columns** and then press Enter.

2. Expand and review the topics that display. This information is a good review of the content in this chapter related to columns and also introduces some new information.

3. Open **w04D_Council_News**. From the **Format** menu, click **Columns**. In the **Columns** dialog box, experiment with the different preset column formats displayed. Use the Help pane to assist you as you experiment with different column formats.

4. Close your document without saving changes. Close Help and then close Word.

chapterfive

5 Using Charts, Special Effects, and Styles

In this chapter, you will: complete these projects **and** practice these skills.

Project 5A **Creating a Chart**	**Objectives** • Create a Chart with Microsoft Graph • Format a Chart • Add Special Text Effects

Project 5B **Creating and Using Styles**	**Objectives** • Use Existing Styles • Create and Modify New Styles • Modify the Document Window

Project 5C **Creating an Outline**	**Objective** • Create an Outline

Project 5D **Creating a Program Outline**	**Objective** • Create an Outline Using the Outline View and the Outlining Toolbar

University Medical Center

The University Medical Center (UMC) is a premier patient-care and research institution serving Orange Beach, Florida. To maintain UMC's sterling reputation, the Office of Public Affairs (OPA) actively promotes UMC's services, achievements, and professional staff. The OPA staff interacts with the media, writes press releases and announcements, prepares marketing materials, develops public awareness campaigns, maintains a speakers bureau, and conducts media training for physicians and researchers. The UMC will soon be announcing successful results of a clinical trial of a new surgical technique, so this announcement will be a high priority for the OPA staff for the next several weeks.

©Photosphere Images Ltd.

Making Professional Documents with Charts and Styles

Charts are visual representations of numeric data. Chart data is often easier to understand than textual data. Pie charts, which show the contributions of each piece to the whole, and column charts, which make comparisons among related numbers, are commonly used charts. Word features make it easy to design an effective chart.

Character, paragraph, and list styles provide a way to quickly apply formatting instructions to text. Character styles are applied to individual characters, paragraph styles are applied to entire paragraphs, and list styles are applied to bulleted or numbered lists. Word contains pre-defined styles, and you can also create your own styles.

Word also enables you to create and edit multiple-level outlines to organize an overview about a topic.

In this chapter, you will create and format charts. You will learn how to use existing styles and to create and modify new styles. Finally, you will create multilevel outlines.

Project 5A **Nutrition Flyer**

Graphical representation of numbers helps a reader understand the implications and trends in a visual manner that is easier to interpret than lists of numbers. Using the Microsoft Graph program, you can add attractive charts to documents and reports.

In Activities 5.1 through 5.8, you will edit a nutrition flyer for the University Medical Center Nutrition Unit. You will add a chart to the flyer showing the results of a nutrition survey and format the chart to make it visually appealing. You will also use special formatting features to give your flyer a professional look. Your completed document will look similar to Figure 5.1. You will save your document as *5A_Nutrition_Flyer_Firstname_Lastname.*

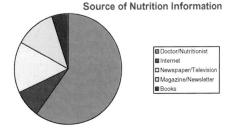

Figure 5.1
Project 5A—Nutrition Flyer

Objective 1
Create a Chart with Microsoft Graph

Charts are often used to make a set of numbers easier to understand. There are two ways to create a chart in Word using a built-in feature called **Microsoft Graph**. The easiest and most direct is to create a table with the data, and then create the chart directly from the table. You can also start Microsoft Graph and fill in the data in a table-like structure called a **datasheet**. There are 14 types of charts available in Word, each with a different purpose. The most commonly used are column, bar, pie, line, and area charts, as described in Figure 5.2.

Chart Types Available in Word

Purpose of Chart	Chart Type
Show comparison among data	Column, Bar
Show proportion of parts to a whole	Pie
Show trends over time	Line, Area

Figure 5.2

Activity 5.1 Creating a Chart from a Word Table

1 On the Standard toolbar, click the **Open** button. Navigate to the location where the student files for this textbook are stored. Locate **w05A_Nutrition_Flyer** and click once to select it. Then, in the lower right corner of the **Open** dialog box, click **Open**.

The w05A_Nutrition_Flyer file opens.

2 From the **File** menu, click **Save As**. In the **Save As** dialog box, navigate to the location where you are storing your files, creating a new folder for this chapter if you want to do so.

3 In the **File name** box, type **5A_Nutrition_Flyer_Firstname_Lastname** and then click **Save**.

4 Locate the table in the middle of the document, and then in the table, click anywhere to position the insertion point. From the **Table** menu, point to **Select**, and then click **Table**.

The table is selected, as shown in Figure 5.3. When creating a chart from a Word table, arrange the table so that the category labels form the first column and headings form the first row.

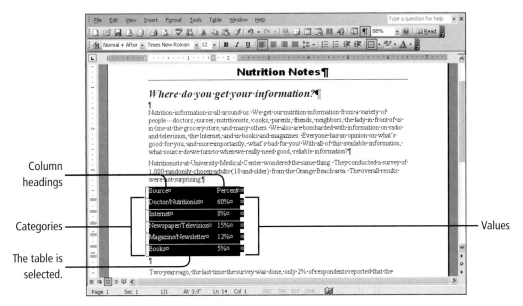

Column headings

Categories

The table is selected.

Values

Figure 5.3

5 From the **Insert** menu, point to **Picture**, and then click **Chart**.

The Microsoft Graph program displays a three-dimensional column chart surrounded by a slashed border and a Datasheet table. New toolbars also display.

Alert!

If the Datasheet Disappears

If you click outside the chart, the datasheet will disappear, and the chart will no longer be in edit mode. To return to edit mode, double-click the chart. If the datasheet still does not display, from the View menu, click Datasheet.

6 Look at Figure 5.4, and take a moment to become familiar with the parts of a chart with which you will be working.

The heading of the second column in the table—*Percent*—displays along the **category axis** (or x-axis). A **scale** of percentage values—from 0% to 60%—displays along the **value axis** (or y-axis). This scale is calculated by the Microsoft Graph program. The four categories from the first column are displayed in a **legend**, which relates the categories to the data in the chart. The chart graphic displays in the **plot area**; everything outside the plot area is the **chart area**. The table values have been copied to a datasheet, which is where future changes or additions to the data will be recorded. See Figure 5.4.

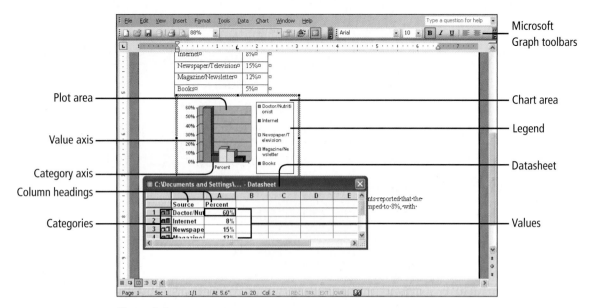

Plot area

Value axis

Category axis

Column headings

Categories

Microsoft Graph toolbars

Chart area

Legend

Datasheet

Values

Figure 5.4

Note — Chart Defaults

If your chart does not look similar to the chart shown in Figure 5.4, it is because the default chart settings have been modified. Changing the chart default can be something as simple as changing the chart type for new charts, to custom changes of individual chart elements. Changes to the chart defaults should not interfere with completing the following activities, although your screens will look different from the ones in the book.

7 On the Standard toolbar, click the **Save** button 🖫.

Activity 5.2 Adding a Chart Title

Add a title to a chart to help the reader understand the topic of the chart's data.

1 From the **Chart** menu, click **Chart Options**. If necessary, in the **Chart Options** dialog box, click the **Titles tab**. Alternatively, right-click on the chart area and click Chart Options from the shortcut menu.

2 Click in the **Chart title** box and type **Source of Nutrition Information**

After a few seconds, the new title displays in the Preview area. See Figure 5.5.

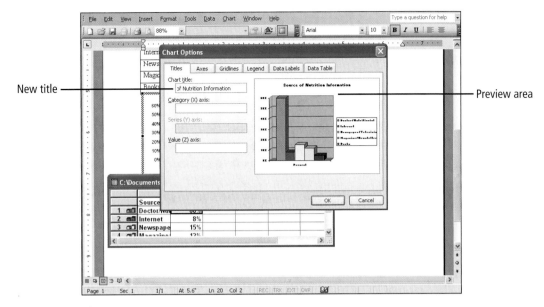

New title

Preview area

Figure 5.5

3 At the bottom of the **Chart Options** dialog box, click **OK**. Click in the datasheet to remove the selection box from the title.

The title is added to the chart, and the size of the chart area is reduced, as shown in Figure 5.6.

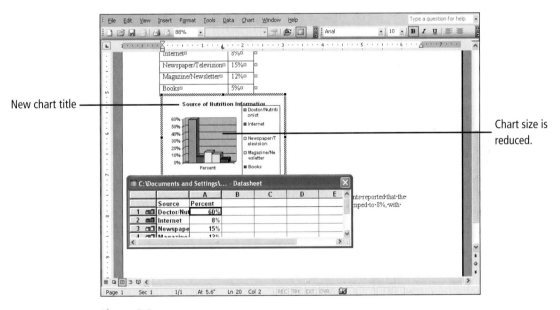

New chart title

Chart size is reduced.

Figure 5.6

4 On the Standard toolbar, click the **Save** button.

Objective 2
Format a Chart

When you create a chart, it contains only the chart in default format and a legend. You can make changes to colors and backgrounds, change the size and page location of the chart, and add chart titles. Unless you have changed the default chart type, each new chart you create will be a ***column chart***, which is used to compare data. Thus, if you need a pie chart or a line chart, you will need to change the chart type.

Activity 5.3 Changing the Chart Type

The purpose of a chart is to graphically depict one of three types of relationships—a comparison among data, the proportion of parts to a whole, or trends over time. The data in your chart shows the parts of a whole, which is most effectively illustrated using a ***pie chart***.

1 Be sure that two toolbars display at the top of your screen. If only one toolbar row is displayed on your screen, at the right end of the Standard toolbar, click the **Toolbar Options** button , and then click **Show Buttons on Two Rows**.

The Microsoft Graph Standard and Formatting toolbars are displayed in separate rows.

2 On the Standard toolbar, click the **Chart Type button arrow** .

A menu of chart type buttons displays. See Figure 5.7.

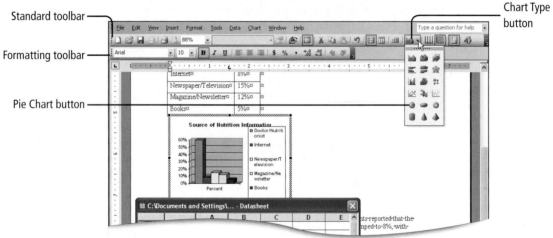

Standard toolbar

Formatting toolbar

Pie Chart button

Chart Type button

Figure 5.7

3 Move the pointer over the chart buttons and take a moment to look at the buttons and ScreenTips.

Notice that the buttons depict the type of chart with which they are associated.

4 From the **Chart Type** menu, click the **Pie Chart** button .

The chart changes into a pie chart, but only the first row of information is charted, as indicated by the icon in the datasheet. See Figure 5.8.

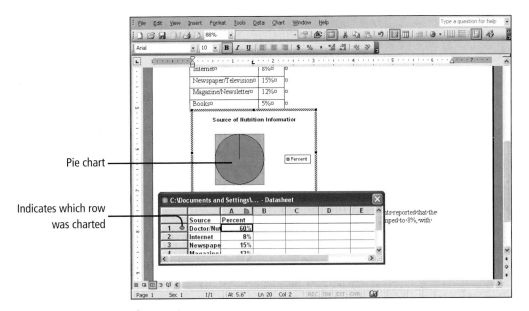

Pie chart

Indicates which row was charted

Figure 5.8

More Knowledge — Two Ways of Displaying Chart Data

Charts can be displayed by row or by column. The difference can be very important. In a column chart, for example, changing the display from Rows to Columns switches the contents of the legend and the category (x) axis. In a pie chart this difference is particularly important. If you choose to display your data by rows, only the data in row 1 of the datasheet is displayed. If your data is in column format, you need to change the orientation of the chart to make the chart useful.

5 On the Standard toolbar, click the **By Column** button.

The chart displays all the data, and icons in each row of the datasheet show that a pie slice has been added for each row. All of the slices together add up to 100 percent. See Figure 5.9.

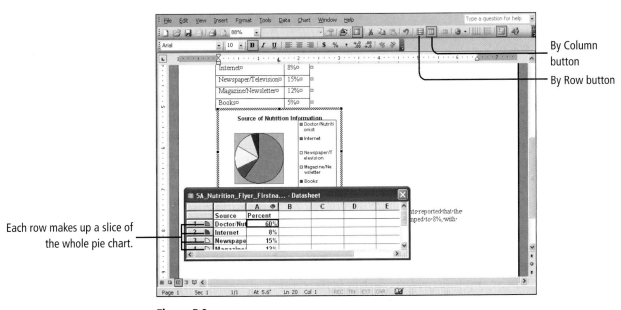

By Column button

By Row button

Each row makes up a slice of the whole pie chart.

Figure 5.9

6 On the Standard toolbar, click the **Save** button 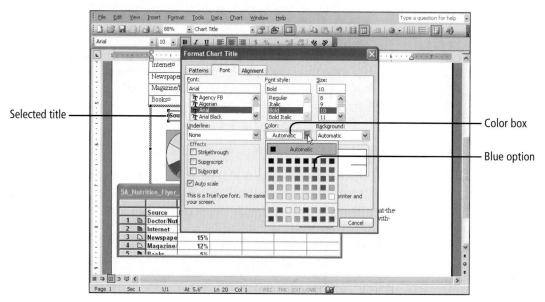.

Activity 5.4 Formatting Chart Text

You can format any text on a chart, including the title, axis titles, and text in legends.

1 On the chart, click anywhere in the title *Source of Nutrition Information*.

A box with a gray border and sizing handles surrounds the title, indicating that the title is selected. You may have to click the title a second time to select it.

2 From the **Format** menu, click **Selected Chart Title**.

The Format Chart Title dialog box displays.

3 If necessary, on the **Format Chart Title** dialog box, click the **Font tab**.

Font options and a limited set of Effects are available in this dialog box.

4 Click the **Color arrow** to display the color palette, as shown in Figure 5.10.

Selected title

Color box

Blue option

Figure 5.10

5 In the second row, click the sixth color—**Blue**—and then click **OK**.

The title is changed to blue. See Figure 5.11.

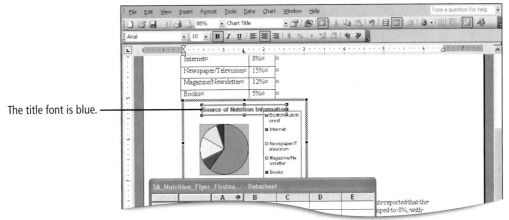

The title font is blue.

Figure 5.11

6 Click to select the legend. From the **Format** menu, click **Selected Legend**.

The Format Legend dialog box displays.

7 In the **Format Legend** dialog box, under **Font style**, click **Regular**, and then click **OK**.

The legend text changes from bold to regular, as shown in Figure 5.12.

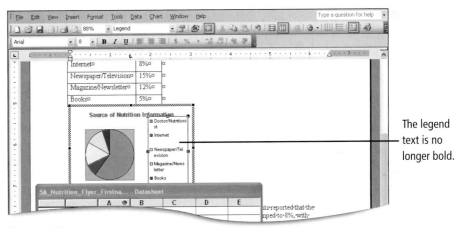

The legend text is no longer bold.

Figure 5.12

8 On the datasheet, click in the title bar.

The Close button, which had been hidden while the datasheet was inactive, displays.

9 On the datasheet title bar, click the **Close** button ☒.

The datasheet closes, but the chart remains active.

10 On the Standard toolbar, click the **Save** button 🖫.

Activity 5.5 Resizing and Centering a Chart

You can resize both the chart area and the individual chart elements. You can also position the chart on your page relative to the left and right margins.

1 With the chart selected, drag the handle in the middle of the right border to approximately **5 inches on the horizontal ruler**.

Notice that the selection box stretches as you drag to the right. See Figure 5.13.

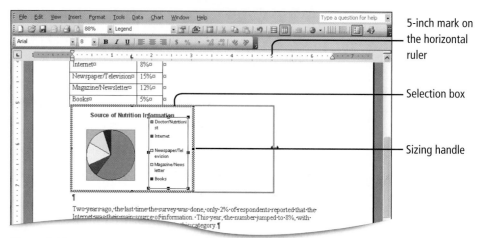

Figure 5.13

2 Release the mouse button.

Notice that the text in the legend has expanded to display the widest entry, although the title may still be cut off.

3 Move the pointer over the chart title and drag it to the right, near the edge of the chart box, as shown in Figure 5.14.

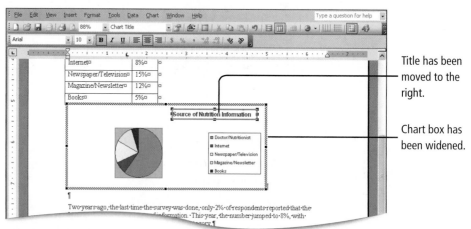

Figure 5.14

4 With the chart selected, drag the handle in the middle of the bottom border down to approximately **8 inches on the vertical ruler**.

The chart box is about 3 inches high. The legend and title size also increase, and the legend text may wrap.

5 Move the pointer to one of the corners of the plot area, which is the area used for the pie.

A ScreenTip displays identifying the plot area.

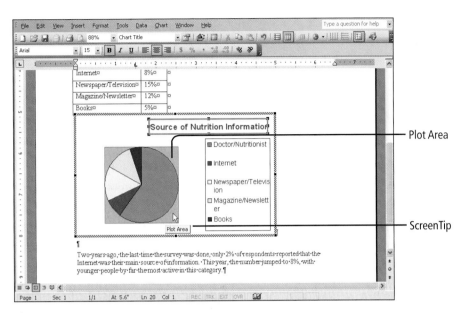

Figure 5.15

6 Click once to select the plot area. Using the sizing handle in the lower right corner of the plot area, drag down and to the right until the chart is near the lower border of the chart box.

7 Using the sizing handle in the upper left corner of the plot area, drag up and to the left until the plot area is about 0.5 inch from the top border of the chart box.

Notice in Figure 5.16 that the legend text increases in size proportionally.

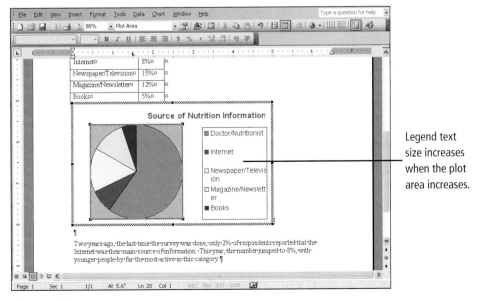

Figure 5.16

8 Click once on the legend. On the Formatting toolbar, click the **Font Size button arrow** 10 ▾, and then click **9**. If necessary, using the legend sizing handles, resize the legend box so that the text for each item displays on one line.

9 Click once on the plot area outside the pie. From the **Format** menu, click **Selected Plot Area**.

The Format Plot Area dialog box displays.

10 Under **Border**, click the **None** option button. Under **Area**, click the **None** option button.

This will remove the box and shading surrounding the pie. Compare your Format Plot Area dialog box with Figure 5.17.

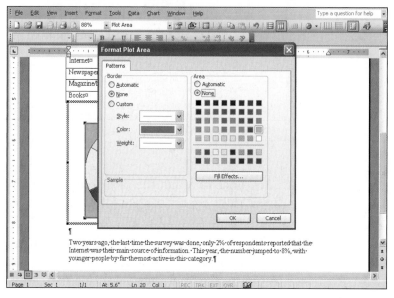

Figure 5.17

11 At the bottom of the **Format Plot Area** dialog box, click **OK**.

The plot area border and shading are removed.

12 Click in the document outside of the chart area to deselect the chart. Click once on the chart to select it. On the Formatting toolbar, click the **Center** button ▤.

The chart area is centered horizontally on the page, as shown in Figure 5.18.

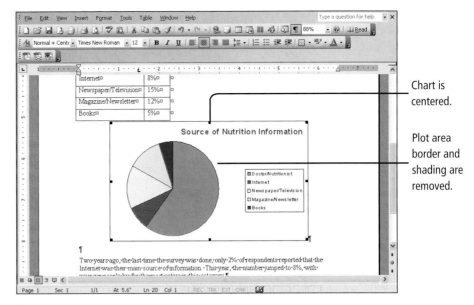

Chart is centered.

Plot area border and shading are removed.

Figure 5.18

13 In the table, click anywhere to position the insertion point. From the **Table** menu, point to **Delete**, and then click **Table**.

The table is removed, but the chart retains its data because the data is stored in the datasheet associated with the chart.

14 On the Standard toolbar, click the **Save** button ![save icon].

Objective 3
Add Special Text Effects

Word provides a number of methods to format text in a distinctive manner. For example, magazines and books sometimes use a large first letter to begin the first paragraph of an article or chapter. This is referred to as a ***drop cap***. The first letter can be three or four times taller than the rest of the text, which gives the text a finished look. Other distinctive text formatting is accomplished by adding a shadow effect, applying special underlining, or reducing the spacing between the letters.

Activity 5.6 Creating a Drop Cap

A drop cap gives text a professional look, but use it only once in an article or chapter.

1 Press [Ctrl] + [Home] to move to the top of the document. In the paragraph beginning *Nutrition information* select the letter *N* at the beginning of the paragraph.

2 From the **Format** menu, click **Drop Cap**.

The Drop Cap dialog box displays. Under Position, notice that the default is *None*, and there are two other options. The ***Dropped*** position enlarges the letter and places it into the text, as illustrated by the small example. The ***In margin*** position places the enlarged letter in the left margin. See Figure 5.19.

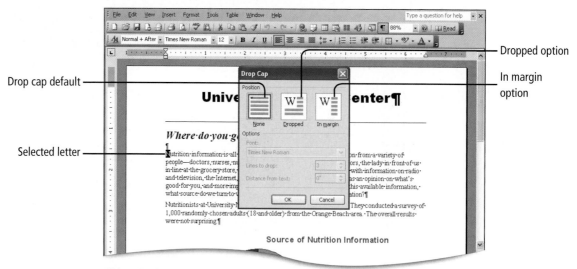

Figure 5.19

3 Under **Position**, click **Dropped**.

4 Under **Options**, click the **Lines to drop spin box up arrow** to change the line height of the drop cap to **4** lines.

Compare your Drop Cap dialog box with Figure 5.20.

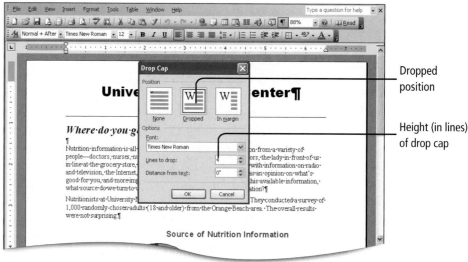

Figure 5.20

5 In the **Drop Cap** dialog box, click **OK**.

The drop cap is inserted in the text, and resize handles display around its border indicating that it is selected.

6 On the Formatting toolbar, click the **Font Color button arrow** [A▾], and from the displayed palette in the second row, click the sixth color—**Blue**.

The drop cap color changes to blue.

7 Click anywhere in the document to deselect the drop cap.

Compare your screen with Figure 5.21.

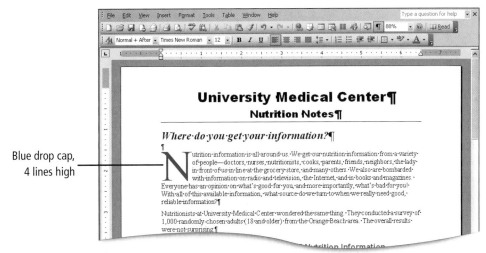

Blue drop cap, 4 lines high

Figure 5.21

8 On the Standard toolbar, click the **Save** button .

Activity 5.7 Adding a Shadow to a Title

Special text effects, such as shadows, are effective when used sparingly. Use the Font dialog box to add text effects and also to change several font characteristics at the same time.

1 Move to the top of the document. Move the pointer into the left margin to the left of the first line of text. When the pointer changes to a white arrow, click once to select the entire line.

2 From the **Format** menu, click **Font**.

The Font dialog box displays.

3 If necessary, at the top of the **Font** dialog box, click the **Font tab**.

In this dialog box, you can change many font characteristics, and a Preview window at the bottom of the dialog box will reflect the changes you make to the selected text. See Figure 5.22.

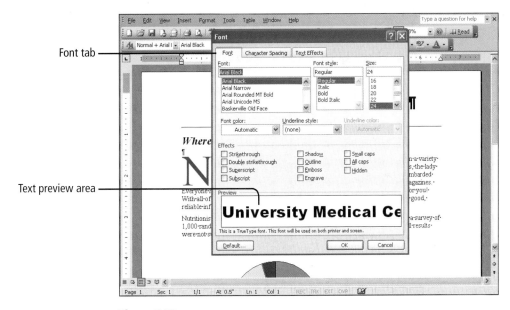

Font tab

Text preview area

Figure 5.22

4 In the **Font** dialog box, under **Font style**, click **Bold**.

Notice that the text in the preview box is shown in bold.

5 In the **Size** box, select **24** and type **32**

The 32-point font size is not an option in the Size list. If you want a font size that does not appear in the list, you can type it in the Size box.

6 Click the **Font color arrow**, and then in the second row, click **Blue**.

Blue is the sixth color in the second row. If you pause your mouse pointer over the colors, a ScreenTip displays the name of each color.

7 Under **Effects**, select the **Small caps** check box.

8 Under **Effects**, select the **Shadow** check box.

The changes to the text are reflected in the Preview box, as shown in Figure 5.23.

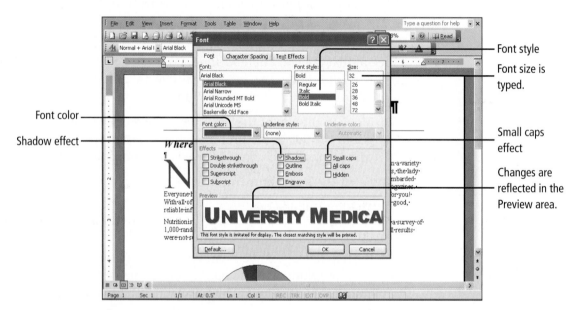

Font style

Font size is typed.

Font color

Shadow effect

Small caps effect

Changes are reflected in the Preview area.

Figure 5.23

9 At the bottom of the **Font** dialog box, click **OK**, and then click anywhere to deselect the title and view the changes you have made. Compare your screen with Figure 5.24.

Figure 5.24

10 Move the pointer into the left margin to the left of the subtitle line, *Nutrition Notes*. When the pointer changes to a white arrow, drag down to select the subtitle, the divider line, and the heading *Where do you get your information?*

The second and third lines of the document are selected.

11 On the Formatting toolbar, click the **Font Color** button, which should have retained its previous usage of blue. If not, click the arrow on the right of the Font Color button and click the same color you used for the title and the drop cap. Click anywhere to deselect the text.

The top three lines of the document are blue, along with the drop cap and the title of the chart, as shown in Figure 5.25.

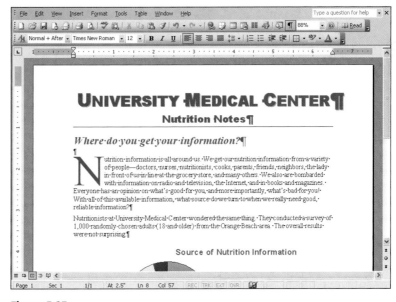

Figure 5.25

12 On the Standard toolbar, click the **Save** button.

Activity 5.8 Modifying Character Spacing

Increasing or decreasing font size changes the size of the letters and the spacing between the letters proportionally. You can make the text look denser by condensing (decreasing) the space between characters, which does not affect the font size. You can also expand (increase) the space between characters. This technique is useful to make text completely fill a page or to make text that is a little too long for a page or a text box fit precisely.

1 Move the pointer into the margin to the left of the paragraph beginning *Nutrition information*. When the pointer changes to a white arrow, drag down to select that paragraph and the next one.

When you use this method to select a paragraph containing a drop cap, the paragraph marker above the drop cap is also selected, as shown in Figure 5.26. Notice the spacing of the letters in the selected paragraphs.

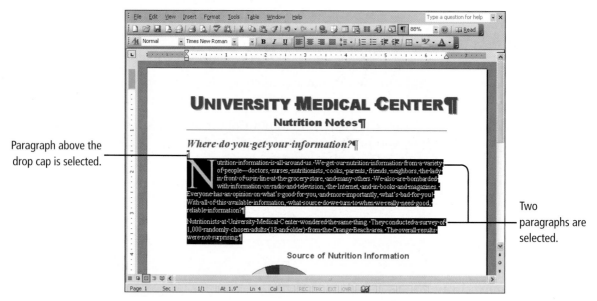

Paragraph above the drop cap is selected.

Two paragraphs are selected.

Figure 5.26

2 From the **Format** menu, click **Font**.

The Font dialog box displays.

3 At the top of the **Font** dialog box, click the **Character Spacing tab**.

In this dialog box you can adjust the scale, spacing, and position of characters, and a Preview window at the bottom of the dialog box will reflect changes made to the selected text.

4 Look at the Preview box and notice the spacing. Click the **Spacing arrow**. From the displayed list, point to **Condensed**, and then watch the Preview area as you click.

The *By* box to the right of the *Spacing* box displays *1 pt*. This means that the characters are moved 1 point closer together.

5 To the right of the **Spacing** box, click the **By spin box up arrow** to change the spacing to **0.3 pt**.

This will move the characters about a third of a point closer. Recall that a point is ¹⁄₇₂ of an inch. Compare your dialog box with Figure 5.27.

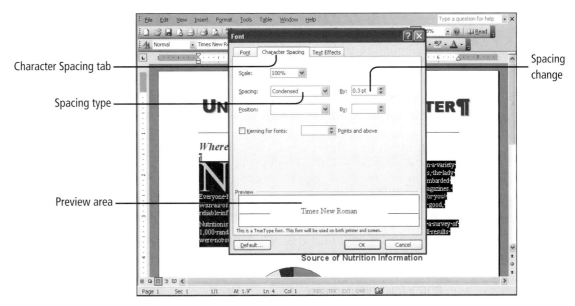

Character Spacing tab

Spacing type

Preview area

Spacing change

Figure 5.27

6 At the bottom of the **Font** dialog box, click **OK**. Click anywhere to deselect the text.

Notice how much the text is condensed. The first paragraph, which was seven lines long, is now six lines long, but the font size remains unchanged. Compare the selected text in Figure 5.26 to the text in Figure 5.28.

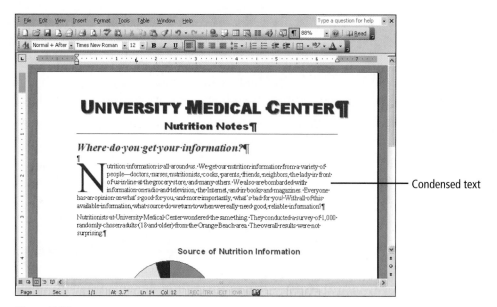

Figure 5.28

7 From the **View** menu, click **Header and Footer**. On the Header and Footer toolbar, click the **Switch Between Header and Footer** button 🖳.

8 On the **Header and Footer** toolbar, click the **Insert AutoText** button Insert AutoText ▾, and then click **Filename**.

The file name is inserted in the footer.

9 On the **Header and Footer** toolbar, click the **Close** button Close.

10 On the Standard toolbar, click the **Save** button 🖫.

11 On the Standard toolbar, click the **Print Preview** button 🔍. Take a moment to check your work. On the Print Preview toolbar, click the **Close Preview** button Close.

12 Make any necessary changes to your document. When you are satisfied, on the Standard toolbar, click the **Print** button 🖨. Close the document.

End You have completed Project 5A ————————————

Project 5B Medical Records

Businesses often develop a uniform appearance for procedure and policy manuals that includes headings to help organize the material and make it easier for a user to find information. Microsoft Word includes a set of predefined styles with several heading levels, or you can create your own styles to use in your documents.

In Activities 5.9 through 5.17, you will edit a section of a medical center Policy and Procedure manual by applying new and existing styles. Your completed document will look similar to Figure 5.29. You will save your document as *5B_Medical_Records_Firstname_Lastname.*

Medical Center Policy and Procedure Manual

Topic: Official Medical Records

Policy and Procedure Manual Location: Section 1, Medical Center Administration

Section 1.4, Medical Records Policy and Procedure

Section 1.4.1, Integrated Central Medical Records System

I. Purpose:
> The purpose of this policy is to provide guidance to *Medical Center* physicians, both faculty and staff, in the development and maintenance of an integrated, central medic[al] documentation will be develope[d] receives assessment or treatmen[t] unit. All documentation will be st[...] This makes it a more efficient an[d] patient, and also better serves the[...]

II. Definitions:
> A. Integrated Medical Record – [...] the documentation and diagn[osis] and those received from othe[r]
> B. Centralized Medical Records [...] unique medical records of all [...] business functions.
> C. Official Medical Record – A [...] current centralized system an[d] system includes those medica[l] Family Practice Center, Pedia[...] Women's Center, Plastic Surg[ery]
> D. Office/Shadow Records – Me[...] centralized medical records s[ystem] Official medical record.

III. Policy:
> It is the policy of *Medical Cen[ter]* medical records system and to [...] order to support patient care, [...] functions of the organization acc[...]
> A. All original internal and exte[r] Medical Records to be assem[bled] medical record.

5B_Medical_Records_Firstname_Lastna[me]

> B. Appropriately document the encounter within the patient's Official medical record.
> C. Discourage the creation or use of Office/Shadow medical records.

IV. Procedure:
> Whenever possible, the patient's *Official medical record will be made available for each patient encounter with Medical Center physicians.*
> A. All documentation should either occur directly within the Official medical record in accordance with applicable policies or should be forwarded to Medical Records after completed.
> B. Any external patient information received should be appropriately reviewed by the responsible provider and forwarded to Medical Records.

5B_Medical_Records_Firstname_Lastname

Figure 5.29
Project 5B—Medical Records

Objective 4
Use Existing Styles

A **template** is a model for documents of the same type, and it stores information that determines the basic structure for a document in Word. The template information includes document settings such as page layout, fonts, special formatting, and styles. A **style** is a group of formatting commands that Word stores with a specific name, which you can retrieve by name and apply to text. Unless you select a specific template, all new Word documents are based on the **Normal template**—stored in your computer as *Normal.dot*.

The Normal template contains a small set of built-in styles that you can use to format text with one action instead of three or four. The default settings for the Normal template include such formatting as Times New Roman font, font size of 12 pt., single spacing, left alignment, 1" top and bottom margins, and 1.25" left and right margins. Styles are added to text using either the Style button in the Formatting toolbar, or the Styles and Formatting task pane. There are four types of styles, as shown in Figure 5.30.

Word Style Types

Style Type	Purpose
Paragraph style	Controls the formatting of a paragraph, including line spacing, indents, alignment, tab stops, font type, and size.
Character style	Affects the selected text within a paragraph, including font style, font size, bold, italic, and underline.
Table style	Formats border type and style, shading, cell alignment, and fonts in a table.
List style	Formats font style, font size, alignment, and bullet or number characteristics in lists.

Figure 5.30

Activity 5.9 Displaying Styles

You can display the styles available for paragraphs on the left side of a document and show all of the available styles in a task pane on the right side of the document.

1 On the Standard toolbar, click the **Open** button 📂. Navigate to the location where the student files for this textbook are stored. Locate and open **w05B_Medical_Records**. Save the file as **5B_Medical_Records_Firstname_Lastname**

2 On the left edge of the horizontal scroll bar, click the **Normal View** button 📄.

The document changes to Normal View. Recall that Normal view gives you more area in which to type, but does not display graphics or the edges of the page. It also enables you to see the styles used for each paragraph. Page breaks are indicated by a dotted line.

3 From the **Tools** menu, click **Options**. Be sure the **View tab** is selected. See Figure 5.31.

View tab

Normal View button

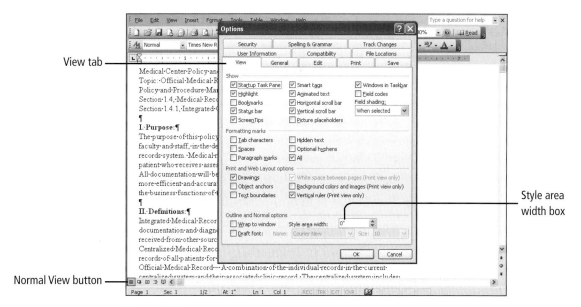

Figure 5.31

Note — Is Your Style Area Already On?

If the last person to use the computer left the style area on, you may see it when you switch to Normal View. If this is the case, perform Steps 6 and 7 to verify that your style area is the right size.

4 At the bottom of the **View tab**, under **Outline and Normal options**, click the **Style area width spin box up arrow** until the width is **0.6"**.

5 In the lower right corner, click **OK**.

A style area opens at the left side of the document, and the style name for each paragraph displays. All of the paragraphs in this document use the default Normal style, except the section headings, which use a style named *Subheading*—a style created for this chapter. See Figure 5.32.

Style area

Subheading style

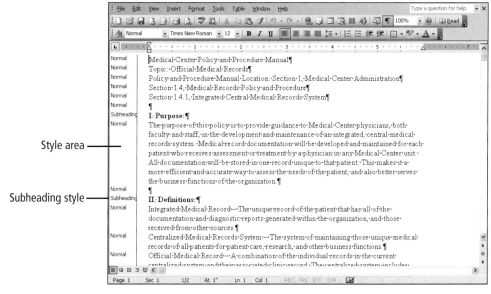

Figure 5.32

6 On the left side of the Formatting toolbar, click the **Styles and Formatting** button.

The Styles and Formatting task pane displays. The style of the paragraph that contains the insertion point is shown in the box at the top of this pane and is bordered in blue in the list of available styles.

7 If the right edge of the text is hidden behind the task pane, on the Standard toolbar, click the **Zoom button arrow** 100% , and then click **Page Width**.

8 In your document, click to place the insertion point anywhere in the line that begins *II. Definitions*.

In the style area on the left, notice that this paragraph has the *Subheading* style applied. In the Styles and Formatting task pane, notice that the *Subheading* style is selected.

9 In the **Styles and Formatting** task pane, under **Pick formatting to apply**, examine the list of style names. If necessary, at the bottom of the **Styles and Formatting** task pane, in the **Show** box, click the arrow, and then click **Available formatting**.

The built-in styles, plus the *Subheading* style that was created for this chapter, are listed. See Figure 5.33.

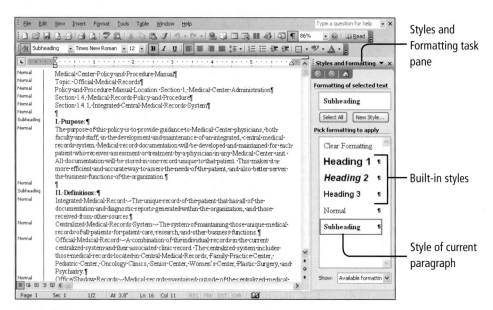

Figure 5.33

Note — Style Names Do Not Print

Although the style area looks like it is part of the document, it is not. It does not print, and there is no method to print the style names as shown on the screen.

10 On the Standard toolbar, click the **Save** button 🖫.

Activity 5.10 Working with Default Styles

Four styles are included with every document created with the Normal template, which is the default template in Word. The four styles include three heading styles and the Normal style. The Subheading style was created for this chapter. Your version of Word may display other styles that have been added to the default template.

1 At the top of the document, click to position the insertion point in the first line, which begins *Medical Center Policy.*

This is the document title. To apply a paragraph style, you need only position the insertion point somewhere in the paragraph—you do not need to select the entire paragraph.

2 In the **Styles and Formatting** task pane, under **Pick formatting to apply**, click **Heading 1**.

The Heading 1 style is applied to the title. The Heading 1 style includes a font size of 16 and bold font style. Notice that the *Heading 1* name in the Styles and Formatting task pane has the same character formatting—the style name also acts as a style preview, as shown in Figure 5.34.

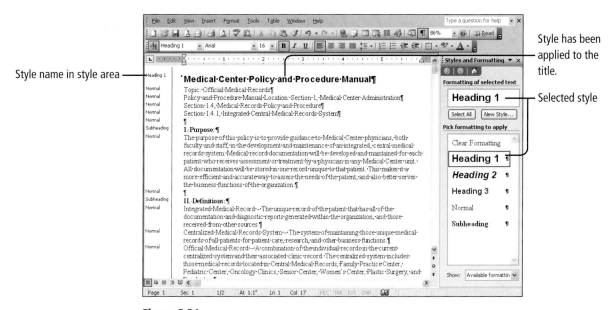

Style name in style area

Style has been applied to the title.

Selected style

Figure 5.34

3 Position the insertion point in the next line, beginning *Topic: Official.*

4 In the **Styles and Formatting** task pane, under **Pick formatting to apply**, click **Heading 2**.

The Heading 2 style includes a font size of 14, smaller than Heading 1, and bold and italic font style.

5 Position the insertion point in the next line, beginning *Policy and Procedure Manual.*

6 In the **Styles and Formatting** task pane, under **Pick formatting to apply**, click **Heading 3**.

The Heading 3 style includes font size of 13 and bold font style, as shown in Figure 5.35.

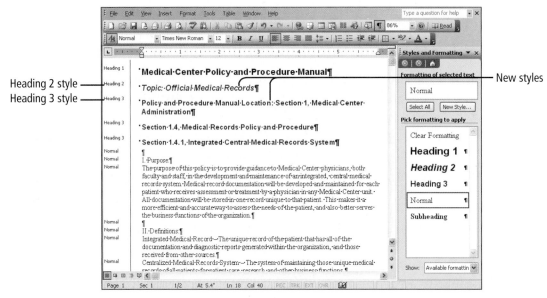

Heading 2 style
Heading 3 style
New styles

Figure 5.35

7 Move the pointer to the left of the line beginning *Section 1.4, Medical.* When the pointer changes to a white arrow, drag down to select that paragraph and the next one, beginning *Section 1.4.1, Integrated.*

8 In the **Styles and Formatting** task pane, under **Pick formatting to apply**, click **Heading 3**.

Notice that you can apply styles to more than one paragraph at a time.

9 Click to position the insertion point in the next line, beginning *I. Purpose.* In the **Styles and Formatting** task pane, under **Pick formatting to apply**, click **Heading 3**.

10 Click to position the insertion point in the line beginning *II. Definitions.* In the **Styles and Formatting** task pane, under **Pick formatting to apply**, click **Heading 3**.

11 On the Standard toolbar, click the **Save** button ![Save icon].

Activity 5.11 Clearing Styles

You can remove all formatting from a document or from selected text in a document, which removes any styles that were applied.

1 If necessary, position the insertion point in the line beginning *II. Definitions.*

2 In the **Styles and Formatting** task pane, under **Pick formatting to apply**, click **Clear Formatting**.

The Heading 3 style is removed, and the paragraph reverts to the Normal style. Notice that in task pane list, *Normal* is bordered.

3 Click to position the insertion point in the line beginning *I. Purpose.*

4 In the **Styles and Formatting** task pane, under **Pick formatting to apply**, click **Clear Formatting**.

The Heading 3 style is removed, and the paragraph reverts to the Normal style, as shown in Figure 5.36.

Paragraphs revert to Normal style.

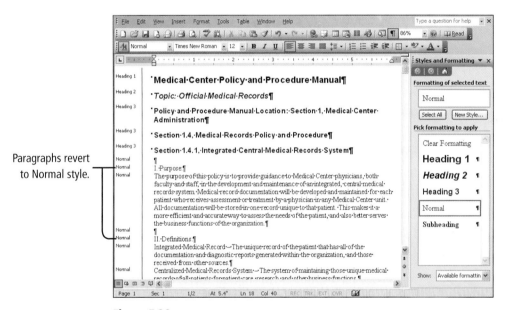

Figure 5.36

5 Move the pointer into the left margin to the left of the paragraph beginning *I. Purpose.* When the pointer changes to a white arrow, click once.

6 Move the pointer into the left margin to the left of the paragraph beginning *II. Definitions.* When the pointer changes to a white arrow, hold down Ctrl and click once.

Two nonadjacent paragraphs are selected, as shown in Figure 5.37.

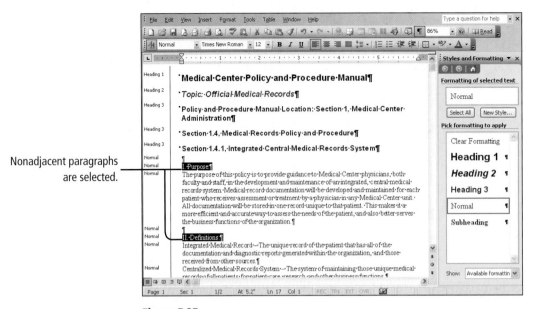

Nonadjacent paragraphs are selected.

Figure 5.37

7 In the **Styles and Formatting** task pane, under **Pick formatting to apply**, click **Subheading**.

The Subheading style is restored to both paragraphs.

8 On the Standard toolbar, click the **Save** button ⊟.

Objective 5
Create and Modify New Styles

By default, only a few styles are included with the Normal template, but you can create your own styles based on formats that you use often. For example, if you always type your name or company name in a distinctive manner (e.g., for example, bold, Verdana font, font size 14), you can create that as a style and apply it when needed. After you have created a style, you can modify it to suit your changing needs. One of the strengths of using styles is that it enables you to change all instances of a style throughout a document at the same time.

Activity 5.12 Creating and Applying Paragraph Styles

When you need to match special formatting guidelines to complete a document, you can use paragraph styles that will enable you to perform several formatting steps with a single click.

1 Move the pointer to the left of the line beginning *The purpose of this policy*. When the pointer changes to a white arrow, drag down to select the entire paragraph. Alternatively, you can double-click in the paragraph margin to select it.

2 On the Formatting toolbar, click the **Italic** button [I].

3 From the **Format** menu, click **Paragraph**. If necessary, click the **Indents and Spacing tab**.

4 Under **General**, click the **Alignment arrow**, and then click **Justified**.

5 Under **Indentation**, click the **Left spin box up arrow** to set the left indent at **0.5"**.

6 Under **Indentation**, click the **Right spin box up arrow** to set the right indent at **0.5"**.

Compare your Paragraph dialog box with Figure 5.38.

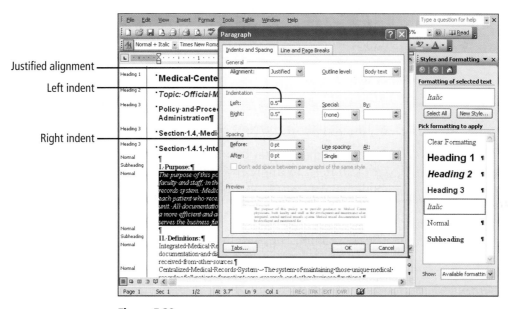

Justified alignment ——

Left indent ——

Right indent ——

Figure 5.38

7 At the bottom of the **Paragraph** dialog box, click **OK**.

The changes you made are reflected in the paragraph, and the paragraph remains selected.

8 With the paragraph still selected, in the **Styles and Formatting** task pane, under **Formatting of selected text**, click **New Style**.

The New Style dialog box displays.

9 In the **New Style** dialog box, under **Properties**, in the **Name** box, type **Intro**

A style formatting list displays under the preview window, as shown in Figure 5.39.

New style name ———

Selected paragraph ———

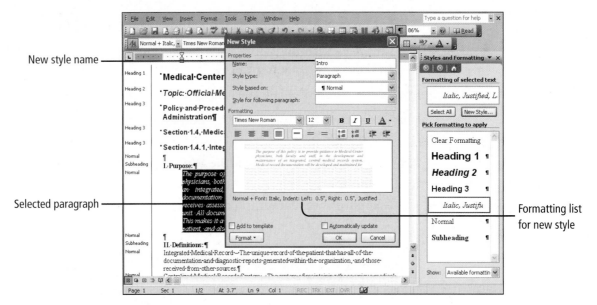

——— Formatting list for new style

Figure 5.39

10 At the bottom of the **New Style** dialog box, click **OK**.

Even though you just created a style using the selected paragraph, you still need to apply the style. A temporary style displays the modifications you have made.

11 In the **Styles and Formatting** task pane, click the **Intro** style.

The new style is applied to the selected paragraph.

More Knowledge — Creating Styles Using the Style Box

There is a shortcut method to create styles using the Style box. Make the desired changes to a paragraph. In the Formatting toolbar, click once in the Style box. Type the name of the new style and press Enter. The new style is created and applied to the current paragraph. There are limitations to this method of creating styles. You can create only paragraph styles, and you have less control over the style than you have when creating a style in the New Style dialog box.

---

12 Scroll down and, near the end of the first page, click to place the insertion point in the paragraph beginning *It is the policy.* In the **Styles and Formatting** task pane, click the **Intro** style.

The paragraph changes to the new style, with both margins indented, the text justified, with italic font style. See Figure 5.40.

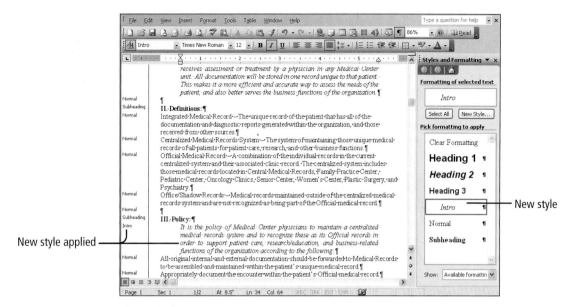

New style applied

New style

Figure 5.40

13 Scroll down and click to place the insertion point in the paragraph beginning *Whenever possible* near the end of the document. In the **Styles and Formatting** task pane, click the **Intro** style.

The paragraph changes to the new style.

14 On the Standard toolbar, click the **Save** button 🔲.

Activity 5.13 Creating and Applying List Styles

Styles can be created for lists and then applied to any text, which will change the text to match the list characteristics of the style.

1 Near the end of the document, move the pointer to the left of the line beginning *All documentation should*. When the pointer changes to a white arrow, drag down to select the last two paragraphs.

2 On the Formatting toolbar, click the **Numbering** button 📄.

The two paragraphs are numbered.

3 From the **Format** menu, click **Bullets and Numbering**. In the displayed **Bullets and Numbering** dialog box, click the **Numbered tab**.

4 From the **Bullets and Numbering** dialog box, click the option with capital letters, as shown in Figure 5.41. If that option is not displayed, at the bottom of the Bullets and Numbering dialog box, click the Reset button.

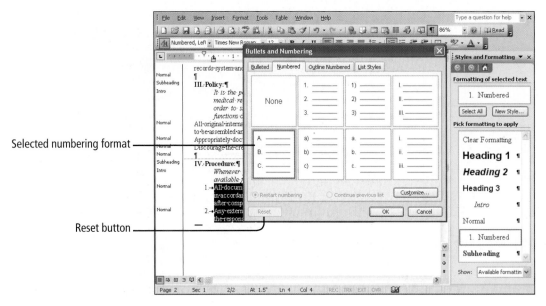

Selected numbering format

Reset button

Figure 5.41

5 At the bottom of the **Bullets and Numbering** dialog box, click **OK**.

The numbers change to letters.

6 From the Formatting toolbar, click the **Increase Indent** button ▤.

The selected list items are indented to the right.

7 In the **Styles and Formatting** task pane, under **Formatting of selected text**, click **New Style**.

The New Style dialog box displays.

8 In the **New Style** dialog box, under **Properties**, in the **Name** box, type **Points**

9 In the **New Style** dialog box, under **Properties**, click the **Style type arrow**, and then click **List**.

The list options display in the New Style dialog box, as shown in Figure 5.42.

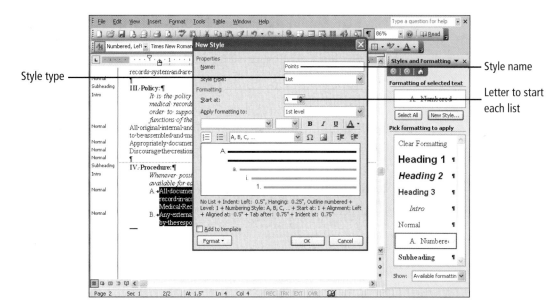

Style type ——

Style name ——

Letter to start each list ——

Figure 5.42

10 At the bottom of the **New Style** dialog box, click **OK**.

The list changes to the new style, and the new style name is displayed in the list of styles in the Styles and Formatting task pane. Notice in Figure 5.43 that the new list style also displays a small icon indicating the style type.

11 In the **Styles and Formatting** task pane, click the **Points** style.

Even though you just created a style using the selected paragraph, you still need to apply the style. When you apply a list style, the style displays in the Style box on the Formatting toolbar and in the Styles and Formatting task pane, but still displays Normal in the styles area. See Figure 5.43.

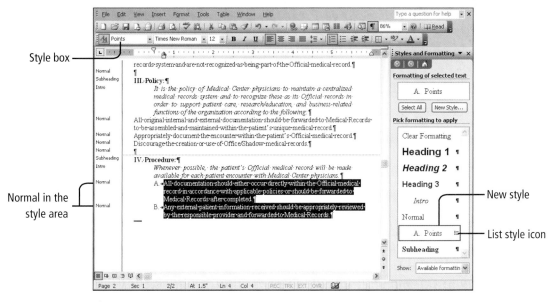

Style box ——

Normal in the style area ——

New style ——

List style icon ——

Figure 5.43

12 Scroll up in the document. In each paragraph containing text that uses the Normal style, position the insertion point, and then in the **Styles and Formatting** task pane, click the **Points** style.

Your document should look similar to Figure 5.44.

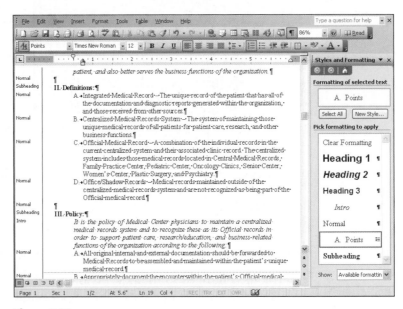

Figure 5.44

13 On the Standard toolbar, click the **Save** button.

Activity 5.14 Creating and Applying Character Styles

Character styles are applied to selected text within a paragraph; they do not affect the formatting of the entire paragraph.

1 In the **Styles and Formatting** task pane, under **Formatting of selected text**, click **New Style**.

The New Style dialog box displays.

2 In the **New Style** dialog box, under **Properties**, in the **Name** box, type **Med Center**

3 Under **Properties**, click the **Style type arrow**, and then click **Character**.

Under Formatting, the character options display in the New Style dialog box.

4 In the **New Style** dialog box, under **Formatting**, locate the two boxes with arrows.

From the first box, you can select a font, and from the second box you can select a font size.

5 Click the **Font Size button arrow** and then click **14** points.

6 In the **New Style** dialog box, under **Formatting**, click the **Bold** button **B**.

7 In the **New Style** dialog box, under **Formatting**, click the **Font Color button arrow** **A·**, and in the third row, click the first color—**Red**. Compare your dialog box with Figure 5.45.

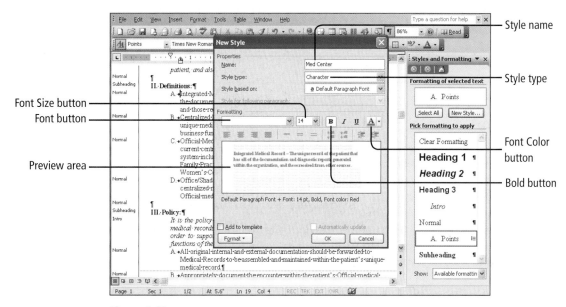

Figure 5.45

8 At the bottom of the **New Style** dialog box, click **OK**. Scroll to the top of the document.

The style is added to the Styles and Formatting task pane list, but the style has not been used to modify any text. Notice that the symbol on the right of the new style is a small *a*, which indicates a character style.

9 In the paragraph beginning *The purpose of this policy*, in the first sentence, select *Medical Center*.

10 In the **Styles and Formatting** task pane, click the **Med Center** style. Click on the text you just formatted to deselect the text.

The three formatting changes you made in the New Style dialog box are applied. See Figure 5.46.

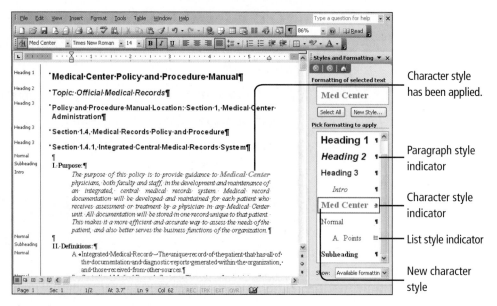

Figure 5.46

11 In the same paragraph, in the fifth line, select **Medical Center**. In the **Styles and Formatting** task pane, click the **Med Center** style.

12 Locate *Medical Center* in the Intro style paragraphs following *III. Policy* and *IV. Procedure*, and apply the **Med Center** style to both, as shown in Figure 5.47.

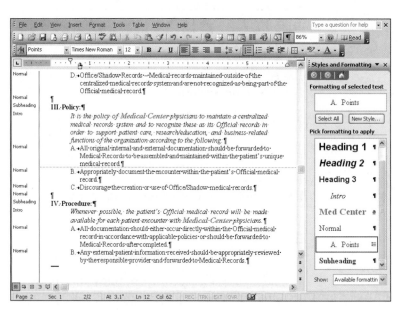

Figure 5.47

13 On the Standard toolbar, click the **Save** button.

Activity 5.15 Selecting and Modifying Styles

If you want to change a style, you can select all instances of the style, and then modify all of the paragraphs at once.

1 In the **Styles and Formatting** task pane, pause the mouse pointer over the **Subheading** paragraph style. Click the arrow on the right of the **Subheading** style.

A short menu displays, as shown in Figure 5.48. Here you can select, delete, or modify this style.

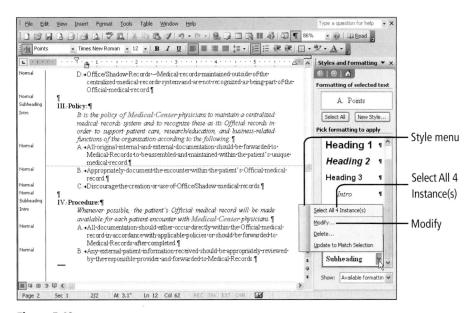

Style menu

Select All 4 Instance(s)

Modify

Figure 5.48

2 From the displayed menu, click **Select All 4 Instance(s)**.

All four of the Subheading style paragraphs are selected. While not required to change all of the paragraphs at once, selecting all of the instances helps you see where the style is used in the document.

3 Click the arrow on the right of the **Subheading** style again. From the displayed menu, click **Modify**.

The Modify Style dialog box displays.

4 In the **Modify Style** dialog box, under **Formatting**, click the **Italic** button $\boxed{I}$.

5 Near the bottom of the **Modify Style** dialog box, select the **Automatically update** check box.

The Automatically update feature enables you to change all of the paragraphs using the same style, and the style itself, by selecting and modifying only one paragraph. Compare your dialog box with Figure 5.49.

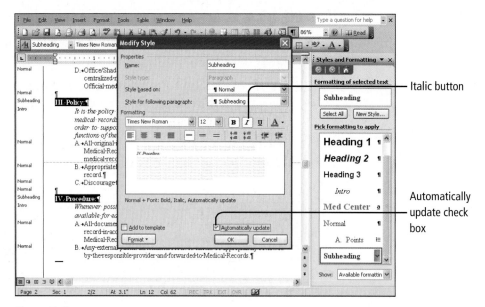

Figure 5.49

6 At the bottom of the **Modify Style** dialog box, click **OK**.

All of the paragraphs using the Subheading style are changed, as shown in Figure 5.50.

Subheading style has been changed.

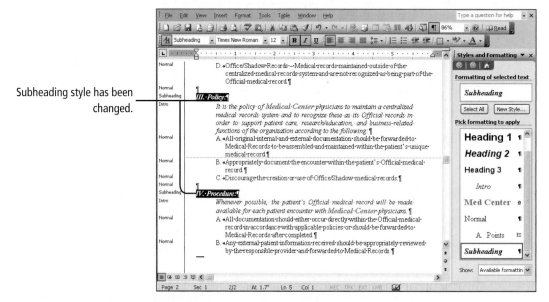

Figure 5.50

7 In the **Styles and Formatting** task pane, pause the mouse pointer over the **Med Center** character style. Click the arrow on the right of the **Med Center** style.

8 From the displayed menu, click **Modify**.

The Modify Style dialog box displays.

9 In the **Modify Style** dialog box, under **Formatting**, click the **Font Size button arrow**, and then click **12** points.

Compare your dialog box with Figure 5.51.

Font size is
changed.

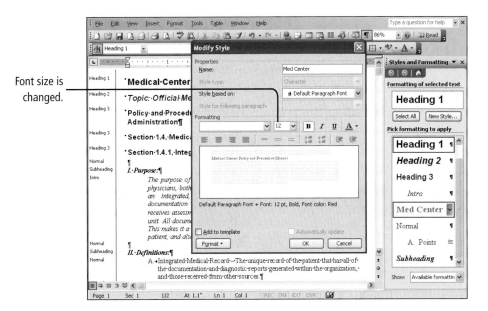

Figure 5.51

10 At the bottom of the **Modify Style** dialog box, click **OK**.

All of the text using the Med Center style is changed.

11 From the **Tools** menu, click **Options**. If necessary, click the **View tab**. Under **Outline and Normal options**, click the **Style area width spin box down arrow** until the style area width is **0"**. At the bottom of the **Options** dialog box, click **OK**. Alternatively, drag the vertical line on the right side of the style area to the left edge of the document window.

The style area on the left side of the screen closes.

12 On the Standard toolbar, click the **Save** button .

Objective 6
Modify the Document Window

When you are working in Print Layout View, the gap between pages can take up a large portion of the screen, particularly when you are working on a laptop computer. You can minimize the gap between the pages so you can see more of your document, yet still maintain the visual advantage of seeing the edges of the paper. You can also split the window so that you can view two parts of a document at the same time. This is especially useful in long documents when you need to see pages at the beginning of the document and pages at the end of the document at the same time.

Activity 5.16 Hiding Spaces Between Pages

1 In the **Styles and Formatting** task pane, in the title bar, click the **Close** button .

2 On the left edge of the horizontal scroll bar, click the **Print Layout View** button . If necessary, set the Zoom to 100%.

The document changes to Print Layout View.

3 Scroll down until the break between the two pages is in view in the middle of your screen.

Notice how much of the screen is unused. You can see that a large portion of the screen contains blank white or gray space.

4 Move the pointer into the gray area between the two pages.

The pointer changes to a Hide White Spaces pointer, as shown in Figure 5.52.

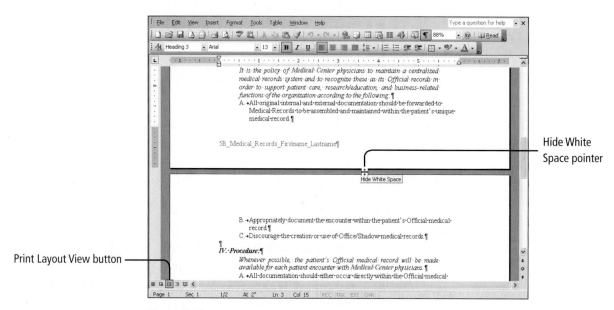

Figure 5.52

5 With the pointer positioned between the pages, click once.

Notice that the gap is closed, and the text appears to be on one continuous page, with a line showing the page breaks, as shown in Figure 5.53. Notice also that the footer area is hidden. The headers and footer areas are removed from the display, although both will still print.

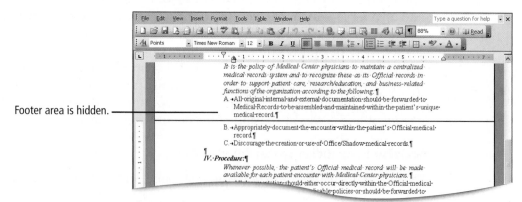

Figure 5.53

6 Move the pointer over the black line between the two pages and click.

The gap between the pages displays again.

Activity 5.17 Splitting the Window

1 At the top of the vertical scroll bar, above the arrow, locate the small gray bar, called a **split box**, and then move the pointer over the split box.

The pointer changes to a Resize Pointer, an up- and down-pointing arrow, as shown in Figure 5.54.

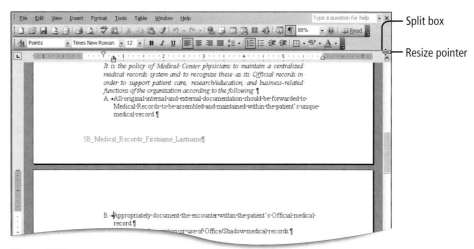

Figure 5.54

2 With the Resize pointer displayed, drag about half way down the screen and release the mouse button.

The window splits in two, with a separate vertical and horizontal scroll bar for each portion of the window, as shown in Figure 5.55.

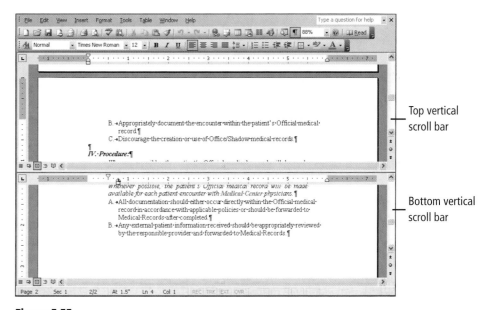

Figure 5.55

3 Use the top vertical scroll bar to scroll to the top of the document.

4 Use the bottom vertical scroll bar to scroll to the last section of the document, beginning with the *IV. Procedure* heading.

You can work on one part of the document while viewing another part, and you can cut or copy and paste between the two windows. If you are working in one window, you will need to click in the other window to make it active.

5 In the upper window, move the pointer slightly below the horizontal scroll bar until the Resize pointer displays.

6 Double-click or, alternatively, drag the bar to the top of the screen.

The second window is closed.

7 From the **View** menu, click **Header and Footer**. On the Header and Footer toolbar, click the **Switch Between Header and Footer** button 🗗.

8 On the **Header and Footer** toolbar, click the **Insert AutoText** button Insert AutoText ▾, and then click **Filename**. On the **Header and Footer** toolbar, click the **Close** button Close.

9 On the Standard toolbar, click the **Save** button 🖫.

10 On the Standard toolbar, click the **Print Preview** button 🔍. Take a moment to check your work. On the Print Preview toolbar, click the **Close Preview** button Close.

11 Make any necessary changes to your document, and then, on the Standard toolbar, click the **Print** button 🖨.

12 On the far right edge of the menu bar, click the **Close Window** button ✕.

End You have completed Project 5B ──────────────

Project 5C Policy Outline

Outlines can help you organize the content of a document and provide a structure for writing. Microsoft Word has a built-in outline format that can be applied to documents.

In Activities 5.18 through 5.19, you will create a multilevel outline for a portion of a medical center policy manual. The manual will have eight sections, but the outline you will create will be for the Medical Center Facilities and Services section. Your completed document will look similar to Figure 5.56. You will save your document as *5C_Policy_Outline_Firstname_Lastname*.

MEDICAL CENTER POLICY AND PROCEDURE MANUAL

I. MEDICAL CENTER ADMINISTRATION
II. FACULTY POLICIES
III. STAFF POLICIES
IV. MEDICAL CENTER FACILITIES AND SERVICES
    A. Equipment Center
        1. Equipment Center Overview
        2. Checkout Procedures
        3. Equipment Purchases
        4. Equipment Repair
    B. Medical Communications
        1. Medical Communications Overview
        2. Medical Illustration Policies and Procedures
        3. Waiver Procedures
    C. Medical Center Libraries
        1. Graduate Library Policy and Procedures
        2. Medical Library Policy and Procedures
    D. Space and Facilities
        1. Medical Center Space Inventory
        2. Storage in Corridors
        3. Vacated Space
        4. Environmental Services
        5. Facilities Maintenance
        6. Cleanup Procedures
V. FINANCIAL MANAGEMENT
VI. HUMAN RESOURCES
VII. SAFETY AND SECURITY
VIII. FORMS

5C_Policy_Outline_Firstname_Lastname

Figure 5.56
Project 5C—Policy Outline

Objective 7
Create an Outline

An *outline* is a list of topics for an oral or written report that visually indicates the order in which the information will be discussed, and the relationship of the topics to each other and to the total report. Outlines are used in planning situations to organize and rearrange information. The most basic outline is a numbered list, which has only one outline level. Word provides up to nine levels in an outline.

Activity 5.18 Creating a Multilevel Outline

The first step in creating an outline is to define the outline format.

1 On the Standard toolbar, click the **Open** button. Navigate to the location where the student files for this textbook are stored. Locate and open **w05C_Policy_Outline**. Save the file as **5C_Policy_Outline_Firstname_Lastname**

2 Click to position the insertion point to the left of the second line, which begins *Medical Center Administration*. Using the scroll bar, scroll down to the end of the document, hold down the Shift key, point to end of the last line, and then click again.

All of the text, with the exception of the title, is selected.

3 On the **Format** menu, click **Bullets and Numbering**. In the displayed **Bullets and Numbering** dialog box, click the **Outline Numbered tab**. Click the second option in the first row.

The Bullets and Numbering dialog box should look like Figure 5.57. If the second option in the first row does not match the figure, see Step 4.

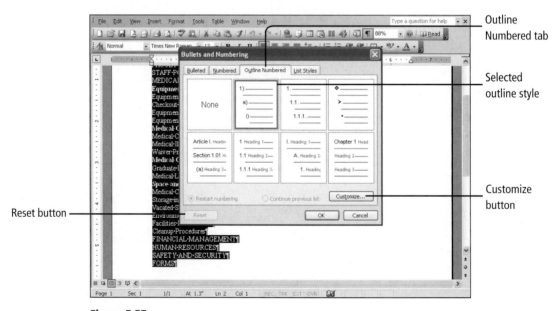

Outline Numbered tab

Selected outline style

Customize button

Reset button

Figure 5.57

4 Locate the **Reset** button at the bottom of the **Bullets and Numbering** dialog box. If the **Reset** button is active (dark), click it, and then click **Yes** when prompted to restore the default settings. If the **Reset** button is light gray, the button is inactive.

If someone has adjusted the outline settings on your computer, it is a good idea to restore the outline default settings.

5 In the lower right corner of the **Bullets and Numbering** dialog box, click the **Customize** button.

The Customize Outline Numbered List dialog box displays. Under Number format, the Level starts at 1 by default. All formatting that you do will affect only the selected outline level.

6 Under **Number format**, in the **Number style** box, click the arrow, and then click **I, II, III** from the list. In the **Number format** box, place the insertion point to the right of the parenthesis mark and press Bksp. Type a period.

Notice the format displayed in the Preview area.

7 Under **Number format**, in the **Number position** box, click the arrow, and then click **Right** from the list. Under **Text position**, click the **Indent at spin box up arrow** to set the indent at **0.3"**.

In a formal outline, the Roman numerals should align on the decimal. These numbers need a little extra space to fit properly. Compare your Customize Outline Numbered List dialog box with Figure 5.58.

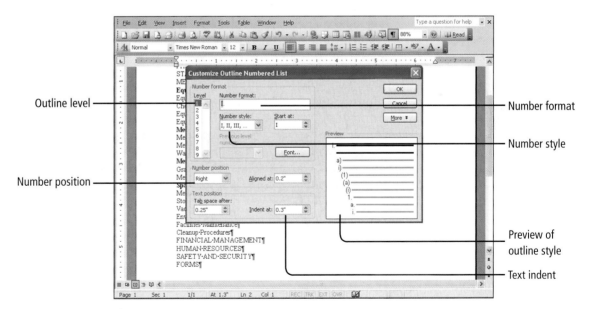

Outline level

Number position

Number format

Number style

Preview of outline style

Text indent

Figure 5.58

8 Under **Number format**, in the **Level** box, click **2**. In the **Number style** box, click the arrow, and then click **A, B, C** from the list. In the **Number format** box, place the insertion point to the right of the parenthesis mark and press Bksp. Type a period.

Compare your Customize Outline Numbered List dialog box with Figure 5.59.

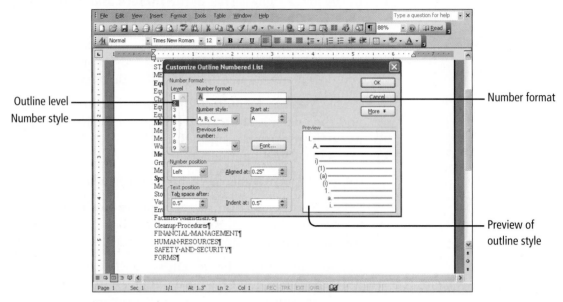

Outline level
Number style
Number format
Preview of outline style

Figure 5.59

9 Under **Number format**, in the **Level** box, click **3**. In the **Number style** box, click the arrow, and then click **1, 2, 3** from the list. In the **Number format** box, place the insertion point to the right of the parenthesis mark and press Bksp. Type a period.

Compare your Customize Outline Numbered List dialog box with Figure 5.60.

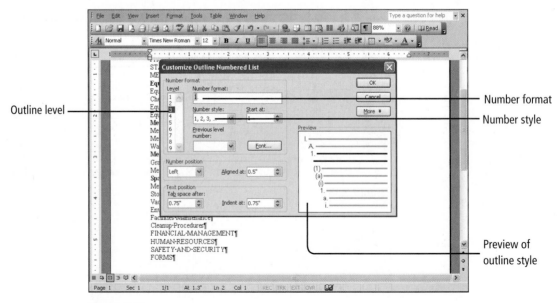

Outline level
Number format
Number style
Preview of outline style

Figure 5.60

10 In the upper right corner of the **Customize Outline Numbered List** dialog box, click **OK**. Hold down `Ctrl` and press `Home`.

The outline is created, but all items are at the top level—not visually indented to show different levels. See Figure 5.61.

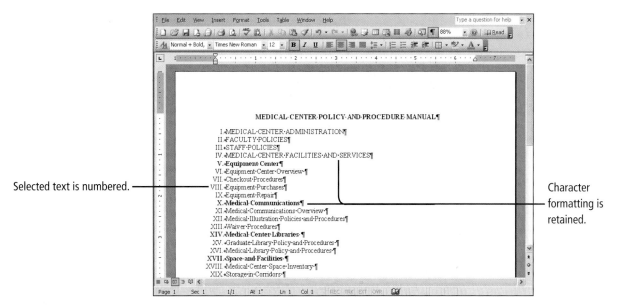

Selected text is numbered.

Character formatting is retained.

Figure 5.61

11 On the Standard toolbar, click the **Save** button 🖫.

Activity 5.19 Setting Outline Levels

After you set up a list as a multilevel outline, you can use the Increase Indent and Decrease Indent buttons on the Formatting toolbar to change outline levels. In this activity, you will set the lines shown in all caps at outline Level 1, the entries shown in bold at outline Level 2, and the entries shown in Normal text at outline Level 3.

1 Click to position the insertion point anywhere in the paragraph beginning *V. Equipment Center*.

You do not need to select the entire paragraph to change the outline level.

2 On the Formatting toolbar, click the **Increase Indent** button 📐.

The line is indented 0.25 inch, and the number changes from *V* to *A*, a second-level outline entry. See Figure 5.62.

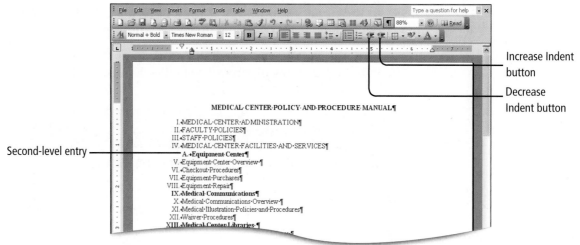

Increase Indent button

Decrease Indent button

Second-level entry

Figure 5.62

3 Move the pointer into the left margin to the left of the next line beginning *Equipment Center Overview*. When the pointer changes to a white arrow, drag down to select that paragraph and the next three.

Four lines are selected.

4 On the Formatting toolbar, click the **Increase Indent** button [image] twice.

All four lines become third-level outline entries, as shown in Figure 5.63.

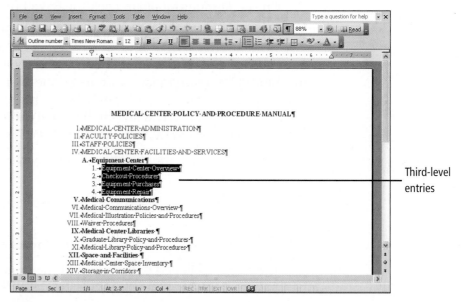

Third-level entries

Figure 5.63

5 Continue setting outline levels for the remainder of the document. Recall that text in all caps retains its first-level setting, text in bold should be set at the second level, and normal text should be set at the third level. Use the **Increase Indent** button [image] once on the bold text and twice on the normal text.

6 On the Standard toolbar, click the **Show/Hide** button ¶ to hide the nonprinting characters.

Compare your outline with Figure 5.64. Notice that the first-level entries align on the decimal points, not the left margin. This is the proper format of a formal outline.

First-level entry ——
Second-level entry ——
Third-level entry ——

First level aligned on the decimal points ——

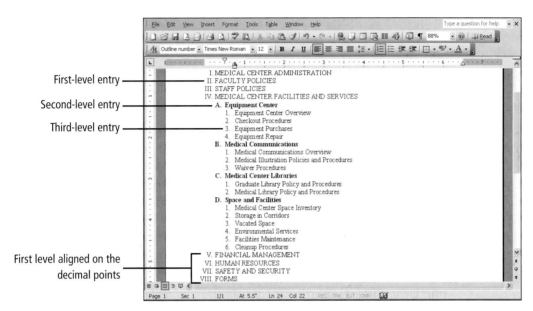

Figure 5.64

7 On the Standard toolbar, click the **Show/Hide** button ¶ to display the nonprinting characters again. From the **View** menu, click **Header and Footer**. On the Header and Footer toolbar, click the **Switch Between Header and Footer** button.

8 On the **Header and Footer** toolbar, click the **Insert AutoText** button Insert AutoText ▾, and then click **Filename**. On the **Header and Footer** toolbar, click the **Close** button Close.

9 On the Standard toolbar, click the **Save** button.

10 On the Standard toolbar, click the **Print Preview** button. Take a moment to check your work. On the Print Preview toolbar, click the **Close Preview** button Close.

11 Make any necessary changes to your document, and then, on the Standard toolbar, click the **Print** button.

12 On the far right edge of the menu bar, click the **Close Window** button ⊠.

End You have completed Project 5C

Project 5D Fitness

The Outline View enables you to use the Outlining toolbar to quickly create an outline based on heading styles. This outline can be rearranged, and heading levels can be changed with the click of a button.

In Activities 5.20 through 5.21 you will use the Outline View and the Outlining toolbar to create an outline for a summer fitness program at the University Medical Center. You will format existing text using the Outline toolbar, and you will modify and rearrange the outline. Your completed document will look similar to Figure 5.65. You will save your document as *5D_Fitness_Program_Firstname_Lastname.*

Summer Sports and Fitness Program

The University Medical Center will off a full range of sports, fitness, and dance programs beginning after Memorial Day. The following programs are offered to all Medical Center staff and their families at no cost.

Sports

Competitive sports will be offered in the mornings this summer. Slots fill up very quickly, especially for golf and tennis.

Golf

All rounds will be played on the University golf course on Monday and Wednesday mornings, except the week of the tournament. All participants will play in foursomes. Tee times will be at 6 a.m., 8 a.m., and 10 a.m.

Tennis

Matches will be played on the tennis courts at the IM building. If demand is great enough, the courts behind Married Housing will also be available. Court times will be assigned in one hour blocks on Monday or Thursday mornings. Players need to specify whether they are interested in singles, doubles, or mix

Rowing

There were not a lot of people interested in two- and this summer only kayak racing will be offered. The ti determined.

Fitness

Swimming

All swimming events will be held at the Natatorium t pool will be used most of the summer by the high sch Summer Quest program. Free swimming will be avai Swimmersize classes will be held at noon on Monday The number of fitness programs has been increased b sessions last summer.

Aerobics

The aerobics program has not been finalized.

Martial Arts

The martial arts program has not been finalized.

5D_Fitness_Firstname_Lastname

Kickboxing

Kickboxing has become extremely popular with young adults and additional classes will be considered. The classes are currently scheduled on Wednesday evening and Saturday morning.

Dance

Jazz and Tap

West Coast Swing

Ballroom Dance

5D_Fitness_Firstname_Lastname

Figure 5.65
Project 5D—Fitness

Objective 8
Create an Outline Using the Outline View and the Outlining Toolbar

When you display a document in Word's Outline View, Word treats each paragraph as a separate topic to which you can apply either Heading or Body Text styles. Word's built-in Heading 1 style represents the highest heading level, called Level 1, in an outline.

Activity 5.20 Creating an Outline Using the Outlining Toolbar

An outline created using the Outline View and the Outlining toolbar enables you to look at sections of a document, and move all of the text under a heading by clicking that heading.

1 On the Standard toolbar, click the **Open** button 📂. Navigate to the location where the student files for this textbook are stored. Locate and open **w05D_Fitness**. Save the file as **5D_Fitness_Firstname_Lastname**

2 To the left of the horizontal scroll bar, click the **Outline View** button 📄. To the left of the Formatting toolbar, click the **Styles and Formatting** button 🄰.

The document displays in Outline View. The Outlining toolbar displays under the Formatting toolbar and the Styles and Formatting task pane displays on the right of the screen.

3 Display the style area on the left of the screen by displaying the **Tools** menu, and then clicking **Options**. Click the **View tab**. Under **Outline and Normal options**, click the **Style area width spin box up arrow** until the style area width is **0.5"**. At the bottom of the **Options** dialog box, click **OK**.

In Outline View, each paragraph is considered a topic, and will be preceded by a symbol. If the paragraph does not have a Heading style, it is considered **body text**, and the symbol is a small box called a **topic marker**. Compare your screen with Figure 5.66.

Styles and Formatting button

Topic marker

Outline View button

Outlining toolbar

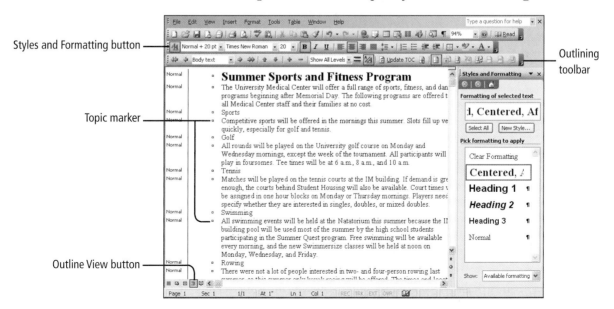

Figure 5.66

4 Click to position the insertion point in the fifth line of the document, which contains only the word *Sports*. In the Styles and Formatting task pane, under **Pick formatting to apply**, click **Heading 1**.

The paragraph changes to the Heading 1 style. The outline level, Level 1, displays in the Outline Level box. An open plus symbol, called an ***Expand button***, replaces the topic marker to the left of the paragraph, as shown in Figure 5.67. The expand button indicates that there is lower-level text associated with this heading, which in this instance is the remaining text in the document.

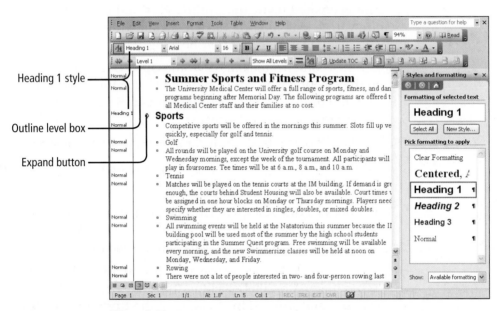

Heading 1 style
Outline level box
Expand button

Figure 5.67

5 Scroll down and click to position the insertion point in the line that contains only the word *Fitness*. Press F4—the Repeat key. Repeat this process to change the *Kickboxing* line to a **Heading 1** style. Alternatively, click the Heading 1 style in the Styles and Formatting task pane.

The F4 button repeats the immediately-preceding command, in this instance the application of the Heading 1 style.

6 Hold down Ctrl and press Home. Position the insertion point in the eighth line of the document, which contains only the word *Golf*.

Notice that this line currently uses the Normal style, and has a topic marker on the left.

7 On the Outlining toolbar, click the **Demote** button ➡.

The paragraph changes to a Heading 2 style. The outline level is Level 2, as shown in Figure 5.68. All of the text following the word *Golf*, up to but not including the next heading, is also demoted and is treated as subordinate text to the *Golf* heading. The Demote and Promote buttons can be used to set the outline level of existing text, or you may find it faster to use the Styles and Formatting task pane along with the F4 key.

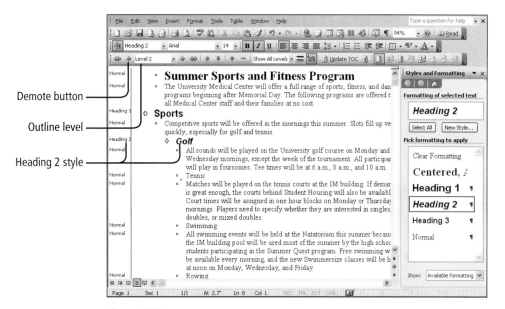

Demote button

Outline level

Heading 2 style

Figure 5.68

8 Click to position the insertion point in the line that contains only the word *Tennis*. In the **Styles and Formatting** task pane, under **Pick formatting to apply**, click **Heading 2**.

9 Scroll down and position the insertion point in the line that contains only the word *Swimming*. Press F4. Continue this process to the end of the document, changing *Rowing*, *Aerobics*, and *Martial Arts* to a **Heading 2** style. Hold down Ctrl and press Home.

Compare your document with Figure 5.69.

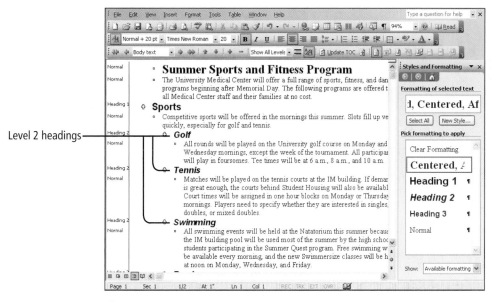

Level 2 headings

Figure 5.69

10 On the Standard toolbar, click the **Save** button.

Activity 5.21 Modifying an Outline in Outline View

In Outline View, you can change heading levels, rearrange headings in an existing outline, and show only the parts of the outline you want to see. You can also enter new text in the outline.

1 To the left of the *Swimming* heading, click the **Expand** button.

The heading, along with all of its subordinate text (and headings if there were any) are selected, as shown in Figure 5.70.

Move Down button

Expand button
Selected heading and
subordinate material

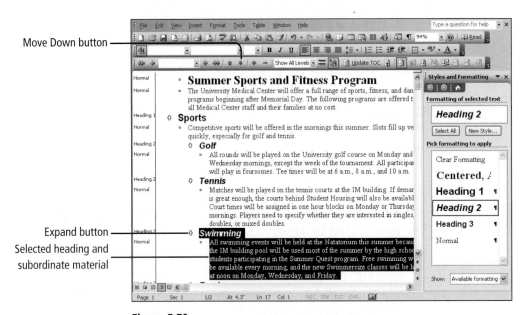

Figure 5.70

2 Scroll down until you can see the end of the document. On the Outlining toolbar, click the **Move Down** button [⬇].

The Swimming heading and the subordinate paragraph move down one topic (paragraph).

3 Click the **Move Down** button [⬇] twice more.

The *Swimming* heading and related text are moved to the *Fitness* section, as shown in Figure 5.71.

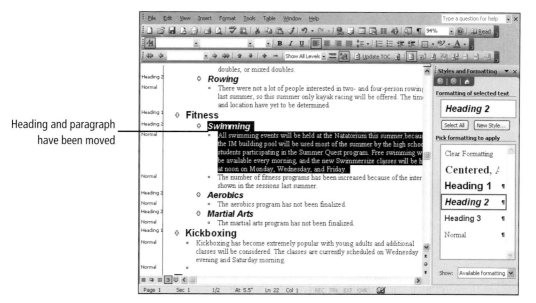

Heading and paragraph have been moved

Figure 5.71

4 Click to position the insertion point in the *Kickboxing* heading.

On the Outlining toolbar, click the **Demote** button.

The Kickboxing heading changes from a Heading 1 style to a Heading 2 style, and from Level 1 to Level 2. It is now subordinate to (a lower level than) the Fitness heading. See Figure 5.72.

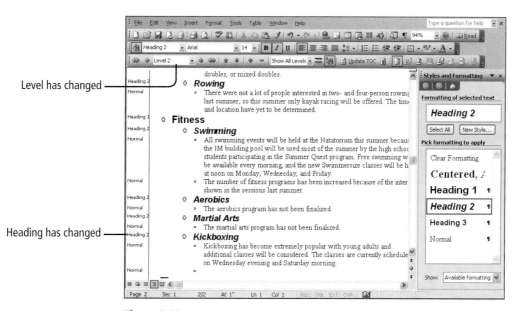

Level has changed

Heading has changed

Figure 5.72

5 Hold down Ctrl and press Home. Hold down Ctrl and press A to select the entire document. On the Outlining toolbar, click the **Show Level button arrow** Show All Levels, and then click **Show Level 2**. Click anywhere to deselect the text.

Everything at Level 2 and higher is displayed, as shown in Figure 5.73. Headings underlined with wavy lines indicate that subordinate body text exists, but is currently hidden from view. In this manner, you can view the overall sections of your report (or presentation) without the clutter of the remaining text.

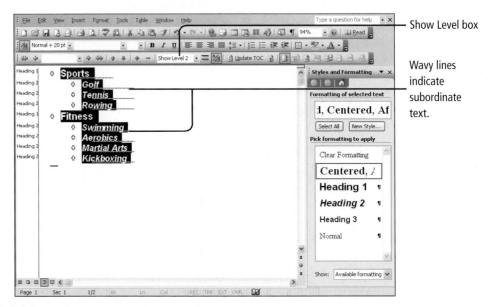

Figure 5.73

6 On the Outlining toolbar, click the **Show Level button arrow** Show Level 2, and then click **Show All Levels**.

The headings and body text are all displayed.

7 Near the top of the document, position the pointer over the **Expand** button to the left of the *Sports* heading. Double-click the **Expand** button.

All of the subordinate headings and text associated with the *Sports* heading are hidden—this is referred to as being **collapsed**. The Fitness heading is not affected. See Figure 5.74.

The heading is collapsed.

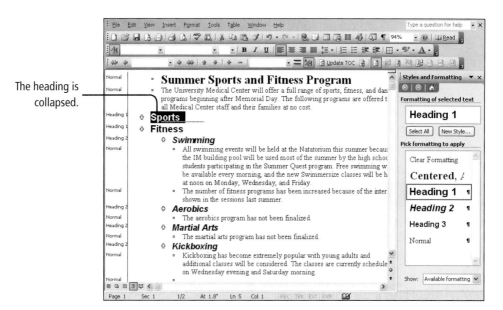

Figure 5.74

8 Press `Ctrl` + `End` to position the insertion point at the end of the last line of the document, and then press `Enter`. Click the **Promote** button twice. Type **Dance**

A new Level 1 heading is created.

9 Press `Enter`. Click the **Demote** button and type **Jazz and Tap**

A new Level 2 heading is created.

10 Press `Enter` and type **West Coast Swing** Press `Enter` again and type **Ballroom Dance**

The Dance heading now has three Level 2 headings under it. The Level 2 headings have no subordinate headings or text, indicated by a **Collapse button** to the left of each, as shown in Figure 5.75.

New Level 1 heading ——
Collapse buttons ——

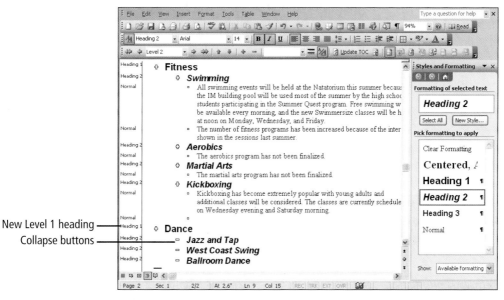

Figure 5.75

11 To the left of the Formatting toolbar, click the **Styles and Formatting** button to close the Styles and Formatting task bar. To the left of the horizontal scroll bar, click the **Print Layout View** button . Hold down Ctrl and press Home.

Compare your document with Figure 5.76.

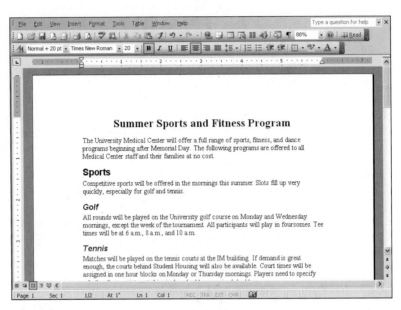

Figure 5.76

12 From the **View** menu, click **Header and Footer**. On the Header and Footer toolbar, click the **Switch Between Header and Footer** button.

13 On the **Header and Footer** toolbar, click the **Insert AutoText** button `Insert AutoText`, and then click **Filename**.

The file name is inserted in the footer.

14 On the **Header and Footer** toolbar, click the **Close** button `Close`.

15 On the Standard toolbar, click the **Save** button.

16 On the Standard toolbar, click the **Print Preview** button. Take a moment to check your work. On the Print Preview toolbar, click the **Close Preview** button `Close`.

17 Make any necessary changes to your document. When you are satisfied, on the Standard toolbar, click the **Print** button.

18 On the menu bar, click the **Close** button, saving any changes.

End **You have completed Project 5D**

Summary

In this chapter, you used the Microsoft Graph program to create a chart from data displayed in a table. After the chart was created, you modified the elements of the chart by adding a title, changing the chart type, changing the font size and color and changing the size and placement of the chart in your document.

Some new character effects were demonstrated, including adding a drop cap to the first letter in the first paragraph of a document, adding a shadow effect to a title, and changing the character spacing in a paragraph.

Styles were introduced as a method to apply uniform formatting to long documents to achieve a consistent appearance. You practiced how to apply existing styles, set new styles, and modify styles for paragraph, character, and list style formats.

Techniques for modifying the Word window were demonstrated, including splitting a window so you can see the top and bottom of a document at the same time, and hiding the white space when you are in Print Layout view so that more text displays on the screen.

Finally, you practiced using a multilevel outline by modifying the outline format and applying it to text in a document. You also created an outline in the Outline View, and practiced changing ouline levels and moving blocks of text by move outline headings.

In This Chapter You Practiced How To

- Create a Chart with Microsoft Graph
- Format a Chart
- Add Special Text Effects
- Use Existing Styles
- Create and Modify New Styles
- Modify the Document Window
- Create an Outline
- Create an Outline Using the Outline View and the Outlining Toolbar

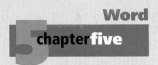

Concepts Assessments

Matching Match each term in the second column with its correct definition in the first column by writing the letter of the term on the blank line in front of the correct definition.

_____ **1.** A built-in feature of Word that is used to create charts.

_____ **2.** A type of chart that shows comparison among data.

_____ **3.** A type of chart that shows trends over time.

_____ **4.** A type of chart that shows the proportion of parts to the whole.

_____ **5.** A table-like structure that is part of the Microsoft Graph program in which you can enter the numbers used to create a chart.

_____ **6.** The chart element that relates the data displayed to the categories.

_____ **7.** The area on a chart where the graphic (pie or column) is placed, which can be resized by using sizing handles.

_____ **8.** A text effect that adds a silhouette behind the letters.

_____ **9.** A group of formatting commands that are stored with a specific name and can be retrieved and applied to text.

_____ **10.** A type of style that controls the font, font size, and font style applied to individual characters.

_____ **11.** The default Word template.

_____ **12.** A list of topics that visually indicates the order in which information in an oral or written report will be presented and the relationship of the topics to each other.

_____ **13.** The dialog box used to create an outline.

_____ **14.** In the Styles and Formatting task pane, the term that describes the items listed under _Pick formatting to apply_.

_____ **15.** An enlarged letter positioned at the beginning of text and displayed on several lines.

A Bullets and Numbering

B Character style

C Column

D Datasheet

E Drop cap

F Legend

G Line

H Microsoft Graph

I Normal

J Outline

K Pie

L Plot area

M Shadow

N Style

O Style names

Fill in the Blank Write the correct answer in the space provided.

1. The data along the bottom of a chart displays in the
_____ axis.

2. The numbers along the left side of a chart display in the
_____ axis.

3. The numbers on the left side of a chart are called a(n)
_____ because they display a range of numbers.

4. A large first letter used to begin the first paragraph in a chapter or
article is known as a _____.

5. Increasing or decreasing the space between letters is accomplished
by changing the _____ spacing.

6. The information that determines the basic structure and format
of a document is known as a _____.

7. To change the line spacing, indents, alignment, and tab stops, you
could change the _____ style.

8. A quick way to create a new style is to set the style, and then type
a name in the _____ box.

9. An item in an outline can be moved to a lower level by clicking the
_____ button.

10. In the Styles and Formatting task pane, you can click the arrow
at the right end of a selected style and choose _____
to change the style.

Project 5E — Service Area

Objectives: *Create a Chart with Microsoft Graph, Format a Chart, Add Special Text Effects, Use Existing Styles, Create and Modify New Styles, Modify the Document Window, and Create an Outline.*

In the following Skill Assessment, you will create and modify a pie chart that shows the geographic distribution of patients in the University Medical Center service area. Your completed document will look similar to the one shown in Figure 5.77. You will save your document as *5E_Service_Area_Firstname_Lastname.*

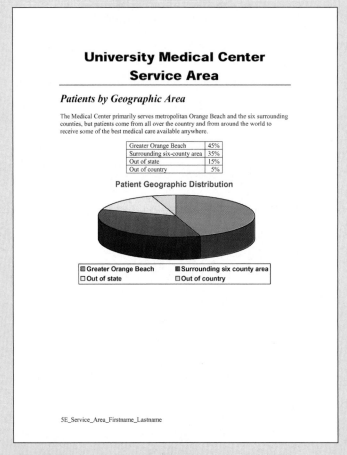

Figure 5.77

1. On the Standard toolbar, click the **Open** button. Navigate to the location where the student files for this textbook are stored. Locate and open **w05E_Service_Area**. Save the file as **5E_Service_Area_Firstname_Lastname**

2. In the table, click anywhere to position the insertion point in the table. From the **Table** menu, point to **Select**, and then click **Table**.

(Project 5E–Service Area continues on the next page)

(Project 5E–Service Area continued)

3. From the **Insert** menu, point to **Picture**, and then click **Chart**. The Microsoft Graph program displays and the data from the table displays in the datasheet.

4. Be sure that your Standard and Formatting toolbars are displayed on two rows. (If only one toolbar row is displayed on your screen, at the right end of the toolbar, click the Toolbar Options button, and then click Show Buttons on Two Rows.)

5. Click anywhere inside the **datasheet**, and then on the datasheet title bar, click the **Close** button. On the Chart toolbar, click the **By Column** button. Recall that the data must be displayed by column before you can change the default column chart into another type of chart.

6. On the Chart toolbar, click the **Chart Type arrow**, and then in the fifth row, click the second button—the **3-D Pie Chart**. Use the ScreenTip to help identify the chart type. The chart display changes to a pie chart. On the Standard toolbar, click the **Save** button.

7. From the **Chart** menu, click **Chart Options**. If necessary, in the Chart Options dialog box, click the Titles tab. Alternatively, right-click on the chart and click Chart Options from the shortcut menu. Click in the **Chart title** box, type **Patient Geographic Distribution** and then click **OK**.

8. Right-click the **Chart Title** and from the shortcut menu click **Format Chart Title**. In the **Format Chart Title** dialog box, click the **Font tab**. The font displayed is Arial, Bold, 10 pt. Click the **Color arrow**. From the displayed palette, in the second row, click the sixth color—**Blue**. Click **OK**.

9. Right-click the **Legend** and from the shortcut menu click **Format Legend**. In the **Format Legend** dialog box, click the **Placement tab**, and then click the **Bottom** option button. From this dialog box, you can move the legend to different areas on the chart. Click **OK**.

10. Drag the lower right sizing handle of the chart box down and to the right until the right edge of the chart area is at approximately **6 inches on the horizontal ruler** and the lower edge of the chart is at approximately **6 inches on the vertical ruler**.

11. Right-click in the **Plot Area**—the gray area behind the pie chart—and click **Format Plot Area** from the shortcut menu. Under **Border**, click **None**. Under **Area**, click **None**, and then click **OK**.

12. Click in the body of the document to close the Microsoft Graph program and return to the document window. Click on the chart once to select it, and then on the Formatting toolbar click the **Center** button to center the chart on the page. Compare your screen with Figure 5.77.

(Project 5E–Service Area continues on the next page)

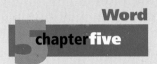
(Project 5E–Service Area continued)

 13. From the **View** menu, display the Header and Footer toolbar, switch to the footer, and then, on the Header and Footer toolbar, click **Insert AutoText**. From the displayed list, click **Filename**. Close the Header and Footer toolbar.

14. On the Standard toolbar, click the **Save** button, and then click the **Print Preview** button to see the document as it will print. Click the **Print** button, and then close the file, saving changes if prompted to do so.

End You have completed Project 5E ——————————————

Project 5F—Child Care

Objectives: *Add Special Text Effects, Create an Outline, and Modify the Document Window.*

In the following Skill Assessment, you will format a multilevel outline of the topics for a child care symposium that is being held by the University Medical Center. You will also add a drop cap to the title. Your completed document will look similar to the one shown in Figure 5.78. You will save your document as *5F_Child_Care_Firstname_Lastname.*

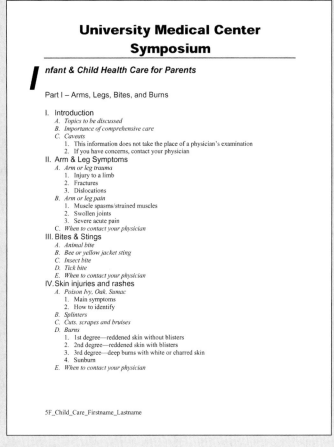

Figure 5.78

1. On the Standard toolbar, click the **Open** button. Navigate to the location where the student files for this textbook are stored. Locate and open **w05F_Child_Care**. Save the file as **5F_Child_Care_Firstname_Lastname**

2. Be sure the document is in **Print Layout View**. If necessary, change the Zoom setting to Page Width. Move the mouse pointer to the top edge of the document until you see the *Hide White Space* pointer, and then click. This will maximize your viewing area.

(**Project 5F**–Child Care continues on the next page)

(Project 5F–Child Care continued)

3. Notice that the lines in the body of the document are formatted in three ways—Arial 14 pt., Times New Roman italic 12 pt., and Times New Roman 12 pt. (no emphasis). Select the line *Infant & Child Health for Parents*. From the **Format** menu, click **Drop Cap**. In the **Drop Cap** dialog box, under **Position**, click **In margin**. Under **Options**, change the **Lines to drop** box to **2**, and then click **OK**.

4. Near the top of the document, click to position the insertion point to the left of *Introduction*. Use the scroll bar to view the end of the document, position the pointer to the right of the last word in the document, hold down Shift, and then click to select all the text from *Introduction* to the end.

5. With the text still selected, on the **Format** menu, click **Bullets and Numbering**. If necessary, in the Bullets and Numbering dialog box, click the Outline Numbered tab. In the first row, click the second **Outline Numbered** box. At the bottom of the **Bullets and Numbering** dialog box, check to see if the **Reset** button is active (not gray), and if it is, click it, and then click **Yes** when prompted to restore the default settings.

6. In the lower right, click the **Customize** button. Under **Number format**, in the **Number style** box, click the arrow, and then click **I, II, III** from the list. In the **Number format** box, place the insertion point to the right of the parenthesis mark and press Bksp. Type a period. Under **Number format**, in the **Number position** box, click the arrow, and then click **Right** from the list. Under **Text position**, click the **Indent at spin box up arrow** to set the indent at **0.3"**. The first level of the outline format is set.

7. Under **Number format**, in the **Level** box, click **2**. In the **Number style** box, click the arrow, and then click **A, B, C** from the list. In the **Number format** box, place the insertion point to the right of the parenthesis mark and press Bksp. Type a period. The second level of the outline format is set.

8. Under **Number format**, in the **Level** box, click **3**. In the **Number style** box, click the arrow, and then click **1, 2, 3** from the list. In the **Number format** box, place the insertion point to the right of the parenthesis mark and press Bksp. Type a period. In the upper right corner of the **Customize Outline Numbered List** dialog box, click **OK**.

9. Hold down Ctrl and press Home. On the Standard toolbar, click the **Save** button. Click to position the insertion point to the left of the paragraph beginning *II. Topics to be discussed* and drag down to select the next two lines, ending with *IV. Caveats*. (The Roman numerals will not be selected.) On the Formatting toolbar, click the **Increase Indent** button. These items become A.–C. Recall that the Increase Indent button is used to move items in an outline to a lower level.

(Project 5F–Child Care continued)

10. Move the pointer into the selection area to the left of the paragraph that begins *II. This information* and select that line and the following line. On the Formatting toolbar, click the **Increase Indent** button twice. These two lines are changed to the third level in the outline and become 1.–2.

11. Locate and select the remaining lines displayed in Times New Roman 12 pt. italic and set them to outline level two. (Hint: Hold down Ctrl and select each italic line.) Click Increase Indent once to get the result A. B. C. and so forth. Use the same technique to locate and select the remaining lines displayed in Times New Roman without emphasis, and then set them to outline level three (click Increase Indent twice to get the result 1. 2. 3. and so forth). Compare your document with Figure 5.78.

12. From the **View** menu, display the Header and Footer toolbar, switch to the footer and then, on the Header and Footer toolbar, click **Insert AutoText**. From the displayed list, click **Filename**. Close the Header and Footer toolbar.

13. On the Standard toolbar, click the **Save** button, and then click the **Print Preview** button to see the document as it will print. Click the **Print** button, and then close the file, saving changes if prompted to do so.

 You have completed Project 5F

Project 5G—Art Program

Objectives: *Use Existing Styles and Create and Modify New Styles.*

In the following Skill Assessment, you will format an informational flyer about the University Medical Center arts program. You will use existing styles, create new styles, and modify a style. Your completed document will look similar to the one shown in Figure 5.79. You will save your document as *5G_Art_Program_Firstname_Lastname.*

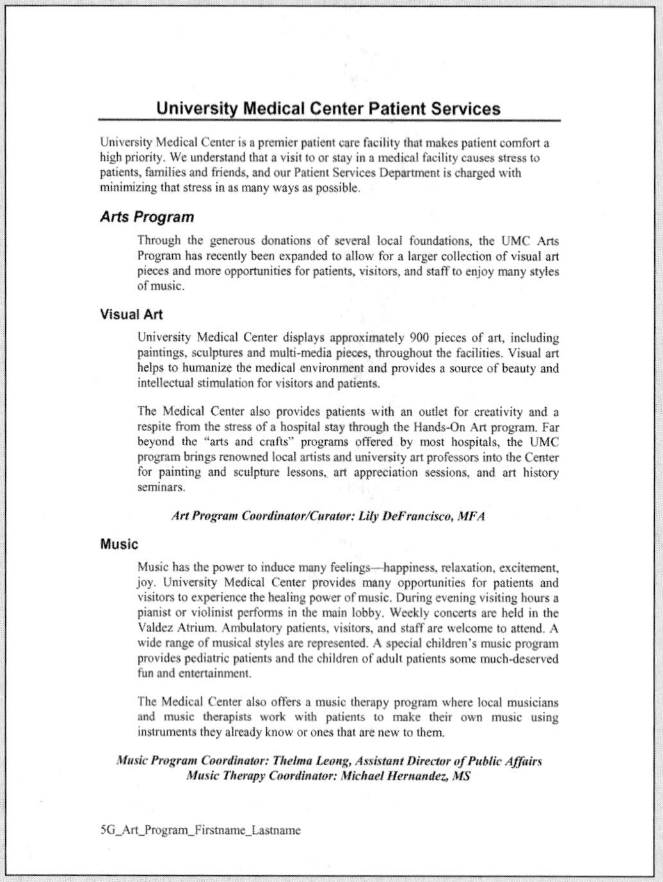

University Medical Center Patient Services

University Medical Center is a premier patient care facility that makes patient comfort a high priority. We understand that a visit to or stay in a medical facility causes stress to patients, families and friends, and our Patient Services Department is charged with minimizing that stress in as many ways as possible.

Arts Program

Through the generous donations of several local foundations, the UMC Arts Program has recently been expanded to allow for a larger collection of visual art pieces and more opportunities for patients, visitors, and staff to enjoy many styles of music.

Visual Art

University Medical Center displays approximately 900 pieces of art, including paintings, sculptures and multi-media pieces, throughout the facilities. Visual art helps to humanize the medical environment and provides a source of beauty and intellectual stimulation for visitors and patients.

The Medical Center also provides patients with an outlet for creativity and a respite from the stress of a hospital stay through the Hands-On Art program. Far beyond the "arts and crafts" programs offered by most hospitals, the UMC program brings renowned local artists and university art professors into the Center for painting and sculpture lessons, art appreciation sessions, and art history seminars.

Art Program Coordinator/Curator: Lily DeFrancisco, MFA

Music

Music has the power to induce many feelings—happiness, relaxation, excitement, joy. University Medical Center provides many opportunities for patients and visitors to experience the healing power of music. During evening visiting hours a pianist or violinist performs in the main lobby. Weekly concerts are held in the Valdez Atrium. Ambulatory patients, visitors, and staff are welcome to attend. A wide range of musical styles are represented. A special children's music program provides pediatric patients and the children of adult patients some much-deserved fun and entertainment.

The Medical Center also offers a music therapy program where local musicians and music therapists work with patients to make their own music using instruments they already know or ones that are new to them.

Music Program Coordinator: Thelma Leong, Assistant Director of Public Affairs
Music Therapy Coordinator: Michael Hernandez, MS

5G_Art_Program_Firstname_Lastname

Figure 5.79

1. On the Standard toolbar, click the **Open** button. Navigate to the location where the student files for this textbook are stored. Locate and open **w05G_Art_Program**. Save the file as **5G_Art_Program_Firstname_Lastname**

2. To the left of the horizontal scroll bar, click the **Normal View** button. From the **Tools** menu, click **Options**. Be sure the **View tab** is selected. At the bottom of the **View tab**, under **Outline and Normal options**, click the **Style area width spin box arrows** as necessary until the width is **0.6"**. Click **OK**.

(Project 5G–Art Program continues on the next page)

(Project 5G–Art Program continued)

3. On the left side of the Formatting toolbar, click the **Styles and Formatting** button. If the right edge of the text is hidden behind the task pane, on the Standard toolbar, click the Zoom button arrow, and then click Page Width.

4. Click anywhere in the first line, *University Medical Center Patient Services*. In the **Styles and Formatting** task pane, under **Pick formatting to apply**, click **Heading 1**. Click anywhere in the line *Arts Program*, and then click **Heading 2**. Click in the line *Visual Art*, and then click **Heading 3**. Scroll down the page, click in the line *Music*, and then click **Heading 3**. You have now completed applying existing heading styles to the major headings in this document.

5. Scroll to the top of the document, locate the paragraph beginning *Through the generous*, and then triple-click in the paragraph to select it. From the **Format** menu, click **Paragraph**. If necessary, click the **Indents and Spacing tab**. Under **General**, click the **Alignment arrow**, and then click **Justified**. Under **Indentation**, click the **Left spin box up arrow** to set the left indent at **0.5"**. Under **Spacing**, click the **Before spin box up arrow** to set the Before spacing to **6 pt**. Click the **After spin box up arrow** to set the After spacing to **12 pt**. Click **OK**.

6. With the paragraph still selected, in the **Styles and Formatting** task pane, under **Formatting of selected text**, click the **New Style** button. In the **New Style** dialog box, under **Properties**, in the **Name** box, type **Para** and then click **OK**. In the **Styles and Formatting** task pane, click the **Para** style. Recall that after you create a style, you must click it to apply the style to the selected paragraph.

7. Click in the first paragraph under *Visual Art* that begins *University Medical Center*, and then from the **Styles and Formatting** task pane, under **Pick formatting to apply**, click **Para**. Click in the next paragraph that begins *The Medical Center*, and then click **Para**. Scroll down until the paragraphs under the *Music* heading are displayed on your screen. Move the mouse pointer to the left margin until it changes to a white selection arrow, and then drag to select the first two paragraphs under *Music*, beginning with *Music has the power*. From the **Styles and Formatting** task pane, click **Para**.

8. Just above the *Music* heading, select the one-line paragraph that begins *Art Program Coordinator*. In the **Styles and Formatting** task pane, click the **New Style** button. In the displayed **New Style** dialog box, under **Properties**, in the **Name** box, type **Contact** In the **New Style** dialog box, under **Formatting**, click the **Bold** button, the **Italic** button, and the **Center** button. Click **OK**. In the **Styles and Formatting** task pane, click the **Contact** style to apply the style to the selected paragraph.

(Project 5G–Art Program continues on the next page)

(Project 5G–Art Program continued)

9. Scroll down and select the last two paragraphs in the document, beginning with *Music Program Coordinator*. From the **Styles and Formatting** task pane, click **Contact** to apply the style to the selected paragraphs.

10. Hold down Ctrl and press Home. Click in the heading at the top of the document—*University Medical Center Patient Services*. On the Formatting toolbar, click the **Center** button. From the **Format** menu, display the **Borders and Shading** dialog box, and if necessary, click the **Borders tab**. Under **Style**, be sure the single line at the top of the Style area is selected. Click the **Width arrow**, and then click **1½ pt**. In the **Preview** area, click the **bottom** of the graphic to apply the line under the paragraph. Click **OK**.

11. From the **Format** menu, display the **Paragraph** dialog box. Under **Spacing**, change the **After** box to **12 pt.**, and then click **OK**.

12. In the **Styles and Formatting** task pane, click the **New Style** button. Under **Properties**, in the **Name** box, type **Title 1** and then click **OK**. In the **Styles and Formatting** task pane, click **Title 1** to apply the style to the title at the top of the document.

13. On the **Styles and Formatting** task pane's title bar, click the **Close** button. From the **Tools** menu, click **Options**. On the **View tab**, under **Outline and Normal options**, in the **Style area width** box, select the number, type **0** and then click **OK**.

14. To the right of the horizontal scroll bar, click the **Print Layout View** button. Compare your document with Figure 5.79. From the **View** menu, display the Header and Footer toolbar, switch to the footer, and then, on the Header and Footer toolbar, click **Insert AutoText**. From the displayed list, click **Filename**. Close the Header and Footer toolbar.

15. On the Standard toolbar, click the **Save** button, and then click the **Print Preview** button to see the document as it will print. Click the **Print** button, and then close the Print Preview. Close the file, saving changes if prompted to do so.

End You have completed Project 5G ——————————————

Project 5H — Daily Patients

Objectives: *Create a Chart with Microsoft Graph and Format a Chart.*

In the following Performance Assessment, you will create a column chart that shows the number of patients treated daily at University Medical Center by service provided. Your completed document will look similar to the one shown in Figure 5.80. You will save your document as *5H_Daily_Patients_Firstname_Lastname.*

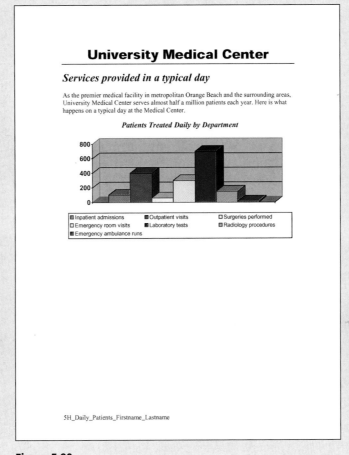

Figure 5.80

1. On the Standard toolbar, click the **Open** button. Navigate to the location where the student files for this textbook are stored. Locate and open **w05H_Daily_Patients**. Save the file as **5H_Daily_Patients_Firstname_Lastname**

2. Click anywhere in the table. Display the **Table** menu, point to **Select**, and then click **Table**. From the **Insert** menu, point to **Picture**, and then click **Chart**.

(Project 5H–Daily Patients continues on the next page)

(Project 5H–Daily Patients continued)

3. Be sure that two toolbar rows are displayed. If only one toolbar row is displayed on your screen, at the right end of the toolbar, click the Toolbar Options button, and then click Show Buttons on Two Rows.

4. Click in the **datasheet**, and then, on the datasheet title bar, click the **Close** button. Right-click in the white area of the chart, and then, from the shortcut menu, click **Chart Options**. Click the **Titles tab**. Click in the **Chart title** box, type **Patients Treated Daily by Department** and then click **OK**. On the Standard toolbar, click the **Save** button.

5. Scroll down so that you can see the 7-inch mark on the vertical ruler. Position the pointer over the right middle sizing handle on the outside border of the chart and drag to the right to approximately **6 inches on the horizontal ruler**. Point to the bottom middle sizing handle and drag down to approximately **6.5 inches on the vertical ruler**. Refer to Figure 5.80 as a guide.

6. Right-click the **Legend**, from the shortcut menu click **Format Legend**, and then click the **Font tab**. Change the **Size** box to **10** and the **Font style** box to **Regular**. Click the **Placement tab**, and then click **Bottom**. Click **OK**.

7. Right-click the **chart title**, and then, from the shortcut menu, click **Format Chart Title**. Click the **Font tab**. Under **Font**, scroll the list and click **Times New Roman**. Change the **Font style** box to **Bold Italic**, the **Size** box to **14**, and then click **OK**.

8. Click anywhere outside the selected chart to close the Microsoft Graph program and return to the document window. Click on the chart once to select it, and then, on the Formatting toolbar, click the **Center** button to center the chart on the page. Compare your screen with Figure 5.80.

9. Scroll as necessary to view the entire table, and then click in the table. From the **Table** menu, point to **Delete**, and then click **Table**. Recall that the data is now incorporated in the underlying datasheet that is represented by the chart—the table is no longer needed.

10. From the **View** menu, display the Header and Footer toolbar, switch to the footer, and then, on the Header and Footer toolbar, click **Insert AutoText**. From the displayed list, click **Filename**. Close the Header and Footer toolbar.

11. On the Standard toolbar, click the **Save** button, and then click the **Print Preview** button to see the document as it will print. Click the **Print** button, and then close the Print Preview. Close the file, saving changes if prompted to do so.

End You have completed Project 5H ——————————

Project 5I — Specialties

Objectives: *Add Special Text Effects, Create an Outline, and Modify the Document Window.*

In the following Performance Assessment, you will format the outline for an index of specialties available at University Medical Center. You will also apply a special text effect to the title. Your completed document will look similar to the one shown in Figure 5.81. You will save your document as *5I_Specialties_Firstname_Lastname.*

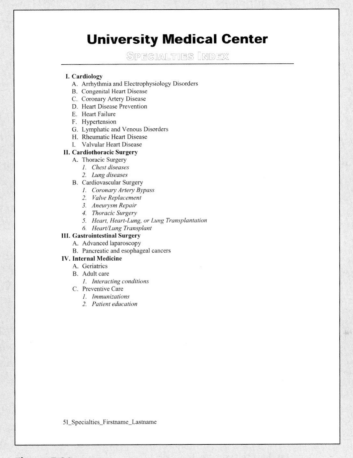

Figure 5.81

1. On the Standard toolbar, click the **Open** button. Navigate to the location where the student files for this textbook are stored. Locate and open **w05I_Specialties**. Save the file as **5I_Specialties_Firstname_Lastname**

2. Open the header. Select the line *Specialties Index*. From the **Format** menu, display the **Font** dialog box. Under **Effects**, select the **Outline** check box and the **Small caps** check box. Click the **Character Spacing tab**. Click the **Spacing By up spin arrow** to display **0.5 pt**. Click **OK**. Close the header.

(Project 5I–Specialties continues on the next page)

(Project 5I–Specialties continued)

3. If necessary, click the Print Layout button, and then change the **Zoom** setting to **Page Width**. Move the mouse pointer to the top edge of the document until you see the **Hide White Space** pointer, and then click. This will maximize your viewing area.

4. Click to position the insertion point to the left of *Cardiology*. Use the scroll bar to move to the end of the document, and, at the end of the last word, hold down Shift and click to select all but the title lines in the document.

5. From the **Format** menu, display the **Bullets and Numbering** dialog box, and then click the **Outline Numbered tab**. In the first row, click the second option. Check to see if the **Reset** button is active or grayed. If it is active, click it, and then click **Yes** to reset the selected outline format.

6. Click the **Customize** button. In the **Customize Outline Numbered List** dialog box, in the **Number style** box, display the list and click **I, II, III**. In the **Number format** box, replace the parenthesis mark with a period. Change the **Number position** box to **Right**. Under **Text position**, change the **Indent at** box to **0.3"**.

7. Under **Number format**, in the **Level** box, click **2**. In the **Number style** box, click **A, B, C** from the list. In the **Number format** box, replace the parenthesis mark with a period.

8. Under **Number format**, in the **Level** box, click **3**. In the **Number style** box, click **1, 2, 3** from the list. In the **Number format** box, replace the parenthesis mark with a period. Click **OK**.

9. Hold down Ctrl and press Home to move to the top of the document. Save your changes. Select the items labeled *II*. through *X*. and click the **Increase Indent** button. These items display as specialties under *Cardiology*.

10. Click anywhere in the line *Thoracic Surgery* and click the **Increase Indent** button. Select the next two lines—*III. Chest diseases* and *IV. Lung diseases*—which are formatted in italic. Click the **Increase Indent** button twice.

11. Continue to format the outline. Items that are not bold or italic are Level 2 items. Items formatted in italic are Level 3 items. (Hint: Use Ctrl to select multiple lines, and then apply the indent formatting.) Compare your document with Figure 5.81.

12. Display the **View** menu and click **Header and Footer**. Switch to the footer area, click the **Insert AutoText** button, and then click **Filename**. Close the Header and Footer toolbar.

(Project 5I–Specialties continues on the next page)

(Project 5I–Specialties continued)

 13. Click the **Save** button, and then click the **Print Preview** button to see the document as it will print. Click the **Print** button, and then close the Print Preview. Close the file, saving changes if prompted to do so.

End You have completed Project 5I

Project 5J — Annual Report

Objectives: *Use Existing Styles, Create and Modify New Styles, Create an Outline Using the Outline View and the Outlining Toolbar.*

In the following Performance Assessment, you will format a draft outline of the annual report for the University Medical Center Foundation by using and creating styles and creating an outline. Your completed document will look similar to the one shown in Figure 5.82. You will save your document as *5J_Annual_Report_Firstname_Lastname.*

ANNUAL REPORT, DRAFT OVERVIEW

University Medical Center Foundation

Introduction

University Medical Center in the Community

This section will outline the programs and services UMC provides to the community. It will include a section of "quick facts" with statistics such as number of patients treated, number of procedures, etc.

How UMC Foundation Impacts the Center

This section will introduce the programs funded by the Foundation and how those programs serve the community.

Section I

H. J. Worthington Hospice

- Overview of the purpose of the hospice and the care provided to terminally ill patients
- Overview of operating expenses
- Narrative overview
- Pie chart showing department expenses as percentage of total

This section will include two quotes from patient family members on their experience with the hospice's programs and staff.

University Medical Center Health Careers Scholarship Fund

- Overview of why the scholarship was established
- Amount of the scholarship
- Overview of criteria for selection of recipient
- Short description of the qualifications of past two years' recipients
- Quotes from past two years' recipients

This section will include two quotes from recipients of University Medical Center scholarships.

University Medical Center Cancer Center Fund

- Overview of the Cancer Center
- Founding date
- Purpose
- Overview including types of state-of-the-art treatments, number of patients treated, support programs
- Overview operating expenses
- Percentage of expenses funded by the Foundation

This section will include a quote from one of the Center's physicians regarding the state-of-the-art treatments available at the center.

5J_Annual_Report_Firstname_Lastname

Figure 5.82

(Project 5J–Annual Report continues on the next page)

(Project 5J–Annual Report continued)

1. On the Standard toolbar, click the **Open** button. Navigate to the location where the student files for this textbook are stored. Locate and open **w05J_Annual_Report**. Save the file as 5J_Annual_Report_Firstname_Lastname

2. To the left of the horizontal scroll bar, click the **Outline View** button. To the left of the Formatting toolbar, click the **Styles and Formatting** button. Set the Zoom to 100% if the text on the screen seems too large.

3. Display the style area on the left of the screen by displaying the **Tools** menu, and then clicking **Options**. Click the **View tab**. Under **Outline and Normal options**, click the **Style area width spin box up arrow** until the style area width is **0.5"**. At the bottom of the **Options** dialog box, click **OK**.

4. Click to position the insertion point in the second line of the document, which contains only the word *Introduction*. In the Styles and Formatting task pane, under **Pick formatting to apply**, click **Heading 1**.

5. Scroll down and click to position the insertion point in the line that contains only *Section I*. Press F4—the Repeat key. Alternatively, click the Heading 1 style in the Styles and Formatting task pane.

6. Position the insertion point in the third line of the document, which begins *How UMC Foundation*. On the Outlining toolbar, click the **Demote** button.

7. Position the insertion point in the line that begins *University Medical Center in the Community*. In the **Styles and Formatting** task pane, under **Pick formatting to apply**, click **Heading 2**.

8. Use the same procedure to apply a **Heading 2** style to the other three lines that use an italic font style. Hold down Ctrl and press Home.

9. To the left of the third line, which begins *How UMC Foundation*, click the **Expand** button.

10. On the Outlining toolbar, click the **Move Down** button twice.

11. On the Outlining toolbar, click the **Show Level button arrow**, and then click **Show Level 2**. Click anywhere to deselect the text. Only Level 1 and Level 2 headings display; the remaining text is hidden from view so that you can see only the Level 1 and 2 headings.

12. Click to position the insertion point in the line that begins *H. J. Worthington*. On the Outlining toolbar, click the **Expand** button to expand only that section of the document.

13. Near the top of the document, position the pointer over the **Expand** button to the left of the line that begins *How UMC Foundation*. Double-click the **Expand** button to expand that section. This is another way to expand the text under a single section.

(Project 5J–Annual Report continues on the next page)

(Project 5J–Annual Report continued)

14. On the Outlining toolbar, click the **Show Level button arrow**, and then click **Show All Levels**.

15. To the left of the horizontal scroll bar, click the **Print Layout View** button. To the left of the Formatting toolbar, click the **Styles and Formatting** button to close the Styles and Formatting task pane. Compare your document with Figure 5.82.

16. Display the **View** menu and click **Header and Footer**. Switch to the footer area, click the **Insert AutoText** button, and then click **Filename**. Close the Header and Footer toolbar.

17. Click the **Save** button, and then click the **Print Preview** button to see the document as it will print. Close the Print Preview. Click the **Print** button, and then close the file, saving changes if prompted to do so.

End You have completed Project 5J ——————————————

Project 5K — Growth

Objectives: *Create a Chart with Microsoft Graph and Format a Chart.*

In the following Mastery Assessment, you will create a two-column chart for a University Medical Center report to show how staff levels have increased to keep up with the growing population of Orange Beach. Your completed document will look similar to the one shown in Figure 5.83. You will save your document as *5K_Growth_ Firstname_Lastname*.

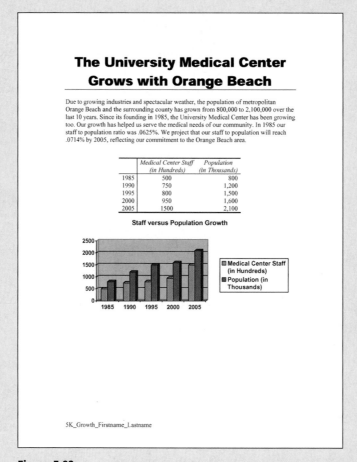

The University Medical Center Grows with Orange Beach

Due to growing industries and spectacular weather, the population of metropolitan Orange Beach and the surrounding county has grown from 800,000 to 2,100,000 over the last 10 years. Since its founding in 1985, the University Medical Center has been growing too. Our growth has helped us serve the medical needs of our community. In 1985 our staff to population ratio was .0625%. We project that our staff to population will reach .0714% by 2005, reflecting our commitment to the Orange Beach area.

	Medical Center Staff (in Hundreds)	Population (in Thousands)
1985	500	800
1990	750	1,200
1995	800	1,500
2000	950	1,600
2005	1500	2,100

Staff versus Population Growth

5K_Growth_Firstname_Lastname

Figure 5.83

1. **Start** Word. From your student files, open **w05K_Growth**. Save the file with the name **5K_Growth_Firstname_Lastname** in the same location as your other files. In the same manner as you have done in previous documents, display the footer and insert the **AutoText** filename.

2. Select the entire table, display the **Insert** menu, point to **Picture**, and then click **Chart**. Close the datasheet. If necessary, click the Toolbar Options button, and then click Show Buttons on Two Rows to display both toolbars.

(Project 5K–Growth continues on the next page)

(Project 5K–Growth continued)

3. On the Chart toolbar, click the **By Column** button. To make a year-by-year comparison between staff and population, the data needs to be displayed by column.

4. Right-click in the white area of the chart, and then click **Chart Options**. In the **Chart title** box, type **Staff versus Population Growth** and then click **OK**.

5. Scroll so that you can view the 7-inch mark on the vertical ruler. Position the pointer over the right middle sizing handle of the chart and drag to approximately **6 inches on the horizontal ruler**. Point to the bottom middle sizing handle and drag down to approximately **7 inches on the vertical ruler**. Refer to Figure 5.83 as a guide.

6. Click in the body of the document to return to the document window. Click on the chart once to select it, and then, on the Formatting toolbar, click the **Center** button. Compare your screen with Figure 5.83.

7. Save the completed document. Preview the document, and then print it.

End You have completed Project 5K ─────────────────────

Project 5L — Speakers

Objectives: *Add Special Text Effects, Modify the Document Window, Create an Outline, and Apply and Modify Styles.*

In the following Mastery Assessment, you will format a speaker directory for the University Medical Center. You will apply an outline format that uses styles, modify one of the styles, add a special text effect to the opening paragraph, and modify the document window as you work. Your completed document will look similar to the one shown in Figure 5.84. You will save your document as *5L_Speakers_Firstname_Lastname.*

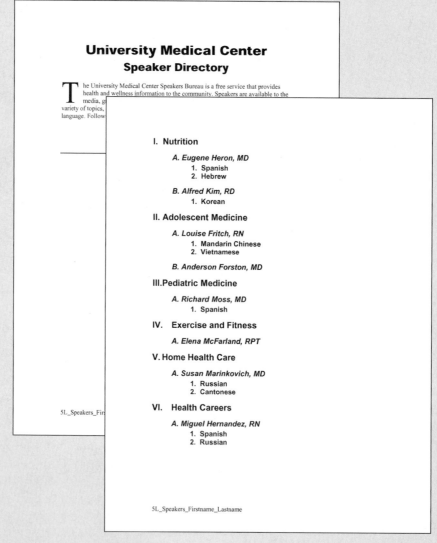

Figure 5.84

(**Project 5L**–Speakers continues on the next page)

(Project 5L–Speakers continued)

1. Start Word. From your student files, open **w05L_Speakers**. Save the file with the name **5L_Speakers_Firstname_Lastname** in the same location as your other files. In the same manner as you have done in previous documents, display the footer and insert the **AutoText** filename.

2. Position the insertion point in the paragraph beginning *The University Medical Center*. From the **Format** menu, open the **Drop Cap** dialog box, and then, under **Position**, click **Dropped**. Under **Options**, click the **Distance from text spin box up arrow** to add **0.1"** extra spacing between the drop cap and the text to its right. Click **OK**.

3. If necessary, change the Zoom setting to Page Width. Move the mouse pointer to the top edge of the document until you see the **Hide White Space** pointer, and then click.

4. Select the two paragraphs beginning *Ricardo*, which will include the phone number under his name. From the Formatting toolbar, change the selected lines to **14 pt.**, **Bold**, and **Italic**, and then **Center** the text.

5. Starting with *Nutrition*, select all of the remaining text through the end of the document. From the **Format** menu, display the **Bullets and Numbering** dialog box, and then click the **Outline Numbered tab**. In the second row, click the third option. Check to see if the **Reset** button is active or grayed. If active, click it to restore the original settings to this outline choice. This outline uses the I. A. 1. format you have practiced and combines it with the Heading 1, 2, 3, styles. Click **OK**.

6. Scroll up to view the result. A new page was created starting with *Nutrition*. Click in the paragraph that begins *II. Eugene Heron, MD* and click the **Increase Indent** button once. In this manner, the speakers need to be indented to Level 2. Listed under Dr. Heron are two languages—*II. Spanish* and *III. Hebrew*. Select these paragraphs and click the **Increase Indent** button twice. In this manner, the languages for each speaker need to be indented to Level 3. Continue down the page and indent the speaker names to Level 2 and the languages to Level 3. Compare your screen with Figure 5.84 to verify the outline levels.

7. On the Formatting toolbar, click the **Styles and Formatting** button. In the **Styles and Formatting** task pane, under **Pick formatting to apply**, scroll down the list, point to and then click the arrow to the right of **Heading 3**, and then click **Select All 10 Instance(s)**. Click the arrow again and click **Modify**. In the **Modify Style** dialog box, under **Formatting**, locate the second row of buttons. Point to the third button from the right to display the ScreenTip **Decrease Paragraph Spacing**. Click this button twice. Watch the preview window to see how the space before and after the example is decreased. Select the **Automatically Update** check box, and then click **OK**.

(Project 5L–Speakers continues on the next page)

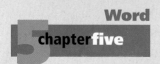

(Project 5L–Speakers continued)

8. Scroll the page to see the results. Close the **Styles and Formatting** task pane. Position the pointer at the top edge of the document and click the **Show White Space** pointer. Compare your screen with Figure 5.84.

9. Save the completed document. Preview the document, and then print it.

 End **You have completed Project 5L** ——————————————————

Project 5M—Outline

Objectives: *Add Special Text Effects, Use Existing Styles, and Create an Outline.*

Outlines can help you organize information when you are writing research papers for your classes. In this Problem Solving exercise, you will create your own outline for a research paper on a topic of your choice. You will also use some of the styles you have practiced and apply some special text effects. You will save your outline as *5M_Outline_Firstname_Lastname*.

1. Select a topic for your paper. It can be a paper for another class, something you are interested in researching, or a topic related to the use of computers.

2. Enter the title of your research paper and apply the **Heading 1** style. **Center** the heading.

3. Under the title, type **Outline** Apply the **Heading 2** style and **center** this subheading. Select the *Outline* subheading and, from the **Font** dialog box, apply the **Outline** effect. Click the **Character Spacing tab** and expand the spacing to **1.0"**. Press [Enter] to move to any empty line.

4. Open the **Bullets and Numbering** dialog box. Click the **Outline Numbered tab** and, as practiced in the chapter, set the outline Level 1 format to I. II. III., set the Level 2 format to A. B. C., and set the Level 3 format to 1. 2. 3. Click **OK**.

5. Write your outline, using the **Increase Indent** button to position topics at the second or third level of the outline as appropriate. Include at least four Level 1 headings, at least two Level 2 headings under each major topic, and two instances of Level 3 headings somewhere in the outline.

6. Proofread your outline and remove any spelling, grammar, or typographical errors. In the footer area and using the **AutoText** button, insert the **Filename**. Save the document.

7. Print the document, and then close the file, saving changes if prompted to do so.

End **You have completed Project 5M** ─────────────────

Project 5N — Personal Styles

Objective: *Create and Modify New Styles.*

The University Medical Center is issuing a press release about an upcoming health information series. In this Problem Solving exercise you will create new styles and apply them to the press release that has been written announcing this program. You will save the article as *5N_Press Release.*

1. Locate and open **w05N_Press Release**. Save it as **5N_Press_Release_Firstname_Lastname** with your other files. As you have with previous files, display the footer area and insert the **AutoText** filename.

2. Display the **Styles and Formatting** task pane. If necessary, change the view to **Normal**. Use the **Options** dialog box to display the **Styles area** on the left side of the window.

3. Using the skills you have practiced in this chapter, create a paragraph style named **PR** that is all **caps**, **Arial Black**, **18 pt.** and apply it to *Press Release*.

4. Create another paragraph style using font and paragraph styles of your own choice and apply it to the article headline that begins *The New Health*. Name the style **News Headline**.

5. Create a character style that is **Bold**, **Italic**, and **Red** and name it **UMC** Apply the **UMC** character style to all occurrences of *University Medical Center* in the body of the document—but not in the article headline.

6. Save the document, print it, and then close the file.

 End **You have completed Project 5N**

Downloading More Charting Tools

In this chapter you practiced using the Microsoft Graph program to create column charts, pie charts, and a line chart. There are other charting tools available as downloads from the Microsoft online support site.

1. Be sure that you are connected to the Internet. Open Word and, in the **Type a question for help** box, type **chart types** and press Enter.

2. In the Search Results task pane, click **Timeline**. A Template window opens on your screen with a Timeline chart displayed. Click the **Next arrow** at the bottom of the window to browse through the 10 templates that are available.

3. Click the **Previous** button until the screen returns to the Timeline template.

4. If you are working in a lab, check to be sure you can download files. If it is permitted, click the **Download** button. The template displays with instructions telling you how to use the template.

5. Follow the instructions and practice using the Timeline chart template you downloaded. Fill in the timeline with significant events in your life over the course of the time displayed. Follow the instructions to replace dates on the timeline as needed.

6. When you are done, close the file without saving changes, and then close Word.

Styles in Word 2003 Help

Using styles can be very helpful if you need to format a large document. In this chapter you were introduced to the basics of how to create and apply styles. You can learn more about styles by reviewing some of the Word Help topics on the subject. One helpful technique when you are formatting a large document is to specify that one paragraph style follow another. For example, you may want a body text style to always follow a Heading 3 style.

1. Start Word. In the **Type a question for help** box, type **Styles**. Scroll through the list of topics that displays in the Search Results task pane.

2. From this list of help topics, click *Specify that one paragraph style follow another* and read the results. Print these instructions if you want.

3. In a blank document write two brief paragraphs. Format the first paragraph with a style of your choosing. Modify the style so it is followed by another specific paragraph style—not the Normal style. Using the Help instructions, update the style applied to the first paragraph to test the change. The style of the second paragraph should change if it was done correctly.

4. Review some of the other Help topics related to styles, printing any that interest you. Test some of the other instructions to learn more about applying styles.

5. Close the Help task pane, close your document without saving the changes, and then exit Word.

chaptersix

Working on a Group Project

In this chapter, you will: complete these projects and practice these skills.

Project 6A **Creating a Document from a Template**	**Objective** • Create a Document Using a Template

Project 6B **Preparing a Document for Distribution to Others**	**Objectives** • Review and Modify Document Properties • Use Comments in a Document • Track Changes in a Document

Project 6C **Comparing Different Versions of a Document**	**Objectives** • Circulate Documents for Review • Compare and Merge Documents

The Management Association of Pine Valley

The Management Association of Pine Valley is an employers' group providing legal services, training, human resources consulting, and organizational development to member companies. Members are small and mid-size companies with 1 to 1,000 employees. Although most services come from the association's staff of experts, some services are outsourced. The association will also assist its members in procuring needed services from other organizations.

Working on a Group Project

The process of creating documents is often a team effort. The people who need to review a document may be in the same office, in different cities, or even in different countries. After a document has been created, it is often necessary for several people to review it. Word includes several features that enable you to keep track of changes made to the original document and to add comments to the text. Changes made by others can be accepted or rejected by the document's author.

When no central network is available, documents can be distributed as attachments to email messages. If time is short and people are working on different copies of the same document, you can compare and merge them, using the Track Changes feature to accept or reject changes.

Project 6A **Memo**

Templates contain predefined document formats that can be used to save time and to create a consistent look for similar documents. Templates exist for resumes, memos, letters, reports, brochures, faxes, and several other document types.

The Management Association of Pine Valley

Memo

To: David Rosenberg, Siena Madison

From: Deepa Patel, Director of Human Resource Counseling

CC: Satarkta Kalam, Director of Labor Relations Services

Date: August 19

Re: Document Reviews

We will be working on two documents this week to present as part of a package to our members at next month's Human Resources Conference. Bill Newson finished the first drafts before he left on vacation. I would like you to read them carefully and give me your opinions. You can edit the documents I send you, but be sure you turn on the Track Changes feature in Word. I will need your edits by Friday.

6A_Memo_Firstname_Lastname

In Activities 6.1 through 6.2, you will use a template to create a memo for a team working on an upcoming conference for The Management Association of Pine Valley. You will replace existing text and replace placeholder text used to reserve areas of the document for specific kinds of information. Your completed document will look similar to Figure 6.1. You will save your document as *6A_Memo_Firstname_Lastname*.

Figure 6.1
Project 6A—Memo

Objective 1
Create a Document Using a Template

A ***template*** is a model for documents of the same type; it is a predefined structure that contains the basic document settings, such as fonts, margins, and available styles. Unless otherwise specified, every Word document is based on the default Normal template. A document template can also store document elements such as headers, greetings, text blocks, and company logos. Word provides document templates for memos, resumes, and other common business documents. Other templates can be built using ***wizards***, which ask you for information about the type of document you want to create. Document templates use a .dot file extension.

Activity 6.1 Creating a Memo Using a Template

1 Start Microsoft Word. From the **File** menu, click **New**.

The New Document task pane opens, as shown in Figure 6.2. If another Word document is open, it still displays in the document window.

On my computer option —————

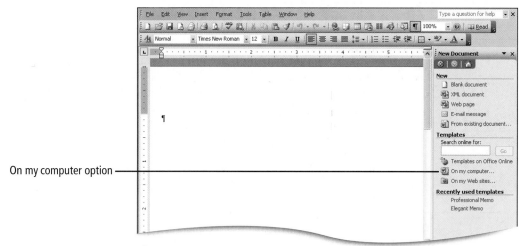

Figure 6.2

2 In the **New Document** task pane, under **Templates**, click **On my computer**.

The Templates dialog box displays. Notice the template categories displayed in the tabs at the top of the dialog box.

3 In the **Templates** dialog box, click the **Memos tab**, and then click the **Professional Memo** icon.

A preview of the memo displays in the Preview area. Under Create New, you have the option of creating a new document based on the Professional Memo template or of creating a new, customized template (document model) by modifying the existing template. See Figure 6.3.

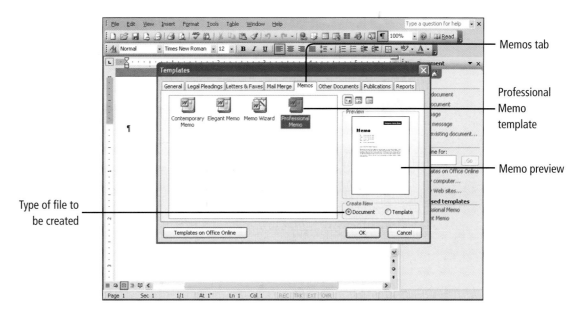

Memos tab

Professional Memo template

Memo preview

Type of file to be created

Figure 6.3

More Knowledge — Templates on the Web

If you are connected to the Internet, you can click the *Templates on Office Online* button at the bottom of the Templates dialog box. This will give you access to hundreds of available templates for Word, Excel, Access, and PowerPoint. The Word templates will display the Word icon that appears on the left side of the Word title bar. Available Word templates on the Web include a performance review, a net worth calculator, many styles of calendars, and even a timeline diagram.

4 At the bottom of the **Templates** dialog box, click **OK**. On the Standard toolbar, click the **Zoom button arrow** 100% ▼, and then click **Page Width**.

The Professional Memo template displays, and the new document is unnamed. See Figure 6.4. The small black squares in the left margin are part of the template and display when paragraphs are formatted with a style that keeps paragraphs together rather than splitting them across pages. You need not be concerned with styles in this project.

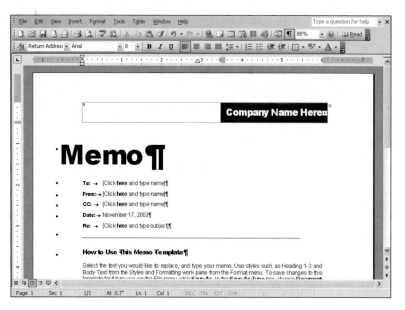

Figure 6.4

5️⃣ Be sure that you can see the nonprinting characters displayed on your screen. If necessary, on the Standard toolbar, click the Show/Hide ¶ button **¶** to display the formatting characters.

6️⃣ On the Standard toolbar, click the **Save** button 🖫. In the **Save As** dialog box, navigate to the location where you are storing your projects for this chapter, creating a new folder for Chapter 6 if you want to do so. In the **File name** box, type **6A_Memo_Firstname_Lastname** and then click **Save**.

Word saves the file as a document with a .doc extension, and the formatting is based on the template.

Activity 6.2 Replacing Placeholder Text and Customizing the Memo

Sample text and ***placeholder text*** display in a document created from a template. Placeholder text reserves space for the text you will insert; it looks like text, but cannot be edited—it can only be replaced. You will edit all or some of this text and replace it with your personalized content.

1️⃣ At the top of the document, select the title **Company Name Here**. Type **The Management Association of** and then press Shift + Enter. Type **Pine Valley** to complete the company name. On the Formatting toolbar, click the **Center** button ▦.

Because this placeholder title is formatted as a one-row table with two cells, the title is centered in the table's cell. Recall that pressing Enter while holding down Shift creates a manual line break, but keeps all of the text in the same paragraph with the same paragraph formatting. See Figure 6.5.

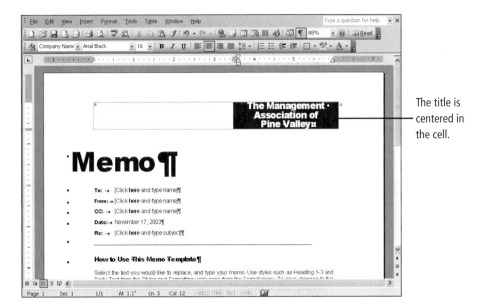

The title is centered in the cell.

Figure 6.5

[2] In the **To** line, click **[Click here and type name]**.

Notice that a single click selects the entire placeholder text. Placeholder text cannot be edited and behaves more like a graphic than text. See Figure 6.6.

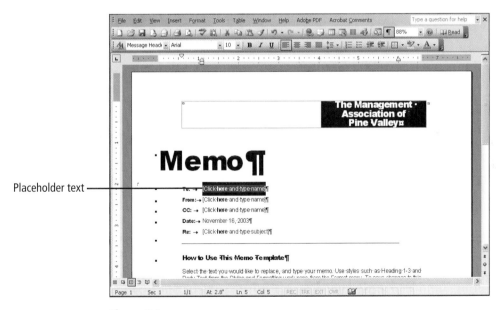

Placeholder text

Figure 6.6

[3] Type **David Rosenberg, Siena Madison**

The text you typed replaces the placeholder text.

[4] In the **From** line, click **[Click here and type name]**. Type **Deepa Patel, Director of Human Resource Consulting**

5 In the **CC** line, click **[Click here and type name]**. Type **Satarkta Kalam, Director of Labor Relations Services**

6 In the **Date** line, select the existing date and type **August 19**

This replaces the default date, which is the current date.

7 In the **Re** line, click **[Click here and type subject]**. Type **Document Reviews**

Compare your document with Figure 6.7. You can see that using a predefined memo template saves you time in creating the basic parts of a memo.

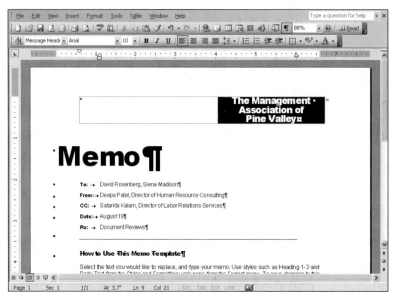

Figure 6.7

8 If necessary, scroll down to view the middle portion of the document. Select the line **How to Use This Memo Template** and press Delete.

9 Select the paragraph that begins *Select the text you would like*. Type

We will be working on two documents this week to present as part of a package to our members at next month's Human Resources Conference. Bill Newson finished the first drafts before he left on vacation. I would like you to read them carefully and give me your opinions. You can edit the documents I send you, but be sure you turn on the Track Changes feature in Word. I will need your edits by Friday.

Compare your memo with Figure 6.8.

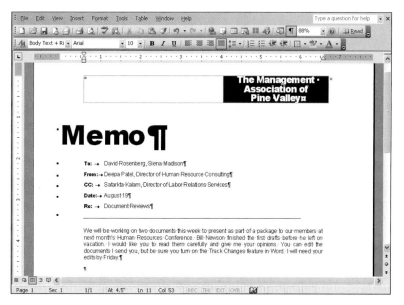

Figure 6.8

chapter six

10 From the **View** menu, click **Header and Footer**. On the Header and Footer toolbar, click the **Switch Between Header and Footer** button 🔁.

11 Press Delete twice to remove the page number that was included as part of the template. On the **Header and Footer** toolbar, click the **Insert AutoText** button Insert AutoText ▾. Point to **Header/Footer** and click **Filename**.

The file name is inserted in the footer.

12 On the Header and Footer toolbar, click the **Close** button Close.

13 On the Standard toolbar, click the **Save** button 🖫.

14 On the Standard toolbar, click the **Print Preview** button 🔍. Take a moment to check your work. On the Print Preview toolbar, click the **Close Preview** button Close.

15 Make any necessary changes to your document. When you are satisfied, on the Standard toolbar, click the **Print** button 🖨. Close the document, saving changes if you are prompted to do so.

End You have completed Project 6A

Project 6B Exit Interview

Microsoft Word records information about every document, such as document size, word count, date and time last edited, and author. This information is available to you from the Properties dialog box. When a document is edited by several people, changes and comments, along with the name of the person making each change or comment, can be displayed using the Track Changes feature.

In Activities 6.3 through 6.11, you will edit a draft document to be distributed to member businesses of The Management Association of Pine Valley, and you will look at the document summary. The draft document has been completed by one person; edits and comments have been added by another. You will make changes to the document and add more comments, and then you will accept or reject each of the changes. Your completed document will look similar to Figure 6.9. You will save your document as *6B_Exit_Interview_ Firstname_Lastname.*

DRAFT: Exit Interviews – Voluntary Separation

Exit interviews with employees who are voluntarily leaving the organization are useful to determine why an employee has decided to leave and to find opportunities for improving the organization's overall employee relations.

When conducting an exit interview, the interviewer should be relaxed and open to encourage honest feedback. The employee should be treated with respect and given time to discuss concerns and ask questions.

Sample questions for an exit interview include:

- What did you like most about your job?
- What did you like least about your job?
- What made you decide to leave this job?
- Do you feel adequate training was provided for you to do your job?
- Do you think your supervisor treated you and others fairly and reasonably? explain.
- Were you given access to information for promotional opportunities withir organization?
- Do you believe you were given honest consideration for promotion?
- Do you feel your contributions were appreciated by your supervisor, co-w organization?
- Did you have the appropriate tools (equipment and resources) to do your j
- Do you believe your salary matched the job you were doing?
- Were you satisfied with the employee benefits? (Ask for details if necessa
- Was the physical environment comfortable and did it allow for productivit
- Was the job presented to you realistically at the time you were hired?

The organization should have strict confidentiality rules in place. These processes explained to the employee so they feel comfortable speaking freely, especially reg negative feedback.

For the exit interview information to be useful to the organization, the information interviews should be analyzed and summarized at least annually. Compare the inf turnover statistics for a period of time to identify trends. Appropriate feedback sh supervisors and managers while protecting the identity of employees who gave th

6B_Exit_Interview_Firstname_Lastname

Filename: 6B_Exit_Interview_Firstname_Lastname.doc
Directory: C:\Student
Template: C:\Documents and Settings\Bob\Application
                    Data\Microsoft\Templates\Normal.dot
Title: DRAFT: Exit Interviews
Subject: Student Name
Author: Bill Newsom
Keywords: Exit Interviews, Fall Conference
Comments: Draft copy of the Exit Interviews handout for the Fall conference.
Creation Date: 9/5/2003 9:02:00 PM
Change Number: 10
Last Saved On: 9/5/2003 11:40:00 PM
Last Saved By: Siena Madison
Total Editing Time: 133 Minutes
Last Printed On: 9/6/2003 2:38:00 AM
As of Last Complete Printing
    Number of Pages: 1 (approx.)
    Number of Words: 300 (approx.)
    Number of Characters: 1,713 (approx.)

Figure 6.9
Project 6B—Exit Interview

Objective 2
Review and Modify Document Properties

Document properties—recorded statistics and other related information, such as the date the document was created, the date it was last modified, where the file is stored, and the author's name—are updated each time the document is modified.

Additionally, you can add document summary information to the properties area. You can give the document a title or a subject, and you can add the name of the company for which the document was created. Keywords can be added, which can help when searching for a document in Windows. The document properties also can be printed.

Activity 6.3 Viewing the Summary

1 On the Standard toolbar, click the **Open** button. Navigate to the location where the student files for this textbook are stored. Locate and open **w06B_Exit_Interview**. Save the file as **6B_Exit_Interview_Firstname_Lastname**

2 On the Standard toolbar, click the **Zoom button arrow** `100%`, and then click **Page Width**. If necessary, on the Standard toolbar, click the Show/Hide ¶ button to display formatting marks.

Alert!

Check Your Screen

Changes were made to this document and comments have been added. Your screen may display the changes, or they may be hidden. The Reviewing toolbar may or may not be displayed. If the changes are displayed, they may be shown as multicolored text and balloons in the right margin of the document or just multicolored text in the document. Do not be concerned about the arrangement of your screen or the toolbar configuration at this point.

3 From the **File** menu, click **Properties**. If necessary, click the General tab.

The document's Properties box displays, with the document name in the title bar. The General tab displays the type of document, file location, and file size. The creation date and date last modified also are displayed, as shown in Figure 6.10.

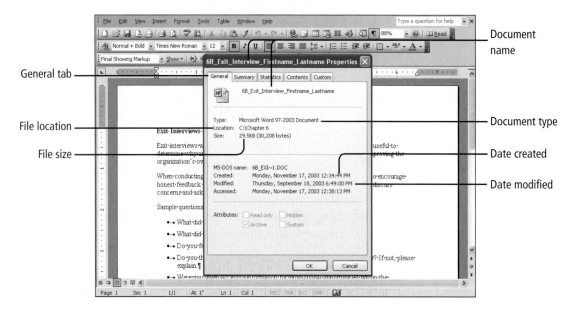

Figure 6.10

4 In the **Properties** box, click the **Summary tab**.

The name in the Author box is the name of the person who originally registered the Office software, although the name can be changed at any time. The name in the Company box is the name of the last entry in that box; it will stay that way for each new document until it is modified. These two boxes are the only ones that are filled in automatically. See Figure 6.11.

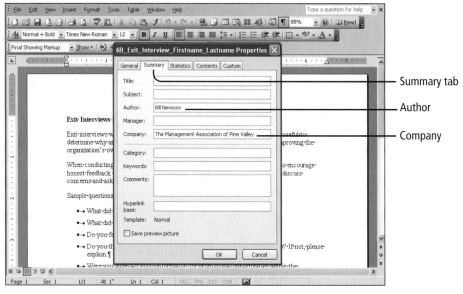

Figure 6.11

5 In the **Properties** box, click the **Statistics tab**.

The Statistics tab expands on the information in the General tab, displaying the last time the document was printed, how many revisions have been made to the document, and how many minutes the document has been open—referred to as ***editing time***. Editing time is not an exact measurement of actual time on task, because the document may have been left open overnight with no editing, and the time would still be added to the total. Document statistics are also displayed. See Figure 6.12.

Statistics tab

Number of revisions

Last time printed

Editing time

Document statistics

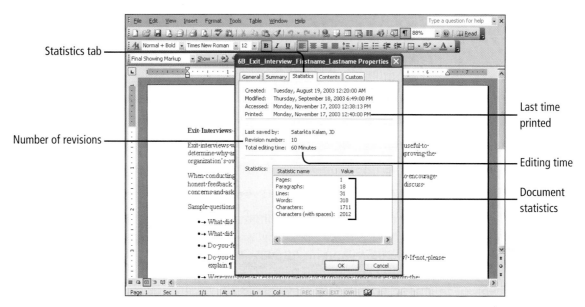

Figure 6.12

Activity 6.4 Editing the Summary and Printing the Document Properties

Editing summary information and adding more information can make the document easier to find using the Windows search feature. It also enables you to make notes about the document for future reference.

1 In the **Properties** box, click the **Summary tab**.

2 On the **Summary** sheet, in the **Title** box, delete the existing text, and then type **DRAFT: Exit Interviews**

3 In the **Keywords** box, type **Exit Interviews, Fall Conference**

4 In the **Comments** box, type **Draft copy of the Exit Interviews handout for the Fall conference.**

Compare your screen with Figure 6.13.

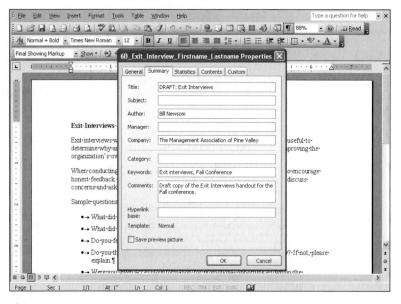

Figure 6.13

5 In the **Subject** box, type your name.

6 At the bottom of the **Properties** box, click **OK**.

7 On the Standard toolbar, click the **Save** button 🖫.

Activity 6.5 Checking Word and Paragraph Counts

Some documents written for magazines or newsletters have word count or line count limits. Word enables you to open a toolbar that keeps track of the number of words, lines, and even characters in a document.

1 From the **Tools** menu, click **Word Count**.

The Word Count dialog box displays, as shown in Figure 6.14. These are the same statistics that were displayed in the Statistics sheet of the document's Properties box.

Show Toolbar button ——

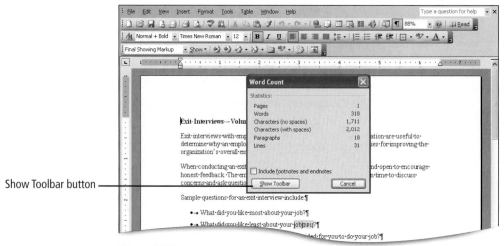

Figure 6.14

2 At the bottom of the **Word Count** dialog box, click **Show Toolbar**.

The Word Count toolbar displays.

3 At the bottom of the **Word Count** dialog box, click **Cancel**.

4 In the Word Count toolbar, click the **Word Count Statistics** button <Click Recount to view>.

The list of statistics displays, as shown in Figure 6.15. Notice the number of words in the document.

Word Count toolbar ———

Word Count Statistics button ———

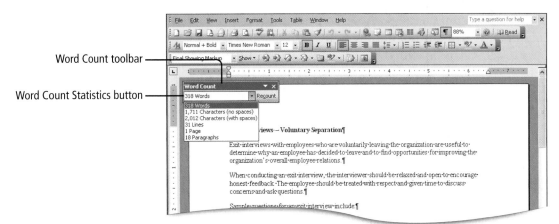

Figure 6.15

5 Click to position the insertion point to the left of the first line of the document, beginning *Exit Interviews*, closing the displayed list. Type **DRAFT:** and then press Space.

Notice that the Word Count Statistics box displays *<Click Recount to view>*.

6 In the Word Count toolbar, click the **Recount** button Recount.

The Word Count Statistics box displays the new number of words—319—in the document.

7 Leave the Word Count toolbar open for the following activities. On the Standard toolbar, click the **Save** button.

Objective 3
Use Comments in a Document

A ***comment*** is a note that an author or reviewer adds to a document. Word displays the comment in either a balloon-type graphic in the margin of the document or in a reviewing pane at the bottom of the document. Comments are a good way to communicate when more than one person is involved in the editing process.

Comments are like sticky notes attached to the document—they can be seen and read, but they do not print. When more than one person adds comments, each person's comments are displayed in a different color. The author's initials are also displayed in the comment box. Comments can be edited, and more than one author can edit the same comment.

Activity 6.6 Adding a Comment

Comments can be added at a specific location in a document or to a selection of text.

1 From the **Tools** menu, click **Options**, and then click the **Track Changes tab**.

The Options dialog box displays. See Figure 6.16.

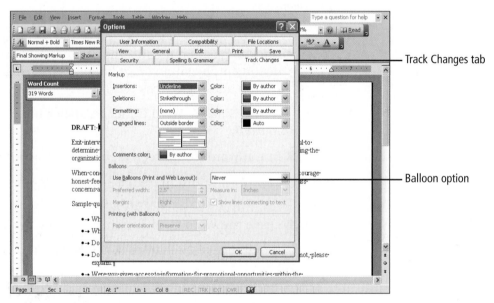

Figure 6.16

2 Under **Balloons**, click the **Use Balloons (Print and Web Layout) arrow**, and then click **Always**.

When the Track Changes feature is active, this action will cause Word to always display comments and deletions in the right margin in a balloon when the document is displayed in Print Layout or Web Layout views.

More Knowledge

In the Track Changes tab of the Options dialog box, you can change the width of the balloons. You can also set the balloons to display in the left margin.

3 In the **Options** dialog box, click the **User Information tab**.

4 Under **User information**, write down the current name and initials so that you can restore them when this project is completed. In the **Name** box type **Siena Madison** and in the **Initials** box type **SFM**

The name and initials will be used when comments are added and changes are made to the document. Compare your dialog box with Figure 6.17.

User Information tab ———
Name ———
Initials ———

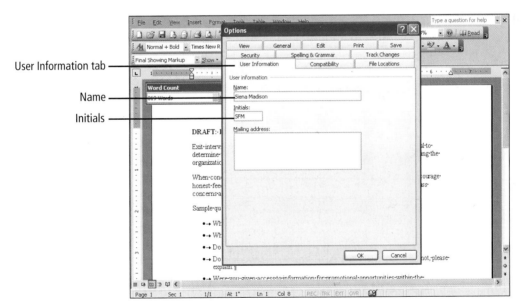

Figure 6.17

Note — Restoring Word Settings

When you are using a computer that is used by more than one person, and you make a change to Word settings, it is always good practice and common courtesy to restore the setting when you are finished.

5 Click **OK** to close the **Options** dialog box. From the **View** menu, point to **Toolbars**. Examine the list to see if the **Reviewing** toolbar is displayed (checked). If it is not checked, click it; if it is checked, click outside the menu to close it.

The Reviewing toolbar displays.

6 On the Standard toolbar, click the **Zoom button arrow** 100% ▾, and then click **Page Width**. Be sure that you are in **Print Layout** view, and if necessary, from the View menu, click Print Layout.

The window adjusts to make more space for the balloons. On small screens, such as those on laptop computers, the text may be almost too small to read.

7 Select the paragraph near the top of the document that begins *Sample questions*. If necessary, drag the Word Count toolbar away from the Reviewing toolbar. From the Reviewing toolbar, click the

Insert Comment button 🖼️. Type **I think this list covers the necessary topics very well!**

The new comment displays in the right margin. The initials *SFM* appear at the beginning of the comment, followed by the number *1*, which means that this is the first comment in the document. See Figure 6.18.

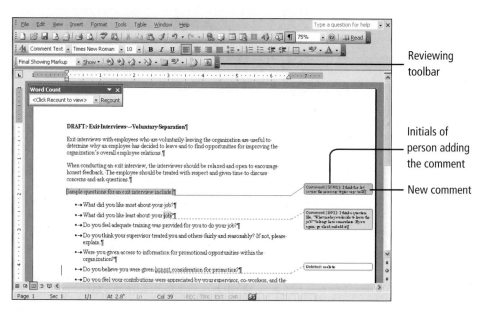

Figure 6.18

8 Click to position the insertion point at the end of the first (title) line of the document that begins *Draft Exit Interviews*. From the Reviewing toolbar, click the **Insert Comment** button. Type **Should there be a separate form for salaried vs. hourly employees?**

The last word of the line is highlighted, and the comment displays in the right margin. This comment is now *SFM1*, and the other comment you added changes to *SFM2*, as shown in Figure 6.19.

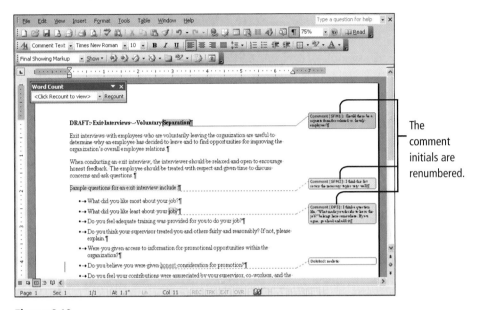

The comment initials are renumbered.

Figure 6.19

9 On the Standard toolbar, click the **Save** button.

Activity 6.7 Reading Comments Using the Reviewing Pane

You can view comments in a reviewing pane at the bottom of the screen as well as in balloons in the margin. The advantage to using the reviewing pane is that you can jump from comment to comment and read text that is sometimes too small to read in the margin.

1 On the Word Count toolbar, click the **Recount** button.

Notice that the document word count has not changed. Comments do not affect document statistics.

2 On the Reviewing toolbar, click the **Reviewing Pane** button.

The reviewing pane displays at the bottom of the screen. The comment closest to the insertion point displays in the pane. The reviewing pane also includes the full name of the person who added the comment and the date and time of the comment, as shown in Figure 6.20.

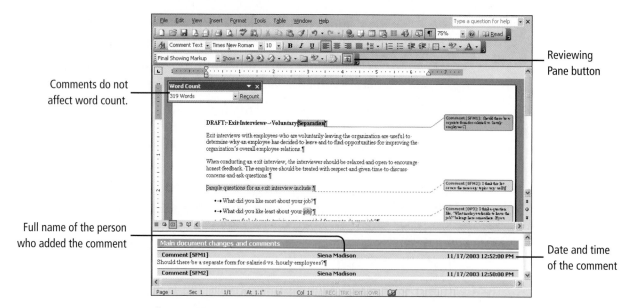

Comments do not affect word count.

Full name of the person who added the comment

Reviewing Pane button

Date and time of the comment

Figure 6.20

3 In the upper window of your screen, use the vertical scroll bar to scroll down to the bottom of the document. Click to place the insertion point anywhere in the last paragraph, which has a comment attached.

The comment associated with this paragraph displays in the reviewing pane.

4 In the reviewing pane, use the small vertical scroll bar to scroll up. Click the comment labeled *SFM2*.

The upper window moves to display the selected comment so that the screen and reviewing pane comments match, as shown in Figure 6.21.

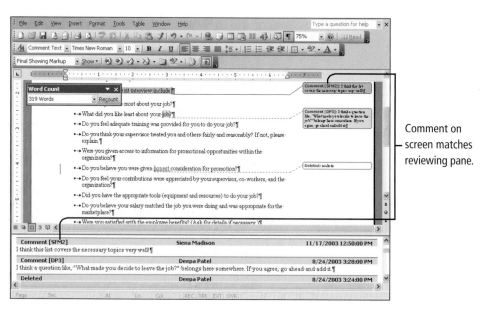

Comment on screen matches reviewing pane.

Figure 6.21

5 From the **View** menu, point to **Toolbars**, and then click **Word Count** to close the Word Count toolbar.

6 On the Standard toolbar, click the **Save** button 🖫.

Activity 6.8 Editing a Comment

Comments can be edited in the balloons or in the reviewing pane. You can also add a response to someone else's comment.

1 In the reviewing pane, in comment *DP3*, select the words *a question like*, press Delete, and then type **the following question:**

Be sure you remove the comma from the original text and add the colon to the end of the new text. Notice that the text is also changed in the balloon. Your reviewing pane should look like Figure 6.22.

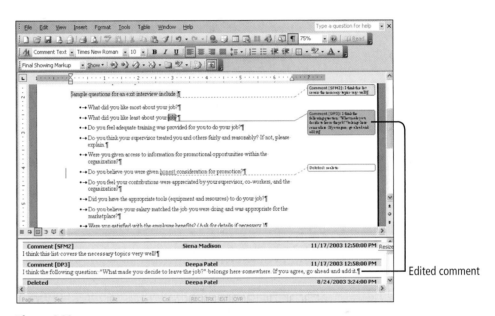

Edited comment

Figure 6.22

2 In the reviewing pane, in comment *DP3*, place the insertion point at the end of the comment and press Enter.

A second line is added to the comment made by another person.

3 In the reviewing pane, in the new line for comment *DP3*, type **I agree. Let's add this question. Siena**

Because the comment is being edited by someone other than the comment author, signing your name lets everyone know who responded to comment. See Figure 6.23.

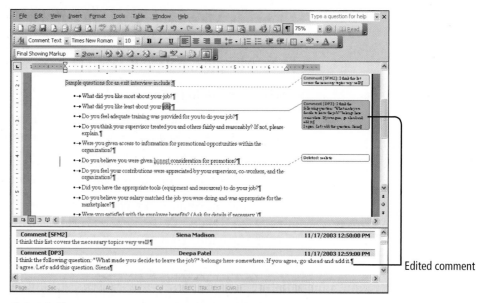

Figure 6.23

4 On the Reviewing toolbar, click the **Reviewing Pane** button [image].

The reviewing pane closes.

5 On the Standard toolbar, click the **Save** button [image].

Objective 4
Track Changes in a Document

The ***Track Changes*** feature in Word provides a visual indication of deletions, insertions, and formatting changes in a document. If the document is edited by more than one person, the changes are in different colors for each new reviewer. After the document has been reviewed by the appropriate individuals, the author can locate the changes and accept or reject the edits.

Activity 6.9 Turning on Track Changes

While viewing a document with the Track Changes feature active, the document can be displayed in final form, showing what the document would look like if all suggested changes were accepted. Comments are also hidden.

1 Hold down [Ctrl] and press [Home].

The insertion point moves to the beginning of the document.

2 On the Reviewing toolbar, click the **Display for Review button arrow** [Final Showing Markup] and click **Final**.

All comments and marked changes are hidden, and the document displays as it will print if all of the changes are accepted. See Figure 6.24.

Display for Review button —

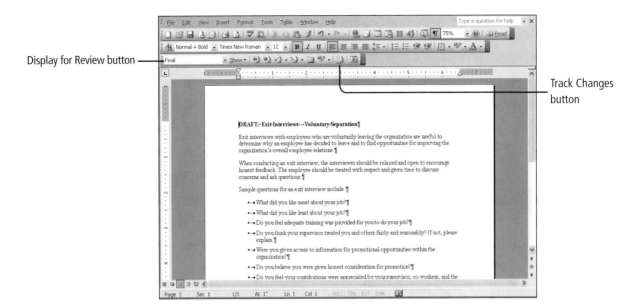

Track Changes
button

Figure 6.24

3 On the Reviewing toolbar, click the **Display for Review button arrow** `Final Showing Markup`, and then click **Final Showing Markup**.

All changes to the document, such as deletions, insertions, and formatting modifications are displayed. Comments also are displayed.

4 From the Reviewing toolbar, click the **Track Changes** button.

Track Changes is turned on, and any changes you make to the document will be visually indicated in the right margin and in the text. Notice that *TRK* is dark on the status bar.

5 Position the insertion point at the end of the second bullet point, beginning *What did you like least*. Press Enter.

A bullet point is added to the list, and a line displays to the left of the new line, indicating that a change has been made to the document at this location.

6 Type **What made you decide to leave this job?**

Notice that the inserted text is displayed with a different color and is underlined. The short vertical black line positioned in the left margin indicates the point at which a change has been made, but not what type of change. The type of change—formatting as a bullet point—is indicated in a balloon in the right margin.

7 Point to the new bullet point.

A ScreenTip displays, showing who made the change and when. See Figure 6.25.

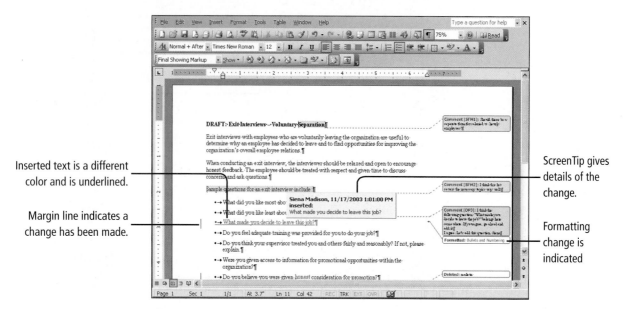

Inserted text is a different color and is underlined.

Margin line indicates a change has been made.

ScreenTip gives details of the change.

Formatting change is indicated

Figure 6.25

---

8 Scroll down and locate the bullet point beginning *Do you believe your salary.* Select *and was appropriate for the marketplace.* Do not select the question mark. Press Delete.

The selected text is deleted, and the deleted text is displayed in a balloon to the right of the line. A dotted line points to the location of the deleted text, as shown in Figure 6.26.

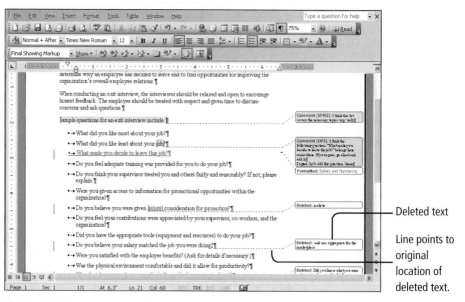

Deleted text

Line points to original location of deleted text.

Figure 6.26

---

9 On the Standard toolbar, click the **Save** button 🔲.

Activity 6.10 Locating Changes in a Document

You can locate changes and comments in the order they appear in the document, or you can display only comments and changes by selected reviewers.

1 Hold down Ctrl and press Home to move to the top of the document.

On the Reviewing toolbar, click the **Next** button ⬎.

The insertion point moves to the first change or comment in the document. See Figure 6.27.

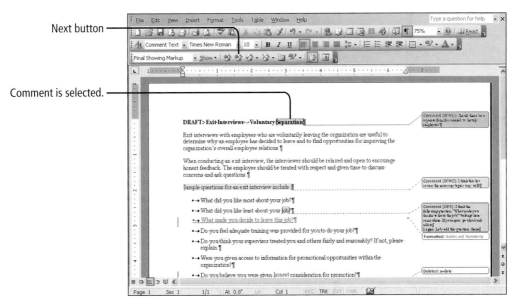

Next button

Comment is selected.

Figure 6.27

2 On the Reviewing toolbar, point to the **Next** button ⬎, and then watch your screen as you click the button five times.

The comments and changes are highlighted in the order they display in the document. The deletion of the word *realistic* is selected.

3 On the Reviewing toolbar, click the **Next** button ⬎ again.

The next comment or change is selected, in this case the insertion of the word *honest*. When the change was made, the word *realistic* was selected, and *honest* was typed to replace it. Deleting text and then inserting new text are treated as two separate changes to the document.

4 On the Reviewing toolbar, click the **Show button arrow** Show ▾. Take a moment to study the available options.

You can display only comments, insertions and deletions, or formatting changes, or a combination of those changes. You can also display only the changes or comments by a specific reviewer.

5 In the **Show** menu, point to **Reviewers**.

A list of all of the reviewers who have made changes to the document displays, as shown in Figure 6.28.

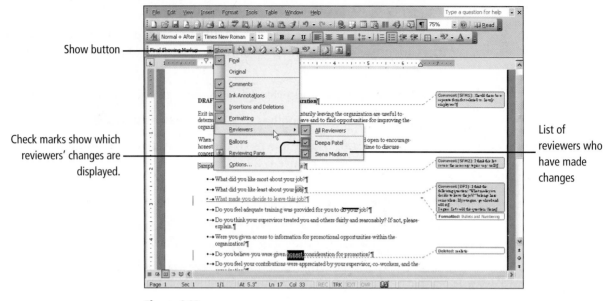

Figure 6.28

Show button (label pointing to Show button)

Check marks show which reviewers' changes are displayed. (label)

List of reviewers who have made changes (label)

6 From the **Reviewers** list, click **Deepa Patel**.

This action hides Deepa Patel's comments. Because only two reviewers made changes to the document, only those of Siena Madison are now displayed in the document.

7 Click the **Show button arrow** Show ▾ again, and then point to **Reviewers**.

Notice that the check box for Deepa Patel is cleared, as shown in Figure 6.29.

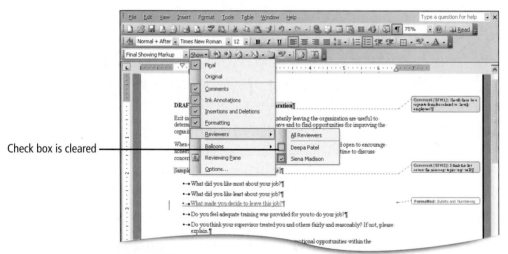

Check box is cleared (label)

Figure 6.29

8 From the **Reviewers** list, click **All Reviewers**.

All of the comments and changes are once again displayed.

9 On the **Reviewing** toolbar, click the **Track Changes** button .

The Track Changes feature is turned off. Notice that *TRK* is gray on the status bar. Changes made from this point on will not be marked, but existing changes and comments still display in the document.

10 On the Standard toolbar, click the **Save** button.

Activity 6.11 Accepting or Rejecting Changes in a Document

When all of the reviewers have made their suggestions and added their comments, the author must decide which changes to accept and which to reject, and which comments to act on. Unlike changes, comments are not accepted or rejected. The author reads the comments, decides whether any action is necessary, and then removes them.

1 Hold down Ctrl and press Home to move to the top of the document. On the Reviewing toolbar, click the **Next** button.

The insertion point moves to the first comment in the document, which is a comment that will not be acted on.

2 On the Reviewing toolbar, click the **Reject Change/Delete Comment** button.

The comment is deleted, and the insertion point remains at the comment location, as shown in Figure 6.30.

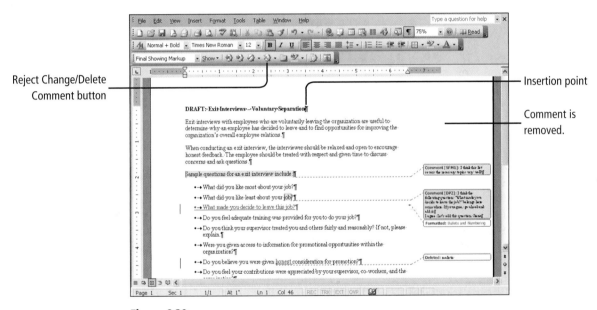

Reject Change/Delete Comment button

Insertion point

Comment is removed.

Figure 6.30

3 On the Reviewing toolbar, click the **Next** button.

The next comment is selected. This comment requires no action and can be removed.

4 On the Reviewing toolbar, click the **Reject Change/Delete Comment** button. On the Reviewing toolbar, click the **Next** button.

The next comment is selected. This comment has already been acted on when the third bullet point was added, so the comment can be removed.

5 On the Reviewing toolbar, click the **Reject Change/Delete Comment** button. On the Reviewing toolbar, click the **Next** button.

The inserted bullet point is highlighted.

6 On the Reviewing toolbar, click the **Accept Change** button.

The change is accepted, and the balloon is removed, as shown in Figure 6.31.

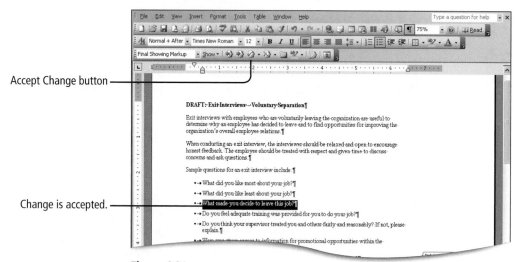

Accept Change button

Change is accepted.

Figure 6.31

7 On the Reviewing toolbar, click the **Next** button.

The deleted word *realistic* in its balloon is selected.

8 On the Reviewing toolbar, click the **Accept Change** button.

Recall that selecting and replacing text is actually two changes—a deletion and an insertion. Notice that the deletion has been accepted, but the insertion is still marked as a change.

9 On the Reviewing toolbar, click the **Next** button to select the insertion. On the Reviewing toolbar, click the **Accept Change** button.

The insertion is accepted.

10 On the Reviewing toolbar, click the **Accept Change button arrow**, and then click **Accept All Changes in Document**.

The remaining changes are accepted. The comment about the last paragraph is all that remains that requires action.

11 On the Reviewing toolbar, click the **Next** button. On the Reviewing toolbar, click the **Reject Change/Delete Comment** button.

The last comment is removed. Because there are no other changes or comments, the extra space in the right margin closes, as shown in Figure 6.32.

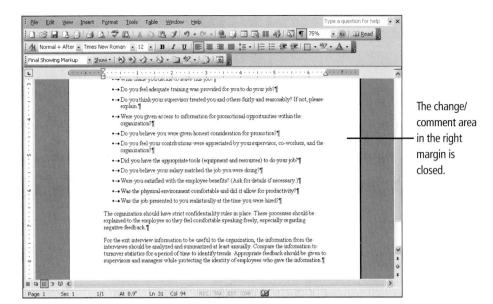

The change/comment area in the right margin is closed.

Figure 6.32

12 From the **Tools** menu, click **Options**, and then click the **User Information tab**. Restore the name and initials that you changed earlier. Click **OK**.

13 From the **View** menu, click **Header and Footer**. On the Header and Footer toolbar, click the **Switch Between Header and Footer** button .

14 On the **Header and Footer** toolbar, click the **Insert AutoText** button Insert AutoText ▾ , and then click **Filename**.

The file name is inserted in the footer.

15 On the **Header and Footer** toolbar, click the **Close** button Close .

16 On the Standard toolbar, click the **Save** button .

17 From the **File** menu, click **Print**. Near the bottom of the **Print** dialog box, click the **Print what arrow**, and then click **Document properties**. Click **OK**.

All of the document properties are printed.

18 On the Standard toolbar, click the **Print Preview** button . Take a moment to check your work. On the Print Preview toolbar, click the **Close Preview** button Close .

19 Make any necessary changes to your document. When you are satisfied, on the Standard toolbar, click the **Print** button . Close the document, saving changes if you are prompted to do so.

End You have completed Project 6B

Project 6C **Insurance**

Documents on which several people collaborate often need to be saved in a universal format that can be edited by reviewers using different word processing programs and that can be attached to emails for review. When reviewed documents are returned, Word has a feature that enables you to compare and merge edited documents.

In Activities 6.12 through 6.15, you will edit an article about health care benefits for the newsletter of The Management Association of Pine Valley. You will save the document in a universal document format and send it to another member of the reviewing team. Then you will compare and merge two versions of the same document. Your completed document will look similar to Figure 6.33. You will save your document as *6C_Insurance_Firstname_Lastname.*

Health Insurance: Preparing for Open Enrollment

In the fall, many companies will be offering open enrollment for health insurance. If you want to make your open enrollment season a success, it is a good idea to do a little groundwork well in advance. This is especially true if you are offering a new, more cost-effective plan with the same company or a more beneficial policy with another company. It is even more important that employees clearly understand the benefits of a new policy (or policy options) that they are not going to like.

Communication is the key to successful—or at least non-acrimonious—changes in employee benefits. Unfortunately, it is the weak link in most companies, at a time when the costs and complexities of health insurance plans make communication even more important.

The following steps need to be implemented well before the open enrollment period begins:

1. Map out changes in the plans, and carefully examine how these changes will affect the employees.
2. Check with the insurance provider to see if any sample guides are available that might help you present the information most effectively.
3. Craft a message to the employees, explaining the differences in the new plan, focusing on the positive provisions. Try to anticipate potential problem areas and defuse them, if possible.
4. Discuss the message with the union or other employee representatives.
5. Send the message to the employees. This is often best done in the summer during the vacation season.
6. Provide regular follow-ups for additional general information and to answer concerns that have been voiced.

The messages need to be well crafted, presenting the information in a positive light. Don't oversell one plan or the other—a simple side-by-side comparison is far more effective, and can be designed to slightly favor a particular plan.

6C_Insurance_Firstname_Lastname

Figure 6.33
Project 6C—Insurance

Objective 5
Circulate Documents for Review

Documents created in Microsoft Word are saved in Microsoft's own format, which is indicated by the *.doc* extension on the document name. Some reviewers you work with may not be using Word, and their word processing program may not be able to read a Word document. You can save a Word document in **Rich Text Format (RTF)**, a universal document format that can be read by almost any word processing program. RTF files can be converted back to Word format when the editing process is complete. RTF documents use an *.rtf* extension.

Documents can be distributed as attachments to email messages. After the documents are returned from reviewers, they can be compared and merged.

Activity 6.12 Saving a Document in a Different Format

When you save a Word document as an RTF file, all but the most complex formatting is translated into a format usable by nearly all word processing programs.

1 On the Standard toolbar, click the **Open** button. Navigate to the location where the student files for this textbook are stored. Locate and open **w06C_Insurance**. Save the file as **6C_Insurance_Firstname_Lastname**

2 On the Standard toolbar, click the **Zoom button arrow** `100%`, and then click **Page Width**. Be sure that the nonprinting format marks are displayed, and if necessary, on the Standard toolbar, click the Show/Hide ¶ button to display formatting marks.

3 From the **File** menu, click **Save As**.

The Save As dialog box displays.

4 At the bottom of the **Save As** dialog box, click the **Save as type arrow** and scroll down until you can see **Rich Text Format (*.rtf)**. See Figure 6.34. (The *.rtf* may or may not display, depending on your system setup.)

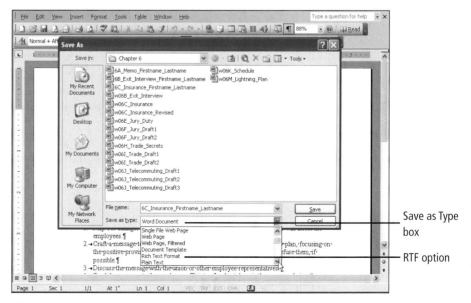

Figure 6.34

5 From the **Save as type** list, click **Rich Text Format (*.rtf)**.

Notice that the file name in the File name box changes to 6C_Insurance_Firstname_Lastname.rtf. The extension may or may not display.

6 At the bottom of the **Save As** dialog box, click **Save**.

The document is saved as an RTF document.

7 From the **File** menu, click **Close**. From the **File** menu, click **Open**. Move to the location of your student files. If necessary, in the Open toolbar, click the **Views button arrow** 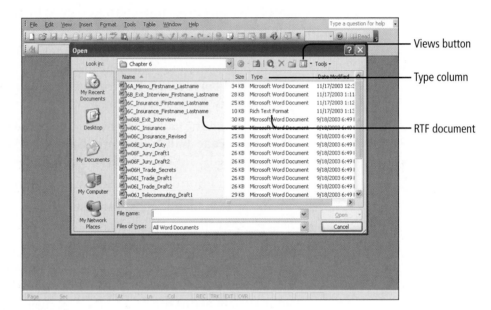, and then click **Details** to view the **Type** column.

The Open dialog box displays, showing a list of your documents, including the RTF file you just saved. The document type is shown in the *Type* column. See Figure 6.35.

Figure 6.35

8 In the **Open** dialog box, click **6C_Insurance_Firstname_ Lastname.rtf**, and then click **Open**.

9 From the **View** menu, click **Header and Footer**. On the Header and Footer toolbar, click the **Switch Between Header and Footer** button.

10 On the **Header and Footer** toolbar, click the **Insert AutoText** button, and then click **Filename**.

The file name is inserted in the footer.

11 On the **Header and Footer** toolbar, click the **Close** button Close .

12 From the **File** menu, click **Save As**. At the bottom of the **Save As** dialog box, click the **Save as type arrow**, scroll, as necessary, and then click **Word Document (*.doc)**.

The file name changes back to 6C_Insurance_Firstname_Lastname.doc, if extensions are displayed.

13 At the bottom of the **Save As** dialog box, click **Save**.

A dialog box displays, indicating that a file of the same name already exists and asking what you want to do, as shown in Figure 6.36.

Replace existing file option ————

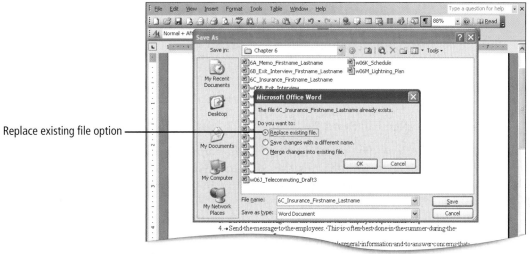

Figure 6.36

14 From the dialog box, click **OK** to replace the existing file.

This Word file that you modified replaces the original RTF version of the same file. If you are not sure what to do when you see this dialog box, you should save the document under a different name.

Activity 6.13 Attaching Documents to an Email Message

Documents can be attached to email messages and sent to others for them to review.

1 From the **File** menu, point to **Send To**.

The *Send To* submenu displays. From this menu, you can send an email, attach the current document to an email, or send a fax. See Figure 6.37.

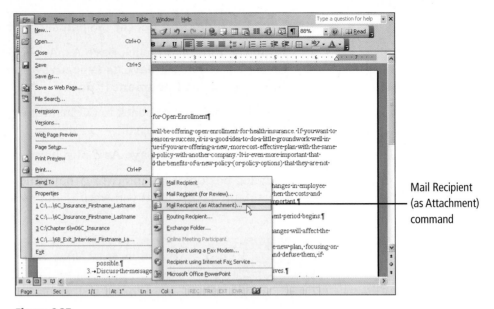

Mail Recipient
(as Attachment)
command

Figure 6.37

▣ From the **Send To** menu, click **Mail Recipient (as Attachment)**.

After a few moments, an email window opens. The name of the document becomes the Subject text, and the name of the document also displays as the attachment name.

Alert!

Does Your Screen Differ?

The appearance of your screen depends on various settings that your system administrator established when Office was installed and how the program has been used most recently. The email window may or may not be maximized, and the elements on the screen depend on the default email program on your computer. If you are using a non-Microsoft mail program, you may have to switch to the program yourself, or this feature may not work at all. Many organizations use Microsoft Outlook or Microsoft Outlook Express as their email program, but yours may differ. In this example, Outlook Express is the active email program.

▣ Click within the white message area in the lower portion of the email window and type **David, Siena:** and press Enter.

▣ Type **Please review this document and return it by Friday.**

▣ In the top of the email window, in the **Subject** box, select the existing text and replace it with **Insurance document for your review**

▣ In the **To** box, type **DRosenberg@mapv.org**

▣ In the **Cc** box, type **SMadison@mapv.org**

This sends a copy of the email and attachment to Siena Madison. Compare your screen with Figure 6.38.

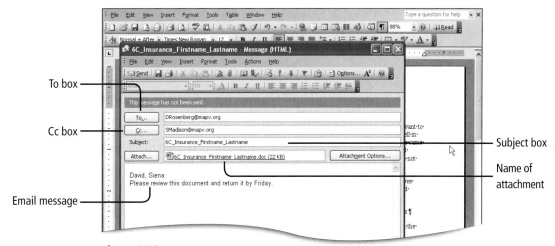

To box

Cc box

Subject box

Name of attachment

Email message

Figure 6.38

8 Because you may or may not have an appropriate email connection at this time, rather than clicking the Send button, display the **File** menu, and then click **Close**. Do not save your changes when prompted.

No email is sent, and your document redisplays.

Objective 6
Compare and Merge Documents

It is not always possible for reviewers to make their comments and edits on a single copy of a document, as you practiced in Project B. When more than one person makes changes to different *copies* of the same document, identifying all the changes can be challenging. Word has a feature that combines the Track Changes feature with a document comparison operation. When you compare two or more documents, the changes are identified, and the Reviewing toolbar is used to decide which changes to accept and which ones to reject. The changes can be stored in the open document, or the combined documents can be saved as a new document.

There are three ways to merge documents, as shown in the table in Figure 6.39.

Three Ways to Merge Reviewed Documents

Type of Merge	Results
Merge	Differences in the documents are displayed as tracked changes in the unopened (baseline) document.
Merge into current document	Differences in the documents are displayed as tracked changes in the open document.
Merge into new document	Changes in both documents are merged into a new, third document, with differences shown as tracked changes.

Figure 6.39

Activity 6.14 Comparing and Merging Documents

To combine documents, you need one of the documents open and the other closed.

1 With your **6C_Insurance_Firstname_Lastname** document open, from the **Tools** menu, click **Compare and Merge Documents**.

The Compare and Merge Documents dialog box displays.

2 If necessary, at the bottom of the **Compare and Merge Documents** dialog box, clear the **Legal blackline** check box. Use the **Look in arrow** to navigate to the location where the student files for this textbook are stored. Locate and select **w06C_Insurance_Revised**.

3 At the bottom of the **Compare and Merge Documents** dialog box, click the **Merge button arrow**.

The three merge commands are listed.

4 From the **Merge** list, click **Merge into current document**.

The documents are compared and merged. The differences between the two documents are displayed as tracked changes in the open document, and the Reviewing toolbar opens. See Figure 6.40.

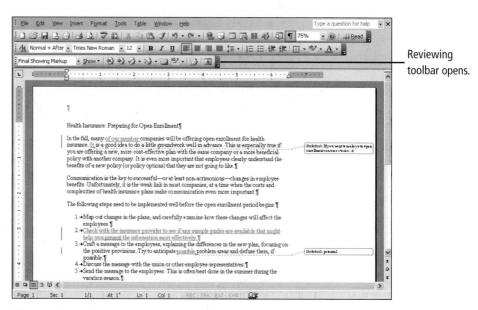

Reviewing toolbar opens.

Figure 6.40

5 On the Standard toolbar, click the **Save** button 🔲.

Activity 6.15 Accepting and Rejecting Merge Changes

Once you have identified the differences between two documents, you need to decide which changes to accept and which to reject.

1 On the Reviewing toolbar, click the **Next** button 🔁.

The inserted text *of our member* is highlighted, as shown in Figure 6.41.

Reject Change/Delete
Comment button

Next button

Accept Change button

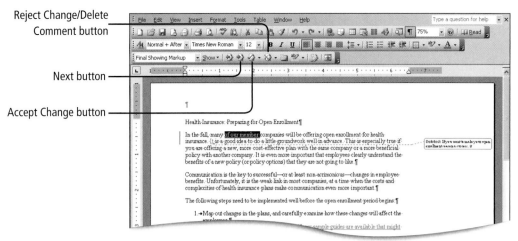

Figure 6.41

2 On the Reviewing toolbar, click the **Reject Change/Delete Comment** button.

The change is removed from the document.

3 On the Reviewing toolbar, click the **Next** button.

The phrase beginning *If you want to make* has been deleted, and the word *It* has been inserted.

4 On the Reviewing toolbar, click the **Reject Change/Delete Comment** button.

The inserted text is removed, but the deleted text has not been addressed yet.

5 On the Reviewing toolbar, click the **Next** button, and then click the **Reject Change/Delete Comment** button.

The deleted text is returned to the document.

6 Click the **Next** button, and then click the **Accept Change** button.

The numbered item is added to the document.

7 Click the **Next** button, and then click the **Reject Change/Delete Comment** button.

The inserted word *possible* is removed.

8 Click the **Next** button, and then click the **Reject Change/Delete Comment** button.

The deleted word *potential* is returned to the document. That was the last tracked change in the document, so the expanded right margin is replaced by the standard document margin, as shown in Figure 6.42.

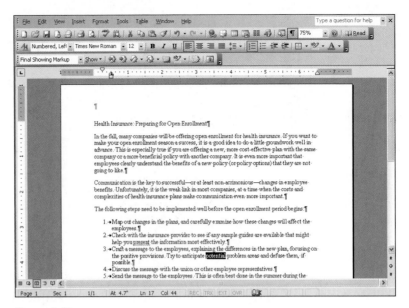

Figure 6.42

9 Click the **Next** button ⏩ once more.

A change was found in the footer—one document had the footer, the other did not.

10 Click the **Accept Change** button 🖉▾. On the **Header and Footer** toolbar, click the **Close** button Close.

The footer is kept in the document.

11 On the Standard toolbar, click the **Save** button 🖫.

12 On the Standard toolbar, click the **Print Preview** button 🔍. Take a moment to check your work. On the Print Preview toolbar, click the **Close Preview** button Close.

13 Make any necessary changes to your document. When you are satisfied, on the Standard toolbar, click the **Print** button 🖨. Close the document, saving changes if you are prompted to do so, and close Word.

End You have completed Project 6C

Summary

Businesses and organizations standardize document formats to give their printed materials a consistent look. Templates set up a document's structure, including page formatting, font, font size, margins, and indents. Templates are useful because they give all documents of a similar type the same look.

Business documents often are composed through a collaborative effort; that is, many individuals contribute text and ideas to the document. Word offers a number of collaboration tools. Document properties are statistics and document information that are stored with a document and can be used for document identification. These include the date the document was created and the date it was last modified. Summary information is also available and can include the document name, title, subject, and company. Information on the document category, keywords for document searches, and comments can also be added. Document statistics, such as word and line counts, enable you to keep within document guidelines.

When documents are exchanged between reviewers, comments can be added and edited, and changes can be tracked. Comments are identified by reviewer and can be added anywhere in the document, although they are not included in the final print version. The Track Changes option also enables the reader to see who made changes and exactly what changes were made. Once all of the comments have been added, and the changes by various reviewers are completed, the changes can be accepted or rejected, and the comments can be deleted.

While many companies provide a file server for quick access to group documents, it is often expedient to send document copies via email. Documents can be sent as attachments to email messages, and these documents can be compared and merged when the reviews are complete. Rich Text Format (RTF) is available if you need to send the document to someone using a word processor other than Microsoft Word.

In This Chapter You Practiced How To

- Create a Document Using a Template
- Review and Modify Document Properties
- Use Comments in a Document
- Track Changes in a Document
- Circulate Documents for Review
- Compare and Merge Documents

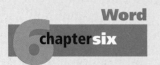

Concepts Assessments

Matching   Match each term in the second column with its correct definition in the first column by writing the letter of the term on the blank line in front of the correct definition.

____ **1.** Statistics and related information about a document, including file size and location, author, title, and subject.

____ **2.** The template on which most documents are based; it contains the default Word document settings.

____ **3.** The document property that shows the title, author, company, subject, and keywords for a document.

____ **4.** A small, bordered shape in the right margin that displays a change or comment.

____ **5.** A toolbar that keeps track of document statistics.

____ **6.** A template set up with the elements necessary for a specific document type, such as a memo, resume, or letter.

____ **7.** An area at the bottom of the screen that displays comments and tracked changes.

____ **8.** A note attached to a document.

____ **9.** The process by which documents are compared and differences are displayed as tracked changes in the unopened (baseline) document.

____ **10.** The Word feature that enables you to see which reviewer made edits or added comments to a document.

____ **11.** A universal document format that can be read by nearly all word processing programs.

____ **12.** The command that compares two documents and creates a new document to display the differences.

____ **13.** Text in a document created using a template; this text can be replaced but not edited.

____ **14.** The toolbar button that highlights the first change or comment following the insertion point.

____ **15.** A step-by-step program that asks you questions and then sets up a document based on your answers.

A Balloon

B Comment

C Document properties

D Document template

E Merge

F Merge into new document

G Next button

H Normal template

I Placeholder text

J Reviewing pane

K RTF

L Summary

M Track Changes

N Wizard

O Word Count

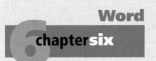

Fill in the Blank Write the correct answer in the space provided.

1. Document template files have a(n) _____ extension.

2. The _____ toolbar enables you to track, accept or reject changes, and delete comments.

3. _____ text is selected with a single click.

4. Microsoft Word files use a(n) _____ extension, which may or may not display depending on your system setup.

5. Adding Keywords to the _____ tab of the Properties dialog box is useful when you use the Windows Search command.

6. In the Properties dialog box, the _____ tab displays a document's word and line count.

7. On the Reviewing toolbar, click the Display for Review button arrow, and then click _____ to hide tracked changes and comments.

8. Rich Text Format documents use a(n) _____ extension.

9. To attach an open document to an email message using Word, click the _____ command from the File menu.

10. When using Track Changes, balloons are displayed in the _____ margin.

Project 6D — Jury Duty Memo

Objective: *Create a Document Using a Template.*

In the following Skill Assessment, you will create a memo for The Management Association of Pine Valley. The memo will involve the review of a draft of a company policy regarding jury duty. Your completed document will look similar to the one shown in Figure 6.43. You will save your document as *6D_Jury_Duty_Memo_Firstname_Lastname.*

Figure 6.43

1. From the **File** menu, click **New**. In the **New Document** task pane, under **Templates**, click **On my computer**.

2. In the **Templates** dialog box, click the **Memos tab**, and then click the **Memo Wizard** icon. At the bottom of the **Templates** dialog box, click **OK**.

3. Examine the first **Memo Wizard** dialog box. Notice the sequence line on the left side, with the *Start* box highlighted in green. At the bottom of the dialog box, click **Next**.

(Project 6D – Jury Duty Memo continues on the next page)

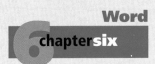

(Project 6D–Jury Duty Memo continued)

4. In the *Style* **Memo Wizard** dialog box, click the **Contemporary** option button. Click **Next**.

5. In the *Title* **Memo Wizard** dialog box, accept *Interoffice Memo* as the title text by clicking **Next**.

6. In the *Heading Fields* **Memo Wizard** dialog box, if necessary, click to select (place a check mark in) the **Priority** check box. In the first three text boxes, substitute the following text, and then click **Next**. (Note that if another student has recently completed this exercise on the computer at which you are seated, the information may already be filled in.)

    Date: **December 17**
    From: **Satarkta Kalam, JD**
    Subject: **Jury Duty Position Paper**

7. In the *Recipient* **Memo Wizard** dialog box, in the **To** text box, type **William Newson** and then click **Next**.

8. In the *Closing Fields* **Memo Wizard** dialog box, if necessary, select the **Attachments** check box, and then click **Next**.

9. In the *Header/Footer* **Memo Wizard** dialog box, under **Which items would you like in the footer for all pages?**, if necessary, clear the **Date** and **Page Number** check boxes, and then click **Next**.

10. In the *Finish* **Memo Wizard** dialog box, click **Finish** to display the customized memo. If the **Office Assistant** displays, click **Cancel** to close it.

11. On the Standard toolbar, click the **Save** button. Navigate to the location where the student files for this textbook are stored. Save the file as **6D_Jury_Duty_Memo_Firstname_Lastname**

12. Select the entire line **Cc: [Click here and type names]** and press Delete.

13. Click **[Click here and type your memo text]**. Type the following:

    The policy memo on Jury Duty that we sent out last year may be causing us some problems. I've heard that at least two unions are preparing grievances against our client companies on this issue. I am attaching a copy of the old policy. I'll send you a draft of a possible update for your review this afternoon.

14. From the **View** menu, click **Header and Footer**. On the Header and Footer toolbar, click the **Switch Between Header and Footer** button.

15. In the footer area, position the insertion point at the end of *Confidential*, and then press Enter. On the **Header and Footer** toolbar, click the **Insert AutoText** button, and then click **Filename**. Because of special formatting in the template, the file name overlaps the marked footer area; however, this will print properly.

(Project 6D–Jury Duty Memo continues on the next page)

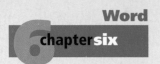

(Project 6D–Jury Duty Memo continued)

16. On the **Header and Footer** toolbar, click the **Close** button.

17. On the Standard toolbar, click the **Save** button.

18. On the Standard toolbar, click the **Print Preview** button. Take a moment to check your work. On the Print Preview toolbar, click the **Close Preview** button.

19. Make any necessary changes to your document. When you are satisfied, on the Standard toolbar, click the **Print** button. Close the document, saving any changes.

 You have completed Project 6D ————————————————

Project 6E — Jury Duty

Objectives: *Use Comments in a Document, Track Changes in a Document, and Compare and Merge Documents.*

In the following Skill Assessment, you will edit an employee leave policy for jury duty. You will work with the document summary. You will add comments, track changes, and then accept or reject the changes and remove the comments. Your completed document will look similar to the one shown in Figure 6.44. You will save your document as *6E_Jury_Duty_Firstname_Lastname.*

1. Start Word. On the Standard toolbar, click the **Open** button. Navigate to the location where the student files for this textbook are stored. Locate and open **w06E_Jury_Duty**. Save the file as **6E_Jury_Duty_Firstname_Lastname**

2. On the Standard toolbar, click the **Zoom button arrow**, and then click **Page Width**. If necessary, on the Standard toolbar, click the Show/Hide ¶ button to display formatting marks.

3. From the **Tools** menu, click **Options**, and then click the **Track Changes tab**. Under **Balloons**, click the **Use Balloons (Print and Web Layout) arrow**, and then click **Always**.

4. In the **Options** dialog box, click the **User Information tab**. Note the name and initials and restore them when Project 6F is completed. Under **User information**, in the **Name** box, type **Satarkta Kalam, JD** and in the **Initials** box, type **SK** Click **OK**.

5. From the **View** menu, point to **Toolbars** and if necessary, click **Reviewing** to activate the Reviewing toolbar.

(Project 6E–Jury Duty continues on the next page)

(Project 6E–Jury Duty continued)

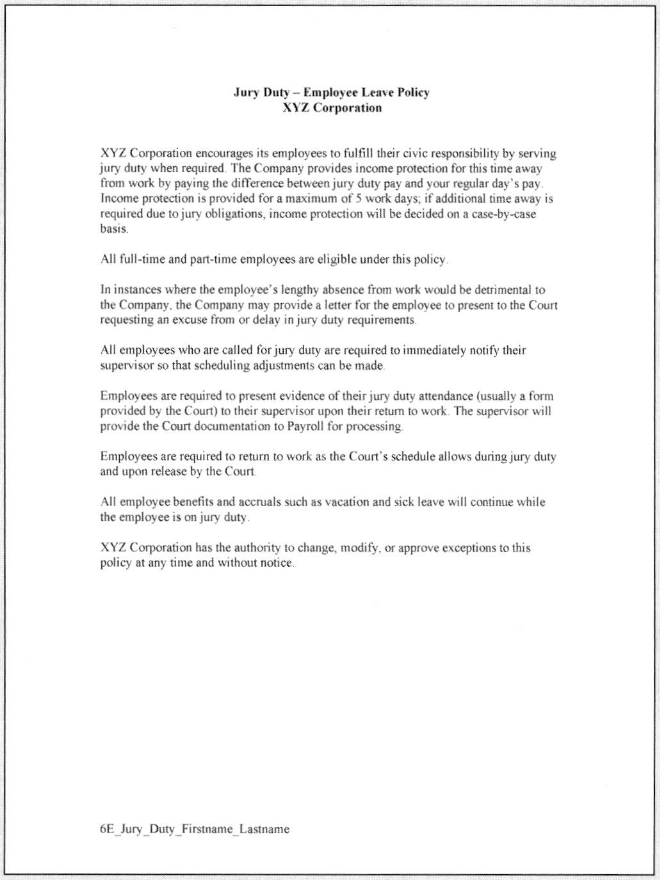

Jury Duty – Employee Leave Policy
XYZ Corporation

XYZ Corporation encourages its employees to fulfill their civic responsibility by serving
jury duty when required. The Company provides income protection for this time away
from work by paying the difference between jury duty pay and your regular day's pay.
Income protection is provided for a maximum of 5 work days; if additional time away is
required due to jury obligations, income protection will be decided on a case-by-case
basis.

All full-time and part-time employees are eligible under this policy.

In instances where the employee's lengthy absence from work would be detrimental to
the Company, the Company may provide a letter for the employee to present to the Court
requesting an excuse from or delay in jury duty requirements.

All employees who are called for jury duty are required to immediately notify their
supervisor so that scheduling adjustments can be made.

Employees are required to present evidence of their jury duty attendance (usually a form
provided by the Court) to their supervisor upon their return to work. The supervisor will
provide the Court documentation to Payroll for processing.

Employees are required to return to work as the Court's schedule allows during jury duty
and upon release by the Court.

All employee benefits and accruals such as vacation and sick leave will continue while
the employee is on jury duty.

XYZ Corporation has the authority to change, modify, or approve exceptions to this
policy at any time and without notice.

6E_Jury_Duty_Firstname_Lastname

Figure 6.44

6. Near the top of the document, locate the sentence that begins *The Company provides income protection*. Hold down Ctrl and click anywhere in the sentence to select it. From the Reviewing toolbar, click the **Insert Comment** button. Type **This phrase could cause trouble.**

7. In the lower portion of the page, select the sentence that begins *Employees are required to return to work*. From the Reviewing toolbar, click the **Insert Comment** button. Type **This is another controversial section.** On the Standard toolbar, click the **Save** button.

8. Hold down Ctrl and press Home. From the Reviewing toolbar, click the **Track Changes** button to turn the feature on. On the Reviewing toolbar, click the **Display for Review button arrow**, and then click **Final Showing Markup**. This will display the changes within the document.

(Project 6E–Jury Duty continues on the next page)

(Project 6E–Jury Duty continued)

9. In the paragraph that begins *In instances where the employee*, double-click *lengthy* and press Delete.

10. In the same paragraph, position the insertion point after *from* near the end of the paragraph. Press Space, and then type **or delay in**

11. In the paragraph that begins *All employees who are called*, select *who are* and press Delete.

12. On the **Reviewing** toolbar, click the **Track Changes** button to turn off Track Changes.

13. Hold down Ctrl and press Home to move to the top of the document. On the Reviewing toolbar, click the **Next** button.

14. On the Reviewing toolbar, click the **Reject Change/Delete Comment** button to delete the first comment.

15. On the Reviewing toolbar, click the **Next** button, and then click the **Accept Change** button to accept the insertion.

16. On the Reviewing toolbar, click the **Next** button, and then click the **Reject Change/Delete Comment** button to delete the second comment. Repeat this procedure to accept any changes and remove any other comments in the document.

17. From the **View** menu, click **Header and Footer**. On the Header and Footer toolbar, click the **Switch Between Header and Footer** button.

18. On the **Header and Footer** toolbar, click the **Insert AutoText** button, and then click **Filename**.

19. On the **Header and Footer** toolbar, click the **Close** button.

20. On the Standard toolbar, click the **Save** button.

21. On the Standard toolbar, click the **Print Preview** button. Take a moment to check your work. On the Print Preview toolbar, click the **Close Preview** button.

22. Make any necessary changes to your document. When you are satisfied, on the Standard toolbar, click the **Print** button.

23. From the **Tools** menu, click **Options**, and then click the **User Information tab**. Restore the name and initials that you changed earlier. Click **OK**. Close the file, saving any changes.

End You have completed Project 6E

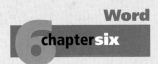

Project 6F—Jury Final

Objectives: *Review and Modify Document Properties, Circulate Documents for Review, and Compare and Merge Documents.*

In the following Skill Assessment, you will finalize edits on two different drafts of the employee leave policy for jury duty. You will work with the document summary and print the summary. You will also compare, merge, and respond to tracked changes in the two draft documents to produce a final document. Your completed document will look similar to the one shown in Figure 6.45. You will save your document as *6F_Jury_Final_Firstname_Lastname.*

Jury Duty – Employee Leave Policy
XYZ Corporation

XYZ Corporation encourages its employees to fulfill their civic responsibility by serving jury duty when required. The Company provides income protection for this time away from work by paying the difference between jury duty pay and your regular day's pay. Income protection is provided for a maximum of 5 work days; if additional time away is required due to jury obligations, income protection will be decided on a case-by-case basis.

All full-time and part-time employees are eligible under this policy.

In instances where the employee's absence from work would be detrimental to the Company, the Company may provide a letter for the employee to present to the Court requesting an excuse from or delay in jury duty requirements.

All employees who are called for jury duty are required to immediately notify their supervisor so that scheduling adjustments can be made.

Employees are required to present evidence of their jury duty attendance (usually a form provided by the Court) to their supervisor upon their return to work. The supervisor will provide the Court documentation to Payroll for processing.

Employees are required to return to work as the Court's schedule allows during jury duty and upon release by the Court. Employees required to be in court for any part of a day will not be required to work the remainder of that day.

All employee benefits and accruals such as vacation and sick leave will continue while the employee is on jury duty.

XYZ Corporation has the authority to change, modify, or approve exceptions to this policy at any time and without notice.

Afternoon and night shift employees shall have the option of choosing to be excused from the shift either immediately before or immediately after the day of jury duty.

6F_Jury_Final_Firstname_Lastname

Figure 6.45

1. On the Standard toolbar, click the **Open** button. Navigate to the location where the student files for this textbook are stored. Locate and open **w06F_Jury_Draft1**. Save the file as **6F_Jury_Final_Firstname_Lastname**

2. On the Standard toolbar, click the **Zoom button arrow**, and then click **Page Width**. If necessary, to display formatting marks on the Standard toolbar, click the Show/Hide ¶ button.

(Project 6F–Jury Final continues on the next page)

(Project 6F–Jury Final continued)

3. From the **File** menu, click **Properties**. If necessary, click the **Summary tab**.

4. In the **Summary** sheet, in the **Author** box, type your name.

5. In the **Summary** sheet, type the following in the indicated boxes:

Title	**Jury Duty Final**
Keywords	**Jury, Leave**
Comments	**Final Draft of the Jury Duty policy statement document**
Company	**The Management Association of Pine Valley**

6. At the bottom of the **Properties** box, click **OK**. On the Standard toolbar, click the **Save** button.

7. From the **File** menu, click **Save As**. At the bottom of the **Save As** dialog box, click the **Save as type arrow**, scroll down, and then click **Rich Text Format**. At the bottom of the **Save As** dialog box, click **Save**.

8. From the **File** menu, click **Print**. Near the bottom of the **Print** dialog box, click the **Print what arrow**, and then click **Document properties**. Click **OK** to print the document properties. Notice that the document type is .rtf.

9. From the **File** menu, click **Close**. From the **File** menu, click **Open**. If necessary, move to the location of your student files. Check to see that the document type is visible, and if necessary, click the Views button arrow in the upper right corner of the dialog box, and then click Details. In the **Open** dialog box, click the *Word document* **6F_Jury_Final_Firstname_Lastname**, and then click **Open**.

10. From the **Tools** menu, click **Compare and Merge Documents**. In the displayed dialog box, navigate to the location where the student files for this textbook are stored. Locate and select **w06F_Jury_Draft2**.

11. At the bottom of the **Compare and Merge Documents** dialog box, click the **Merge button arrow**. If necessary, at the bottom of the **Compare and Merge Documents** dialog box, clear the **Legal blackline** check box. From the **Merge** list, click **Merge into current document**.

12. On the Standard toolbar, click the **Save** button.

13. On the Reviewing toolbar, click the **Next** button, and then click the **Accept Change** button to accept the deletion of *lengthy*.

14. On the Reviewing toolbar, click the **Next** button, and then click the **Accept Change** button to accept the insertion of the sentence beginning *Employees required to be in court.*

(Project 6F–Jury Final continues on the next page)

(Project 6F–Jury Final continued)

15. On the Reviewing toolbar, click the **Next** button, and then click the **Reject Change/Delete Comment** button to reject the deletion of *and without notice.*

16. On the Reviewing toolbar, click the **Next** button, and then click the **Accept Change** button to accept the addition of the paragraph beginning *Afternoon and night shift.*

17. On the Standard toolbar, click the **Save** button.

18. From the **View** menu, click **Header and Footer**. On the Header and Footer toolbar, click the **Switch Between Header and Footer** button. Click the **Insert AutoText** button, and then click **Filename**.

19. On the **Header and Footer** toolbar, click the **Close** button.

20. On the Standard toolbar, click the **Print Preview** button. Take a moment to check your work. On the Print Preview toolbar, click the **Close Preview** button. Make any necessary changes to your document. When you are satisfied, on the Standard toolbar, click the **Print** button.

21. If you are using your own computer and have it set up to use Word for email, from the **File** menu, point to **Send To**.

22. From the **Send To** menu, click **Mail Recipient (as Attachment)**. In the open area in the bottom part of the email window, type your name and press Enter.

23. Type **Please review this document over the weekend and return it by Monday.**

24. In the top of the email window, in the **Subject** box, select the existing text and type **Jury Duty document**

25. In the **To** box, type your email address.

26. If you are sure you have an appropriate email configuration, click the **Send** button; otherwise, from the **File** menu, click **Close** and do not save your changes. If necessary, check your email to make sure the document arrived.

End You have completed Project 6F ──────────────────────

Project 6G — Trade Fax

Objectives: *Create a Document Using a Template and Circulate Documents for Review.*

In the following Performance Assessment, you will create a fax to a company about an enclosed trade secret and nondisclosure agreement. Your completed document will look similar to the one shown in Figure 6.46. You will save your document as *6G_Trade_Fax_Firstname_Lastname.*

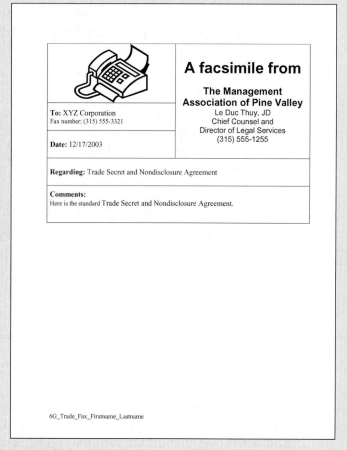

A facsimile from

**The Management
Association of Pine Valley**
Le Duc Thuy, JD
Chief Counsel and
Director of Legal Services
(315) 555-1255

To: XYZ Corporation
Fax number: (315) 555-3321

Date: 12/17/2003

Regarding: Trade Secret and Nondisclosure Agreement

Comments:
Here is the standard Trade Secret and Nondisclosure Agreement.

6G_Trade_Fax_Firstname_Lastname

Figure 6.46

1. From the **File** menu, click **New**. In the **New Document** task pane, under **Templates**, click **On my computer**.

2. In the **Templates** dialog box, click the **Letters & Faxes tab**, and then click the **Business Fax** icon. At the bottom of the **Templates** dialog box, click **OK**. If you do not have the same business fax template as the one displayed in Figure 6.46, use a similar one and adjust your responses accordingly.

(Project 6G–Trade Fax continues on the next page)

(Project 6G–Trade Fax continued)

3. Save the document as **6G_Trade_Fax_Firstname_Lastname**

4. Replace the **To** placeholder with **XYZ Corporation**

5. Place the insertion point after *Fax number* and type **(315) 555-3321**

6. Replace the **Business name** placeholder with **The Management Association of Pine Valley**

7. Replace the **Contact information** placeholder with the following:

   **Le Duc Thuy, JD
   Chief Counsel and
   Director of Legal Services
   (315) 555-0155**

8. Replace the **Regarding** placeholder with **Trade Secret and Nondisclosure Agreement**

9. In the **Comments** box, on the line below *Comments*, type **Here is the standard Trade Secret and Nondisclosure Agreement.**

10. Use **Insert AutoText** to insert the file name in a footer, and then close the footer.

11. On the Standard toolbar, click the **Save** button. Preview the document, and then print it.

12. Save and close the document.

End You have completed Project 6G ——————————————————

Project 6H — Trade Secrets

Objectives: *Use Comments in a Document and Track Changes in a Document.*

In the following Performance Assessment, you will add comments and make changes to a trade secrets and nondisclosure agreement policy statement, and then you will accept or reject changes. Your completed document will look similar to the one shown in Figure 6.47. You will save your document as *6H_Trade_Secrets_Firstname_Lastname*.

1. On the Standard toolbar, click the **Open** button. Navigate to the location where the student files for this textbook are stored. Locate and open **w06H_Trade_Secrets**. This file contains comments and changes that have been made with the Track Changes feature turned on. Save the file as **6H_Trade_Secrets_Firstname_Lastname**

2. On the Standard toolbar, click the **Zoom button arrow**, and then click **Page Width**. If necessary, on the Standard toolbar, click the Show/Hide ¶ button to display formatting marks.

(Project 6H–Trade Secrets continues on the next page)

(Project 6H–Trade Secrets continued)

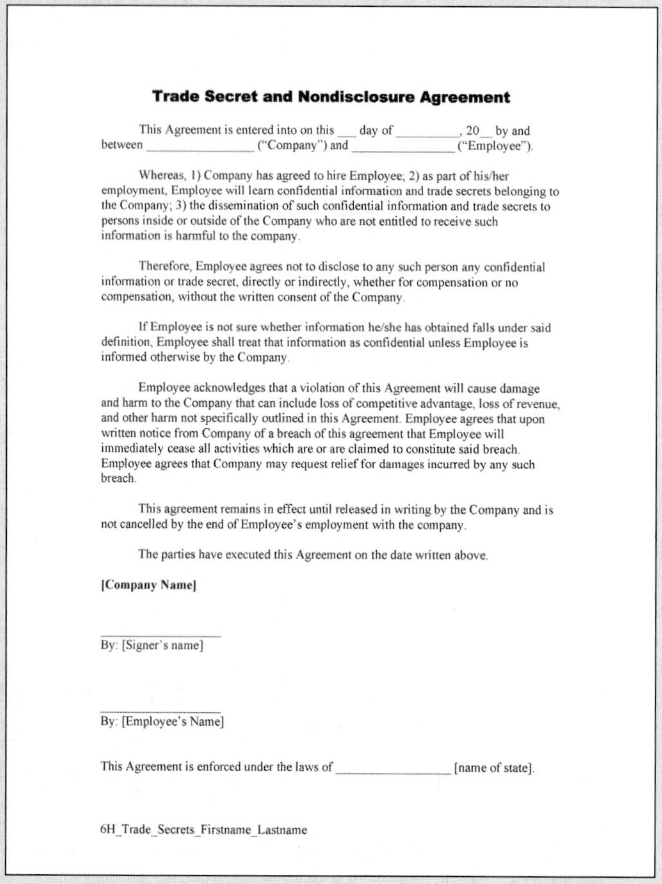

Trade Secret and Nondisclosure Agreement

This Agreement is entered into on this ___ day of _____, 20__ by and
between _____ ("Company") and _____ ("Employee").

Whereas, 1) Company has agreed to hire Employee; 2) as part of his/her
employment, Employee will learn confidential information and trade secrets belonging to
the Company; 3) the dissemination of such confidential information and trade secrets to
persons inside or outside of the Company who are not entitled to receive such
information is harmful to the company.

Therefore, Employee agrees not to disclose to any such person any confidential
information or trade secret, directly or indirectly, whether for compensation or no
compensation, without the written consent of the Company.

If Employee is not sure whether information he/she has obtained falls under said
definition, Employee shall treat that information as confidential unless Employee is
informed otherwise by the Company.

Employee acknowledges that a violation of this Agreement will cause damage
and harm to the Company that can include loss of competitive advantage, loss of revenue,
and other harm not specifically outlined in this Agreement. Employee agrees that upon
written notice from Company of a breach of this agreement that Employee will
immediately cease all activities which are or are claimed to constitute said breach.
Employee agrees that Company may request relief for damages incurred by any such
breach.

This agreement remains in effect until released in writing by the Company and is
not cancelled by the end of Employee's employment with the company.

The parties have executed this Agreement on the date written above.

[Company Name]

_____
By: [Signer's name]

_____
By: [Employee's Name]

This Agreement is enforced under the laws of _____ [name of state].

6H_Trade_Secrets_Firstname_Lastname

Figure 6.47

3. From the **Tools** menu, click **Options**, and then click the **Track Changes tab**. Turn on balloons for all tracked changes.

4. In the **Options** dialog box, click the **User Information tab**. Note the name and initials and restore them when Project 6I is completed. Under **User information**, in the **Name** box, type **David Rosenberg** and in the **Initials** box, type **DR**

5. Right-click on any toolbar and if necessary, click Reviewing to display the toolbar. Turn on **Track Changes** (the button will display as orange when the feature is turned on and as blue when the feature is turned off).

6. Select the title (the first line of the document). Change the font to **Arial Black** and the font size to **14**.

7. In the paragraph that begins *Therefore, Employee agrees*, position the insertion point after the space following the word *confidential*. Type **or proprietary** and press Space.

(Project 6H–Trade Secrets continues on the next page)

(Project 6H–Trade Secrets continued)

8. In the paragraph that begins *Employee acknowledges that a violation*, near the end of the paragraph, position the insertion after the space following the word *request*. Type **equitable** and press Space.

9. Save the document. Hold down Ctrl and press Home to move to the beginning of the document. On the Reviewing toolbar, click the **Next** button, and then click the **Accept Change** button to accept the formatting change to the title. Press the **Next** button again, and then click the **Accept Change** button to accept the deletion of *4*.

10. Move to the next change, an insertion of *3*, and accept it. Move to the next change, the insertion of *or proprietary*, and accept it.

11. Move to the next change and click the **Reject Change/Delete Comment** button to reject the deletion of the paragraph beginning *If Employee is not sure*.

12. Move to the next change. Accept the insertion of *equitable*. Leave the comment at the end of the document for the next reviewer to read. Turn off **Track Changes**.

13. Use **Insert AutoText** to insert the file name in a footer, and then close the footer. In the **Reviewing** toolbar, click the **Display for Review arrow** and click **Final** to show the document without the comment in the margin.

14. If you are not going to do Project 6I, from the **Tools** menu, click **Options**, and then click the **User Information tab**. Restore the name and initials that you changed earlier. Click **OK**.

15. Save the document. Preview and print the document. Close all documents, saving any changes.

End You have completed Project 6H

Project 6I — Trade Final

Objectives: *Review and Modify Document Properties and Compare and Merge Documents.*

In the following Performance Assessment, you will change the document properties for a trade secrets and nondisclosure agreement policy statement, and then you will compare and merge two drafts of the same documents. Your completed document will look similar to the one shown in Figure 6.48. You will save your document as *6I_Trade_Final_Firstname_Lastname*.

1. On the Standard toolbar, click the **Open** button. Navigate to the location where the student files for this textbook are stored. Locate and open **w06I_Trade_Draft1**.

(Project 6I–Trade Final continues on the next page)

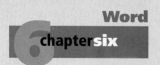

(Project 6I–Trade Final continued)

Trade Secret and Nondisclosure Agreement

This Agreement is entered into on this _____ day of _____, 20__ by and between _____ ("Company") and _____ ("Employee").

Whereas, 1) Company has agreed to hire Employee; 2) as part of his/her employment, Employee will learn confidential information and trade secrets belonging to the Company; 3) the dissemination of such confidential information and trade secrets to persons inside or outside of the Company who are not entitled to receive such information is harmful to the company.

Therefore, Employee agrees not to disclose to any such person any confidential information or trade secret, directly or indirectly, whether for compensation or no compensation, without the written consent of the Company.

If Employee is not sure whether information he/she has obtained falls under said definition, Employee shall treat that information as confidential unless Employee is informed otherwise by the Company.

Employee acknowledges that a violation of this Agreement will cause damage and harm to the Company that can include loss of competitive advantage, loss of revenue, and other harm not specifically outlined in this Agreement. Employee agrees that upon written notice from Company of a breach of this agreement that Employee will immediately cease all activities which are or are claimed to constitute said breach. Employee agrees that Company may request relief for damages incurred by any such breach.

This agreement remains in effect until released in writing by the Company and is not cancelled by the end of Employee's employment with the company.

The parties have executed this Agreement on the date written above.

[Insert Company Name]

_____
By: [Signer's name]

_____
By: [Employee's Name]

This Agreement is enforced under the laws of _____.
[Name of State]

6I_Trade_Final_Firstname_Lastname

Figure 6.48

2. From the **Tools** menu, click **Options**, and then click the **Track Changes tab**. Under **Balloons**, be sure the **Use Balloons (Print and Web Layout)** box indicates **Always**. If necessary, change the **Zoom** to **Page Width** and turn on the formatting characters.

3. From the **Tools** menu, click **Compare and Merge Documents**. Navigate to the location where the student files for this textbook are stored. Locate and select **w06I_Trade_Draft2**.

4. At the bottom of the **Compare and Merge Documents** dialog box, click the **Merge button arrow**. From the **Merge** list, click **Merge into new document**. All differences between the two versions are displayed in an unnamed document, leaving the original documents unchanged.

5. Save the new document on your screen as **6I_Trade_Final_Firstname_Lastname**

(Project 6I–Trade Final continues on the next page)

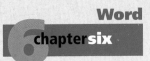
(Project 6I–Trade Final continued)

6. On the Reviewing toolbar, click the **Next** button. All of the changes appear to be selected, but this is an indication that the document margins have changed, as shown in the first balloon. Click the **Accept Change** button to accept the new margins.

7. Move to the next change, which is inserted underlines to make the black lines longer, and accept the change. Repeat the procedure for the other three line changes.

8. Move to the next change, in which the word *Insert* was inserted, and accept the change.

9. On the Reviewing toolbar, click the **Next** button, and then click the **Accept Change button arrow**. Click **Accept All Changes in Document** to accept the remainder of the changes. If necessary, delete any remaining comments.

10. Create a footer, use **Insert AutoText** to insert the file name, and then close the footer. Save the document.

11. From the **File** menu, click **Properties** and move to the **Summary** sheet, if necessary.

12. In the **Summary** sheet, type the following in the indicated boxes:

Author	**your name**
Title	**Trade Secrets Policy Statement**
Comments	**Final Draft of the Trade Secrets and Nondisclosure Agreement policy statement**
Company	**The Management Association of Pine Valley**

13. Save your work. Preview the document and print it if you are satisfied with the way it looks.

14. From the **Tools** menu, click **Options**, and then click the **User Information tab**. Restore the name and initials that you changed earlier. Click **OK**. Close all documents, saving any changes.

End You have completed Project 6I

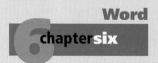
Project 6J — Telecommuting

Objectives: *Compare and Merge Documents and Review and Modify Document Properties.*

In the following Mastery Assessment, you will compare and merge three drafts of a proposed Telecommuting Policy for The Management Association of Pine Valley. To merge three documents, you compare and merge two of them, and then compare the third document to the merged document. Your completed document will look similar to the one shown in Figure 6.49. You will save your document as *6J_Telecommuting_Firstname_Lastname*.

Filename: 6J_Telecommuting_Firstname_Lastname
Directory: C:\Chapter 6
Template: C:\Documents and Settings\Robert L. Ferrett\Application
                   Data\Microsoft\Templates\Normal.dot
Title: Telecommuting Policy
Subject:
Author: Deepa Pate
Keywords:
Comments: Firstname I
Creation Date: 9/4/2003 1.
Change Number: 9
Last Saved On: 12/29/2003
Last Saved By: Deepa Pate
Total Editing Time: 10 Minutes
Last Printed On: 12/29/2003
As of Last Complete Printing
    Number of Pages: 2 (approx.)
    Number of Words: 768
    Number of Characters: 4,38

Sample Telecommuting Policy
The Management Association of Pine Valley

Many companies believe that offering their employees the option to telecommute is mutually
beneficial for the employer and the employe
reduced costs for office space, ability to recr
employment opportunities for the physically
morale. Employees incur fewer expenses for
family needs.

It is important, however, that the company h
implementation and employee acknowledge
sample policy follows.

XYZ Company Telecommuting Policy

The term telecommute means paid employm
conventional office, generally from the empl
is not the same as a home-based business or
This telecommuting policy does not apply to
other than the company's office, such as emp
people who are in the field every day.

Telecommuting is an option offered by the c
part of both the company and the employee.
employment. This policy applies to full-time
or in a trial period are not eligible.

Employees who wish to participate in the tel
Telecommuting Application and Agreement
Agreement, including reporting problems wi
completed according to their work rules.

Supervisors and managers will identify the j
Supervisors and managers are responsible fo
requirements, certifying attendance of teleco
completed according to the employee's work

Telecommuters are required to perform only
alternate work site. While telecommuting is
personal obligations, telecommuting is not to
provide dependent care during work hours. I
ensure appropriate arrangements so that wor

Telecommuters are subject to the same performance appraisal process as other employees. If a
telecommuter's performance should decline and the supervisor believes this is due to the
employee's participation in the program, the telecommuting schedule will be modified or
terminated as appropriate to bring performance back to the required level. Telecommuters are
governed by the same policies that apply to other employees regarding work schedules and hours
of work.

Participation in the program is voluntary. Employees may request participation in the program at
any time; however, permission is granted based on the operational needs of the company.

Decisions on whether a position is suitable for the work to be performed from an alternate
location will be based on job content, not title or work schedule. Other factors in considering
approval of a telecommuting schedule include the employee's record of conduct and attendance
and ability to work without supervision; whether the employee's absence from the office will
adversely affect others; and, whether the employee requires access to tools and materials that
cannot be moved from the office.

On occasion, an employee who was previously scheduled to telecommute may be required to
report to the office. The business needs of the company will take priority in such cases, but every
attempt will be made to give the employee reasonable notice that they must report to the office.

Supervisors have the right to certify that work is being performed at the alternate work site
according to this agreement, and to ensure the accuracy of time sheets and attendance records.
The company has put in place approved methods for doing so which include occasional
supervisory phone calls to the employee and scheduled visits to the alternate work site.
Employees must be available by telephone during all regularly scheduled business hours.

The company and the employee will work together to ensure that the home office or alternate
work site is equipped as necessary for the employee to conduct business. The company will not
reimburse employees for home maintenance or utility costs associated with working at home.
Home work areas must be in compliance with all building codes. Only hardware and software
procured and approved by the company will be installed on company-owned computers.

It is the sole responsibility of the employee to determine the Federal and State tax implications of
working from an alternate site.

6J_Telecommuting_Firstname_Lastname

6J_Telecommuting_Firstname_Lastname

Figure 6.49

(Project 6J–Telecommuting continues on the next page)

(Project 6J–Telecommuting continued)

1. Start Word. From your student files, open **w06J_Telecommuting_ Draft1**. Save the file with the name **6J_Telecommuting_Firstname_ Lastname** in the same location as your other files from this textbook. In the same manner as you have done in previous documents, create a footer and insert the **AutoText** filename.

2. Compare and merge the document **w06J_Telecommuting_Draft2** into the current document. In the displayed box, be sure the first option— **Your document**—is selected, and then click **Continue with Merge**.

3. Accept changes until you reach the deletion of *means*. Reject the change from *means* to *is defined as*. Reject the deletion of the sentence that begins *It is the sole responsibility*. Accept all other changes and click Save.

4. Compare and merge the **w06J_Telecommuting_Draft3** document into the current document on your screen. Accept the default and click **Continue with Merge**. At the bottom of the document, reject the deletion of the sentence that begins *It is the sole responsibility*. Accept all other changes and save the document.

5. In the document summary, type **Telecommuting Policy** as the **Title**, **Deepa Patel** as the **Author**, and **The Management Association of Pine Valley** as the **Company**. Type your name in the **Comments** box.

6. Save the completed document. Preview and print the document, and then print the document properties. Save and close the document.

 End You have completed Project 6J ───────────────────────

Project 6K — Schedule

Objectives: *Use Comments in a Document, Track Changes in a Document, Review and Modify Document Properties, and Circulate Documents for Review.*

In the following Mastery Assessment, you will edit a document regarding training sessions and seminars that has already been edited extensively by a colleague. You will make changes, and then print the document displaying all of the changes and comments. Your completed document will look similar to the one shown in Figure 6.50. You will save your document as *6K_Schedule_Firstname_Lastname*.

1. Start Word. From your student files, open **w06K_Schedule**. Save the file with the name **6K_Schedule_Firstname_Lastname** in the same location as your other files. In the same manner as you have done in previous documents, display the footer and insert the **AutoText** filename.

(Project 6K–Schedule continues on the next page)

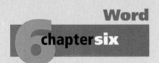

(Project 6K–Schedule continued)

Management Association
Training Sessions and Seminars

Human Resource Management
Role playing, group exercises and case studies cover a wide range of human resource issues and management techniques. Learn to develop workplace diversity programs, prepare for a changing workforce, and discuss legislation affecting HR departments in organizations of all sizes. Recruiting, pre-employment testing, training, compensation and performance management will also be covered.

Presenter: Deepa Patel
3 days Member cost: $650 Non-member cost: $995

Preparing Your Organization's Affirmative Action Plan
It takes constant vigilance to be sure your organization's AAP meets all current requirements. The Management Association keeps up to date on all new regulations for you and helps you update your AAP through this important seminar. Learn how to conduct analysis and develop best practices to assure a diverse workplace. Prepare for compensation and compliance audits and implement remedies for violations.

Presenter: Deepa Patel
2 days Member cost: $600 Non-member cost: $800

Information Technology Cost Management
Information Technology (IT) managers are required to demonstrate a return on technology investment and keep costs down while increasing productivity. However, many IT managers aren't trained in the details of budgets, cost accounting, and overall financial management. This seminar will help you develop and manage an IT budget that is right for your organization, identify areas for cost reduction, and communicate with the organization's finance team. Effective purchasing techniques and outsourcing will also be covered.

Presenter: Michael Romano
2 days Member cost: $600 Non-member cost: $800

Information Technology Basics for Managers
Managers in today's companies need to be able to communicate easily with IT staff to effectively manage projects, implement processes and improve productivity. In this seminar you will learn the basic workings of an IT department and the meanings common IT vocabulary (for example, CRM, legacy systems, TCP/IP, etc.). We will help you identify and measure the value of IT programs and how to include these in your department budget. The important subject of creating and managing a team to implement an IT project is also covered extensively.

Presenter: David Rosenberg
2 days Member cost: $700 Non-member cost: $850

6K_Schedule_Firstname_Lastname

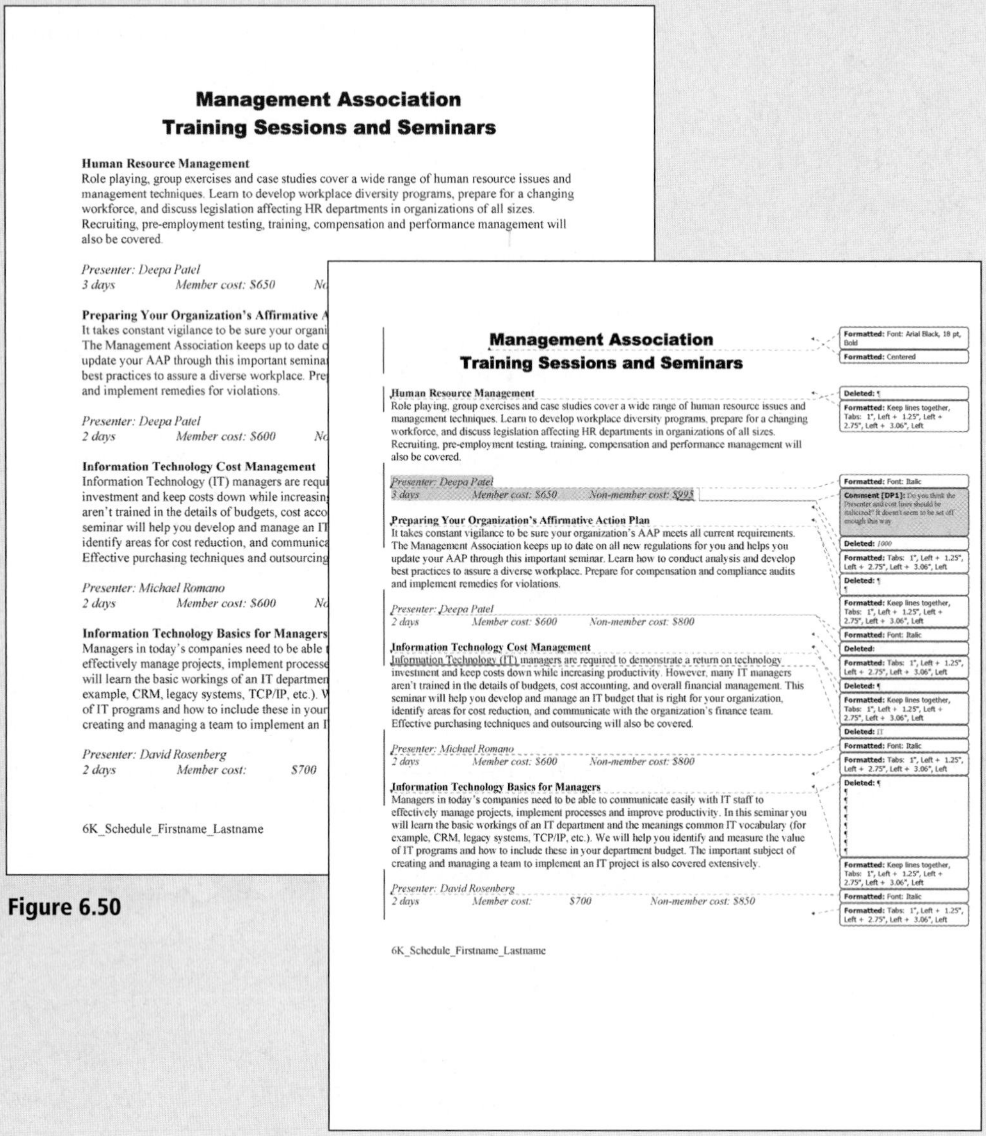

Figure 6.50

2. Turn on the Reviewing toolbar and, if necessary, turn on **Track Changes**. If necessary, turn on balloons for all tracked changes.

3. At the end of each Training Session description, the name of the Presenter is listed, followed in the next line by the date and cost. Go through the document and make all of these line pairs **Italic**. This will add additional tracked changes, but in a different color to identify you as a new reviewer.

(Project 6K–Schedule continues on the next page)

(Project 6K–Schedule continued)

4. In the middle of page 1, locate the first line following the *Information Technology Cost Management* heading, select *IT* (the first word in the sentence), and then replace it with **Information Technology (IT)**

5. Scroll down to examine the numerous changes to the document. To print these tracked changes, from the **Print** dialog box, click the **Print what** arrow, and then click **Document showing markup**. Under **Page range**, click the **Pages** option button, and then in the **Pages** box, type **1** so that only the first page prints. Click **OK**.

6. On the Reviewing toolbar, click the **Display for Review arrow**, and then click **Final** to see what the final document will look like. Print only the first page.

7. In the document summary, add your name and the current date to the **Comments** area. Change the **Title** to **Training Sessions and Seminars** and change the **Company** to **The Management Association of Pine Valley**

8. If your email system is set to do so, send the document as an email attachment to a friend or to yourself. Save your changes and close the document.

 End **You have completed Project 6K** ————————————————

Project 6L — Resume

Objectives: *Create a Document Using a Template and Review and Modify Document Properties.*

Your resume is the first thing a prospective employer sees. Two things are important in an effective resume: the look of the document and the information about yourself. A professional-looking resume will give you a much better chance of having the potential employer take the time to read about your qualifications. In this project, you will create and save your resume as *6L_Resume_Firstname_Lastname*.

1. Create a new document using the **Professional Resume** template in the **Other Documents tab** of the **Templates** dialog box. Save the document as **6L_Resume_Firstname_Lastname**

2. At the top of the resume, enter your address and phone number as indicated by the placeholder text.

3. Write an objective for a job you are considering now or in the future after you have completed more education.

4. Replace the information in the various categories with your own information. If you have had only one job, delete the other job headings and their associated information.

5. Under *Education*, add any certificates or degrees you have. If you have not yet earned a certificate or degree, enter the expected date of certificate completion or graduation. Add any honors you have received, and/or your grade point average if it is above 3.0 on a 4.0 scale. Be sure you include your major, if you have one.

6. Add any interests where indicated, and then delete the *Tips* section, unless you have a category you would like to add (such as Public Service).

7. Go to the **Document Properties** dialog box and add your name in the **Author** box and the name of this document in the **Title** box. Type your college name for the **Company** name. In the **Comments** area, add the current date. Save your work and close the document. You might want to keep this file and update it whenever appropriate.

End You have completed Project 6L

Project 6M — Lightning

Objectives: *Use Comments in a Document and Review and Modify Document Properties.*

In this project, you will add and edit comments in a draft copy of a lightning action plan document. You will save the document as *6M_Lightning_Firstname_Lastname.*

1. Locate and open **w06M_Lightning**. Save it as **6M_Lightning_Firstname_Lastname** with your other files. As you have with previous files, display the footer area and insert the **AutoText** filename.

2. Turn on the **Reviewing** toolbar and open the **reviewing pane**.

3. Display the Properties sheet, write down the existing **User Information**, and then change the user information to your name and initials.

4. Look through the document and add two comments on any topic of your choice.

5. Respond to the comments of Satarkta Kalam as if you were a member of the team working on the document and knew the answers to his questions. Search the Web to find a site with information about lightning safety for outdoor workers and add a sentence about the site. Add a hyperlink to a word or phrase in the new sentence that will take the reader to the site you have found.

6. Restore the **User Information** to the original name and initials. Save the document, print it, and then close the file.

End **You have completed Project 6M** ——————————————

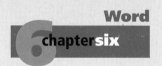

Word
chapter six

On the Internet

Downloading a Template from the Office Web Site

In this chapter you created a professional-looking memo using a template that was stored on your computer. Many templates are installed with Microsoft Office, but one that is exactly right for your purpose may not be included. Microsoft has an Internet site that makes many additional templates available.

1. Be sure that you are connected to the Internet. Open Word. In the **New Document** task pane, under **Templates**, click **Templates on Office Online**.

2. On the Templates page of Microsoft Office Online, scroll down to see the categories of templates that are available to you. Click on some of the categories to see what you can download.

3. Click the **Back** button until the screen returns to the Template page.

4. Under the **Health Care and Wellness** category, click **Diet and Exercise**. Click one of the templates that looks interesting to you. Make sure you select one that has the Word icon to the left of the template name. This list also includes Excel, PowerPoint, and Access templates. Notice the template is previewed on the screen.

5. If you are working in a lab, check to make sure you can download files. If it is permitted, click the **Download Now** button. The template displays with instructions explaining how to use the template.

6. Follow the instructions and practice using the template you downloaded.

7. When you are done, close the file without saving changes and then close Word. Remember that even though you have not saved your changes, the template is now available on the computer.

Sending a Document for Review

In this chapter you practiced sending an email with a document attached. You can learn more about sending documents for review by examining some of the Word Help topics on the subject. Word includes a reviewing feature that makes the process much more interactive than attaching an email. When you send a document using the *Mail Recipient (for Review)* command instead of the *Mail Recipient (as Attachment)* command, the program keeps track of your messages, flags them, and turns on the Track Changes feature when the document is returned.

1. Start Word. In the **Type a Question for Help** box, type **mail for review** and press Enter.

2. Examine the list of topics that displays in the Search Results task pane. From this list of help topics, click **About sending a file for review** and read the results. At the top of the Help window, click the **Show All** button, and then print these instructions if you want.

3. In a blank document, write two brief paragraphs about how and when you might use email to work collaboratively on a document. In the Search Results pane, click **Send a document in e-mail**, and then click **Send a document for review**. Notice the restrictions on the email programs that will work for this procedure.

4. If you are using one of these email programs and have permission to do so, follow the instructions to create and send this document to a friend. In the email message, ask the friend to make several changes and send the message back.

5. When you get the message back, in the Search Results pane, click **End a review cycle**. Read the instructions. End the review cycle and respond to the tracked changes.

6. Close the Help window and the Help task pane, close your document without saving the changes, and exit Word.

Word 2003 Task Guide

Each book in the *GO! Series* is designed to be kept beside your computer as a handy reference, even after you have completed all the activities. Any time you need to recall a sequence of steps or a shortcut needed to achieve a result, look up the general category in the alphabetized listing that follows and then find your task. To review how to perform a task, turn to the page number listed in the second column to locate the step-by-step exercise or other detailed description. Additional entries without page numbers describe tasks that are closely related to those presented in the chapters.

Word Task	Page	Mouse	Menu Bar	Shortcut Menu	Shortcut Keys
Align, center	86	on Formatting toolbar	Format | Paragraph | Indents and Spacing tab, Alignment	Right-click, Paragraph | Indents and Spacing tab, Alignment	Ctrl + E
Align, justify	86	on Formatting toolbar	Format | Paragraph | Indents and Spacing tab, Alignment	Right-click, Paragraph | Indents and Spacing tab, Alignment	Ctrl + J
Align, left	86	on Formatting toolbar	Format | Paragraph | Indents and Spacing tab, Alignment	Right-click, Paragraph | Indents and Spacing tab, Alignment	Ctrl + L
Align, right	86	on Formatting toolbar	Format | Paragraph | Indents and Spacing tab, Alignment	Right-click, Paragraph | Indents and Spacing tab, Alignment	Ctrl + R
Arrow, insert and format	185	on Drawing toolbar	Format | Auto-Shape | Colors and Lines tab	Right-click arrow, Format | AutoShape	
AutoComplete, use	34				Begin typing the first few letters of a month (or other AutoComplete text); when a ScreenTip displays, press Enter
AutoCorrect, record entries	121		Tools | AutoCorrect Options | AutoCorrect tab		
AutoCorrect, use shortcuts	124				Type shortcut text and press Enter, Spacebar, or Tab, or add punctuation mark
AutoFormat, table	222	on Tables and Borders toolbar	Table | Table AutoFormat	Select table, right-click, Table AutoFormat	
AutoShape, insert	187	AutoShapes ▾ on Drawing toolbar	Insert | Picture | AutoShapes		

Word Task	Page	Mouse	Menu Bar	Shortcut Menu	Shortcut Keys
AutoText, insert	126		Insert | AutoText		Begin typing the first few letters of AutoText text; when a ScreenTip displays, press `Enter`
AutoText, insert in header or footer	119	`Insert AutoText ▾` on Header and Footer toolbar	Insert | AutoText		
AutoText, record entries	126		Tools | AutoCorrect Options | AutoText tab		Select, `Alt` + `F3`
Border, add to paragraph	271	⊞ ▾ on Formatting toolbar	Format | Borders and Shading | Borders tab, Box		
Border, insert custom	264		Format | Borders and Shading | Borders tab, Custom		
Browse, select browse object	301	◉ on vertical scroll bar, select object on palette, use ⤓ for next object			
Browse, by comment	301	◉ on vertical scroll bar, 🖼	Edit | Go To, Comment		`Ctrl` + `G`
Browse, by edits	301	◉ on vertical scroll bar, ✎			
Browse, by endnote	301	◉ on vertical scroll bar, 📑	Edit | Go To, Endnote		`Ctrl` + `G`
Browse, by field	301	◉ on vertical scroll bar, {a}	Edit | Go To, Field		`Ctrl` + `G`
Browse, by footnote	301	◉ on vertical scroll bar, 📄	Edit | Go To, Footnote		`Ctrl` + `G`
Browse, by graphic	301	◉ on vertical scroll bar, 🖼	Edit | Go To, Graphic		`Ctrl` + `G`
Browse, by heading	301	◉ on vertical scroll bar, 📋	Edit | Go To, Heading		`Ctrl` + `G`
Browse, by page	301	◉ on vertical scroll bar, ▢	Edit | Go To, Page		`Ctrl` + `G`
Browse, by section	301	◉ on vertical scroll bar, 🗗	Edit | Go To, Section		`Ctrl` + `G`
Browse, by table	301	◉ on vertical scroll bar, ▦	Edit | Go To, Table		`Ctrl` + `G`
Browse, find	301	◉ on vertical scroll bar, 🔍	Edit | Find		`Ctrl` + `F`
Browse, go to	301	◉ on vertical scroll bar, →	Edit | Go To		`Ctrl` + `G`

Word Task	Page	Mouse	Menu Bar	Shortcut Menu	Shortcut Keys
Bulleted list, create	109	on Formatting toolbar	Format | Bullets and Numbering	Select text, right-click,Bullets and Numbering	
Bulleted list, customize	114		Select list, Format | Bullets and Numbering | Bulleted tab; select style and then click Customize	Select list, right-click,Bullets and Numbering | Bulleted tab; select style and then click Customize	
Character style, create for selected character(s)	372	Apply formatting and then click New Style; in Style type box, click Character			
Chart, add title	342		Activate chart, Chart | Chart Options | Titles tab	Activate chart; right-click chart area, Chart Options | Titles tab	
Chart, center	348	on Formatting toolbar	Format | Paragraph | Indents and Spacing tab, Alignment		Ctrl + E
Chart, change type	344	on Graph Standard toolbar	Activate chart, Chart | Chart Type	Activate chart; right-click chart area, Chart Type	
Chart, close datasheet	347	on datasheet title bar on Standard toolbar when the datasheet is open	View | Datasheet	Activate chart; right-click, Datasheet	
Chart, create from table	340		Activate table, Insert | Picture | Chart		
Chart, display datasheet	341		Activate chart, View | Datasheet		
Chart, edit	341	Double-click chart	Activate chart, Edit | Chart Object | Edit	Double-click chart; right-click chart, Chart Object | Edit	
Chart, format text	346	on Graph Standard toolbar	Activate chart, Format | Selected <object>	Activate chart; right-click text, Format <object>	
Chart, graph by column	345	on Graph Standard toolbar	Activate chart, Data | Series in Columns		
Chart, graph by row	345	on Graph Standard toolbar	Activate chart, Data | Series in Rows		
Chart, resize	348	Drag a selection handle	Activate chart, Format | Object | Size tab	Double-click chart; right-click chart, Format Object	
Chart, select	341	Click chart			
Clip art, insert	172	on Drawing toolbar in task pane and then click Clip Art	Insert | Picture | Clip Art		

Word Task	Page	Mouse	Menu Bar	Shortcut Menu	Shortcut Keys
Clip art, resize	179	Drag sizing handle on Picture toolbar	Select picture, Format | Picture | Size tab	Right-click image, Format Picture | Size tab	
Clip art, wrap text around	176	on Picture toolbar on Drawing toolbar, Text Wrapping	Select picture, Format	Right click image, Format Picture | Layout tab	
Clipboard, clear	289	Clear All in Clipboard task pane			
Clipboard, clear individual items	296	Click arrow next to item in Clipboard, click Delete		Right-click item in Clipboard, Delete	
Clipboard, collect and paste	289, 296	Display Clipboard task pane, or multiple objects; in new location(s), click objects on Clipboard to paste or Paste All	Collect objects on Clipboard using Edit | Copy; Edit | Cut; then paste in new location	Display Clipboard; right-click objects in document, Copy or Cut; right-click objects in Clipboard and Paste	Ctrl + C (copy) or Ctrl + X (cut)
Clipboard, collect from other documents	292	Display Clipboard, document selections to Clipboard	Collect objects on Clipboard using Edit | Copy; Edit | Cut	Display Clipboard; right-click objects in documents, Copy or Cut	Ctrl + C (copy) or Ctrl + X (cut)
Clipboard, display task pane	289	in any task pane and then click Clipboard	Edit | Office Clipboard		Ctrl + F1, and click Clipboard Ctrl + C twice
Close, document	292	on menu bar	File | Close		Ctrl + F4 or Ctrl + W
Close, file	48	on menu bar	File | Close		Ctrl + F4 or Ctrl + W
Close, header or footer	26	Close on Header and Footer toolbar Double-click in text area of document			
Close, print preview	34	Close or			
Collect and paste, multiple selections	289, 296	Display Clipboard task pane, or multiple objects; in new location(s), click objects on Clipboard to paste or Paste All	Collect objects on Clipboard using Edit | Copy; Edit | Cut; then paste in new location	Display Clipboard; right-click objects in document, Copy or Cut; right-click objects in Clipboard, Paste	Ctrl + C (copy) or Ctrl + X (cut)
Columns, balancing breaks	269		Insert | Break, Continuous		

Word Task	Page	Mouse	Menu Bar	Shortcut Menu	Shortcut Keys
Columns, change number	266	on Standard toolbar	Format | Columns		
Columns, insert break	269		Insert | Break, Column break		
Command, repeat	390				`F4`
Comment, delete	451	on Reviewing toolbar		Right-click comment balloon or comment in reviewing pane, and then click Delete Comment	
Comment, insert	442	on Reviewing toolbar	Insert | Comment		`Alt` + `Ctrl` + `M`
Comment, modify	445	Click in comment balloon or in reviewing pane, edit text			
Comment, read in reviewing pane	443	on Reviewing toolbar; click in text that has a comment, and then read in reviewing pane			
Copy	102	on Standard toolbar	Edit | Copy	Right-click selected text, Copy	`Ctrl` + `C`
Create, new document	33	Start Word (opens blank document) on Standard toolbar Click *Create a new document* in Getting Started task pane Click *Blank document* in New Document task pane	File | New		`Ctrl` + `N`
Create, new folder	28	in Open or Save As dialog box			
Create, new table	203	on Standard toolbar	Table | Insert | Table		
Cut	99, 104	on Standard toolbar	Edit | Cut	Right-click selected text or object, Cut	`Ctrl` + `X`
Date and time, insert in header or footer	120	on Header and Footer toolbar	Insert | Date and Time		`Alt` + `Shift` + `D` and `Alt` + `Shift` + `T`
Delete, text	39, 97		Edit | Clear | Contents		`Bksp` or `Delete`
Display, ScreenTip	13	Point to a screen element			
Display, toolbar	4		View | Toolbars	Right-click any toolbar, click toolbar name	
Display/hide, task pane	9		View | Task Pane		`Ctrl` + `F1`

Word Task	Page	Mouse	Menu Bar	Shortcut Menu	Shortcut Keys
Document, accept merge changes	461	on Reviewing toolbar			
Document, attach to email message	457		File | Send To | Mail Recipient (as Attachment)		
Document, create new	33	Start Word (opens blank document) on Standard toolbar Click Create a new document in Getting Started task pane Click Blank document in New Document task pane	File | New		Ctrl + N
Document, reject merge changes	461	on Reviewing toolbar			
Document, save	34		File | Save		Ctrl + S
Document, save in another format	455		File | Save As; change *Save as type* to another format		
Documents, compare and merge	459		Tools | Compare and Merge Documents		
Drag-and-drop, turn off/on	104		Tools | Options | Edit tab		
Drawing canvas, hide	182		Tools | Options | General tab		
Drop cap, create	351		Format | Drop Cap		
Em dash, insert	128		Insert | Symbols | Special Characters tab		Alt + Ctrl + −
Email, document as attachment	457		File | Send To | Mail Recipient (as Attachment)		
Endnote insert	130		Insert | Reference | Endnote		Alt + Ctrl + F
Exit Word	31		File | Exit		Alt + F4
File, close	48	on menu bar	File | Close		
File, view properties	435		File | Properties		
Find and replace text	95	on Select Browse Object palette and then click Replace tab	Edit | Replace		Ctrl + H
Folder, create new	28	in Open or Save As dialog box			

Word Task	Page	Mouse	Menu Bar	Shortcut Menu	Shortcut Keys
Font, apply bold or italic style	47	**B** *I*	Format | Font, Font style	Right-click and then click Font	Ctrl + B or Ctrl + I
Font, apply underline	47	U	Format | Font, Underline	Right-click and then click Font	Ctrl + U
Font, change	44	Times New Roman ▾ on Formatting toolbar	Format | Font	Right-click and then click Font	
Font, change size	44	12 ▾ on Formatting toolbar	Format | Font, Size	Right-click and then click Font	
Font, color	274	A ▾ on Formatting toolbar	Format | Font, Font color	Right-click and then click Font	
Font, effects	275		Format | Font, Effects, select effect	Right-click and then click Font	
Footnote, insert	130		Insert | Reference | Footnote		Alt + Ctrl + F
Format Painter	94	on Standard toolbar (double-click to apply repeatedly)			Ctrl + Shift + C and Ctrl + Shift + V
Format, paragraph	366		Format | Paragraph	Paragraph	
Formatting marks, display/hide	17	¶ on Standard toolbar	Tools | Options | View tab, Formatting marks		
Graphic image, move	181	Drag image; and on Standard toolbar	Edit | Cut Edit | Paste	Right-click image, Cut, and then right-click at new location and choose Paste	Ctrl + X and Ctrl + V Select image, ← → ↑ ↓
Header or footer, add to document	26	Double-click in a header or footer area on a page (only if header or footer is not empty)	View | Header and Footer; position insertion point in header or footer area and then enter text		
Header or footer, close and return to document	26	Close on Header and Footer toolbar Double-click in text area of document			
Header or footer, insert date and time	120	on Header and Footer toolbar	Insert | Date and Time		Alt + Shift + D and Alt + Shift + T
Header or footer, insert page numbers	117	on Header and Footer toolbar	Insert | Page Numbers		Alt + Shift + P

Word Task	Page	Mouse	Menu Bar	Shortcut Menu	Shortcut Keys
Header or footer, switch between	26	⊞ on Header and Footer toolbar			
Help, display in Word	51	⊙ on Standard toolbar Click the *Type a question for help* box; type text and press [Enter]	Help | Microsoft Office Word Help		[F1]
Help, hide Office Assistant	8		Help | Hide the Office Assistant	Right-click Office Assistant and then click Hide	
Help, show Office Assistant	51		Help | Show the Office Assistant		
Hide/Show, space between pages (Print Layout View)	377	Point between pages to display Hide/Show White Space pointer, and then click	Tools | Options | View tab, White space between pages		
Hyperlink, graphic	282	⬚ on Standard toolbar	Insert | Hyperlink	Right-click and then click Hyperlink	[Ctrl] + [K]
Hyperlink, modify	283	⬚ on Standard toolbar	Insert | Hyperlink	Right-click and then click Edit Hyperlink	[Ctrl] + [K]
Hyperlink, text	279	⬚ on Standard toolbar	Insert | Hyperlink	Right-click and then click Hyperlink	[Ctrl] + [K]
Indent, decrease left indent	197	⬚ on Formatting toolbar	Format | Paragraph | Indents and Spacing tab, Left	Right-click, Paragraph | Indents and Spacing tab | Left	[Ctrl] + [Shift] + [M]
Indent, first line	93	♡ on ruler	Format | Paragraph | Indents and Spacing tab, Special	Right-click, Paragraph | Indents and Spacing tab, Special	
Indent, hanging	136	⬚ on ruler	Format | Paragraph | Indents and Spacing tab, Special	Right-click, Paragraph | Indents and Spacing tab, Special	[Ctrl] + [T]
Indent, increase left indent	197	⬚ on Formatting toolbar Drag Left Indent marker on ruler	Format | Paragraph | Indents and Spacing tab, Left	Right-click, Paragraph | Indents and Spacing tab | Left	[Ctrl] + [M]
Indent, left	93	⬚ hanging	Format | Paragraph | Indents and Spacing tab, Left	Right-click, Paragraph | Indents and Spacing tab, Left	
Insert mode, toggle between overtype/insert	40	Double-click OVR in status bar			[Insert]
Insert, clip art	172	⬚ on Drawing toolbar ▼ in task pane, then click Clip Art	Insert | Picture | Clip Art		[Ctrl] + [F1], then choose Clip Art

Word Task	Page	Mouse	Menu Bar	Shortcut Menu	Shortcut Keys
Insert, text box	182	⬚ on Drawing toolbar	Insert | Text Box		
Keyboard shortcut	9				Press and hold down the first key, such as Ctrl, and then press the second key (if any), such as F1
Line spacing	88	≡▾ on Formatting toolbar	Format | Paragraph | Indents and Spacing tab, Line spacing	Right-click, Paragraph | Indents and Spacing tab, Line spacing	Ctrl + 1 (single) Ctrl + 2 (double) Ctrl + 5 (space and one half)
List style, create for selected list	369	Apply formatting and then click New Style button in Styles and Formatting task pane; in Style type box, click List			
Margins, set	84	Double-click at right of ruler and then click	File | Page Setup | Margins tab		
Markup, show/hide	446	Final Showing Markup ▾ on Reviewing toolbar	View | Markup		
Memo, create from template	428	Click *On my computer* on New Document task pane, and then click Memos tab	File | New, *On my computer*, click Memos tab		
Memo, replace placeholder text	430	Click in a placeholder and then type			
Menu bar, use	9	Click menu name and then click a command			Alt + underlined letter on menu and then underlined letter of command
Menu, display full	9	Double-click menu name in menu bar Wait a few seconds after displaying menu Click expand arrows at bottom of menu	Tools | Customize | Options tab, Always show full menus		
Menu, display full always	9		Tools | Customize | Options tab, Always show full menus	Right-click any toolbar and then click Customize; on Options tab, select Always show full menus	
Menu, use keyboard shortcut shown on menu	9				Press and hold down the first key, such as Ctrl, and then press the second key (if any), such as F1

Word Task	Page	Mouse	Menu Bar	Shortcut Menu	Shortcut Keys
Merge, accept changes	461	on Reviewing toolbar			
Merge, documents	460		Tools | Compare and Merge Documents		
Merge, reject changes	461	on Reviewing toolbar			
Move, graphic image	181	Drag image; and on Standard toolbar	Edit | Cut and Edit | Paste	Right-click image, Cut, and then right-click at new location and choose Paste	Ctrl + X and Ctrl + V. Select image ← → ↑ ↓
Move, text	99, 104	and on Standard toolbar. Drag selected text to new location	Edit | Cut Edit | Paste	Right-click selected text, Cut, and then right-click at new location and choose Paste	Ctrl + X and Ctrl + V
Navigate, down, a line at a time	13	at the bottom of vertical scroll bar			↓
Navigate, up/down, screen at a time	13	Click in gray area above/ below scroll box on vertical scroll bar			Page Up PageDown
Navigate, to beginning of current line	16	Click at beginning of line			Home
Navigate, to beginning of document	16	Drag vertical scroll bar to top, click before first line			Ctrl + Home
Navigate, to beginning of next word	16	Click at beginning of next word			Ctrl + →
Navigate, to beginning of previous word	16	Click at beginning of previous word			Ctrl + ←
Navigate, to end of current line	16	Click at end of line			End
Navigate, to end of document	16	Drag vertical scroll bar to lower end, click after last line			Ctrl + End
Navigate, up a line at a time	13	at the top of the vertical scroll bar			↑
Normal view, display	18	in lower left corner of Word window	View | Normal		Alt + Ctrl + N
Numbered list, create	110	on Formatting toolbar	Format | Bullets and Numbering	Select text, right-click Bullets and Numbering	

Word Task	Page	Mouse	Menu Bar	Shortcut Menu	Shortcut Keys
Open, existing document	8	on Standard toolbar More or document name in Getting Started task pane	File | Open File | document name at bottom of File menu		Ctrl + O
Outline entry, collapse	395	on Outlining toolbar Double-click Collapse indicator			
Outline entry, demote	390	on Outlining toolbar		Increase Indent	Tab or Alt + Shift + →
Outline entry, expand	392	on Outlining toolbar Double-click Expand indicator			
Outline entry, move up	392	on Outlining toolbar			In Outline View, drag Expand/ Collapse button up
Outline entry, move down	392	on Outlining toolbar			In Outline View, drag Expand/ Collapse button down
Outline entry, promote	395	on Outlining toolbar		Decrease Indent	Shift + Tab or Alt + Shift + ←
Outline view, display	18	in lower left corner of Word window	View | Outline		Alt + Ctrl + O
Outline, set numbering	382		Format | Bullets and Numbering | Outline Numbered tab	Bullets and Numbering | Outline Numbered tab	
Page break, insert manual	130		Insert | Break, Page break		Ctrl + Enter
Page numbers, different on first page	117	on Header and Footer toolbar	File | Page Setup | Layout tab		
Page numbers, format in header or footer	117	on Header and Footer toolbar			
Page numbers, in header or footer	117	on Header and Footer toolbar	Insert | Page Numbers		Alt + Shift + P
Page setup	34	Double-click left or right of ruler	File | Page Setup		

Word Task	Page	Mouse	Menu Bar	Shortcut Menu	Shortcut Keys
Paragraph style, create for selected paragraph	366	Apply formatting, and then click New Style button in Styles and Formatting task pane; Normal ▾ on Formatting toolbar; type a new name and then press Enter			
Paragraph, border	271	on Formatting toolbar	Format | Borders and Shading | Borders tab, Box		
Paragraph, decrease left indent	112	on Formatting toolbar	Format | Paragraph | Indents and Spacing tab, Left	Right-click, Paragraph | Indents and Spacing tab, Left	Ctrl + Shift + M
Paragraph, increase left indent	112	on Formatting toolbar	Format | Paragraph | Indents and Spacing tab, Left	Right-click, Paragraph | Indents and Spacing tab, Left	Ctrl + Shift + M
Paragraph, format	366		Format | Paragraph	Paragraph	
Paragraph, hanging indent	136	on ruler	Format | Paragraph | Indents and Spacing tab, Special	Right-click, Paragraph | Indents and Spacing tab, Special	Ctrl + T
Paragraph, indent first line	93	on ruler	Format | Paragraph | Indents and Spacing tab, Special	Right-click, Paragraph | Indents and Spacing tab, Special	
Paragraph, Indent left margin	88	on ruler	Format | Paragraph | Indents and Spacing tab, left	Right-click, Paragraph | Indents and Spacing tab, Left	
Paragraph, line spacing	88	on Formatting toolbar	Format | Paragraph | Indents and Spacing tab, Line spacing	Right-click, Paragraph | Indents and Spacing tab, Line spacing	Ctrl + 1 (single) Ctrl + 2 (double) Ctrl + 5 (space and one half)
Paragraph, shading	273		Format | Borders and Shading | Shading tab		
Paragraph, spacing	90, 112		Format | Paragraph | Indents and Spacing tab, Before/After	Right-click, Paragraph | Indents and Spacing tab, Before/After	
Paste	99	on Standard toolbar Click item in Office Clipboard	Edit | Paste	Right-click, then choose Paste	Ctrl + V
Paste options	99	after Paste			
Picture, insert	124	on Drawing toolbar then choose	Insert | Picture | From File		Ctrl + F1 and then choose Clip Art
Picture, resize	179	Drag sizing handle; on Picture toolbar	Format | Picture | Size tab	Right-click image, Format Picture | Size tab	

Word Task	Page	Mouse	Menu Bar	Shortcut Menu	Shortcut Keys
Picture, wrap text around	176	[icon] on Picture toolbar; Draw ▾ on Drawing toolbar, Text Wrapping	Format | Picture | Layout tab	Right-click image, Format Picture | Layout tab	
Preview, as Web page	285		File | Web Page Preview		
Print Layout view, display	18	[icon] in lower left corner of Word window	View | Print Layout		Alt + Ctrl + P
Print, document	31, 48	[icon] on Standard toolbar	File | Print		Ctrl + P
Print, document properties	437		File | Print; click Print what, and then click Document properties		
Print, from preview	187	[icon] on Print Preview toolbar			
Print, preview	34	[icon] on Standard toolbar	File | Print Preview		Ctrl + F2
Reading Layout view, close	18	🕮 Close on Reading Layout toolbar			
Reading Layout view, display	18	[icon] in lower left corner of Word window; 🕮 Read on Standard toolbar	View | Reading Layout		
Redo an action (after Undo)	106	[icon] ▾ on Standard toolbar	Edit | Redo		Ctrl + Y
Research	293	[icon] on Standard toolbar, type a search topic and select a source	Tools | Research		Alt + click word(s)
Reviewing pane, show/hide	443	[icon] on Reviewing toolbar			Alt + Shift + C (hide only)
Ruler, display/hide	84		View | Ruler		
Save, document	34	[icon]	File | Save		Ctrl + S
Save, document (new name, location, or type)	28		File | Save As		F12
Save, document as Web page	286		File | Save as Web Page		
Save, document in another format	455		File | Save As; change *Save as type* to another format		

Word Task	Page	Mouse	Menu Bar	Shortcut Menu	Shortcut Keys
ScreenTip, display	13	Point to a screen element			
Sort, paragraphs	136	▲↓ or ▼↓ on Tables and Borders toolbar	Table | Sort		
Spelling and Grammar, check entire document	23	☑ on Standard toolbar	Tools | Spelling and Grammar, then choose an action for each suggestion		F7
Spelling and Grammar, check individual errors	21			Right-click word or phrase with red or green wavy underline and then choose a suggested correction or other action	
Spelling and Grammar, turn on/off features	21		Tools | Options | Spelling & Grammar tab, then choose Check spelling as you type and/or Check grammar as you type		
Start Word	4	🎚 start on Windows task-bar and then locate and click Microsoft Office Word 2003	Start | All Programs | Microsoft Office | Microsoft Office Word 2003		
Statistics, view properties	435		File | Properties | Statistics tab		
Style area, display (Normal View)	360		Tools | Options | View tab, Style area width (increase)		
Style area, hide (Normal View)	362	Drag style areas vertical border to left edge of window	Tools | Options | View tab, Style area width (set to 0)		
Style, apply	363, 365, 371	Normal ⏷ on Formatting toolbar Click Style in Styles and Formatting task pane			
Style, clear	365	Normal ⏷ on Formatting toolbar, and then click *Clear Formatting* Click *Clear Formatting* in Styles and Formatting task pane			
Style, modify	376	In Styles and Formatting task pane, point to style, click arrow, and then click Modify		Right-click style in Styles and Formatting task pane, and then click Modify	
Styles and Formatting task pane, display/hide	360	🅰🅰 on Formatting toolbar	Format | Styles and Formatting		Ctrl + F1, then choose Styles and Formatting
Summary, view or edit properties	435, 437		File | Properties | Summary tab		

Word Task	Page	Mouse	Menu Bar	Shortcut Menu	Shortcut Keys
Symbols, insert	128		Insert | Symbols | Special Characters tab		
Tab stops, clear	195	Drag tab stop off ruler	Format | Tabs, Clear or Clear All		
Tab stops, dot leaders	197		Format | Tabs, Leader		
Tab stops, format	195		Format | Tabs, Set		
Tab stops, move	200	Drag markers on ruler	Format | Tabs, Set		
Tab stops, set	192	⌊ on ruler; click to cycle tab types, then click ruler	Format | Tabs, Set		
Tab stops, use	197				Tab while typing
Table, align	218	Select table, ▤ or ▤ or ▤ on Formatting toolbar	Table | Table Properties | Table tab	Right-click, Table Properties, Table tab	
Table, align cells	223	▤ ▾ on Tables and Borders toolbar	Table | Table Properties | Cell tab	Right-click in cell, Cell Alignment	
Table, AutoFormat	222	▤ on Tables and Borders toolbar	Table | Table AutoFormat	Select table, right-click, Table AutoFormat	
Table, change border	215	▤ ▾ on Tables and Borders toolbar	Format | Borders and Shading | Borders tab	Right-click, Borders and Shading | Borders tab	
Table, column width	208	Drag column boundary	Table | Table Properties | Column tab, Preferred width	Right-click in column, Table Properties | Column tab, Preferred width	
Table, convert from text	219		Table | Convert | Text to Table		
Table, create new	203	▤ ▾ on Standard toolbar	Table | Insert | Table		
Table, delete	351		Click in table, Table | Delete | Table		
Table, format cell text	211	Formatting toolbar			
Table, insert column	209	▤ ▾ arrow on Tables and Borders toolbar, Insert Columns to the Left or Insert Columns to the Right	Table | Insert | Columns to the Left or Columns to the Right	Right-click in selected column, Insert Columns	
Table, insert row	206	▤ ▾ arrow on Tables and Borders toolbar, Insert Rows Above or Insert Rows Below	Table | Insert | Rows Above or Rows Below	Right-click to left of row, Insert Rows	
Table, merge selected cells	223	▤ on Tables and Borders toolbar	Table | Merge Cells	Right-click in selected cells, Merge Cells	

Word Task	Page	Mouse	Menu Bar	Shortcut Menu	Shortcut Keys
Table, move between cells	203	Click in cell			Tab, Shift + Tab, → ← ↑ ↓
Table, select	218	Click table move handle in Print Layout view	Table | Select | Table		Alt + 5
Table, shading cells	213	⬛ ▾ on Tables and Borders toolbar	Format | Borders and Shading | Shading tab	Right-click in selected cells, Borders and Shading | Shading tab	
Tables and Borders toolbar, display		⬛ on Standard toolbar	View | Toolbars | Tables and Borders	Right-click in any toolbar, click Tables and Borders	
Task pane, display/hide	9		View | Task Pane		Ctrl + F1
Template, find on Web	429	Click *Templates on Office Online* on New Document task pane	File | New, *Templates on Office Online*		
Template, use to create document	428	Click *On my computer* on New Document task pane	File | New, *On my computer*		
Text box, insert	182	⬛ on Drawing toolbar	Insert | Text Box		
Text box, move	184	Drag border; ✂ and ⬛ on Standard toolbar	Edit | Cut and Edit | Paste	Right-click border, Cut, then right-click at new location and choose Paste	Ctrl + X and Ctrl + V ← → ↑ ↓
Text box, resize	184	Drag sizing handle	Format | Text Box | Size tab	Right-click border, Format Text Box | Size tab	
Text, align	86	▤ ▤ ▤ ▤	Format | Paragraph | Indents and Spacing tab, Alignment	Right-click, Paragraph | Indents and Spacing tab, Alignment	Ctrl + L (left) Ctrl + E (center) Ctrl + R (right) Ctrl + J (justify)
Text, cancel selection	42	Click anywhere in document			
Text, change font	44	Times New Roman ▾ on Formatting toolbar	Format | Font	Right-click and then click Font	
Text, change font size	44	12 ▾ on Formatting toolbar	Format | Font	Right-click and then click Font	
Text, character spacing	356		Format | Font | Character Spacing tab	Font | Character Spacing tab	
Text, copy	102	⬛ on Standard toolbar	Edit | Copy	Right-click selected text, Copy	Ctrl + C
Text, delete	39, 97		Edit | Clear | Contents		Bksp or Delete
Text, drop cap	351		Format | Drop Cap		
Text, enter	34	Click to place insertion point and then type text			

Word Task	Page	Mouse	Menu Bar	Shortcut Menu	Shortcut Keys
Text, find and replace	95	[icon] on Select Browse Object palette and then click Replace tab	Edit | Replace		Ctrl + H
Text, move (cut)	99, 104	[icon] and [icon] on Standard toolbar Drag selected text to new location	Edit | Cut Edit | Paste	Right-click selected text, Cut, click at new location, and choose Paste	Ctrl + X Ctrl + V
Text, new paragraph or blank line	34				Enter once or twice
Text, overtype/ insert	40	Double-click OVR in status bar, then type			Insert and then type
Text, paste	99	[icon] on Standard toolbar	Edit | Paste	Right-click and then choose Paste	Ctrl + V
Text, paste options	99	[icon] after pasting			
Text, select	42	Drag over text			Click at beginning, Shift + click at end of selection
Text, select consecutive lines	42				Shift + ↑ or ↓
Text, select consecutive paragraphs	42				Shift + Ctrl ↑ or ↓
Text, select entire document (including objects)	42	Triple-click [icon] in selection bar	Edit | Select All		Ctrl + A
Text, select line	42	Click [icon] next to line in selection bar			
Text, select one character at a time	42				Shift + → or ←
Text, select one word at a time	42, 97				Shift + Ctrl + → or ←
Text, select paragraph	42	Triple-click in paragraph Double-click [icon] in selection bar next to paragraph			
Text, select sentence	42				Ctrl + click sentence
Text, select word	42	Double-click word			
Text, shadow effect	353		Format | Font | Font tab, Shadow	Font | Font tab, Shadow	

Word Task	Page	Mouse	Menu Bar	Shortcut Menu	Shortcut Keys
Text, small caps effect	354		Format | Font | Font tab, Small Caps	Font | Font tab, Small Caps	Ctrl + Shift + K
Thesaurus	299	[icon] on Standard toolbar, select Thesaurus in Research task pane	Tools | Language | Thesaurus	Right-click a word, Synonyms | Thesaurus	Shift + F7
Toolbar, display	4		View | Toolbars	Right-click any toolbar, click toolbar name	
Toolbars, show on one or two rows	4	[icon] on Standard or Formatting toolbar, Show Buttons on One Row / Two Rows	Tools | Customize | Options tab, Show Standard and Formatting toolbars on two rows View | Toolbars | Customize | Options tab, Show Standard and Formatting toolbars on two rows	Right-click any toolbar and then click Customize; on Options tab, select or clear Show Standard and Formatting toolbars on two rows	
Track changes, accept change	452	[icon] on Reviewing toolbar			
Track changes, locate next change	449	[icon] on Reviewing toolbar			
Track changes, reject change	451	[icon] on Reviewing toolbar			
Track changes, reviewers	449	Show ▾ on Reviewing toolbar; click Reviewers and then click All Reviewers or a reviewer's name			
Track changes, show settings	449	Show ▾ on Reviewing toolbar			
Track changes, show/hide markup	446	Final Showing Markup ▾ on Reviewing toolbar	View | Markup		
Track changes, turn on/off	446	Show ▾ on Reviewing toolbar	Tools | Track Changes	Right-click a tracked change, and then click Track Changes	Ctrl + Shift + E
Undo an action	106	[icon] on Standard toolbar	Edit | Undo		Ctrl + Z
View, Normal	18	[icon] in lower left corner of Word window	View | Normal		Alt + Ctrl + N
View, Outline	18	[icon] in lower left corner of Word window	View | Outline		Alt + Ctrl + O
View, Print Layout	18	[icon] in lower left corner of Word window	View | Print Layout		Alt + Ctrl + P

Word Task	Page	Mouse	Menu Bar	Shortcut Menu	Shortcut Keys
View, Reading Layout	18	[icon] in lower left corner of Word window [icon] Read on Standard toolbar	View | Reading Layout		
View, Web Layout	18	[icon] in lower left corner of corner of Word window	View | Web Layout		
Web Layout view, display	18	[icon] in lower left corner of Word window	View | Web Layout		
Web page, save document	286		File | Save as Web Page		
Window, remove split	379	Double-click split bar between panes Drag split bar up	Window | Remove Split		
Window, split	379	Drag split box (above vertical scroll bar)	Window | Split		
WordArt, alignment	262	[icons] on WordArt toolbar			
WordArt, change shape	262	[icon] on WordArt toolbar			
WordArt, character spacing	262	[icon] on WordArt toolbar			
WordArt, display toolbar	262	Click the WordArt image	View | Toolbars | WordArt		
WordArt, edit text	262	Edit Text... on WordArt toolbar		Right-click WordArt, Edit Text	
WordArt, format	262	[icon] on WordArt toolbar	Format | WordArt	Right-click WordArt, Format WordArt	
WordArt, gallery	262	[icon] on WordArt toolbar			
WordArt, insert	260	[icon] on Drawing toolbar	Insert | Picture | WordArt		
WordArt, same letter heights	262	[icon] on WordArt toolbar			
WordArt, text wrapping	262	[icon] on WordArt toolbar	Format WordArt | Layout tab	Right-click WordArt, Format WordArt | Layout tab	
WordArt, vertical text	262	[icon] on WordArt toolbar			

Word Task	Page	Mouse	Menu Bar	Shortcut Menu	Shortcut Keys
Word count, check	438	`<Click Recount to view>` on Word Count toolbar	Tools | Word Count View | Toolbars | Word Count		Ctrl + Shift + G, and then Enter
Word count, recheck	439	`Recount` on Word Count toolbar	Tools | Word Count View | Toolbars | Word Count		Ctrl + Shift + G, and then Enter
Zoom, magnify or shrink the view of a document	19	`100%` arrow on Standard toolbar and then choose a display percentage Click in Zoom box `100%` and then type a percentage	View | Zoom		
Zoom, maximum page width	19	`100%` arrow on Standard toolbar and then choose Page Width	View | Zoom, Page Width		

Aligned left The most common alignment, with the left edge of the text straight, and the right edge uneven.

Aligned right The right edge of the text is straight, and the left edge is uneven.

Alignment The placement of paragraph text relative to the left and right margins.

Anchor Indicates that an object is attached to the nearest paragraph.

AutoComplete A Word feature that assists in your typing by suggesting words or phrases.

AutoCorrect A feature that corrects common typing and spelling errors, and can also be used as a shortcut for typing commonly used text.

AutoFormat, Table Uses predefined formats to create a professional-looking table.

AutoText A feature that stores commonly used text and graphics for easy retrieval.

Body text Text in the Outline View that does not use a heading style.

Bullet A symbol used at the beginning of each item in a bulleted list.

Bulleted list A group of items formatted in a similar manner, and preceded by a symbol, called a bullet.

Category axis (x-axis) The horizontal axis along the bottom of a chart that displays labels.

Cell The intersection of a row and column in a table.

Center alignment Text is spaced equally between the left and right margins.

Character style Style that contains a set of instructions for changing a group of formatting characteristics, such as font and font size, for text only. All changes are applied together.

Chart A graphic representation of numbers in a worksheet used to display comparisons, change over time, contributions to the whole, or some other relationship that is easier to understand with a picture.

Chart area The part of the chart that displays the chart graphic.

Clip A media file, such as sound, art, animation, or movies.

Clip art Graphic images included with the Microsoft Office program or obtained from other sources.

Clipboard Shortcut term for the Office Clipboard.

Collapse button An open minus symbol to the left of a heading in an outline indicating that no text or lower-level headings are associated with the heading.

Collapsed Subordinate headings and text associated with a heading are hidden.

Collect and paste Microsoft Office feature that enables you to place up to 24 objects in the Office Clipboard, and then paste them as needed, and in any order.

Column chart A graph with vertical columns that is used to make comparisons among related numbers.

Comment A note attached to a document. By default, comments do not print.

Copy Send a graphic or block of text to the Office Clipboard, while also leaving it in its original location.

Copyright Laws that protect the rights of authors of original works, including text, art, photographs, and music.

Cut Send a graphic or block of text to the Office Clipboard and remove it from its original location.

Datasheet A special table that holds chart data. Each chart has its own datasheet.

Desktop publisher A program, such as Microsoft Publisher, that is used to create newsletters, posters, greeting cards, and even Web pages.

Document properties Statistics and related information about a document, including file size and location, author, title, and subject.

Dot leader A series of dots preceding a tab; often used between a text entry and a page number in a table of contents.

Double-click The action of clicking the left mouse button twice in rapid succession.

Drag Hold the left mouse button down over selected text or a graphic element and move it by moving the mouse; also, to hold down the left mouse button and move over text to select it.

Drag-and-drop A method of moving text and graphics from one location to another by selecting it and then clicking and holding the mouse button and moving the text.

Drawing canvas A work area for creating and editing complex figures created using the drawing tools.

Drop cap The first letter (or letters) of a paragraph, enlarged and either embedded in the text or placed in the left margin.

Dropped Drop cap position embedded in the text, rather than in the margin.

Edit Make changes to the text or format of a document.

Editing time How many minutes the document has been open. Editing time is not an exact measurement of actual time on task.

Em dash A long dash that separates distinct phrases in a sentence. It is about four times as long as a hyphen.

Endnote A reference placed at the end of a section or the end of the document.

Expand button An open plus symbol to the left of a heading in an outline indicating that there is text associated with the heading. If double-clicked, it acts as an on/off button to display subordinate text.

Floating image A graphic that moves independently of the surrounding text.

Font A set of characters with the same design and shape.

Font styles Bold, italic, and underline used to enhance text.

Footer Area reserved at the bottom of each page for text and graphics that appear at the bottom of each page in a document or section of a document.

Footnote A reference placed at the bottom of a page.

Format text The process of establishing the overall appearance of text in a document.

Formatting marks Characters that display on the screen, but do not print, indicating where the Enter key, the Spacebar, and the Tab key were pressed. Also called nonprinting characters.

Formatting toolbar Contains buttons for some of the most common formatting tasks in Word. It may occupy an entire row or share a row with the Standard toolbar.

Hanging indent A paragraph where the first line extends to the left of the rest of the lines in the same paragraph. Hanging indents are often used for bibliographic entries.

Header Area reserved for text and graphics that appear at the top of each page in a document or section of a document.

Horizontal scroll bar Enables you to move left and right in a document that is wider than the screen.

Hyperlink Text that you click to go to another location in a document, another document, or a Web site. Hyperlinks are often a different color (usually blue) than the surrounding text, and are often underlined.

In margin Drop cap position with the letter in the margin, rather than embedded in the text.

Inline image A graphic that acts like a character in a sentence.

Insert mode The mode in which text moves to the right to make space for new characters or graphic elements.

Insertion point A blinking vertical line that indicates where text or graphics will be inserted.

Justified alignment Both the left and right margins are straight (aligned). Text in books and magazines is nearly always justified.

Keyboard shortcut A combination of keys on the keyboard, usually using the Ctrl key or the Alt key, that provides a quick way to activate a command.

Legend A key in a chart that identifies the data series by color.

Line spacing The distance between lines of text in a paragraph.

List style Formats font style, font size, alignment, and bullet or number characteristics in lists.

Manual column break An artificial end to a column used to balance columns or to provide space for the insertion of other objects.

Margin The white space at the top, bottom, left, and right sides of a page.

Masthead The large title at the top of a newsletter.

Menu A list of commands within a category.

Menu bar The bar beneath the blue title bar that lists the names of menu categories.

Microsoft Graph A subprogram built into Microsoft Office that is used to create charts.

Navigate To move within a document.

Nonprinting characters Characters that display on the screen, but do not print, indicating where the Enter key, the Spacebar, and the Tab key were pressed. Also called formatting marks.

Normal template The template on which most documents are based, which contains the default Word document settings.

Normal View A simplified view of a document that does not show graphics, margins, headers, or footers.

Numbered list A group of items formatted in a similar manner, with each item preceded by a number. Numbered lists are used for items that have some relationship (chronological or sequential).

Office Clipboard A memory area that can hold up to 24 graphics or blocks of text. Items are placed in the Office Clipboard when the Cut or Copy features are used.

Outline A list of topics for an oral or written report that visually indicates the order in which the information will be discussed, as well as the relationship of the topics to each other and to the total report.

Outline view A document view that shows headings and subheadings, which can be expanded or collapsed.

Overtype mode A mode for entering text in which existing text is replaced as you type.

Paragraph style Style that contains a set of instructions for changing a group of formatting characteristics in a paragraph, such as font, font size, line spacing, and indentation. All changes are applied together.

Paste Insert an object from the Office Clipboard into a document.

Pie chart A graph in the shape of a pie that is used to show the contribution of each part to the whole.

Placeholder text In a document created using a template, text that can be replaced but not edited.

Plot area The portion of a chart occupied by the chart graphic—a pie or columns. It does not include the title or legend areas.

Point A measurement of the size of a font. There are 72 points in an inch, with 10–12 points being the most commonly used font size.

Print Layout view A view of a document that looks like a sheet of paper. It displays margins, headers, footers, and graphics.

Pt. Abbreviation for point in terms of font size.

Reading Layout View Displays easy-to-read pages that fit on the screen.

Recognizer A purple dotted underscore beneath a date or address indicating that the information could be placed into another Microsoft Office application program such as Outlook.

Reference The source of information, taken verbatim or paraphrased, from another location, usually indicated by a mark or a number. References can be placed at the bottom of each page (footnote) or the end of the section or document (endnote).

Reviewing pane An area at the bottom of the screen that displays comments and tracked changes.

Rich Text Format (RTF) A universal document format that can be read by nearly all word processing programs.

Right-click The action of clicking the right mouse button.

Rotate handle Rotates an image clockwise or counter-clockwise.

Ruler Displays the exact location of paragraph margins, indents, and tab stops.

Sans serif font A font with no lines or extensions on the bottoms of characters; usually used for titles or headlines.

Scale The range of numbers in the data series that controls the minimum, maximum, and incremental values on the value axis of a chart.

ScreenTip A small box, activated by holding the pointer over a button or other screen object, that displays the name of a screen element.

Scroll box Provides a visual indication of your location in a document. It can also be used with the mouse to drag a document up and down.

Selecting text Highlighting text so that it can be formatted, deleted, copied, or moved.

Separator character A character used to identify column placement in text; usually a tab or a comma.

Serif font A font that contains extensions or lines on the ends of the characters; usually the easiest type of font to read for large blocks of text.

Shortcut menu A context-sensitive menu that displays commands relevant to the selected object.

Sizing handle A small square or circle in the corners and the middle of the sides of a graphic that can be used to increase or decrease the size of the graphic.

Small caps Text format, usually used in titles, that changes lowercase text into capital letters using a reduced font size.

Spin box arrow The up and down arrows in an option box that enable you to increase or decrease a value incrementally.

Split box The short gray bar at the top of the vertical scroll bar that can be dragged to split the screen and as a result display two different parts of the document.

Standard toolbar Contains buttons for some of the most common commands in Word. It may occupy an entire row or share a row with the Formatting toolbar.

Status bar A horizontal bar at the bottom of the document window in Microsoft Word that provides information about the current state of what you are viewing in the window, including the page number, and whether overtype or track changes are on or off.

Style A set of formatting characteristics that is stored in one shortcut command. All formatting characteristics, such as font, font size, and indentation, are applied together.

Tab stop A mark on the ruler bar to which the insertion point will jump when the Tab key is pressed.

Table Rows and columns of text or numbers, used to organize data and present it effectively.

Table style Formats border type and style, shading, cell alignment, and fonts in a table.

Task pane Displays commonly used commands or utilities available for use with the current task.

Taskbar Displays the Start button and any open documents. The taskbar may also display shortcut buttons for other programs.

Template Predefined document structures defining the basic document settings, such as font, margins, and available styles.

Thesaurus A language tool that helps add variety to your writing by suggesting synonyms (words that have the same meaning) for words that you select.

Title bar Displays the program icon, the name of the document, and the name of the program. The Minimize, Maximize/Restore Down, and Close buttons are grouped on the right side of the title bar.

Toggle switch A button, such as the Numbering or Bold button, that turns on with a click, and then off with another click.

Toolbar A row of buttons that activate commands, such as Undo or Bold, with a single click of the left mouse button.

Toolbar Options Button that enables you to see all of the buttons associated with a toolbar. It also enables you to place the Standard and Formatting toolbars on separate rows or on the same row.

Topic marker A small open square symbol to the left of body text in an outline.

Track Changes A feature in Word that provides a visual indication of deletions, insertions, and formatting changes in a document.

Value axis (y-axis) The vertical line on the left side of the chart that displays the numeric scale for numbers in the selected data.

Vertical scroll bar Enables you to move up and down in a document.

Web browser Software that enables you to use the Web and navigate from page to page and site to site.

Web Layout View A document view that shows how the document would look if viewed with a Web browser.

Wizard template A step-by-step program that asks you questions and then sets up a document based on your answers.

Word wrap Automatically moves text from the right edge of a paragraph to the beginning of the next line as necessary to fit within the margins.

WordArt A Microsoft Office drawing tool that enables you to turn text into graphics.

Zoom To get a closer view of a document, or to see more of the document on the screen.

Index

Symbols